Organizational Change

Fourth Edition

This book is dedicated to Tupper Cawsey,

our dear and wonderful friend, colleague, and extraordinary educator.

He passed away, but his positive impact continues to reverberate in those he touched.

Thank you, Tupper.

Gene and Cynthia

Sara Miller McCune founded SAGE Publishing in 1965 to support the dissemination of usable knowledge and educate a global community. SAGE publishes more than 1000 journals and over 600 new books each year, spanning a wide range of subject areas. Our growing selection of library products includes archives, data, case studies and video. SAGE remains majority owned by our founder and after her lifetime will become owned by a charitable trust that secures the company's continued independence.

Los Angeles | London | New Delhi | Singapore | Washington DC | Melbourne

Organizational Change

An Action-Oriented Toolkit
Fourth Edition

Gene Deszca
Wilfrid Laurier University

Cynthia Ingols
Simmons University

Tupper F. Cawsey
Wilfrid Laurier University

Los Angeles | London | New Delhi
Singapore | Washington DC | Melbourne

FOR INFORMATION:

SAGE Publications, Inc.
2455 Teller Road
Thousand Oaks, California 91320
E-mail: order@sagepub.com

SAGE Publications India Pvt. Ltd.
B 1/I 1 Mohan Cooperative Industrial Area
Mathura Road, New Delhi 110 044
India

SAGE Publications Ltd.
1 Oliver's Yard
55 City Road
London EC1Y 1SP
United Kingdom

SAGE Publications Asia-Pacific Pte. Ltd.
18 Cross Street #10-10/11/12
China Square Central
Singapore 048423

Printed in the United States of America

Library of Congress Cataloging-in-Publication Data

Names: Deszca, Gene, author. | Ingols, Cynthia, author. | Cawsey, T. F., author/

Title: Organizational change : an action-oriented toolkit / Gene Deszca, Wilfrid Laurier University, Canada, Cynthia Ingols - Simmons College, USA, Tupper F. Cawsey - Wilfrid Laurier University, Canada.

Other titles: Organisational change

Description: Fourth Edition. | Thousand Oaks : SAGE Publications, [2019] | Revised edition of Organizational change, [2016] | Includes bibliographical references and index.

Identifiers: LCCN 2019013498 | ISBN 9781544351407 (paperback)

Subjects: LCSH: Organizational change.

Classification: LCC HD58.8 .C39 2019 | DDC 658.4/06—dc23

LC record available at https://lccn.loc.gov/2019013498

Acquisitions Editor: Maggie Stanley
Editorial Assistant: Janeane Calderon
Production Editor: Gagan Mahindra
Copy Editor: Lynne Curry
Typesetter: C&M Digitals (P) Ltd.
Proofreader: Rae-Ann Goodwin
Indexer: Mary Mortensen
Cover Designer: Candice Harman
Marketing Manager: Sarah Panella

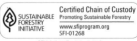

SFI label applies to text stock

19 20 21 22 23 10 9 8 7 6 5 4 3 2 1

BRIEF CONTENTS

DETAILED CONTENTS

PREFACE TO THE FOURTH EDITION

Difficult to see. Always in motion is the future.[1]

The world has continued to churn in very challenging ways since the publishing of the third edition of this text. Uneven and shifting global patterns of growth, stubbornly high unemployment levels in many parts of the world, increasing income inequality, and serious trade disputes that threaten to transform trade patterns are severely stressing our highly interconnected global economy. The massive credit crisis of a decade ago was followed by unprecedented worldwide government stimulus spending and low interest rates to promote growth, which, in turn, have resulted in escalating public debt, exacerbated in some nations through tax cuts. These combine to threaten the capacity of national governments to respond to future economic difficulties.

In addition, wars, insurrections and civil insurrections in parts of Africa, the Ukraine, the Middle East, and Asia have sent masses of people searching for safety in new places. Simultaneously, deteriorating international relationships involving major powers, fears of global pandemics (Ebola and MERS), and the staying power of radical Islamist groups such as al-Qaeda and ISIS affiliates, Boko Haram and Jemaah Islamiyah have shaken all organizations in affected regions—big or small, public or private. Escalating concerns related to global warming, species extinctions, and rising sea levels are stressing those who recognize the problems in governments and organizations of all shapes and sizes, as they attempt to figure out how to constructively address these emerging realities. Add to these elements the accelerating pace of technological change and it's easy to see why we, at times, feel overwhelmed by the turbulence, uncertainty, and negative prognosis that seem to define the present.

But, all is not doom and gloom. Progress on human rights and gender equity, reductions in extreme poverty and hunger, declining rates of murder and violent crime, improving rates of literacy and life expectancy, and increasing access to information and knowledge through affordable digital resources provide evidence that progress is being made on some fronts. The growing public willingness to tackle very difficult environmental and social issues now, not later, are combining with innovative technologies, creative for-profit and not-for-profit organizations, and forward-thinking politicians and leaders from all walks of life. Supportive public policies are combining with public and private initiatives to demonstrate that we can make serious progress on these issues, *if* we collectively choose to act in constructive and thoughtful manners locally, regionally, and globally. These factors have also made us, your authors, much more aware of the extreme influence of the external environment on the internal workings of all organizations.

---

[1] Spoken by Yoda in the movie *The Empire Strikes Back*

As we point out in our book, the smallest of firms needs to adapt when new competitive realities and opportunities surface. Even the largest and most successful of firms have to learn how to adapt when disruptive technologies or rapid social, economic, political and environmental changes alter their realities. If they fail to do so, they will falter and potentially fail.

Our models have always included and often started with events external to organizations. We have always argued that change leaders need to scan their environments and be aware of trends and crises in those environments. The events of the past two years have reinforced even more our sense of this. Managers must be sensitive to what happens around them, know how to make sense of this, and then have the skills and abilities that will allow them to both react effectively to the internal and external challenges *and* remain constant in their visions and dreams of how to make their organizations and the world a better place to live.

A corollary of this is that organizations need a response capability that is unprecedented because we're playing on a global stage of increasing complexity and uncertainty. If you are a bank, you need a capital ratio that would have been unprecedented a few years ago, and you need to be working hard to understand the potential implications of blockchain technologies, regulatory changes, and changing consumer preferences on the future of banking. If you are a major organization, you need to design flexibility and adaptability into your structures, policies, and plans. If you are a public-sector organization, you need to be sensitive to how capricious granting agencies or funders will be when revenues dry up. In today's world, organizational resilience, adaptability, and agility gain new prominence.

Further, we are challenged with a continuing reality that change is endemic. All managers need to be change managers. All good managers *are* change leaders. The management job involves creating, anticipating, encouraging, engaging others, and responding positively to change. This has been a theme of this book that continues. Change management is for everyone. Change management emerges from the bottom and middle of the organization as much as from the top. It will be those key leaders who are embedded in the organization who will enable the needed adaptation of the organization to its environment. **Managers of all stripes need to be key change leaders.**

In addition to the above, we have used feedback on the third edition to strengthen the pragmatic orientation that we had developed. The major themes of action orientation, analysis tied with doing, the management of a nonlinear world, and the bridging of the "knowing–doing" gap continue to be central themes. At the same time, we have tried to shift to a more user friendly, action perspective. To make the material more accessible to a diversity of readers, some theoretical material has been altered, some of our models have been clarified and simplified, and some of our language and formatting has been modified.

As we stated in the preface to the first edition, our motivation for this book was to fill a gap we saw in the marketplace. Our challenge was to develop a book that not only gave prescriptive advice, "how-to-do-it lists," but one that also provided up-to-date theory without getting sidetracked by academic theoretical complexities. We hope that we have captured the management experience with change so that our manuscript assists all those who must deal with change, not just senior executives or organization development specialists. Although there is much in this book for the senior executive and organizational development specialist, our intent was to create a book that would be valuable to a broad cross section of the workforce.

Our personal beliefs form the basis for the book. Even as academics, we have a bias for action. We believe that "doing is healthy." Taking action creates influence and demands responses from others. While we believe in the need for excellent analysis, we know that action itself provides opportunities for feedback and learning that can improve the action. Finally, we have a strong belief in the worth of people. In particular, we believe that one of the greatest sources of improvement is the untapped potential to be found in the people of all organizations.

We recognize that this book is not an easy read. It is not meant to be. It is meant as a serious text for those involved in change—that is, all managers! We hope you find it a book that you will want to keep and pull from your shelf in the years ahead, when you need to lead change and you want help thinking it through.

Your authors,
Gene, Cynthia, and Tupper

Note on Instructor Teaching Site

A password-protected instructor's manual is available at study.sagepub.com/cawsey4e to help instructors plan and teach their courses. These resources have been designed to help instructors make the classes as practical and interesting as possible for students.

PowerPoint Slides capture key concepts and terms for each chapter for use in lectures and review.

A Test Bank includes multiple-choice, short-answer, and essay exam questions for each chapter.

Video Resources for each chapter help launch class discussion.

Sample Syllabi, Assignments, and Chapter Exercises as optional supplements to course curriculum.

Case Studies and teaching notes for each chapter facilitate application of concepts in real world situations.

ACKNOWLEDGMENTS

We would like to acknowledge the many people who have helped to make this edition of the book possible. Our colleagues and students and their reactions to the ideas and materials continue to be a source of inspiration.

Cynthia would like to thank her colleagues at the School of Business, Simmons University, Boston, Massachusetts. In particular, she would like to thank Dr. Stacy Blake-Beard, Deloitte Ellen Gabriel Chair of Women and Leadership, and Dr. Paul Myers, senior lecturer, who each contributed a case to this fourth edition of the book. In addition, Paul graciously read and gave feedback on other cases and parts of the text, suggesting ways to bring clarity to sometimes muddled meanings. Alissa Scheibert, a Simmons library science student, conducted in-depth research for a number of chapters. Dr. Erin Sullivan, research director, and Jessica L. Alpert, researcher, Center for Primary Care, Harvard Medical School, contributed two cases to this edition of the book and I am very grateful for their contributions. Jess Coppla, a former Healthcare MBA student leader and author of one of the cases, will someday be CEO of a healthcare organization. . . . I'm just waiting to see which one. Colleagues Gary Gaumer, Cathy Robbins, Bob Coulum, Todd Hermann, Mindy Nitkin, and Mary Shapiro were wonderful cheerleaders throughout the many hours of my sitting, writing, and revising in my office: thank you all!

Managers, executives, and front-line employees that we have known have provided insights, case examples, and applications while keeping us focused on what is useful and relevant. Ellen Zane, former CEO of Tufts Medical Center, Boston, is an inspiring change leader; her turnaround story at the Tufts Medical Center appeared in the second edition of this book and was published again in the third edition; it continues to be on the Sage website for use by faculty. Cynthia has also been fortunate to work with and learn from Gretchen Fox, founder and former CEO, FOX RPM: the story of how she changed her small firm appeared in the second edition of the book and the case continues to be available through Harvard Business Publishing (http://hbr.org/product/fox-relocation-management-corp/an/NA0096-PDF-ENG). Noah Deszca, a high school teacher, was the prime author of the Travelink Solutions case, an organization that underwent significant changes while he was working there. Katharine Bambrick, a former student of Gene's and the CEO of the Ontario Trillium Foundation and the former CEO of Food Banks Canada, is another of the inspiring leaders who opened their organizations to us and allowed us to learn from their experiences, and share it with you. The Food Banks case appeared in the third edition of this book and is one of the additional cases that are available on this book's website.

Special thanks to Paige Tobie for all her hard work on the instructors' resources. She is a gem to work with.

As with the previous editions, our partners Bertha Welzel and Steve Spitz tolerated our moods, our myopia to other things that needed doing, and the early mornings and late nights spent on the manuscript. They helped us work our way through ideas and sections that were problematic, and they kept us smiling and grounded when frustration mounted.

Our editors at SAGE have been excellent. They moved the project along and made a difficult process fun (well, most of the time). Thank you, Maggie Stanley, our acquisitions editor, for keeping us on task and on time (or trying to keep us on time. . .). We appreciate your style of gentle nudges. Thank you to Janeane Calderon, our editorial assistant who was constantly on top of the various parts of the book and helped us push through to the end. Copyeditor Lynne Curry found stray commas and inconsistencies throughout the book: thank you for fixing the problems. Gagan Mahindra, Production Editor, kept us wonderfully focused on the details of production: thank you!

Finally, we would like to recognize the reviewers who provided us with valuable feedback on the third edition. Their constructive, positive feedback and their excellent suggestions were valued. We thought carefully about how to incorporate their suggestions into this fourth edition of the book. Thank you Mulugeta Agonafer of Springfield College, Brenda C. Barnes of Allen College, C. Darren Brooks of Florida State University, Robert Dibie of Indiana University Kokomo, Jonathan E. Downs of MidAmerica Nazarene University, Alexander C. Heckman of Franklin University, Scott Elmes McIntyre of University of Houston – Clear Lake, Frank Novakowski of Davenport University, Pamela R. Van Dyke of Southern Methodist University, Jack Wilson of the United States Naval Academy, and Diana J. Wong-MingJi of Eastern Michigan University.

In short, our thanks to all who made this book possible.

CHAPTER ONE

CHANGING ORGANIZATIONS IN OUR COMPLEX WORLD

Chapter Overview

- The chapter defines organizational change as "planned alteration of organizational components to improve the efficiency and effectiveness of organizations."
- The orientation of this book is to assist change leaders—and potential change managers—in becoming effective in their change activities.
- The social, demographic, technological, political, and economic forces pushing the need for change are outlined.
- Four types of organizational change are discussed: tuning, adapting, reorienting, and re-creating.
- Four change roles found in organizations are described: change initiators, change implementers, change facilitators, and change recipients and stakeholders. The terms *change leader* and *change agent* are used interchangeably and could mean any of the four roles.
- The difficulties in creating successful change are highlighted, and then some of the characteristics of successful change leaders are described.

Organizations fill our world. We place our children into day care, seek out support services for our elderly, and consume information and recreational services supplied by other organizations. We work at for-profit or not-for-profit organizations. We rely on organizations to deliver the services we need: food, water, electricity, and sanitation and look to governmental organizations for a variety of services that we hope will keep us safe, secure, well governed, and successful. We depend on health organizations when we are sick. We use religious organizations to help our spiritual lives. We assume that most of our children's education will be delivered by formal educational organizations. In other words, organizations are everywhere. Organizations are how we get things done. This is not just a human phenomenon as it extends to plants and animals: look at a bee colony, a reef, a lion pride, or an elephant herd and you'll see organizations at work.

And these organizations are changing—some of them declining and failing, while others successfully adapt or evolve, to meet the shifting realities and demands of their environments. What exactly is organizational change? What do we mean when we talk about it?

DEFINING ORGANIZATIONAL CHANGE

When we think of organizational change, we think of major changes: mergers, acquisitions, buyouts, downsizing, restructuring, the launch of new products, and the outsourcing of major organizational activities. We can also think of lesser changes: departmental reorganizations, installations of new technology and incentive systems, shutting particular manufacturing lines, or opening new branches in other parts of the country—fine-tuning changes to improve the efficiency and effectiveness of our organizations.

In this book, when we talk about organizational change, we refer to planned alterations of organizational components to improve the effectiveness or efficiency of the organization. Organizational components are the organizational mission, vision, values, culture, strategy, goals, structure, processes or systems, technology, and people in an organization. When organizations enhance their effectiveness, they increase their ability to generate value for those they serve.

The reasons for change are often ambiguous. Is the change internally or externally driven? In July 2018, Tim Hortons (a Canada-based coffee restaurant chain) announced that it was aiming to open 1,500 new stores in China in the next decade.[1] This is in addition to expansion efforts involving the United States, the Philippines, Britain, Mexico, the Middle East, and Spain. Tim Horton's has a network of approximately 3,900 outlets in Canada and another 900 elsewhere. It has also been busy revising its menu to shore up flattening same-store sales, adding Wi-Fi access, undertaking major store remodeling, and making changes to its sustainability and corporate social responsibility initiatives. What is driving these changes? The executives reported that they were undertaking these actions in response to competitive pressures, customer needs, market opportunities, and the desire to align their efforts with their values. For Tim Hortons, the drivers of change are coming from both the internal and external environment. Dunkin' Donuts, a much larger U.S.–based chain with similarities to Tim Hortons' business model and competitive pressures, seems to have been pursuing similar adaptive responses.[2] It is essential for managers to be sensitive to what is happening inside and outside the organization and adapt to those changes in the environment.*

Note that, by our definition and focus, organizational change is intentional and planned. Someone in the organization has taken an initiative to alter a significant organizational component. This means a shift in something relatively permanent. Usually, something formal or systemic has to be altered. For example, a new customer relations system may be introduced that captures customer satisfaction and reports it to managers; or a new division is created and people are allocated to that division in response to a new organizational vision.

Simply doing more of the same is not an organizational change. For example, increasing existing sales efforts in response to a competitor's activities would not be classified as an organizational change. However, the restructuring

---

*Tim Hortons and Burger King announced their $12.5 billion merger on August 26, 2014, forming the third largest quick-service restaurant in the world. They have maintained these two distinct brands post-merger, but have taken advantage of synergies by leveraging their respective strengths and geographic reach.

of a sales force into two groups (key account managers and general account managers) or the modification of service offerings would be, even though these changes could well be in response to a competitor's activities rather than a more proactive initiative.

Some organizational components, such as structures and systems, are concrete and thus easier to understand when contemplating change. For example, assembly lines can be reordered or have new technologies applied. The change is definable and the end point clear when it is done. Similarly, the alteration of a reward system or job design is concrete and can be documented. The creation of new positions, subunits, or departments is equally obvious. Such organizational changes are tangible and thus may be easier to make happen, because they are easier to understand.

When the change target is more deeply imbedded in the organization and is intangible, the change challenge is magnified. For example, a shift in organizational culture is difficult to engineer. A change leader can plan a change from an authoritarian to a more participative culture, but the initiatives required to bring about the change and the sequencing of those initiatives are trickier to get a hold of than more concrete change initiatives. Simply announcing a new strategy or vision does not mean that anything significant will change since "you need to get the vision off the walls and into the halls."[3] A more manageable way to think of such a culture change is to identify concrete changes that reinforce the desired culture. If management alters reward systems, shifts decision making downward, and creates participative management committees, then management increases the likelihood that it will create cultural change over time. Sustained behavioral change occurs when people in the organization understand, accept, and act. Through their actions, the new vision or strategy becomes real.[4]

The target of change needs to be considered carefully. Often, managers choose concrete tangible changes because they are easiest to plan for and can be seen. For example, it is relatively easy to focus on pay and give monetary incentives in an attempt to address employee morale. But the root cause of these issues might be managerial styles or processes—much more difficult to recognize and address. In addition, intervening through compensation may have unanticipated consequences and actually worsen the problem. An example of this can be found in the story below.

CHANGE AT A SOCIAL SERVICE AGENCY

In a mid-sized social service agency's family services division, turnover rates climbed to more than 20%, causing serious issues with service delivery and quality of service. The manager of the division argued that staff were leaving because of wages. According to him, children's aid societies' wages were higher and staff left to join those organizations. Upon investigation, senior management learned of morale problems arising from the directive, non-inclusive management style of the manager. Instead of altering pay rates, which would have caused significant budgetary and equity problems throughout the organization, senior management replaced the manager and moved him to a project role. Within months, turnover rates dropped to less than 10% and the manager decided to leave the agency.[5]

In this example, if the original analysis had been accepted, turnover rates might have declined since staff may have been persuaded to stay for higher wages. But the agency would have faced financial challenges due to higher labor costs as well as a festering morale problem.

THE ORIENTATION OF THIS BOOK

The focus, then, of this book is on organizational change as a planned activity designed to improve the organization's effectiveness. Changes that are random (occur simply due to chance) or unplanned are not the types of organizational change that this book will explore, except, insofar, as they serve as the stimulus for planned change initiatives. Similarly, changes that may be planned but do not have a clear link to attempts to improve organizational effectiveness are not considered. That is, changes made solely for personal reasons—for personal gain, for example—fall outside the intended focus of this book.

> There is a story of two stonecutters. The first, when asked what he was doing, responded, "I am shaping this stone to fit in that wall." The second, however, said, "I am helping to build a cathedral."

The jobs of the two stonecutters might be the same, but their perspectives are dramatically different. The personal outcomes of satisfaction and organizational commitment will likely be much higher for the visionary stonecutter than for the "just doing my job" stonecutter. Finally, the differences in satisfaction and commitment may well lead to different organizational results. After all, if you are building a cathedral, you might be more motivated to stay late, to take extra care, to find ways to improve things, and to help others when help is needed.

In other words, the organizational member who has a broader perspective on the value of his or her contributions and on the task at hand is likely to be a more committed and capable contributor. As a result, we take a perspective that encourages change leaders to take a holistic perspective on the change and to be widely inclusive in letting employees know what changes are needed and are happening.

If employees have no sense of the intended vision and see themselves as "just doing a job," it is likely that any organizational change will be difficult to understand, be resisted, and cause personal trauma. On the other hand, if employees "get" the vision of the organization and understand the direction and perspective of where the organization is going and why, they are more likely to embrace their future role—even if that future means they leave the organization.[6]

This book is aimed at those who want to be involved in change and wish to take positive actions. We encourage readers to escape from passive, negative change recipient positions and to move to active and healthy roles—those of change initiators, facilitators, and implementers. Readers may be in middle manager roles or may be students hoping to enter managerial roles. Or, they may be leaders of change within an organization or a subunit. The book is also intended for the informal leaders in organizations who are driving change, sometimes in spite of their bosses. They might believe that their bosses "should" be driving the change but don't see it happening, and so they see it as up to them to make change happen regardless of the action or inaction of their managers.

This book has an action, "how to do it" emphasis. Nothing happens unless we, the people, make it happen. As someone once said, "The truth is—the cavalry isn't coming!" There will be no cavalry charging over the hill to save us. It is up to us to make the changes needed. At the same time, this "how-to" orientation is paired with a focus on developing a deep understanding of organizations. Without such an understanding, what needs to be changed, and what the critical success factors are, change efforts will be much more difficult. This twin theme, of knowing both how to do it and what to do, underpins the structure of this book and our approach to change. To paraphrase Zig Ziglar, "It's not what happens to you that matters. It's how you respond that makes a difference."[7]

Change capability is a core managerial competence. Without skills in change management, individuals cannot operate effectively in today's fluctuating, shifting organizations.[8] Senior management may set the organizational direction, but, in this decentralized organizational world, it is up to managers and employees to shift the organization to accomplish the new goals and objectives. To do this, change-management skills are paramount. In many organizations, those managers are looked to for insights, innovative ideas, and initiatives that will make a positive difference in their firms. Investigate firms such as Google, Cisco, Marriott, St. Jude Children's Hospital, Deloitte, and others listed among the 100 best to work for here and offshore, and you will find many examples of firms embracing these practices.[9] They do so with a realistic appreciation for the fact that change management is often more difficult than we anticipate. We believe, as do Pfeffer and Sutton, that there is a Knowing–Doing gap.[10] Knowing the concepts and understanding the theory behind organizational change are not enough. This book is designed to provide practicing and prospective managers with the tools they will need to be effective change agents.

Environmental Forces Driving Change Today

Much change starts with shifts in an organization's environment. For example, government legislation dealing with employment law pushes new equity concerns through hiring practices. Globalization means that marketing, research and development, production, and other parts of an organization (e.g., customer service's call centers) can be moved around the world and/or outsourced. International alliances form and reform. These and related factors mean an organization's competition is often global in nature, rather than local. New technologies allow purchasing to link to production within an integrated supply chain, changing forever supplier–customer relationships. Concerns over global warming, sustainability, and environmental practices give rise to new laws, standards, and shifts in consumer preferences for products and firms that exhibit superior environmental performance. A competitor succeeds in attracting an organization's largest customer and upsets management's assumptions about the marketplace. Each of these external happenings will drive and push the need for change. These factors are summed up in the acronym PESTEL. PESTEL factors include political, economic, social, technological, ecological/environmental, and legal factors that describe the environment of an organization.

These are not simply private sector realities. Not-for-profits, hospitals, schools, and governments all experience these environmental challenges as the world shrinks and the seeming pace of change accelerates and increases in complexity. Not-for-profits or NGOs (nongovernmental organizations) and various governmental bodies respond to hunger in war-torn Somalia and Syria; public universities and hospitals respond to for-profit competitors. Governments around the world deal with issues related to enhancing their economic competitiveness and attracting employers, hopefully in sustainable and socially responsible ways. No one is immune.

Sometimes organizations are caught by surprise by environmental shifts, while other organizations have anticipated and planned for new situations. For example, management may have systems to track the perceived quality and value of its products versus its competition's. Benchmarking data might show that its quality is beginning to lag behind that of a key competitor. These environmental scanning and early warning systems allow for action before customers are lost or provide paths to new customers and/or new services. Toyota had such systems in place, but management appears to have responded inadequately.

DID TOYOTA OR GM KNOW ABOUT THE SAFETY DEFECTS?

Misreading the Environment and Associated Risks

On April 5, 2010, the U.S. government's transportation department stated it would seek $16.4 million from Toyota for not notifying the government about potential accelerator pedal problems. "In taking the step, federal authorities are sending the strongest signal yet that they believe the carmaker deliberately concealed safety information from them."[11]

Did Toyota know about these deficiencies and respond by denying they existed and covering up? If so, this is an example of an inappropriate organizational response to environmental stimuli.

The same question could be asked of General Motors concerning ignition switch problems in the Cobalt and other brands. By GM's admission, they first became aware of this problem in 2001. It was the subject of a technical service bulletin in 2005, but there was no recall until 2014, in the aftermath of multiple deaths and injuries, mounting public scrutiny, and lawsuits. The global recall totaled 2.6 million vehicles by May 2014: there have been humiliating U.S. congressional hearings, CEO Mary Barra has publicly apologized, and GM is sought immunity from the courts for lawsuits related to periods before its 2009 bankruptcy. To say this had the potential to undermine confidence in GM and its brand would be a gross understatement and points to the danger of failing to act and implement needed changes in a timely manner.[12]

It's beyond the scope of this book to provide an in-depth treatment of all of the various trends and alterations in the environment. However, we will highlight below some of the important trends to sensitize readers to their environments. As is always the case, organizations find themselves influenced by fundamental forces: changing social, cultural, and demographic patterns; spectacular technological achievements that transform how we do business; concerns about the physical environment and social responsibility that are producing demands for changes in our products and business practices; a global marketplace that sends us competing worldwide and brings competition to our doorsteps; political and legal forces that have the potential to transform the competitive landscape; continued political uncertainty in many countries that has the potential to introduce chaos into world markets; the aftermath of the economic turmoil that rocked the world economy in 2008; and trade wars in 2018 that promoted further uncertainty.

RESPONSES TO THE EXTERNAL ENVIRONMENT CAN ESCALATE RISKS

The financial crisis of 2008 occurred because banks failed to comprehend the risks they took with asset-backed securities and other derivatives. Incentive systems drove bankers to take on excessive risks for excessive profits. They denied the evidence presented to them, and when the bubble burst, the results were catastrophic. For example, when warned by his chief risk officer, who proposed shutting down the mortgage business in 2004, the head of Lehman Brothers threatened to fire him! This rush for profits drove many banks. Chuck Prince, the head of Citigroup at the time, just before the credit markets seized up in August 2007, said, "As long as the music is playing, you've got to get up and dance. We're still dancing."[13]

Clearly bankers misread both the ethical and business implications of what was going on inside their firms. Either there was collective myopia at work with respect to mounting evidence of excessive risk from very credible sources,[14] or the rewards and short-term performance pressures were such that they chose not to attend to the warning clouds.

The Changing Demographic, Social, and Cultural Environment

Age Matters. The social, cultural, and economic environment will be dramatically altered by demography. Demographic changes in the Western world and parts of Asia mean that aging populations will gray the face of Europe, Canada, China, and Japan.[15] The financial warning bells are already being sounded. Even before the huge government deficits of 2009 and beyond that Western nations have been digging themselves out from under, Standard & Poor's predicted that the average net government debt-to-GDP ratio for industrialized nations will increase from 33% in 2005 to 180% by 2050, due to rising pension and health care costs,[16] if changes are not undertaken. In 2013 and 2016 they reported modest progress had been made on this debt challenge, but the problems and related societal challenges have certainly not gone away.[17]

Although the United States will age less quickly, Europe and Japan will face a dependency crisis of senior citizens requiring medical care and pension support. By 2050, the median age in the United States is projected to be 41 versus approximately 50 in Europe. The United States will keep itself younger than Europe through immigration and a birth rate that is close to replacement level,[18] though even here growth assumptions have come under question as the rate of immigration has declined in the aftermath of the economic slowdown and questions around emigration policies remain highly politicized. Even with this influx, if nothing changes, it is estimated the U.S. governmental debt-to-GDP ratio will grow to 472% of GDP by 2050, due mainly to pension and health care costs.[19] Aging European countries will be around 300–400% of GDP, despite older populations, due to more cost-efficient approaches in these areas. On the high side, Japan is predicted to reach 729%. The European Union's population is projected to peak in 2025 at around 470 million and then begin to decline, while the United States reaches 335 million in 2020 and continues to grow thereafter to 398 million in 2050. The decline in the European Union would occur much earlier if it were not for immigration.

Throughout the world, fertility rates are falling and falling fast.[20] In 1974, only 24 countries had fertility rates below replacement levels. By 2009, more than 70 countries had rates below 2.1. In some countries, the swings are dramatic. The fertility rate in Iran dropped from 7 in 1984 to 1.9 in 2009, a huge shift.

Some see a close tie between female education, fertility rates, and economic growth. When economies are poor, the fertility rate is high and there are many young dependents relying on working adults and older siblings for sustenance. When fertility rates drop, there is a bulge of people, meaning the ratio of working adults to dependents increases, leading to an increase in per capita wealth. Mexico and China are examples of this currently. When this bulge ages, dependent, nonworking seniors become a larger percentage of the population, so these advantages tend to disappear over time, as incomes rise and fertility rates fall.[21] As discussed above, this has happened and is happening in Europe and Japan. India, Africa, and Mexico are examples of areas with a smaller proportion of dependents (the young and the old) relative to their working populations, and this is something referred to as an economic dividend. However, it is only a dividend if the population has the skills and abilities needed, and there are infrastructure and policies in place to support employment—something many developing nations are finding very challenging.[22]

These demographic shifts can take decades to work their way through, and the economic implications for organizations are significant. Imagine 400 to 500 million relatively wealthy Americans and the impact that will have on

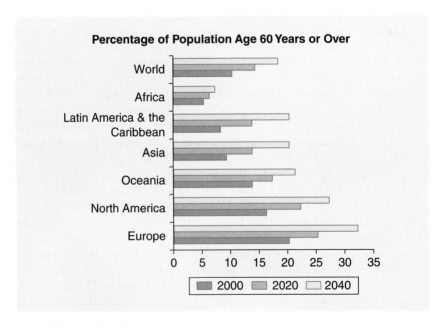

Percentage of Population Age 60 Years or Over

Source: U.N. Population Division.

global economic power, assuming that pension and health care challenges are effectively managed. Consumer spending in developing countries is expected to grow to $44.8 trillion by 2030, eclipsing the $19.2 trillion in North America and Europe.[23] Also imagine the impact of a graying Europe and Japan's declining workforce. Some estimates put the fiscal problems in providing pensions and health care for senior citizens at 250% of national income in Germany and France.[24]

Pension costs can become a huge competitive disadvantage at the company level too. At General Motors, there were 2.5 retirees for every active worker in 2002. These so-called "legacy" costs were $900 per vehicle at that time due to pension and health care obligations. These costs rose to $1,800 by 2006[25] and retired employee–related costs were one of the key reasons that GM sought bankruptcy relief in 2009. Debt relief certainly alleviated the immediate pressure, but as the number of retired to active GM employees continues to grow, this challenge is not going away.[26]

Companies appear to be ill prepared to deal with this aging population.[27] Both private and public sector employers are waking up to these pressures and attempting to bring about changes to their pension programs that will be more sustainable, but the journey will not be easy. Public pushback to reductions in pension income and other entitlement programs has been strong, and even relatively modest proposals for shifts to policies such as increasing the age of retirement by a year or two have faced widespread resistance. This is resistance that scares politicians because these are also people who are most likely to vote and who are also feeling vulnerable as they find their savings are insufficient to sustain their lifestyle.[28]

An aging population also provides new market opportunities—would you have predicted that the average age of a motorcycle purchaser would be over 49? That's Harley-Davidson's experience.[29] With aging populations, organizations can expect pressures to manage age prejudice more effectively. Subtle discrimination based on age will not be accepted. Innovative solutions will be welcomed by aging members of the workforce and an increasing necessity for employers. See the story below.

OLDER WORKERS CAN'T BE IGNORED

"The day is coming when employers are going to embrace the value of older workers. They don't have a choice," writes Kerry Hannon. Demographic and fiscal realities are making the retention of older members of the workforce escalate in importance and give rise to the innovations in working relationships, from full time to flexible work relationships and contract positions. Some employers are realizing the benefits that these employees can bring with them and are recognizing the importance of investing in them before their knowledge walks out the door. Employers that fail to adjust their approach to older employees could find themselves seriously at risk as U.S. labor markets reflect the demographic realities.[30]

KPMG has publicly recognized the benefits, noting that "older workers tend to be more dedicated to staying with the company, a plus for clients who like to build a relationship with a consultant they can count on to be around for years."[31]

Other demographic issues will provide opportunities and challenges. In the United States, Latinos will play a role in transforming organizations. The numbers of Latinos jumped from 35.3 million during the 1990s, to 55.4 million or 17.4% of the population in 2014 (up from 13% in 2000), making them the largest ethnic/racial group in the United States. They are also much younger (29 versus the national average age of 37.2), and 65.6% of its members have been born in the United States. Significantly, the largest growth often is in "hyper-growth" Latino destinations such as Nevada and Georgia,[32] some of which have seen an increase of more than 300% in Latino populations since 1980. The immigration component of this growth rate was adversely affected by the U.S. economic downturn and improvements in the Mexican economy, but it is predicted to continue upward due to domestic population growth, difficult conditions in other parts of Latin America, and the impact that a return to economic health in the United States will have on immigration.

One of the outcomes of hyper-growth in certain urban areas has been an imbalance of Latino males and females. In the non-Latino population, the ratio of males to females is 96:100. In the Latino population, ratios as high as 118:100 are seen in the hyper-growth destinations.[33] While the specific implications for businesses are unclear, the general need for response and change is not. Notions of cultural norms (including those around English literacy and dominant language used) and markets could be shattered by such demographic shifts.

There have also been significant demographic shifts in Europe and parts of Asia, as people move from disadvantaged areas (economic, social, and political) in search of greater opportunities, security, and social justice. These trends are likely to continue, and as in the United States, they provide both challenges and opportunities. For countries like France and Austria, they help to moderate the effects of an aging population by providing new entrants to the workforce and new customers for products and services. However, they also represent integration challenges in terms of needed services and there has been a backlash from some groups, who see them as both an economic and social threat. Resistance to immigration reform in the United States, the tightening of emigration rules in Canada, the rise of anti-immigration political parties in Western Europe, and the January 2019 shut-down of the U.S. federal government over the disputed wall on the U.S.-Mexico border are evidence of this.

Our assumptions about families and gender will continue to be challenged in the workplace and marketplace of the future. Diversity, inclusiveness, and equity issues will challenge organizations with unpredictable results. The heated debates that occurred in the United States in 2006 concerning legislation related to illegal or undocumented immigrants, temporary workers, and family unification continue to provoke passionate positions and no resolution as of 2019. In Europe, debate around these topics has given rise to some electoral success by what used to be fringe parties in Sweden, France, and Italy (to name three), and isolated examples of violence.[34] Some nations have implemented laws around certain religious practices (typically associated with dress and visible symbols in schools and workplaces) that are viewed by many as discriminatory.[35] Matters related to same-sex marriage, gender identity, and gender equity continue to be challenging for many organizations, as laws and behavioral norms related to what is acceptable slowly evolve. The front-page coverage devoted to the drafting by the St. Louis Rams of Michael Sam, the first openly gay professional football player, testifies to the attention and emotions these matters can generate.[36] In too many parts of the world they represent life and death issues.

The same is true for matters of gender violence, as seen in the rise of the #MeToo movement in the United States and other parts of the world. Bad behavior is being exposed, attitudes are changing, and governments and organizations are beginning to alter policies and procedures in meaningful ways. Reactions to the reported behaviors of Harvey Weinstein (film producer), Roger Ailes (Fox News chairman), and many others attest to this. Christine Blasey Ford and Brett Kavanaugh's 2018 Supreme Court hearing concerning allegations of gender violence attracted over 20 million viewers[37] and the strength of subsequent responses suggest public concerns and demands for action on gender-related matters are increasing.

In some nations, employment- and human rights-related legislation have gone a long way toward advancing the interests and acceptance of diversity, by providing guidance, rules of conduct, and sanctions for those who fail to comply. However, issues related to gender, race, and diversity still need to be attended to by organizations. Participation and career advancement rates and salary level differences continue to attract the attention of politicians, the public, and the courts. Further, they constrain the development of talent in organizations and have adverse consequences on multiple levels—from the ability to attract and retain to performance and attitudinal outcomes that can, in turn, influence the culture and work climate of the firm.[38]

What happens when this boils over? In 2014 the intense news coverage and disciplining of Donald Sterling, the owner of the Los Angeles Clippers NBA franchise, for racist comments made during a private conversation, point to the extreme distress it caused members of the team and the reputational and brand consequences his behavior had on the franchise and the league itself. Only the swift actions of NBA Commissioner Adam Silver contained the damage, facilitated the sale of the franchise, and clearly signaled what was expected of owners.[39]

Risks in this area are not just related to the actions of senior management. Social media exposure extends the risks to all levels of the firm, where postings from organizational members can and do go viral with adverse consequences (more will be said about this later). Employees in the United States have certain protections when it comes to discussing working conditions with others online. In the case of fast-food restaurants, this has manifested itself into a very public national campaign to increase the minimum wage from $7.50 to $15.00 per hour. This campaign began on social media and is now giving rise to pay increases by some firms and minimum wage increases at the state level.[40] Firms are finding they must respond very carefully, in part because of the public's connection to a workforce where matters of age, gender, race, ethnicity, and economic fairness are very visible.[41] When employee postings go over the line on matters of race, gender, diversity, and equity, firms need to act and be seen to be acting quickly and appropriately in order to control damage.[42]

Being viewed as proactive and progressive in these areas can create advantages for firms in terms of attraction, retention, and the commitment levels of employees and customers. Firms such as TD Bank communicate this commitment very publicly and have been recognized as one of the best employers by Diversity Inc., Corporate Knights, and the Human Rights Campaign.[43]

Multinational corporations, such as IBM, view workforce diversity management as a strategic tool for sustaining and growing the enterprise.[44] That doesn't mean it is easy. Google has sought to increase the diversity of its workforce for several years. In May 2014 it publicly recognized its current lack of diversity (30% women, 2% black, and 3% Hispanic), and committed itself to aggressively address this through significant external and internal initiatives geared to attracting more individuals from these groups to technical careers and Google.[45] Smaller and medium-size firms (particularly tech start-ups) are increasingly recognizing the importance of this, as they attempt to scale their operations.

Race, gender, age, and diversity-related challenges multiply once organizations extend their footprints internationally. Differing rules, regulations, cultural norms, and values add to the change leadership challenges that need to be managed, as people learn to work with one another in efficient, effective, and socially appropriate ways. Think of the workforce challenges that a North American, Brazilian, or Indian firm needs to address when establishing its presence in a different part of the world. How will they deal with norms and values in these areas that run contrary to their core values? This is not just an issue for larger organizations. Increasingly, smaller firms find themselves facing international challenges as they seek to grow. These come in many forms—from managing virtual, globally dispersed teams and supply chains, to dealing with the complexities of joint ventures. While the challenges can seem daunting, an increasing number of small and midsize companies are succeeding on the global stage. A study of 75 such firms highlights the strategies and tactics that have produced positive results. Change leadership skills in these firms play a critical role in their survival and success.[46]

The Physical Environment and Social Responsibility Matters

Concerns over global warming, the degradation of the environment, sustainability, and social responsibility have escalated societal pressure for change at the intergovernmental, governmental, multinational and national corporate, and community levels. Accountability for what is referred to as the "triple bottom line" is leading firms to issue audited statements that report on economic, social, and ecological performance with the goal of sustainability in mind.[47] The 2013 fire and building collapse involving garment suppliers in Bangladesh (1,100 workers killed) and the 2014 spread of the Ebola virus in West Africa intersected with questions about the role of multinational corporations in the health and safety of people in developing countries.

The 2010 pictures of BP's oil well gushing millions of gallons into the Gulf of Mexico combined with pictures of oil-coated pelicans, drought, extreme heat, storm-related flooding, and disappearing ice masses reinforce the message that action is urgently needed. While the Paris Agreement on Climate Change was hailed as a breakthrough, the United States decision to withdraw from it has cast into doubt the future of coordinated global abatement efforts. However, the increasing frequency of extreme weather events (e.g., floods, storms, droughts, extreme heat events) and their human impact will cause the pressure for action to intensify in the years ahead. The question is more a matter of how quickly the intensifying pressure for action will reach a tipping point and will that tipping point come in time? The growing number of credible reports expressing serious concerns over the future of seaside metropolises such as Miami due to sea level rises, the increasing frequency of storms, and imminent threats to its water supply will hopefully hasten that tipping point and advance needed changes before it is too late.[48]

There is also mounting evidence of the advantages that can accrue to organizations that think about these issues proactively and align their strategies and actions with their commitment to sustainability and corporate social responsibility.[49] Reported benefits range from increased employee commitment to positive customer reactions and improved financial performance. The reputational damage firms incur when they are found to have failed to behave responsibly can be severe (e.g., Volkswagen's falsification of diesel emissions tests).[50]

New Technologies

In addition to responding to environmental and demographic changes in the workplace and marketplace, organizations and their leaders must embrace the trite but true statements about the impact of technological change. Underpinning technological change is the sweeping impact that the digitization of information is having. The quantity of data available to managers is mind-boggling. It is estimated that digital data will grow from 400 billion gigabytes of Web-enabled data in 2013 to 40 trillion gigabytes by 2020.[51] The explosion in the amount of data available will be aided by the impact of inexpensive nano-scale microelectronics that will allow us to add sensors and collection capacity to just about anything. The use of *data mining* methodologies and artificial intelligence is becoming increasingly common in organizations that seek to transform data into information.[52] The following list of technological innovations points to the breadth of changes we can anticipate. This is not the stuff of science fiction. In most of these areas, applications are already present and costs are declining rapidly:

- Software that writes its own code, reducing human error

- Health care by cell phone, laptop, and app

- Vertical farming to save space and increase yield[53]

- The Internet of Things, cloud technology, and crowd sourcing are providing access to massive data pools that can be translated into useful information and action.

- The automation of knowledge work

- Advanced robotics, from industrial applications to surgery

- Wearable computing, from basic data gathering to human augmentation and computer–brain interfaces

- Autonomous and near autonomous vehicles

- Next-generation genomics, from agricultural applications to substance production (e.g., fuel) and disease treatment applications

- Renewable energy and energy storage breakthroughs that will change energy access and cost equations

- 3-D printing for applications as varied as the production of auto parts and human body parts

- Advanced materials (e.g., nano technology) for a host of applications that will result in dramatic reductions in weight and improvements in strength, flexibility, and connectivity

- Advanced oil and gas exploration and recovery technologies[54]

- The use of blockchain technologies and cyber currencies is likely to change the way we undertake and securely record transactions on digital ledgers that can't be tampered with. These can be used to record and track the ownership those assets over time, execute contracts, transfer ownership rights and obligations, and make payments, to name a few of the potential applications.

Technology has woven our world together. The number of international air passengers rose from 75 million in 1970 to an estimated 3.7 billion in 2016.[55] The cost of a 3-minute phone call from the United States to England dropped from more than $8 in 1976 to less than $0.06 in 2014 when VoIP (voice over Internet protocol) is used for a call to a landline or cell phone. When both the sender and receiver have the appropriate software (e.g., Skype, WhatsApp) then the cost goes to 0. The number of transborder calls in the United States was 200 million in 1980.[56] Estimates of the numbers today are in the tens of billions. VoIP has disrupted traditional long-distance telephone markets dramatically, and the proliferation of alternative communication channels, including SMS texting, BBM (Blackberry Messenger), Facebook, and their equivalents on other platforms have transformed the communication landscape. The number of cell phones in use totaled 6.8 billion in 2013, meaning one for almost every person alive.[57] In 2017, there were an estimated 2.32 billion smartphone users, meaning access to digital information and apps for everything from weather forecasts to online purchasing and the transfer of funds. Even those without access to a bank or smartphone can transfer cash safely and securely on a regular cell phone in some developing parts of the world—Google "M-Pesa" for an example of this.[58]

Our embrace of digital technology and connectedness has opened the world to us and made it incredibly accessible, but it has come with costs. Security concerns related to viruses and hacking have also escalated, and serious breaches are a common occurrence. The Ponemon Institute estimates that in the United States alone, 110 million adults had their personal information exposed by hackers during a 12-month period in 2013. In September 2018 Facebook reported that 50 million of its accounts were directly affected by a hack.[59] The cost to firms responding to these threats and breaches are in the billions, and that doesn't include the damage done to customer trust and loyalty. Costs related to online fraud and identity theft are in the billions (some put the estimates in excess of $100 billion) and growing rapidly. These issues will not go away any time soon.[60] Issues related to the loss of privacy, industrial espionage, and sabotage involving both firms and government agencies have also become common.[61] On a business-to-business level, supply chains woven together through software allows them to operate effectively and efficiently, while at the same time opening them to risks.[62]

With the Internet, students around the globe can access the same quality of information that the best researchers have if it is in the public domain (which is increasingly the case) and if their government hasn't censored access to it. At the same time, the technology that has made the world smaller has also produced a technological divide between haves and have-nots that has the potential to produce social and political instability. Aspects of the gap are closing, as is seen in the growth of cell phones, smartphones, and Internet access in the developing world. Laptops and tablets are now available at well under $100, and the cost in India has dropped to below $50.[63] Lack of access to clean water, sufficient food, and needed medication is less likely to be tolerated in silence when media images tell people that others have an abundance of such resources and lack the will to share. Events such as the Arab Spring, Occupy Wall Street, the 2014 election of Narendra Modi as India's prime minister, and the 2017 Women's March point to the power this technology has in mobilizing public interest and action. Technology transforms relationships. Facebook, LinkedIn, Twitter, and their equivalents keep us connected, 19% of U.S. newlyweds in 2017 were reported to have met online, and people have even been found attempting to text in their sleep.[64]

THE NEW CHANGE TOOL ON THE BLOCK

Social media has fundamentally altered thinking about change management. It has changed how information is framed, who frames it, and how quickly it migrates from the few to the many. It can stimulate interest, understanding, involvement, and commitment to your initiative, and it can also be used to create anxiety and confusion, and used to mobilize opposition and resistance. It can create communities of shared interest, but it can also serve to isolate communities when they choose to only search out information that confirms their view of the situation. The one thing it can't be is being ignored!

Our purpose is not to catalogue all new and emerging technologies. Rather, our intent is to signal to change leaders the importance of paying attention to technological trends and the impact they have on organizations, now and in the future. As a result of these forces, product development and life cycles are shortened, marketing channels are changing, and managers must respond in a time-paced fashion. Competitors can leapfrog organizations and drop once-market-leaders into obsolescence through a technological breakthrough. The advantages of vertical integration can vanish as technical insights in one segment of the business drive down the costs, migrate the technology through outsourcing to other segments, or otherwise alter the value chain in ways that had not been anticipated.

Is this overstating the importance of paying attention to how rapidly technological and social change can alter the competitive landscape? BlackBerry went from creating and dominating the smartphone business to less than 3% market share in five years. Dramatic downsizing and reinvention became the order of the day as the BlackBerry executives searched for new paths and renewed market relevance; it took them years to regain their competitive footing as a cybersecurity software and connected cars firm.[65] Now shift your thoughts to the automotive sector. What will the emergence of self-driving electric vehicles mean for manufacturers and their suppliers and distributors? What will they mean for city planners, urban transit, and the taxi driver? Prototypes are currently driving on the streets of Mountain View, California, and elsewhere. Expectations are that these sorts of vehicles will be for sale by 2020.[66] The watchword for change leaders is: be aware of technological trends and be proactive in considering how to respond to organizationally relevant ones.

Political Changes

The external political landscape of an organization is a reality that change leaders need to pay attention to and figure out how to engage. Even the largest of multinationals has minimal impact on shaping the worldwide geopolitical landscape and the focus of governing bodies.[67] However, if they are attentive and nimble, their interests will be better served.

The collapse of the Soviet Empire gave rise to optimism in the West that democracy and the market economy were the natural order of things, the only viable option for modern society.[68] With the end of communism in Russia, there was the sense that there was no serious competitor to free-market democracy and the belief existed that the world would gradually move to competitive capitalism with market discipline.

Of course, this optimism was not realized. Nationalistic border quarrels (India–Pakistan, for example) continue. Some African countries have become less committed to democracy (Zimbabwe and Ethiopia). Nation-states have dissolved into microstates (Yugoslavia and Sudan) or had portions annexed as in the case of Crimea. While American power may still be dominant worldwide, September 11, 2001 (9/11) demonstrated that even the dominant power cannot guarantee safety. Non-nation-states and religious groups have become actors on the global stage. The Middle East, north and central parts of Africa, the Ukraine, Venezuela, and Central Asia continue to be in turmoil, creating political and economic uncertainty.

Changes in the economic performance of nations have also altered the geopolitical landscape. Growth in China and India, though it has slowed, continues to advance much more than twice the rate of the developed world.[69] They led the world out of the 2007–2008 crash, and in some periods have been joined by other African and Asian nations that are experiencing more rapid economic growth than the developed world. However, progress in the developing world has slowed in the face of global concerns related to protectionism, trade wars, and constrained capital flows[70]. Grinding poverty rates, though improving, are still the reality for hundreds of millions of people who live in these areas.[71]

As organizations become global, they need to clarify their own ethical standards. Not only will they need to understand the rules and regulations of each country, they will also have to determine what norms of conduct they will work to establish for their organizational members, and what constitutes acceptable and unacceptable behavior. Peter Eigen, chairman of Transparency International, states, "Political elites and their cronies continue to take kickbacks at every opportunity. Hand-in-glove with corrupt business people, they are trapping whole nations in poverty and hampering sustainable development. Corruption is perceived to be dangerously high in poor parts of the world, but also in many countries whose firms invest in developing nations."[72] Left unaddressed, political corruption can become embedded in organizations. Transparency International finds bribery most common in public works and construction and arms and defense corporations as compared with agriculture.[73] The accounting and governance scandals of 2001 to 2002 (Enron and WorldCom), followed by an almost uninterrupted series of major ethical lapses in global financial services/banking, pharmaceutical, and government sectors (to name just three), have created public demands for transparency, accountability, regulations with teeth, and heightened expectations that firms should be expected to behave in socially responsible manners. Some companies, Hewlett-Packard, H&M, Tesco, Loblaw, and Apple, for example, have responded by requiring that they and the participants in their supply chain adhere to a set of specified ethical standards. Further, they are committed to working with their suppliers to ensure they reach these standards.[74]

The politics of globalization and the environment have created opportunities and issues for organizations. The United States' Obama administration was committed to the introduction of new green energy initiatives, but the election of Donald Trump has placed U.S. progress in this area in doubt.

The desire to reduce the world's dependence on foreign oil and coal has meant subsidy programs for new technologies and opportunities for businesses in those fields. It has also led to an explosion of energy recovery methods, such as fracking, which bring with them their own ethical issues. Some organizations are restructuring themselves to seize such opportunities. For example, Siemens has reorganized itself into three sectors—industry, energy, and health care—to focus on megatrends.[75] Senge and his colleagues argued that the new environmentalism would be driven by innovation and would result in radical new technologies, products, processes, and business models.[76] The rapid rates of market penetration for such technologies and the decline in their costs are evidence that Senge was right.

The politics of the world are not the everyday focus for all managers, but change leaders need to understand their influence on market development and attractiveness, competitiveness, and the resulting pressures on boards and executives. Firms doing business in jurisdictions such as Russia, China, and Argentina know this all too well. Issues related to climate change, water and food security, power, urbanization/smart cities, public transport, immigration, health care, education, trade, employment, and our overall health and safety will continue to influence political discussion and decision making at all levels—from the local to the international context. A sudden transformation of the political landscape can trash the best-laid strategic plan. The growth of populist and anti-global sentiments in Europe and the United States has demonstrated how political surprises (e.g., the Brexit vote in the UK and the election of Donald Trump) can quickly disrupt existing relationships (e.g., alliances, markets, supply chains) and create high levels of uncertainty as to what lies ahead. It's been argued that the rise of these movements is attributable to the declining size of the middle class in many countries, the massing of wealth by elites, and the declining sense in parts of the population that a positive future is available, given current conditions and trends.[77]

Successful change leaders will have a keen sense of the opportunities and dangers involved in global, national, and local political shifts. If they are behaving in a manner consistent with corporate social responsibility, they will also have a keen sense of the opportunities and dangers related to the issues themselves.

The Economy

In 2007, the world economy crashed into financial crisis and appeared headed for a 1930s depression. Trillions of dollars of asset-backed paper became valueless, seemingly overnight. Investors and pension funds lost 20% of their value. Global stock markets shrank by $30 trillion, or half their value.[78] The American housing market, which provided an illusory asset base, collapsed and led to the credit crisis. Firms that were chastised for having too much cash on hand and were seen as missing opportunities suddenly became the survivors when credit vanished. At the individual firm level, the economic crisis led to layoffs and bankruptcies. Firms saw their order books shrink and business disappear. Entire industries, such as the automotive industry, were overwhelmed and certain large automotive manufacturers might have vanished if not for government bailouts. An example of the impact on one small firm is shown in the story below.

THE IMPACT OF THE 2007–2009 RECESSION ON A SMALL BUSINESS

Serge Gaudet operates a wholesale and retail drapery and window blind business in the small Canadian town of Sturgeon Falls, Ontario. The world economic crisis suddenly became real when banks would no longer extend him credit. In his words, "I had signed orders, contracts in hand, and my bank refused my line of credit so that I could buy the inventory. How was I to finance this deal? I had the contract and it was with a government hospital. Surely, this was creditworthy? What else could I do?"

Mr. Gaudet managed through the crisis by negotiating newer, tougher terms with his bank. But the lack of credit was not his only problem. "Normally, I bid on requests for proposals and win a reasonable percentage of them," he reported. "Suddenly, there was nothing to bid on. Nothing. Every institution that was going to buy blinds was waiting—waiting for government aid that was very slow in coming. It was touch-and-go whether I could last until new contracts came in."

Mr. Gaudet's story is typical of the situation faced by many small businesses as they struggled through the economic crisis of 2007–2009. Many did not survive. Those that did were able to do so because they had low overhead and debt.[79] As of 2019, Mr Gaudet continues to successfully operate his business.

Governments responded to the economic crisis with Keynesian abandon. G20 countries ran huge deficits as governments tried to stimulate their economies out of recession. America's federal deficit hit 83% of GDP in 2009, and the overall debt to GDP went from 62% in 2007 to 99% in 2012.[80] In December 2010, economists were talking about a slow recovery in America and an almost nonexistent one in Europe, and they were right.[81] Economists also predicted that China would have an 8.6% GDP growth and 11.1% investment growth, with significant growth also predicted for India, the BRICS nations and other parts of the developing world (in particular, Africa). While growth in these economies has not been as robust as expected during the 2010s, most (with the exception of Russia) performed relatively well until around 2016 when significant economic headwinds emerged. These headwinds have varied in nature from country to country (e.g., declining foreign direct investment, serious and credible corruption allegations leading to political uncertainty, growing protectionism). However, most economists believe there has been a shift in the economic order of the world toward the developing world and that is not about to reverse. Initiatives such as China's One Belt and One Road initiative and its involvement in African development reinforce this.[82]

As slower rates of growth in the developed world became the norm, frustration was building within those countries amongst those who were feeling marginalized and left behind economically. Their economic concerns were coupled with growing fears about immigration, unfair trade, societal norms, and their place in society. While Donald Trump's "Make America Great Again" campaign provides a window on the U.S. context, Brexit in the UK, and the rise of nationalistic governments elsewhere, for example, Austria, Italy, and Turkey, suggest that this is not an isolated phenomenon. Though Keynesian solutions were quickly applied to triage the 2008 crisis, budgetary discipline at the national level in many countries has been missing in action in the 2018 period. Budgetary deficits are ballooning in a number of countries at a time when most economists would suggest we should be saving for a rainy day, creating escalating risk for a financial crash.[83] For example, the Congressional Budget Office predicts the U.S. deficit to rise to $1 trillion by 2020 and 148% of GDP by 2047.[84] This suggests the economic fallout that will accompany the next downturn will be exacerbated due to our level of indebtedness.

The lessons from the economic crisis and subsequent developments are centered on risk management and capacity building. In a world where everything is interconnected, organizations need to be able to respond quickly. In order to do so, organizations need the capacity to weather numerous challenges. Ideally, organizations will incorporate the mechanisms to anticipate these challenges and adapt their management and leadership practices to hold the underlying social fabric of the firm. In many situations, these anticipatory mechanisms will not be available and organizations will need to rely on their ability to adapt and change as the environment shifts.

See **Toolkit Exercise 1.2** to practice thinking about environmental forces facing your organization and their implications.

THE IMPLICATIONS OF WORLDWIDE TRENDS FOR CHANGE MANAGEMENT

The economic globalization of the world, the demographic and social shifts around the globe, technological changes, environmental and ecological pressures, and the upheaval and political and economic uncertainties around the world form the reality of organizational environments. Predicting specific short-run changes is a fool's errand. Nevertheless, change leaders need to have a keen sense of just how these seemingly external events impact internal organizational dynamics. "How will external changes drive strategy and internal adjustments and investments?" has become a critical question that change leaders need to address. For example, the rise of the sharing economy has disrupted traditional business structures of the hotel and taxi business. Airbnb and Uber have both capitalized on globalization trends and technological innovations to improve access to information relevant to travelers, increase social trust, and through these mechanisms change the way that people travel.[85]

In 2002, Barkema, Baum, and Mannix predicted that certain macro environmental changes would change organizational forms and competitive dynamics and, in turn, lead to new management challenges.[86] They captured three **macro changes** facing us today: digitization of information; integration of nation states and the opening of international markets; and the geographic dispersion of the value chain. These are leading to the globalization of markets. This globalization, in turn, will drive significant shifts in organizational forms and worldwide competitive dynamics. Table 1.1 summarizes Barkema and colleagues' article. Column 1 outlines those three macro changes, column 2 the new organizational forms and competitive dynamics arising from them, and column 3, the new management challenges that arise from these.

The early decades of the 21st century suggest accelerated change in comparison to the latter part of the 20th century. Diversity, synchronization and time-pacing requirements, decision making, the frequency of environmental discontinuities, quick industry life cycles and in consequence product and service obsolescence, and competency traps all suggest greater complexity and a more rapid organizational pace for today and tomorrow. As such, middle managers will play increasingly significant roles in making change effective in their organizations in both evolutionary and revolutionary scenarios. Barkema et al. argue that much change today deals with mid-level change—change that is more than incremental but not truly revolutionary. However, increasing rates of disruption in retail, finance/banking, technology, manufacturing, mining, media, insurance

Table 1.1   New Organizational Forms and Management Challenges Based on Environmental Change

Macro Changes and Impacts	New Organizational Forms and Competitive Dynamics	New Management Challenges
• Digitization leading to faster information transmission, lower-cost information storage and transmission • Integration of nation states, and opening of markets • Geographic dispersion of the value chain • All leading to globalization of markets	• Global small and medium-sized enterprises • Global constellations of organizations (i.e., networks) • Large, focused global firms • All leading to spread of autonomous, dislocated teams; digitally enabled structures; intense global rivalry; and running faster while seeming to stand still	• Greater diversity • Greater synchronization requirements • Greater time-pacing requirements • Faster decision making, learning, and innovation • More frequent environmental discontinuities • Faster industry life cycles • Faster newness and obsolescence of knowledge • Risk of competency traps where old competencies no longer produce desired effects • Greater newness and obsolescence of organizations

Source: Adapted from Barkema, H. G., Baum, J. A. C., & Mannix, E. A. (2002). Management challenges in a new time. *Academy of Management Journal*, 45(5), 916–930.

and other sectors is challenging this assumption and giving rise to the belief that if we don't disrupt ourselves, our competitors will.[87]

Four Types of Organizational Change

Organizational changes come in different shapes and sizes: mergers, acquisitions, buyouts, downsizing, restructuring, outsourcing the human resource function or computer services, departmental reorganizations, installations of new incentive systems, shutting particular manufacturing lines or opening new branches in other parts of the world, and the list goes on. All of these describe specific organizational changes. The literature on organizational change classifies such changes into two types, episodic or discontinuous change and continuous change. That is, change can be dramatic and sudden—the introduction of a new technology that makes a business obsolete or new government regulations that immediately shift the competitive landscape. Or, change can be much more gradual, such as the alteration of core competencies of an organization through training and adding key individuals.

Under dramatic or episodic change, organizations are seen as having significant inertia. Change is infrequent and discontinuous. Reengineering programs are examples of this type of change and can be viewed as planned examples of injecting significant change into an organization. On the other hand, under continuous change, organizations are seen as more emergent and self-organizing, where change is constant, evolving, and cumulative.[88] Japanese automobile manufacturers have led the way in this area with *kaizen* programs focused on encouraging continuous change. In the technology sectors, collaborative approaches, facilitated by social networks that extend beyond corporate boundaries and even crowd sourcing, are giving rise to continuous change models for organizational adaptation, growth, and renewal.[89]

A second dimension of change is whether it occurs in a proactive, planned, and programmatic fashion or reactively in response to external events. Programmatic or planned change occurs when managers anticipate events and shift their organizations as a result. For example, Intel, a multinational semiconductor chip maker headquartered in California, anticipates and encourages a cycle of computer chip obsolescence.[90] As a result, the organization has been designed to handle this obsolescence. Alternately, shifts in an organization's external world lead to a reaction on the part of the organization. For example, the emergence of low-cost airlines has led to traditional carriers employing reactive strategies, such as cutting routes, costs, and service levels in an attempt to adapt.[91]

Nadler and Tushman combine these two dimensions in a useful model illustrating different types of change (see Table 1.2). They define four categories of change: tuning, adapting, redirecting or reorienting, and overhauling or re-creating.

Tuning is defined as small, relatively minor changes made on an ongoing basis in a deliberate attempt to improve the efficiency or effectiveness of the organization. Responsibility for acting on these sorts of changes typically rests with middle management. Most improvement change initiatives that grow out of existing quality-improvement programs would fall into this category. Adapting is viewed as relatively minor changes made in response to external stimuli—a reaction to things observed in the environment, such as competitors' moves or customer shifts. Relatively minor changes to customer servicing caused by

Table 1.2 Types of Organizational Change

	Incremental/Continuous	Discontinuous/Radical
Anticipatory	**Tuning** Incremental change made in anticipation of future events Need is for internal alignment Focuses on individual components or subsystems Middle-management role Implementation is the major task For example, a quality improvement initiative from an employee improvement committee	**Redirecting or Reorienting** Strategic proactive changes based on predicted major changes in the environment Need is for positioning the whole organization to a new reality Focuses on all organizational components Senior management creates sense of urgency and motivates the change For example, a major change in product or service offering in response to opportunities identified
Reactive	**Adapting** Incremental changes made in response to environmental changes Need is for internal alignment Focuses on individual components or subsystems Middle-management role Implementation is the major task For example, modest changes to customer services in response to customer complaints	**Overhauling or Re-creating** Response to a significant performance crisis Need to reevaluate the whole organization, including its core values Focuses on all organizational components to achieve rapid, system-wide change Senior management creates vision and motivates optimism For example, a major realignment of strategy, involving plant closures and changes to product and service offerings, to stem financial losses and return the firm to profitability

Source: Adapted from Nadler, D. A., & Tushman, M. (1989, August). Organizational frame bending: Principles for managing reorientation. *Academy of Management Executive, 3*(3), 196.

reports of customer dissatisfaction or defection to a competitor provide an example of this sort of change, and once again, responsibility for such changes tends to reside within the role of middle managers.

Redirecting or reorienting involves major, strategic change resulting from planned programs. These frame-bending shifts are designed to provide new perspectives and directions in a significant way. For example, a shift in a firm to develop a customer service organization and culture would fall in this category. Finally, **overhauling or re-creation** is the dramatic shift that occurs in reaction to major external events. Often there is a crisis situation that forces the change—thus, the emergence of low-cost carriers forced traditional airlines to re-create what they do. Likewise, the credit crisis bankrupted General Motors and forced a complete overhaul and downsizing of the company.

The impact of the change increases as we move from minor alterations and fine-tuning to changes that require us to reorient and re-create the organization. Not surprisingly, reorienting and re-creating an organization is much more time-consuming and challenging to lead effectively. These activities also have a greater impact on individuals who must reorient themselves. Regardless of difficulty, the financial crisis and recession of 2008–2009 forced companies to react. While there are no data that we know of to confirm this, anticipatory organizational change does not seem to be sufficient to prepare organizations for the dramatic shift in the global business environment presented by 2008–2009. While planning can help organizations think about risk and opportunities, it was their awareness and adaptive capacity that allowed firms to respond and survive the crisis. The escalating interest in heightening adaptive capacities within organizations reflects the importance of this.[92]

An examination of the history of British Airways provides a classic example of a single organization facing both incremental and discontinuous change while both anticipating issues and being forced to react.[93]

BRITISH AIRWAYS: STRATEGIC AND INCREMENTAL CHANGE

Todd Jick's case study describes the crisis of 1981. British Airways' (BA's) successful response in the 1980s was revolutionary in nature. During that period, BA revolutionized its culture and its view of the customer with outstanding results. In the 1990s, BA entered a period of slow decline as the systems and structures at BA became increasingly incongruent with the new deregulated environment and the successful competitors that were spawned by that environment.

Major upheavals in international travel pushed BA into a reactive mode following 9/11, and the results of management's attempts to develop new strategies were unclear for a considerable period. A strike in the summer of 2003 created more uncertainty for the firm.[94] The dramatic rise in oil costs during 2007 and 2008 forced BA to cut costs and implement a merger with Iberia. These strategic moves to cut costs were matched by more incremental internal actions to limit the wages of cabin

staff to match those of its competitors. These changes led to limited strike action in 2010 and a negotiated resolution in 2011, which was facilitated by the arrival of new chief negotiators on both sides—Keith Williams, BA's new president, and Len McCluskey, the union's new general secretary. Fleet renewal (their first Airbus A380 was put into service in 2013), along with ongoing changes to systems, processes, and procedures were undertaken in and around that time.[95]

Roll the clock forward to 2018 and new and recurring strategic and operational challenges have emerged that BA must manage. These include issues related to Brexit, aggressive competitors, labour challenges, data security, and other IT related issues (e.g., the IT failure that grounded 75,000 people for days in May 2017).[96] These mark the continuance of their change journey, marked by both strategic and incremental change initiatives.

Nadler and Tushman raise this question: "Will incremental change be sufficient or will radical change be necessary in the long run?" Suffice it to say that this question has not been answered. However, the Japanese provided a profound lesson in the value of incremental, daily changes. Interestingly enough, it was a lesson the Japanese industrialists learned from North American management scholars such as Duran and Deming. If one observes employee involvement and continuous improvement processes effectively employed,[97] one also sees organizational team members that are energized, goal directed, cohesive, and increasingly competent because of the new things they are learning. Such teams expect that tomorrow will be a little different from today. Further, when more significant changes have to be embraced, these teams are likely to be far less resistant and fearful of them because of their earlier experiences with facilitating change within group structures. Organizational change is part of daily life for them.

Many think of incremental/continuous change and discontinuous/radical change as states rather than a perspective or a spectrum of change size. From an organization's point of view, a departmental reorganization might seem incremental. However, from the department's perspective, it may seem discontinuous and radical. As Morgan puts it,

> A mythology is developing in which incremental and quantum change are presented as opposites. Nothing could be further from the truth. . . . True, there is a big difference between incremental and quantum change when we talk of results (but) incremental and quantum change are intertwined. As we set our sights on those 500% improvements, remember they're usually delivered through 5, 10, and 15% initiatives.[98]

The perception of the magnitude of the change lies in the eye of the beholder. Incremental changes at the organizational level may appear disruptive and revolutionary at a department level. However, as noted earlier, those who are accustomed to facing and managing incremental change on a regular basis will likely view more revolutionary changes in less threatening terms. Those who have not faced and managed change will be more likely to view even incremental changes as threatening.

Organizational members need to learn to accept and value the perspectives of both the adaptor (those skilled in incremental change) and the innovator (those skilled in radical change).[99] As a change agent, personal insight regarding your abilities and preferences for more modest or more radical change is critical. The secret to successful organizational growth and development over time lies in the capacity of organizational members to embrace both approaches to change at the appropriate times and to understand that they are, in fact, intertwined.[100]

Planned Changes Don't Always Produce the Intended Results

To this point, it is clear that change—from simple fine-tuning to radical reconstruction—is a necessary prerequisite to organizational survival. However, successful change is extremely difficult to execute as the scope and complexity increases. Many types of change initiatives have failed: reengineering, total quality management, activity-based costing, joint optimization, strategic planning, and network structures.[101] If change leaders were to fully consider the failure rates when designing interventions or acquisitions, fear would trump action. As one manager put it, "The opportunity has turned out to be 10 times what I thought it would be. The challenges have turned out to be 20 times what I thought they were!"[102]

Fortunately or unfortunately, inaction and avoidance are no solution. Maintaining the status quo typically does not sustain competitive advantage, particularly in troubled organizations. Delays and half-hearted efforts that begin only after the problems have become critical increase costs and decrease the likelihood of a successful transformation. As Hamel and Prahalad put it, "No company can escape the need to re-skill its people, reshape its product portfolio, redesign its process, and redirect resources."[103] Organizations that consistently demonstrate their capacity to innovate, manage change, and adapt over the years are the ones with staying power.[104]

Hamel and Prahalad believe that restructuring and reengineering, on their own, do little to increase the capabilities of the firm. These two Rs increase profitability and can enhance competitiveness but "in many companies . . . re-engineering (and restructuring) . . . are more about catching up than getting out in front."[105] Hamel and Prahalad argue that companies need to regenerate their strategy and reinvent their industry by building their capacity to compete. These transformations and realignments that result are sustained marathons, not quick fixes. Skilled change leaders provide a coherent vision of the change and do all that they can to help people adapt and embrace the changes with realistic expectations. When change recipients understand that things will often get worse before they get better, but also believe that the benefits are well worth the effort, change initiatives are more likely to be sustained.[106] For example, as costs rise in China, the environment is shifting manufacturing elsewhere, including a rebirth of manufacturing in the United States. This trend demands a continuing evolution of strategy as well as reshaping of supply chains to alter ingrained overseas production practices that have evolved over the past 15 years—changes that manufacturing and supply chain managers may have difficulty adjusting to.[107]

Radical solutions both terrify and fascinate managers. Often managers are comfortable with relatively small technological fixes as the source of products, services, efficiency, and effectiveness. However, they tend to fear interventions that seem to reduce their control over situations, people, and outcomes. When organizations embrace technology but not people, they pay a steep price. They reduce the likelihood that the change will produce the desired results and they fail to take advantage of the collective capacity of organizational members to improve operations, products, and services. To say the least, this practice is extremely wasteful of human capacity and energy, causing them to atrophy over time. Investment in infrastructure alone is insufficient,[108] and as a result, increasing attention is being directed toward matters such as employee engagement, commitment and organizational agility (the ability to rapidly and successful adapt to changing conditions).[109]

ORGANIZATIONAL CHANGE ROLES

Without a sense of vision, purpose, and engagement, it is easy to become a passive recipient of change. As a passive recipient, you see yourself as subject to the whims of others, as relatively helpless, perhaps even as a victim. As a passive recipient, your self-esteem and self-efficacy may feel as if they are under attack.[110] Your perception of power and influence will diminish and you will feel acted on. Years ago, Jack Gordon talked about aligning employees. That is, once top management has decided on the strategic direction, employees need to be aligned with that direction. We cannot help but think that if you are the recipient of change, "being aligned" just won't feel very good.[111]

Who are the participants in organizational change? Many employees will step up and make the change work. They will be the **change implementers**, the ones making happen what others, the **change initiators**, have pushed or encouraged. Change initiators, or champions, also frame the vision for the change and/or provide resources and support for the initiative. Or, employees can be on the receiving end of change, **change recipients**. Some employees will play a role in facilitating change—**change facilitators** won't be the ones responsible for implementing the change, but they will assist initiators and implementers in the change through their contacts and consultative assistance.

Of course, one person might play multiple roles. That is, a person might have a good idea and talk it up in the organization (change initiator); take action to make the change occur (change implementer); talk to others to help them manage the change (change facilitator); and, ultimately, be affected by the change too (change recipient). In this book, we use the terms **change leader** and **change agent** interchangeably. Change initiators, change implementers, and change facilitators are different roles than played by the change leader or agent. At any given moment, the person leading the change may be initiating, implementing, or facilitating. Table 1.3 outlines the roles that people play in organizational change.

Change Initiators

Change initiators get things moving, take action, and stimulate the system. They are the ones seeking to initiate change to make things better. They identify the need for change, develop the vision of a better future, take on the change tasks, and champion the initiative. Change initiators may face considerable risk in the organization. To use a physical metaphor, action creates movement, movement creates friction, and friction creates heat! And creating heat may help or hurt one's career. Change initiators need to take calculated actions and be prepared to undertake the work needed to create and support the powerful arguments and coalitions to effect change in organizations from the top or the middle of the organization.

Change initiators will find useful aids for change in this book. We, as authors, cannot supply the passion and powerful vision needed by initiators, but we can point out the requirements of successful change: planning, persuasion, passion, and perseverance. And we can provide frameworks for analysis that will enhance the likelihood of successful change.

Change initiators need to be dogged in their desire and determination. Those who succeed will earn reputations for realistic, grounded optimism, for a good sense of timing, and for not giving up. If nothing else, the opposition may tire in the face of their persistence. Better yet are those who have the uncanny ability to creatively combine with others into a coalition that turns resisters into allies and foot draggers into foot soldiers and advocates for change.

Change Implementers

Many would-be and existing managers find themselves as change implementers. Others, including their bosses, may initiate the change, but it is left to the

Table 1.3 Managerial Roles and Organizational Change

Roles	Role Description
Change leader or agent	The person who leads the change. He or she may play any or all of the initiator, implementer, or facilitator roles. Often, but not always, this person is the formal change leader. However, informal change leaders will emerge and lead change as well. (Note: In this book, change leader and change agent are used interchangeably.)
Change initiator	The person who identifies the need and vision for change and champions the change and advocates for it in the organization.
Change implementer	The person who has responsibility for making certain the change happens, charting the path forward, nurturing support, and alleviating resistance.
Change facilitator	The person who assists initiators, implementers, and recipients with the change-management process. Identifies process and content change issues and helps resolve these, fosters support, alleviates resistance, and provides other participants with guidance and council.
Change recipient	The person who is affected by the change. Often the person has to change his or her behavior to ensure the change is effective.

implementers to make it work. This role is critical. Pfeffer argues that effectiveness doesn't come from making the critical decision but rather from managing the consequences of decisions and creating the desired results.[112] As he says, "If change were going to be easy, it would already have happened." The change implementer's role is important and needed in organizations. Without it, there is no bridge to the desired end state—no sustained integrated approach.[113]

Change implementers will find much in this book to assist them. They will find guidance in creating and increasing the need for the changes that change initiators are demanding. They will find tools for organizational diagnosis and for identifying and working with key stakeholders. And they will find concepts and techniques to facilitate the internal alignment of systems, processes, and people; improve their action plans and implementation skills; and help them sustain themselves during the transition.

At the same time, we encourage and challenge change implementers to stay engaged, to stay active, and to initiate change themselves. Oshry identifies the dilemma of "middle powerlessness," where the middle manager feels trapped between tops and bottoms and becomes ineffective as a result.[114] Many middle managers transform their organizations by recognizing strategic initiatives and mobilizing the power of the "middles" to move the organization in the direction needed.

Change Facilitators

Today's complex organizational changes can fail because parties lock into positions or because perspectives get lost in personalities and egos. In such cases, an outside view can facilitate change. Change facilitators understand change processes and assist the organization to work through change issues. As such, they sometimes formally serve as consultants to change leaders and teams.

However, many of those who act as change facilitators do so informally, often on the strength of their existing relationships with others involved with the change. They have high levels of self-awareness and emotional maturity and are skilled in the behavioral arts—using their interpersonal skills to work with teams or groups.

In this book, change facilitators will discover frameworks that will help them to understand change processes. With these frameworks, they will be able to translate concrete organizational events into understandable situations and so ease change. And their knowledge and interpersonal skills will provide change perspectives that will allow managers to unfreeze their positions.

Common Challenges for Managerial Roles

Table 1.4 highlights common sources of difficulty that change initiators, implementers, and facilitators face when attempting to implement planned changes. While there are external factors that can frustrate progress in unanticipated and undesirable directions, this table focuses on ways in which change leaders act as their own worst enemies, self-sabotaging their own initiatives. They stem from predispositions, perceptions, and a lack of self-awareness. The good news is that they also represent areas that a person can do something about if he or she becomes self-aware and chooses to take the blinders off.

Change Recipients

Change recipients are those who find themselves on the receiving end of change. Their responses will vary from active resistance, passivity, to active support,

Table 1.4   Common Managerial Difficulties in Dealing With Organizational Change

1. Managers are action oriented and assume other rational people will see the inherent wisdom in the proposed change and will learn the needed new behaviors. Or, managers assume that they will be able to replace recalcitrant employees.

2. Managers assume they have the power and influence to enact the desired changes, and they underestimate the power and influence of other stakeholders.

3. Managers look at the transition period activities as a cost, not an investment that increases the prospects for success and reduces failure risks.

4. Managers are unable to accurately estimate the resources and commitment needed to facilitate the integration of the human dimension with other aspects of the change (e.g., systems, structures, technologies).

5. Managers are unaware that their own behavior, and that of other key managers, may be sending out conflicting messages to employees and eventually customers.

6. Managers find managing human processes unsettling (even threatening) because of the potential emotionality and the difficulties they present with respect to prediction and quantification.

7. Managers simply lack the capacity (attitudes, skills, and abilities) to manage complex changes that involve people. When those managing the change get defensive, the minds of others tend to close rather than open.

8. Managers' critical judgment is impaired due to factors related to overconfidence[115] and/or groupthink.

depending upon their perceptions of the change, its rationale, and its impact. When people feel acted upon and with little or no voice or control in the process, dissatisfaction, frustration, alienation, absenteeism, and turnover are common responses to demands for change.[116] This book provides guidance that will help recipients to better understand what is happening to them and their organizations. Further, it will identify strategies and approaches that will help change recipients to take an active role and increase the amount of control they have over organizational events.

Regardless of your role in the organization—change recipient, change implementer, change initiator, or change facilitator—this book contains useful tools. Change recipients will understand what is happening to them and will learn how to respond positively. Change implementers will develop their capacity to use tools that increase their effectiveness, and change initiators will learn to take more effective actions to lever their change programs. Change facilitators will find themselves with new insights into easing organizational change.

See **Toolkit Exercise 1.3** to think about change roles you've played in the past.

Gary Hamel of Harvard talks about "leading the revolution"—anyone can play the change game. Anyone can seek opportunities, ask questions, challenge orthodoxies, and generate new ideas and directions! And in doing so, individuals from virtually anywhere in an organization (or even outside of it) can become change leaders.[117] The leadership that started Facebook and Google came from dorm rooms. The local heroes nominated by CNN viewers and profiled on their network come from all walks of life.[118] Change leaders foment action. They take independent action based on their analysis of what is best for the long-term interests of their organizations or even society, and they recognize the many faces of change and the crucial next steps necessary to meet their long-term change goals. Finally, they recognize who needs to play what roles in order to advance needed change. As such, at different points in time they fulfill the roles of change initiator, implementer, and facilitator, depending upon the needs of the situation, their skills and abilities, and their beliefs about what is required at a point in time to advance the change.

THE REQUIREMENTS FOR BECOMING A SUCCESSFUL CHANGE LEADER

Successful change leaders balance keen insight with a driving passion for action. They have that sensitivity to the external world described above and will be skilled anticipators of that world. They have a rich understanding of organizational systems—their system in particular and the degree to which continuous or strategic changes are appropriate. They understand themselves, their influence, and image in their organizational context. They have special personal characteristics— a tolerance for ambiguity, emotional maturity, self-confidence, comfort with power, a keen sense of risk assessment, a need for action and results, and persistence grounded in reasoned optimism and tenacity. Finally, while they are curious and have a strong desire to learn, they also have a deep and abiding distrust of organizational fads and recognize the negative impact of fad surfing in organizations.[119] Change leaders who see the world in simple, linear terms will have more difficulty creating effective change.[120]

Change leaders understand the rich tapestry that forms the organizational culture. They understand the stakeholder networks that pattern organizational life. They recognize the impact and pervasiveness of organizational control systems (organizational structures, reward systems, measurement systems). They know and can reach key organizational members—both those with legitimate power and position and those with less recognizable influence. And they understand which tasks are key at *this* point in time given *this* environment and *this* organizational strategy.[121]

Successful change leaders know their personal skills, style, and abilities and how those play throughout the organization. Their credibility is the bedrock on which change actions are taken. Because change recipients will often be cynical and will examine how worthy the leaders are of their trust, change leaders must be aware of their personal blind spots and ensure these are compensated for whenever needed.

Change leaders also embrace the paradoxes of change:[122]

They are involved in both driving change and enabling change. Change leaders understand the need to persist and drive change through their organization. Without such determination, organizational inertia will slow change and other organizations will race ahead. At the same time, change leaders recognize that getting out of the way might be the most helpful management action to be taken. When those around a manager are following a passion, the best thing might be to help in whatever way possible or to provide resources to make things happen.

They recognize that resistance to change is both a problem and an opportunity. Change resistance happens in planned change. Overcoming such resistance is frequently necessary to make progress. However, change leaders recognize that there are often good reasons for resistance—the person resisting is not just being difficult or oppositional; he or she often knows things or has perspectives that cast doubt on the wisdom of a particular change initiative. Change leaders need to recognize this and work actively to overcome this paradox.

Good change leaders focus on outcomes but are careful about process. Far too often, change programs get bogged down because a focus on results leads change implementers to ignore good process. At the same time, too much attention to process can diffuse direction and lead to endless rituals of involvement and consultation. Good change leaders learn how to manage this balance.

Change leaders recognize the tension between getting on with it and changing directions. The environment is always changing. Leaders can always modify their objectives and respond to the environment. But, if this is done repeatedly, they never settle on a design and direction, and as a result, will fail to get things done. Keeping the focus on the long-term direction while making adjustments can make sense. The trick is to understand and balance this tension.

Change leaders understand the need to balance patience and impatience. Impatience may prove very helpful in overcoming inertia and fear, generating focus, energizing a change, and mobilizing for action. However, patience can also prove a valuable tool in reducing tension and establishing focus and direction, by providing time for people to learn, understand, and adjust to what is being proposed.

Finally, today's change leader knows that in today's global competition, what matters is not the absolute rate of learning, but rather the rate of learning compared to the competition. And if your organization doesn't keep pace, it loses the competitive race.

SUMMARY

This chapter defines organizational change as a planned alteration of organizational components to improve the effectiveness or efficiency of the organization. The forces that drive change today are classified under PESTEL: political, economic, social, technological, ecological/environmental, and legal. Four types of organizational change—tuning, reorienting, adapting, and re-creating—are outlined. Finally, the nature of change leaders is discussed and some of the paradoxes facing them are examined.

This chapter outlines the change roles that exist in organizations: change initiator, change implementer, change facilitator, and change recipient. Change leaders or agents could be any of the four roles, initiator, implementer, facilitator, or recipient.

Finally, the chapter outlines a summary checklist and critical questions that change leaders need to consider when thinking through matters related to how to change and what to change. See **Toolkit Exercise 1.1** for critical thinking questions for this chapter.

KEY TERMS

Organizational change—for the purposes of this book, organizational change is defined as a planned alteration of organizational components to improve the effectiveness of the organization. By organizational components, we mean the organizational mission and vision, strategy, goals, structure, process or system, technology, and people in an organization. When organizations enhance their effectiveness, they increase their ability to generate value for those they are designed to serve.

Change management—is based in a broad set of underlying disciplines (from the social sciences to information technology), tends to be strategy driven, with attention directed to whatever factors are assessed as necessary to the successful design and implementation of change.

PESTEL factors—the political, economic, social, technological, and ecological/environmental, and legal factors that describe the environment or context in which the organization functions.

Macro changes—large-scale environmental changes that are affecting organizations and what they do.

Tuning—defined as small, relatively minor changes made on an ongoing basis in a deliberate attempt to improve the efficiency or effectiveness of the organization.

Adapting—viewed as relatively minor changes made in response to external stimuli—a reaction to things observed in the environment such as competitors' moves or customer shifts.

Redirecting or reorienting—major, strategic change resulting from planned programs. These frame-bending shifts are designed to provide new perspectives and directions in a significant way.

Overhauling or re-creation—the dramatic shift that occurs in reaction to major external events. Often there is a crisis situation that forces the change.

Incremental/continuous changes— organizational changes that are relatively small in scope and incremental in nature. They may stem from the fine-tuning of existing practices or represent an incremental adaptation to environmental changes. Depending on the perspective of the change recipient, incremental change can be perceived as discontinuous/radical change.

Discontinuous/radical changes—changes that are broad in scope and impact and that may involve strategic repositioning. They usually occur in anticipation of or reaction to major environmental changes and are discontinuous in that they involved changes that are *not* incremental in nature and are disruptive to the status quo.

Change implementer—the person responsible for making certain the change happens, charting the path forward, nurturing support, and alleviating resistance.

Change initiator—the person who identifies the need and vision for change and champions the change.

Change recipient—the person who is affected by the change. Often the person who has to change his or her behavior to ensure the change is effective.

Change facilitator—the person who assists initiators, implementers, and recipients with the change-management process. Identifies process and content change issues and helps resolve these, fosters support, alleviates resistance, and provides other participants with guidance and council.

Change leader or **change agent—**these two terms are used interchangeably in the text to describe those engaged in change initiator, implementer, or facilitator roles. All those involved in providing leadership and direction for the change fall within their broad coverage.

END-OF-CHAPTER EXERCISES

TOOLKIT EXERCISE 1.1
Critical Thinking Questions

The URLs for the videos listed can be found in two places. The first spot is next to the exercise and the second spot is on the website at **study.sagepub.com/cawsey4e.**

1. Did You Know 2019 — 6:13 minutes

    https://www.youtube.com/watch?v=bTM06NZOyDQ&t=3s

    This video helps us visualize the rate of technical change in the environment.

    - Choose one fact and discuss how it may impact change initiatives for an organization you're familiar with.

    - Which fact listed do you think will have the most long-term implications for organizations in the future?

    - Find a video that outlines ecological and environmental changes and consider their implications for you and organizations you're familiar with

    - Brainstorm other political, economic, social, technological, environmental/ecological, and legal factors that you think may be true in 5 years, 15 years, and 25 years and consider their implications for individuals, organizations and society.

(Continued)

(Continued)

2. IBM Study: Making Change Work—2:57 minutes

   https://www.youtube.com/watch?v=2ol9zYw4Chg&t=8s

   The video discusses an IBM study that only 60% of change projects succeed. It discusses factors that seem to increase the chances for success.

   - List reasons (both in the video as well as those not mentioned) that explain why change projects often fail.

   - Can you think of similar instances of change project failure from your own experience?

   - What are the main takeaways about how to increase the success of a change initiative?

3. Individually or in groups, pick a product or service and then go to the Web and explore what technological and/or geopolitical changes are occurring that could seriously disrupt existing organizations in that sector. Then pick an organization that would be affected and identify the changes you'd undertake to help it adapt and thrive.

   For example, if you owned a taxi firm in New York City, how would you prepare for the potential arrival of self-driving cars?

*Please see **study.sagepub.com/cawsey4e** for a downloadable template of this exercise.*

TOOLKIT EXERCISE 1.2

Analyzing Your Environment

Select an organization you are familiar with. What are the key environmental issues affecting this organization? List the factors under each subheading and their implications for the organization.

Factors	Proactive Implications	Reactive Implications
Political		
Economic		
Social		
Technological		
Ecological/Environmental		
Legal		

Please see **study.sagepub.com/cawsey4e** *for a downloadable template of this exercise.*

TOOLKIT EXERCISE 1.3

Change Roles in Your Organization

Think about organizations that you are familiar with—organizations for which you have worked, schools you've attended, and organizations you've volunteered for such as a baseball league or a church.

Think about changes, large or small, that have taken place in those organizations. Take a moment to describe a situation when you filled each of the change roles (Return to Table 1.4 on page 28 for definitions of each role). How did the role feel? What did you accomplish in the role?

- When did you play the role of a change initiator?

- When did you play the role of a change implementer?

- When did you play the role of a change facilitator?

- When did you play the role of a change recipient?

*Please see **study.sagepub.com/cawsey4e** for a downloadable template of this exercise.*

CHAPTER TWO

HOW TO LEAD ORGANIZATIONAL CHANGE: FRAMEWORKS

Chapter Overview

- In this chapter we discuss frameworks that illustrate the process of how to create organizational change; in Chapter 3 we examine what aspects of an organization might need to be changed. Change leaders must understand and do both.

- We present six models that provide dissimilar and complementary insights into the process of planned, purposeful change:

  1. The first model is a basic step model, that is, the leader takes an organization through step 1 before step 2; this is Lewin's three-stage model.

  2. Kotter's eight stages of organizational change provide a highly structured, finish-one-stage-before-the-next-stage approach to change.

  3. The third model is Gentile's *Giving Voice to Values* methodology, which supports individuals taking effective ethical action when a situation so demands.

  4. The fourth model is Duck's five-stage model that focuses on people and the range of their emotional responses to change.

  5. Fifth, there is a modified version of Beckhard and Harris's change-management model that concentrates on process issues.

  6. We end this chapter with the Change Path, our four-stage model that concentrates on process issues and is used as a guiding framework throughout the book. The four stages of this model are Awakening, Mobilization, Acceleration, and Institutionalization.

     Just as an athlete needs different types of training and equipment to play and succeed at different sports (think of the difference between a professional baseball player and a downhill skiing professional), so too does the change leader need different frameworks to apply to specific situations.

- These models will help change leaders articulate their approach to leading organizational change and provide guideposts for instituting that change.

Sweeping demographic changes, technological advances, geopolitical shifts, and demands to be sensitive to our physical environment are combining with concerns for security and organizational governance to generate significant pressure for organizational change. Awareness of the political, economic, sociological, technological, ecological/environmental and legal aspects of any organization's external environment forewarns managers for the need to pay attention to multiple factors. Furthermore, it alerts managers to attend to their organizations' environmental contexts and to decide whether they need to take some action as a result.

McDonald's has been one of many organizations that scanned its environment and made changes to its products as a result of shifts in its environment. The recession of 2008–2009 put pricing pressure on the restaurant business. McDonald's responded with a continuous stream of new products. Since 2004, it has introduced the snack wrap, several salads, specialty coffees, and, most recently, the Angus burger, a 1/3-lb. burger.[1] These product innovations have led to increases in store sales and improved profits. Recently, McDonald's has embraced the "green movement" with major initiatives in the areas of sustainability and corporate social responsibility, and public reporting of their progress. They also piloted the placement of charge points for electronic vehicles in one store in 2009, and this initiative has now been extended to a few other locations.[2] One trend that has challenged McDonald's creativity is the "eat local" movement, where consumers are encouraged to eat locally grown foods. In the international market, McDonald's has created a variety of partnerships to create a more localized experience for its consumers. McDonald's now offers Red Bean Pie in Hong Kong, a Parmigiano Reggiano burger in Italy, and Caldo Verde soup in Portugal.[3] In the United States, McDonald's has tried to use a message about locally grown foods in its advertising. At first it was slow to commit to using verifiable metrics to support these claims,[4] but it has improved in this area over the years. To make these product decisions, McDonald's managers had to evaluate environmental shifts and assess their relevance to the organization's strategy and the probability of its continued effectiveness.[5]

In the early 2000s scientific evidence linked childhood obesity in the United States with kids eating fast-food meals that were loaded with calories, sodium, sugar, and saturated fats. McDonald's Happy Meals was one such example. By 2018, in partnership with the Alliance for a Healthier Generation, McDonalds had set goals to improve the nutrition and limit the calories in its Happy Meals in the United States. Simultaneously, the fast-food giant analyzed how it could enact its corporate mission: "to be our customers' favorite place and way to eat and drink." In January, 2019, McDonald's announced that they, too, would add bacon to their menu: customers could buy cheesy bacon fries (cheese and bacon were added to their iconic french fries), a Big Mac Bacon burger, and a Quarter Pounder Bacon burger. Bacon, they noted, earned 17,000 mentions a day on U.S. online platforms and the company wanted to get on board with the trend. McDonald's executives examined the bacon trend and decided that product changes were necessary.

If one takes the McDonald's example and generalizes it to all managers, then changes in the external environment provide powerful clues about how an organization's products and services need to change—quickly. In 2019, the rapidity of changes in the marketplace makes acquiring and diagnosing data and then acting on the data immediately a demanding skill set for organizational leaders.

Each person has ideas about how organizations work. For some, this model is explicit—that is, it can be written down and discussed with others. However, many managers' views of organizational functioning are complex, implicit, and based on their personal experiences. Deep knowledge and intuition, so-called tacit knowledge, about the functioning of an organization is invaluable. However, tacit knowledge is personal, often difficult to communicate, and almost impossible to discuss and challenge rationally. As a result, this book takes an explicit approach and provides ways to articulate unspoken models of how organizations work and to use several models to think systematically about how to change an organization.

DIFFERENTIATING *HOW* TO CHANGE FROM *WHAT* TO CHANGE

The complexity of change can be simplified somewhat by recognizing that there are two distinct aspects of organizational change that must be addressed. Managers must decide both *How* (process) to lead organizational change and *What* (content) to change in an organization. The example below highlights the difference between the how and what of change. Imagine that you are the general manager of a major hotel chain and you received the following customer letter of complaint:

A LETTER OF COMPLAINT

Dear Sir:

As a customer of yours, I wanted to provide you with our experiences at ATMI, your London, England, hotel.* I have reflected on my experience and decided to provide you with feedback—particularly given your promise on your website—the Hospitality Promise Program.

My wife and I arrived around 10 p.m. after a flight from North America and the usual tiring immigration procedures, baggage check, and finding our way to your hotel. The initial greeting was courteous and appropriate. We were checked in; the desk person asked if we wished a room upgrade. After I clarified that this would cost money, I declined that proposal.

We then went to our room on the 3rd floor, I believe, and discovered it was a disaster, totally not made up. I phoned the switchboard and was put through to reception immediately.

There were profuse apologies and we were told that someone would be up immediately with another key.

Within 5 minutes, someone met us with a key to a room on the 5th floor, a quick, fast response. However, when we got to the new room, it was not made up!

Again I phoned the switchboard. The operator said, "This shouldn't have happened. I will put you through to the night manager." I said that was not necessary, I just wanted a room. However, the operator insisted and I was put through to the night manager. Again, there were profuse apologies and the manager said, "This shouldn't have happened, I will fix this and get right back to you." I indicated that I just wanted a room—I didn't want the organization fixed, just a room. The manager repeated, "I will get right back to you."

We waited 5, 10, 15 minutes. Inexplicably, the manager did not return the call even though he said he would.

---

*The hotel name is disguised.

(Continued)

Finally, around 20 minutes later, I phoned switchboard again. I said we were waiting for a room and that the night manager had promised to call me back. The operator said, "This is probably my fault as I was doing work for the assistant manager." I did not and do not understand this part of the conversation but again, I was told that they would call right back. Again, I repeated, "I just need a room."

I waited another 5 minutes—it was now 11 p.m. and we were quite tired—there was no return phone call.

My wife and I went down to reception, waited, and after a brief time were motioned forward by the person who registered us initially. I explained that we needed a room. He said, "You were taken care of. You got a room." I stated that "No, I did not have a room, I just had two rooms that were not made up and we needed a clean one for the night."

Again, there were profuse apologies. The reception person then said, "Excuse me, just for a moment, so I can fix this." I said, "Really, I just would like a room." The person at the reception desk went around the corner and began to berate someone working there. This went on for several minutes. He then returned to his station, called me forward again, apologized again, and located a third room for us. As well, he gave us coupons for a complimentary breakfast.

This third room was made up. It was "more tired" than the previous rooms, but it was clean and we were delighted to find a spot to sleep.

In the middle of the night, as is the norm in many places, the invoice was delivered to our room. To our surprise, a £72 charge was added to the price of the room for a "room change."

Of course, early the next morning, I queued up to discuss this charge. The same reception person was still on duty. He motioned me forward and then immediately left to open up all the computer stations in the reception area. He had a tendency to not make eye contact. This may have been a cultural phenomenon or it may have been his dismay at having to deal with me again. I cannot say.

I showed him the invoice. He said, "Oh, there will be no charge for that room." I said that I was concerned as the invoice did show the charge. He said, "It is taken care of." I said, "Regardless, I would like something to prove that there would not be another charge to my credit card." After one further exchange and insistence on my part, he removed the charge from my invoice.

My wife and I had a pleasant breakfast and appreciated it being complimentary.

We thought that you would want to know of our experience. Customer service is a critical part of the hospitality industry and I am certain that ATMI would wish feedback on experiences such as these.

I am interested in such things and look forward to your reply.

Yours truly,

The list of things done poorly and the organizational issues that exist at this hotel are extensive. Identifying this list of *what* needs attention is relatively easy. The desk clerk has twice assigned rooms that were unmade. This indicates that the system used to record and track information on the condition of the rooms is either nonexistent or not working properly. One wonders if someone is responsible for monitoring the housekeepers' performance. There are managerial issues—a manager promises to get back to a customer and doesn't. There are organizational culture issues—the excuses by the switchboard operator and yelling by the reception person. There are further system issues as indicated by the £72 charge for a room change. There are some service training issues—the responses by the receptionist were variable. He was quick to send up a second room key but left the customer standing while he turned on computers. He was reluctant to reverse the extra room charge. There is some hint that there might be other cultural issues that are pertinent.

However, it is not clear *how* the general manager should proceed with needed changes. First off, how accurate is the letter? Can the general manager accept it, or does he have to investigate? Assuming the letter reflects the experiences of more than one unhappy customer, then the general manager still faces the "how" question. If the computer system for tracking room availability does not exist, then it is relatively straight forward to buy and install one. However, if the system exists but is not being used, how does the general manager get the staff to use the system effectively? Closer supervision and training might work, but who can do that and who will pay for it? Even more difficult are the organizational and cultural issues. The norm among employees appears to be to make excuses and to "berate" others when things go wrong. A manager can tell employees that these behaviors are inappropriate, but how does one persuade employees not to respond abusively? And how will the general manager know if and when the changes are implemented? Is there a system in place to track customer and employee satisfaction? Are these several systems worth the cost they impose on the organization?

Clearly, managers must know what needs to change. However, how to go about making change requires careful thought and planning. The models below may help you to think about the process of change and how to make it happen.

THE PROCESSES OF ORGANIZATIONAL CHANGE

Many leaders know what they need to achieve, but they just don't know how to get there. An examination of competitors' initiatives and accomplishments, customers' behavior, and other data from environmental scans will provide cues as to what is needed, but moving one's organization to successfully address these factors and related opportunities is difficult.

Why is it so difficult to accomplish organizational change?

There is a web of tightly woven factors that make organizational change difficult. However, one common cause might lie in practices that were effective in the past and that are no longer appropriate; this can be called the "failure of success." Organizations learned what worked and what didn't. They developed systems that exploited that knowledge and established rules, policies, procedures, and decision frameworks that capitalized on previous successes. Further, they developed patterned responses (habits), assumptions, attributions, and expectations that influenced the ways employees thought about how the world worked.[6] These beliefs and ingrained responses formed a strong resistant force, which encouraged people and their organizations to maintain old patterns regardless of feedback that they were no longer appropriate. In many respects, this is where the questions of what to change and how to change intersect.

Charles Handy describes some of these dilemmas by examining the pattern of success over time.[7] As he so aptly said, too often "by the time you know where you ought to go, it's too late" (p. 50). He describes a sigmoid curve that outlines where one should begin changing and where it becomes obvious that one needs to change (see Figure 2.1). This curve depicts the outcomes of a system as a curve that increases during early-stage development and growth phases, flattens at maturity, and shifts into decline over time. Consider the path tracked by successful technological innovations. Once an innovation demonstrates its value to key early adopters, then sales take off. As others see the benefits of the innovation, they adopt it as well. Patents and proprietary knowledge provide some protection, but over time competitors launch similar products, profit margins become squeezed, and sales growth slows due to increased competition and the level of market saturation. This leads to a flattening of the curve, referred to as the maturity phase. Decline follows as the market becomes increasingly saturated and competitive, and this decline accelerates with the arrival of a new, disruptive innovation that attracts customers away from the existing product or service. Think of what happened to the VCR players when DVD players arrived on the scene. Consider how prices fell for DVD players in the face of competition. Now, video streaming has eclipsed the market for DVDs. DVDs are becoming obsolete as more companies offer streaming services.

The time to introduce change is at point B when the system is growing. The dilemma is that in the short run, the costs are likely to be greater than the benefits. It is only when the new changes are adopted and the system is working well that the outcomes' curve turns upward again. One dilemma is that the costs of change are real and include adding people and shifting production lines, while the benefits of change are uncertain. Managers believe the changes will improve productivity and profits, but that may not occur. By holding off investing in change, an organization may improve its profits in the short run. However, if environmental conditions continue to change and the organization fails to adjust in a timely fashion, executives can quickly find themselves lagging behind their competitors, scrambling to adapt, and running to catch up. If management waited too long to adapt, then an organization may find it impossible to do so. The escalating rate of change, combined with the frequency and magnitude of disruptions being experienced by firms point to the dangers of being laggards!

By the time the system reaches point A, the need for change is obvious, but it may also be too late for the organization to survive without experiencing significant trauma. Positive planned change needs to be commenced sooner in the process—before things deteriorate to a crisis or disaster stage. Unfortunately, change typically comes with costs that appear to lessen the positive outcomes in the short run. As many know, convincing anyone that they should incur costs, make investments, and initiate changes now for long-run benefits is a difficult selling task, particularly if things are going well. This is depicted as the shaded space between the solid and dotted lines beginning at point B in Figure 2.1. The costs of change appear certain and are tangible. But the benefits are uncertain and often vaguely defined. The time after point B is a time of two competing views of the future, and people will have difficulty abandoning the first curve (the one they are on) until they are convinced of the benefits of the new curve. In concrete terms, creating change at point B means convincing others about the wisdom of spending time and money now for an uncertain future return.

In the following pages we present six models for thinking about and changing organizations. These models are both discrete and complementary. Below is an overview of what you will find in these models.

- Lewin's model is simple, making it useful for communicating the overall change process to participants.

- Kotter's provides a detailed map of the change process in terms of what each step needs to achieve (i.e., the key success factors of a change initiative), which is useful for planning and implementing.

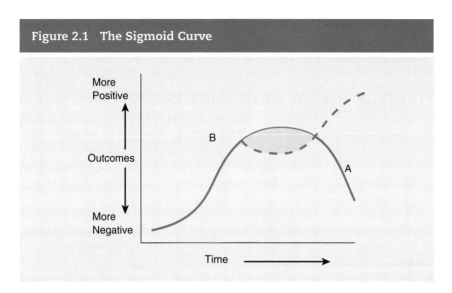

Figure 2.1 The Sigmoid Curve

Source: Adapted from Handy, C. (1994). *The age of paradox* (p. 50). Boston, MA: Harvard Business School Press.

- Gentile provides individual-level guidance for pushing back and responding skillfully and effectively to people and situations that contradict a person's values; this approach may or may not make systemic change, but it often allows an individual to change an unethical situation.

- Duck offers guidance for people and the emotional issues associated with organizational change.

- Beckhard and Harris provide an action-oriented overview that indicates the sets of activities that should be completed within the steps Kotter identified (roughly).

- The Change Path Model maps sets of activities within a systems-level view (following Lewin) that also reflects organizational-level factors (e.g., operations, control, and measures).

The models have more similarities than differences.

- Each is a process model (i.e., they all depict *how* change should happen).

- Two are descriptive (Lewin and Duck), three are prescriptive (Kotter, Gentile, and Beckhard and Harris), and our Change Path Model combines both.

- One is system-level (Lewin); three are organizational-level (Kotter, Beckhard and Harris, and our Change Path Model); and two are individual-level (Gentile and Duck).

- The models describe many of the same processes, but describe them at varying levels of granularity and with different lenses (e.g., emotions with Duck, managerial tasks with Kotter).

Organizational change most often requires changing at three levels: individual, team or unit, and the organization. Learning and applying more than one model will give the change agent a large set of tools to work with.

(1) STAGE THEORY OF CHANGE: LEWIN

Our first model is a basic step model. Sixty years ago, Kurt Lewin[8] wrote about the problem of how to bring about change. He described a three-stage model of change:

Unfreeze → Change → Refreeze

Lewin stated that we need to understand the situation and system as a whole as well as the component parts that make up the system. Before change can occur, an unfreezing process must happen within that system. Unfreezing focuses on the need to dislodge the beliefs and assumptions of those who need to engage in systemic alterations to the status quo. The unfreezing process might occur because of some crisis. For example, new competitive products that are attacking the major profit centers of a private enterprise might be a sufficient shock to the organization to "unfreeze" patterns. In this example, the balance in the system must be disrupted or broken in order to permit conditions for change to develop. Some top managers even talk about "creating a crisis" in order to develop the sense of urgency around the need for change.[9]

When this unfreezing occurs, the people who are embedded in the systems become susceptible to change. Systems and structures, beliefs, and habits become fluid and thus can shift more easily. Once the change has been completed, these systems, structures, beliefs, and habits can refreeze in their new form.

To illustrate Lewin's model, refer back to the Letter of Complaint and examine the comments below.

Unfreeze

Will this letter of complaint be sufficient to "unfreeze" the general manager and move him to action? If this is a single letter, it is highly unlikely that change will occur. If complaints are common for this hotel, this might be seen as just one more letter in a pile—background noise in running the hotel. The letter suggests that this might be an airport hotel in London, England. The location of the hotel might be such that customer service shortfalls might not make a difference to occupancy rates, whereas minimizing costs would be crucial to the hotel's profitability. In all the above scenarios, no unfreezing would take place.

However, this letter may represent an initiative that captures managerial attention and promotes action. The general manager might be facing declining occupancy and view this letter as a signal of where problems lie. A comparison with other hotels on measures of profitability and customer satisfaction might demonstrate a dramatic need for change that the letter foreshadowed. In this situation, the general manager's views on the existing system are more likely to be unfrozen, and he would be ready for change.

Note that the unfreezing must take place at many levels. The general manager might be ready for change, but the employees at the reception desk might think things are just fine. Their perceptions need unfreezing as well! The integration and interdependence of systems and people require us to think about the unfreezing of the organizational system as a whole.

Change

Assume that the general manager accepts the need to improve the system that indicates that rooms are ready for occupancy. He must decide what else needs to change to bring about the needed improvements. He could begin by hiring a quality-control person who is charged with inspecting and certifying all rooms before they are entered into the system as "ready to use." Some computer programming may be needed to flag rooms when they are ready, and the quality-control person must be responsible for managing that flag subsystem. The quality-control person will have to be recruited, hired, and trained if management cannot promote an appropriate internal person. Once the room-quality system has been designed and procedures are in place, all receptionists will have to be trained. This change could be a participatory process with the involvement of staff; or, the general manager could have it designed and order its implementation. Either way, the change process would be complex, involving a number of people and systems.

During this phase, there would be considerable uncertainty. The new system could be ready before the quality-control person is hired and trained. Or, the reverse could be true: the person may be hired and trained, but the room-quality system is not ready. Employees might see opportunities to improve what is being proposed and make suggestions regarding those improvements. Regardless of the specifics, the organization will be in flux as the general manager analyzes the organization's problems and decides how he will implement changes: in other words, the manager will need to decide who will do what, when, where, why, and how.

Refreeze or More Appropriately Re-gell

Once the changes are designed and implemented, employees will need to adapt to those changes and develop new patterns and habits. The new flag system will alter how those at reception and in housekeeping do their work. They may informally ask the quality-control person to check certain rooms first as these are in higher demand. The general manager will follow up to see how the system is working and what people are doing. New reporting patterns need to be established, and the quality-control person might begin passing on valuable information to hotel maintenance and housekeeping regarding the condition of particular rooms. At this point, the system settles into a new set of balances and relative stability. With this stability comes refreezing, as the new processes, procedures, and behaviors become the new "normal" practices of the organization.

What do we mean by this notion of relative stability and predictability that comes with refreezing? It stems from the observation that organizational systems, composed of tasks, formal systems, informal ways of behaving, and individuals, develop over time an interdependent state of balance called *homeostasis*. Perturbations or shifts in one part of the system are resisted, or swings away from balance are countered and balance is regained. As suggested earlier, managers may introduce change initiatives only to have those initiatives fail because of existing systems, processes, or relationships that work against the change. Planned changes in structures and roles may be seen as decreasing the power and influence of certain individuals or groups, and these groups may react in complex ways to resist change. For permanent change, new structures and roles are needed and new points of balance or homeostasis developed.

The image of a spider's web can help to depict the phenomenon. That is, view the organization as a complex web of systems, relationships, structures, assumptions, habits, and processes that are interconnected and interdependent over time. Altering one strand of the web is not likely to alter the patterns significantly. To do that requires a breaking of many interconnected items—the "unfreezing" in Lewin's terms.

This simple model has stood the test of time. Change agents find it useful both because of its simplicity and because it reminds us that you can't expect change unless the system is unfrozen first! We may need other, more complex models of the organization to think through what must be unfrozen and changed, but Lewin forces us to recognize the rigidity that comes with stability and interconnectedness within existing systems, relationships, and beliefs.

However, several concerns prevent us from wholeheartedly embracing this model. First, the model oversimplifies the process of change and suggests that change is linear. The reality is that change tends to be complex, interactive, and emergent. Second, the creation of the need for change deserves more attention. It is not merely a matter of moving individuals away from their assumptions about the current state. Rather, they need to have a vision of a future desirable state. Finally, the model implies that refreezing is acceptable as a frame of mind. This seems problematic because it implies that change is a discrete event, rather than a continuous process. In today's rapidly changing world, organizations find that pressures to adapt mean they are never "refrozen"—and if they are, they are in trouble.

Organizations that freeze too firmly may fail to thaw in time, when new markets and customers appear. They may refuse to incorporate feedback in making useful changes. Continuous improvement programs may appear faddish, but they reflect a realistic view of what is needed in a dynamic environment because they enhance an organization's adaptive capacity. Thus, there is concern with the image created by the word *refreeze*, as this is likely too static a condition for long-term organizational health. In discussions with managers, we find the phrase **"re-gelling"** to have appeal as a state between total fluidity of a liquid and the excess rigidity of a solid. Since Lewin articulated his framework of organizational change in the early 1950s, it is likely that he, too, would have modified his framework for change.

(2) STAGE MODEL OF ORGANIZATIONAL CHANGE: KOTTER

This second model describes a highly structured step-by-step process that overcomes the problem of simplification of Lewin's model. In 1996, Harvard Business School Professor John Kotter published *Leading Change*.[10] His eight-stage process argues that an organization must successfully go through each phase in sequence. For example, failing to establish a sense of urgency throughout an organization (step 1), may explain a leader's inability to communicate effectively a vision for change (step 4). Kotter's framework helps managers know what they should do, when they should take specific actions, and when and how they are ready to move to the next stage.

Kotter's Eight-Stage Process

1. **Establish a sense of urgency:** In older, well-established organizations a sense of complacency may have set in. Leaders need to illustrate the threats to the system and move enough organizational members from a sense of invulnerability to vulnerability.

2. **Create a guiding coalition:** Select a significant number of people (10 to 50) who have titles and lead divisions and departments, have the respect of their colleagues, and relevant knowledge. This group should be aligned and know that change is needed.

3. **Develop a vision and strategy:** People need an overarching dream of an inspiring future. From this vision comes the implementation plans and steps.

4. **Communicate** the change vision: Capture the hearts and minds of most employees by communicating through multiple channels and multiple times the vision for change.

5. **Empower employees** for broad-based action: Large numbers of employees need to embrace the vision and then organizational structures, human resources systems, and a myriad of other internal organizational mechanisms need to support, rather than block, the change.

6. **Generate short-term wins:** Large-scale organizational change may take three to five years and yet employees need to see evidence of successful change within 18 months (p. 11). Highlight short-term gains to keep employees motivated.

7. **Consolidate gains and produce more change:** Since it takes years for organizational change to become a part of an organization's DNA, many leaders stop too soon. Keep pressing forward until the change seeps into the deepest recesses of an organization.

8. **Anchor new approaches** in the culture: Make sure that the change is embedded in the organization's cultural norms and values.

The heightened need for agility in the face of escalating rates of change, the challenge of closing the gap between the current mode of operation and the desired future state, and collateral challenges related to managing the transition have caused Kotter to offer additional advice in this area. Goods, services and the value promise still need to be delivered upon as the changes are pursued. To "accelerate" the process (Kotter's words), he recommends a new strategy designed to augment his original eight steps.

Kotter sees these accelerators as concurrent and always at work, energized by a volunteer army and nested in a flexible and agile network. His eight accelerators are (1) create a sense of urgency around a single, big opportunity; (2) build and maintain a guiding coalition; (3) formulate a strategic vision and develop change initiatives designed to capitalize on the big opportunity; (4) communicate the vision and the strategy to create buy-in and attract a growing volunteer army; (5) accelerate movement toward the vision and the opportunity by ensuring the network removes barriers; (6) celebrate visible, significant short-term wins; (7) never let up—keep learning from experience and don't declare victory too soon; and (8) institutionalize strategic changes in the culture.[11]

(3) GIVING VOICE TO VALUES: GENTILE

The third model focuses on the ethical implications of organizational change. Pick up any newspaper or magazine and one finds stories about personal, corporate, or governmental malfeasance; accounts of injustice; and reports of individual violence against peers and society's vulnerable members. An underlying issue in most of these situations is an organizational climate that does not effectively manage individual and group behavior. Take the multiple scandals at Wells Fargo. In April, 2018, the bank agreed to pay $1 billion to settle U.S. federal government probes into its mistreatment of consumers. The settlement covered problems in Wells Fargo's auto-lending and mortgage divisions. In 2017, the bank had revealed that its employees had forced customers who took out car loans to buy unwanted insurance. Other employees imposed inappropriate charges for locking in interest rates on new home loans. In October, 2016, CEO John Stumpf resigned abruptly, as pressure mounted from the public and lawmakers.

With numerous examples of corruption and fraud, educator and research scholar Mary Gentile decided to develop *Giving Voice to Values*, a program, at first for business students, to support people's development of confidence and skills that would allow them to speak and act their values—effectively—when faced with a situation that runs counter to their principles. Gentile's *Giving Voice to Values* (GVV) curriculum[12] takes people through a learning process that prepares them to expect values conflicts and provides the tools to intervene when they perceive wrongdoing. (See https://www.darden.virginia.edu/ibis/initiatives/giving -voice-to-values/ for cases and other teaching tools for the GVV curriculum).

The GVV curriculum focuses on the practical application of skills needed to push back and respond skillfully and effectively to people and situations that contradict a person's values. The GVV curriculum consists of three parts that represent the process individuals need to work through to advocate for the need to change: the clarification and articulation of one's values; post-decision-making analysis and implementation plan; and the practice of speaking one's values and receiving feedback.

1. **Clarification and articulation of one's values:** The GVV curriculum invites participants to consider the notion that there is a universality of values and some researchers, such as Martin Seligman and Rushworth Kidder, have found a commonality of core values across cultures and religions. Kidder, who conducted a cross-cultural survey, identified a "list of five widely shared values: honesty, respect, responsibility, fairness, and compassion" (p. 30). The first step requires participants to articulate their values and the impact of acting on those values. This exercise encourages participants to take their often implicit principles and make them explicit and public, an important first step in bringing about change.

2. Post-decision-making analysis and implementation plan: The GVV curriculum requires participants to examine case studies of protagonists who have been clear about their values and have effectively voiced their principles in difficult situations (all GVV cases are available through the website). The protagonists of GVV cases have concluded what is right, and the cases walk readers through their thinking and actions—to a point: then readers are invited to figure out what the protagonist might do to voice her values effectively. For example, in the "Not Even an Option" case, readers meet Ajith, a pharmaceutical representative in a developing country. Ajith is clear that paying bribes is not an option for him (read his story at the end of this chapter). And, yet, it seems that he and his company will not succeed unless he succumbs to societal norms and pays bribes to government officials to review and accept his company's registrations for the drugs. Participants analyze Ajith's situation and ask, given Ajith's unwillingness to pay bribes, what should he do and say, and to whom? These situations start from the point where the protagonist knows his values and what is right for him to do. GVV is, then, a curriculum about taking actions post decision making.

The analytical work can be further subdivided into three parts. First, participants engage in a stakeholder analysis. This is not the traditional "stakeholder analysis" that encourages a utilitarian weighing and making of trade-offs, but rather is an effort to understand how to effectively influence key people. Second, people need to anticipate how stakeholders might respond to the protagonist's questioning of the stakeholders' actions. Gentile calls this the "reasons and rationalization" that a protagonist might expect from others. And, third, Gentile asks, what levers can a protagonist use to persuade stakeholders to join the protagonist's vision?

3. The practice of speaking one's values and receiving feedback: One of the central tenets of GVV is the importance of "pre-scripting." As noted above, the GVV cases often invite readers to decide to whom the protagonist should talk and what she should say. Gentile believes that participants' practice in speaking their values after they have analyzed a situation "is both a cognitive exercise as well as a behavioral and emotional one" (p. 173). Participants write out a script, speak the script in front of another participant, and receive feedback from a third participant—an observer who acts as a peer coach to the participant who is articulating the script. Delivering a script challenges participants to articulate often vaguely formed ideas, which deepens their sense that they will take action in difficult, future situations.

GVV and Organizational Change

An assumption of this GVV training is that prepared individuals will speak up and in their speaking up people will change the course of events in units, organizations, or even societies. The GVV cases provide numerous examples of people shifting the direction of their organizations. In the Helen Drinan case, for example, Drinan pushes back and speaks up when it seems that a CEO of a hospital system will be let off the hook even though several women have accused the CEO of sexual harassment.[13] The publicity surrounding this case led the attorney general of Massachusetts to note the problems with governance of the hospital system; eventually the Catholic Diocese of Boston was pushed to sell its hospitals. The point is this: When people think tactically and strategically about how to most effectively create change around a values conflict, the person or group can be successful. Sometimes this process involves speaking up and at other times the process involves gathering data, asking questions, building a coalition, and/or making alliances with key people. The point of the GVV curriculum is to prepare people to expect conflicts in values and then to take effective action for individual and organizational change.

(4) EMOTIONAL TRANSITIONS THROUGH CHANGE: DUCK

The fourth model captures the people and their emotional responses to the change process. In *The Change Monster: The Human Forces That Fuel or Foil Corporate Transformation and Change*,[14] consultant Jeanie Daniel Duck argues that organizational change evolves in a fairly predictable and manageable series of phases that she calls the "Change Curve." This Change Curve is a "simplification and an approximation" of complex, ambiguous, and volatile human emotions that accompany all types of organizational change, from externally driven mergers and acquisitions to internally planned and managed new programs.

Duck's Five-Stage Change Curve

1. **Stagnation** occurs when people have their heads in the sand and have an insufficient sense of threat from the external world. This can only end with a forceful demand for change from the external environment, such as a merger or acquisition, or from internal pressures for change from a strong internal leader. It is the leader's role to push people to see the truth of their situation and to wake them up.

2. **Preparation** begins with a dramatic announcement of change from an internal person, such as the CEO, or from an external force, such as an announcement of a takeover. Immediately, some people feel anxious or jittery; others may be hopeful that needed change is coming; while still others will retreat to cynicism and will not take the announcement seriously. When this rush of emotion occurs, productivity often goes down.

   This phase requires a tremendous amount of planning and operational work by the leaders. In addition, organizational leaders must be aligned for the planned change to succeed.

3. **Implementation** is when the journey begins. It includes designing new organizational structures, job descriptions, and lots of other detailed plans. However, operational changes are not enough: Implementation also requires changing people's mindsets and work practices—in other words, people's emotional maps and habits.

4. **Determination** kicks in when people realize that the change is real and they will need "to live their work lives differently" (p. 30). Duck argues that "people long for an excuse to quit the hard path of transformation," requiring leaders to recognize this emotional trap and to pursue the new vision with high energy and enthusiasm.

5. **Fruition** is the time when the hard work pays off and the organization seems new. "The employees feel confident in themselves; they're optimistic and energized, and they're able to get their work done with less hassle, in less time, and with better results" (p. 34). Leaders need to make sure that this basking in the satisfaction of the change does not lead to napping and future stagnation.

In 1969, Elizabeth Kübler-Ross observed and wrote in *On Death and Dying* about the five predictable emotional stages in terminally ill patients: denial, anger, bargaining, depression, and finally acceptance. She later said that these observable stages apply to children whose parents are going through divorce and to people who experience traumatic losses, such as parents whose child dies. Although Duck does not reference Kübler-Ross, Duck focuses on predictable human emotional responses to organizational change. In reality, people embrace change differently and at dissimilar speeds; Duck argues, however, that individuals go through similar emotional responses to change. It is the savvy leader who monitors his own emotional response to change, anticipates and articulates underlying negative and positive emotional responses to change in others, and then pulls the group through the negative to excitement and satisfaction with the new order.

(5) MANAGING THE CHANGE PROCESS: BECKHARD AND HARRIS

The fifth model of change, outlined by Beckhard and Harris,[15] has a strong **focus on process**. Building on the work of Kurt Lewin, Beckhard and Harris propose a process model that begins with an assessment of why change is needed. Here the forces for and against change are analyzed and understood. A thorough understanding of the organization and its stakeholders will assist in this analysis.

Following the recognition of the need for change, leaders are faced with the task of defining and describing a desired future state in contrast to an organization's present reality. This process is called a **gap analysis**. This second step in the change process involves both determining the need for change and creating a powerful change vision A desired future state allows leaders to identify the gap between the present and the future and how they propose to close the gap. This is one of the most important steps in the Beckhard and Harris Model and one that change leaders need to attend to.

The discussion of how to get from the present to a desired future state represents the action or implementation state. The final step in the change process is to **manage the transition**. Beckhard and Harris provide a useful elaboration of how the process of change occurs. What is not so clear is how to bring the various stages of the model to life, in order to see change through to a successful outcome. The Change Path Model addresses this matter.

(6) THE CHANGE PATH MODEL: DESZCA AND INGOLS

Extracting from the preceding models, years of consulting work, and decades of teaching and talking with managers and executives about change, the

Change Path Model combines process and prescription: There is more detail and direction than Lewin and less instruction than Kotter. We recommend that managers also use Gentile's model to act effectively, especially if there is a conflict in values. Duck reminds us about the all too often neglected side of change: the emotional impact of change. Finally, Beckhard and Harris[16] remind us of the power of a well-executed analysis of the gap between the current mode of operation and the desired state. (Figure 2.2 sets out the change Path Model.)

Step 1: The first process is **Awakening**, which begins with a Critical Organizational Analysis (like Beckhard and Harris). Leaders need to scan continuously both their external and internal environments and understand the forces for and against any particular organizational shift. The most powerful drivers for change tend to originate outside organizations. These forces range from new legislation, new products launched by competitors, new population trends, to new technologies; in fact, it is usually an interlocking web of external factors that make environmental shifts so challenging for organizations to respond to effectively. Leaders *also* need to understand deeply what is going on inside their own organizations. For example, are people with critical competencies leaving the organization? If yes, why is the turnover rate disturbingly high?

Managers need *data* from all significant parts of their organization and stakeholders to understand the dynamics internal to their institutions. Once external and internal data is compiled, leaders need to examine their organizations' situation and talk about how the new challenges from the external and internal environments impact their institutions. Chapter 3 addresses how to diagnose an organization's problems and Chapter 4 focuses on identifying and clarifying the need for change, assessing the organization's readiness for change, and developing the vision for the change.

Step 2: The second step in the process is **Mobilization**, which includes several significant actions. The determination of what specifically needs to change and the vision for change are further developed and solidified by additional analyses and by engaging others in discussions concerning what needs to change and nurturing their participation in the change process. Many assume that the need for change is easily recognizable, obvious, and evident from the environment. Sometimes this occurs, but often it is not the case. For example, if bankruptcy risks are rising or if profits have declined, some people in the organization may believe things must change, but others may not, thinking that what is needed is to simply stay the course until conditions improve. However, once change leaders are convinced of the need for change, it is their job to convince others from the top of the organization to the frontline staff.

Change leaders also need to recognize that there is often a lag between what they know, as the results of their assessments, and what is known by others in different parts of the organization. This lag in information requires change leaders to engage others through multiple communication channels, so that they become convinced of the importance of changing now and not continuing to operate as they have in the past.

The development of the analysis of the present state and the definition of a desired future state leads to the solidification of the gap analysis—an image of the differences between where an organization presently is and where it needs and wants to go. A manager, for example, might have data that employee morale is low. To take appropriate action to improve employee morale, managers need to understand the root causes of the problem. Is it the pay system? Is it the performance appraisal system? Is the problem found across the organization, or is it confined to certain divisions? The answers to these and other questions may suggest different courses of action. In Chapter 3, several frameworks are described for readers to develop a sophisticated checklist for organizational diagnosis. The gap analysis allows change leaders to clearly address the questions of why change is needed and what needs to change. Being able to clearly and succinctly communicate this, along with the vision for the change, is critical to building shared understanding and support for the change in the organization. Think of this as the value of a clear, succinct, and compelling "elevator pitch" of what you have in mind and why it is worth undertaking.

The analyses of (a) formal structures, systems, and processes; (b) the power and cultural dynamics of the organization; (c) the various stakeholders; (d) the recipients of the change; and (e) the change agents themselves, all help to complete an understanding of the situation and the gaps that need attention. In addition to identifying the gaps that must be addressed, these analyses also help change leaders to understand how the existing situation can be leveraged in order to increase the prospects for success. For example, change leaders need to consider how existing systems and processes can be used to advance the change and how influence can be exercised and support built for the undertaking. Further, they need to assess how their own skills and abilities are best deployed to advance the changes.

Step 3: Acceleration involves action planning and implementation. It takes the insights gained in earlier chapters and translates them into the development and activation of a detailed plan for action, in order to bring the change to life. Appropriate tools are deployed to manage the plan, build momentum, and manage the transition. People are systematically reached out to, engaged and empowered to advance the change. Needed new knowledge, skills, abilities, and ways of thinking are developed in others to support the change. Finally, small wins and the achievement of milestones along the way need to be celebrated.

While the stages of the change process, including acceleration, are depicted as linear and straightforward, the reality is usually quite different. Managing change while operating the organization is like changing the tire on a moving car. Conditions can change in unanticipated ways and change leaders need to be able to learn and adapt their understanding of the situation and what is needed as they go. The way the change is communicated, the specifics of the change, and its implementation may also need to be adapted for different parts of the organization to help them better understand and implement the change within their specific contexts (e.g., production vs. marketing). Transition management plays an important part in doing just that.

Figure 2.2   The Change Path Model

Awakening
Chapter 4

1. Identify a need for change and confirm the problems or opportunities that incite the need for change through collection of data.
2. Articulate the gap in performance between the present and the envisioned future state and spread awareness of the data and the gap throughout the organization.
3. Develop a powerful vision for change.
4. Disseminate the vision for the change and why it's needed through multiple communication channels.

Mobilization
Chapters 5 through 8

1. Make sense of the desired change through formal systems and structures and leverage those systems to reach the change vision (Chapter 5).
2. Assess power and cultural dynamics at play and put them to work to better understand the dynamics and build coalitions and support to realize the change (Chapter 6).
3. Communicate the need for change organization-wide and manage change recipients and various stakeholders as they react to and move the change forward (Chapter 7).
4. Leverage change agent personality, knowledge, skills and abilities, and related assets (e.g., reputation and relationships) for the benefit of the change vision and its implementation (Chapter 8).

Acceleration
Chapter 9

1. Continue to systematically reach out to engage and empower others in support, planning, and implementation of the change. Help them develop needed new knowledge, skills, abilities, and ways of thinking that will support the change.
2. Use appropriate tools and techniques to build momentum, accelerate, and consolidate progress.
3. Manage the transition; celebrate small wins and the achievement of milestones along the larger, more difficult path of change.

Institutionalization
Chapter 10

1. Track the change periodically and through multiple balanced measures to help assess what is needed, gauge progress toward the goal, and to make modifications as needed and mitigate risk.
2. Develop and deploy new structures, systems, processes and knowledge, skills and abilities, as needed, to bring life to the change and new stability to the transformed organization.

Step 4: Institutionalization involves the successful conclusion of the transition to the desired new state. This is aided by the sophisticated monitoring of progress along the way, including the assessment of when the changes have been incorporated into the fabric of the organization. Measurement can play a very useful role in this area. Understanding the impact of the particular organizational changes we are trying to achieve depends on our ability to measure such change and this sets the stage for future change initiatives. Measurement and data also play very important roles in earlier phases of the change process.

APPLICATION OF THE CHANGE PATH MODEL

Let's return to the hotel guest's letter presented earlier in this chapter and use it as an opportunity to apply the Change Path process model to an organization that appears to need to change.

Awakening: Why Change?

The general manager might have very good reasons for interpreting the letter as a signal not to change. The hotel already might be in the midst of a computer systems modification and be overwhelmed with this change. Or, the general manager may have a tracking system that indicates that most hotel guests are very satisfied and that this is an unusual occurrence. Or, the general manager may be under pressure to reduce costs and views change as leading to increased costs. Or, the general manager might see himself as exiting the organization and does not want to put the time and energy into changing systems.

On the other hand, the general manager may have the opposite reaction. The letter could trigger the manager to note inefficient processes that cause higher costs (i.e., it is more costly to clean a room twice or have to return to a room to deliver missing towels). If this letter were sent to Trip Advisor, Yelp, or other travel-related websites, then the hotel could experience the loss of customers and a damaged reputation, particularly if there were other unhappy customers who expressed dissatisfaction with the hotel.

Even if the general manager accepts the need for change, the employees might not. At this point in time, they know nothing about the letter. They may feel that their performance is good and no change is needed. They might have a department manager who doesn't follow up on directives and, thus, they could believe that no action is necessary. Or, they might be new to their jobs and be poorly trained in customer service.

The challenge for the change leader is to articulate "why change" and their initial vision for the change to key stakeholders in ways that they will understand and move them to positive actions.

Mobilization: Activating the Gap Analysis

The present state of the hotel operations has several dimensions that could be addressed. The following gaps might exist:

- A gap in information between room readiness and the information that the desk clerk has

- A gap between what the hotel's managers say they will do and what they actually do

- A gap between the appropriate bill and the bill given to the customer

- A gap between the desired interpersonal relationships between employees and customers and that which exists

- A gap between the desired handling of hotel guests and that which occurs

Each of these gaps could require different action plans for change. Careful analysis will demonstrate that there are underlying issues that need to be dealt with. For example, if the organization's culture has evolved to one that is not focused on customer care and relationships, the individual gaps might be difficult to correct without a systematic approach. This gap analysis, then, needs to be used by change leaders to further develop and frame the vision for change. This vision plays a critical role in helping others understand the gap in concrete terms by contrasting the present state with the desired future state.

Taking an organization through the process of change requires going through predictable stages of change. Some organizational change experts, such as Kotter (1996)[17] and Duck (2001),[18] argue that a leader must successfully take the organization through each stage before moving to the next stage. While our experiences suggest that context matters and we challenge a rigid prescription of stages of change, we do believe that there is a predictable beginning, middle, and end process of change, and these set the stage for future pressures for change. Things don't stand still.

Acceleration: Getting from Here to There

In this phase, specific actions are undertaken to advance the implementation of the desired changes. Several planning tools can be used (see Chapter 9). If the general manager in the hotel case decided that the issue to be tackled is computer systems, then the implementation plan and actions might include the following steps:

- Discuss the need for change, the gap analysis, and the vision for change with involved staff to develop a consensus concerning the need for action.

- Form a users' task force to develop the desired outcomes and usability framework for a new computer system.

- Contact internal information systems specialists for advice and assistance on improving the hotel's information system.

- Identify the costs of systems changes and decide which budget to draw on and/or how to fund the needed systems' changes.

- Work with the purchasing department to submit a "request for proposal," promoting systems' suppliers to bid on the proposed system.

- Contact human resources to begin staffing and training plans.

- Implement the plans.

This list of sample tasks lays out the actions needed to accomplish the change. In Chapter 9, we identify tools that help in planning. For example, there are tools to assign responsibilities for different aspects of projects and others for contingency plans. Other tools illustrate how to manage during the transition.

Organizations usually don't stop what they are doing because they are changing! In the hotel, for example, rooms will need to be made up, allocated, and assigned while the information system is being modified. In particular, receptionists will need to ensure a seamless transition from the old to the new system. In many system changes, parallel systems are run until the bugs in the new system are found and corrected. Hotel receptionists need to be trained on the new system. How and when that will be done in this implementation phase is part of the managerial challenge during the transition state.

Institutionalization: Using Data to Help Make the Change Stick

The final aspect of the model deals with the measurement of change and the metrics used in that measurement. How will the general manager know that the changes implemented are working? Managers can measure inputs easily, such as the number of hotel receptionists who are trained on the new system. But management will also need to track the number of times rooms are misallocated. This is a more difficult problem because the staff could be motivated to prevent accurate reporting from such a system if the results could put the staff in a negative light. Chapter 10 talks about measurement and control methods that can assist change managers in navigating the path forward.

Models improve change managers' abilities to plan and implement organizational change and to predict outcomes. The Change Path Model provides a practical framework that lays out a linear process for change. This model, like others, risks having change managers oversimplify their challenges. Cause–effect analysis is complex because organizations are nonlinear, complex entities and the constantly shifting external environment impacts an organization's customers and resources. An overreliance on superficial thinking can lead to errors in judgment and unpleasant surprises. Organizations are more surprising and messier than people often assume.

Coordination and control of change may appear fairly straightforward. However, the reality is that organizations often undertake multiple change projects simultaneously. For example, a factory may be shifted toward a continuous improvement process while other parts of the organization are being restructured. Different managers are working on separate change projects to make things better. Under such complexity, control is difficult and likely involves multiple layers of authority and systems. Difficult yes, but coordination and integration of efforts toward shared goals can be accomplished when approached carefully, thoughtfully, and empathetically. See **Toolkit Exercise 2.2** to examine a change initiative through the Change Path process and differentiate between the how and what of change.

SUMMARY

This chapter differentiates what to change from how to change and uses several models to explicitly consider how to change. Successful change management requires attention to both process and content. The Change Path Model serves as the organizing framework for the chapter sequence is laid out using the model. See **Toolkit Exercise 2.1** for critical thinking questions for this chapter.

KEY TERMS

How to change—relates to the process one uses to bring about change

What to change—relates to the assessment of what it is that needs to change—in other words, the content of the change

Sigmoid curve—describes the normal life cycle of something including an initial phase, a growth phase, deceleration, and decline

Lewin's Model of Change: Unfreeze → Change → Refreeze

Unfreezing—the process that awakens a system to the need for change—in other words, the realization that the existing equilibrium or the status quo is no longer tenable

Change—the period in the process in which participants in the system recognize and enact

new approaches and responses that they believe will be more effective in the future

Refreeze (or re-gel)—the change is assimilated and the system reenters a period of relative equilibrium

Kotter's Eight-Stage Change Process

Establish a sense of urgency—upend complacency in order to communicate the need for change

Create a guiding coalition—a team of a significant number of people (10 to 50) who have titles, lead divisions and departments, and have the respect of their colleagues and relevant knowledge to lead the change

Develop a vision and strategy—an overarching dream of an inspiring future and how to get there

Communicate, communicate, communicate—capture the hearts and minds of most employees

by communicating through multiple channels and multiple times the vision for change

Empower employees—helping employees embrace the vision and support necessary structural mechanisms

Generate short-term wins—highlight short-term gains to keep employees motivated

Consolidate gains and produce more change—continue pressing forward until the change seeps into the deepest recesses of an organization

Anchor new approaches—embed the changes in the organization's cultural norms and values

Gentile's Giving Voice to Values

Clarification and articulation of one's values—articulation of one's own values and the impact of acting on those values, making implicit principles explicit

Post-decision-making analysis and implementation plan—understanding

how to voice opinions in difficult situations

The practice of speaking one's values and receiving feedback—pre-scripting situations in order to practice voicing values

Duck's Five Phases of People's Reaction Model

Change Curve—a simplification of the complex, often volatile, human emotion that accompanies change

Stagnation—occurs when people have an insufficient sense of threat or challenge from the external world

Preparation—requires a tremendous amount of planning and operational work and alignment of leaders

Implementation—includes designing new organizational structures, job descriptions, and lots of other detailed plans as well as changing people's mindsets and work practices

Determination—motivation to continue the long path to transformation

Fruition—is the time when the hard work pays off and the organization seems new

Beckhard and Harris's Change-Management Process

Focus on process—is key to this model with a step-by-step prescription for change

Gap analysis—describing a desired future state in contrast to an organization's present reality

Manage transition—the final step in the process key to a successful change initiative

The Change Path—Cawsey-Deszca-Ingols

Awakening—the stage of the process in which the need for change is determined and the nature of the change or vision is characterized in terms others can understand

Mobilization—the identification of the distance between the desired future state and the present state at which the system operates

Acceleration—the stage of the process in which plans are developed for bridging the gap between the current mode of operation and the desired future state and the means by which the transition will be managed. A key part of this stage includes action planning and implementation.

Institutionalization—the process of making the change inherent in organizational processes. Also, a consideration of how to measure change and what measures will be used to help identify where the organization is and the level of success achieved.

END-OF-CHAPTER EXERCISES

TOOLKIT EXERCISE 2.1

Critical Thinking Questions

The URLs for the videos listed below can be found in two places. The first spot is next to the exercise and the second spot is on the website at study.sagepub.com/cawsey4e.

A visit to the following website will provide the reader with numerous videos, cases and other materials related to the Giving Voice to Values curriculum.

https://www.darden.virginia.edu/ibis/initiatives/giving-voice-to-values/

1. **Giving Voice to Values:**

   Please read at the end of this chapter: "Not an Option to Even Consider: Contending with Pressures to Compromise," and consider the following questions:

   - Who are the important stakeholders that Ajith needs to work with?

   - What are the main arguments that Ajith will need to counter? In other words, what are the reasons and rationalizations that Ajith should expect to encounter with the different stakeholders?

   - What levers can Ajith pull to increase the chances that Laurent's drugs will be registered? In other words, what power and/or influence does Ajith have to get what he wants?

- Gentile talks about the importance of Giving Voice to Values to frame and address ethical issues and change. Meet in small groups and discuss an issue organizations have to deal with that has conflict of values imbedded in it. Would positive change be advanced if we were to adopt the methodology recommended by Gentile?

2. Kotter's Eight-Step Organizational Change Model: Sydney Boone, Ayushmaan Baweja, and Steven Thomsen—12:57 minutes

   https://www.youtube.com/watch?v=LxtF4OXzhyI

   This video delves more deeply into Kotter's process model of change.

   - What are the key lessons you learned from the video?

   - How do they help you think about the process of leading change?

   - Compare this approach with the Change Path Model. What are their similarities and differences, and how would you work with both models if you were leading change?

*Please see **study.sagepub.com/cawsey4e** for a downloadable template of this exercise.*

TOOLKIT EXERCISE 2.2

Analyzing a Change Process through
the Change Path Model

Part I

Interview a manager at any level who has been involved in change with his or her organization. Ask the person to describe the change, what he or she was trying to accomplish, and what happened. Use the following questions as guides for the interview.

- How was the desired change identified? What were the reasons for the change?

- Describe the gap between the organization's current performance and the desired future state.

- What was the vision for the change? How was that vision communicated throughout the organization?

- How were the formal structures, systems, and processes involved in the change?

- How were the recipients of change and other key stakeholders engaged in order to get them on board with the change?

- What tools and trainings were used as the change was implemented, and how did the leadership make the change stick?

- What challenges surfaced that weren't accounted for in the original change plan?

- What were the results of the change process? Did the results reflect the original vision? How was measurement used to facilitate change at different stages of the process?

Part II

After the interview, describe the process of the change by answering the following questions that are related to *how* they managed the process:

- How did the manager work to make things happen?

- Who was involved?

- How did they persuade others?

- What resources did they use?

- Also describe *what* was being changed? Why were these things important? How did these changes help the organization?

- As you reflect back on the interview, which do you feel was more important to the impact of the change: how things were changed, that is, process, or what was changed?

*Please see **study.sagepub.com/cawsey4e** for a downloadable template of this exercise.*

"NOT AN OPTION TO EVEN CONSIDER:" CONTENDING WITH THE PRESSURES TO COMPROMISE (A)[†]

By Heather Bodman, Researcher, and Cynthia Ingols, Professor of Practice

School of Business, Simmons University, Boston, MA

Ajith sighed as he hung up the phone. Once again, the health ministry had failed to move his registration application forward so that his company, Laurent Pharmaceuticals, could begin selling prescription medications in the Southeast Asian state of Kamaria. Though this new delay wasn't entirely unexpected, Ajith, a seasoned pharmaceutical executive, was still disappointed. Ajith's primary goal ever since arriving in Kamaria a year earlier to serve as director of operations and chief resident representative overseeing Laurent's in-country businesses, had been to obtain these registrations. Laurent's existing businesses included personal care products and over-the-counter medications. Laurent hoped to enter the pharmaceutical and vaccine markets but without the registrations, Ajith knew that the firm could not enter the market, restricting the firm's ability to grow the small but promising Kamarian business.

His disappointment was not only due to the delays themselves, but also to the reasons for them. The products that Laurent Pharmaceuticals intended to introduce specifically addressed growing major health concerns in the country. Ajith suspected that if his application could get past the first gatekeeper and into the hands of the health ministry's review committees, he could make a compelling case for introducing Laurent's products into Kamaria and dramatically improving the health of its citizens. Yet other companies appeared to be getting priority over Laurent. "What was quite amazing to us at the time was that companies who came with files six months later or three months later, were getting registrations extremely quickly," Ajith recalled. How were his competitors achieving these results? "They were basically bribing the gatekeeper and their files quickly ended up in the review committees, and they then probably met up with the review committee people and starting doing the same," Ajith realized. "They were getting quite a few registrations, so what we finally saw was that all sorts of registrations were coming through for our competitors and none for us."

Every day, the pressures on Ajith increased. Both his commitment to uphold the official policy of the company, which stated that compromise was unacceptable, and his strong sense of personal integrity—a source of professional and personal pride for Ajith—were being tested. Externally, the competitive pressures were mounting as other companies' mangers compromised and obtained registrations. Internally, Ajith's Laurent managers were becoming impatient with the obstacles to progress and were beginning to think that policy or no policy, compromise was the only way forward. Ajith disagreed, but he knew that he needed to articulate a better way.

To make matters worse, further difficulties had arisen in the over-the-counter market that Ajith also oversaw in Kamaria. Laurent Pharmaceuticals produced a widely used over-the-counter painkiller under the brand name Theradil. At first, this product was quite successful in Kamaria, achieving over 50% market share

---

[†] This case was prepared by Heather Bodman under the supervision of Professor Cynthia Ingols of Simmons University School of Business. This case was inspired by interviews and observations of actual experiences but names and other situational details have been changed for confidentiality and teaching purposes.

by 2008. But Ajith had recently begun to notice that Theradil's market share was eroding. Cheap, locally produced imitation products of inferior quality had begun to pop up in the pain relief market, decreasing Laurent's market share considerably. In investigating further, Ajith discovered that the factories producing the fake Theradil were run by former generals of the Kamarian army, who had been awarded these factories as rewards for their years of service and as spoils of war. Any attempt to shut them down could further impact Laurent Pharmaceuticals' ability to operate in Kamaria, and could potentially pose personal dangers for Ajith, due to the powerful nature of the individuals who ran these operations.

Ajith remained calm in the face of these challenges, reflecting that "these were standard issues that go with the terrain of operations in this part of the world, and especially the developing nations." Still, he acknowledged, "the situation after one year of operations in Kamaria was grim." How could he obtain registrations for the pharmaceutical products without compromising his integrity? And what strategies could he use to combat the growing problem of imitation Theradil without impacting Laurent's ability to do business in Kamaria?

HISTORICAL CONTEXT

Kamaria is a small, single-party state located in Southeast Asia. A former European colony, Kamaria suffered through decades of brutal civil war in the 20th century and finally achieved independence in 1987. Though it remained a closed market through the end of 1998, Kamaria began to open its markets to the outside world the following year, establishing a small private sector dominated by small- and medium-sized businesses and encouraging foreign-owned enterprises to set up local operations. By 2008, Kamaria was recognized as a fast-growing and export-driven emerging economy. The government of Kamaria was seeking to use their new status on the world stage to negotiate favorable trade agreements with the UK, the United States, and other developed nations to ensure the continued success of their exports. As in other developing countries, however, corruption was a problem that impaired Kamaria's ability to attract significant foreign direct investment, in spite of the attractiveness of its rapidly growing markets and manufacturing sector. Another issue facing Kamaria in trade agreements was the general lack of control they exerted over intellectual property, which was a concern to Western companies across a diverse set of industries, from entertainment and electronics to consumer goods and pharmaceuticals.

Laurent Pharmaceuticals was originally founded in the late 18th century as the first compounding pharmacies were beginning to appear throughout Europe. During the 19th century, Jean-Philippe Laurent inherited the firm and under his leadership, the company expanded into industrial manufacturing of chemical agents and early forms of pharmaceutical products. Though business suffered during the turbulent first half of the 20th century, Laurent recovered and became one of the first manufacturers of antibiotics, developing into one of the leading manufacturers of antibiotics and vaccines in the world by the 1970s. Today, they have evolved into a multinational, research-driven pharmaceutical and chemical company with operations in over 40 countries, including the United States, the UK, the EU, Australia, and dozens of emerging and developing nations. Producing and selling prescription medications for a variety of indications, as well as over the counter medications and personal care products, Laurent Pharmaceuticals is now one of the largest pharmaceutical companies in the world, earning $42 billion in revenues worldwide in 2008.

GROWING A BUSINESS

In 1988 Ajith began his career in marketing, working for a large multinational firm in his home region of South Asia. After moving to Laurent Pharmaceuticals in 2000, he accepted several international posts, which took him to the Middle East and East Africa. Working in these challenging markets honed his talent for management of in-country operations in developing countries, attracting the attention of Laurent's regional management is Southeast Asia.

In 2008, Ajith was recruited to serve as director of operations for Laurent's business in Kamaria.

Initially, Ajith managed Laurent's operations in Kamaria from Singapore, introducing over-the-counter medications and personal care products. In a short period of time, Laurent achieved a 50% market share in the lucrative pain relief market in Kamaria on the strength of its huge Theradil brand, an over-the-counter analgesic, creating a small but profitable (approximately $60,000 USD annually) operation. The next step in growing Laurent's Kamarian business was to enter the pharmaceutical market. To facilitate this new venture, Ajith was tasked with starting up a local office in Kamaria:

> Basically, when I went down to Kamaria, my first task, besides setting up the office, was to try and meet with the ministry of health officials and prepare all the registration files for all the vaccines that we needed to register and all the antibiotics we needed to register and accelerate the registration process.

> By about mid-2006, we had set up operations and we had started building a small team. We had probably about 15 to 20 medical delegates on board now, who were mostly qualified doctors—medical doctors—who were on the team as medical delegates. The pay that they were getting in government hospitals was pretty low, and I think that they saw this as an attractive option for them.

At the time, doctors in the state-run hospitals in Kamaria could expect to make approximately $30 USD per month. Ajith noted, "I think they were all finding it quite difficult to exist with that income." Doctors who became medical delegates to international pharmaceutical companies like Laurent could expect to start at $70–$100 USD per month, and could potentially earn as much as $200 a month if they were successful. "They had to make a call at that time," Ajith said, "and make a decision as to what they wanted to do." Doctors could not work for the hospitals and the pharmaceutical companies at the same time, "but they had the option of moving out anytime they wanted back into being doctors, and some of them saw this as a short-term measure to collect some cash."

By the time Laurent Pharmaceuticals entered the Kamarian market, there were already approximately 30 competitors operating in Kamaria, including companies based in the United States, Europe, South Korea, and India, along with many local firms. "The Korean and Indian companies all had similar portfolios in terms of products to what we had. There were also Kamarian competitors, but very much in the lower-end product categories, like over-the-counter medicines, not in the high end vaccine and antibiotics businesses." Though competition was healthy, the market was booming.

In part, this rapidly growing market was fueled by growing health concerns in Kamaria, as Ajith explains:

> There were two major health issues in Kamaria at the time. The first one was Hepatitis B. Hepatitis B in Kamaria has almost a 10% carrier rate, which means 1 in 10 Kamarians are prone to Hepatitis B. And the second big issue that was rising rapidly in Kamaria was resistance to antibiotics. Antibiotic resistance had now reached close to 18%, which meant that lots of frontline antibiotics were no longer effective amongst close to 20% of Kamaria's population. So most of the drugs that we were trying to register were high end vaccines for Hepatitis B and also the better antibiotics that we had in our portfolio, because Laurent has always been a world leader in both vaccines and in antibiotics and continues that leadership today. So, we knew the need was there, we knew the consumer problem was there, and we also knew that our products were significantly superior in delivering the remedial action compared to the drugs that we were getting registered.

Pharmacists, Ajith noted, were a key population that Laurent needed to reach in order to make any progress against antibiotic resistance. "I don't think too many Kamarian pharmacists know what it is to deliver a prescription and not under-deliver a prescription, and also educate consumers of the need for giving the full antibiotic dose as opposed to under-dosing themselves."

It would not be possible for Ajith to undertake such a marketing campaign himself until he was able to convince the Kamarian government to issue registrations for Laurent Pharmaceuticals products:

> We were quite perturbed because it had taken close to one year that we'd been there, and we were struggling to get anywhere with registrations. It was becoming more and more clear that if we needed registrations that we had to be ready to compromise, and that the Korean companies were compromising, and the Indian companies were compromising, and some of the other European companies were compromising.

Compromising was not an acceptable solution for Ajith, however:

> It was extremely clear to me that that was not an option for us to even consider. That was a very clear integrated policy in the company and we practiced that in almost every market where we operated. However, I must mention that if left up to some of the managers, they would also compromise. Now for example, at the time I was running Kamaria for Laurent, the guy who was running [a major competitor] was compromising. So having an integrity principle is one thing, but deciding whether to practice it or not, depending on the pressure you are getting from the company, is another thing. I can tell you that I was getting quite a lot of pressure from my regional head and

from the global operations people because they were seeing very little for progress in growing the Kamaria business.

At the same time, problems were brewing in the previously robust over-the-counter business that Laurent Pharmaceuticals was operating in Kamaria.

> We realized that sales of our brand of pain reliever, Theradil, were beginning to crash down rapidly. We had probably about 50% of the market in Kamaria for pain relievers, and we were suddenly seeing a massive decline from a 50–55% share down to about a 30% share, and when we began to investigate this further, we found that there were close to 12 brands of fake imitation Theradil in our market.

Testing of samples of the fake Theradil products revealed that consumers who purchased these brands were being seriously underdosed—at best, the imitation pain relievers contained 72% of the minimum standard dose of the active ingredient, with the most inferior substitutes containing just 36% of the standard dose.

To address the imitation Theradil problem, Ajith hired a law firm to investigate these issues and made a disquieting discovery.

> Almost all the 11 fake Theradils that were available in different parts of Kamaria were manufactured by factories formerly owned by the Kamarian government which were run by the then-generals of the Kamarian army. These generals had been given a pharmaceutical factory each, as compensation or recognition of their great contribution to the success of the Kamarian war at the time. In different parts of Kamaria, each of these guys had their little companies and it doesn't cost much to get a printer and develop your own artwork ripping off the competition.

With their government connections, Ajith knew that it would be difficult to put pressure on these factory owners to shut down their operations, particularly since, as Ajith observes, they made no attempt to hide what they were doing.

> Most of these companies were putting their factory addresses at the bottom of the pack. The detectives didn't have to do too much detection to figure out what was happening, because this was a reasonably flagrant violation. Anyway, they probably knew that they were sort of above the law at the time and could get away with it, so they probably didn't worry too much about that.

By the time Ajith uncovered the extent of the Theradil problem, eight submissions of registration paperwork to the ministry of health for Laurent antibiotics and vaccines had now been missed. "We were now having a sales decline in our base business, and not having the opportunity to grow the potential business, and that was very much the situation we were in," Ajith recalled.

DEVELOPING RELATIONSHIPS

In the course of launching the office in Kamaria in 2008, Ajith had recruited a dedicated local management team. This team oversaw the staff of doctors and supervised all other aspects of day-to-day operations of Laurent in Kamaria. Ajith's commitment to accountability and transparency in his organization were inspirational to his staff. Determined to fit in with his staff, Ajith began learning the Kamarian language, and only stopped conducting meetings in Kamarian when his staff expressed their desire to practice their English with him instead. He also plied his team for their expertise on a wide range of issues involving local customs and traditions, gaining insight into the tightly-knit culture of Kamaria. This expertise helped shape the vision Ajith was forming of what Laurent could offer the Kamarian consumer once the pharmaceutical registrations were approved.

At the same time, Ajith had been working closely with the French embassy in Kamaria as Laurent's operations were ramping up. In recent discussions with embassy officials, Ajith observed that the upcoming trade negotiations were a frequent topic of speculation, with strong opinions on all sides of the debate. Some embassy officials felt that the government of Kamaria was simply too corrupt to be considered a good free trade partner. Others saw great potential in Kamaria, and supported Europe's participation in free trade agreements with Kamaria, but worried about the weak protections in Kamaria for intellectual properly. Still others advocated for totally open trade, arguing that once Kamaria entered the global market, market forces would require the government to behave differently or risk losing their lucrative export position.

TAKING ACTION

Ajith sat at his desk and pondered his options. He did not want to compromise, but unless he took some action, he knew that his management would give up on Kamaria and he would have to leave. In fact, some members of his legal team went so far as to suggest that it would be in his best interest to leave Kamaria, due to concerns about the reaction from the powerful factory owners about the investigations into the production of imitation Theradil. But Ajith was not willing to give up quite so easily. He knew that Laurent's products, particularly the vaccines and antibiotics, could make a real, long-term difference in addressing the growing health concerns for the people of Kamaria, and this motivated him to pursue a creative solution. Surely there was a path forward that did not involve either compromising or turning a blind eye to illegal competition, and Ajith felt that he was up to the challenge.

What resources could he use to motivate the Kamarian government to review his submissions and issue registrations? Who were the stakeholders that Ajith needed to involve? What levers could he use to address the growing problem with fake Theradil? And how could he address these issues without compromising his values and the values of his company?

CHAPTER THREE

WHAT TO CHANGE IN AN ORGANIZATION: FRAMEWORKS

Chapter Overview

- Change leaders need to understand both the process of making organizational modifications (the *how* to change as outlined in Chapter 2) and the ability to diagnose organizational problems and take actions to change an organization.

- Determining what needs changing requires clear organizational frameworks. Change leaders need to comprehend the complexity and interrelatedness of organizational components: how analysis needs to occur at different organizational levels, and how organizations and their environments will shift over time, requiring further analysis and action.

- This chapter outlines several frameworks that one can use to analyze organizational dynamics:

  (1) Nadler and Tushman's Congruence Model balances the complexity needed for organizational analysis, and the simplicity needed for action planning and communication, and provides the overarching structure for this book;

  (2) Sterman's Systems Dynamics Model views the nonlinear and interactive nature of organizations;

  (3) Quinn's Competing Values Model provides a framework that bridges individual and organizational levels of analysis;

  (4) Greiner's Phases of Organizational Growth Model highlights organizational changes that will—inevitably—occur over time in organizations, from their infancy to maturity; this model is particularly useful for entrepreneurs who sometimes need to be reminded that change needs to occur, even in their small start-up organizations; and

  (5) Stacey's Complexity Theory is introduced to highlight the interactive, time-dependent nature of organizations and their evolutionary processes.

- Each framework aids a change agent in diagnosing a particular kind of organizational issue and suggests remedies for what ails an institution.

In Chapter 2, we considered the process of change (the Change Path). In this chapter, we deal with what aspects of an organization to change. Differentiating the process from the content is sometimes confusing, but the rather unusual example below will highlight the difference.

Bloodletting is a procedure that was performed to help alleviate the ills of mankind. . . . In the early 19th century, adults with good health from the country districts of England were bled as regularly as they went to market; this was considered to be preventive medicine.[1]

The practice of bloodletting was based on a set of assumptions about how the body worked—bloodletting would diminish the quantity of blood in the system and thus lessen the redness, heat, and swelling that was occurring. As a result, people seemed to get better after this treatment—but only in the short term. The reality was that they were weakened by the loss of blood. As we know today, the so-called science of bloodletting was based on an inaccurate understanding of the body. It is likely that bloodletting professionals worked to improve their competencies and developed reputations based on their skills in bloodletting. They worked hard at the *how* aspects of their craft. Advances in medicine prove that they did not really understand the consequences of *what* they were doing.

Bruch and Gerber differentiate *the what* and *the how* in a leadership question—"What would be the right action to take?"—and a management question—"How do we do it right?"[2] They analyzed a strategic change program at Lufthansa that took place from 2001 to 2004. This program generated more than €1 billion in continuing cash flow. The *how* questions focused on gaining acceptance of the change: focusing the organization, finding people to make it happen, and generating momentum; and the *what* questions were analytical, asking what change was right, what should be the focus, and what can be executed given the culture and situation. Bruch and Gerber concluded that a focus on implementation was not sufficient. A clear grasp of the critical needs, the change purpose or vision, was also essential.[3]

The two foundational models of this book are the Change Path Model (Chapter 2) and the Nadler and Tushman's Congruence Model (Chapter 3). The latter helps in the analysis of what is going on in an organization and what components of an organization need to be changed. That is, it is the "what to change" model. In any organizational change, both process (how to) and content (what) are important. Thus, we embed the Nadler and Tushman model in the four-stage Change Path Model. Nadler and Tushman help us to understand what gaps exist between where the organization is and where we want the organization to be. Like all models, the Nadler and Tushman's Congruence Model captures organizational reality from one perspective; consequently, Chapter 3 describes four additional organizational models designed to assist change leaders in their thinking about organizations and the reality that they represent.

For strengths, the Nadler and Tushman's Congruence Model gives us a comprehensive picture of an organization, its component parts, and how they fit together. That is, it asks us to examine organizational tasks (the work of the organization), people, informal organization (often thought of as the culture), and the formal organization (structures and systems) in the context of an organization's external environment, resources, history, and other inputs. Organizations are dynamic and highly interactive with their constantly changing environments. Change one aspect of an organization and other things are affected. Change the compensation system, for example, and we expect employee motivation and efforts to change as well—which they might or might not do.

Our second model in this chapter, Sterman's Systems Dynamics Model, helps us to understand underlying dynamics in complex systems and to see potential unanticipated consequences before they happen. Sterman asks managers to discard their linear, rational, causative view of organizations and to expand their perspectives to complex, interactive, multi-goal viewpoints. Note that this perspective is at the individual level. If we focus only at that individual level, we will miss major environmental factors and/or organizational-level matters.

Our third model of this chapter, Quinn's Competing Values Model, reminds us to think of the individual and organizational levels. This model captures much of the dual reality. It categorizes organizations into four cultural types with matching roles and skills needed to effectively operate in each of the organizational cultures.

So, we know that we need to have a process to change (the Change Path helps). We need to know what to change (Nadler and Tushman help). We need to understand how systems are interactive and dynamic (Sterman helps). And we need to think about levels of analysis: individual and organizational (Quinn helps). But, we also know that both the internal and external environment changes over time, too.

In order to help us think about time, our fourth model, Greiner's Phases of Organizational Growth Model, helps. Greiner posits a series of predictable stages that occur in the life of an organization. While the empirical evidence to support this model is weak, many managers find this prescriptive stage model helpful in thinking about organizations and how they change over time and grow.

Finally, our fifth model recognizes just how complex organizational systems are. Stacey's Complexity Theory provides a set of propositions about organizations that helps us to capture the implications of intricacies and convolutions.

Keeping a clear line of sight on what needs to change is *not a "one shot" activity*, conducted only at the commencement of an initiative. This is particularly true for initiatives that are not simple and straight forward. Analyses are, by their nature, premised on assessments of factors that can and do shift over time. Sometimes, those shifts are slow to evolve while at other times, such as the financial meltdown in 2008 or the imposition of tariffs in 2018, they are swift and profound.

Analyses, including the questioning of the underlying assumptions that ground them, need to be updated throughout the course of a change initiative. By tracking changing conditions, adjustments can be made along the way. When Target entered Canada, evidence suggests it assumed that replicating what it did in the United States would lead to success. That assessment was faulty. Twenty-three months after entering Canada, they exited, taking a $5.4 billion loss. One of the main causes of this was tied to Target's failure to adapt its supply chain to the Canadian context—something that was arguably preventable.[4]

Further, the analyses attached to a change initiative need to drill down into the different parts of an organization in order to assess what specifically needs to change in each area to support the overall change program. One size does not fit all.

In summary, to be a successful change leader we need to understand both how to change (i.e., a focus on process) and what to change (i.e., an analysis of organizational problems). We need to know that organizations are dynamic, they can be viewed at different levels of analysis (from individual to group to organizational), they change over time, and they are complex. Each model described in this chapter builds our conceptual toolkit to better lead change.

OPEN SYSTEMS APPROACH
TO ORGANIZATIONAL ANALYSIS

Organizations interact with their environments in complex and dynamic ways. This **open systems perspective** is based on the following assumptions:[5] Open systems exchange information, materials, and energy with their environments. As such, a system interacts with, and is not isolated from, its environment.

- A system is the product of its interrelated and interdependent parts and represents a complex set of interrelationships rather than a chain of linear cause–effect relationships.

- A system seeks equilibrium: when it is in equilibrium, it will only change if some energy is applied.

- Individuals within a system may have views of the system's function and purpose that differ greatly from the views held by others.

- Things that occur within and/or to open systems (e.g., issues, events, forces) should not be viewed in isolation, but rather should be seen as interconnected, interdependent components of a complex system.

The adoption of an open systems perspective allows managers to identify areas of misalignment and risk between the external environment and the organization's strategy and structure. Open systems analysis helps practitioners to develop a rich appreciation for the current condition of an organization and plausible alternatives and actions that could improve it. For example, when people, products, or services within systems have operated without considering their environment for extended periods of time, they risk becoming seriously incongruent with the external environment.[6] Or, if an environment changes rapidly, the results can prove disruptive and, in some cases, disastrous for an organization. Consider how the innovations and actions at Apple and Google disrupted the smartphone market in ways that left Blackberry and Nokia scrambling to revive and reinvent themselves as relevant technology providers. Innovation by one company led to significant disruption and change for other organizations. Disruptions can shake organizations to their foundations, and they also have the potential to sow the seeds for renewal (hence the term *creative destruction*, coined by Joseph Schumpeter[7]).

In summary, organizations should not be analyzed as if they exist in a bubble, isolated from their environments. But rather, organizations should be analyzed as to how effectively and efficiently they garner resources from the external environment and transform these resources into outputs that the external environment welcomes. Nadler and Tushman's Congruence Model does just that.

(1) NADLER AND TUSHMAN'S CONGRUENCE MODEL

In this book, the Nadler and Tushman model is used as a framework to assist in structuring change leaders' organizational analysis. The model has a reasonably complete set of organizational variables and presents them in a way that encourages straightforward thinking. It specifically links environmental input factors to the organization's components and outputs. As well, it provides a useful classification of internal organizational components and shows the interaction among them. Nadler and Tushman's model is one example of an open systems model.

Nadler and Tushman[8] provide a conceptual scheme that describes an organization and its relationship to its external environment. The Congruence Model is based on the principle that an organization's performance is derived from four fundamental elements: tasks (or the work of the organization), people, formal organization (structure and systems), and informal organization (part of which is the "culture"). The more congruence there is among these four components, and the more aligned they are with the external environmental realities and the strategy of the organization, then the better the organization's performance will be in the external marketplace—whether it is the quality of services for at-risk youths offered by a local school board, or a new electric vehicle an automobile firm hopes will achieve market acceptance.[9] An adaptation of their model is depicted in Figure 3.1. This model is used as a framework for this book. Inputs are transformed to outputs, and the feedback links make the model dynamic and the components highly interdependent.

History and Environment

From its start-up phase, leaders of an organization make choices concerning where they want to locate themselves, what they want to do, and which resources they want to buy, access, or otherwise develop and deploy. These historical decisions set the stage for future actions and outcomes, and which human, technological, and capital resources they subsequently seek from the environment. The history of an organization provides insights into how it evolved its mission, culture, strategy, and approach to how it organizes and manages itself. 3M's early experience, for example, as a near bankrupt mining company set the stage for a sustained culture that highly values flexibility and innovation as keys to its resilience and success.

In addition to history and resources, external environmental factors play a huge role in influencing what organizations choose to do. These include political, economic, social, technological, ecological, and legal factors (PESTEL factors). For example, if a competitor launches a more attractive product/service, if new environmental regulations are enacted that create risk or opportunity for your products/services, or if an attractive new foreign market is emerging due to changing economic and demographic conditions, organizations will need to consider such environmental factors and trends as they decide upon their strategic approach. All organizational leaders must deal with an organization's history and recognize the impact and constraints, as they deal with the current external environment and seek to align their resources with the strategy to produce the desired results. In thinking about what to change, all inputs may be sources of opportunity and constraint.

For change leaders, an ability to analyze the organization's external environment and see implications for action in the organization is a central change skill.

Strategy

An analysis of the organization's competencies, strengths, and weaknesses, in light of the environmental threats and opportunities, leads to the strategy that organizational leaders decide to pursue. Strategic choices lead to the allocation

Figure 3.1 Nadler and Tushman's Organizational Congruence Model

Source: From Nadler, D. A., & Tushman, M. L. (1989). Organizational frame bending: Principles for managing reorientation. *Academy of Management Executive,* III(3), 194–204.

of resources. Sometimes the strategy is consciously decided. At other times, it is a reflection of past actions and market approaches that the organization has drifted into. When there is a gap between what leaders say their strategy is and what they do (i.e., the actual strategy in use), one needs to pay close attention to the strategy in use. In Chapter 4, we discuss strategy in depth.

For change leaders, the change strategy is a critical focus of their analysis. What are the purposes and objectives of the planned change in the context of the organizational strategy? Is it of the fine-tuning variety, to better align resources with the strategy, remove an obstacle, and more effectively deliver the desired results, or does the change involve something much more substantial, including changes to the strategy itself?

The Transformation Process

The next elements of the model are what Nadler and Tushman define as the transformation process. This is where the organization's components are combined to produce the outputs. They include the work to be done, the formal structures, systems and process, the informal organization, and the people.

Work

The work is the basic tasks to be accomplished by an organization and its subunits in order to carry out the organization's strategy. Some of these tasks are key success factors that the organization must execute in order to successfully implement its strategy. An organization's work may be described in a very discrete way, listing, for example, the duties of a particular position, or, at the polar extreme, the basic functions such as marketing. Tasks may be nested in teams, requiring coordination and integration; be separated and independent from one another or configured in some other way. The tasks may be designed to require a wide range of sophisticated skills and abilities or require a narrow set of basic skills. The work may require sophisticated judgment and decision making or require people to follow standardized procedures. Existing task designs reflect past decisions concerning what needs to be done and how best to do things. These designs often reflect cultural beliefs in the organization and are, to a degree, a matter of choice. Chapter 5 deals with how the work is formally structured and organized.

In change situations, change leaders should think through the necessary shifts in key tasks in order to carry out the change initiative. This will assist in developing a specific gap analysis and change plan.

The Formal Organization

The formal organization includes the "organizational architecture, a term that describes the variety of ways in which the enterprise formally structures, coordinates, and manages the work of its people in pursuit of strategic objectives."[10] Once tasks are identified and defined, they are grouped to form reporting relationships, the formal organizational chart of roles, responsibilities, departments, divisions, and so on. The purpose of a structure is to enable efficient and effective task performance. The formal systems of an organization are the mechanisms that help the organization accomplish its work and direct the efforts of its employees. These include an organization's human resource management systems (recruitment and selection, reward and compensation, performance management, training and development); information systems; measurement and control systems (e.g., budget, balanced scorecard); production systems; and so forth. Chapter 5 deals with designed systems and structures.

Change leaders need to understand how the formal systems and structures influence people's behaviors and how structures can be used to facilitate change. Often formal systems, such as budgeting systems, need to be used to gather data for change.

The Informal Organization

The informal relationships among people and groups in the organization, the informal way things get done, and the norms accepted by organizational members reflect the way the culture manifests itself in the organization. While managers define the work necessary to accomplish the strategy and then structure those tasks in formal ways, many things occur that are unplanned, unanticipated, and/or evolve over time. For example, friendly relationships between individuals often ease communications; groups form and provide support or opposition for the accomplishment of tasks; and individuals and teams adapt procedures to make things easier or more productive.* The informal system will include an organization's culture, the norms or understandings about "how we do things around here," values (e.g., about the importance of customer service), beliefs (for example, about why the organization is successful), and managerial style (a "tough boss" style, for example). It will also reflect the informal leadership and influence patterns that emerge in different parts of the organization.

Culture is a product of both the organization's history and its current organizational leadership. It acts as a control system in the sense that it defines

---

* For an interesting perspective on the relational aspect of an informal system, see either M. Hutt, et al., "Defining the Social Network of a Strategic Alliance," *Sloan Management Review 41*, no. 2 (2000): 51–62, or D. Krackhardt and J. R. Hanson, "Informal Networks: The Company Behind the Chart," *Harvard Business Review 74*, no. 4 (1993): 104–111.

acceptable and unacceptable behaviors, attitudes, and values and will vary in strength and impact, depending upon how deeply held and clearly understood the culture is. Other elements of the informal organization that are important to analyze when considering how to create change include power relationships, political influence, and decision-making processes. Chapter 6 deals with informal systems, power, and culture.

Change leaders need to make explicit the oftentimes implicit norms and behaviors of individuals and groups. Identifying the currently useful and dysfunctional norms and dynamics is a critical change agent activity.

People

The people in an organization perform tasks using both the organization's designed systems and structures, and the informal cultural processes that have evolved. It is important that the attitude, knowledge, and skills of each person match the individual's role, and that their responsibilities and duties match the organization's needs. Understanding the individuals in the organization and how they will respond to the proposed change will be significant in managing the change process. The role of stakeholders and change recipients is discussed in Chapters 4, 6, and 7.

Within every organization, certain key individuals are critical to its success. Often, we think of the formal leaders as those who are most important in terms of accomplishing the mission, but others may be crucial. These people might have special technical skills or might be informal leaders of a key group of employees. People such as these, acting as change leaders, are described in Chapter 8.

Change leaders need to understand the impact of proposed changes on the organization's employees. Further, they need to identify key leaders in the organization who can facilitate the needed changes.

Outputs

The outputs of an organization are the services and products it provides to generate profitability or, especially in the case of public sector and nonprofit organizations, to meet mission-related goals. Additional outputs are also important: the satisfaction of organizational members, the growth and development of the competencies of the organization and its members, and customer satisfaction (to name just three). These outputs need to be defined and measured as attentively as profitability, return on investment (ROI), or numbers of clients served.

The above model reflects how one would look at the organization as a whole. However, this same approach can be adapted to look at internal parts of an organization that supply inputs or services for another part of the enterprise. The level of success of the organization in producing desired outputs becomes part of the feedback loop and a new input to the organization. In a well-functioning organization, feedback will provide input when contemplating modifying the strategy or internal alignments. Chapter 10 focuses on the measurement of change.

Change leaders need to recognize that "what gets measured is what gets done." They need to select key measures that will track the change process.

In their work, Nadler and Tushman make three critical statements. First, the system is *dynamic*. This means that a diagnosis of how the organization should operate will change over time if external or internal conditions change or if different concerns and objectives emerge. Second, the *"fit"* or congruence between components is significant in diagnosing why the organization performs well or poorly. And third, *the better the fit is among organizational components and their alignment with the environment, the more effective the organization is.* The organizational change challenge is to align the system's components to respond to changing external and internal conditions.

The System is Dynamic

When an organization's environment shifts, so must its diagnosis, in order to identify the changes needed to effectively realign its people, formal systems and processes, tasks, and culture to that environment and produce the desired outcomes. For example, when inflation was running at 1,100% per year in Brazil,[11] the influence of financial executives soared because financial management played a pivotal role in sustaining firms. When inflation slowed and stabilized in the range of 10% to 20%, power shifted away from finance and toward sales, marketing, and production. If the external environment alters significantly, the internal organization needs to change also. While this may seem like a statement of the obvious, it often goes unobserved in practice. Managers develop patterns of thinking about organizational performance that served them well in the past, but over time these patterned approaches may impair their ability to see when conditions have changed, and a different approach is needed. Since the external environment is dynamic, the internal systems also need constant tuning, or even, at times, transformation.

The "Fit" Between and Among Organizational Components Is Critical

Nadler and Tushman argue that there are many different ways to think about the components of an organization. However, they choose to focus their model on four major components: "1) the task, 2) the individuals, 3) the formal organizational arrangements, and 4) the informal organization."[12]

A change agent needs to understand these four components of an organization and how they fit together and influence one another. Congruence is a measure of how well components fit together. For example, executives in an organization who restructure and ignore the knowledge and skills of people who will fill the newly created jobs do so at some risk. Restructured organizations with newly defined jobs either require the retraining of employees, or the hiring of new employees with the requisite skills. Or, if managers create structures and jobs to fit the competencies of key people and then those people leave, there may be a significant loss of fit between the structural components and the new key people.

Organizations With Good Fit Are More Effective Than Those With Poor Fit

Nadler and Tushman argue that effective organizations have excellent "fit" or "congruence" between components. Further, they argue that the strategy needs to flow from an accurate assessment of the environment and respond to, or take advantage of, changes occurring in that environment. Similarly, the strategy needs to fit the organization's capabilities and competencies, or the organization needs to develop capabilities and competencies that are aligned with the strategy. If all of these are not aligned reasonably well with the strategy, the organization will be less effective than it could have been. Inside the organization, the four components (tasks, people, designed structure and systems, and culture) must fit each other. For example, if an organization hires motivated, highly skilled individuals and assigns them routine tasks without challenge or decision-making opportunities, those individuals will likely be bored. There will be a lack of fit and productivity will suffer. Or, if the strategy demands the adoption of new technology and employees are not provided with the necessary training, fit is lacking. Within categories, elements might not fit. For example, an organization might decide to "empower" its employees to improve performance. If it fails to adjust the supervisory approach and reward system to reinforce the desired behaviors, or if the culture of the organization is one of mistrust, this lack of fit could easily lead to a failure of the empowerment strategy.

Overall, lack of fit leads to a less effective organization. Good fit means that components are aligned with the strategy and the strategy is effectively aligned with what is going on in the environment.

For many managers, the notion of fit is easiest to understand as they follow the flow from strategy to key tasks to organizing those tasks into formal structures and processes to accomplish the desired objectives. This is a rational approach to management and appeals to one's logic. At the same time, the reality of organizations often means that what appears to management as logical and necessary is not logical to employees. Managerial logic may be viewed by employees as against their interests or unnecessary. Peters recognizes the importance of the so-called nonrational aspects of organizations.[13] He argues that managers should tap into the power of teams to accomplish results and that individuals can be challenged to organize themselves to accomplish tasks. Thus, while fit is easiest to picture in logical terms, change agents need to consider it in terms of the informal system and the key individuals in the change process who will influence its success.

In a typical scenario, changes in the environment may require leaders to rethink the organization's strategy. This, in turn, results in changes in key tasks and how managers structure the organization to do those tasks. In developing a new strategy and in redesigning an organization's systems and structures, managers need to become aware of and understand the influence of key individuals and groups.

Why Should Those Advocating for Change Care?

Nadler and Tushman's Congruence Model helps practitioners in three ways. First, it provides a template to assist in an organizational analysis. Second, it gives one a way of thinking about the nature of the change process—environmental factors tend to drive interest in the organization's strategy, which, in turn, propels the transformational processes. These, then, influence the results. Third, the congruence framework emphasizes that, for organizations to be effective, a good fit among all elements in the process is required from environment to strategy through to the transformation process. Fit is also necessary within the transformation process; this is a constant challenge for incremental change initiatives such as continuous improvement programs. An emphasis on the internal fit between organizational components often focuses on efficiency. An emphasis on the external fit between the organization and its environment is an effectiveness focus. See **Toolkit Exercise 3.2** to practice examining a situation through Nadler and Tushman's model.

An Example Using Nadler and Tushman's Congruence Model

Over the past several years, Dell Computers has transformed itself. Dell made its name by selling low-cost computers directly to customers. The company was renowned for an efficient supply chain that allowed it to receive payment for its computers before it incurred the cost of building them. The Dell story outlines the company's attempt to reorient itself.

DELL COMPUTERS REORIENTS ITSELF[14]

For years, Dell focused on being the low-cost, efficient producer of computers. As one report put it, "Dell long stuck with its old playbook of cranking out PCs as efficiently as possible."[15] Dell had focused on making the computer a commodity and sold online using generic parts. Dell focused on optimizing the business it already had while the market shifted. Its competitors, Hewlett-Packard, IBM, Apple, and others, marketed newer, sleeker laptops with better Internet capabilities using retail stores for distribution.

In 2007, company founder Michael Dell returned as CEO after three years of relative distance from operations. He replaced his senior management team, added new products and services, and focused on what customers wanted. However, the marketplace was changing radically as smartphones and similar products became the hot, new focus.

The troubles for Dell had begun when the market shifted. Growth in the corporate market lessened while the consumer sector flourished. As well, developing markets overseas became critical—markets that were less willing to buy over the Internet and use direct delivery. Additional processing power became less critical, and consumers demanded special features and more attractive machines. Dell saw the clear need to alter what it was doing. A diagnosis of what would work led to an overhaul of its products and the company.

After taking over, Michael Dell responded to the marketplace. He set up mechanisms to get customers' input. He shifted Dell's distribution strategy to sell in retail outlets, too. This required a shift in mindset for Dell managers as they had to establish new distribution systems and manage their relationships with retailers. New machine designs were created and new hardware, including smartphones, were offered. Dell began selling mini-notebooks to appeal to overseas markets. And the company responded to changes in the corporate sector by providing systems solutions, not just computers.

To implement his strategy, Michael Dell installed a new senior management team. One of his first moves was to hire Ron Garriques, the executive who introduced Motorola's Razr phone, as head of Dell's consumer business. Garriques shut down work on the Mantra, a standard line of Dell products. As well, he stopped the introduction of Dell specialty stores and developed relationships with retailers. Product design became a new, central focus.

Michael Dell also brought in Brian Gladden from GE. Gladden believed that Dell needed to be restructured, that its systems and processes were not sophisticated enough for a company of its size. One major move was to shift how Dell focused on external markets by organizing around market segments, such as consumers, corporations, small- and mid-sized businesses, and governments and educational buyers.

Culture change was necessary to shift Dell to a more responsive, flexible company. Group leaders had clear financial targets but were given significant discretion in determining how to achieve these targets.

New products were developed and Dell began selling what in 2010 was the world's thinnest notebook. Design and style were emphasized, along with "tech appeal." Smartphones were also introduced, but Dell announced it was exiting this product category in December 2012 as they continued to search for a strategy that would work in this very competitive sector.

While Dell Inc. remained one of the leading companies in the technology industry, key financial ratios from 2006 and 2010 illustrate its problems: profit margins fell from 6.5% in 2006 to 2.7% in 2010. In 2006 Dell reported revenue growth at 13.6%; in 2010 the company reported a 13.4% decline in revenue.[16] Ever-the-optimist CEO Michael Dell said the business climate was improving and "repeated his expectations for a 'powerful' hardware refresh cycle beginning next year (2010)."[17] Somewhere in the 2011–2013 period, Michael Dell decided to take his eponymous company (#51 on Fortune 500 list in 2014) private. He had concluded that further changes were needed and that being a publicly listed firm was getting in the way of accomplishing the longer-term objectives. By November 2013, he celebrated his public to private deal with 350 employees in Silicon Valley. As one of the world's richest men, Dell mixed in "his 16% ownership, valued at more than $3 billion, and another $750 million in cash, with $19.4 billion from Silver Lake Partners (a private equity firm) for a 75% stake in Dell Inc."[18]

Dell has not faded from the scene. In 2013 it was the world's largest shipper of monitors and in 2015 Dell was the third largest PC vendor.[19] At the same time, it continued to actively diversify its revenue streams through its servers, networking, software, and services. Its activities in cloud computing are notable. In 2016 Dell announced the acquisition of EMC Corp. (an enterprise and cloud storage firm) for an estimated $64 billion in cash and shares.[20] This allowed Dell to become a much more significant competitor in this growing market. In July 2018, Dell undertook some financial reengineering and announced that it intended to once again become a publicly traded company.[21] This was likely done to provide his private equity partners with path to exit and to provide Dell with greater access to capital and public exposure.

Time will tell if the transformations undertaken within Dell Inc. will lead to sustained success.

During its rapid growth years in the 1990s, Dell provided unrivalled service to its markets. Corporations wanted reliable equipment with good prices and excellent service. Dell provided this with online ordering and fast delivery. Its manufacturing, inventory management, and distribution systems were designed to deliver built-to-order PCs at a low cost. Speed of production became critical in order to minimize the delay between customer order and shipment to that customer. Relationships in the market were with customers, not retailers. While major clients (governments, etc.) had clout, as long as Dell delivered quality products and provided good technical service, the clients were satisfied. The key tasks, to use Nadler and Tushman's terminology, were production and distribution.

During this growth phase, Dell's organization was aligned well with its market. Internally, the production orientation fit those market needs. Systems were designed for efficiency and simplicity. There was no need for retail management. Inventories were minimized as Dell built to order, leveraging its effective supply chain. Finances were simple because customers paid as they ordered and before Dell incurred the costs of production. Dell's management team excelled at getting efficiencies from this system, and the results showed for many years.

As the market shifted, the Dell organization became increasingly out of sync with the marketplace. Dell's strategy was no longer a good fit as the marketplace shifted away from corporate demand to consumers, from machine power to design, from hardware to software and the Internet, from America to other nations. The clean, straightforward organization that Dell had built could not meet the more complex market expectations.

Note how Michael Dell responded. All components of the company changed. First, the strategy shifted. Design was emphasized. Retailers became key parts of the distribution network. Product variety increased. With that strategic shift, the key success factors or critical tasks changed. Design became more important. Management of retail distribution became crucial and introduced an entirely new set of skills at Dell. As the product range increased, skills in the introduction and timing of new products became more important. To manage this, the company was reorganized into four divisions, each focused on one major customer segment. Financial systems would need to be overhauled to manage this complexity. New formal and informal networks were established as the company's focus changed. Key executives were replaced by others with the skill sets demanded by this new strategy. In short, a new state of congruency was sought so that the internal operations fit the new strategy better.

When these strategies were found to be producing results too slowly in the eyes of investors and analysts, Dell decided to cease being a publicly traded firm and go private in 2013. They did this in order to have more freedom to execute their longer-term strategies away from the public glare. It downsized and reorganized and continued to actively pursue product and service diversification and growth though product and service innovations. The acquisition of EMC in 2016 was particularly noteworthy. It fit well with Dell's strategy to greatly enhance their capacities in growing areas of cloud data storage, cloud computing, and related enterprise services.

Dell's shifts in market focus (products, services, markets, channels), acquisitions, legal structure (public vs private), and internal realignments over time provide an excellent example of how the Nadler and Tushman model's notion of congruency can be used to help us understand and analyze organizations, the resultant outcomes produced, and what needs to change in order to achieve the desired outcomes. At the time of the writing of this book, it is too early to tell if Dell's most recent initiatives will yield desired results.

Nadler and Tushman's model enables a change agent to think systematically about the organization. It serves as a checklist to ensure practitioners consider the critical components that must be matched with the strategy and environmental demands. Since the system is dynamic, the environment, the people, the competition, and other factors change over time, and part of that change is due to how the components interact with each other. Second, the fit between organizational components is critical. Dell's products, organization, systems, and culture had become misaligned with the emerging environment in and around the 2010–2013 period. Finally, organizations with good fit are more effective than those with poor fit because they will be able to more efficiently and effectively transform inputs into outputs. The moves that Michael Dell made improved the fit and led to a modest turnaround in sales and margins in the short term, but subsequent competitive challenges caused him to recognize that much more is needed—hence the move to take the company private so that needed changes could be made away from the glare of stock market pressures for short-term results.

Like any living entity, an organization survives by acting and reacting effectively to its external environment. Unless it adjusts with appropriate changes to its approach and, when needed, its strategy, it reduces its capacity to thrive. When one part of the organization is changed, then other parts also need to adapt to maintain the congruence that leads to effectiveness. Whether Dell and his team have made enough savvy changes for the long term will be demonstrated by the company's future performance. Critical to this will be Dell's ability to innovate and change in the face of shifts in its environment.

Evaluating Nadler and Tushman's Congruence Model

Are the assumptions made by Nadler and Tushman's Congruence Model reasonable ones? For example, should strategy always dictate the organization's structure and systems? While that is one of the traditional views of how to achieve organizational effectiveness, it is not unusual to see the reverse where changes in the structures and systems drive alterations to strategy. For example, FedEx used its systems and expertise that it built to deliver packages to its own customers to provide logistical services to other companies. Amazon got into the cloud storage business by taking advantage of its capability to run large server farms. Thus, the implied direction of the Nadler and Tushman model is appropriate, but any analysis must recognize how dynamic and interactive organizational factors are. For many change agents, particularly those in middle management, the strategy of their organizations will be a given and their role will be to adapt their parts of the transformation process to better achieve those strategic directions. In doing so, they may also seek to influence what goes on in other parts of the organization because of how things in one part of the organization impact on the achievement of their objectives. This task is made easier when the objectives are shared.

Alternatively, change agents may attempt to influence the strategy directly (e.g., participation in a strategic task force) and/or indirectly (initiate activities that lead to the development of new internal capacities, learning, awareness, and interest that make new strategies viable).

Has the importance of fit been overstated? Probably not. For example, in an investigation into the mixed results achieved by total quality management (TQM) initiatives, Grant, Shani, and Krishnan found that "TQM practices cannot be combined with strategic initiatives, such as corporate restructuring, that are based on conventional management theories. The failure of one or both programs is inevitable."[22] Thus, they found that the strategy, the structure, and new TQM processes need to fit with each other. Another example of issues of fit emerged following September 11, 2001, when the U.S. government created the Department of Homeland Security, which combined 22 government entities. However, reports subsequently emerged that suggested the secretary of the department had few levers needed to do his job: the formal structure had been created, but not the systems and processes that were necessary to give him leverage to be successful.[23] In both of these examples, a lack of alignment undermined the efforts to effectively change these organizations.

The need for change may not always be identified by looking at an organization's environment. Problems surface in a variety of ways. There might be problems in the organization's outcomes or outputs, indicating that some aspect of performance needs to be addressed. Further, there is the question of the magnitude of the change. The organization may decide to change its strategy, its culture, or some other core element. Generally, the more fundamental the change, the more other elements of the organization will need to be modified to support the desired change. For example, a change to one aspect of an organization may create a domino effect, requiring other changes to structure, systems, culture, and people.

MARY BARRA, GM, AND THE NEED FOR REALIGNMENT

Mary Barra, GM's CEO who was appointed in 2014, is living with this challenge. While alignment had improved significantly since emerging from bankruptcy in 2009, as evidenced by positive product reviews and improvements in sales and profitability, GM's leaders found themselves dealing with legacy cultural issues. For example, ignition switch design defects that resulted in 124 deaths had not been addressed for a decade. Internal investigations and congressional hearings reported that there was an organizational culture that promoted silence on such issues.

Barra acted on the dysfunctional aspects of GM's culture. She fired 15 executives found to have been involved with the situation, spoke about it with greater candor than ever before, and instituted a corporate-wide change initiative called "Speak up for Safety."[24]

She has affirmed that more recalls are likely as they search through their files: She stated that an "aggressive stance on product recalls is the new norm at GM" and that it is unacceptable for employees to stay silent on safety issues. She also focused GM's attention on innovation, particularly in the area of electric and self-driving vehicles, and on diversity in its workforce. It was ranked #1 out of 200 global firms in its efforts to achieve gender equity in 2018. Barra states, "You need the right people, the right culture and the right strategy. To be truly great, your team must have diversity of thought and be willing to collaborate constructively. Your company culture should empower and inspire people to relentlessly pursue the company vision – always with integrity."[25]

Finally, does better fit always increase the likelihood of effectiveness? This depends upon the measure of effectiveness. In the short run, fit focused on efficiency might mean increased profits as the organization reduces costs and becomes efficient. However, an innovation measure might show that fit focused primarily on efficiency has led to declining creativity. Efficiency is important but so is the development of appropriate adaptive capacities in an organization. It can be argued that in the long run, tight congruence in a stable environment leads to ingrained patterns inside the organization. Individuals and organizations develop formal systems and structures, as they should, but these can lead to ritualized routines and habits. Such patterns can be change resistant and can be hugely ineffective when the environment changes. Dell Computers suffered from this prior to Michael Dell's reintroduction in 2007. If the pace of change an organization must deal with is rapid, then an overemphasis on getting congruence "just right" can lead to delays that put the health of the firm at risk. In a rapidly changing environment, approximations are appropriate: don't make it perfect; get it acceptable and move on. Nevertheless, for most analytical purposes, the assumption that an increasing fit is a good objective is appropriate.

As with other congruence or alignment-oriented models, the Nadler and Tushman model must deal with the criticism that "too much emphasis on congruence potentially (could have) an adverse or dampening effort on organizational change."[26] The key lies in balancing the need for flexibility and adaptability with the need for alignment. This balance point shifts as environmental conditions and organizational needs change. To emphasize the dynamic nature of organizations, we next examine Sterman's Systems Dynamics Model.

(2) STERMAN'S SYSTEMS DYNAMICS MODEL[27]

As discussed, Nadler and Tushman's Congruence Model acknowledges the dynamic nature of systems as the authors focus on the importance of alignment. In contrast, Sterman's model, below, focuses on the interplay of dynamic forces of the environment, managerial decisions, and actions of others. Sterman believes that managers should handle increased complexity by increasing the number of variables that they consider. The dynamic nature of the variables and the interactions among the variables over time may lead to counterintuitive results.

Sterman argues that managers often take a linear view of the world—a rational, causative model where managers identify a gap between what is and what is desired, make a decision, and take action, expecting rational results. If sales are low, management might increase advertising, thinking that sales will flow. However, because of how the variables interact with one another, this linear view can be inaccurate and limiting. What management may get are counterintuitive results that are often change resistant. If Company A, for example, increases its advertising, then Companies B, C, and D may increase their advertising as well. The result may be increased costs and static revenues. Managers may fail to anticipate the side effects of their decisions, and how their actions lead to competitive responses.

The dynamics described above at the organizational level can also play out at the national and international levels. The trade war between the United States and China that began in 2018 caused some analysts to urge caution out of concern that it could, paradoxically, make China a stronger competitor. Their assessment was that tariff pressures could give rise to unanticipated innovations and competitive responses in China's industries that could, in turn, end up hurting firms in the West.[28]

Consider the following example. Managers change the incentive structure for employees, anticipating that this will lead to higher productivity. However, employees might see increased productivity as leading to layoffs (if we produce more, they will need fewer of us), and thus resist increasing outputs. Or, employees will begin to focus on quantity and neglect crucial quality concerns. This, in turn, creates negative customer reactions that cause management to create new control systems around quality. Such control systems take additional paperwork and effort that increase costs and potentially defeat the original objective of increasing productivity.

Another point Sterman makes is that many problems result from time lags and delays, inventories and buffer stocks in the system, and attribution errors. Thus, another possible outcome, in our above example, is that employees may increase their efforts to generate new sales as the result of the changed rewards. However, there could be a significant lag before sales increase. Some sales cycles take months and even years before producing results. Thus, management's initial observation might be that the change in the reward system did not work. Small changes in demand may get exaggerated because of inventory buffers that automatically adjust. And finally, humanity's need to attribute cause might mean that managers assume causal links that don't exist.

Sterman's model heightens the awareness of the complexity involved with change and the challenges involved in developing alignments that will produce desirable results in the short and long term and not result in unpleasant surprises. As such, Sterman's model builds on the work of Argyris and Schön,[30] identifying the importance of organizational analysis through double-loop and triple-loop learning. Single loop is essentially adaptive learning within the organization's operation. Internal data are assessed and modifications are made, but the original objectives are not questioned. Double-loop learning goes beyond making incremental modifications and challenges the assumptions, standards, policies, values, and mode of operation that gave rise to the standards and objectives. Triple-loop learning extends this analysis and exploration of possibilities further and questions the underlying rationale for the organization and why it exists. Triple-loop learning is also consistent with the work of Senge[31] on how organizations should be designed and managed in order to enhance organizational learning, innovation, and change.

In Figure 3.2, decisions lead to side effects as well as intended effects. These interact with the environment and the goals of others to create a more complex set of outcomes than were anticipated.

At McDonald's at the beginning of the 21st century, management decided to increase the number of corporate-owned stores and decrease costs. In the short term, this led to improved results: higher sales and improved profits. However, it also led to a decreased focus on store cleanliness as stores reduced staff. With more stores, overall revenues increased. With less time and effort focused on cleanliness, operating costs decreased and, in turn, increased profits. However, over time, customers became aware of the lack of cleanliness and stopped going to McDonald's. These unintentional side effects created more pressure for short-term profits due to a decline in sales. The cycle would repeat until management became aware of this self-defeating cycle.[32]

When a firm lowers its prices to increase market share and profitability, management may do so without thinking through the implications of its decisions. Its actions may lead to competitor responses that lower prices further and

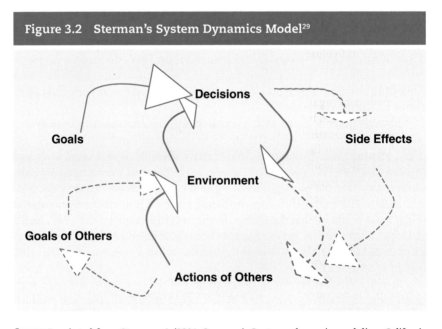

Figure 3.2   Sterman's System Dynamics Model[29]

Source: Reprinted from Sterman, J. (2001, Summer). Systems dynamic modeling. *California Management Review*, 43(4). Copyright ©2001, by The Regents of the University of California.

sweeten sales terms and conditions (e.g., no interest or payments for 12 months or improved warranties) in an effort to respond to its competitors and win back market share. Thus, the planned advantages coming from the price cuts may end up adding a few new sales, shrink margins, condition customers to see the product in primarily price terms, and lock the organization into a price-based competitive cycle that is difficult to escape.[33]

Sterman cautions managers to avoid the trap of thinking in a static, simplistic way. Increasingly, successful managers are resorting to systems thinking and more complex, nonlinear modeling to improve their diagnostic skills. *The Economist* argues, "Better understanding is the key" to improved productivity.[34] The promise of "big data" is that it will allow us to engage in much more sophisticated modeling of what is going on and why, so that more accurate assessments and effective courses of action can be undertaken. However, being awash in increasing mounds of data won't help unless we learn how to model it in ways that more accurately reflect the complexity of what is going on, including the lag effects our actions in one area can have on other areas.

In doing a diagnosis, managers need to recognize their assumptions and values that underlie their implicit understanding of organizational dynamics and the nature of the environment and the market place. Picture marketing people in a meeting with operations or R&D people and you can imagine the value clashes. Marketing people are often externally oriented while operations people are concerned with internal dynamics. A model by Quinn helps to frame these issues and points to the value of a diversity of perspectives when approaching organizational and environmental analysis.

(3) QUINN'S COMPETING VALUES MODEL

How managers think about organizations will largely determine what they think needs changing. The level of analysis that a manager examines can range from the individual to team to department to organization. A psychologist, for example, analyzes individuals and small groups and suggests changes at that level. In contrast, an economist uses econometric models to analyze on the organizational or societal level. Quinn provides a model that bridges the individual, team, department, and organizational levels and encourages change agents to think about the interaction between the systems at these levels.[35]

Quinn's Competing Values Model outlines four frames relevant to organizations. Each frame is based on a set of values and assumptions about the organization and how it works. Quinn argues that two dimensions underlie and help define these four frames: an internal-external dimension and a control-flexibility dimension. That is, underlying the perceptions of organizations are assumptions about the importance of the inside versus the outside of the organization and the need for control versus the need for adaptability. Plotting these two dimensions forms four quadrants, each of which provides a different "frame" or view of the organization. The Competing Values Model is portrayed in Figure 3.3.

As a manager, do you think about the organization in internal terms and how it operates? Or, do you think of the organization's environment and the fit between that environment and the organization? Do you focus your attention on how the organization adapts and changes? Or, is your emphasis more on ensuring that the direction is under control and that people do what is needed? Quinn argues that these dimensions form the four value orientations: Open Systems View, Rational Economic View, Internal Process View, and Human Resources View. Further, he states that while all orientations are needed in an organization, each person will tend to operate from one quadrant more than the others. As well, because the values underlying each quadrant are in conflict, individuals will have difficulty having a "natural" perspective from more than one quadrant. Individuals will tend to adopt one set of internally consistent values and find their views in conflict with or competing with those individuals with perspectives from other quadrants.

One of the strengths of Quinn's model is that it links individual and organizational levels of analysis. That is, managers can examine an organization's processes and determine whether they are focused on external adaptation, internal adaptation, and so forth. At the same time, Quinn suggests managerial roles and skills that are needed for each quadrant. To increase the focus on a quadrant, one needs to have managers develop the competencies needed and design systems to reinforce those skill behaviors. Of specific interest to change leaders are those skills that help with change processes. (See Chapter 8 on change leaders for more on this.)

Quinn labels the internal/flexibility quadrant the Human Resources View of organizations. Similarly, the external/flexibility quadrant is the Open Systems View, the external/control quadrant is the Rational Economic View, and the internal/control quadrant is the Internal Processes View. Each of these quadrants can be associated with a particular way of thinking about organizations

Figure 3.3 Competing Values Model and Change

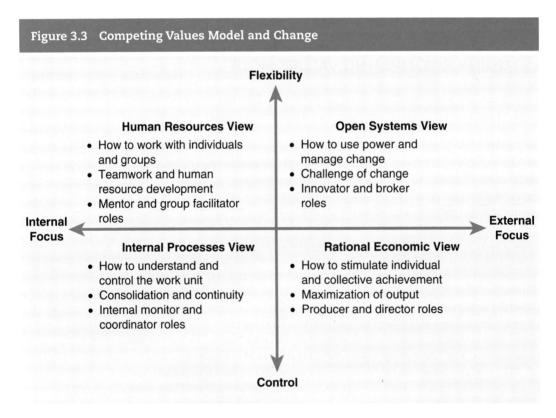

Source: Quinn, R. E., Bright, D., Faerman, S. R., Thompson, M. P., & McGrath, M. R. (2003). Becoming a master manager. New York: John Wiley & Sons.

with roles that managers need to play and skill sets managers can learn that enable them to play the roles.[36]

Every organization needs to attend to all four quadrants to know what is going on internally while also understanding its external environment. It needs to control its operations and yet be flexible and adaptable. At the same time, too much emphasis on one dimension may be dysfunctional. That is, organizations and leaders need to be flexible, but too much flexibility can bring chaos. Conversely, too much control can bring rigidity and paralysis. In the end, organizations need to balance these in ways that are congruent with their external environmental realities.

Each quadrant provides a value orientation needed in organizations and suggests managerial roles and skills that will support those value orientations. For example, Quinn argues that innovator and broker roles are needed in the Open Systems quadrant. The innovator roles demand an understanding of change, an ability to think creatively to produce change, and the development of risk-taking. The broker role involves the development and maintenance of a power and influence base, the ability to negotiate solutions to issues, and the skills of persuasion and coalition building. Care must be taken not to be trapped into adopting one view and ignoring alternate perspectives. Too much focus on internal stability led IBM to miss the PC revolution for many years. Too much focus on the external world led many dot-coms to spin out of control in the technology boom of the early 2000s, and many bitcoin inspired block chain initiatives to do the same in the 2018 period.[37]

Quinn's model can be used in several ways: to characterize an organization's dominant culture, to describe its dominant tasks, to portray the focus of its reward systems, or to describe a needed shift in task emphasis or in the types of people that it must recruit. To refer again to the Dell example, the company was striving to become more consumer oriented while maintaining its production efficiencies. Because these two value orientations are not joined easily, change leaders will know that the concurrent development of these two initiatives will require careful management.

Quinn's model provides both a framework that bridges individual and organizational levels of analysis and a framework to understand competing value paradigms in organizations. While these perspectives are useful, they suggest a relatively static situation, not a dynamic one that Sterman argues for. In particular, Quinn's framework does not encourage managers to consider possible changes that occur in organizations over time. Greiner's model, described below, provides a framework for predicting the stages of change that occur within organizations over time as they grow from entrepreneurial ventures to multidivisional, multinational entities.

(4) GREINER'S MODEL OF ORGANIZATIONAL GROWTH

As discussed in Chapter 1, the magnitude of organizational changes can vary markedly—from small, evolutionary changes to large, revolutionary ones.[†] Evolutionary shifts are, by definition, less traumatic for organizational members

---

[†] The determination of the size of the change is, of course, somewhat dependent upon organizational level and perspective. An incremental change, according to a CEO, may well be viewed as transformational by the department head that is directly affected by the change.

and less disruptive to the organization. Since they typically involve small, incremental shifts in existing systems and behaviors, they are easier to plan and execute. However, they may not be what the organization needs in order to maintain health and vitality. For incremental, evolutionary change, the challenge might be convincing people of the need and tweaking systems and processes to reinforce the desired outcomes. For disruptive, revolutionary change, the issue may well be keeping the organization operating while making significant alterations to how the organization views the world, its strategy, and how it goes about transforming inputs into outputs that its customers desire.

Greiner believes that organizations pass through periods of relative stability and incremental change, punctuated periodically by the need for radical transformations of practices.[38] During the periods of relative stability, organizations tend to be in equilibrium, and evolutionary approaches to change are adopted in order to incrementally improve practices. Then a crisis occurs, such as the rapid growth of the enterprise or the introduction of a disruptive technology by a competitor, and the crisis demands revolutionary change. In the "crisis of leadership" stage, the founding leader of an entrepreneurial adventure may be pushed aside for the hiring of professional managers. Greiner describes these alternating periods of evolutionary and revolutionary change as natural as an organization grows over time.[‡] Figure 3.4 outlines Greiner's model.

In Greiner's view, over time, managers will change their views on how to operate a business incrementally. These become less effective as conditions change and the business becomes increasingly less well aligned or congruent with its internal and external realities. (In Nadler and Tushman's terms, the organizational strategy and/or the transformational components—task, formal organization, informal organization, and people—become increasingly out of sync with the environment.) Once the pressure builds sufficiently, it produces the need for more radical transformations of the organization. Pressures build until a breaking point is reached and change is forced. Will the organization adapt to the radical changes needed or will its decline become inevitable?[39] This relatively rapid and discontinuous change over most or all domains of organizational activity is referred to by Greiner as the revolutionary change period.[40]

As shown in Figure 3.4, Greiner outlines a model of typical stages of growth in an organization. He suggests that these patterns are progressive and logical as the organization grows. Greiner is prescriptive in that he claims the organization must pass through these crises in order to grow and develop. The transitions may be caused by a variety of issues: the death of the founder; the need for a functional organization to develop specialties; the emergence of disruptive market forces and/or technologies; the need to decentralize into divisions to keep closer to the customer; and, finally, the need to become more flexible to enable the organization to use the potential of all employees.

This framework is appealing because of its straightforwardness, logic, and simplicity. However, the model is suggestively prescriptive. Not all organizations

---

[‡] Eisenhardt believes that organizations can force incremental change by "time pacing"—setting up targets and deadlines that require regular periodic change. See S. Brown and K. Eisenhardt, "The Art of Continuous Change: Linking Stacey's Complexity Theory and Time-Paced Evolution in Relentlessly Shifting Organizations," *Administrative Science Quarterly 42*, no. 1 (1997): 1–34, or K. Eisenhardt and B. N. Tabrizi, "Accelerating Adaptive Processes: Product Innovation in the Global Computer Industry," *Administrative Science Quarterly 40*, no. 1 (1995): 84–110.

Figure 3.4 Greiner's Five Phases of Organizational Growth

Source: Reprinted with permission from Greiner, L. (1972, July-August). Evolution and revolution as organizations grow. *Harvard Business Review.*

follow Greiner's patterns. In today's world, a small entrepreneurial venture may become a global competitor of reasonable size by using the Internet and collaborating with partners around the world. In other words, organizations need not develop as Greiner claims. The model does not seem open to the possibility of the broker organization, one that makes money by connecting organizations to each other. Nevertheless, the framework is valuable in highlighting many of the crises faced by organizations and in relating those crises to the growth stages of the organization. The model reinforces the notion of the competing values that managers must keep in an appropriate state of dynamic tension. For example, as managers move from the crisis of autonomy to growth through delegation, there should be a shift in values and perspectives, from control to flexibility in Quinn's terms.

In the Dell example, the company shifted from a control and functional specialty stage to one where the company was organized into relatively autonomous divisions focused on customer segments. While Greiner's model suggests that certain tensions predominate during different growth phases, such tensions might not vanish. As such, Dell may continue to struggle with balancing the previously successful efficiency focus that its managers held with its need for flexibility and adaptiveness.

While Greiner's model is prescriptive, it captures many of the issues faced by organizations both in responding to growth and in dealing with the human side of organizational change. Too often, managers are trapped by their own perspectives. They fail to recognize that regardless of who has what title or authority, others will see things differently and have different criteria to judge potential outcomes. An important key in identifying what to change is to embrace multiple perspectives, recognizing that each comes with its own biases and orientation on what needs to be done. By developing an integrated, comprehensive assessment process and being conscious of one's own biases and preferences, the change leader is likely to achieve a holistic understanding of what change will produce the necessary realignment for organizational success.

(5) STACEY'S COMPLEXITY THEORY

Many models of organizational change rely on a gap analysis as the description of what needs to change,[41] just as this book does. While this has the advantage of simplicity, change agents need to move beyond this to recognize the importance of interdependence and interrelationships.[42] This chapter began by describing organizations as open systems, and frameworks have been presented for analysis that can account for the dynamic, multilevel, time-dependent nature of organizations. As well, change leaders have been encouraged to recognize that different situations require different levels of analysis, and the appropriate analytic tools are dependent on that level. The importance of moving away from seeing change in primarily simple, rational, cause-and-effect terms should not be underestimated. Change leaders must learn how to cope with complexity and chaos as realities.

Another branch of organizational theorists argues that organizations are complex, paradoxical entities that may not be amenable to managerial control. In this theory, called Stacey's Complexity Theory, Stacey[43] identifies the following as the underlying propositions (adapted below):

- Organizations are webs of nonlinear feedback loops that are connected with other individuals and organizations by webs of nonlinear feedback loops.

- These feedback systems can operate in stable and unstable states of equilibrium to the point at which chaos ensues.

- Organizations are inherently paradoxical. On one hand, they are pulled toward stability by forces for integration and control, security, certainty, and environmental adaptation. On the other hand, they are pulled toward instability by forces for division, innovation, and even isolation from the environment.

- If organizations give in to the forces for stability, they become ossified and change impaired. If they succumb to the forces for instability, they will disintegrate. Success is when organizations exist between frozen stability and chaos.

- Short-run dynamics (or noise) are characterized by irregular cycles and discontinuous trends, but the long-term trends are identifiable.

- A successful organization faces an unknowable specific future because things can and do happen that were not predicted and that affect what is achieved and how it is achieved.

- Agents within an organization can't control, through their actions, analytic processes and controls, the long-term future. They can only act in relation to the short term.

- Long-term development is a spontaneous, self-organizing process that may give rise to new strategic directions. Spontaneous self-organization is the product of political interaction combined with learning in groups, and managers have to pursue reasoning through the use of analogy.

- It is through this process that managers create and come to know the environments and long-term futures of their organizations.

Some complexity theorists would argue that the managed change perspective that underpins this book is fundamentally flawed. They would do so because it focuses on management of complexity and renewal through environmental analysis and programmatic initiatives that advance internal and external alignment, and through them the accomplishment of the goals of the change. Those who adopt a complexity perspective would view the change leader's job as one of creating conditions and ground rules that will allow for innovation and efficiency to emerge through the encouragement of the interactions and relationships of others.

Advocates believe this approach can unleash energy and enthusiasm and allow naturally occurring patterns to emerge that would otherwise remain unseen (i.e., they self-organize into alignment). Vision and strategy are still valued by complexity theorists because they can supply participants with a sense of the hoped-for direction. However, they are not viewed as useful when they attempt to specify the ultimate goal.

A close review of the complexity ideas, though, shows that this perspective is not far from the one advocated by this book. This book adopts an open systems perspective and argues that the environment is characterized by uncertainty and complexity and that organizations are more likely to be successful over time if they develop adaptive capacities. This means that openness to new ideas and flexibility need to be valued and that organizations need to learn how to embrace the ideas, energy, and enthusiasm that can be generated from change initiatives that come from within the organization. The book recognizes the value that teams (including self-managed teams) can contribute to successful change, from needs assessment to the development of initial ideas and shared vision through to strategy development and implementation. Further, it acknowledges that too much standardization and reduction of variance could drive out innovation. Finally, it notes that greater uncertainty and ambiguity gives rise to greater uncertainty over how things will ultimately unfold, thereby highlighting the importance of vision and strategy as directional beacons for change initiatives as opposed to set directives or rules.

An important idea that comes from Stacey's Complexity Theory is that small changes at key points early on can have huge downstream effects. But can one predict with any certainty where those changes and leverage points will be or what downstream results will emerge as the result of actions we take today? Often the answer is no. Motorola likely had no clear idea where wireless technology would take the world when it began work on cellular phone technology in the 1960s. Likewise, Monsanto probably had little sense of the magnitude of the marketplace resistance that would build for genetically modified seeds when its research and development program was initiated in the 1980s.

We may not be able to predict precisely what will transpire over the long term, but we can make complex and uncertain futures more understandable and predictable if we do our homework in an open systems manner, look at data in nonlinear as well as linear terms, engage different voices and perspectives in the discussion, and rigorously consider different scenarios and different approaches to envisioning what the future might look like.

When organizations do this, they are likely to get a sense of what is possible from a visionary, directional, and technological perspective. Further, through the engagement and involvement of many, change leaders are in a strong position to initiate change with a shared sense of purpose. They are also more likely to have identified critical actions and events that must occur and where some of the potentially important leverage and resistance points exist. As a result, they are more aware of how things may unfold and are in a stronger position to take corrective or alternative action as a result of their ongoing monitoring and management of the process.[44] As well, change agents will recognize the importance of contingency planning as unpredictable, unplanned events occur.

It may not be possible to predict absolute outcomes. However, it is possible to generally predict where an organization is likely to end up if it adopts a particular strategy and course of action. The identification of the direction and the initial steps allow an organization to begin the journey. Effective monitoring and management processes allow leaders to make adjustments as they move forward. The ability to do this with complex change comes about as the result of hard work, commitment, a suitable mindset (e.g., openness and flexibility), relevant skills and competencies, appropriate participation and involvement approaches, access to sufficient resources, and control and signaling processes. In the end, the authors of this book subscribe to the belief that "Luck is the intersection of opportunity and preparation."[45]

SUMMARY

In this chapter, change agents learned about five different organizational models that will help them to develop a well-grounded sense of what needs to change in an organization. This book uses Nadler and Tushman's model as its main framework. The model focuses on achieving congruence among the organization's environment, strategy, and internal organizational components to achieve desired outcomes. In addition, it helps managers categorize the complex organizational data that they must deal with. It examines the tasks, people, structures, and culture of organizations. Finally, it fits neatly into a process approach to organizational change, helping to merge what needs to be changed with the process of how change might occur.

While the book relies on both Nadler and Tushman's framework and the Change Path Model, change leaders must be particularly sensitive to the dynamic nature of organizations, to the need for multiple levels of analysis, and to the shifts that organizations make over time. Sterman's, Quinn's, and Greiner's models take a systems' perspective and are presented to reinforce subtle differences in focus. As well, we discuss Stacey's Complexity Theory. This theory challenges a simple goal-oriented approach that many change managers might take and encourages an emergent view of organizations.

Change leaders must recognize the assumptions and biases underlying their analysis and whether the assumptions they make limit their perspectives on needed change. Their diagnosis should recognize the stage of development of the organization and whether it is facing evolutionary, incremental change, or, at the other end of the change continuum, revolutionary, strategic change. By developing an in-depth and sophisticated understanding of organizations, change leaders will appreciate what has to be done to enhance an organization's effectiveness. See **Toolkit Exercise 3.1** for critical thinking questions for this chapter.

KEY TERMS

Open systems perspective—considers the organization as a set of complex, interdependent parts that interacts with the external environment to obtain resources and to transform the resources into outputs.

Models of Organizations

Nadler and Tushman's Congruence Model—views organizations as composed of internal components (tasks, designed structures and systems, culture, and people). The model states higher effectiveness occurs when the organization is congruent with its strategy and environment. This model forms the framework for this text.

Sterman's Systems Dynamics Model—describes organizations as interactive, dynamic, and nonlinear as opposed to the linear, static view that many individuals hold of organizations.

Quinn's Competing Values Model—describes organizations as based on opposing values: flexibility versus control and external versus internal. These two dimensions lead to four competing views of organizations: the Human Resources View, the Open Systems View, the Rational Economic View, and the Internal Process View.

Greiner's Model of Organizational Growth—hypothesizes that organizations move through five states of growth followed by five stages of crisis.

Stacey's Complexity Theory—argues that organizations are webs of nonlinear feedback loops that connect individuals and organizations that can lead to self-organization and alignment among parts.

END-OF-CHAPTER EXERCISES

TOOLKIT EXERCISE 3.1

Critical Thinking Questions

The URLs for the videos listed below can be found in two places. The first spot is next to the exercise and the second spot is on the website at **study.sagepub.com/cawsey4e.**

1. How Organizations Change: Henrik Marten—7:07 minutes

   https://www.bing.com/videos/search?q=how+organizations+change%3a+henrik+marten&docid=608043414918531403&mid=3133A011A1B9CC647A6A3133A011A1B9CC647A6A&view=detail&FORM=VIRE

   Presentation by H. Marten on how learning is necessary for organizational change.

   - Explain Marten's key takeaways about how an organization can best learn.

   - Discuss any change experience you've had and how it may compare to Marten's description of organizational learning.

2. Eddie Obeng: Smart Failure for a Fast-Changing World—12:33 minutes

   https://www.youtube.com/watch?v=EjSuaeVfE9I

   Obeng talks about our ever-changing world, how our learning has changed and the importance of smart failures.

   - Describe how you perceive failure.

   - Describe how others you've worked with in the past have dealt with failure in themselves as well as people around them.

   - Discuss how you might begin changing an organization to treat failure as learning, as Obeng describes in the video.

*Please see **study.sagepub.com/cawsey4e** for access to the videos and downloadable template of this exercise.*

TOOLKIT EXERCISE 3.2

Analyzing Your Organization Using Nadler and Tushman's Congruence Model

Use the congruence model to describe your organization or any organization you are familiar with.

1. Describe the key input factors that influence the organization:

   a. The external environment (the PESTEL factors include political, economic, social, technological, ecological and legal factors).

   b. The organization's history (including its culture) and the resources it has access to.

2. What is the strategy of the organization? Is it in line with the organization's environmental inputs and its history (including its culture) and resources?

3. Are the components of the transformation processes well aligned with the input factors and the strategy? These elements include the following:

   a. The work

   b. The formal organization

   c. The people

   d. The informal organization (part of which is the culture that manifests itself in different parts of the organization)

   e. How they interact with one another in ways that influence the outputs produced by the organization

4. What outputs are being achieved? Are these the desired outputs?

5. When you evaluate your organization's outputs at the individual, group, and organizational levels, what issues should the organization address?

6. Are there any aspects of how your organization works that you have difficulty understanding? If so, identify the resources you would need to access to help with this analysis.

7. Use your answers to fill in the visual model.

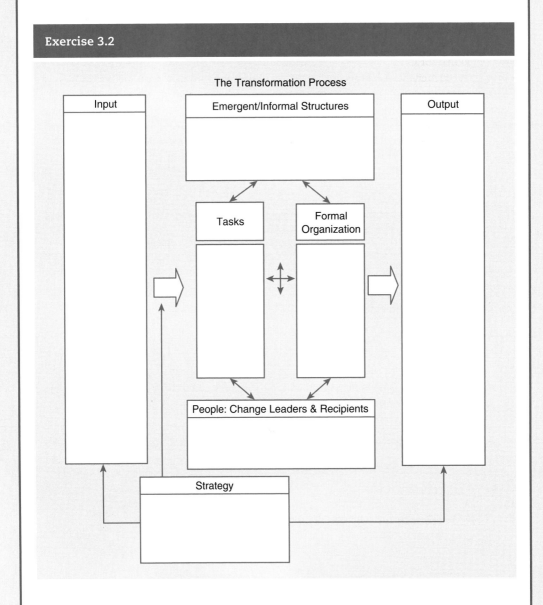

SARAH'S SNACKS

By Paul Myers, PhD

School of Business, Simmons University, Boston, MA

Sarah Woodley, CEO and Founder of Sarah's Snacks, sat at her desk preparing to meet with her executive team. It had been eighteen months since the company adapted a consultant's recommendation to change the company from a functional organization to a process-based one. Despite expectations that performance would improve, little had changed. The extended length of time it took to introduce new products cost the company market share as competitors more quickly came out with flavors that better matched emerging consumer trends. Production delays due to supply shortages led to stockouts at some of the largest supermarket customers. The organizational changes were intended to resolve these problems as well as create efficiencies that would reduce overall costs. Woodley needed her team to determine why the company was not yet seeing those results and to help her decide whether they needed to make additional changes.

COMPANY BACKGROUND

Sarah's Snacks was a producer of organic popcorn, pretzels, tortilla chips, and other snack foods. Woodley launched the company in 1995 by selling hand-packed bags of varieties of popcorn kernels grown in her native Indiana at local farmer's markets. From its modest beginnings, the company had become one of the top ten independent producers of organic snacks in the United States. Years of steady revenue growth as the company expanded its product line and entered new geographic markets confirmed that the strategy of offering a broad line of organic products with distinctive flavors aligned with what customers were looking for.

Over time, however, new entrants into their product categories cut into sales and made price a more important factor to consumers. At the same time, because of growing demand for organic ingredients, the cost of supplies was rising. This resulted in profit margins being squeezed. To help investigate what might be done to reverse this trend and other performance issues, Woodley hired a consultant to advise her. After analyzing the situation, his recommendation was that the company redesign how it operates to make better use of information technology to integrate its business processes. He provided a plan for the initial steps the company should take to implement the solution.

Formal Organization

Sarah's Snacks operated as a functional organization, which meant activities were divided between departments where employees with similar skills worked together. Those functional areas included purchasing, product development, operations, marketing and sales, accounting, and information technology (see diagram below). Each department was led by a director who typically had two or three direct reports responsible for managing others. Roles and duties were clearly spelled out in detailed job descriptions. Departments set goals independently of each other, and employees were evaluated and rewarded based on their individual performance. Promotions were typically within department, and employees seldom moved between functional areas. The company had no formal training process. While the company had a single information technology infrastructure, many departments used their own applications to record transactions and manage data.

Work

Production workers operated the largely automated production lines and were responsible for assessing quality. Horizontal coordination across functions, including information flows, occurred on a limited basis. For instance, after the product development team came up with new snacks, their involvement ended after they passed the specifications on to the manufacturing group to determine how to produce them. Except for the product development group, most work was done independently and without much collaboration.

Informal Organization

The culture at Sarah's Snacks was integrally linked with Woodley's core belief in the importance to health and wellness of eating organic products. Even at the top levels of the company, success was defined as meeting customers' desires for snacks they could feel good about eating. This mission drove everything the company set out to do and represented a set of values that motivated employees seeking to serve a higher purpose. One employee noted that "most of us are here as much out of the sense that we're doing good as for a paycheck." Most employees regarded their co-workers as a family, and Woodley reinforced this sense in how she interacted with them. To the extent anyone thought about customers, it was as snack consumers with whom they would never directly interact. The predominant management style was characterized by benevolence and a high degree of trust; the executive team tended to smooth over conflict in search of reaching consensus on decisions.

People

In most functional areas, Sarah's Snacks hired people based on their knowledge and skills rather than their psycho-social profile on such factors as adaptability or learning orientation. Some of its non-production staff joined the company soon after college graduation and had worked for no other employer. Sixty percent of employees were women, including a majority of the executive team. More than half of the employees had worked at the company for over ten years, and a few had been there almost since the start.

ORGANIZATIONAL CHANGE

In line with the consultant's advice, the first order of business in changing the organization focused on how work was done. Woodley assigned her executive team the task of identifying key business processes. These included order fulfillment, which encompassed everything from taking orders from customers to receiving payment; product development, including analyzing market needs, moving from concept to prototype, market testing, and manufacturing and equipment design; procurement, which incorporated activities related to acquiring supplies, such as inputting purchase orders, receiving goods, and accounts payable.

The next step identified how the processes could be redesigned and integrated across functions using information technology. This began with considering the perspective of the customer, then eliminating non-value adding steps, and finally devising new ways of organizing the work across functional lines. Doing so created new process flows of information supported by an integrated set of databases and portals that were part of an off-the-shelf system purchased by the company. The consultant had advised that to meet an aggressive implementation schedule, decisions at this important phase would need to be made quickly. Senior managers within the functional groups shared responsibility for process redesign. Often there was disagreement about the best solution; after long discussions, they generally took the approach that garnered the most support.

The company took an incremental but accelerated approach to implementation by starting with the procurement process; other processes followed soon after. The changes focused exclusively on how work was done; no other organizational changes were made. They affected all employees at the company, although some more than others and manufacturing workers least of all. The new processes required employees to learn new ways of doing things, including how to use the new information technology system intended to replace existing applications. They also meant many employees needed to work with others in different departments for the first time. In addition, a key element of moving to a process-based organization was adopting a new, broader, internally focused view of who a customer was. Employees now had to think about whom the recipient of their work was and focus on the quality and timeliness of what they were sending.

RESULTS

Implementing the new process designs proved more difficult than expected. The company had undertaken rolling out additional processes before the preceding ones had been completed. Many employees continued to rely on the old processes rather than adopting the new ways of doing things, which they regarded as both confusing and ineffective. They also continued to use existing applications that had not yet been retired, often failing to enter data in the new system. Most of these omissions were not discovered and rectified until weeks later. Employees found the new system difficult to learn, and it was much easier to do things the way they always had.

As the key processes were being implemented, administration of the practices that were not affected continued unchanged. Annual reviews of non-production employees relied on existing performance plans since managers were too busy with the process redesigns to revise them. One consequence of the process changes was that a number of management positions were eliminated. Those who were laid off received two weeks' notice and the promise of positive recommendations to their potential

new employers. At the same time, recruitment and hiring of new employees continued unabated in order to replace essential ones who had left the company rather than deal with the effects of the process changes.

Based on the consultant's guidance, Woodley had anticipated cost savings of 10%-15% from reducing errors and rework, experiencing fewer stockouts, and eliminating most legacy software applications. She also expected a reduction of up to 30% in the time from conceiving a new product to producing and selling it. After a year and a half of effort, none of these outcomes had been achieved. Woodley wondered what had gone wrong and whether there was anything she could do about it.

ASSIGNMENT QUESTIONS

1. How well did Sarah's Snacks fit Nadler and Tushman's congruence model before it began its organizational change?

2. Why have the changes at Sarah's Snacks not produced the expected results?

3. What do you recommend Woodley do? Which of your recommendations can be implemented in the short term, and which are longer term solutions?

4. How does the Change Path Model help you analyze what should have happened at 18 months and what should happen now?

Sarah's Snacks Organization Chart

BUILDING AND ENERGIZING THE NEED FOR CHANGE

Chapter Overview

This chapter asks the question, "Why change?"

- It develops a framework for understanding the need for change based on making sense of external and internal organizational data, and the change leaders' personal concerns and perspectives.
- The chapter describes what makes organizations ready for change and provides a questionnaire to rate an organization's readiness.
- It outlines how change leaders can create awareness for change.
- Finally, the chapter outlines the importance of the change vision and how change leaders can create a meaningful vision that energizes and focuses action.

In Chapter 2, we discussed the concept of unfreezing as a precondition to change. How can an organization and its people move to something new if their current mindset and response repertoire are not open to alternative paths and actions?

You are in a large auditorium filled with people when suddenly you smell smoke and someone yells, "Fire!" You leap to your feet, exit the building, and call 911.

This situation above is straightforward. A crisis makes the **need for change** clear and dramatic. It demands an immediate response and the required action is understood—even more so if the institution has taken fire-safety planning seriously. Most people know the key actions: Where to exit? How to avoid panic? Who should be notified? Who should do the notifying?

However, in many situations, the need for change is vague and appropriate action is unclear. For example, even in an emergency, if there have been no "fires" for a considerable period but there have been false alarms, people may have become complacent, warning systems might be ignored or even have been deactivated due to improper maintenance, and emergency action plans forgotten. A parallel to this might explain the lack of action prior to the mortgage meltdown in the United States in 2007 and the contagion it caused in global financial markets. Some economists and financial experts had raised alarms as early as 2003[1] (including the FBI in 2004[2]) over flawed financial practices and regulations. However, their warnings about the need to regulate mortgage lenders were ignored. The prevailing perspective within the Bush administration was that regulations needed to be minimized because they got in the way of free markets and the generation of personal wealth. Before the meltdown, the need for change was evident to only a few people. In addition, powerful financial institutions and their executives had huge incentives to ignore such warnings and silence those in their own firms who were raising alarms. Self-interest, blind spots, and/or misguided views of the greater good can sometimes blind people to strengths, weaknesses, opportunities, and risks. It is a primary reason for the rise in the importance of risk management and the requirements around risk reporting that publicly traded firms must comply with.[3]

Past experiences may cause people to become not only complacent but also cynical about warnings. If false alarms have been regular occurrences, people will come to ignore them. If employees are told that there is a crisis when similar alerts in the past have proven to be false alarms, they will tend to discount the warning. If people are busy and they don't want to be sidetracked, they won't prepare for events that they think aren't going to happen. Remember the press reports concerning the H1N1 flu pandemic in the summer and fall of 2009 and how they changed by the winter of 2010? In the fall, there was a sense of panic, with people lining up overnight to get inoculated. By February, journalists were writing that the World Health Organization (WHO) had overstated the threat, as they had with Bird Flu. As such reports multiply and become the fodder for watercooler and Internet conversations, will the public take WHO warnings as seriously next time?[4] Concerns related to creating complacency may help to explain the careful way that WHO framed the warnings related to the outbreaks of Ebola in West Africa and the SARS-like virus in Saudi Arabia in 2013–2014.[5]

When leaders are perceived to cry "wolf" too often, who will take them seriously when the threat comes to fruition? However, when risks manifest themselves into reality, the blaming always begins with whether or not warning signs were ignored. Such were the responses following both the Sandy Hook School Shooting, in Newtown, Connecticut, in December 2012, and the bombing at the Boston Marathon in April 2013. This, in turn, may lead us to treat symptoms rather than underlying causes, as we look for quick solutions and misinterpret correlations for causality. Even trained professionals can miss obvious cues, as in the story below.

A few years ago, my father was in intensive care, hooked to a heart monitor. Shortly after I arrived to visit him, the emergency alarm went off, but no one responded. I ran for help but was told not to worry—the alarm goes off all the time—just hit the reset button. The health care professionals had clearly adjusted their behavior to discount false alarms, but needless to say, I was left feeling anything but secure concerning the quality of the system designed to monitor the need for change in my dad's treatment. What if it hadn't been a false alarm? (G. Deszca)

Change agents need to demonstrate that the need for change is real and important. Only then will people unfreeze from past patterns. This is easier said than done. From 2008 through to the winter and spring of 2009, General Motors (GM) struggled to convince the United Auto Workers Union (UAW) that they needed significant financial concessions to survive. The UAW initially took the position that GM had signed a deal and should live up to it. However, the collapse of consumers' demand for automobiles in the summer of 2008 led to fears of bankruptcy. Political pressure from the U.S. and Canadian governments on both GM and their employee unions in the United States (the UAW) and Canada (the CAW or Canadian Auto Workers) escalated in the wake of bailout requests. As a result of this pressure, the UAW abandoned its position that "We have done our share." Concessions followed during the next nine months, covering everything from staffing levels, pay rates, health care benefits to pensions.[6] The CAW followed suit, shortly thereafter. When it comes to raising alarms concerning the need for change, it is sometimes tough to know when and how to get through to people. With GM, it took going to the edge of the precipice and beyond. They had to go bankrupt!

Many change-management programs fail because there is sustained confusion and disagreement over (a) why there is the need for change and (b) what needs changing. Ask organizational members—from production workers to VPs—why their organization is not performing as well as it could and opinions abound and differ. Even well-informed opinions are often fragmentary and contradictory. Individuals' perspectives on the need for change depend on their roles and levels in the organization, their environments, perceptions, performance measures and incentives, and the training and experience they have received. The reactions of peers, supervisors, and subordinates as well as an individual's own personality all influence how each person looks at the world. When there has been no well-thought-out effort to develop a shared awareness concerning the need for change, then piecemeal, disparate, and conflicting assessments of the situation are likely to pervade the organization.[7]

Look at the responses of different constituencies to the big issues of our day. Take air quality. The adverse effects of poor air quality on public health are well documented. However, if you review the ongoing debate concerning the urgency of the problem and how we should go about addressing it, you will see various stakeholders with different vested interests and perspectives, and how they marshal evidence to advance their points of view and protect their positions. As a result, meaningful problem solving is delayed or sidetracked. Appropriate analyses, actions, and interventions are delayed, with predictable consequences, unless a disaster, very visible near disaster, or a seismic shift in public opinion occurs that galvanizes attention and precipitates action.

People often see change as something that others need to embrace and take the lead with. One hears, "Why don't they understand?" "Why can't they see what is happening?" or "They must be doing this intentionally." But stupidity, blindness, and maliciousness are typically not the primary reasons for inappropriate or insufficient organizational change. Differences in perspective affect what is seen and experienced. As the attributions of causation shift, so too do the beliefs about who or what is the cause of the problems and what should be done.[8] A common phenomenon called responsibility diffusion often occurs around changes. Responsibility diffusion happens when multiple people are involved and everyone stands by, assuming someone else will act.[9]

In terms of the change-management process, the focus of this chapter is on the "Awakening" box contained in Figure 4.1. To address this, change leaders need to determine the need for change and the degree of choice available to them and/or the organization about whether to change. Further, they need to develop the change vision and they need to engage others in these conversations so that a shared understanding develops. Without these in hand, they are in no position to engage others in conversations about the path forward.

Figure 4.1   The Change Path Model

Awakening
Chapter 4
1. Identify a need for change and confirm the problems or opportunities that incite the need for change through collection of data.
2. Articulate the gap in performance between the present and the envisioned future state, and spread awareness of the data and the gap throughout the organization.
3. Develop a powerful vision for change.
4. Disseminate the vision for the change and why it's needed through multiple communication channels.

Mobilization
Chapters 5 through 8
1. Make sense of the desired change through formal systems and structures, and leverage those systems to reach the change vision (Chapter 5).
2. Assess power and cultural dynamics at play, and put them to work to better understand the dynamics and build coalitions and support to realize the change (Chapter 6).
3. Communicate the need for change organization-wide and manage change recipients and various stakeholders as they react to and move the change forward (Chapter 7).
4. Leverage change agent personality, knowledge, skills and abilities, and related assets (e.g., reputation and relationships) for the benefit of the change vision and its implementation (Chapter 8).

Acceleration
Chapter 9
1. Continue to systematically reach out to engage and empower others in support, planning, and implementation of the change. Help them develop needed new knowledge, skills, abilities, and ways of thinking that will support the change.
2. Use appropriate tools and techniques to build momentum, accelerate and consolidate progress.
3. Manage the transition, celebrating small wins and the achievement of milestones along the larger, more difficult path of change.

Institutionalization
Chapter 10
1. Track the change periodically and through multiple balanced measures to help assess what is needed, gauge progress toward the goal, and to make modifications as needed and mitigate risk.
2. Develop and deploy new structures, systems, processes and knowledge, skills, and abilities, as needed, to bring life to the change and new stability to the transformed organization.

This chapter asks change leaders, be they vice presidents, line operators, or volunteers at their local food bank, to seek out multiple perspectives as they examine the need for change. There is typically no shortage of things that could be done with available resources. What, then, gets the attention and commitment of time and money? What is the compelling reason for disrupting the status quo? Are there choices about changing and, if so, what are they? In many cases, it is not clear that change is needed. In these cases, the first step is for leaders to make a compelling case for why energy and resources need to be committed to a particular vision. Addressing these concerns advances the unfreezing process, focuses attention, and galvanizes support for further action.

But recognizing the need and mobilizing interest are not sufficient—a change leader also needs to communicate a clear sense of the desired result of the change. Change leaders do this by developing a compelling vision of the change. It conveys to others what life will look like after it is implemented. The vision for change seldom arrives fully formed and more often than not emerges through the engagement of others. This approach to creating momentum is the focus of the latter half of this chapter.

UNDERSTANDING THE NEED FOR CHANGE

The change process won't energize people until they begin to understand the need for change. People may have a general sense that things are amiss or that opportunities are being missed, but they will not mobilize their energies until the need is framed, understood, and believed. An organization may have amassed data on customers, production processes, suppliers, competitors, organization financials, and other factors, but nothing will happen until someone takes the information and communicates a compelling argument concerning the need for change. Advancing the change agenda is aided by being able to address the following questions:

DEVELOPING AN ASSESSMENT FOR THE NEED FOR CHANGE

1. **What do you see as the need for change and the important dimensions and issues that underpin it?** What external and internal data either confirms or contradicts your assessment for the need for change? How much confidence do you have in the data and why should others have confidence it? In what ways is the appraisal for the need for change grounded in a solid organizational and environmental assessment?

2. **How have you investigated the perspectives of internal and external stakeholders?** Who has a stake in the matter of change and do you understand their perspectives on the need for change? People's perspectives of organizational life are often determined by their role and their level in the organization. How many people have you talked with in marketing, operations, HR, and so forth? How many middle and

upper middle managers have you talked with? What external stakeholders, such as customers and vendors, have you talked with or surveyed?

3. **How can the different perspectives be integrated in ways that offer the possibility for a collaborative solution?** How can you avoid a divisive "we/they" dispute?

4. **How have you communicated the message concerning the need for change? Have you done so in ways that have the potential to move the organization to a higher state of readiness for and willingness to change?** Or have your deliberations left change recipients feeling pressured into doing something they don't agree with, don't understand, or fear will come back to haunt them?

The challenges at this stage for change leaders are to develop the information they need to assess the situation, develop their views on the need for change, understand how others see that need, and create awareness and legitimacy around the need for change when a shared awareness is lacking. To make headway on these questions and challenges, change leaders need to seek out and make sense of external data, the perspectives of stakeholders, internal data, and their own personal concerns and perspectives. (Figure 4.2 outlines these factors.)

Seek Out and Make Sense of External Data

Change leaders should scan the organization's external environment to gain knowledge about and assess the need for change. Getting outside one's personal perceptual box helps to avoid blind spots that are created by **"closed-loop learning."**[*][10] Change agents may make incremental improvements and succeed in improving short-term results. However, change leaders may not be doing what is needed to assess the risks and opportunities and to adapt to the environment over the long term.[11] Executives tend to spend too little time reflecting on the external environment and its implications for their organizations.[12]

Figure 4.2 Developing Your Understanding of the Need for Change

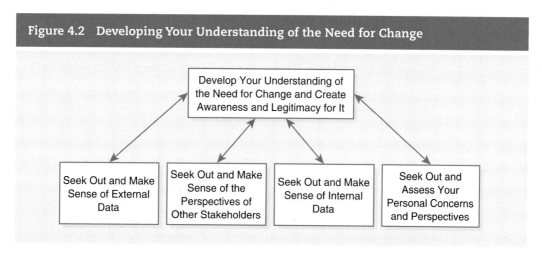

---

[*] Closed-loop learning is learning that focuses on current practices and perspectives rather than developing a deeper understanding of the complex interactions underpinning the situation, including the impact of the external environment.

An organization that is experiencing an externally driven crisis will feel the sense of urgency around the need for change. In this case, the change initiator's task will be easier.[13] This crisis can be used to mobilize the system and galvanize people's attention and actions. Without this, many within the organization may not perceive a need for change even though the warning clouds or the unaddressed opportunities may be keeping the change leader awake at night.

The value of seeing organizations as open systems cannot be underestimated. This analytic approach and the learning it promotes play an important role in the development of awareness, improved vision, and flexibility and adaptability in the organization.[14] Often the question for the change leader becomes "Which external data do I attend to?" A change agent can drown in information without a disciplined approach for the collection, accumulation, and integration of data. Consider how complex the innocuous-sounding task of benchmarking can become.[15] The absence of a disciplined approach to data gathering may mean that time is wasted, that potentially important data go uncollected or are forgotten, or the data are never translated into useful information for the organization.

Some sources for data will be concrete (trade papers, published research, and news reports), while others will be less tangible (comments collected informally from suppliers, customers, or vendors at trade shows). Data collection can take a variety of forms: setting aside time for reading, participating in trade shows and professional conferences, visiting vendors' facilities, and/or attending executive education programs. Just as important, the change leader should consider engaging others in processes related to framing the questions, identifying and collecting data, and systematically interpreting the results in a timely fashion. This makes the task more manageable, increases the legitimacy of the data and the findings, builds awareness and understanding of the need for change, and creates a greater sense of ownership of the process.

Working without awareness of the external environment is the equivalent of driving blind. And yet it happens all the time. For a variety of reasons, ranging from a heavy workload or a sense of emergency, to complacency or arrogance, organizational leaders can be lulled into relying on past successes and strategies rather than investigating and questioning. In so doing, they risk failing to develop an organization's capacity to adapt to a changing environment.[16]

Seek Out and Make Sense of the Perspectives of Stakeholders

Change leaders need to be aware of the **perspectives of key internal and external stakeholders** and work to understand their perspectives and reasons for supporting or resisting change. This will inform and enrich a change agent's assessment of the need for change and the dynamics of the situation, and allow them to frame their approaches in ways that have a greater chance of generating needed support. Without such work, it is impossible to accurately assess perceptions of the situation and frame responses to questions that will resonate with those stakeholders—questions such as why change and what's in it for me?[17]

Externally, these stakeholders may include suppliers, bankers, governmental officials, customers, and alliance and network partners. Internally, the stakeholders will include those individuals who are directly and indirectly affected by the change. If the change involved a reorganization of production processes, the internal stakeholders would include a long-list of managers: production supervisors; union officials; human resource personnel with recruitment and training responsibilities; finance folks with budget and control tasks; sales and marketing managers with customer service implications and IT implications; and engineering managers.

The point of view of the person championing the need for change will likely differ from the perspectives of other stakeholders. What is interesting and important to those stakeholders will vary, and this will affect what data and people they pay attention to and what they do with the information. If the change leader hopes to enlist their support or at least minimize their resistance, the leader needs to capture and consider their perspectives and the underlying rationale.[18] Particular stakeholders may still remain ambivalent or opposed to the change, but not seeking them out and listening is likely to make things worse. Why create resistance if you don't have to?

All of this highlights the importance of doing preparatory analysis and having a purposeful discussion with affected stakeholders and those who understand their perspectives and can potentially influence them. It will increase the change leader's awareness and sensitivity to the context, inform and strengthen the analysis, and indicate blind spots and alternative explanations and paths.

CHANGE VISION AT AN INSURANCE FIRM

When a North American insurance firm acquired one of its competitors, the senior manager in charge of integrating the acquisition was determined to have every employee understand the need for change, the new vision, and its implications. On the day the deal was announced, she made a live presentation (along with the CEO and other key officials) to employees at the head office of the acquisition and streamed the meeting live to all of the acquisition's branch offices and facilities, as well as into the parent organization. She honored the acquisition's senior management team, who were present, communicated the reasons for the acquisition and its implications for change, took questions, and encouraged employees to contact her with questions or concerns. She set up a special website and phone line to answer questions in a timely and direct manner and followed this with visits to all the offices, key customers, and suppliers over the next two months. She held two town-hall meetings with employees over the next year to communicate the status of integration activities and reduce anxiety.

An integration team from the acquiring firm was deployed to the acquired firm the day the deal was announced. After introducing themselves and their mandate, the integration team presented specific initiatives with staff to align key systems and processes and develop strategic and tactical plans. Leaders from the integration team visited key groups at all levels in the acquired organization to discuss the need for change, to discuss their current position in the marketplace, and to review how the roles and responsibilities were currently organized. Integration team members communicated what they knew, listened hard, and made firm commitments to get back with answers by specific dates. The integration team honored those commitments, including the communication of the new organization's strategic and tactical plans and clarification of each person's employment status, within 90 days of the acquisition. Like the senior manager responsible for the integration of the acquisition, the integration team communicated candidly, listened, and adjusted to assessments of the need for change and the strategic path forward, based upon what they learned. The team's approach tapped into the emotional needs of "acquired" employees, reducing their anxieties, instilling hope for the future, and illustrating that their views and concerns were heard. Employee surveys, low absentee and turnover rates, and performance data confirmed this.[19]

The change agents for the insurance firm did their homework when developing and communicating the need for change. They openly engaged stakeholders in dialogue, listened and responded with care and consideration, and then proceeded to the next stage in the change process. Too many executives underestimate the need for communication and the importance of it being two-way. There can never be too much top-level communication and support, but unfortunately, there is often far too little listening. A rule of thumb for managers is to talk up a change initiative at least three times more than you think is needed and listen at least four times as much as you think you should![20] One change leader states that messages need to be communicated 17 times before they get heard![21]

Seek Out and Make Sense of Internal Data

It is no surprise that change leaders need to pay careful attention to internal organizational data when developing their assessment of the need for a particular initiative. Change agents who command internal respect and credibility understand the fundamentals of what is going on within a firm. Change leaders need to know what can be inferred from internal information and measures, how these are currently being interpreted by organizational members, and how they may be leading the firm down the wrong path. Some of this will be in the form of so-called hard data—the sort that can be found in the formal information system and it is often numeric in nature (e.g., customer retention and satisfaction, service profitability, cycle time, and employee absenteeism). Other valuable information will be soft data, the intuitive information gathered from walking around the building and work areas and having discussions with critical stakeholders. For example, do employees generally pick up litter such as candy wrappers, or is that task left exclusively to the janitorial staff? The former often indicates widespread pride and feelings of ownership in an organization.

Seek Out and Assess Your Personal Concerns and Perspectives

"Know thyself" is a critical dictum for change leaders. Change agents need a good understanding of their strengths and weaknesses, attitudes, values, beliefs, and motivations. They need to know how they take in information and how they interpret and make decisions. They need to recognize their preferences, prejudices, and blind spots. As change agents expand their self-awareness, they are freer to ask questions and seek help when they need it.[22]

"I think it's a combination of how self-aware people are and how honest they are. I think if someone is self-aware, then they can always continue to grow. If they're not self-aware, I think it's harder for them to evolve or adapt beyond who they already are."

Tony Hsieh, CEO, Zappos.com, Inc.[23]

During the Cuban Missile Crisis, October 1962, Collins and Porras report that President Kennedy was incredibly comfortable with expressing what he did not know and asking many questions before passing judgments.[24] This led to informed decision making that may have saved the world from World War III.

Many change leaders have difficulty publicly owning the fact that they do not have all the answers and demonstrating a real interest in listening and learning. They likely have noticed that someone who communicates more confidence in their judgment tends to be responded to more positively than a person who is more cautious—particularly if the audience is predisposed to that point of view. However, behavioral economists have found that this can lead to serious errors of judgment. For example, those individuals in the media who are most self-assured in their judgment are significantly less accurate than those who are more nuanced in their assessments. We may love their bravado and certainty, which helps explain their frequent appearances on TV, but beware of putting too much trust in their conclusions![25] In 2002–2003 Vice President Dick Cheney's confidence in Saddam Hussein and Iraq's possession of weapons of mass destruction was absolute, and yet, U.S. forces found very few.

Reputations for skill, judgment, and success develop over time, and this development is aided by a greater willingness to look, listen, and learn before committing to a course of action. As Daniel Kahneman and his colleagues have noted, dangerous biases creep into important decision making and these need to be guarded against. Taking steps that keep you open to learning and testing your assumptions can help you avoid decision traps and greatly benefit the quality of the final choice.[26] These actions reinforce the value of looking before you leap. People will build trust in your judgment, knowing that you've done your homework and considered the situation seriously, and show others that a little humility in one's judgment never hurts.[27]

NEW LEADERSHIP AT MICROSOFT

With the selection of Satya Nadella as its CEO in February 2014, Microsoft signaled a departure from the loudness of Steve Ballmer and a return to someone more like Bill Gates in his skill set and approach to management. Nadella is very competent technically and managerially and has demonstrated this over the years at Microsoft as he has successfully led change initiatives, most recently at the Cloud and Enterprise group. People report that he has done so by asking questions, listening, and engaging and energizing participants in ways that allow them to get out of their comfort zone and succeed. Those who have worked with him say he is honest, inclusive, authentic, and caring—generating success by thoughtfully nurturing the involvement and commitment of those around him.[28]

Whenever we, the authors, work with groups of university students, or managers and executives who are attempting organizational change, we caution them not to assume that their perspectives are held by all. They often fail to understand the impact of their own biases, perspectives, and needs and how they differ from those of others involved in a change initiative. They believe that they understand the situation and know what must change; this attitude can create significant barriers to accomplishing the change objectives. The strength of their concerns combined with their lack of self-awareness creates blind spots and causes them to block out dissenting perspectives. When change leaders talk to stakeholders, they may receive polite responses and assume that this implies a commitment to action. Statements such as "That's an interesting assessment" are taken as support rather than as neutral comments. Change leaders' inability to read subtle cues or misinterpret legitimate concerns as resistance, rather than thoughtful feedback, leads them astray.

In an extreme attempt to protect himself and his followers from his personal shortcomings and cult-like reputation, Nehru, one of the founding fathers of modern, independent India, used an alias when he wrote the following about himself in a prominent publication in 1937. The backdrop was the struggle for independence from Britain, which was achieved 11 years later.

What lies behind that mask of his, what desires, what will to power, what insatiate longings? Men like (Nehru) with all their capacity for great work, are unsafe in democracy . . . every psychologist knows that the mind is ultimately a slave to the heart and logic can always be made to fit in with the desires and irrepressible urges of a person. . . . (Nehru's) conceit is already formidable. It must be checked. We want no Caesars.[29]

—Nehru writing in the press about himself, using an alias

Nehru's deep commitment to India's independence did not blind him to how his own ego and the burgeoning hero worship that he was experiencing might impair the goal of a democratic India that would need an electorate that exercised thoughtful discourse and informed decision making. As such, he publicly noted the trend toward hero worship and its intoxicating impact on himself and his followers.

This section asks change leaders to consider their readiness for leading a change initiative and the roles that they will play in the process. It asks change agents to assess their skills, abilities, and predispositions to assess and guide the change. In Chapter 8, change agents will again be asked to look in a mirror and assess their predispositions toward various change agent roles. See **Toolkit Exercise 4.2** to understand and diagnose a need for change.

ASSESSING THE READINESS FOR CHANGE

Understanding the need for change and creating a vision for change are closely linked. Diagnosing where an organization is in the present moment is a prerequisite for figuring out its future direction. Beckhard and Harris[30] argue that addressing the question "Why change?" is a necessary precondition to being able to define the desired future state or the vision. If the question of "Why change?" is never meaningfully addressed, no one should expect the emergence of any sense of a shared vision. The answer to "Why?" is a prerequisite to the "What?" and the "How?" of change.

While dissatisfaction with the status quo by senior managers is certainly very helpful in advancing change, it is unlikely to be a *sufficient* condition. Spector[31] argues that the creation of dissatisfaction among others is needed. This dissatisfaction can be developed by sharing competitive information, benchmarking the organization's performance against others, challenging inappropriate behaviors through highlighting their impact, developing a vision for the future that creates frustration with the present state, and simply mandating dissatisfaction if one has the clout. Being dissatisfied with the status quo helps to ready the organization for change. That readiness depends on previous organizational experiences, managerial support, the organization's openness to change, its exposure to disquieting information about the status quo, and the systems promoting or blocking change in the organization.

Change initiators may understand the need for change, but other key stakeholders may not be prepared to recognize that need or believe it is strong enough to warrant action. Newspaper accounts of the failure to react in time are all too common (e.g., Chrysler in the auto industry,[32] Target (Canada) and Kmart in retailing,[33] Yahoo and BlackBerry in the digital world[34]). Though a litany of reasons is offered in the press, two common themes emerge: (1) Management failed to attend to the warning clouds or the opportunities that were clearly visible, often well in advance; and (2) when management took actions, they did too little too late. Past patterns of success can lead to active inertia (doing more of the same), flawed environmental scanning and assessments, and other factors that will be discussed later in the chapter that sabotage organizational members' capacity to successfully adapt.[35]

Organizational readiness for change is determined by the previous change experiences of its members; the flexibility and adaptability of the organizational culture; the openness, commitment, and involvement of leadership in preparing the organization for change; and member confidence in the leadership. It is also influenced by the organizational structure, the information members have access to, reward and measurement systems, resource availability, and the organization's flexibility and alignment with the proposed change.[36] This theme goes back to Chapter 3's discussion of Nadler and Tushman's Congruence Model and the importance of alignment. Readiness is advanced when organizational members can see how the existing misalignment is getting in the way of producing better outcomes and believe that the needed realignment can be achieved. An organization's readiness for change will influence its ability to both attend to environmental signals for change and listen to internal voices saying that change is needed.[37]

Previous experiences affect **individual readiness for change**. If organizational members have experienced more gain than pain from past change initiatives, they will be more predisposed to try something new. However, there is also the risk that they may resist changes that divert them from initiatives that have worked in the past.

If previous change experiences have been predominantly negative and unproductive, employees tend to become disillusioned and cynical ("we tried and it didn't work" attitude).[38] However, under the right conditions, this situation may produce increased resolve concerning the need for change. (Reactions to past change experiences will be discussed further in Chapter 7.)

Writers regularly report that the development and maintenance of top management's support is crucial to change success.[39] If senior managers are visibly supporting the initiative, are respected, and define and tie their success to the change initiative, then the organization is likely to be receptive to change. However, it is not unusual to find differences of opinion concerning change at the senior management level, so a lack of initial support is a reality that many change leaders must navigate. The beginning of any change journey can feel quite lonely, because though you and a few others have become convinced of the need for change, others may have quite different opinions about the need or not yet have given the matter much thought. This includes senior management. Perhaps more troubling situations than the lack of visible support occur when senior management assures change agents of support but fails to provide it at crucial moments because it isn't one of their priorities or they choose to engage in passive forms of resistance.

Organizations that have well-developed external scanning mechanisms are likely to be aware of environmental changes. Cultures and systems that encourage the collection and objective interpretation of relevant environmental, competitive, and benchmark data tend to be more open to change and provide members of the organization with the information they need to provoke their thinking concerning the need for change.[40] If the culture supports environmental scanning and encourages a focus on identifying and resolving problems rather than "turf protection," organizations will be more open to change.

READYING AN ORGANIZATION FOR CHANGE

Armenakis and his colleagues[41] identified factors for readying an organization for change. Their list includes the following:

1. The need for change is identified in terms of the gap between the current state and the desired state.

2. People believe that the proposed change is the right change to make.

3. The confidence of organizational members has been bolstered so that they believe they can accomplish the change.

4. The change has the support of key individuals the organizational members look to.

5. The "what's in it for me/us" question has been addressed.

Holt was concerned about an organization's readiness for change and developed a scale based on four beliefs among employees: They could implement a change, the change is appropriate for the organization, leaders are committed, and the proposed change is needed.[42] Judge and Douglas were also interested in calibrating an organization's readiness for change and utilized a rigorous approach to identify **eight dimensions related to readiness**:

1. Trustworthy leadership—the ability of senior leaders to earn the trust of others and credibly show others how to meet their collective goals

2. Trusting followers—the ability of nonexecutives to constructively dissent or willingly follow the new path

3. Capable champions—the ability of the organization to attract and retain capable champions

4. Involved middle management—the ability of middle managers to effectively link senior managers with the rest of the organization

5. Innovative culture—the ability of the organization to establish norms of innovation and encourage innovative activity

6. Accountable culture—the ability of the organization to carefully steward resources and successfully meet predetermined deadlines

7. Effective communications—the ability of the organization to effectively communicate vertically, horizontally, and with customers

8. Systems thinking—the ability of the organization to focus on root causes and recognize interdependencies within and outside the organization's boundaries.[43]

Table 4.1 contains a readiness-for-change questionnaire. It reflects the questions and issues raised in this section and provides another method for helping change leaders assess an organization's readiness for change.[44] By considering what is promoting and inhibiting change readiness, change agents can take action to enhance readiness—a change task in and of itself. For example, if rewards for innovation and change are seen to be lacking, or if employees believe they lack the needed skills, steps can be taken to address such matters. When considering rewards, remember these include intrinsic as well as extrinsic rewards. The impact of rewards on judgment and behavior needs to be considered carefully, because it can be complicated. For example, excessive rewards for success or excess punishment for failure are more likely to produce unethical behavior.[45] Alternatively, intrinsic rewards and moderate levels of equitable extrinsic rewards that are nested in teams can heighten information sharing, motivation, and commitment.[46] More will be said about this in later chapters. Change readiness must be consciously developed, aligned with supportive systems and structures, and then put to use as a source of competitive advantage. Developing change readiness is an important matter in both public and private organizations.[47]

Table 4.1 Rate the Organization's Readiness for Change

Readiness Dimensions	Readiness Score
Previous Change Experiences	
1. Has the organization had generally positive experiences with change?	Score 0 to +2
2. Has the organization had recent failure experiences with change?	Score 0 to −2
3. What is the mood of the organization: upbeat and positive?	Score 0 to +2
4. What is the mood of the organization: negative and cynical?	Score 0 to −3
5. Does the organization appear to be resting on its laurels?	Score 0 to −3
Executive Support	
6. Are senior managers directly involved in sponsoring the change?	Score 0 to +2
7. Is there a clear picture of the future?	Score 0 to +3
8. Is executive success dependent on the change occurring?	Score 0 to +2
9. Are some senior managers likely to demonstrate a lack of support?	Score 0 to −3

(Continued)

Table 4.1 (Continued)	
Readiness Dimensions	**Readiness Score**
Credible Leadership and Change Champions	
10. Are senior leaders in the organization trusted?	Score 0 to +3
11. Are senior leaders able to credibly show others how to achieve their collective goals?	Score 0 to +1
12. Is the organization able to attract and retain capable and respected change champions?	Score 0 to +2
13. Are middle managers able to effectively link senior managers with the rest of the organization?	Score 0 to +1
14. Are senior leaders likely to view the proposed change as generally appropriate for the organization?	Score 0 to +2
15. Will the proposed change be viewed as needed by the senior leaders?	Score 0 to +2
Openness to Change	
16. Does the organization have scanning mechanisms to monitor the internal and external environment?	Score 0 to +2
17. Is there a culture of scanning and paying attention to those scans?	Score 0 to +2
18. Does the organization have the ability to focus on root causes and recognize interdependencies both inside and outside the organization's boundaries?	Score 0 to +2
19. Does "turf" protection exist in the organization that could affect the change?	Score 0 to –3
20. Are middle and/or senior managers hidebound or locked into the use of past strategies, approaches, and solutions?	Score 0 to –4
21. Are employees able to constructively voice their concerns or support?	Score 0 to +2
22. Is conflict dealt with openly, with a focus on resolution?	Score 0 to +2
23. Is conflict suppressed and smoothed over?	Score 0 to –2
24. Does the organization have a culture that is innovative and encourages innovative activities?	Score 0 to +2
25. Does the organization have communications channels that work effectively in all directions?	Score 0 to +2
26. Will the proposed change be viewed as generally appropriate for the organization by those not in senior leadership roles?	Score 0 to +2
27. Will the proposed change be viewed as needed by those not in senior leadership roles?	Score 0 to +2
28. Do those who will be affected believe they have the energy needed to undertake the change?	Score 0 to +2

Readiness Dimensions	Readiness Score
29. Do those who will be affected believe there will be access to sufficient resources to support the change?	Score 0 to +2
Rewards for Change	
30. Does the reward system value innovation and change?	Score 0 to +2
31. Does the reward system focus exclusively on short-term results?	Score 0 to –2
32. Are people censured for attempting change and failing?	Score 0 to -3
Measures for Change and Accountability	
33. Are there good measures available for assessing the need for change and tracking progress?	Score 0 to +1
34. Does the organization attend to the data that it collects?	Score 0 to +1
35. Does the organization measure and evaluate customer satisfaction?	Score 0 to +1
36. Is the organization able to carefully steward resources and successfully meet predetermined deadlines?	Score 0 to +1

The scores can range from –25 to +50.

If the organization scores below 10, it is not likely ready for change and change will be very difficult.

- The higher the score, the more ready the organization is for change.
- If the score is below 10, the organization is not likely ready for change at the present.
- To increase readiness, change agents can use the responses to the questions to help them identify areas that need strengthening and then undertake actions to strengthen the readiness for change.

Change is never "simple," but when organizational factors supportive of change are in place, the task of the change agent is manageable.

The purpose of this tool is to raise awareness concerning readiness for change. Change agents can modify it to better reflect the realities of their organization and industry.

Source: Adapted from Stewart, T. (1994, February). "Rate your readiness to change" scale. Fortune, 106–110; Holt, D. (2002). Readiness for change: The development of a scale. *Organization Development Abstracts,* Academy of Management Proceedings, and Judge, W., & Douglas, T. (2009).Organizational change capacity: The systematic development of a scale. *Journal of Organizational Change Management, 22*(6), 635–649.

Heightening Awareness of the Need for Change

When an organization is open to change, thinking individuals will still want to critically assess the evidence concerning the need for change. The change leader may experience blanket resistance and defensiveness, or may experience more localized opposition. Individuals may recognize the need for change in some departments and functions but be resistant to recognizing the need for change as it gets closer to home. If they see only the unraveling of what they've worked to accomplish and/or unpleasant alternatives ahead for them, they will be very reluctant to embrace change proposals. Even when the need for change is broadly recognized, action does not necessarily follow.

FROM BAD TO WORSE:
GARBAGE SERVICES IN NAPLES, ITALY

Naples, Italy, has lived with a garbage problem for years. Poor management, organized crime, and ineffective political leadership allowed the matter to fester and escalate. In 2008, worldwide coverage of the problem drew attention and political promises for action, as 55,000 tons of uncollected garbage filled city streets, and 110,000 to 120,000 tons awaited treatment in municipal storage sites. Though the streets are now cleaner, resolution has been slow and suspect. Untold tons of irresponsibly (some would argue criminally) handled waste continue to reside in illegal landfills that dot the countryside, or they have been shipped elsewhere for questionable "disposal." The results have fouled the environment, endangered health, seriously harmed Naples' economy, and required deployment of the army in 2008 and 2011 to deal with uncollected garbage.[48] In November 2013, the legacy created by decades of mismanagement and corruption erupted very publicly yet again—this time in the form of burning trash heaps on the outskirts of Naples that were producing toxic fumes and threatening water quality and food safety in the region.[49]

In the story above, the need for change seems obvious. However, the politicians of the city and other levels of government were reluctant to take the difficult steps needed to deal with the problems. Clearly, Naples and her citizens were not yet prepared to undertake the type of change needed.

Once change leaders understand the need for change, they can take different approaches to heighten the awareness of the need throughout the organization. Change leaders can do the following:

1. Make the organization aware that it is in or near a crisis.

2. Identify a transformational vision based on higher-order values.

3. Find a transformational leader to champion the change.

4. Take the time to identify shared goals and work out ways to achieve them.

5. Use information and data to raise awareness of the need for change.

1. The first method is a form of shock treatment and involves *making the organization aware that it is in or near a crisis.* Many of the dramatic turnaround stories that are reported are successful because the actions of people were galvanized and focused by the necessity for action. In the face of crisis, people find it difficult to deny the need to change and to change *now.* When the crisis is real, the issue will be one of showing others a way out that they will follow if they have confidence in its viability, given that the alternatives are far from attractive.[50]

At times, managers will be tempted *to create a sense of urgency* to change and mobilize staff around a change initiative that may—or may not— be fully justified. Creating a sense of crisis when one does not really exist must be approached with care.[51] If mishandled, it may be viewed as manipulative and result in heightened cynicism and reduced commitment. The change leader's personal credibility and trustworthiness are then at stake. The reputation developed in and around change initiatives casts a long shadow, for better or worse. The currencies that change agents use are credibility and trustworthiness. These take a long time to develop and can be quickly squandered.[52]

An extension of the crisis approach is the "burn or sink your boats." In this case, the change leader takes the process one step further and cuts off any avenue of retreat. That is, there is no going back. This approach is based on the belief that this will lead to increased commitment to the selected course of action. While it may aid in focusing attention, this approach can increase risks: (a) individuals may resent being forced into a situation against their will; or (b) it may produce compliant and even energized behavior in the short term due to the absence of alternatives, but it can give rise to undesirable long-term consequences if the actions come to be viewed as inappropriate or unfair. Consequences can include elevated levels of mistrust, reduced commitment, and poor performance.[53]

CREATING URGENCY AT NEW YORK CITY'S METROPOLITAN TRANSIT AUTHORITY (MTA)

In October 2012, Hurricane Sandy left huge challenges for NYC's MTA. MTA used the sense of urgency to motivate staff to think in creative ways to get the most essential job done. The priority was to get the city connected and moving after the storm. Despite there being no emergency handbook for this kind of situation, the MTA was able to get partial service up within days and full lines running within a week.[54]

In the wake of Hurricane Sandy, the transit system was underwater in many areas, infrastructure had been destroyed, and virtually nothing was running. The crisis faced by Joseph Leader, the subway's chief maintenance officer, and all the other executives and staff, was both real and devastating. They knew tough decisions were needed around the alignment and coordination of resources and that a huge amount of work would be required to get the city's transit system operational. A competent and highly motivated staff, combined with the powerful shared goal of getting the trains moving, allowed them to mobilize, sort out what needed to be done, and act—even in the absence of protocols.

Urgency is straightforward when there is an event such as Sandy. However, it can prove more difficult when it evolves more slowly, such as deteriorating market conditions, or in the case of not-for-profits such as government agencies, deteriorating service standards or relevance to the public. With the right use of data and influence approaches, people can be woken up. Creating a sense of social and political urgency through advocacy approaches has proven powerful in the public arena, as seen in the pressure for change in the U.S. Department of Veterans Affairs.[55] Likewise, approaches that disrupt existing perspectives, challenge past learning, and hasten the adoption of new perspectives through creating a sense of urgency have been shown to help new product development teams get out of ruts and become more effective, though they do have to guard against information and knowledge loss in the process.[56]

2. A second approach to enhancing people's awareness of the need for change is by *identifying a transformational vision based on higher-order values*, such as the delivery of superb service and responsiveness to customers' needs. Transformational visions tap into the need for individuals to go beyond themselves, to make a contribution, to do something worthwhile and meaningful, and to serve a cause greater than themselves. These appeals can provide powerful mechanisms to unfreeze an organization and create conditions for change. In addition, transformational visions pull people toward an idealized future and a positive approach to needed change.

Cynics in an organization may reject these visionary appeals for several reasons. They may see them as superficial, naive, ill-advised, off-target, or designed simply to serve the interests of those making the pronouncements. If organizational members have previously heard visionary pronouncements, only to see them ignored or discarded, they may believe the most recent iteration is simply the current "flavor of the week" approach to change.

Change agents need to be committed to following through on the actions that underlie the visionary appeals. If they are not, then they should stop rather than contribute to the build-up of organizational cynicism and alienation that accompanies unmet expectations. Nevertheless, the power of truly transformational visions should not be underestimated. How else do we understand the response to the visionary perspectives provided by change leaders such as Mahatma Ghandi and Nelson Mandela?

3. A third approach to enhancing the need for change is through *transformational leadership*. Leadership in general and transformational leadership, in particular, continue to command attention in the change literature—not surprising, given its stature in Western culture and mythology.[57] From George Washington to Adolf Hitler, from Nelson Mandela to Saddam Hussein, we elevate heroes and condemn villains.

The same is true for the corporate world. Steve Jobs's resuscitation of Apple, Anne Mulcahy's transformation of Xerox, Thomas Tighe's work at Direct Relief International, Oprah Winfrey's growth of a media empire, Richard Branson's entrepreneurial initiatives at Virgin, and Elon Musk's development of PayPal, SpaceX, and the Tesla automobile are examples of the work of successful transformational leaders. The appeal of charismatic and transformational individuals is powerful. In addition to effectively framing the change vision as noted above, they have the capacity to create strong, positive personal connectedness and a willingness to change in followers that often overrides the followers' personal concerns. However, corporate scandals (e.g., Bernie Ebbers of WorldCom, Bernie Madoff of Madoff Investment Securities, Angelo Mozilo of Countrywide Financial, and John Stumpf of Wells Fargo) remind people of the risks of idolizing transformational exemplars. Even GE's Jack Welch's image took a beating with published reports of his divorce battles and the size and nature of his retirement package.[58] Caution is needed if you are relying on charisma to induce followers to change an organization. Charismatic appeals can prove powerful and helpful, but there are good reasons for people to be suspicious of charismatic appeals because history demonstrates that personal magnetism is not always directed toward desirable outcomes.

It is important to note that many leaders are very effective change agents without being particularly charismatic. Some of those who have proven to be most influential in nurturing long-term organizational success have been much quieter in their approach.[59] Such a list would include Meg Whitman, CEO of HP; Satya Nadella, CEO of Microsoft; Warren Buffett of Berkshire Hathaway; Michael Latimer, president and CEO of OMERS, a large Canadian pension fund; Ursula Burns, CEO of Xerox; and Ellen Kullman, CEO of DuPont.

4. A fourth way of stimulating awareness of a need for change is by *taking the time to identify shared goals and working out ways to achieve them.* Finding common areas of agreement is a very useful way to avoid resistance to change. Instead of focusing on what might be lost, examine the risks of not taking action. What will be gained by taking action can create momentum for change. This is often achieved by having people seriously consider their long-term interests (rather than their immediate positions) and the higher-order goals that they would like to pursue. Shared interest in and commitment to higher-order goals can provide a powerful stimulus for commitment and mobilization.

5. Fifth, *information and data can be used* to raise awareness of the need for change. In many respects, this is the inverse of the command-and-control approach to change, because it seeks to build awareness and support through information rather than edict. Reluctance to change may be a result of lack of information, or confusion about conflicting sources of information. This can be overcome with a well-organized communications campaign that provides employees with needed information, such as best practices in a specific area; benchmark data about the practices and approaches of others; visits to other organizations to see and hear about their practices; or competitive data on the specific topic.[60] Research on effective organizations can provide a compare-and-contrast picture to an organization's current mode of operation and that process can stimulate discussion and facilitate change.

MISGUIDED APPROACH TO CHANGE

In October, 2018, Sears filed for bankruptcy. Founded in St. Louis in 1928, Sears had been a retailing giant, with thousands of stores across the USA. Hard-hit by the e-commerce revolution in retailing, Sear's billionaire CEO Eddie Lampert decided to reengineer the company's finances rather than do the hard-work of organizational change. Since 2005 Lampert spent $6 billion to buy back Sears' own shares in an effort to support its stock price. William Lazonick, a retired University of Massachusetts' Economics Professor and an expert in share repurchasing, argues that if Lampert had used the $6 billion to reduce its debt burden and/or provide capital to modernize stores, then Sears just *might* have stayed out of bankruptcy court.

Once again, the change agent's credibility is crucial. If employees are suspicious of the motives of the change agent, the accuracy of the information, or there has been a history of difficult relationships, then the information will be examined with serious reservations. When employees come to accept the information and related analyses, the ground is fertile for the development of a shared sense of the need and the vision for change.

Factors That Block People From Recognizing the Need for Change

Giving voice to the need for change can create awareness in employees. However, future directions are not always obvious and an organization's history and culture can be strong impediments to new pathways. It took Hewlett-Packard a number of years of poor performance, problematic acquisitions, and related stumbles under different CEOs (most notably Carly Fiorina) until they recognized that cobbling in poorly fitting acquisitions to boost market share, and focusing primarily upon efficiency and cost reduction by playing with structures and product/service portfolios, would not reverse the fortunes of their business. Meg Whitman, the retired CEO of eBay, stepped into this very difficult situation and led the revitalization of storied HP by valuing its roots, leading the conversation around the need for change, working to create a sense of urgency and hope, and taking actions to remove some of the obstacles in the way.

REVERSING THE DEATH SPIRAL AT HEWLETT-PACKARD

Hewlett-Packard had demonstrated commitment over the years to the belief that long-term success was grounded in the "'HP Way"—a cultural perspective that celebrated technical expertise, flexibility, and innovation; placed high value on their collegial, teamwork-based environment; saw employees as their most important resource; and had a strong customer orientation and commitment to act with integrity at all times. However, in 1999, following a period of lackluster performance, HP hired Carly Fiorina as their CEO. Fiorina's top-down leadership style put results as the number one priority and arguably devalued employees. Her autocratic and aggressive style left her workforce demoralized. The ill-conceived merger with Compaq and a number of other major actions, such as the restructuring of the enterprise into a more hierarchical one, generated sustained, deepening disappointment on the performance front.

It could be argued that Fiorina suffered from tunnel vision concerning how to act on the need for change and manage the path forward. This blocked her from realizing how to value what was there, respond constructively to the challenges they faced, and modify her management style to facilitate needed changes. The results of her actions demoralized members of the firm, generated significant turnover, and adversely affected the entire organization.

Following Fiorina's dismissal in 2005 and subsequent flawed efforts to get things back on track, the board appointed Meg Whitman as CEO in 2011. At that point, many believed HP was operating on borrowed time. A number of the members of the senior management team were reported to have been very unhappy with her appointment. Whitman was an outsider, and some of them had been jockeying for the top job.

Whitman knew that hard choices were needed. These included making major changes to her senior management team to get rid of infighting and promote much-needed cooperation and constructive engagement. Major job cuts (34,000) had to be made to address cash flow and market realities. However, she also clearly signaled a return to the organization's roots, by restoring funding and executive support for what was then a gutted and demoralized R&D function, symbolizing their commitment to innovation. She made the need for change salient to organizational members and highlighted a sense of urgency. The enterprise was restructured to better align it with the emergent strategy, and she reinforced the importance of having a clear customer focus. Further, she created a vision for the future that offered employees reasons for hope and regenerated shared commitment through the focus on teamwork, collaboration, excellence in execution, and shared celebrations of success. Changes of this magnitude do not happen overnight. HP's impressive return to cultural and financial health by 2014 (stock price up 300% since 2011; being recognized as one of the 100 top employers in Canada in 2014) show that they were well on their way.[61] There were drops in revenue, profit and unit performance in 2015 and 2016, but these had rebounded nicely by 2017. Its share price was approximately 2.2 times its 2016 low by January 2019.[62]

All too often, strategists will introduce a new direction and seek to change the organizational culture without attending to the question of the impact of cultural artifacts on the desired change.[63] Cultural artifacts are the stories, rituals, and symbols that influence employees' attitudes and beliefs; they are important because they help to define and give life to the culture. If change agents continue to tie themselves to those artifacts, they may reinforce the old culture they wish to change. However, being dismissive of the past can also be problematic because it may signal that things done in the past are no longer valued. The challenge is: how do you value the past and its positive attributes without trapping yourself in the past? In 1994, Bethune and Brenneman faced this challenge when they tackled the turnaround of Continental Airlines, taking the firm from near bankruptcy and the worst customer service ratings in the industry to success on all fronts over the next decade.[64] One of the major reasons that they were successful in implementing a turnaround was their introduction of new cultural artifacts that highlighted customer service as a key corporate value.

CULTURAL CHANGE AT CONTINENTAL AIRLINES

A new reward system was put into place at Continental that focused on improved service. Performance-reward systems, in and of themselves, are not necessarily cultural artifacts, but this new reward system contrasted with past practices. It was tied directly to corporate performance, and the financial rewards were paid in a separate check to employees to draw attention to the relationship between performance and rewards. This reward system not only reinforced a new value at Continental, but it also became a symbol to employees of the importance of high levels of performance in the new Continental, as opposed to the acceptance of poor performance, as had been the case in the old Continental. In addition, stories were told throughout Continental about how the new CEO told jokes to employees, answered questions honestly, and was an all-around good guy to work for. These and numerous additional artifacts replaced old ones that had reinforced bureaucracy and the acceptability of poor performance and that had led to unbelievably low employee morale.[65] They succeeded in sustaining positive changes in customer service and fleet performance over the years, and their financial performance reflected their success in this very competitive industry. In 2009, *Fortune* magazine named Continental the world's most admired airline, and the World Airline Awards recognized it as the best North American airline.[66] In 2010 United Airlines acquired Continental.

Both the Continental and HP examples show that the existing culture can impair organizational members' capacity to either recognize the urgency of the need for change, or believe that there is the organizational will to constructively respond. Even if organizational members recognize the need, culture can impede their ability to take appropriate actions until things occur that weaken the existing beliefs and open the way to new thinking about the organization, the current situation, and its leadership. When this occurred at Continental and HP, the door was opened to meaningful change. Actions that created reasons for hope and reinforced the development and strengthening of new cultural beliefs ensured that the organization would continue its journey in a positive direction and wouldn't regress to old patterns.

Culture can get in the way of recognizing the need for change in poorly performing firms. However, it can represent an even more difficult barrier in successful firms. Consider Unilever, which had great brands and a long history in emerging markets and yet was falling behind competitors in those same markets. They knew they needed to change something but were mentally locked into the business practices that had become sources of disadvantage.[67] In 2004, they finally recognized the sources of the problem and by 2006 were reaping the benefits in terms of renewed growth and profitability. Unilever's performance was adversely affected by the 2008 recession, along with all their major competitors, but their renewed competitive capacities facilitated their recovery by 2010 and led to all-time share price highs in 2014.[68] Sull argues that organizations trapped in their past successes often exhibit lots of activity (this was true for Unilever), but the outcome is "active inertia," because they remain essentially unchanged.[69] Even when organizations recognize that they need to change, they fail to take appropriate actions. He believes this occurs because

- **Strategic frames**, those mental models of how the world works become blinders to the changes that have occurred in the environment;

- **Processes** harden into routines and habits, becoming ends in themselves rather than means to an end;

- **Relationships** with employees, customers, suppliers, distributors, and shareholders become shackles that limit the degrees of freedom available to respond to the changed environment; and

- **Values**, those deeply held beliefs that determine corporate culture, harden into dogma, and questioning them is seen as heresy.

During periods of financial difficulty, senior management may become polarized in their positions, isolate themselves from data they need, and incorrectly assess the need for change. Senior management may prevent critical information from surfacing as they self-censor, avoid conflict, and/or are unwilling to solicit independent assessments as they attempt to preserve cohesion and commitment to a course of action.[70] These are conditions that lead to groupthink[†] and can result in disastrous decisions that flow from the flawed analysis.[71]

[†] Groupthink is "a mode of thinking that people engage in when they are deeply involved in a cohesive in-group, when the members' striving for unanimity overrides their motivation to realistically appraise alternative courses of action." Retrieved December 2010 from http://wps.prenhall.com/wps/media/objects/213/218150/glossary.html.

Change agents need to be vigilant and take actions to ensure that groupthink does not cloud a team's capacity to assess the need for change. If change agents are dealing with a cohesive team exhibiting the characteristics of groupthink, the agent needs to take action with care, considering how to make the group aware of factors that may be clouding its judgment. Change agents who attempt to alert such teams to these realities are often dealt with harshly, since "shooting the messenger" is a speedy way for teams to protect themselves from difficult data. Strategies for avoiding groupthink include the following:

- Have the leader play an impartial role, soliciting information and input before expressing an opinion.

- Actively seek dissenting views. Have group members play the role of devil's advocate, challenging the majority's opinion.

- Actively pursue the discussion and analysis of the costs, benefits, and risks of diverse alternatives.

- Establish a methodical decision-making process at the beginning.

- Ensure an open climate for discussion and decision making, and solicit input from informed outsiders and experts.

- Allow time for reflection and do not mistake silence for consent.[72]

Additional factors that obstruct managerial judgment over the need for change and the inability to develop constructive visions for future action have been highlighted in both the business and academic press. Ram Charan and Jerry Useem summarized such factors in their 2002 *Fortune* magazine article on the role executives play in organizational failures:

- They have been softened by past success.

- They see no problems or at least none that warrant serious change. This can be both internal and external blindness.

- They fear the CEO and his or her biases more than competitors.

- They overdose on risk and play too close to the edge. This is often tied to systems that reward excessive risk taking.

- Their acquisition lust clouds their judgment.

- They listen to Wall Street more than to employees and others who have valuable insights they should attend to.

- They employ the "strategy du jour"—the quick-fix flavor of the day.

- They possess a dangerous corporate culture—one that invites high-risk actions.

- They find themselves locked in a new economy death spiral—one that is sustained and accelerating.

- They have a dysfunctional board that fails in its duties around governance.[73]

Developing a well-grounded awareness of the need for change is a critical first step for change leaders when helping organizations overcome inertia, rein in high-risk propensities, address internal and external blind spots, disrupt patterns of groupthink, and view their environment in ways that open organizational members to change.

So far, this chapter has outlined the variety of perspectives that will exist regarding the need for change. It emphasizes that the perspective of the change leader may not be held by others and that often change leaders need to develop or strengthen the need for change before trying to make specific changes. One of the ways to enhance the perceived need for change and begin to create focused momentum for action is to develop a clear and compelling new vision.

DEVELOPING A POWERFUL VISION FOR CHANGE

A *vision* is an idealized view of the future. A manager may, for example, have a three-year vision for her career, which, once the next desired-for management level is reached, will require a new vision. The new vision clarifies the actions that the manager will need to take in the future to reach her following career goal. For example, the manager may need to earn an MBA degree to have the skills that are needed for the subsequent level of management responsibilities. Visions, then, foreshadow the type and direction of actions. Just as visions can set direction and action for individuals, visions are also needed for teams, departments, and organizations. When organizations are undergoing massive change, a new vision can provide a powerful pull on employees to participate positively in the change process and the actions that will come.[74] As Simons says, "Vision without task is a dream world and task without vision is drudgery."[75]

Change leaders use visions to create and advance the mental pictures people have of the future. Developing a new vision is a key part of defining a future state: the change leader needs to articulate the gap between where an organization is today and where it wishes—ideally— to go in the future.

Understanding the foundational components of **organizational vision** is important. In an ideal world, it is closely connected to the mission of the organization and informs the core philosophy and values of the institution. It addresses such questions as "What does this organization stand for?" From this should flow the strategies, goals, and objectives of the organization.[76] When change leaders have fully developed a change process, the strategies, goals, and objectives flow from the vision and will address three essential questions for an enterprise:

What business are we in?

Who are our target customers and what is our value proposition to them?

How will we deliver on our value proposition?

Change agents often create "sub-visions" in different department units to generate emotional energy and directional clarity for a large-scale organizational change. These allow the overall new vision to be adapted to reflect how it manifests itself within specific areas of the organization. If FedEx's overriding commitment to its customers for its express service is "absolutely, positively overnight," then a change leader's vision concerning a logistics support initiative might deal with enhancing accuracy in package tracking to reduce error rates to below .00001%.

Beach states,

> Vision is an agenda of goals . . . vision is a dream about how the ideal future might be . . . it gives rise to and dictates the shape of plans . . . vision infuses the plan with energy because it gives it direction and defines objectives. Even the most unassuming vision constitutes a challenge to become something stronger, better, different.[77]

In short, a vision can mobilize and motivate people[78] and have a positive impact on performance and attitudes.[79]

Change leaders need to know *how* to develop a vision. Jick outlines three methods for creating a vision: (a) leader-developed, (b) leader-senior team-developed, and (c) bottom-up visioning.[80] As the name suggests, a **leader-developed vision** is done largely in isolation from others. Once it has been created, it is announced and shared with others in the organization. **Leader-senior team-developed vision** casts a broader net. Members of the senior team are involved in the process of vision formation. Once completed, it is then shared with others. **Bottom-up visioning**, or an employee-centric approach, is time-consuming, difficult, *and* valuable in facilitating the alignment of organizational members' vision with the overall **vision for change**. If an executive leader can articulate a compelling vision that captures a broad spectrum of organizational members' hearts, then a leader-developed vision is likely appropriate. If, on the other hand, employees are diverse and have mixed feelings about upcoming changes, then the change agent's job will be difficult and a bottom-up approach may be helpful. If employees both "get it" (i.e., the vision) and "want to get it," subsequent support for change will prove much easier to develop, leverage, and implement.[81] This is particularly important when cultural changes are involved.[82]

What does it take to develop an effective change vision? According to Jick, good change visions are clear, concise, easily understood.[83] They are

- Memorable
- Exciting and inspiring
- Challenging
- Excellence centered
- Stable but flexible
- Implementable and tangible

The process of creating a vision statement encourages change agents to dream big. Paradoxically, when visions become too grand and abstract, they can cease to have much impact. Alternatively, they may provide guidance that energizes and mobilizes individuals to undertake initiatives that unintentionally work at cross purposes to other initiatives that have been embarked upon or that may even have the potential to put the organization at risk.[84]

FOOD BANKS CANADA

Food Banks Canada is the national body that plays a leadership role with its 450 affiliated nonprofit food banks across the country and 10 provincial associations. Its corporate vision is to relieve hunger in Canada every day by raising food and funds to share with food banks nationally, delivering program and services to Canadian food banks, and influencing public policy to create longer term solutions. To help them convey this message they adopted the slogan "a Canada where no one goes hungry." This slogan provides guidance that underpins the vision for specific change initiatives that do the following: promote increased food donations from national and regional organizations (e.g., supermarkets, food producers); advance coordination and cooperation among local food banks and the provincial bodies; enhance press and community awareness of food bank initiatives and hunger issues; build support in the corporate community; and influence relevant governmental organizations and departments on matters related to hunger and food security.

These initiatives grew out of restructuring and revitalization initiatives by the food bank community around 2006. At that time the new CEO and other staff members were recruited, the board and its governance processes were restructured, branding activities for the national organization were undertaken, and the approaches to advocacy and outreach were revitalized. As the result of these initiatives, Food Banks Canada has improved its reputation with government, national private sector organizations (e.g., grocery chains and food manufacturers), and affiliated local food banks as a credible and respected national voice on hunger issues, and an effective deliverer of related services. Donations (food, money, and related services such as trucking) are significantly stronger now. Awareness levels related to domestic hunger have also increased. The release of their data-rich annual publication, *Hunger Counts*, now generates significant media attention and commentary by the sorts of individuals who can make a difference.[85]

Lipton provides a pragmatic view of what makes for an effective vision statement. He argues that it needs to convey three key messages: (a) the mission or purpose of the organization, (b) the strategy for achieving the mission, and (c) the elements of the organizational culture that seem necessary to achieving the mission and supporting the strategy.[86] He believes a vision will be more likely to fail when the following occurs:

- Actions of senior managers are incongruent with the vision. They fail to "walk the talk."

- It ignores the needs of those who will be putting it into practice.

- Unrealistic expectations develop around it that can't possibly be met.

- It is little more than limited strategies, lacking in a broader sense of what is possible.

- It lacks grounding in the reality of the present that can be reconciled.

- It is either too abstract or too concrete. It needs to stimulate and inspire, but there also needs to be the sense that it is achievable.

- It is not forged through an appropriately messy, iterative, creative process requiring a combination of "synthesis and imagination."

- It lacks sufficient participation and involvement of others to build a consensus concerning its appropriateness.

- Its implementation lacks "a sense of urgency . . . and measurable milestones."[87]

Lipton's list provides change leaders with a set of factors to consider when developing and operationalizing their vision for change. Are their actions aligned with the vision? Have they considered the needs of those who will be putting it into practice? If not, Lipton would argue that you are lowering the motivational and directional value the change vision can provide. Conversely, if these elements are present, the power of the change vision is enhanced.

Visions need to paint pictures that challenge the imagination and enrich the soul. Too many vision statements are insipid and dull. Too often they represent generic pap—right-sounding words but ones devoid of real meaning, designed for plaques and outside consumption and not rooted in the heart of the organization. By trying to say everything or appeal to everyone, they say nothing and appeal to no one.[88] Table 4.2 contains the Handy-Dandy Vision Crafter, a cynical view of how some organizational vision statements are developed. While many statements may end up containing words similar to those in the model, the Handy-Dandy Vision Crafter ignores the hard work and the difficult creative process and activities that organizations go through to develop a vision statement that they are truly committed to. In many ways, the process of developing a new vision is as important as the vision itself. However, too many vision statements read as if the Vision Crafter had been used to create them.

Table 4.2   The Cynics' Handy-Dandy Vision Crafter

Just fill in the blanks with the words that best suit your needs!

We strive to be the: _____

(Premier, Leading, Preeminent, World-class, Dominant, Best of class . . .)

Organization in our industry. We provide the best in: _____.

(Committed, Caring, Innovative, Expert, Environmentally friendly, Reliable, Cost-effective, Focused, Diversified, High-quality, On-time, Ethical, High-value-added . . .)

(Products, Services, Business Solutions, Customer-oriented Solutions . . .)

To: _____

(Serve Our Global Marketplace; Create Customer, Employee, and Shareholder Value; Fulfill Our Covenants to Our Stakeholders; Exceed Our Customers' Needs; Delight Our Customers . . .)

Through _____ employees

(Committed, Caring, Continuously Developed, Knowledgeable, Customer-focused . . .)

In the Rapidly Changing and Dynamic: _____

(Industry, Society, World)

Sometimes a quick statement, a slogan, can serve as a vision proxy. Consider the following statements:

- Every life deserves world-class care: Cleveland Clinic

- Think differently: Apple Computers

- Saving people money so they can live better: Walmart

- Inspire the world, create the future: Samsung

- To organize the world's information and make it universally accessible and useful: Google

- The greatest tragedy is indifference: Red Cross

- Grace, space, pace: Jaguar

- Play on: Lego

- Until every child is well: Boston Children's Hospital

These slogans are tied to statements of mission and vision, and they provide messages that are clear to employees and customers alike. They are meant to reflect underlying values that the organization holds dear and can help provide continuity with the change vision. Consider, for example, the one adopted by the Cleveland Clinic: Every life deserves world-class care. If you were to take the words at their face value and were an associate there, change initiatives that facilitate access for the poor at the Cleveland Clinic are more likely to be viewed as positive change initiatives than ones focused solely on improving profitability, because they have the potential to be consistent with what the organization is all about.

The slogan "Quality is job #1" was used by Ford to symbolize its determination to improve quality in the 1980s. In the aftermath of quality and safety concerns that buffeted Ford, the automaker successfully used these words, with an accompanying concerted program of action, to refocus employee and public perceptions of the importance of quality to Ford and, ultimately, the excellence of its products. This major initiative spanned several years and was ultimately successful in taking root in the minds of employees and the public. However, the Ford Explorer/Firestone controversy in 2000[89] concerning vehicle stability in emergency situations reopened public questions of Ford's commitment to quality and safety and put extreme internal and external pressure on Ford and Bridgestone, Firestone's parent organization, to restore the public trust. The lesson to draw from Ford's experience is that an image built on a vision that took years to develop can be shattered quickly. Ford appears to have learned from the experience and their recent slogan, "Drive Further," is intended to address customer concerns around quality by committing to deliver products that are up to the challenge.

GM is relearning this lesson now, due to its decade-long failure to address an ignition switch problem that has resulted in a number of deaths, lawsuits, and the recall of approximately 18 million cars in North America in 2014. CEO Mary Barra has worked hard to get out in front of this horrible situation, be transparent with the internal and external investigations, take concerted action to address the issue, and restore public confidence that inaction, such as this, will not recur under her watch at the GM.[90]

Johnson & Johnson's response to the 1982 Tylenol deaths and tampering of bottles scare[91] and Procter & Gamble's[92] response to inappropriate competitive intelligence activities related to hair care products provide two examples of how clear vision can help organizations develop initiatives that respond effectively to potentially damaging events. In the case of Tylenol, this best-selling brand was pulled from store shelves until the company was confident it had effectively addressed the risk of product tampering, at the cost of tens of millions of dollars. In the Procter & Gamble situation, when the CEO found out, he fired those involved, informed P&G's competitor that it had been spied upon, took appropriate action with respect to knowledge that P&G had inappropriately gained, and negotiated a multimillion-dollar civil damage payment to the aggrieved competitor. The actions of these two firms demonstrated their commitment to their respective visions of how they should operate and reinforced public and employee confidence in the firms and what they stood for.[‡]

Compare Procter & Gamble's and Johnson & Johnson's responses with Toyota's initial reactions to safety concerns in 2009 and 2010. The Toyota vision in 2010 was to become the most successful and respected car company in each market around the world by offering customers the best purchasing and ownership experience. However, one wonders if the desire to become the largest and most successful auto firm got in the way of the vision for respect that would be linked to quality and the willingness to put the needs of customers ahead of the company's own. The response to safety concerns was initially slow and defensive, and Toyota paid a very heavy price in lost sales and damaged reputation and brand.[93] It was ranked the seventh most admired company in the world by *Fortune* in 2010, dropped to 33 for 2011 and 2012, and is slowly regaining ground, landing 29th on the list in 2013.[94]

As noted earlier, companies can be trapped by the existing vision of their organization.[95] Goss, Pascale, and Athos argue that (a) narrow definitions of what the company is about, (b) failure to challenge the accepted boundaries and assumptions of the company, and (c) an inability to understand the context leads to inadequate or mediocre visions. They show the problems that can occur when a vision is achieved—now what? Once the vision is achieved, motivation is lost. It is a bit like a team whose vision was to "make it to the Super Bowl"—it is at a distinct disadvantage when playing against a team whose vision is to "win the Super Bowl."

Once the vision is clear, the issue becomes one of enactment by employees. *Storytelling* is a technique employed by change leaders to communicate a vision and mobilize awareness and interest. Because people identify with and remember stories, change agents can use stories in several ways: to create contextual awareness of how an organization got to its problematic condition; to demystify data; to clarify a change initiative and why a particular course of action makes sense; to relieve or increase tension and awareness; and finally, to instill confidence.[96] The multiple uses of stories make storytelling a critical skill for change leaders. Some have referred to this as ways to increase the "stickiness" of the message and enhance its meaningfulness. To increase the stickiness,

---

[‡] Johnson & Johnson's credo can be found at http://www.jnj.com/connect/about-jnj/jnj-credo/. Procter & Gamble's mission, vision, and values can be found at http://www.pg.com/en_US/downloads/media/PVP_brochure.pdf.

Cranston and Keller recommend framing the stories five different ways. By this they mean not stopping the message for change after the traditional data-based approach that either demonstrates shortfalls (here is how we're falling behind and need to improve) or opportunities. In addition to this, they recommend also framing the stories in terms of the impact of the vision on society, the customer, the work team, and the individuals. Which messages are you more likely to remember—stories about positive impacts on you, your work team, your customers, and society, or ones that speak solely to 5% improvements to margins and 10% increase in sales levels?[97]

Wheatley argues that one must "get the vision off the walls and into the halls."[98] She claims that people are often trapped by a mechanical view of vision, one that is limited to only a directional component of vision. She argues that vision should be viewed as a field that touches every employee differently and is filled with eddies and flux and shifting patterns. This view emphasizes the need to understand how each individual "sees" or "feels" the vision. As Beach says, "Each member of the organization has his or her own vision."[99] Somehow, these individual visions need to be combined into an overall sense of purpose for the organization. The active engagement and involvement of employees in the development, communication, and enactment of the vision for change is a strategy that has been effectively used to advance the creation of a shared sense of purpose.[100] Twenty-six centuries ago, Lao Tzu observed that "the best change is what the people think they did themselves."

THE DIFFERENCE BETWEEN AN ORGANIZATIONAL VISION AND A CHANGE VISION

While the rules for crafting a vision remain the same, the focus of the vision shifts depending upon the level and position of the change leader. Different parts of the organization will focus the vision for their areas in ways that reflect the aspirations for their part of the enterprise. They should be aligned with the overarching vision but differentiated in ways that generate meaning and energy for those involved with that part of the organization. *Whereas the corporate vision is about the long-term future, the change vision is shorter term in its perspective, and more specific as to the targets for change, the tangible outcomes to be achieved, and the anticipated impact.* In other words, it is focused on the specific changes to be implemented. By definition, they are designed to contribute to the vision of the organization but are focused in their scope, and often require the cooperation of others to bring them to fruition.[101]

This is easy to understand if subunits, such as divisions, are involved with different products and/or services and/or different markets. However, it also holds for other functions within the organization, such as manufacturing, marketing, or accounting services. For example, a staff support function such as HR will have a change focus that is largely internal to the organization, because that is where most of its customers and services lie. However, a vision for change focused on improving HR's ability to successfully recruit and retain external talent would involve an external focus plus the needed alignment of internal systems and processes to produce the desired results for the organization. If you are an organization needing to scale your operations rapidly, change initiatives that facilitate the recruitment, development, and retention of talented employees takes on added urgency—something firms such as Infosys and Tata Consulting, know all too well.[102] In 2014, Infosys reported they were planning to add 3,500 employees to two of their Indian development centers and were striving to keep their attrition rate at 12% or lower. To promote their image as a desirable employer, they had, among many internal and external initiatives, undertaken specific outreach initiatives to educational institutions and had distributed 10,000 electronic notebooks to students studying in government schools in regions near the two development centers.[103]

Change leaders' goals are advanced when they develop compelling messages that appeal to the particular groups of people critical to the change initiative. However, in practice, there will be tensions between the changes proposed and what other parts of the organization are attempting to accomplish. For example, the sales force may be focused on how quickly it is able to respond to customers with the products they require, while manufacturing may be rewarded for how efficiently it is able to operate rather than how quickly it is able to respond to customers' orders. These tensions need to be recognized and managed so that the needed changes do not flounder, and various approaches for handling this will be addressed in subsequent chapters.

When change leaders develop their vision for change, they are challenged with the question of where to set the boundaries. A narrower, tighter focus will make it easier to meet the test of Jick's characteristics of an effective vision for a specific target audience, but it may also reduce the prospects for building alliances and a broad base of support across an organization. As the need for change extends to strategic challenges and the culture of a firm, this issue of building a broad constituency for the change becomes increasingly important. Two questions must be answered: First, where, if anywhere, do common interests among stakeholders lie? Second, can the vision for change be framed in terms of the common interest without diverting its purpose where it no longer delivers a vision that will excite, inspire, and challenge?

This was a challenge that Dr. Martin Luther King met superbly. In 1963, King stood on the steps of the Lincoln Memorial and delivered his famous "I Have a Dream" speech on the 100th anniversary of the publishing of the Emancipation Proclamation by President Lincoln. This was a critical point in the Civil Rights Movement, and Dr. King succeeded in seizing that moment by enunciating a compelling vision that embraced a large coalition. Attention to the coalition is apparent in his words:

> The marvellous new militancy which has engulfed the Negro community must not lead us to distrust all white people, for many of our white brothers, as evidenced by their presence here today, have come to realize that their destiny is tied up with our destiny and their freedom is inextricably bound to our freedom. We cannot walk alone.

Dr. King then went on to set out a vision in language all would understand: "I have a dream that one day this nation will rise up and live out the true meaning of its creed: We hold these truths to be self-evident: that all men are created equal."[104]

A broadly stated vision will potentially appeal to a broader range of people and engage a more diverse group in a change process. For example, the National Campaign to Prevent Teen Pregnancy appealed to a broad range of groups, from Catholics who opposed abortion to Planned Parenthood who accepted abortion.[105] Regardless of their specific positions, all groups wanted to prevent teen pregnancy. However, each of these groups had different ideas about the strategies for prevention. The risk of a broad vision is that its appeal to particular groups may either be watered down, or the coalitions attracted to it may subsequently fall apart when the vision gets translated into action.

Coalitions that develop around a common vision can be surprising. Who would have thought that Ted Olson, a prominent conservative lawyer, and David Boies, a prominent liberal lawyer, who had faced off in the courts over the hanging chads in the 2000 U.S. presidential election, would become co-councils in the successful litigation to defeat the Defense of Marriage Act and California's Proposition 8, that culminated in a decision in their favor in the Supreme Court of the United States?[106] Likewise, the ability for environmentalists and conservative Republicans to forge a common cause around the reduction of fossil fuel consumption is not something many expected, but it now exists. Though their perceptions of the underlying rationale for the need for change are different, they identified a common vision for change:

REDUCING FUEL CONSUMPTION AS A COMMON VISION

Environmentalists and groups of conservative Republicans are stepping up a campaign to promote alternative-fuel vehicles and wean the USA from dependence on foreign oil. While conservatives are still skeptical about links between autos and global warming, they have concluded that cutting gasoline consumption is a matter of national security.

Right-leaning military hawks—including former CIA Director R. James Woolsey—have joined with other conservative Republicans and environmental advocates such as the Natural Resources Defence Council to lobby Congress to spend $12 billion to cut oil use in half by 2025. Their vision is to end America's dependence on foreign oil, build a sustainable energy system, and, in the process, create millions of jobs. The alliance highlights how popular sentiment is turning against the no-worries gas-guzzling culture and how alternative technologies such as gas–electric hybrids are finding increasingly widespread support in the United States.

"I think there are a number of things converging," said Gary L. Bauer, a former Republican presidential candidate and former head of the Family Research Council who has signed on to a strange-bedfellow coalition of conservatives and environmentalists called Set America Free. "I just think reasonable people are more inclined right now to start thinking about ways our country's future isn't dependent on . . . oil from a region where there are a lot of very bad actors."[107]

EXAMPLES OF VISIONS FOR CHANGE

In the past, visions have generally been viewed as aspirational organization-level statements. However, change programs can benefit from a clear sense of direction and purpose that vision statements provide. The most powerful visions tap into people's need to be part of something transformative and meaningful. Mundane but important change programs involving restructuring or profit-focused issues need clear, concise targets.

Here are some examples of organizational change visions:

IBM—Diversity 3.0

IBM has a long history of commitment to diversity and has consistently taken the lead on diversity policies long before it was required by law. It began in the mid-20th century, grounded in Equal Opportunity Legislation and compliance (Diversity 1.0). We moved forward to Diversity 2.0 in the 1990s with a focus on eliminating barriers, and understanding regional constituencies and differences between the constituencies. As our demographics changed, we adapted our workplace to be more flexible and began our focus on work-life integration. In addition, over the past 5 years, we've introduced IBM's Values, which links to our diversity work.

This strong foundation brings us to where we are today—Diversity 3.0. This is the point where we can take best advantage of our differences—for innovation. Our diversity is a competitive advantage and consciously building diverse teams helps us drive the best results for our clients.[108]

Tata's Nano: From Vision to Failed Project

Ratan Tata's 2003 Vision to his engineering team, led by 32-year-old star engineer Girish Wagh, was this:

> Create a $2,000 "people's car." It has to be safe, affordable, all weather transportation for a family. It should adhere to regulatory requirements, and achieve performance targets such as fuel efficiency and acceleration.

The result of this vision was Nano, a compact "city car," that was to appeal to motorcycle and scooter riders. The rear-engine hatchback was launched in 2008 in India for one lakh rupees, or approximately US$2,500. It got 50 miles to the gallon and sat up to five people. Unfortunately, there were delays in manufacturing and early instances of the Nano catching fire (Tata maintained that it was foreign electrical equipment that was placed on top of their exhaust system that caused the fires). In March 2012, Mr. Tata stated that the original vision for the Nano had been achieved, and that the vision had now shifted to further upgrading and refinement of the product.[109] In 2018, Cyrus Mistry, chair of the Tata Group, called the Tata Nano a failed project and production ended in May.[110]

Change Vision for the "Survive to 5" Program

Save the Children, World Vision, UNICEF and other not-for-profits, have taken up the challenge posed by the World Health Organization, to reduce child mortality by two-thirds, by 2015. Mortality rates had been reduced by 41% between 1990 and 2011, but the refugee crises that have been created by wars and environmental disasters were complicating efforts, giving rise to a call for the United Nations for a redoubling of efforts.[111] Vision: We believe all children should live to celebrate their fifth birthday.

The Survive to 5 campaign supports Millennium Development Goal 4—to reduce child mortality by two thirds by 2015 and save the lives of over 5 million children under 5 who are dying of preventable and treatable diseases.[112]

In order to help reduce preventable deaths, Survive to 5 will work in countries where basic health care is inaccessible to large numbers of children. Working with government and private sector health care systems, we will develop policy environments that are conducive to community-based care and train a cadre of local health care workers to increase health care coverage and ensure linkages and referrals to facilities for more complicated cases. Research shows that simple interventions—including vaccines, oral rehydration therapy, antibiotics for pneumonia and sepsis and medicine to treat malaria—could save some two-thirds of the children who currently do not survive. Clean practices at birth and improved immediate newborn care, such as breastfeeding and special care for low birth weight babies would also contribute to saving young lives.[113]

Change Vision for "Reading Rainbow"

In 2014, LeVar Burton used the crowdsourcing website "Kickstarter" for a campaign to raise $5 million. The short-term change vision was to work together to bring back the "Reading Rainbow" show to PBS, and provide free access to it in 7,500 classrooms.

This change vision was linked to a broader vision of leveraging the existing free Reading Rainbow app and make its existing and future content available for free, to each and every web- connected child, by developing a web-enabled Reading Rainbow for the home, create a classroom version with the tools teachers need, and subsidize the cost so it is available to schools for free.[114]

Change Vision for a Large South African Winemaker[§]

Every brandcrafters, every day, will search for opportunities for improvement and work cooperately with one another to bring these improvements to life in real time—not the distant future. These actions will allow us to work more effectively together, make our work more pleasant and meaningful, allow us to produce better wine, heighten our pride in what we do, and collectively celebrate becoming the best-in-class producer in term of quality and cost by 2023. We will know we are making progress by listening to our brandcrafters, working with them to improve their satisfaction and commitment, tracking the number and the quality of the improvement initiatives we undertake, celebrating our efforts to improve and ultimately, our achievement of best-in-class quality and cost by 2023.

When reading the above statement, it is important to know that this specific change program focuses on the actual production of the wine and does not involve the farmers who grow the grapes, nor the downstream marketing, sales and distribution staff. It was initiated by senior production staff, in response to senior management's recognition of its eroding position in terms of cost and quality. The vision for change statement was developed with high levels of employee involvement. Brandcrafters is the term used to describe all those

---

[§] Courtesy of Mr. Mpsheboshego Ngwato Malesela, Engineer, MBA, and the firm's operational excellence manager.

directly involved in the production and bottling of wine. Agreed-to metrics are in place to track progress on all the fronts mentioned in the vision for change.

Change Vision for the Procurement System in a Midsize Manufacturing Firm[**]

> We believe that providing reliable and cost-effective procurement services is critical to the future survival and success of our organization. We will develop and deploy a computer-based process that will provide accurate and repeatable information to procurement so that those involved will be able to eliminate purchasing errors, make more knowledgeable purchase decisions, and through these actions reduce costs and increase the profitability and effectiveness of the organisation. This change will completely eliminate rework on the bill of materials and will enhance the effectiveness and efficiency of the procurement process, quoting and planning phases. We will know we have succeeded in bringing this change to life by the measures we use to track progress, including error rates, costs, time savings, and user satisfaction.

This change initiative was undertaken by the firm's senior design engineer, who saw the need to improve the efficiency and effectiveness of the procurement system. His firm manufactured products for the construction industry. The vision for change statement evolved from the input of those in the organization who generate and use the bills of material. IT staff assisted in the development of the new process, though much of the coding was done by the design engineer who had worked to develop an intimate knowledge of both the existing and desired process. The estimated time to fully execute the change, including training, was six months. Before and after measures were used to track progress.

Visions for change are the starting point for a chain: vision → objectives → goals → activities.[††] To make the change vision tangible, change agents need to specify measurable goals for their change efforts. The research on goal setting has been quite clear on the benefits of SMART (specific, measurable, attainable, relevant, and time-bound) goals.[115] The provision of direction with measurable results for feedback galvanizes many people to pursue desired aims. This is easy to say, but defining the right measurable goals is not straightforward. Perhaps a critical task is to persuade a key stakeholder to view the change positively. How does one assess when such attitudes are beginning to change and capture the progress? Identifying interim goals, indicators of progress, and key milestones that demonstrate progress toward the end goals of the change vision are challenges that will be dealt with in subsequent chapters. See **Toolkit Exercise 4.3** to practice writing a vision statement, then move on to **Toolkit Exercise 4.4** to combine your understanding for the need for change and your newly crafted vision statement.

[**] Courtesy of Mr. Andro Ventor, B.Eng (Mechanical), MBA, and Senior Design Engineer with the midsize manufacturing firm supplying the construction industry.

[††] We use the following definitions. *Mission* means the overall purpose of the organization. *Vision* means the ultimate or ideal goal pursued. Thus, for a social service agency, the mission might be to look after the homeless and improve their health outcomes. The vision could be to eradicate homelessness and related health issues in the community by 2020. The change vision related specifically to accommodations might then be to provide access to safe, affordable housing for 60% of the homeless in the community within the next three years.

SUMMARY

In summary, change occurs when there is an understanding of the need for change, the vision of where the organization should go, and a commitment to action. Change leaders need to address the question "Why change?" and develop both a sound rationale for the change and a compelling vision of a possible future. Unfreezing organizational members is advanced when these have been effectively executed.

The rationale for change emerges from a sound understanding of the situation: the external and internal data that point to a need for change, an understanding of the perspectives of critical stakeholders in the organization, internal data in the organization that affects any change, and the personal needs and abilities of the change leaders themselves. Critical in this is an understanding of the organization's readiness for change and the awareness of the need for change throughout the organization. Finally, the chapter discusses the creation of powerful visions and how to develop a specific change vision.

In addition to creating appealing visions of the future and demonstrating a compelling need for change, change agents need to understand the particular contexts of the major individuals in the change events. These stakeholders, or key players, will have an impact on the change situation, so their motives and interests need to be analyzed. Likewise, the impacts of formal structures, systems, and processes on the change need to be assessed and understood. The next two chapters explore these topics. See **Toolkit Exercise 4.1** for critical thinking questions for this chapter.

KEY TERMS

Need for change—the pressure for change in the situation. This need can be viewed as a "real" need, that demonstrated by data and facts, and a "perceived" need, that seen by participants in the change.

Developing a perspective on the need for change is aided by (a) seeking out external data, (b) seeking out the perspective, (c) seeking out data internal to the organization, and (d) reflecting upon personal concerns and perspectives of the change leader.

Perspectives of key internal and external stakeholders—the unique point of view of important participants in the change process. Understanding this perspective is critical to recognizing why this stakeholder supports or resists change.

Readiness for Change

Organizational readiness for change—the degree to which the organization as a whole perceives the need for change and accepts it.

Individual readiness for change—the degree to which the individual perceives the need for change and accepts it.

Readying an organization for change—can be done through the use of a variety of strategies, including (a) creating a crisis, (b) developing a vision that creates dissatisfaction with the status quo in the organization, (c) finding a champion-of-change leader who will build awareness of the need for change and articulate the vision for change, (d) focusing on common or superordinate goals, and (e) creating dissatisfaction with the status quo through education, information, and exposure to superior practices and processes of both competitors and non-competitors. Different strategies have different strengths and weaknesses associated with them.

Eight dimensions related to readiness—trustworthy leadership, trusting followers, capable champions, involved middle management, innovative culture, accountable culture, effective communications, and systems thinking.

Strategic frames—the mental models or sets of assumptions held by change participants about how the world works. These can block the recognition for the need for change.

Vision

Vision for change—the idealized view of the short-term future after a specific change has been enacted. Change visions are more specific than organizational visions and have some element of a time constraint.

Organizational vision—the idealized view of the future. The vision needs to be (a) clear, concise, easily understood; (b) memorable; (c) exciting and inspiring; (d) challenging; (e) excellence centered; (f) stable but flexible; and (g) implementable and tangible.

Leader-developed vision—developed directly by the change leader.

Leader–Senior-team-developed vision—developed by the senior management group in conjunction with the change leader.

Bottom-up visioning—engages a broader spectrum of organizational members in the vision framing process. The change vision is developed through the active participation of those responsible for implementing the change, including those on the front line.

A CHECKLIST FOR CHANGE: CREATING THE READINESS FOR CHANGE

1. What is the "objective" need for change? That is, what are the consequences to the organization of changing or not changing? Are people aware of these risks?

2. Are organizational members aware of the need for change? Do they feel the need for change, or do they deny its need? How can they be informed?

3. Remember that individuals are motivated toward change only when they perceive the benefits as outweighing the costs. How can you, as a change leader, help employees see the benefits as outweighing the costs?

4. If individuals believe the benefits outweigh the costs, do they also believe the probability of success is great enough to warrant the risk-taking, including the investment of time and energy that the change will require?

5. What change alternatives are people predisposed to? What are the costs, benefits, and risks that make them attractive? How should these alternatives be addressed by the change leader?

END-OF-CHAPTER EXERCISES

TOOLKIT EXERCISE 4.1
Critical Thinking Questions

The URL for the video listed below can be found in two places. The first spot is next to the exercise and the second spot is on the website at **study.sagepub.com/cawsey4e.**
Consider the questions that follow.

1. David Logan: Tribal Leadership—16:36 minutes

   https://www.ted.com/talks/david_logan_on_tribal_leadership

   This video focuses on five kinds of tribes that people naturally form and how they influence behavior.

   • Describe Logan's theory on tribes.

   • Compare Logan's ideas with tribes you've been a part of in the past.

   • Reflect on how Logan's idea of Tribal Leadership may affect how to approach change.

2. There are lots of great examples of leaders communicating their vision for change, such as Martin Luther King, Nelson Mandela, Malala Yousafzai, Steve Jobs, Howard Schultz, Indra Nooyi, and Melinda Gates.

   • Go to the Web and find a powerful vision for change speech that resonates with you. What is it about the one you selected that resonates with you?

   • Does it share the characteristics of an effective vision statement outlined in the text?

*Please see **study.sagepub.com/cawsey4e** for a downloadable template of this exercise.*

TOOLKIT EXERCISE 4.2

Developing the Background to Understand the Need for Change

As suggested earlier in this book, a careful diagnosis is essential for successful organizational change. Much of this diagnosis is needed to understand the need for change that the organization faces and then to engage and persuade organizational members concerning the need for change.

1. Consider an example of an organizational change that you are familiar with or are considering undertaking. What data could help you understand the need for change?

2. Have you:

    a. Understood and made sense of external data? What else would you like to know?

    b. Understood and made sense of the perspectives of other stakeholders? What else would you like to know?

    c. Understood and assessed your personal concerns and perspectives and how they may be affecting your perspective on the situation?

    d. Understood and made sense of internal data? What else would you like to know?

3. What does your analysis suggest to you about the need for change?

*Please see **study.sagepub.com/cawsey4e** for a downloadable template of this exercise.*

TOOLKIT EXERCISE 4.3

Writing a Vision for Change Statement[116]

Think of an organization you are familiar with that is in need of change. If you were the change leader, what would be your vision statement for change?

1. Write your vision statement for the change you are striving for.

2. Evaluate your vision. Is it:

    - Clear, concise, and easily understood?

    - Memorable?

    - Exciting and inspiring?

    - Challenging?

    - Excellence centered?

    - Stable and yet flexible?

    - Implementable and tangible?

3. Does the vision promote change and a sense of direction?

4. Does the vision provide the basis from which you can develop the implementation strategy and plan?

5. Does the vision provide focus and direction to those who must make ongoing decisions?

6. Does the vision embrace the critical performance factors that organizational members should be concerned about?

7. Does the vision engage and energize as well as clarify? What is the emotional impact of the vision?

8. Does the vision promote commitment? Are individuals likely to be opposed to the vision, passive (let it happen), moderately supportive (help it happen), or actively supportive (make it happen)?

9. Now assess your vision on a scale of 1 to 5 (5 being the highest) relative to the factors set out below.

   a. Actions of senior managers are congruent with the vision. They walk the talk.

      1   2   3   4   5

   b. It pays attention to the needs of those who will be putting it into practice.

      1   2   3   4   5

   c. Realistic expectations develop around it that are challenging but can be met.

      1   2   3   4   5

   d. It communicates a broader sense of what is possible.

      1   2   3   4   5

   e. It is grounded in the reality of the present and can be reconciled with it.

      1   2   3   4   5

   f. It is neither too abstract nor too concrete. It has the potential to stimulate and inspire, but it also communicates the sense that it is achievable.

      1   2   3   4   5

   g. It has been forged through an appropriately messy, iterative, creative process requiring a combination of "synthesis and imagination."

      1   2   3   4   5

   h. It has sufficient participation and involvement of others to build a consensus concerning its appropriateness.

      1   2   3   4   5

   i. Its implementation contains "a sense of urgency . . . and measurable milestones."

      1   2   3   4   5

10. Given your assessment of the above items, what would you recommend be done in order to strengthen the value of the change vision?

*Please see **study.sagepub.com/cawsey4e** for a downloadable template of this exercise.*

TOOLKIT EXERCISE 4.4

Putting the Need for Change and the Vision for Change Together

For any change to be successful, the need for change must be real and must be perceived as real. If the organization does not accept the need for change, the chances of anything substantive happening are negligible. Thus, developing the need for change is vital. Understanding the gap between what is and what is desired is important in order to accurately describe the need for change.

Think of the situation you were considering in Exercise 4.2.

1. What is the gap between the present state and the desired future state?

2. How strong is the need for change?

3. What is the source of this need? Is it external to the organization?

4. Is there tangible evidence of the need for change in that there is concrete evidence of the need or a crisis situation that demonstrates the need for change?

5. If the change does not occur, what will be the impact on the organization in the next two to six years?

6. What is the objective, long-range need to change?

People can be motivated by higher-order purposes, things that relate to fundamental values. Change visions can be crucial in capturing support for change and in explaining the nature of change to others. Creating such a change vision is tricky. If one aims too high, it taps into higher values but often fails to link with the specific change project or program. If one aims too low, the vision fails to tap into values that motivate us above and beyond the ordinary. Such a change vision looks like and feels like an objective.

7. Return to the change vision you developed in Exercise 4.2. Does it capture a sense of higher-order purpose or values that underpin the change and communicate what the project is about?

8. Explain how the vision links the need for change.

*Please see **study.sagepub.com/cawsey4e** for a downloadable template of this exercise.*

LEADING CHANGE: THE PHARMACY TEAM

By Jess Coppla, Healthcare MBA, 2018

Simmons University, Boston, MA

INTRODUCTION

Kim could not believe how Joe had just talked *at* an elderly customer. Joe had been rude and abrupt with someone who was clearly confused about his medications. As an employee of Poplar's Drug Store chain, Joe, a pharmacy technician, had been trained in how to approach and interact with customers, but he was not exhibiting the behavior taught in those classes. In her first shift since she had rejoined the pharmacy team at Poplar's Chelsea location, Kim noted other problems among team members: poor communication, high stress levels, inability to balance operational tasks with taking care of customers, a lack of teamwork, and so on. The pharmacist who was on duty, clearly flustered by the backlog of work, was so busy filling prescriptions that he was unaware of Joe's interaction with the customer. After turning to walk away from the counter, another technician bumped directly into Joe, dropping her basket of prescription labels and bottles of medication all over the floor. Obviously upset by what had just transpired, Joe announced to no one in particular that he was taking a bathroom break and stormed out of the pharmacy. No one beside Kim even seemed to notice.

Kim had worked on the Chelsea pharmacy team, the group responsible for prescriptions and over-the-counter medications, for four of the last five years: in fact, she had worked there since her sophomore year in high school. During that time, she knew that the pharmacy team had consistently received low marks in customer service. This dismayed her greatly, because she felt like everyone on the team shared the same goal: helping customers be healthy.

The team members assisting the pharmacist(s) were called "pharmacy technicians." The normal size of the team at the Chelsea store was four plus the lead pharmacy technician. The senior pharmacist on duty was ultimately responsible for the performance of the team, but day-to-day leadership was delegated to the senior technician. Since her return from the nearby Elmwood store, Kim had ideas about how to make things better at Chelsea. A little over a year ago, Kim had transferred to Poplar's nearby Elmwood location where she was promoted, trained, and learned how to become an effective senior technician. Now Kim was back at Chelsea as the senior technician and she was hoping to make changes in how team members approached their work.

Kim envisioned a pharmacy where customers left feeling happy and employees loved coming to work, where a cohesive team delivered a great experience that was reflected in their monthly scorecards. Within hours of her return, however, she observed that nothing had changed in Chelsea since her departure. In fact, if Joe's recent encounter with the elderly customer was any indication, things had gotten worse.

Kim asked herself, how and where should I begin to make changes? What structural changes do I need to make? Or, should I begin with the team's culture, and if so, how? How do I work with the senior pharmacist and staff pharmacists to inspire a shared vision? What about the managers and staff that serviced the other parts of the Chelsea Poplar Drug Store who were responsible for all the other types of products and services the store offered its clients (e.g., over-the-counter drugs, perfume, skin and hair care products, greeting cards, food products, electronic products, etc.)? Did they need to become involved in her change initiative or should she just focus on her team? What changes do we need to make with how we service and treat our customers, Kim asked herself. How will I be received by my team, given that I've just returned? As the second in command after the pharmacist on duty, she knew she needed to talk to Joe and address the situation. A pang of anxiety came over her. For the first time since she embarked on her mission over a year ago, Kim felt nervous. It was at that moment she thought to herself, "What have I gotten myself into?"

BACKGROUND

Poplar's Drug Store had grown its footprint significantly since Kim was hired. Once a small, regional player in Illinois, Poplar's ownership turned its attention to becoming a nationally recognized pharmacy ten years ago. Of particular note were the two very large-scale acquisitions over the past five years, adding more than 1,000 locations and expanding its presence to several more states. Due to acquisitions, Poplar's sales levels had increased dramatically, though profitability had lagged because of integrating, logistics, and rebranding initiatives with the acquisitions. Though there were some 1,000 sq. ft. outlets that were strictly pharmacies, many of the stores were 12,000 to 15,000 sq. ft. in size and Chelsea was one of these. In addition to medically related offerings, the larger stores provided customers with a wide range of beauty care products; household items, such as paper products and cleaning supplies, and food items, including milk, a limited range of meats, fresh fruits, and vegetables.

As it became more of a household name, however, Poplar struggled to hold on to the local vibe and reputation for good customer service it once held. In an effort to standardize business across the fleet of pharmacies, Poplar's management introduced a series of trainings all employees were required to take as well as a monthly scorecard with key performance metrics (KPM) by which each store's performance would be measured. Metrics fell into two

categories: one focused on customer satisfaction and the other on financial health. Customer satisfaction scores were generated from feedback surveys customers completed by filling out an e-survey or by calling a number provided on the bottom of their receipt. Customers completing a survey were given a coupon for a 10% discount on regular priced products. (See Appendix A for an example scorecard.)

PROBLEMS AT THE CHELSEA STORE

Within the very busy, chaotic Chelsea pharmacy, days could get very stressful for Kim and her teammates. Every shift had its own unique challenges and time constraints, but many problems were predictable, too: customers needing prescriptions or over-the-counter, non-prescription medical products that were not in stock; staff not showing up to work; or, so many tasks and responsibilities that staff simply did not have the bandwidth to take care of all the orders and daily tasks within standard operating hours. There were often piles of prescriptions left unfinished from the day before, resulting in long lines of frustrated customers. Despite their dissatisfaction with the Chelsea store, Poplar's was the only conveniently located pharmacy in the community. Kim felt that more customers surely would have left if there were other options. She wondered if improving customer service had been overlooked in the past since the store continued to meet its sales expectations. Considered a "needs improvement" store mainly for its poor performance in customer service, Chelsea's KPM scores had been consistently running in the high 60s when Kim decided to take steps to address the problems. (See example Chelsea scorecard in Appendix B.)

KIM'S CAREER ASPIRATIONS

Although she was 21 years old at the time, juggling a full-time job as a pharmacy technician at Poplar while completing her full, final year of college, Kim yearned to be a leader and to make a difference. She was a fixer, and she wanted to inspire change at her pharmacy for the sake of the patients and the staff alike. Correcting long-standing performance issues and the underlying behaviors that caused them would not be easy, yet Kim felt it was right to try. To do so, she devised a multi-phase career plan that involved leaving the Chelsea store for a short period. Kim was not in a position of power and felt she needed to move into a respected role in order to make changes. Approximately a year ago, she shared her proposed plan with both her senior pharmacist, Will, and with the chain's regional manager. She told them she wanted to become a lead pharmacy technician so that she could play a leadership role and help bring about positive changes. This role functioned as a supervisor within the pharmacy, an intermediary between the pharmacy technicians and the pharmacists and the store manager. The store's current senior technician had notified them that she would be taking a long-term maternity leave in six months.

Will, the senior pharmacist, the store manager, and the regional manager all agreed that Kim was ready to take on more responsibilities. However, they worried that she lacked the experience needed to lead the Chelsea team out of its current state and felt it would be better for her to learn the role by first transferring to another store that was already doing well. That way, she could assist in overseeing a functional team that had no history with her as a friend or co-worker. Kim liked the idea of having a safe place to learn the role and was eager to demonstrate that she was up for the challenge. The regional manager identified a store in Elmwood, a community 30 miles away where she could take on the developmental role of assistant senior pharmacy technician. He did so with the support of the store managers at both pharmacies and the new store's senior technician.

LEARNING HOW TO LEAD CHANGE

While working in the Poplar Drug Store in Elmwood, Kim realized that the recipe for success is hard to bake into a standardized score-card that thousands of stores spread out across the country are expected to follow. The one-size-fits-all approach drove business, but not necessarily culture. The threshold score to "meet expectations" was 77 points out of a possible 100, with up to 50 points earned through customer ratings and the other 50 from sales. In some stores, this created conflict among Poplar's employees who felt at times they did not have ample time to help each customer as quantity of interactions seemed to be valued just as much, if not more, than the quality of them. With the current scorecard structure, stores could somewhat mask issues with customer service if the sales volume was there, which had been the case in Chelsea. Though sales levels accounted for only 50% of a store's score, it was Kim's impression that financial performance played a significantly greater role in determining how stores were assessed, including managerial bonuses. Why else would Chelsea's lower scores have been tolerated for so long by upper level management at Poplar's?

The Elmwood store was a high performer before and during Kim's time there, scoring in the low 90s and earning the designation of "outstanding performer." At first Kim found this ironic since Elmwood was a busier pharmacy with a less tenured staff than Chelsea. She quickly learned that there were key differences between the two pharmacy teams, accounting for their scorecard disparity. Part of what made Elmwood so successful was that everyone on the team knew how to do every task. This alleviated pressure on individuals and created a team environment where the staff knew they could rely on one another to get things done. Additional team-building activities, such as weekly competitions to see who could get the best customer comment or sign up the most customers for flu shots, created a fun atmosphere in Elmwood. The senior pharmacist and the senior pharmacy technician encouraged Kim to have weekly check-ins with each of her technicians as well as take part in team meetings, hiring interviews, and the quarterly performance review process. Kim knew she'd need to bring these practices to Chelsea. Her experience in Elmwood confirmed what she already knew. Scorecards and trainings do not teach passion, empathy, positivity, or trust—leaders do.

The leaders in the Elmwood store, both in the pharmacy and the general merchandise section, shared Kim's vision about how great Poplar could be for its customers. They emulated the passion they wished to see in their teams and led by example. They worked in harmony, offering associates from either section to help the other. Every employee in the store was trained to assist any customer, and coached on the importance of teamwork and great customer service. This was all done *in addition* to the standard training all Poplar employees were required to complete, and the Elmwood team lived out these principles every day. Elmwood even had an unofficial, motivational slogan that Kim found rather clever: "Who puts the U in PopYOUlar?" When an employee was recognized by a customer for a job well done or reached a goal or milestone, their picture was displayed on a bulletin board dubbed The PopYOUlar Wall of Fame. The caption on the board read, "Great job, and thank you! Poplar wouldn't be PopYOUlar without you!" Kim loved this approach and recognized how happy it made the team at Elmwood. She spoke with the senior pharmacist and store manager to learn more about it. They believed that passion must start at the top—if the team doesn't observe genuine enthusiasm in their leader, the shared goals become less important to them and they will pursue their jobs with less fervor. They encouraged Kim to be self-aware and think about how she could show her passion in her work to inspire others.

Over the course of six months, Kim learned the ins-and-outs of the lead pharmacy technician's position, becoming exceptionally proficient in the tasks required for the role. Kim's leadership skills had grown greatly through this experience, training, and the mentorship she had received at Elmwood. She earned a spot on the Wall of Fame for her efforts. Kim felt she was ready to return to Chelsea as lead pharmacy technician and her regional manager and Chelsea's senior pharmacist agreed. Her return to Chelsea was accompanied by challenging performance goals. She was given six months to help Chelsea boost its monthly scores from "needs improvement" to "meets expectations." Kim knew that was a tall order, but she was excited by the challenge. It was both the best thing for her career within Poplar (she had agreed to continue with Poplar following college graduation in three months), and her beloved Chelsea community.

NOW WHAT?

Kim could see Joe walking toward the pharmacy while she was finishing up a transaction with a regular customer. She thanked Mr. Braxton for coming in, took a deep breath, and met Joe at the door.

"Hey Joe, I saw what happened a few minutes ago. Can you tell me a little more about it?" she asked.

"That guy hates this place. He said it was his third time coming in to pick up his prescriptions, which we told him we'd have ready yesterday afternoon. Then he had questions about his medication that I couldn't answer, and was upset when I told him the pharmacist could help him after he was done with his calls. I had to get back to my inventory tasks because unless I order the medications we don't have, we'll get another bad score in 'Item in Stock.' He was yelling at me. I tried to stay calm, but it's hard to excuse yourself when someone won't leave. I had to get away from him."

"That sounds frustrating for both of you," Kim said. She then asked a question to which she felt she already knew the answer. "Who else on the team helps with the inventory?"

"That's a good one, Kim. No one else here is trained in inventory. There's no time for me to teach someone, and there's no one else that wants to learn. It's all on me and without help, it's really hard to get things done."

Kim could hear the exasperation in Joe's voice. She offered, "Why don't I help you with the inventory tasks today, Joe?"

"Really?" Joe's frown eased a bit. "You know Kim, everyone around here is shocked you'd leave as great a store as Elmwood to come back here. I don't think we'll ever be as good as them."

Kim smiled at Joe, although she wondered to herself if he was right. She completed the inventory work before leaving for the night. As she walked out, she considered the magnitude of the work ahead. The clock was ticking on her master plan. She asked herself, "Now what?"

CHAPTER FOUR • BUILDING AND ENERGIZING THE NEED FOR CHANGE   147

APPENDIX A

Example of Monthly Scorecard at Poplar Drug

	Poplar KPM Rating – Example	
	KPM	Target
Customer Satisfaction	Greeted Immediately	5
(Scale 1–5)	Friendly and Attentive	5
	Professional	5
	Received Clear Instructions	5
	Offered Help	5
	Item in Stock	5
	Cleanliness	5
	Timeliness	5
	Would Recommend to Others	5
	Total Satisfaction With Visit	5
Financial Health	Over-the-Counter Sales	25
(Scale 1–25)	Prescription Sales	25
	Overall Monthly Score	**100**
	Rating	**Outstanding Performer**

Rating Scales	
<77	Needs Improvement
77–83	Meets Expectations
84–90	Exceeds Expectations
>90	Outstanding Performer

APPENDIX B

Recent Scorecard at the Chelsea Store

	Poplar KPM Rating – July 2016		
	KPM	Current Score	Target
Customer Satisfaction	Greeted Immediately	2	5
(Scale 1–5)	Friendly and Attentive	3	5
	Professional	3	5

Poplar KPM Rating – July 2016		
KPM	Current Score	Target
Received Clear Instructions	4	5
Offered Help	2	5
Item in Stock	1	5
Cleanliness	2	5
Timeliness	2	5
Would Recommend to Others	2	5
Total Satisfaction With Visit	3	5
Over-the-Counter Sales	22	25
Prescription Sales	20	25
Overall Monthly Score	**66**	**100**
Rating	**Needs Improvement**	

Financial Health (Scale 1–25)

Rating Scales	
<77	Needs Improvement
77–83	Meets Expectations
84–90	Exceeds Expectations
>90	Outstanding Performer

CHAPTER FIVE

NAVIGATING CHANGE THROUGH FORMAL STRUCTURES AND SYSTEMS

Chapter Overview

- This chapter discusses the basics of how organizations structure themselves.

- It outlines how change leaders can diagnose the strengths and weaknesses of existing systems and structures.

- It examines how the formal structure and systems can foster, impair, and facilitate the acceptance of change initiatives.

- It lays out ways to manage systems and structures to gain approval for change initiatives. Formal, coalition-building, and renegade approaches are discussed.

- Finally, it reviews the ways to develop more adaptive systems and structures to increase the likelihood of continuous improvement.

Any discussion of organizational change needs to pay careful attention to the role of formal systems and structures. They influence what gets done, how it gets done, the outcomes that are achieved, and the experiences of the people who come into contact with the organization. While leaders define their organizational systems and structures, the systems and structures—paradoxically—also shape the behavior of organizational leaders and members. Formal systems and structures play important coordination, communication, and control roles, and they influence how decisions are made about change and who is authorized to make changes. Sometimes, systems and structures need to change.

An organization's formal structure is defined by how tasks are formally divided, grouped, and coordinated.[1] **Formal structures** are designed to support the strategic direction of the firm by enhancing order, efficiency, effectiveness, and accountability. They serve as guides and controls on decision-making authority, coordinate and integrate operations, provide direction to internal governance, and attempt to promote desired behaviors and organizational outcomes.[2] The organizational chart is the common document of organizational design.

Formal systems include planned routines and processes such as strategic planning, accounting and control systems, performance management, pay and reward systems, and the information system. Collectively, these set out how things are supposed to be done, the rules and procedures to be followed, how information is collected and disseminated, how individuals are to be compensated, and all the other formalized systems and processes that are used for coordination, integration, and control purposes. They provide the formal infrastructure that operationalizes the organizational structure.

Organizations vary in their need for complexity in their structures and systems, but all require some degree of formalization to be sustainable. These are modified over time as conditions change and they need to bring themselves into alignment with external conditions and the organization's strategy. The corner grocer needs simple systems for accounting, staffing, and managing suppliers, pricing, and inventory. Walmart, on the other hand, requires highly sophisticated systems and structures to efficiently and profitably handle $500 billion in net sales, processed by 2.3 million associates in 11,700 stores that operate in 28 countries.[3] Walmart's sales channels include e-commerce websites in 11 countries, contributing $11.5 billion in online sales in 2017, an increase of 44% over 2016.[4]

One reason that Walmart dominates the consumer retail market is its logistics systems that coordinate all aspects of inventory management, from ordering through to shipping, warehousing, shelving, and final disposition. Its knowledge-management system, Retail Link, provides Walmart and its suppliers with data that allow them to identify emerging opportunities for their products. Their systems are continuously improved in order to better drive business results, and they are demonstrating their ability to effectively extend their technical reach to the world of online retailing. It is systems like this that allow Walmart to satisfy multiple stakeholders and maintain its competitive position in the industry.[5]

This chapter describes the purposes that formal systems and structures play in advancing change. It also provides guidance in identifying the gap between the existing structures and systems, and what is needed to bring about alignment after the change. Figure 5.1 outlines where this chapter fits in the change-management process. This chapter is the first of four that details how change leaders can advance a sophisticated gap analysis and deploy it in pursuit of change. This chapter deals with formal systems and structures, and the chapters that follow will cover the informal aspects of organizations, change stakeholders and recipients, and change leaders themselves.

Change leaders need to develop a deep understanding of how existing structures and systems are currently influencing outcomes and how they are likely to facilitate or impede the proposed changes. Once that understanding is developed, change leaders need to put that system and structural awareness to use to promote and enact change. To advance this agenda, the chapter is divided into four sections:

1. Making sense of organizational structures and systems

2. Diagnosing the strengths and weaknesses of existing systems and structures

3. Understanding how structures and systems influence the approval process of a change initiative and how they then facilitate or hinder the acceptance of change

4. Designing adaptive structures and systems to enhance future change initiatives

Figure 5.1 The Change-Management Process

Awakening
Chapter 4

1. Identify a need for change and confirm the problems or opportunities that incite the need for change through collection of data.
2. Articulate the gap in performance between the present and the envisioned future state, and spread awareness of the data and the gap throughout the organization.
3. Develop a powerful vision for change.
4. Disseminate the vision for the change and why it's needed through multiple communication channels.

Mobilization
Chapters 5 through 8

1. **Make sense of the desired change through formal systems and structures, and leverage those systems to reach the change vision (Chapter 5).**
2. Assess power and cultural dynamics at play, and put them to work to better understand the dynamics and build coalitions and support to realize the change (Chapter 6).
3. Communicate the need for change organization-wide and manage change recipients and various stakeholders as they react to and move the change forward (Chapter 7).
4. Leverage change agent personality, knowledge, skills and abilities, and related assets (e.g., reputation and relationships) for the benefit of the change vision and its implementation (Chapter 8).

Acceleration
Chapter 9

1. Continue to systematically reach out to engage and empower others in support, planning, and implementation of the change. Help them develop needed new knowledge, skills, abilities, and ways of thinking that will support the change.
2. Use appropriate tools and techniques to build momentum, accelerate and consolidate progress.
3. Manage the transition, celebrating small wins and the achievement of milestones along the larger, more difficult path of change.

Institutionalization
Chapter 10

1. Track the change periodically and through multiple balanced measures to help assess what is needed, gauge progress toward the goal, and to make modifications as needed and mitigate risk.
2. Develop and deploy new structures, systems, processes and knowledge, skills, and abilities, as needed, to bring life to the change and new stability to the transformed organization.

MAKING SENSE OF FORMAL STRUCTURES AND SYSTEMS

The structural frame,[6] to use the language of Bolman and Deal, outlines an internal blueprint for how managers assign tasks, roles, and authority to produce products or services for the external marketplace. Wrapped around this structure are all the formal systems and processes that are designed to bring the structure to life and make it possible for the organization to deliver on its strategy and value proposition.

To make sense of structures, it is useful for change leaders to understand and be able to work with core concepts in this area. These are some of the more common elements:[7]

1. *Differentiation:* The degree to which tasks are subdivided into separate jobs or tasks. This concept deals with who does what and asks about the degree to which jobs are specialized and distinctive from one another on both the horizontal and vertical organizational axes. The differentiation of tasks is an early step in the life of an entrepreneurial adventure as it grows from one to two and then three people, with further differentiation of tasks as the number of employees increases. As organizations grow and add more people, tasks are divided and subdivided. Large organizations, as a consequence, are often characterized by highly specialized jobs, leading to silos of similar and separate tasks and job categories.

2. *Integration:* The coordination of the various tasks or jobs into a department or group. This is the extent to which activities are combined into processes and systems, pulling together all the disparate pieces of tasks and jobs into a coherent whole. Small organizations are typically structured in a simple and straightforward manner, organized by functions such as production, accounting/finance, sales and marketing, and human resources. As they grow and become more complex, executives look for more efficient and effective ways to group tasks and activities. Departments or divisions may be organized geographically or by product category, customer segment, or some other hybrid approach such as networks that seem to offer the best way to organize activities at that point in time. Sometimes they may even be spun off as separate, stand-alone entities. In large organizations, such as Boeing, there are integrative roles with people and teams who specialize in coordinating and communicating in order to bring together the disparate parts of the enterprise.

3. *Chain of command:* The reporting architecture in a hierarchical organization. This concept defines how individuals and/or units within an organization report to one another up and down the organizational ladder. It reflects the formal power structure and where decision responsibilities lie within the hierarchy.

4. *Span of control:* The number of individuals who report to a manager. This notion questions the optimal ratio of workers to managers in an organization. Since there is no one correct way to answer this question, part of the art of organizational design is to figure this out, given the culture, strategy, and what needs to be done. An organization that gives managers too little span of control runs the risk of creating a costly and top-heavy administrative structure and encourages its managers to micromanage too few employees. On the other hand, managers who have too many employees reporting to them run the risk of inadequate supervision, feedback, and employee development.

5. *Centralization vs. decentralization:* How and where decision making is distributed in an organizational structure. The more centralized the approach, the more the decision making gravitates to the top of the organization. Conversely, the more decentralized it is, the more the decision making is delegated to lower levels of employees. In general, organizations flatten their hierarchies when they adopt a more decentralized approach and vice versa.

6. *Formal vs. informal:* The degree to which organizational charts exist, are codified, and are followed. This is the extent to which structures and processes of the organization are set down in writing and expected to be followed.[8]

To practice understanding change on existing structures and systems see **Toolkit Exercise 5.2**.

IMPACT OF UNCERTAINTY AND COMPLEXITY ON FORMAL STRUCTURES AND SYSTEMS

Another way of thinking about structural alignment is to begin by reflecting on the environment they operate in. Beginning with the work of Thompson in the 1960s,[9] researchers have explored the impact of uncertainty and complexity on why organizations structure their systems and processes as they do and the impact these configurations have on their capacity to successfully adapt to the environment over time.[10] When examining the structural dimensions, organizations have often been classified into two types: (1) those that are more formal, more differentiated, more centralized, and more standardized; and (2) those that are less formal, less differentiated, more decentralized, and less standardized. The terms that are applied to this organizational typology are *mechanistic* and *organic*. Table 5.1 outlines the characteristics of mechanistic and organic organizational forms as opposite ends of a continuum.[11]

Mechanistic organizations rely on formal hierarchies with centralized decision making and a clear division of labor. Rules and procedures are clearly

Table 5.1 Mechanistic and Organic Organizational Forms

More Mechanistic ⟶	More Organic
Tasks are broken down into separate parts and rigidly defined and assigned	Flexible tasks that are adjusted and redefined through teamwork and participation
High degree of formalization, strict hierarchy of authority and control, many rules	Relatively little formalization, less reliance on a hierarchy of authority and control, few rules, greater participation and decentralization
Narrow span of control with reliance on hierarchies of people in specialized roles	Wide span of control
Knowledge and control of tasks are centralized at the top of the organization, limited decision making at lower levels	Knowledge and control of tasks are decentralized and located throughout the organization; highly decentralized decision making
Communication is vertical	Communication is horizontal and free flowing, with many integrating roles
Simple, straightforward planning processes	Sophisticated environmental scanning, planning, and forecasting, including the use of scenarios and contingency thinking

Source: Adapted from Daft, R. I. (2007). *Organization theory and design* (9th ed., p. 152). Mason, OH: South-Western.

defined and employees are expected to follow them. Work is specialized and routine. Mechanistic organizations tend to be concentrated in industries where the risk of getting it wrong is high. For example, nuclear power suppliers or pharmacy industries will be extremely mechanistic in order to manage the high risk and detailed logistics of their business.

Organic organizations are more flexible. They have fewer rules and procedures, and there is less reliance on the hierarchy of authority for centralized decision making. The structure is flexible and not as well defined. Jobs are less specialized. Communication is more informal, and lateral communications are more accepted. Many start-up companies and companies in creative fields will be more organic, allowing increased communication and flexibility in day-to-day tasks. While it may appear that one structural form is more appealing than the other, both can be effective depending upon their fit with the environment. When efficiency is critical to success and ambiguity and uncertainty are low to moderate, a more mechanistic structure will fit best. However, when an organization's ability to respond to its environment with flexibility and adaptiveness is critical to its success, a more organic structure will make more sense.[12]

FORMAL STRUCTURES AND SYSTEMS FROM AN INFORMATION PERSPECTIVE

A third way of thinking about the impact of systems and structures on how and why firms operate as they do is to look at how they formally manage information. One of the primary purposes of formal structures and systems is to place the right information in the hands of appropriate individuals in a timely fashion so that they can do what is needed. Information technology has been instrumental in allowing organizations to develop structures and systems that are more robust, dynamic, and flexible. Conversely, Atul Gawada reports that doctors hate their computers, reflecting the paradox some feel between the need for consistency and reliability and the need for individual autonomy and professional judgement in matters of analyses and how best to move forward[13] (*New Yorker* article).

Supply chains, distributed manufacturing, flattened hierarchies with empowered workgroups, and networked organizations all owe their growth to improvements in this area. It has let organizations such as Dell to move from mass production models to mass customization, with little productivity loss.[14] However, those who have successfully made the transition have done so by giving very careful attention to the end state and the optimal route for getting there.[15] By extension, technology has also allowed us to think differently about structures and systems when planning and managing organizational change. For example, telecommunication advances mean virtual teams distributed around the globe can be created, meet "face to face," access and share information in real time, and move projects forward in ways that were not possible 10 years ago.

Jay Galbraith defines this as the information-processing view of organizations.[16] If the organization is to perform effectively, there needs to be a fit between the organization's information-processing requirements and its capacity to process information through its structural design choices. The better the fit between these, the more effective the organization will be. As uncertainty increases, the amount of information that must be processed between decision makers during the transformation process increases. The organization must either increase its capacity to handle that information or restructure itself to reduce the need for information handling. Figure 5.2 outlines Galbraith's work.

As uncertainty increases, the traditional vertical information strategies for uncertainty reduction will prove increasingly less effective, and the organization will require methods that either reduce the need for information processing or increase the capacity of the organization to process information.[17] Organizations can reduce their information-processing challenges by adding slack resources to act as buffers (e.g., extra people and inventory) and/or by creating self-contained tasks (e.g., divisions organized around product categories, geography, or customers). For example, extra inventory means that increased variation in demand for a product will be handled by drawing down or increasing inventory levels. Similarly, separating an organization into divisions operating as profit centers means that the divisions may not need to coordinate their activities as much. This reduces the information-processing requirements.

Initially, organizations may attempt to increase their information-processing capacity by using the hierarchy (i.e., vertical communication). That is, if you are uncertain what to do, ask your boss. If the situation becomes repetitive, create a decision rule to guide the decision. If the subordinate knows more about the

Figure 5.2 An Information-Processing View of Organizational Structure

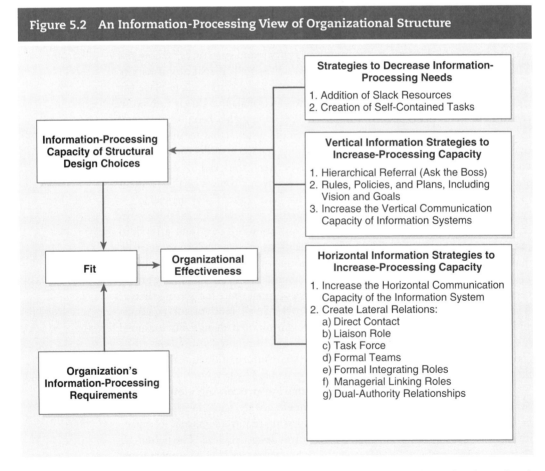

Source: Adapted from Galbraith, J. R. (1977). *Organization design.* Reading, MA: Addison-Wesley; and Daft, R. L. (2003). *Organization theory and design* (8th ed.). Cincinnati, OH: South-Western.

situation than the boss, they can agree on a set of criteria that allows the subordinate to act independently and handle the uncertainty. These represent what Galbraith calls vertical information strategies. A further vertical information strategy is when organizations increase their capacity to process information by investing in vertical information systems (e.g., computer-generated performance reports, decision support systems).

Organizations also can improve their information-processing ability by increasing their horizontal communication capacity (e.g., e-mail systems, intranets, electronic bulletin boards, texting, and various forms of social media). They can increase the capacity to process information horizontally by creating lateral relationships that vary in complexity from something as simple as direct, informal contact, to more formal networks and complex, formal structures such as a matrix that are intended to facilitate the hierarchical and horizontal flow of information.

The role of the information systems is to distribute needed information and get it to the individuals who most need it in a timely manner for decision making. Interdepartmental and interdivisional boundaries and jurisdictional disputes can impede the flow of information. The investigation of the 9/11 tragedy pointed to examples of this.[18] Information was present in various departments and agencies at the federal and state levels that would have assisted in alerting officials to the danger, but communication impediments kept it from being shared and integrated in a timely fashion. Removing impediments is easier said than done in large, complex organizations. Issues such as privacy, data and system security, decision rights (who is supposed to do what with the information), and protection of intellectual property must be sorted out. Questions related to where information resides, in what forms, and who should have access to it need to be tackled before it can be pulled together.

Galbraith identified seven types of lateral relations that will help overcome boundaries that impair information flow. These are listed below:

1. direct contact between affected individuals (e.g., a product designer and a manufacturing engineer)

2. use of individuals in liaison roles to bridge groups

3. multidepartment task forces

4. formal teams

5. integrating roles such as a product manager with cross-departmental authority

6. managerial linking roles (similar to the integrating roles but with more formal decision authority)

7. structures with dual-authority relationships, such as are found in a matrix organization

If the organization is to perform effectively, this model points to the importance of congruence between the firm's strategy, its information-processing requirements (e.g., market and competitive information, operational information), and the information-processing capacity that the firm's design choices promote.

Change leaders need to be aware of the impact of vertical and horizontal information strategies on information flows and organizational performance when assessing what needs to change. Further, sensitivity to these issues needs to extend to the actual management of the change process. This is because even well-managed change will increase uncertainty in the short term, and major changes will significantly increase it for longer periods of time. This will give rise to information-processing needs that change leaders will need to develop and manage.

Research reported by McKinsey and Company point to the value of making greater use of social media technologies and paying more attention to networks to advance change initiatives.[19] When change leaders don't pay sufficient attention to the information-processing needs related to change, the lack of fit may impair the effectiveness of the change initiative. Multiple actions in this area are often needed to support a change initiative — extra resources to increase the capacity to process information, a focus on understanding the goals and purposes, and a significant increase in lateral relations.

Aligning Systems and Structures With the Environment

The structural variables and models outlined above provide change leaders with an introduction to the multiple perspectives they can use when assessing structures and the formal systems that are developed to bring them to life. This can prove helpful when evaluating the internal consistency of structures and systems and their alignment with an organization's strategy, vision, culture, and environment. When cost strategies in a traditional manufacturing context are critical, a more mechanistic approach is often appropriate. When innovation is key, organic approaches provide a better fit with an organization's strategy.[20]

In their quest to improve their performance, there is a tendency for managers to increasingly seek out efficiency improvements. At the same time there is a tendency to avoid potentially valuable innovations that may be more disruptive in the short term.[21] Keeping these in appropriate balance is challenging for change agents as the organization matures.

For change leaders, the importance of this material lies in the fact that organizations need to align their formal structures and systems with their strategy and their environments. In 2008, ITT, an engineering firm serving the energy, transportation, and industrial markets, took a hard look at the alignment of its formal structures. This led ITT to drop its organization-wide performance rating system when management realized it was having an adverse impact on employees in different parts of the company's global operations and was not accomplishing its purpose. For example, a "3" or average on its 5-point rating scale of performance was viewed negatively by its Chinese employees, who saw it as a loss of face. This resulted in increased dissatisfaction and turnover. ITT realigned its formal performance rating system globally to reflect cultural differences and removed this global rating scale. In China, turnover was halved following the change.[22] ITT is not alone in abandoning its existing approach to performance assessment. Microsoft, Dell, IBM, and many other firms have done the same, having concluded that their existing approaches were harmful to advancing the outcomes they hoped to achieve.[23]

In Nadler and Tushman's terminology, there needs to be congruence between the outside world, the strategy, and how the inside world is formally organized. By understanding the nature of the external environment and the organization's strategy, history, and resources, a change leader gains insight into the types of structures and systems that have the most to offer. By understanding the formal organizational arrangements, the leader gains insights on where and how decisions are made and how these can be leveraged to advance change.

Change leaders also need to be aware that even in a fairly mechanistic organization, different departments and divisions may face very different information-processing needs and will therefore need to be structured and managed differently. For example, a firm's R&D department's environment may be more dynamic and uncertain than that faced by the production department. As a result, R&D may need a more organic structure, whereas the production department will benefit from a more mechanistic one that leverages well-developed, standardized processes. Likewise, those involved with the launch of a new product or expansion into a new market will have to deal with higher levels of uncertainty and complexity than those responsible for mature markets, where concerns for structures and systems that enhance efficiency are likely the norm.

Structural Changes to Handle Increased Uncertainty

From a structural perspective, the quest for enhanced organizational efficiency and effectiveness starts by looking at what needs to change in the organization and deciding how best to analyze and allocate the work. These differentiation approaches include aspects such as division of labor and departmentalization. If this has already been done, the challenge usually shifts to a discussion of how to integrate the components so that they can accomplish the intended results. The vertical and horizontal information linkage strategies identified by Galbraith in Figure 5.2 are examples of such integrating approaches. Sorting out the decision rights (who is authorized to make what sorts of decisions) and insuring the flow of appropriate information to those responsible for such decisions is critical to successful alignment.[24]

Boeing's redesigned approach to the development and manufacturing of its aircraft provides an excellent example of the application of structural changes in a very complex business. The aircraft manufacturer realized that it had to change its approach to compete with Airbus, and it did so in its approach to the development of the 787.

BOEING RESTRUCTURES ITSELF

Before the 787, Boeing did all the engineering design work itself. The main reason to change, says Mike Bair, head of the 787 development team, was that the company realized it had to trawl the world and find the best suppliers in order to compete with its main rival in the market for commercial aircraft, the increasingly successful Airbus.

Airbus, a joint European venture involving French, German, British, and Spanish partners, started from scratch. Almost by accident it stumbled on an organizational architecture that, along with generous subsidies, helped it overtake the giant of the business in less than two decades.

Boeing's reorganized commercial plane development operations now look more like the

(Continued)

(Continued)

approach used by Airbus. It scoured the globe for new partners and found some in Europe, some in Japan, and some not far from its home base in the United States. Whereas with the 777 aircraft the company worked with 500–700 suppliers, for the 787 it selected just under 100 "partners."

The difference is not just in the numbers, but in the relationship. Their supplier partners now share greater responsibility for the success of the project. For over six months in 2005, teams of people from the various 787 partners met at Boeing's base in Everett, north of Seattle, to work together on the configuration of the plane—something that until then Boeing had always done by itself. Partners then went back to their own bases, responsible for all aspects of their piece of the puzzle. The partners built their own production facilities for their bits of the aircraft. As Bair said, "It puts a high premium on the choice of partners in the first place."

It also put a high premium on the management of that network of partners. Boeing held a partners' "council meeting" every six weeks and set up a network to facilitate global collaboration that made it possible for designers from all over the world to work on the same up-to-the-minute database.

To further advance communication, collaboration and integration, the company put great faith in videoconferencing and set up high-bandwidth facilities that were in constant use. People came into their offices in the middle of the night to have virtual meetings with colleagues in different time zones. Technically, the 787 is an American plane; but in reality it is a global one.[25]

The 787 was designed to be a breakthrough product, with features that would dramatically improve its performance on all fronts—from fuel consumption to customer comfort. However, breakthroughs with sophisticated new technologies and materials do not come easy. The project was 3½ years late in making it into the hands of its initial customers and development cost ballooned 120% over the original estimate. When the first few planes entered service, performance in areas such as weight and fuel efficiency was found to be wanting. Battery-related fires required the grounding of the plane until they were successfully sorted, creating additional challenges and reputational risk.

However, Boeing was finally on its way to success with the 787 by the end of 2013. In that year, it had carried over 10 million passengers, flown 100 million miles in service, and Boeing had back orders for more than 800 planes. [26] By 2018, total plane orders had reached 1,398, of which 742 had been delivered. The growing pains associated with its supply partners is a distant memory and analysts report that the 787 performance is consistently exceeding performance guarantees which delights its owners.[27]

Then came the crashes of two 737 MAX's (Oct., 2018 and March, 2019).

This example provides a graphic illustration of how Boeing used structural approaches to respond to increasing complexity and ambiguity in its environment. In the aircraft maker's case, this included a revolutionary design. It also included innovations in where and how aircraft design and manufacturing would be undertaken, the role of suppliers, the treatment of intellectual property, and how the process would be managed. Boeing recognized that its past approach was making it uncompetitive. It worked to break down silos and bring its suppliers into the design process as part of a dynamic network. This necessitated a cultural shift toward treating its selected suppliers as trusted partners in the design and manufacturing processes, and it has required the use of information-processing strategies to link it all together.

Boeing's structural and systemic transformations around the 787 were extremely challenging. It logged record advanced orders, but its innovations on the product design and manufacturing fronts resulted in huge cost overruns and more than a 3½-year delay in the delivery of the first planes (outcomes that have been common to Airbus, Bombardier, and other plane manufacturers when they undertook major product innovations). There were serious difficulties getting its global supply chain outsourcing model to work as expected, and a 2-month strike at Boeing exacerbated matters.[28] It entered commercial service in August 2011, but fires related to battery electrical issues grounded the plane for a period in 2013. However, the order backlog has remained strong, pointing to carrier confidence in the 787 and related products that emerge from this platform.

Boeing has demonstrated a willingness to tackle fundamental questions of how to deal with the structural challenges of differentiation and integration to enhance its performance. Wetzel and Buch[29] argue that organizations tend to be more comfortable with increasing both differentiation and integrating mechanisms than with other approaches and tend to overuse these strategies. For example, a need for a specialized response (e.g., the formation of a technical customer support team) leads to a more structurally differentiated organization. This, in turn, leads to a need to integrate more, so that the newly formed technical customer support team is not orphaned in the organization. An alternate strategy would be to decrease the need to differentiate, easing information-processing needs in Galbraith's terms. This could be done by outsourcing the technical customer support function, by undertaking design changes that reduce the need for such customers support, or other such strategies.

Wetzel and Buch believe that it is useful to consider the benefits of a reduction in the amount of structural differentiation in the organization, through such mechanisms as flattened structures, multi-skilled workers, automated processes, and self-managed teams. By reducing their reliance on differentiating structures, organizations can reduce their need for integrating mechanisms. From an information-processing perspective, this falls into the category of strategies to ease information-processing linkage (see Figure 5.2).

One of the ways Boeing attempted to reduce the need for internal differentiation and integrating mechanisms at the enterprise level was through significantly increasing the level of outsourcing of the design and manufacturing of major components (e.g., wings, engines, and fuselage) to trusted supply-chain partners located around the globe, while at the same time reducing the total number of individual suppliers it managed. This was undertaken to increase its flexibility and adaptiveness, reduce cost, and improve quality; however, it was not well managed in the beginning and created major headaches and delays for Boeing.[30] It took them time to learn how to adapt to this new structure at the enterprise level and to handle the increased levels of uncertainty created by a project like the 787 Dreamliner.

Just as Boeing adapted to overcome significant challenges to turn the Dreamliner into a high-performance aircraft, Boeing management must show that it can pull the company through another even more serious crisis that threatens its very survival.

On March 10, 2019, Ethiopian Airlines Flight 302, a Boeing 737 MAX airplane, crashed into the sea, killing all of its passengers and crew. This crash immediately set off alarm bells: on October 29, 2018, Lion Air Flight 610, another Boeing 737 MAX airplane, had crashed off the coastline of Indonesia, killing all on board. Data suggested significant similarities between the two crashes as the 737 MAXes flew erratically in the first minutes of the flight; the pilots asked to return to their respective airports; and the planes crashed soon thereafter. While the investigations are ongoing, there were enough parallels for the U.S. Federal Aviation Authority (FAA) to ground the plane quickly. Soon all Boeing 737 MAX jets were grounded worldwide.

By early April Boeing had swiftly taken a series of steps to manage the situation and to protect itself, as its stock took a 12% shellacking on Wall Street. Boeing CEO Dennis Muilenburg addressed the world through an online video on the company's website, noting that the preliminary report from Ethiopia suggested that there was a software glitch: an "erroneous activation of the Maneuvering Characteristics Augmentation System (MCAS), activated in response to erroneous angle of attack information." Muilenburg declared that its top engineers were working with its customers and the FAA to update the software so that the 737 MAX could safely return to the skies. The software update, said Muilenburg, would be accompanied by updated training and educational materials for pilots around the world (there had been stories that pilots in low-cost airlines, such as Lion Air, had not received adequate training on the 737 MAX and that the instructions for how to deal with the MCAS problems had been written only in English).

How Boeing's leaders deal with this crisis will influence whether or not the company survives these devastating two crashes. While leaders must now fix the software problem as quickly as possible, the larger issue is to figure out how their structures, systems, and processes allowed this problem to go undetected in the developmental and testing stages. What role did their structural arrangements have in allowing the design flaw to go undetected? What were the people issues that might have contributed to the software glitch? These are but two of the hundreds of questions that Boeing's leaders must ask and answer. With some reasonable idea of how the software problems were allowed to enter the 737 MAXes, then the hard work of making organizational changes will need to take place at Boeing.

Making Formal Structural Choices

An organization's design impacts the behavior of its members. In universities, faculty in the schools of management, government, and education may all teach courses on leadership, but these faculties may never speak with one another or teach one another's students. And yet these differentiated faculties may teach the same concepts and use the same textbooks. Similarly, in many large universities, each school or faculty often has its own specialized library and librarians, a costly arrangement. In fact, these diverse libraries might house the same journals and books in different physical locations across a campus or subscribe to the same electronic data sets that provide access to online journals. Faced with significant budget cuts, the Harvard College Library took steps in 2009 to streamline services and foster collaboration with the sharing of research librarians across library facilities. Rather than only looking at cuts to fixed costs and personnel, the library administration chose to "encourage structural efficiency as a means of wringing savings from their ledgers."[31]

Every formal structure and system design has strengths and weaknesses associated with it. Bolman and Deal[32] argue that all organizational designs present structural dilemmas, or insolvable predicaments, that managers must deal with and reconcile. These fundamental design issues confront managers with enduring structural dilemmas: "tough trade-offs with no easy answers."[33] Bolman and Deal define, for example, the differentiation versus integration conundrum as follows:

> The tension between allocating work and coordinating sundry efforts creates a classic dilemma. . . . The more complex a role structure (lots of people doing many different things), the harder it is to sustain a focused, tightly coupled enterprise. . . . As complexity grows, organizations need more sophisticated—and more costly— coordination strategies. Rules, policies, and commands have to be augmented.[34]

Bolman and Deal identify other structural dilemmas. Another, for example, is the *gaps versus overlaps* dilemma. If tasks are not clearly assigned, then they can easily fall through the organizational cracks. If, on the other hand, managers overlap assignments, then they may create "conflict, wasted effort, and unintended redundancies."[35] The point is for change agents to understand these structural dilemmas, know the costs of mismanagement of these structural issues, and analyze if and how a gap has become an organizational liability that needs to change. Once a preferred structural option has been selected, weaknesses related to it can be alleviated and internal alignment improved through the design or modification of the formal policies, processes, structures, and systems.

Change leaders need to understand their organizations' strategy, how the formal structures, systems and processes are aligned with it, and the impact of those arrangements on outcomes. Wischnevsky and Damanpour found that sustained poor performance is likely to produce strategic change, and this, in turn, is likely to drive structural change.[36] This is true at the organizational level, and it is equally true down to the team level.

Change leaders may be faced with this question: "How can the formal structures and systems be modified to enhance the capacity of the organization to deliver on its strategy?" If a change in strategy is needed, how do the formal structures and systems need to be realigned to contribute to the strategic change agenda? Since formal relationships often include *external parties and organizations* (e.g., suppliers, alliance partners), it is important to include them in one's analyses. The Boeing case highlighted this.

At the team or departmental level, change leaders have the option of creating several types of reporting structures, depending upon the need under different conditions. For example, when new perspectives and ideas are sought, brainstorming sessions can be used to promote a free flow of ideas among all members of the group, with no hierarchical impediments. All ideas are equally welcomed. While brainstorming structures are good at generating ideas and engaging broadscale participation, moving to the implementation stage typically requires the concentration of authority and decision making into fewer hands. This could take the form of a team or task force charged with making such decisions, or it could be delegated to a specific individual—more often than not, the manager responsible for the activity.

Mechanistic organizations may need to create structures or processes that allow them to either temporarily or permanently suspend hierarchical practices to advance innovation. The goal is to create spaces in which frank and open dialogue is encouraged, and learning and organizational improvements can be advanced. Continuous improvement teams within call centers, event-debriefing processes used by Special Forces units in the military, and innovation task forces within governments are examples of attempts to encourage reflection and innovation in mechanistic structures. Decisions that lie beyond the authority and responsibilities of those who generate the analyses can then be reviewed by the appropriate senior individuals. Approved initiatives can then be further developed and/or implemented on a broader scale where warranted. This is essentially what occurs at LifeSpring Hospitals.

AN EFFICIENT HIERARCHY WITH WELL-DEVELOPED, STANDARDIZED SYSTEMS AND PROCESSES

Maternity-related deaths total 2 million babies a year in India, but LifeSpring is bringing hope. It is doing so through high quality, no frills pre- and postnatal counselling and delivery at 30–50% of the market price. This is a 50–50 joint venture between the Acumen Fund, a U.S.-based not-for-profit venture philanthropy fund, and HLL Lifecare, a government of India–owned corporation that is the largest manufacturer of condoms in the world. Acumen's investment in this joint venture is $2 million.

LifeSpring is designed for scalability. By 2018 eleven small maternity hospitals (20–25 beds) and eight extension centers were operating, and LifeSpring has plans to raise funds for many more. The Acumen Fund reports that the hospitals are ISO certified. LifeSpring reports they delivered 20,000 babies in the 2015–2017 period and have treated several hundred thousand women with maternity-related issues since inception[37].

The experience of the poor with public hospitals in India has not inspired confidence. Care can be of questionable quality, difficult to access, and sometimes requires bribes. In contrast, LifeSpring hospitals are bright and inviting, and mothers-to-be (plus those who accompany them) have their own private space. Doctors and nurses are in ready attendance, and services include staffed operating rooms in the event that a cesarean section is required. Over 90 standardized procedures have been developed to ensure consistent high-quality care for all and replicability as new hospitals are added. Careful staff selection and training reinforces these quality practices and high standards of care. There is an extensive ongoing commitment to the professional development of medical staff internally and with external bodies. Staff is involved in continuous improvement initiatives to ensure that standards of care and related standardized processes continue to improve. There are also strong commitments to transparency and the building of strong customer relationships through community outreach.[38] In other words, their structure, systems, and processes are all focused on delivering high quality, low cost maternal health through dedicated smaller maternity hospitals that all operate in a similar manner.

How does LifeSpring deliver such consistent, high-quality service to the poor, at 30–50% of the normal cost? The keys lie in clearly focused values, vision, value proposition and strategy, and structures, systems, and processes that are well aligned with the service delivery model. Its scalable, no frills model is supported by high-quality equipment and facilities, the smaller size of its focused hospitals, and a committed, well-trained staff that pursues continuous improvement on an ongoing and systematic basis. Scalability comes from replicating its hospital model (as resources become available) though the application of its structures, systems, and processes.

Change leaders must understand these important points about formal structures:

- There is no one best way to organize.

- Structural decisions should follow strategic decisions because the structure will then be there to support the strategy.

- All structures present leaders with dilemmas that they must manage. Today's trade-off may seem too costly in the future and will suggest a reorganization to fit tomorrow's external environment.

- Once structural choices are made, formal systems, and processes need to be aligned so that weaknesses are addressed and the internal alignment with the strategy is supported.

- Organizational structures shape and impact people's behavior. A task force, for example, that formally brings people together to analyze and report on a particular issue forces its members to cross organizational boundaries and to learn about and collaborate with people beyond their silo.

USING STRUCTURES AND SYSTEMS TO INFLUENCE THE APPROVAL AND IMPLEMENTATION OF CHANGE

Using Formal Structures and Systems to Advance Change

Formal structures and systems must be leveraged, and at times challenged, to advance change. For example, industry-wide standard practices have long inhibited change in the airline industry. At United, American, Air Canada, British Airways, and other traditionally organized air carriers, air routes were organized in what is called a "hub-and-spoke" design. That is, passengers were collected at many points and delivered to a central hub, where they changed planes and were sent out on a different spoke to their final destination. Different types of planes were purchased to service different routes, cabins were divided between business and economy class, and services were very similar across airlines. For many years, this strategy delivered cost savings to the airlines and served them well. Union agreements escalated labor costs over this period as employees sought to share in the success.

However, discount airlines, such as Southwest Air, WestJet, and Ryanair, came along and opted for a different strategic approach. They adopted a single type of plane to ease maintenance challenges, offered a single no-frills service level in the cabin, and structured other aspects of their operations to lower labor and capital costs per passenger mile. Most important, they restructured their air routes to provide point-to-point service, used less expensive airports (where appropriate), and had more efficient schedules that advanced load factors and processes that reduced the time required before the plane was back in the air. The changes they made to the way they structured their activities, as compared with more traditional airlines, were anchored in cultural and strategic differences, and new structures, systems, and processes designed to support the new value proposition. Because of these changes, they were able to fly passengers directly to their destinations at a lower price and, in the case of Southwest, WestJet, and Ryanair, become very profitable in the process. The traditional airlines' structures and systems that were designed to facilitate efficient and effective service delivery became a problem and contributed to the financial challenges that they are continuing to try to overcome by doing things such as launching their own discount services.

Poor financial airline performance in the past has led to growing demands for major improvements from banks, shareholders, pension funds, and other stakeholders. Structural and system realignment to lower labor costs and other cost drivers became key targets of change. Those who sought to resist the changes, such as the airline labor unions, attempted to leverage existing structures and systems to advance their interests. The following example provides a fascinating but different look at the role that existing structures can play in organizational change.

COMPETITIVE EFFICIENCY AT UNITED AIRLINES

One of the ways that the board at United Airlines (UAL) responded to the competitive realities and the disastrous financial results was to use formal processes to replace a number of key executives[39] and charge senior management with responsibility for turning things around in 2002. Staffing arrangements, work rules, and labor costs were among the many areas that attracted the attention of senior management tasked with effecting change. Management analyzed and then used existing systems and structures (including formal judicial components) to advance and legitimize changes to their collective agreements and, by extension, changes to staffing

levels, the organization of work, and related terms and conditions of work.

In response, employee groups enlisted formal (as well as informal) systems and structures to protect their interests—actions that airline executives saw as resisting needed changes. UAL's use of existing structures and systems to effect change was viewed by employee groups as adversarial, generating serious resentment in what was obviously a very difficult context. Despite the dissatisfaction of employees and their representatives with the imposed changes, they were enacted because the formal structures and rules that governed the situation allowed management to do so.

Similar hard-nosed change tactics were employed at Air Canada in 2003 when it entered bankruptcy protection[40] and British Airways in 2010 as it responded to huge financial losses.[41] These examples show the use of existing structures and systems to advance change through the exercise of formal power and authority from the top of the organization and/or through the imposition of action by outside agents such as banks, courts, or regulators.

Approaches that leverage formal structures and systems to advance change do not have to result in a war with one's employees. Rather, their application can be undertaken in a manner that facilitates understanding, builds support (or lessens resistance), and legitimizes change among those who have serious reservations. In 2002, Agilent, an electronic test and measurement business, had to downsize, laying off 8,000 employees.[42] However, management was seen by its employees as having acted responsibly and humanely. Openness and honesty characterized how the financial and strategic issues were approached and how the appropriate systems and structures were applied by the executives. Employees believed all reasonable options were explored and that layoffs were undertaken as a last resort. Those exiting Agilent reported that they were treated with respect and dignity, while those remaining were left with hope for the future of the firm and confidence in the leadership. To go through this level of downsizing and still be ranked #31 on *Fortune*'s 100 Best Companies to Work For in the following period is no small accomplishment!

Agilent continues to be an innovative leader in scientific measurement and a desirable employer. Various awards from around the globe point to its innovativeness, positive employment practices, and corporate citizenship, including being named 2017 company of the year by Instrument Business Outlook.[43] In 2015, it spun off its electronic measurement business, under the name Keysight Technologies. By 2017, Keysight had revenues of $3.32 billion, a net profit of $102 million, employed over 10,000 people, and, according to analysts, a positive financial future. In 2017 Agilent employed 13,500 people, generated sales of $4.5 billion, and had a net profit of $841 million.[44]

Using Systems and Structures to Obtain Formal Approval of a Change Project

Change is made easier when the change leader understands when and how to access and use existing systems to advance an initiative. In larger organizations, **formal approval processes** for major initiatives are often well defined. For example, in universities, significant academic decisions usually require the approvals of department councils, faculty councils, and university senates in the form of formal motions and votes. The change agent's task is to engage in tactics and initiatives that will increase the likelihood of a positive vote for the proposed change through these various formal bodies.

Any significant change initiative will cost money. To maximize the chances of receiving resources for a change initiative, change leaders will need to understand the budget process and how to garner support for the proposed change through departments and individuals who approve the budget. Timing is important. The likelihood of approval, in the short term, is less if the organization is in the middle of the budget cycle and available funds have already been allocated. Efforts to build interest and support should begin well in advance of when significant funds are needed, building to coincide with key decision dates.

Earlier in this book, two dimensions of change were considered: the size of the change and the proactive–reactive initiation dimension. Change projects that are incremental will normally require fewer resources and lower levels of organizational approval. As the change increases in magnitude and strategic importance, change leaders will need to pay attention to formal approval processes, eliciting the support of senior individuals prior to enacting the change. However, exceptions to this general pattern are often found in areas with safety and regulatory compliance implications. In these situations, significant change decisions (e.g., mandated changes to work practices) may be delegated to appropriate frontline staff due to the risk of not responding quickly. Once the urgency abates, decisions may be reviewed by senior managers and other paths adopted. Reactive strategic changes tend to attract everyone's attention because of the risk, visibility, and criticality of such changes to the future of the organization.[45]

When senior decision makers believe the change initiative has significant strategic and/or financial implications and risks, the change will typically require the formal approval of the organization's senior executive team or its board of directors. A savvy change leader knows the approval levels and hurdles associated with different types of changes—that is, at what level does an issue become a board matter, a senior executive decision, or an issue that can be dealt with at a local level? What will they be looking for in the way of analysis and support?

No two organizations will be the same. Organizations in which there are significant negative consequences of failure (e.g., a nuclear power plant or a pharmaceutical manufacturer) will usually require more senior levels of approval for what may appear to be a relatively modest undertaking in a mission-critical area. Likewise, the hurdle levels are likely to be rigorous in organizations with senior managers and/or cultures that have a low tolerance for ambiguity and risk.

Using Systems to Enhance the Prospects for Approval

Change leaders have a variety of factors they need to consider concerning how to leverage the use of existing systems to increase the likelihood of approval.

First, change leaders need to ask themselves if formal approval is required or if the change decision already rests within their span of control. If no approval is required, they may choose to make people aware of their intent and engage them in discussions to increase downstream acceptance. However, why initiate activities that trigger unnecessary formal approval systems and processes when they are not required? Figure 5.3 outlines the various considerations regarding positioning the approval of a change proposal.

In all cases:

a. When there is a decision maker, identify his or her attitude to the change and attempt to work with that person.

b. Demonstrate how the change project relates to the strategy and vision of the organization and the other person's agenda.

c. Use good process to legitimize the change proposal, such as demonstrating that you've engaged in appropriate analyses, exercised due diligence, and consulted with appropriate individuals.

If formal approval is required, change leaders need to demonstrate that the initiative is aligned with the vision and strategy of the organization, advances the organization's agenda, and has benefits that exceed the costs. It will also help if you can show how the change will advance executives' personal agenda if it differs from the above. If the needed changes modify the vision, strategy, or key elements that make up the organization, the change leader will need to demonstrate how such changes will enhance organizational health and have downstream benefits that exceed the costs and risks associated with these significant organizational changes. Included in such a calculation should be the costs and risks of doing nothing.

Another tactic that can assist in obtaining approval through formal systems is to introduce the ideas and rationale behind the change initiatives early, invite dialogue, and seek input. Even though the proposal is not fully developed at this stage, it may be beneficial to familiarize decision makers with key aspects being explored and the underlying logic. This can be particularly important if there are competing ideas under consideration that, if acted upon, would reduce the attractiveness of your change initiative. Awareness precedes understanding which, in turn, precedes trial and acceptance, and the above approach can often help move decision makers along this path. Once others agree with a proposal it becomes harder to change their minds and convince them to change direction.

If changes are more extreme and if there is sufficient time, leaders can frame and introduce the change in ways that increase management's familiarity and comfort with the proposal. They can do this incrementally, using vehicles such as staged agreements on the purpose and scope of the change (e.g., defining the scope of Stage 1, followed by defining the scope of Stage 2 once Stage 1 has been completed, etc.), preliminary studies, task force reviews, consultants' reports, and pilot projects prior to the request for formal approval of the larger initiative. This, in turn, reduces perceived risks, enhances a sense of the benefits, and essentially conditions the organization to embrace (or at least not resist) more fundamental changes to the aligned systems.

If time is of the essence due to a crisis or emerging threats, the change leader can act with urgency and use the danger to focus attention, facilitate approval of the initiative, and generate motivation to proceed. Formal approval

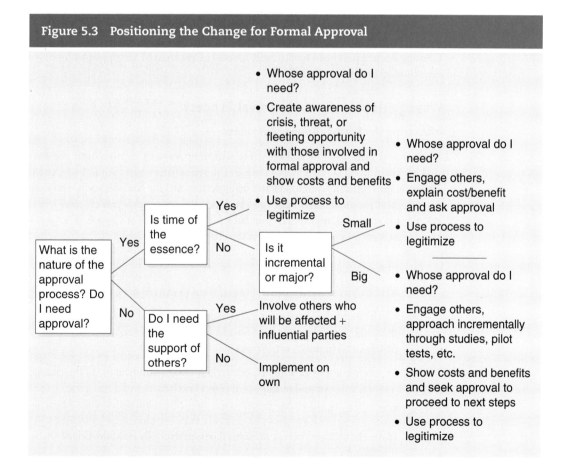

Figure 5.3   Positioning the Change for Formal Approval

processes typically have expedited processes available for dealing with imminent threats and emergencies. One sees this, for example, when there are dangers to health and safety.

When formal approval is required, a change leader will need to know whose agreement is needed. However, if broader acceptance is important before gaining formal approval, then those involved in approval discussions will need to be expanded accordingly. Approval and **acceptance** are generally enhanced when people are involved in the discussion and feel that they have been heard. They are also enhanced when there is the perception that the analysis and discussion around the alignment systems (e.g., vision, strategy, goals, balance scorecards, and strategy maps) have been discussed thoroughly.[46] Acceptance is sometimes increased among the uncommitted and more resistant when they believe that there has been a rigorous review process in place for the assessment of a change. That is, the procedures are thorough and complete. Further, when there is active involvement of those individuals or their representatives in the planning and approval processes, their understanding and acceptance of the change tend to rise. Some may see this as a co-option strategy.

Formal approval systems, therefore, can increase the perception that a change has been assessed appropriately and is worthy of support. However, those who are opposed to a proposal may usurp the process and intentionally erect procedural and approval barriers to an initiative. The oppositions' motives in doing this may be unsullied (the desire for due diligence, due process, and careful review), and they may be firmly convinced that the change is not in the organization's best interests. Or, their motives may be to obstruct out of self-interest. Change leaders will need to carefully assess the motives of the opposition before deciding on how best to respond.

Ways to Approach the Approval Process

Mastering the Formal Approval Process

Howell and Higgins[47] identified three different ways of approaching the formal approval process. The first involves the straightforward rational approach. Proposals are typically developed and brought forward for consideration, and they are reviewed for inclusion on the agenda. Once the proposal is presented and discussed, it is approved, rejected, or sent back for further study or rework. The likelihood of gaining approval is increased when change leaders experience the following:

- Have a well-placed sponsor

- Know their audience members and their preferences

- Understand the power and influence dynamics and the implications of the project for the organization and for those involved in the approval process and in positions of power

- Do their homework with respect to their detailed knowledge of the change project, its scope and objectives, its costs and benefits, and risk areas

- Informally obtain needed approval and support in advance

- Have the change project presented persuasively by an appropriate individual

- Have a good sense of timing concerning when best to bring it forward[48]

- The systems associated with obtaining formal approval for planned changes vary greatly. In organic or entrepreneurial organizations, the process may be loose and idiosyncratic. As organizations mature, even very entrepreneurial firms tend to systematize and formalize the approval processes in order to increase control.

The decision making associated with formal approval processes takes many forms from formal voting by an executive committee to "go/no-go" decisions controlled by an executive. While the exact approval process will be unique to the firm, the level of rigorousness and formality used to assess proposed changes usually varies with the magnitude and cost of the change, the levels of perceived risk, the preferences of those involved with the decision, and the culture and power dynamics at work in the organization.

When the proposed change lies in an area in which much is known, decision makers tend to focus on concrete information (e.g., benchmark data, industry patterns, and performance data). They then use this data to help make a decision.[49] When the changes reside in areas that are inherently ambiguous, attention turns to an assessment of the quality of the analysis and the reputation of the advocate for the proposal. In essence, the decision makers need to decide whether or not they trust the judgment of the change leader and the skills and abilities of the change team.[50]

As organizations mature, they often adopt a staged approval process for changes that are viewed as strategically significant, expensive, wide-reaching in their impact, and potentially disruptive. A staged approach establishes decision approval steps that do not prematurely dismiss ideas worthy of further exploration while controlling the ever increasing commitment of time and resources if the change were to progress to the next stage.[51] The goal is to provide focus through vision and strategic alignment, allow proposed initiatives to be explored and assessed in a rational manner, avoid unpleasant surprises, manage risk, and keep an eye on the portfolio of change initiatives to ensure the organization does not become overwhelmed with initiatives.

As one proceeds through the approval stages, the assessment process becomes increasingly rigorous and the hurdles that must be met before proceeding to the next stage rise. When the process is working well, it should stimulate innovative thinking and initiatives, enhance the quality of assessment, reduce the cycle time from ideation to implementation, and reduce the likelihood of dysfunctional political behavior.

The formal approval process does more than ensure that the decision making concerning change is thorough and reasoned. If the process used to make the decision is viewed as legitimate by others in the organization, this will lend legitimacy to what changes are pursued and enhance acceptance. Sometimes an incremental or staged approval process is used with a major initiative. Staged approaches begin with concept or initial plan assessment, followed by a field experiment or pilot test, possibly a larger field test, and a final review prior to a large-scale adoption. With a staged approach, there are go/no-go decision points and opportunities to fine tune the change, at each stage along the way. When this approach is adopted, the outcomes achieved along the way, the credibility of the findings and the reaction of opinion leaders will play an important part in building support for approval and downstream acceptance by others.

In addition to addressing the traditional hierarchical approach, Howell and Higgins identified two other ways to use system awareness to advance change: strategies based on **creeping commitment** and **coalition building**; and strategies involving simply forging ahead without formal approval.

Encouraging "Creeping Commitment" and Coalition Building

As an alternative to directly pursuing formal approval for a change initiative, change leaders can employ a strategy of creeping commitment (the foot-in-the-door approach[52]) and coalition building. Initiatives such as customer and employee surveys, benchmark data, pilot programs, and other incremental system-based approaches can be used to acclimate organizational members to the change ideas. Such initiatives can be used systematically to clarify the need for change, refine the initiative, address concerns, reduce resistance, show linkages to their agendas, and increase comfort levels. As well, they can create opportunities for direct involvement that will build interest and support for the change within key groups. This, in turn, should reduce pushback and increase the prospects for support if and when formal approval is sought. This strategy also captures commitment by reducing energy that may be spent on other options or directions.

Coalitions can be extremely valuable for building support prior to the formal approval process. Change leaders need to understand key players and behave authentically with them to develop influential coalitions that will support the changes.[53] Often, in technological changes, if key user groups want to adopt new software, management will be more willing to accept the innovation. In other situations, developing the coalition provides the political clout to move the decision in a favorable direction.

The intent of this approach is to create the momentum needed to reach a tipping point[54] that significantly enhances the likelihood of approval. When formal approval is required, the support from key coalition members and stakeholders should make the process more manageable. If the change has been accepted by a coalition of key stakeholders, it may make the approval process all but automatic.

Developing coalitions for change often makes a great deal of sense when seeking formal approval. However, coalition building is not without its risks. This approach takes time and adds complexity (more fingers are in the pie) that may impede the approval process. It can also become quite political and divisive, with coalitions developing in opposition to the change that will need to be managed. Change leaders should avoid getting trapped in tactics that seriously harm relationships, diminish their integrity, and/or compromise long-term objectives.

Bypassing the Formal Approval Process: Just Do It!

The need to seek formal approval can sometimes be bypassed entirely. Peter Grant, a banker who changed the demographic composition of employees at his bank over a 30-year period, never sought formal permission. He understood the systems in his organization and used this awareness to quietly advance a change agenda over 30 years. Through this approach, he dramatically altered the nature of his organization. He would appear to have followed the classic change dictum, "Don't ask, just do it."

PETER GRANT'S "JUST DO IT" APPROACH

Peter Grant was a black manager, one of the few in the firm when he joined. Over his career, he pursued his personal goal of bringing more women and minorities into the firm. Each time he had the opportunity, he hired a qualified minority. And he encouraged others to do the same. Over his career, he was instrumental in having 3,500 talented minority and female members join the organization.[55] When the scope of the change is manageable, defensible, and arguably within their scope of authority, change leaders should seriously consider proceeding on their own without seeking formal approval. Key people, such as supervisors, should be kept sufficiently in the loop so that they are not unpleasantly surprised or left with the belief that someone acted in an underhanded fashion.

When the "just do it" strategy is effectively applied, the dynamics can be powerful. Those who might otherwise be predisposed to oppose the change may not notice it or be lulled into acquiescence as the change proceeds in a lower-key fashion during the initial phases (e.g., data gathering, preliminary experimentation). This approach allows for change refinement, the generation of supportive data, and the building of momentum for change that is difficult to stop.

Howell and Higgins refer to this as the renegade process.[56] It grows out of the premise that it is often easier to gain forgiveness than permission to do something in organizations. This tactic can prove helpful in the early stages of product innovation, but Frost and Egri[57] argue that securing permission is an important contributor to success when social innovations are involved. When using a **renegade approach**, one must be careful not to create enemies unnecessarily or engage in tactics that create long-term damage to your reputation and credibility or the reputation of the firm.

The renegade method does not mean the chaotic introduction of disturbances merely to shake things up. Most organizations are already experiencing enough turbulence. Nor does it mean acting in organizationally naïve ways. Rather, this approach begins with a careful assessment of organizational and environmental factors, including the needs and preferences of key individuals who have the potential to harm or assist the change and the change leader. Finally, it asks change leaders to recognize the power and influence that they have to get things done through launching the initiative on their own and, when the situation is appropriate, to "just do it!" This attitude and propensity toward making these decisions also sets the precedence for similar decisions in the future.

ALIGNING STRATEGICALLY, STARTING SMALL, AND "MORPHING" TACTICS

Gaining approval for change becomes less daunting when you are able to show how the change aligns with the organization's mission, vision, and strategy. When a change plan is being developed, questions of its relationship to these dimensions and its alignment with other existing systems need to be addressed.

If the case can be made that the change initiative adds value over other alternatives *and* fits within the context of the mission, vision, strategy, and significant downstream systems (e.g., information and reward systems, organizational structure), the likelihood of acceptance and adoption of the change is enhanced. If the resources required for the change seem relatively minor relative to the benefits, approval is also more likely. For example, consider a proposed change in the level of customer service offered by call center personnel that has high potential to increase customer satisfaction and significantly reduce the need for callbacks.

The likelihood of approval and acceptance is higher if the only required actions are an additional half day of training, the development of needed support materials, the modification of a couple of decision support screens, the presence of supervisory support, and the modification of performance metrics to reinforce the desired change. In effect, the change leader will have demonstrated that there is little to fear because the change is incremental, is not particularly disruptive in nature, is consistent with the vision and the strategy, and contains benefits that outweigh the costs.

Change leaders often find it is useful to frame changes in ways that reduce the sense of incongruence with existing structures and systems. In general, this approach makes it easier to gain approval because it reduces the sense of disruption and risk that the change will entail. For example, if the end state of a change were to move from mass marketing to relationship-focused, one-to-one marketing, this would be a huge change. The perceived risk can be reduced by breaking the change down into a number of smaller, manageable stages that begin with exploratory research and evaluation, followed by a pilot project, assessment of learning and system alignment challenges, extension to a customer group that was particularly well suited to the approach, and so forth. By starting small and minimizing the incongruence with existing systems, the change leader can move in a systematic fashion in the desired direction, learning, and modifying systems and structures in ways that look incremental in the short term but have significant long-term effects.

As momentum and the critical mass of support build for a revolutionary change that is positioned as incremental, the change may take on a life of its own. When those smaller change elements are added together over time, the cumulative changes will look far more significant in retrospect than they did at any point along the way. The term "morphing" captures the sense of this approach to change because it depicts a slow and steady transformation of the organization over time.[58] Abrahamson refers to this as the "change without pain" approach, though not all recipients would share this sentiment.[59] The earlier example of Peter Grant, who was instrumental in the hiring of 3,500 women and visible minorities at his bank, falls into this category. The lesson is that approval can often be advanced by avoiding the depiction of the change as a marked departure of heroic proportions. An evolving series of ten 5% changes in organizational performance over the course of five years produces a total change of 50% in organizational performance, and that does not include the compounding effects!

See **Toolkit Exercise 5.3** to reflect on an approval process you're familiar with.

THE INTERACTION OF STRUCTURES AND SYSTEMS WITH CHANGE DURING IMPLEMENTATION

Structures and systems not only have an impact on a change leader's ability to gain acceptance for a change project, they can also have a significant impact on the success of the implementation process. When major changes are undertaken, there will be existing systems and structures that change agents have to work with in order to gain approval and proceed. In addition, subsequent alterations to those structures and systems will often be required in order to bring them into alignment with the proposed path forward.

MICROSOFT'S TURNAROUND

When Nadella became the CEO of Microsoft in 2014 and commenced his change initiatives, he and others working on its transformation had to navigate the existing formal structures and systems, in order to create and then deploy the desired structures and systems. Coalitions needed to be built and permission to undertake planned changes needed to be sought within the then existing structures and systems. Nadella's task was made somewhat easier by the fact that Microsoft's board, market analysts, and a large number of existing employees recognized the need for major revitalization.

Nadella's knowledge of the organization combined with his stellar reputation allowed him to engage the organization and move quickly. Actions involved major changes in strategy. These included the following: exiting the smartphone market, ending the war with Apple, Android and Sales Force; entering the Internet of Things and cloud services market;

major investments and acquisitions (e.g., LinkedIn), to speed market success into targeted segments; and possibly most importantly, cultural changes to make it a more inquisitive, inclusive, innovative, empowered, and adaptive learning environment. Changes undertaken also involved product revitalization, the realignment of Microsoft's structures and systems around the new strategy, and the largest layoff in Microsoft's history (18,000). Microsoft's employees' 82% approval rating of Nadella on Glassdoor following these layoffs point to fairly high levels of internal support he enjoyed.[60]

How have things worked out? The changes are proving to be a resounding success. Some things have not met expectations, but many others have clearly made their mark. Microsoft was ranked #2 on Forbes' list of best global companies to work for in 2018, share price in 2018 was triple what it had been in 2014, and sales were up 13.3% over the previous year.[61]

Nadella recognized the necessity of aligning systems and structures with the vision and strategy. He used changes in these areas, in concert with other initiatives, to advance Microsoft's new mission (empower every person and every organization on the planet to achieve more), and the vision for change needed at Microsoft to support that mission. Further, he and others avoided getting bogged down in finger pointing and other defensive tactics when things didn't pan out initially. Such actions can derail progress in even what appears to be a relatively straightforward problem.

Diagnosis of the nature and impact of structures and systems on performance during implementation puts change leaders in a strong position to identify when and where these may present challenges that will need to be managed and where they can be used to facilitate change. The Microsoft and Peter Grant change examples involved approaches that refined and exploited systems (in the best sense of the word) in support of the desired changes.

In summary, change agents need to understand the approval processes for their particular projects. They need to know the key players and how formal the process is. Does it require a vote? Will the go-ahead be authorized at a management or executive meeting? Alternatively, can the change agent act to develop a coalition first, or just act using available resources and power? Further, will there be needs for changes to existing structures and systems to support the underlying change initiative? If so, what are those changes and how should they be executed? In the next section, we will explore the role of systems in change approval, acceptance, and implementation.

USING STRUCTURES AND SYSTEMS TO FACILITATE THE ACCEPTANCE OF CHANGE

Change agents may be tempted to breathe a sigh of relief and relax once a change project is approved. However, gaining formal approval is not the same as gaining generalized acceptance of the change. Too often, the anticipated chorus of excitement fails to materialize and, in its stead, change agents experience begrudging cooperation, or covert or overt resistance. The assumption that approval will automatically lead to acceptance is a dangerous one.

CUSTOMER RELATIONSHIP MANAGEMENT

Complex implementations, failure to yield desired results, and escalating maintenance costs have all marred the reputation of customer relationship management (CRM) programs; 50% of CRM implementations generally fail and almost 42% of CRM software licenses bought end up unused. In 2013, a survey of 352 U.S.-based executives found that failure rates of CRM had risen to 63%. While some fault lies with the vendors, sometimes it is, unfortunately, the business that gets itself in a rut. An analysis of failure implementations found a lack of clear ownership for the initiative 53% of the time followed by a lack of management bandwidth (43%), a lack of executive support (38%), and the lack of a sense that it was an IT priority (38%).[62]

Despite their best intentions, change leaders have less-than-stellar success in bringing approved change to fruition. When major changes are undertaken, approximately 60–70% fall significantly short of their objectives. Since half of the "failures" report achieving some of their objectives, the total failure category lies in the 30–35% range.[63] A poorly thought through change initiative and bad luck can explain some of the lack of success. However, lack of awareness for and acceptance of the change within the organization, lingering doubts and half-hearted commitments at senior levels, confusion as to who is supposed to do what, issues of skill and ability, and lack of time or resources often play significant roles in the lack of success.

Structural and systemic factors in an organization can be used to ease the legitimization and acceptance of a change initiative and provide access to needed resources. They facilitate the assignment of authority and responsibility, provide needed training and bandwidth, publicly affirm commitment and needed resourcing at the senior and middle levels, and ensure that the output of the changes is put to use and not ignored, because they have not been part of past practices. However, they can also derail progress when not properly deployed. The inappropriate delegation of sponsorship, structures that fail to provide sufficient access to needed resources, and the misapplication of systems are three of the most commonly cited mistakes made by top management in change initiatives.[64]

Paul Tsaparis, formerly of Hewlett-Packard, did not make the mistake of underestimating the role that systems and structures can play when undertaking a huge change challenge.

SYSTEMS AND STRUCTURES AT HP (CANADA)

In May 2002, Paul Tsaparis, 42, president and CEO of Hewlett-Packard (Canada) Ltd., began managing the massive integration of Hewlett-Packard and Compaq in Canada. The new 6,800-person organization had annual revenues in excess of $3 billion (Canadian). As is often the case with organizational integration, staff reductions were involved.

Tsaparis approached the integration challenge by getting out and putting a human face on the challenges and changes. He actively communicated the vision and corporate strategy and let people know what was happening to their employment situation as soon as possible. He reassured other key stakeholders (customers, suppliers) that they would not be lost in the shuffle. Tsaparis followed up by deploying organizational structures, systems, and processes that would support HP's strategy, reinforcing the integration change initiative, and increasing the likelihood of longer-term organizational success. Change teams were created to facilitate the implementation of the needed organizational changes and these teams, in turn, required structures, systems, and processes that would support them in the pursuit of their objectives.

Tsaparis remained the president of HP Canada until 2010, when he was promoted to VP of Technology Support for the Americas. He took early retirement in June 2012 and has subsequently served on the board of directors in several organizations, including the Board of York University, where he was appointed chair in 2018. [65]

Tsaparis faced significant cultural, structural, and systemic change challenges. Each organization, HP and Compaq, had its own way of doing things. And many of those systems and structures would have explicit as well as implicit implications—ways of doing things that might not even be written down but were firmly embedded in the habits of organizational members. As a result, the conscious development of structures and systems that would support HP's strategy represented an important step in the building of an infrastructure that would support change and promote acceptance. Conflicting and misaligned structures and systems needed to be identified and addressed so that the resulting web of structures and systems were aligned. Staying true to HP's core values and principles provided critical guidance for the massive change initiative. Tsaparis acted on the belief that the more these are aligned with your own core values, the more likely you, as leader, are to succeed.

Change agents need to understand the effects of structures and systems from the perspective of the person who is on the receiving end of the change—the actual person who will be asked to behave differently. If people do not accept the change, they are unlikely to modify their behavior in the desired direction, no matter how excellent the change project is.

Interestingly, gaining compliance does not necessarily mean attitudes have changed, assuming that attitude change is needed. Attitude change does not always come first. It may well evolve after the change in behavior has been achieved. Changes to systems and structures can be used to promote the desired behavior in individuals through having them live with the new arrangements. For example, when new software goes live and the old software is disabled, individuals have no choice but to work with the new system. When thoughtfully undertaken (i.e., careful analysis and a thoughtful implementation plan), this approach can result in changes in behavior, followed by changes in attitudes in the desired direction over time as people experience their new context.[66]

The *role of physical space in change* deserves highlighting because it sometimes goes underappreciated. Thoughtfully altering the physical space in which people work can change communication and working patterns in ways that promote understanding and facilitate attitudinal changes.[67] Architects and interior designers have long promoted the value of giving this careful consideration.[68] However, one does not always have to wait until there is a major redesign of the physical space. Think of something as simple as sitting patterns in a classroom. Once people find a chair at the beginning of the semester, they tend to return to that space. If the faculty member changes those seating patterns by randomly assigning people to teams that need to sit together, communication patterns will be altered and new relationships formed. The potential value of more modest changes to work space deserves careful attention.

Clarity of purpose and direction, combined with formal processes that facilitate employee involvement and reward desired behavior, can all be used to advance the engagement and involvement of employees in change-related initiatives. However, be careful of approaches that are viewed as heavy handed. A top-down directive that orders change without any consultation may lead to less information sharing, reduced risk-taking, less acceptance of change, and greater employee turnover.[69] The thoughtful use of formal systems and processes can facilitate others' understanding of what is being undertaken (and why) and the sense of legitimacy. Unless the employees buy into the legitimate authority of executives and the legitimacy of the change, they may not accept it and instead may engage in actions that slow, disrupt, or sabotage progress.

Much of the change leaders' difficulty in thinking through the impact of structure on employees' acceptance flows from their assumptions: they see the need for change and the rationale underlying it and believe the change is immensely logical. From that position, it is much too easy to assume that others will see and accept the logic of the change agent! But the logic falls flat for organizational members facing a formal reward system that works against the change or an organizational structure that emphasizes characteristics contrary to the desired change (e.g., a focus on cost controls rather than customer retention).

The passage of time, in conjunction with the use of formal systems, can also influence the acceptance of change. When a change initiative has been the subject of formal discussion and review for an appropriate interval, this gestation period may allow the idea to become more familiar and acceptable. Initiatives that are shocking at first may appear less threatening after a period of reflection. Alternatively, if approval has been granted and there seems to be little activity or visible progress, acceptability and support may diminish.

In summary, systems and structures, properly leveraged and deployed, can play an important role in the speed and rate of acceptance of change. People don't resist all change. Lots of things have the potential to be seen as worth doing, and people tend to respond positively to change initiatives that they understand and believe are worth the effort and risk. The way that systems and processes are deployed will influence the perception of the change.[70]

Developing Adaptive Systems and Structures

The ability of organizations to adapt to change is aided by their ability to learn. Nevis suggests that organizations can be viewed as learning systems that acquire knowledge, disseminate it through the organization, and use that knowledge to accomplish their missions.[71] Learning is facilitated when organizational members do the following:

1. Systematically and deliberately scan their external environment and learn from it

2. Demonstrate the desire to question existing approaches and always improve

3. Have a concern for measurement of performance and shared perceptions of the gap between the current and desired levels of performance

4. Develop an experimental mindset where they try new things

5. Create an organizational climate of openness, accessibility, honesty, and active discussion and debate

6. Engage in continuous education at all organizational levels

7. Use a variety of methods, appreciate diversity, and take a pluralistic view of competencies

8. Have multiple individuals who act as advocates for new ideas and methods and who are also willing to exercise their critical judgment in the review of ideas

9. Have an involved, engaged leadership

10. Recognize the interdependence of units and have a systems perspective

Many of these learning actions are influenced by organizational structures and systems. The presence of formal early-warning systems and opportunity-finding systems advance the scanning capacity of the organization. The presence of a formal strategy and environmental review process, complete with performance metrics, will increase the likelihood that firms will systematically review where they are and where they want to go. Systems that reward innovation and information sharing will increase the prospects for openness and exploration. Systems that fund and reinforce development will open people to continuous education. Likewise, appropriately designed systems and processes can be used to advance diversity and the exploration of new ideas. Finally, systems can be used to increase the prospect that interdependencies are recognized and that a systems perspective is brought to problem solving.

Organizations that are flexible and adaptive have an easier time adjusting to incremental and upending changes than do bureaucratic ones.[72] As the complexity and turbulence of organizational environments increase, more flexible and adaptive systems and structures will be required.[73] Essentially, organizations need to become more "change ready."[74]

In a study of strategic planning in an international nongovernmental development organization, the need for adaptive capacity manifested itself in an interesting way. Rather than opt for an unambiguous course of action, this organization tended to develop multiple strategies that were both ambiguous and ambitious. What looked like strategic drift to outsiders provided managers with flexibility in how they responded to changing conditions. Appropriate ambiguous strategies were used as metaphors to promote consensus and legitimacy with key stakeholder groups and allow for learning and the adjustment of change plans as they proceeded forward.[75]

To cope with turbulence and complexity, organizations are being designed in unconventional ways. These include the increasing use of formal and informal networks to link individuals in the organizations with external individuals and organizations to promote shared initiatives. For example, supply chain networks are increasingly being used to leverage supplier talents in dealing with design and engineering challenges, finding ways to enhance quality, and identifying opportunities for cost reduction. Designer, supplier, producer, and distributor capabilities of different organizations are being brought together in networks to increase flexibility, adaptability, and innovative results. Thus, a product might be designed in Italy, built in Korea from Brazilian materials, and distributed in the United States by a Scandinavian firm. Think IKEA for this type of network.[76] The network partners are held together by market mechanisms such as contracts, just-in-time logistics, shared market intelligence and production systems, shared purposes, and customers' demands rather than by organizational charts and traditional controls.[77]

The need for greater flexibility and adaptiveness is moving organizations away from command and control structures, and giving rise to the increased use of collaborative structures and processes to promote trust, communications, information sharing, and shared ownership of the undertaking. At a micro level, this may come in the form of self-managed work teams, cross-functional teams and task forces, and other approaches that facilitate intra-organizational communication and cooperation. At the organizational level, it may take the form of flattened structures, systems processes, and technologies that promote collaboration (both within and outside the organization), and leadership styles and cultural norms that foster greater collaboration, transparency, and shared sense of purpose.[78]

When people are geographically dispersed and collaboration is needed, virtual teams are increasingly being deployed, along with enabling technologies to allow them to build needed trust and effectively work together. In some organizations, the physical design of office space is being reimagined, in order to bring people from different functions together and promote collaboration, rather than isolate them from one another.[79] One example of a company employing a flatter more democratic structure is Zappos.com. While a democratic system or "holacracy" made up of self-organizing teams has certainly garnered attention, there are doubts as to whether it will become a tried-and-true management structure.[80]

Collaborative relationships and their associated networks are taking new and interesting forms that extend far beyond traditional organizational boundaries. Open-sourced design and development, shared content creation initiatives such as that associated with Wikipedia, customer co-creation, online advisory groups, and other forms of cooperative input and information sharing are creating fascinating opportunities for individuals and organizations of all sizes that did not exist in the past.[81]

In matters of organizational change, the formal use of social technologies and the degree to which they are used to advance the change have been found to contribute to successful implementation.[82] This is not surprising when one thinks of the power of social technologies for communicating information and aligning the interests and efforts of dispersed individuals. Research has found that greater organizational learning and knowledge creation are associated with more organic organizational structures rather than more mechanistic ones.[83] Collaborative networks have been found to be powerful contributors to how people respond to change, but more will be said of this later.[84]

One of the roles of the change agent is to help organizations learn from the past and evolve systems and structures that are likely to help them succeed in the future. Focusing on how organizations acquire knowledge and spread it throughout the organization can be a valuable diagnostic tool in this regard. By facilitating the development of adaptive systems and processes (keeping in mind the competitive realities and the need for congruence with the environment), change agents will succeed in enhancing the capacity of the organization to adjust to change in the future.

SUMMARY

Formal systems and structures influence how change initiatives evolve and succeed. Change leaders need to understand them, how they operate, and how they influence the change process. In addition, change leaders need to know how to manage the approval process for initiatives so that they can work with, through, and/or around them in order to increase the prospects of the change being adopted. Formal systems and structures can be used to advance acceptance and implementation of the change in the organization. And finally, formal systems and structures increasingly need to be flexible and adaptive, to promote learning, and set the stage for needed changes. See **Toolkit Exercise 5.1** for critical thinking questions for this chapter.

KEY TERMS

Formal organizational structure and **systems**—how the organization formally organizes itself to accomplish its mission. Formal structures refer to how the organization's tasks are formally divided, grouped, and coordinated. The structure would include the organizational hierarchy, the structure of any manufacturing operation, and any formal procedures such as the performance appraisal system, as well as other structures. The formal systems are the documented processes of coordination and integration within the organization. Examples include the information, compensation, financial accounting, and human resource systems.

Formal approval process—the formal procedure that change agents must follow for organizational approval of a change project.

Mechanistic organizations—exhibit machinelike qualities. They rely on formal hierarchies with centralized decision making and a clear division of labor. Rules and procedures are clearly defined, and employees are expected to follow them. Work is specialized and routine.

Organic organizations—exhibit organism-like qualities as they are more flexible. They have fewer rules and procedures, and there is less reliance on the hierarchy of authority for centralized decision making. The structure is flexible and not as well defined. Jobs are less specialized. Communication is more informal and lateral communications more accepted.

The **information-processing view of organizations**—considers organizations as information-processing mechanisms. This view argues that the better the fit between the information-processing capabilities of the organization and its environment, the more effective the organization.

Environmental uncertainty—measures the degree of variability of the environment. Duncan suggests two dimensions of uncertainty: degree of complexity of the environment and degree of dynamism.

The formal approval process—the traditional approach in which a person or persons develop a proposal and bring it forward for assessment and formal approval by the appropriate organizational members.

Acceptance of change—the degree to which change participants accept or "buy into" the change that has been implemented.

Creeping commitment—the gradual increase in commitment by change participants toward the change project. Such an increase is often obtained by involving participants in decision making.

Coalition building—the forming of partnerships to increase pressures for or against change.

The renegade approach—when change is initiated without having first obtained formal approval. This is often done in conjunction with creeping commitment and coalition-building tactics. The intent of the approach is that the change is advanced to the point that it cannot easily be reversed by those with formal authority.

Adaptive systems and structures—those that are relatively ready for change compared to others.

CHECKLIST: CHANGE INITIATIVE APPROVAL

1. What does a review of documents related to relevant formal structures and systems reveal about the formal approval process and who has formal authority for approving the change initiative?

2. What are the key points in the process that a change leader needs to pay attention to: timing of meetings, getting on the agenda, cycle time, types of decisions made, and where decisions are made?

   a. How are the relevant systems and structures interconnected? How do they influence one another?

3. Develop a process map that tracks the change idea from start to finish.

   a. What role (and person) has formal authority and decision-making responsibility for this initiative?

   b. What are the decision parameters that are normally applied, and are there zones of discretion available to decision makers?

   c. What are the power and influence patterns around particular systems and structures? Who has direct and indirect influence on how the systems and structures are applied?

   d. How should the change leader manage these formal systems and structures to reduce resistance? And how can they be managed to advance the change initiative?

END-OF-CHAPTER EXERCISES

TOOLKIT EXERCISE 5.1

Critical Thinking Questions

The URLs for the videos listed below can be found in two places. The first spot is next to the exercise and the second spot is on the website at **study.sagepub.com/cawsey4e.**

Consider the questions that follow.

1. How Do Food Banks Help? —1:30 minutes

    https://www.youtube.com/watch?v=IdJnLj-ksVk

    Consider this video from Food Banks Canada.

    - Comment on how a video such as this inspires could be used to inspire a vision for change. If you were a volunteer, what sort of specific vision for change would you want to work toward implementing?

    - How did the video use data to engage listeners?

2. Dr. John Kotter: Accelerate! The Evolution of the 21st Century Organization—6:07 minutes.

    https://www.youtube.com/watch?v=Pc7EVXnF2aI

    In this video, Kotter provides a prescription for how organizations need to structure themselves to be able to evolve successfully today.

    - What do you think of his prescription?

    - Think of an organization you are familiar with (it could be public, private, a not-for-profit, or a branch of government). What are the change implications for it if it were to adopt this approach?

    - What do you think this organization should do to enhance its flexibility and readiness for change?

*Please see **study.sagepub.com/cawsey4e** for a downloadable template of this exercise.*

TOOLKIT EXERCISE 5.2

Impact of Existing Structures and Systems on Change

Think of a change you are familiar with.

1. How did the organization use structures and systems to deal with the uncertainty and complexity in the environment?

   Was this an appropriate response?

   How could the existing structures and systems have been approached and used differently to advance the desired change?

   How did existing structures and systems affect the ability of the change leader to bring about the desired change?

   a. What systems/structures were involved?

   b. How did these systems/structures influence what happened?

      Was this related to how they were formally designed or was this related to how they actually came to be used in practice?

   c. Who influenced how the systems/structures were used, and how did this affect the outcomes that ensued?

2. What role could incremental strategies that were nested with existing systems and structures have played? Would they have really moved the process forward or simply avoided the real changes that needed to be addressed?

3. What role could more revolutionary strategies have played? Would they produce issues related to their alignment with existing systems and structures?

   How would you manage the challenges created by this?

*Please see **study.sagepub.com/cawsey4e** for a downloadable template of this exercise.*

TOOLKIT EXERCISE 5.3

Gaining Approval for the Change Project

Consider a change project in an organization with which you are familiar.

1. What is the approval process for minor change initiatives?

    For major change initiatives?

    Can you describe the processes involved?

    a. If a project requires capital approval, are there existing capital budgeting processes?

    b. If the project needs dedicated staff allocated to it or if it will lead to additions to staff, what are the processes for adding people permanently, and selecting and developing staff?

    c. Does the project alter the way work is organized and performed?

    d. What are the systems and processes used for defining jobs and assessing performance?

    e. Can the project be approved by an individual? Who is that person? What approval power do they have?

2. Are there ways that the perceived risks of the change could have been reduced by the way the change leader staged the project and managed the approval process?

*Please see **study.sagepub.com/cawsey4e** for a downloadable template of this exercise.*

BECK CONSULTING CORPORATION

By Cynthia Ingols, Professor of Practice,
and Lisa Brem, Researcher

*School of Business, Simmons University,
Boston, MA*

As she drove, Beck reflected on all that had transpired in her career since she earned her MBA in 2002. She had started her business, Beck Consulting Corporation (BCC) a year after graduation. Over the next 11 years, her consulting business, which ranged from moving offices to entire companies to new locations, had grown from a one-person consultancy to a successful private company employing 40 people. Beck had reason to feel that she had "made it." But she also felt that she could not simply sit back and savor her success. Her business continued to have opportunities for growth. As Beck explained,

> The real joy for me comes from founding and growing a business. We are a growing company, and we need sparks of excitement that come from change, from going to the next level. Opening new offices, going national or international, expanding the services we offer, going public—all these things would give us as a company more reasons to be proud. People here are invested in the future. We can't get to the future by standing still.

While the business was prospering, its growth posed urgent problems. For the first time, Beck felt she needed to add another layer of management to her organization. In addition, Beck wasn't sure that the compensation and incentive plans currently in place were appropriate for this new layer and she wondered if they needed to develop more formalized work systems and processes. However, she also worried that more

hierarchy and formalization would ruin the carefully constructed culture of independent thinkers at her company.

Beck had built her business by maintaining close contact with both employees and clients. Her vivacious personality, intelligence, and "can-do" attitude set the tone for her company. Beck's personal touch was one of the major motivators for her staff and one of the selling points for the company's services. The central question in Beck's mind was how to grow the business without losing the hands-on style that had made the company successful.

AN EASY WAY TO START A CONSULTING COMPANY

For Marilyn Beck running a relocation company was a perfect fit. She had moved several times in the United States and internationally with her late husband. In 1998, she settled in the Boston area. She earned her MBA part time while holding down a job and raising two children. Throughout the 1990s she held administrative management positions at a variety of Boston law firms. As it happened, a common denominator of all her jobs was moving the office. As Beck recalled,

> All the firms I worked for made major moves, and I ended up managing them. I became something of an expert at it. I preferred the project management aspect of moving rather than the day-to-day maintenance tasks.

In August 2002, at the end of her third year of her part-time MBA program, Beck was ready for a change.

She had become increasingly impatient with the rigid hierarchies she saw in the legal firms where she worked. She felt it took too long to make decisions and that steep hierarchies promoted a lack of accountability. Beck explained:

> One reason I really don't like hierarchies is their lack of immediate decision making. One example that had serious repercussions was when I worked at a law firm and we had a bad snow storm. I wanted to send people home early, but my boss had to go to his boss and on up the chain. By the time I got out of there, I ended up with a seven-hour drive home.

> The other part of it for me, is that I don't automatically respect someone with a title; I'm more interested in a meritocracy. The law firms couldn't give underlings decision making authority because they weren't lawyers. Conversely, I remember a time I was lugging huge water bottles to the cooler and the big, strapping, male lawyers walked right by me—not one stopped to help. Being a partner took precedence over being a person. Those kinds of separations don't make for a cohesive team. I wanted to create a place where I didn't have to live by those rules.

She felt she could be successful if she put all her experience with corporate relocation to work in a consulting business. Beck, however, was not sure how to get started.

In 2003, she had the answer. An office manager from a large Boston law firm called Beck to see if she'd be interested in organizing their upcoming move. The call came as a result of a networking group that Beck had started while she was working for a law firm in Washington D.C. Beck explained the connections that led to her first consulting job:

> I was working for the D.C. satellite office of a large Boston law firm. There was one other Boston firm that also had a satellite office, so I started a lunch group that brought together managers from both companies. I felt as though we dealt with similar issues and could benefit from sharing experiences. I got to know the office manager of the other firm pretty well. A couple of years later, after I'd moved back to Boston, the office manager from the Boston firm happened to be talking to the DC office manager. The Boston office manager was looking for someone to manage the firm's move, and my DC friend immediately recommended me.

> I interviewed for the job along with about eight other people. The hiring manager told me later that even though he'd interviewed people with a lot more experience, he said my interpersonal skills were so strong that they decided to offer the job to me.

The company offered Beck either a full-time one-year contract to move its 950-member workforce, or to serve as an independent contractor. As Beck recalled,

> There I was—wondering how to start consulting and this job dropped in my lap. I decided to go in as an independent contractor. I remember thinking—what easier way to start a consulting company? Of course, I didn't think then of what being a consultant meant. Later, I realized that, in addition to delivering services, I would have to send out invoices, set up a bookkeeping system, and find more clients.

Beck set up shop in her home and worked independently on small projects until 2007 when she accepted a large job at a large, international university that eventually developed into a two-year commitment. She hired several temporary employees to help coordinate the move, but quickly realized that she would need permanent help. Beck hired Susan Smith, a facility management specialist from a large telecommunications company. Smith had a degree in interior design and experience with business furnishings that complemented Beck's business degree and relocation skills. Although Beck was happy to gain an employee with Smith's background, hiring a full-time employee was unsettling. As Beck explained,

> Hiring Susan, my first permanent employee, was the first big milestone for the business. It was the hardest thing I have ever had to do. I was suddenly responsible for someone else—for her family—for her livelihood. It was a combination of worrying about not having enough work for her and having to pay her even if the work wasn't coming in. We sort of got around that. We negotiated an hourly wage, figuring that if I didn't need 40 hours per week consistently, I wouldn't have to pay for it. But in reality, Susan ended up working 50 hours a week from the start and that has never really changed. She is still here—and is vice president of the company.

A LOOSE COLLECTION OF CONSULTANTS

In the fall of 2007, when a large regional bank hired Beck to move its Massachusetts headquarters, Beck hired two more employees. From September 2007 through May 2008, Beck Consulting moved 1,500 people for the bank. From that time on, Beck continued to augment the bank's project management staff, managing various aspects of employee relocation on a permanent basis.

By 2009, the company had seven hourly employees. The base of operations was still Beck's home, although most of the work was done on-site at client facilities. Beck's second employee described this start-up phase:

I started working for Marilyn in 2007. At the time, Beck Consulting wasn't so much a company as a loose collection of consultants. She had one employee—Susan Smith. Mostly, though, Marilyn hired consultants to get the jobs done. Eventually, she hired me as the second employee.

It was interesting working out of someone's house. I feel fortunate to have started that way because I was able to work directly with Marilyn. I got to really understand what she expected and how she worked with clients. At the time she was a project manager running projects instead of the more administrative role she plays now as president of the company. I enjoyed those early days. I felt we were all learning at the same time.

The energy of starting something new and operating on a shoestring was exciting, but Beck felt the need to become established in a Boston location closer to her client base. "People were trying to do business on the streets with their cell phones," she recalled. "It was time we moved downtown."

By December 2010, Beck Consulting had doubled in size, with enough work to keep ten full time employees busy. The company moved to 2,200 square feet of space. Six months later, it increased its office size by another 2,200 square feet. Beck explained the financial risk the company took that year:

> Instead of paying $6,000 a year on rent, we were now paying more than 10 times that amount. It was daunting. But the up side was that our business was expanding as well. By the end of 2011, we had over 20 employees. We had doubled in size in two years.

RELOCATION CONSULTANTS—A NICHE WITHIN THE FACILITY MANAGEMENT INDUSTRY

Before 1980, the term "move consultants" was not in Corporate America's vocabulary.

Most—if not all—moves were performed by employees. Office managers in small to medium-sized firms and facility management teams in large firms typically had the dubious honor of managing and executing a move. In the 1980s, however, as the tidal wave of downsizing swept away corporations, executives found that there was no one left with the expertise and the time to plan a large move. The facility management outsourcing industry gave birth to a small subset of firms that chose to specialize in the high-stress world of corporate relocations.

Another trend in facilities management, called "workforce churn," also fueled the growth of relocation consultants. Churn was the term used to describe the continual movement of employees as a result of expansion, downsizing, redeployment, or a project-oriented workforce. The reasons for the high level of churn rates were increases in industry consolidations, corporate mergers, and the rapid expansion of high-tech firms that used fluid teams to perform projects.

In addition to offering an experienced, cost-efficient team to manage moves, relocation consultants also took the heat of a stressful move off an employee or department. Since two-thirds of employees in charge of a move are either fired or quit soon after the move, hiring a move consultant saved companies the cost of hiring and training new personnel. Beck pointed out that consultants were, for the most part, protected from office politics and made space assignments objectively.

THE BECK WAY

Throughout the 2005-2010 period, Beck experienced growth in number and scope of assignments. She continued to hire project managers in response to the increasing demands of clients. In 2010, Beck promoted Susan, her first employee and right arm, to the position of vice president. This marked a departure from Beck's "loose collection of consultants" and the installation of a rudimentary hierarchy. The bulk of the staff, the project managers, remained on the same level.

The company prided itself on its lack of formal titles and status symbols. As Beck explained,

> I didn't personally do well in hierarchical organizations. I didn't like it, and I chose not to subject other people to it. That's not to say we don't have *any* hierarchy or that we have a totally flat organization. Of course, we do have some hierarchy—we have hierarchy of experience. We have some people who have been in this business for 25 years and some who have been in it for one. The one with 25 years of experience is much more likely to be managing a project than the person with little experience. But we don't use titles, except for Susan and myself. It's not something that's needed internally.

> Despite the lack of titles, it was always clear to the client who to contact if there was a problem. In the beginning they always talked to me; then after I made Susan vice president, she talked to her clients and I kept mine. There was perhaps more internal than external confusion.

Although most of the staff at Beck Consulting were female, Beck asserted that she didn't set out to build an all-female company. The fact was the overwhelming majority of applicants happened to be female. Beck believed the reason for this was that the work lent itself to a traditionally "female" approach to tasks and problem solving. As she explained,

> The way we work is very hands-on. Of course, not all relocation companies work this way. One of our competitors is almost entirely male, and they don't offer the same level of hands-on attention to detail that we do. It's really a different business model.

We are widely known for our incredible ability to coordinate and manage all the details of a move. One of our employees said to me the other day that a lot of what we do is handholding and giving pats on the back. And that really is important. People are traumatized by moves. Even if they are moving to a different floor in the same building, there is something very unsettling about it. We help communicate with people and listen to their concerns. At the same time, we handle a zillion details, from selecting voice/data networks to making sure there are coat hangers in every closet.

Employees at Beck Consulting expressed a strong sense of shared values and prided themselves on their customer-service orientation. As Project Manager Makayla Jones explained,

At Beck, we have a style of working that is tightly focused on customer service. We want the customer to be happy and we want to do a good job. Everyone here is willing to get down and dirty and do whatever it takes to get the job done— whether it's designing office space or crawling around on the floor looking for outlets.

WORKFLOW AT BECK CONSULTING

Client projects at Beck Consulting generally fell into two categories: one-time moves and ongoing facility management. Beck employees were primarily coordinators for one-time moves. They did not actually pick up and move boxes; rather, they set schedules and coordinated the moving company's activities with the activities of other sub-contractors such as security, electricians, and environmental systems. One-time moves involved anything from a small group relocating to another floor, to 2,500 employees moving to a new building

over the course of a single weekend. Beck teams were formed for each job and were disbanded when a job was done.

The ongoing facility work usually entailed at least two people working full time, or nearly full time, on-site at a client's facility. Ongoing work included space planning; inventorying, refurbishment, or procurement of furniture; coordinating new construction and building maintenance; and moving and installing technology. Employees at Beck either worked for several clients and projects at once or were stationed full time on-site as part of the client's facility management team.

Beck and Smith conducted most of the company's marketing, which took the form of networking, nurturing client relationships, following leads, and the occasional write-up in the local press media. Approximately 30% of new jobs came from repeat customers, and most new clients came to Beck Consulting through word-of-mouth. Once a new client was identified, Beck or Smith wrote proposals and conducted negotiations.

Smith maintained a two-month workflow projection based on current jobs and what she and Beck judged to be "in the pipeline." Jobs were assigned to project managers based on their availability and expertise. Employee preferences were taken into account whenever possible. Generally, jobs were given to teams of two or three people. Although one person usually functioned as the primary client contact and maintained a budget and schedule for the project, that person did not have authority over others in the team and did not act as team leader. When the job was completed, members of the team moved on to form new teams around a new project. In large or complex moves, the teams were bigger and Beck or Smith appointed a team leader to manage the overall move. Beck explained the fluid nature of the project manager roles:

People are given projects based mainly on availability. They could be managing a large project this month and put on another project that someone else is running next month. So, a person is not always in charge, nor is he or she always in the position of underling. This structure really makes a difference to how people see their roles.

As Project Manager Makayla Jones explained,

> We don't have politics at Beck. People don't have to vie for position. There's no real hierarchy. People aren't trying to get to the next level, because there is no next level. So, there isn't a sense of competition—just a feeling that we want to do a good job on our projects. We enjoy each other's successes and help out from job to job. There is a lot of camaraderie.

Since most clients wanted to minimize the downtime associated with relocation, the actual moving was done over a short and convenient period of time—usually at night or over a weekend. The team in charge of the move often needed more people to get the job completed on schedule. In particularly large or complex moves, the entire Beck company could be mobilized. As Project Manager Jones explained,

> We think of ourselves as a team— one that needs to work together. Everyone is very good about that. Because even if you're on a two-person team, you may have a large move and you'll need extra help. I've never seen an instance when someone's needed help and no one has come forward. Sure, there are lots of times when you don't know what people are working on, but there are also the times when everyone—even Marilyn—will pitch in and help with a move.

HUMAN RESOURCES

New employees came to Beck Consulting almost exclusively through word-of-mouth. Even in times of low unemployment job markets, the company had never needed to post a help-wanted ad. The company received several unsolicited resumes almost every week. Beck and Smith conducted interviews on an ongoing basis. Most of the resumes came from people with art, architecture, interior design, space planning, or facility management backgrounds. Many had experience as project managers for large companies. Beck felt that despite the word-of-mouth method of hiring, she was diverse in her hiring practices.

Project Manager Steven Brown recalled why he was attracted to Beck Consulting:

> I wanted to work for a small company. I like to keep a balance between my work and personal life and be able, for the most part, to maintain a 40-hour work week. I talked to some people who work for big companies and they had war stories about how many hours they put in. One of the benefits of working at Beck Consulting is that Marilyn and Susan recognize that people have a life outside the office and empower us to manage our own workload and hours.

In the early years of the company, all employees interviewed and approved each new hire. Since the company was so small, Beck wanted to ensure that personalities meshed and that every employee understood and fit into the culture. Project Manager Brown, who was stationed full time at a client site, described a typical Beck Consulting employee:

> We are generally people who can fit in with other people. I like fitting in—I like understanding my client's needs, understanding their organization, and becoming part of it. I keep a reasonable distance while actively taking part in the job and acting in my client's interest. We're chameleons. We can pick up the color of our surrounding environment. It helps to get the job done when you are able to think the way your client thinks.

As the company grew, it was no longer feasible for all employees to be involved in hiring decisions. Instead, new hires met with an ad hoc committee of veteran employees. Project manager Makayla Jones described the hiring process and what she looked for in an applicant:

> Nervous people don't do well here. This is a high stress job. We are usually the last people brought in— after the architect, the builders, and so on. We are also the last people standing there after the move is completed, and we end up taking responsibility for decisions we didn't make. It's also our job to stay on a bit after the move to make sure everyone is settled. Sometime this takes a lot of diplomacy. Lots of people hate their job or hate their company, and the way they express that is to say, "I hate my chair." People will try to gain control over whatever they can. So, we change the chair, the employees are happy, and the project is a success.

> Employees here also need to be comfortable with the lack of formal organizational structure. People come from all kinds of backgrounds. Some, who've come from large organizations with a lot of structure, have a hard time adjusting to the flexibility we have at Beck. We have to work odd hours. We don't have defined roles. And we don't get a lot of formal feedback.

Other than annual reviews conducted by either Beck or Smith, employees were given feedback and direction on a situational basis. Project managers had considerable autonomy over their projects. Jones explained the review process:

> There is a form Marilyn uses for employee reviews, but she just uses it as a guide. I haven't seen her actually fill it out. We are not managed very closely at all. Basically, Marilyn and Susan look at whether we bring our projects in on budget and on time.

At the beginning of a job, they give us a not-to-exceed price based on a scope of work, and then it is up to us to manage the job. We occasionally get feedback from clients through letters or telephone calls. Most times we will ask the client if we can use them as a reference. We get a lot of our jobs through word-of-mouth, so it's important to have a good ongoing relationship with our clients.

Steven Brown described his feelings about the way employees were managed:

> One thing I like more than anything else about this job is that, as far as the client is concerned, I *am* Beck Consulting. We manage ourselves and we represent our own company. I think it's great that I'm a reflection of our company. I've never fully had that feeling before in any other job. It's very satisfying. I have a feeling of ownership without the liability that true ownership would bring.

However, Brown also saw drawbacks to the lack of formal structure:

> I have three people on my team. We are stationed full time at one of our large corporate clients. I am considered the senior person of that team: there is also another project manager and what I'd call a junior person on the team. To the client I am considered the team leader, but at Beck we're all considered to be on the same level. That's where I think there is something lacking in the organization, particularly for junior people who should be receiving regular feedback on their performance from a supervisor. There is some lack of clarity on our parts: our internal roles don't always correspond with our external roles. Most people here seem comfortable with this ambiguity, so I have not made an issue of it.

As one would expect in a service business, payroll and related expenses comprised the largest percentage of expenses. All the project managers at Beck Consulting had the choice of being paid on an hourly *or* salaried basis. Hourly wages and salaries were negotiated individually, with the applicant naming a preferred rate, which Beck compared to other employees in the company with similar experience. Occasionally, Beck researched architectural and design firm employees' pay rates. However, Beck was more concerned with maintaining internal wage parity than comparing with other firms. Most employees chose to be paid hourly. As Beck explained,

> In the early days of the company, people were paid hourly because I wasn't sure we could guarantee full time employment. It was fine with employees—they didn't need the guarantee of a 40-hour salary. Now, paying hourly wages serves as a motivator for people. It's similar to being on a sales force. The employees have some control over how much they make because, in most situations, they can set their schedules. We certainly don't want people working significantly more than 40 hours per week on a regular basis. People know, however, that if they do need to put in that kind of time, they will be paid for it. In certain cases, individuals who are paid hourly make out better on an annual basis than those same individuals would have on salary, so I encourage some people to opt for hourly pay. A few of the people who started out as salaried have eventually asked to go hourly, I have never seen anyone go the other way.

GROWING PAINS

In 2012–2013 many of Beck Consulting's clients experienced growth and mergers, leading the company to double in size from 20 to 40 employees. Up until this point, the company had enjoyed steady, manageable expansion. Project Manager Makayla Jones explained the impact of this growth spurt:

> There was a rough period when we were growing rapidly. We had some growing pains. We went to 40 employees before we had the infrastructure to support them. People were getting hired so quickly. They felt they were thrown into the lion's den without any training. We didn't have time to train, and we weren't able to communicate with each other. On one project a newly hired person did not understand that she needed to report to a project manager for a specific project: the newly hired person did not understand that yesterday's boss could be tomorrow's colleague and yesterday's colleague could be tomorrow's boss. It's hard working in an organization with 38 people when you don't know who some of the new people are.

Quickly, Beck realized that the company needed to change the way it trained new employees:

> It became clear that we could no longer train people just by osmosis. We had to institute a more formal training program, which is basically a mentoring system. New people, regardless of how much work experience they have, are partnered with someone more senior on projects until such time as they can go out on their own.

Jones agreed that the worst of the transition times seemed past:

> As things slowed down a little, we started making time for meetings, and Marilyn and Susan have made an effort to get people to know each other. They tried to shift around the teams to allow people to work with others they hadn't gotten to know

yet. Marilyn started picking names out of a hat and having those people go to lunch with each other. Through all of this rapid growth, Marilyn and Susan have tried to keep up the family atmosphere. For example, they are very tolerant of people's personal lives. Marilyn and Susan try to understand what is going on with everyone and how their personal lives may or may not interfere with their work.

Another way Beck communicated with her growing workforce was a two-hour bi-weekly staff luncheon. All employees attended the meetings—even those stationed off-site. At the meetings, people had a chance to apprise others of particular issues they may have on a project. The company also invited vendors or other experts to give presentations as a way to keep staff up to date on industry issues and new products. The company always paid for lunch, and each meeting concluded with a cake and celebration of staff birthdays.

Growth at Beck Consulting was not only measured in the increased number of client projects and employees. The company was also expanding its capabilities. New employees brought with them a range of skills that Beck Consulting added to its capacities. For example, the company acquired a small interior design firm that had expertise in computer-aided design. Beck Consulting also developed expertise in art collection management. In addition, the company was handling bigger and more complex moving projects that required larger teams of people and a more formal hierarchy to execute. Makayla Jones described the team put in place to conduct the Federal Courthouse move:

> The project was different in that it was more massive than anything I had experienced before. It was the first time we designated an actual team leader, feeling that one person would be most efficient. I was the project leader, and had all the direct client contact. I directed three project managers who worked with the

individual courts. I had to keep the project managers focused, maintain the schedules and budgets, and keep a view of the big picture. It was difficult at first. We had never worked in that kind of a structured team. It caused some tension because previously we'd been equals. But we talked it out and came to an understanding that our roles had to be different for this project. In the end we learned that sometimes we need that kind of structure to get the job done.

For Beck, growth also meant she was forced to step away from project management and the day-to-day oversight of her company. She refocused her role on marketing and public relations. As the company grew, Smith shouldered more and more of the daily responsibility of running the company and supervising employees.

> Marilyn and I play different roles. Marilyn has become a personality—winning awards and being written about in the newspaper. She is now externally focused and involved in the marketing of the company. I am more hands-on, keeping tabs on staffing and the status of projects. Since Marilyn is so much in the public eye and out-of-the office so frequently, I'm not always sure if I should handle Marilyn's clients, if there is an urgent situation.

As Smith and Beck's roles evolved, some employees expressed a sense of ambiguity concerning reporting relationships and authority. As Steven Brown described,

> It's a little hard to say exactly what the reporting structure is here. Clearly Marilyn is the president of the company. I think about her as the overall strategic "picture" person. Susan, I think of more as the general manager/operations director. But I don't feel I have to go to only one of them about a specific problem. They are more like twin managers.

THE FUTURE

As Beck sat at her desk, she felt satisfied that she had built a reputable company, had a great team of people who were happy to work for her, and had a client base that would continue to expand. She knew that some key questions had to be answered in order to meet the future proactively. In what direction should she take the company? What will be the impact of growing from 50 to 100 people? This was very likely to occur in the next year, given the anticipated rate of growth, based in part on the projects they were currently being considered for. How much longer could she pay people on an hourly basis? She was sure that soon she would have to move to a conventional salary model. How would that impact her incentive structure? Beck also felt that she needed to create another layer of management. But should she? What impact would such changes have on teams and leadership of teams?

As Beck became more focused externally, how should she change her role and what should that new role be? Are isolated tensions and ambiguities indicative of systemic problems that could be exacerbated as the company grows? How should Beck Consulting maintain—or change—its structure, culture, and ability to respond quickly and effectively to clients' needs through this period of rapid growth?

STUDY QUESTIONS

1. Draw the current organizational structure of Beck Consulting Corporation (BCC). Have designations for 38 people. How is this organizational chart similar to or different from other organizational charts that you have seen? Next, draw a new organizational chart for BCC with a new layer of management. How many people would you elevate to this new layer of management? Explain your reasoning for the number that you would elevate to the new management roles and note to whom these new managers will report. How do you imagine that this new layer of managers will impact the organizational dynamics within Beck Consulting?

2. What are the advantages and disadvantages of paying professional people on an hourly basis? How should Beck maintain or change her salary model and why? What impact do you imagine a conventional salary model will have on Beck employees? If Beck changes the compensation system from hourly to salary, should she change other aspects of her compensation system?

3. How would you describe the organizational culture at Beck Consulting? How might the purposed new layer of managers impact the organizational culture at BCC? What, if anything, should Beck do if and when she adds a new layer of management?

4. Assume that Beck Consulting chooses to take advantage of current business opportunities and will need to grow to 100 members in the next 9 months in order to respond to the challenges. What changes would you recommend Beck undertake to ensure the continued success of her firm?

CHAPTER SIX

NAVIGATING ORGANIZATIONAL POLITICS AND CULTURE

Chapter Overview

- Change leaders recognize the importance of observing and analyzing the informal components of an organization—power and culture—which are key forces at play within an organization, impacting all stakeholders in the change situation.

- Identifying the power dynamics in an organization is critical to a successful change process. Different sources of power are described, allowing change agents to assess the potential of their power and influence and gain leverage in their organizations, if needed.

- Force field analysis and stakeholder analysis are two tools to advance your understanding of the informal organizational system and how to change it.

- Know yourself as a change leader and stakeholder in the process.

Change leaders' understanding of both the present and desired future state of organizations depends on an analysis of multiple dynamics within organizations. Chapter 5 looked at the formal structures and systems, noting how they impact change initiatives. Chapters 7 and 8 will examine the impact of key individuals in the organization on the change process. This chapter provides the background on the less tangible but no less real aspects of organizations: political dynamics and culture (see Figure 6.1).

It is important to note that in evaluating stakeholders in your organization, you, too, are a stakeholder. To get a full picture of the **informal organization**, it is important to use these political and cultural concepts to evaluate yourself as a part of the system. Be sure to ask yourself how your personality impacts you as a stakeholder and change agent. Evaluate your motivations and understand how you deal with power and how you view your organization's culture.

Figure 6.1   The Change Path Model

Awakening
Chapter 4
1. Identify a need for change and confirm the problems or opportunities that incite the need for change through collection of data.
2. Articulate the gap in performance between the present and the envisioned future state and spread awareness of the data and the gap throughout the organization.
3. Develop a powerful vision for change.
4. Disseminate the vision for the change and why it's needed through multiple communication channels.

Mobilization
Chapters 5 through 8
1. Make sense of the desired change through formal systems and structures, and leverage those systems to reach the change vision (Chapter 5).
2. **Assess power and cultural dynamics at play, and put them to work to better understand the dynamics and build coalitions and support to realize the change (Chapter 6).**
3. Communicate the need for change organization-wide and manage change recipients and various stakeholders as they react to and move the change forward (Chapter 7).
4. Leverage change agent personality, knowledge, skills and abilities, and related assets (e.g., reputation and relationships) for the benefit of the change vision and its implementation (Chapter 8).

Acceleration
Chapter 9
1. Continue to systematically reach out to engage and empower others in support, planning, and implementation of the change. Help them develop needed new knowledge, skills, abilities, and ways of thinking that will support the change.
2. Use appropriate tools and techniques to build momentum, accelerate and consolidate progress.
3. Manage the transition, celebrate small wins and the achievement of milestones along the larger, more difficult path of change.

Institutionalization
Chapter 10
1. Track the change periodically and through multiple balanced measures to help assess what is needed, gauge progress toward the goal, and to make modifications as needed and mitigate risk.
2. Develop and deploy new structures, systems, processes and knowledge, skills, and abilities, as needed, to bring life to the change and new stability to the transformed organization.

If corporate mergers are the ultimate in change-management challenges, then the arrival of a new CEO may also challenge embedded power dynamics and cultural patterns. In December 2000, CEO Jim McNerney arrived at 3M's 28-building, 430-acre, suburban Maplewood, Minnesota campus. Interestingly, McNerney was the first outsider to lead 3M in all of its 98-year history.

YAHOO-TUMBLR MERGER:
POWER AND CULTURAL DIFFERENCES

It was 2007. High-school dropout David Karp founded Tumblr, a blogging service where users own their own pages. It quickly grew due to several factors: young individuals found their voices on the social networking site; like-minded people developed into strong communities; creatives launched Internet memes; and bloggers were offered and accepted numerous book deals. By spring, 2013, when the aging Web pioneer Yahoo bought Tumblr for $1.1 billion in cash, Tumblr had over 108 million blogs and reached 44 million people in the United States and 134 million worldwide. For Marissa Mayer, CEO of Yahoo, buying the social media site was her approach to changing the aging giant Yahoo and bringing in a much-needed young demographic to the company.

Skeptics of the purchase immediately talked about potential problems. Many analysts wondered how Yahoo would be transformed when it was not clear how Tumblr would ever become profitable. Karp had disliked and distrusted advertising and he and other Tumblr executives had not figured out how to monetize its bloggers. In 2012 he had burned through $25 million in cash, and by 2013 investors were not rushing in with additional money at an acceptable valuation. Karp, in other words, needed a savior and in May, 2013, CEO Mayer looked like a potential rescuer for Karp and Tumblr's investors. At the announcement of the purchase for $1.1 billion, Mayer promised not to "screw it up" for Tumblr's users.

The young demographic that Yahoo wanted, however, brought with them a particular culture: an acceptance of sexually explicit content on Tumblr. Advertisers, on the other hand, would not have their ads run on pages that featured pornography. Yahoo needed to figure out a policy that would keep young users on Tumblr while not offending advertisers and Yahoo customers. They never did figure out this cultural clash.

At first California-based Mayer and Yahoo executives had a hands-off approach to Tumblr

and its 175 employees in New York City. By 2015, however, Mayer set a very aggressive target of $100 million in revenue for Tumblr; but, she set this goal with little input from its executives. A year later when the revenue target had not been hit, Mayer abruptly merged Tumblr's ad sales team with Yahoo's under an executive who had little experience or rapport with Tumblr employees. Quickly, Tumblr employees headed for the exit doors. The next year Mayer again reorganized the ad sales teams into two separate groups with chaos and anger following in the wake of the separation. More employees headed for the door.

By spring, 2016, Yahoo and Mayer hinted that the $1.1 billion Tumblr acquisition was a waste of money. At that time Yahoo reduced its overall workforce by 15%, closed offices around the world, and began its search for a private equity or corporate buyer, such as Verizon. Finally, in June, 2017, Verizon announced that it had bought Yahoo and, with it, Tumblr.

A tangle of issues—as many as five to seven—undid this merger. No one figured out how to make money at Tumblr. While Mayer's hands-off policy with a continent between the two companies seemed appropriate at first, it also meant that employees kept their own assumptions and ways of the seeing the world rather than finding useful common ground in a shared culture. When Mayer did step in, people said that it was too little, too late, and too aggressive, particularly around the super-sized revenue goal. Mayer's appointed leaders did not connect with Tumblr's employees who bolted when they did not like Yahoo's actions. There was conflict between Yahoo's leaders and Tumblr's employees who reported being confused at the mixed signals which came from Sunnyvale, California.

In short, Mayer and her team never did the hard work of bringing together two diverse workplaces and workforces into a common culture. Nor did they deal effectively with issues of power and influence.[1]

3M's CEOs usually rise from within, after being steeped in the corporation's culture and philosophy. However, 3M employees found that the new CEO was able to work with those around him.

MCNERNEY ENTERS 3M

Jim McNerney's style has let employees to feel that they, not McNerney, are driving the changes. He was able to introduce data-driven change without forcing his ideas from General Electric onto the organization.

McNerney was able to rely on existing 3M management rather than importing other GE executives. "I think the story here is rejuvenation of a talented group of people rather than replacement of a mediocre group of people," he says. As part of his change plan, he avoids giving orders

and reinforces the 3M culture whenever he can. "This is a fundamentally strong company. The inventiveness of the people here is in contrast with any other place I've seen. Everybody wakes up in the morning trying to figure out how to grow. They really do." This diplomacy generally played well with the 3M faithful. "He's delivered a very consistent message," says Althea Rupert, outgoing chair of Technical Forum, an internal society for all 3M technical people. "There's a sense of speed and a sense of urgency."[2]

In the 3M case, McNerney shows a clear understanding of the players, their perspectives, and their needs, and this made the implementation much easier to accomplish. Perhaps McNerney had no choice. But he did act in ways that involved people, focused their attention and interest, and brought them along rather than attempting to impose an outside set of views.

While the stories of the Yahoo-Tumblr merger and the installation of a new leader within a fully functional 3M are quite different, they demonstrate the impact of power dynamics and the influence of an organization's culture. How change leaders deal with power and behavioral organizational norms and the difficult-to-define, amorphous organizational culture will affect the speed and nature of the change.

When assessing possible responses to change initiatives, leaders need to recognize the impact that individual and organizational history can have. Employees may have had significant experience with change that leads them to be wary. They may have also worked with the existing approaches and have their own perspectives on what change is needed, so ambivalence and concern are natural—particularly in individuals who have demonstrated commitment to the organization and the quality of the outcomes achieved.[3] Some change projects are downsizings in disguise and yet change leaders somehow expect employees to welcome such initiatives with open arms. Surely, such optimism is naïve!

POWER DYNAMICS IN ORGANIZATIONS

Mention the words "organizational politics," and many people roll their eyes, throw up their hands, and say, "I don't want to have anything to do with politics!" The assumption is that organizational politics is inherently dirty, mean-spirited, destructive, and that organizations and their members would be better off without "politics."

Bolman and Deal make a persuasive argument that organizational "politics is the realistic process of making decisions and allocating resources in a context of scarcity and divergent issues. This view puts politics at the heart of decision making."[4] Negotiating, according to Bolman and Deal, is the key process in organizational politics. The marketing department, for example, wants to redesign the organization's website, while the technology folks push back saying, "Not now! We have our hands full as we install the XYZ platform!" In short, organizational politics is the push-and-pull between and among individuals and departments and who gets what resources. There is nothing inherently good or bad about power. Rather, it is the application and purposeful use of power and its consequences that will determine whether it is "good" or "bad."

In fact, the power to do things in organizations is critical to achieving change. Power is a crucial resource used by change agents to influence the actions and reactions of others. The knowledgeable change agent asks multiple power-related questions, such as, What power do I have and what are the sources of my power? What am I authorized to do by virtue of my title and position? What signatory authority and what dollar limits of expenditure does my position have? For example, can I hire someone based on my signature alone, or do I need to obtain approval for the hiring from HR? These questions help change agents to diagnose their formal authority and power.

Individual Power

While organizations confer specific authority and power on particular positions, change agents also need to be perceived as influential. Change agents need to articulate positive beliefs about power—and to be aware of others' perception of their power. There are both internal psychological and external, reality-based roadblocks to exercising power. Clearly, power can be real—one can influence people with knowledge, persuade them by strength of personality and integrity, or use rewards and punishments to direct people's behaviors. But the perception of power is just as important, if not more important, than the actual resources that a manager holds. If others do not believe that a person is influential, then the facts will have little impact until those perceptions are changed. The rookie manager has the same formal power as the experienced one. However, the perception of their power and influence are generally very different. Often the perception that an individual has power to act is all employees need. When individuals have the trust of their CEOs, for instance, they want to maintain that trust and are therefore not likely to use inappropriate influence tactics on their boss.[5]

What gives people power in organizations? Individuals have power because of the position they hold, who they are (character and reputation), and who and what they know. When position, reputation, and expertise combine in one individual, that individual is likely to be powerful. These individual sources of power are classified in Table 6.1.[6]

Departmental Power

In addition to personal influence, departments within an organization may have different levels of power. This power is dependent on the centrality of the work the department does, the availability of people to accomplish important

Table 6.1	Types of Individual Power
Positional Power	• This is the legitimate authority of the title and position; it includes control and access to resources and the ability to formally make decisions and allocate resources. • The formal authority to make decisions is a major source of power.*
Network Power	• Power in this area comes from the quality of the informal and formal network of connections that permits a person to access and pass on valuable information. • People with large networks of colleagues across organizational levels and boundaries have access to more information and are often perceived to be more influential.
Knowledge Power	• Expertise and knowledge is particularly important in some organizations; it is particularly important in such organizations as pharmaceutical and consulting firms. • Expert power is the possession of a body of knowledge essential to the organization; credentials provide independent certification of expertise and increase one's ability to influence. • Information power is clout gained through the flow of facts and data: by creating, framing, redirecting, or distorting information and by controlling who receives the information. • Knowledge power also relates to a person's depth of understanding of how things work in the organization in order to get things done. This relates to both the formal (e.g., how the formal approval process works) and the informal processes (e.g., how power and influence really manifest themselves in the organization) that influence how the organization operates.
Personality Power	• The ability to inspire trust and enthusiasm from others provides many leaders with significant individual power. Sometimes leaders have charisma, a special charm that pulls people to them. • Reputation, which comes from people's experiences with the person, includes reports of success (or failure), and influences personal power.

organizational tasks, and the ability of the department to handle the organization's environment. These can be categorized as follows:

- *Ability to cope with environmental uncertainty:* Departments gain power if they are seen to make the environment appear certain. Thus, marketing and sales departments gain power by bringing in future orders, diminishing the impact of competitors' actions, and providing greater certainty about the organization's future vitality in the marketplace. During times of economic turbulence, finance departments gain power

---

*Another way of looking at this type of power is in terms of "yea-saying" or "nay-saying" power. Yea-saying means that a person can make it happen. For example, he or she could decide who would be hired. Nay-saying power means that a person could prevent something from happening. Thus, nay-saying power would mean that someone could prevent a particular person from being hired but could not decide who would be hired.

through their ability to help the firm navigate its way. Likewise, other departments and functions either enhance or diminish their power based upon their ability to absorb uncertainty and make the world more predictable and manageable for the organization.

- *Low substitutability:* Whenever a function is essential and no one else can do it, the department has power. Think, for example, of the power of human resources departments when no one else can authorize hiring of new personnel or the power of technology departments that often gets to decide what kind of hard- and software a firm will buy and use.

- *Centrality:* Power flows to those departments whose activities are central to the survival and strategy of the organization or when other departments depend on the department for the completion of work. In most large white-collar organizations, systems people have power because of our dependence on the computer and the information derived from it. Close the management information systems and you shut down the organization. Highly regarded and well-developed information systems anchor the success of firms such as Federal Express, Walmart, and Statistics Canada.

Hardy added to our understanding of the sources of power with her classification.[7] She described three dimensions of power:

1. *Resource power*—the access to valued resources in an organization. These include rewards, sanctions, coercion, authority, credibility, expertise, information, political affiliations, and group power. Resource power is very similar to the individual power listed above.

2. *Process power*—the control over formal decision-making arenas and agendas. Examples of process power would be the power to include or exclude an item on a discussion agenda. Nominating committees have significant process power as they determine who gets to sit on committees that make decisions.

3. *Meaning power*—the ability to define the meaning of things. Thus, the meaning of symbols and rituals and the use of language provide meaning power. For example, a shift from reserved parking and large corner offices for executives to first-come parking and common office space can symbolize a significant move away from the reliance on hierarchical power.

Hardy's introduction of process and meaning power adds significantly to the understanding of how one might influence a change situation. Anyone who has tried to get an item added to a busy agenda will understand the frustration of not having process power.

While many sources of power exist, the type of power used by managers can have different effects. Some types of influence are used more frequently than others. One research study found that managers used different influence tactics depending on whether they were attempting to influence superiors or subordinates. Table 6.2 outlines the usage of these **power tactics**. It shows that managers claim they use rational methods in persuading others. The use of overt

Table 6.2 Usage Frequency of Different Power Tactics		
	When Managers Influence Superiors	**When Managers Influence Subordinates**
Most Popular Tactic	Use and give reasons	Use and give reasons
↑	Develop coalitions	Be assertive
	Act friendly	Act friendly
	Negotiate	Develop coalitions
↓	Be assertive	Bargain
Least Popular Tactic	Refer to a higher authority	Refer to higher authority
		Apply sanctions

Source: Kipnis, D., Schmidt, S. M., Swaffin-Smith, C., & Wilkinson, I. (1984, Winter). Patterns of managerial influence: Shotgun managers, tacticians and bystanders. *Organizational Dynamics,* 12(3), 56–67.

power, either by referring something to a higher authority or by applying sanctions, is not a popular tactic.

Change agents, like all managers, need to think of themselves as "politicians."[8] Defining oneself as an organizational "politician" will suggest the need to negotiate, develop coalitions, build and use alliances, deal with the personality of the decision maker, and use contacts and relationships to obtain vital information. Savvy change leaders do not underestimate the need for power and influence in their determination to make something happen.

See **Toolkit Exercise 6.2** to assess different kinds of power.

ORGANIZATIONAL CULTURE AND CHANGE

Organizational culture: What does it mean?

The concept of organizational culture is fairly new. While psychologists talked about group "norms" and social climates in organizations as early as 1939,[9] the concept of "culture" only began to attract organizational behavior researchers in the 1980s and 1990s.[10] Now, the idea is widely used among academics and practitioners alike: A 2014 search on Amazon books by the words "organization culture" yielded a listing of over 47,000 plus books.[11] The widespread use of the term has not, unfortunately, created a standard definition. However, Ed Schein's definition, which has been published in five editions of his book *Organization Culture and Leadership* (1992, 1996, 2004, 2010, and 2016), dominates the field and is quite useful in thinking about the phenomenon. Schein defined culture as follows:

(1) a pattern of shared basic assumptions

(2) that was learned by a group

(3) as it solved its problems of external adaptation and internal integration

(4) that has worked well enough to be considered valid and,

(5) therefore, is taught to new members

(6) as the correct way to perceive, think, and feel in relation to those problems [numbers were added by the authors].

Note the complexity of this definition with its six sub-parts. Schein is concerned with a group and its learning; with how an organization adjusts to the external environment's ever-evolving demands and how internal players respond coherently and in alignment to those challenges; the fact that these ways of behaving are taught to new members "in a socialization process that is itself a reflection of (the) culture"; and that the culture promotes a particular way of thinking and feeling about problems.

How to Analyze a Culture

To assess a culture, Schein identified three levels for analysis. The first level is the visible aspect—or artifacts—of the organization. These include everything from how employees dress and the design of an organization's buildings to its structures and processes. While artifacts are easy to see, their meaning can be difficult to decipher and an observer needs to be careful to ascribe meaning to a single artifact or observation. The second level is an organization's "espoused beliefs and values"; this second level includes an organization's articulated mission, values, and strategy. Most change agents begin to change an organization by starting at this level of culture. The third level is the "basic underlying assumptions" that have become so ingrained and so much a part of a group's thinking and perspective on the world that they are not questioned. Since these assumptions remain largely unarticulated, they are also non-debatable, making them extremely difficult to change. For example, a university faculty may see itself as caring passionately about the quality of the classroom experience, and protect its beliefs by actions that serve to silence anyone who raises questions in this area.

Many founders of organizations explicitly set out to establish a culture that is compatible with their beliefs about how organizations operate best and the values that should be embedded in the organization. For example, Gretchen Fox, founder and former CEO of FOX Relocation Management Corp., Boston, had worked in excessively hierarchical law firms before she started her relocation firm. At law firms she had observed large, physically fit men who were senior partners in the firm and whereby held high-level positions in the organization's hierarchy. These men would ignore low-level women staff as they lifted and carried heavy boxes and bottles of water. For Fox, the human thing for the men to do would have been to help with the heavy lifting. Fox decided then and there that when she built her business, she would establish a flat, non-hierarchical firm. This belief was embedded in the layout of offices (Fox's office was a regular-sized office in a row of offices, leaving the light-filled sunny corner spaces for employees); in the minimal use of titles; in a collective, decision-making process for hiring new employees; and in a rational approach to work that did not involve status in the hierarchy.

As FOX Relocation grew, some of the observable artifacts—such as titles—needed to change to accommodate folks in the external world's understanding of who did what inside the firm. The question became this: What else, if anything, needed to change inside the firm to adapt to its growth and to the external environment while maintaining the integrity of its culture?

Tips for Change Agents to Assess a Culture

A change agent, then, needs to assess a culture at three levels. Such an analysis may lead to innovative ways to change a culture.

1. *Observe the artifacts:* How do people dress? How are offices arranged? What is the space differential for offices between top-level executives and other people who work in the organization? How are parking lots and spaces assigned, and who pays and does not pay for a space? How do members of the organization interact and relate to one another? Where and how are meals eaten? Is there an executive dining room and separate food for executives?

2. *Read documents and talk to people to gain an understanding of an organization's espoused beliefs and values:* What does the organization say about itself on its website and social media platforms? What are the articulated mission, values, and strategy statements? What does it brag about in its press releases? Ask five to ten people: What does this organization value and believe in? What, if any, of its documents have changed in the past five years? How have they changed, and are these changes in alignment with changes in the artifacts of the organization?

3. *Observe and ask people about underlying assumptions:* Since these are often unarticulated and their origins developed years before, it may be difficult for people to express the organization's fundamental suppositions. Observers need to look for clues on fundamental issues: What is the basic orientation to time in terms of past, present, and future? What time units are most relevant for the conduct of the organization's business? For example, colleges and universities orient around the quarter or semesters, units of time that are not relevant to most businesses but would be to bookstores that serve universities and landlords who rent to students. A second example would be the nature of human beings: "Are humans basically good, neutral, or evil, and is human nature perfectible or fixed?" (p. 429).[12] It is important to consider these fundamental issues, and then search for and develop hypotheses about what needs to change to improve the outcomes experienced and how to go about it.

CLASHING WORKPLACE CULTURES*

Training & Careers, Inc. (TCI), a small nonprofit agency, focused on job training and placement for low-income residents included programs in culinary arts, janitorial work, and hotel and hospitality training. Due to financial issues, TCI merged with Careers, Inc. (CI), a national nonprofit that had a similar mission and programs. TCI, headquartered in Boston, had a relaxed and autonomous work culture. Careers, Inc. (CI), headquartered in New York City, had a

(Continued)

(Continued)

regimented and tightly supervised workforce. As the organizations began to merge their operations, they neglected to address the differences in their workforce cultures. TCI was made up of white-collar staff, 25% of whom held a master's degree in social work. TCI was able to attract this talent by offering flexible work schedules, three weeks of paid vacation, and letting the staff out early most Fridays. CI's workforce, on the other hand, attracted largely blue-collar workers who led the janitorial training programs. This workforce had strict time reporting guidelines and few vacation incentives, as their compensation was commensurate with their high school or associate's level education.

As the organizations attempted to merge, TCI experienced significant pushback from its employees as CI eliminated early-release Fridays and proposed cutting vacations. TCI moved away from staff autonomy by adopting CI's time clock system, which required employees to punch in and out each day. Because the leaders of the two organizations did not sufficiently understand the cultural differences and take these into account during the merger, TCI experienced a 43% turnover of frontline staff following the merger. Remaining staff were disgruntled and openly sought other job opportunities outside the organization.

_____

* The names and locations of the organizations are disguised.

This vignette suggests three levels of organizational culture. The time clock system, requiring employees to punch in and out each day, is an artifact that was present in one of the organizations, but not the other. The espoused beliefs and values were discernable in the comparable missions and programs of the two organizations and pointed to potential friction points. Further, the underlying assumptions of who to hire and how to manage them suggests differences at the third level of culture. At Careers Inc., executives believed that staff needed to be tightly controlled and supervised to make sure that they did a day's work. By contrast, the underlying assumption of TCI was that staff accepted lower pay in return for more autonomy and time off perks. When this assumption was challenged, the results were disastrous.

To create one organization and one culture, the executives at CI required all of its employees to use the time clock, punching in and out daily. In making this requirement, CI executives sent a signal about their core beliefs about the nature of human beings and how they should be managed.

TOOLS TO ASSESS THE NEED FOR CHANGE

Individuals choose to consider and adopt a proposed organizational change—or choose not to. Sometimes they do this willingly and other times they choose reluctantly, either feeling forced or mixed about their decisions. This perspective is valuable when thinking about increasing the success of organizational change, for it is at the individual level that people decide to change. Their choices depend on their views of the situation and how it impacts their lives.

In the recent past, many change programs have been focused on cost cutting, including the downsizing of the number of employees in an organization. People are bright. They understand what is happening. And if a program will cost them their jobs, why would you expect them to be enthusiastic and positive? Such resistance demonstrates the point that individuals will choose to cooperate or not depending on their personal circumstances and their assessment of how the change will impact them personally. Individuals will adopt or accept change only when they think that their perceived personal benefits are greater than the perceived costs of change. This can be summarized as follows:

CHANGE OCCURS WHEN

Perceived Benefits of Change > Perceived Cost of Change

This simple formula highlights several things. First, change agents have to deal with both the reality of change and its perceptions. Again, perception counts as much as reality. Second, in many situations, the costs of changing are more evident than the benefits of change. In most change situations, first the costs are incurred and then the benefits follow. The perceived benefits of change depend on whether people think the benefits are likely—that is, the probability of the change being successful in ways that count for them. As well, the benefits of change depend on the state of happiness or dissatisfaction with the status quo. Interestingly, people also tend to focus on the consequences of the change rather than the consequences of remaining the same. The more dissatisfied people are, the more they as individuals will be willing to change. The **change equation** can be modified to capture this as follows:

CHANGE OCCURS WHEN

Dissatisfaction × Benefits × Success > Cost

Where

    Dissatisfaction = Perception of dissatisfaction with the status quo
    Benefits = Perception of the benefits of change
    Success = Perception of the probability of success
    Cost = Perceived cost of change

Thus, change agents need to build the case for change by increasing the dissatisfaction with the status quo by providing data that demonstrate that other options are better, demonstrating that the overall benefits are worth the effort of the change, and showing that the change effort is likely to succeed. When discussing these factors with others, it's useful to extend the assessment beyond the rational, "head-related" factors such as cost savings, market share, improved profitability, and competitive advantage. The assessment should extend to "heart-related" matters, such as the human impact of the change on employees, work teams, the department/division, customers and the community. *Doing your homework, engaging others in conversations about the change, and early successes are important parts of the change agent's toolkit in the early stages of a change initiative.*

It is important to differentiate between the costs and benefits to the organization and the costs and benefits to individuals. Too often, change leaders focus on the organizational benefits and miss the impact at the individual level. The earlier example highlighted this. If an individual sees that the change will increase profits and result in job loss, why would a manager expect support? It takes very secure people who feel they have alternatives and are being equitably treated to be positive under these circumstances even if they believe the change is needed for the organization.

Table 6.3 captures this. It contrasts the impact on individuals with the impact on the organization to predict the resulting support for a change initiative. The purpose of Table 6.3 is to encourage change leaders to avoid the trap of assuming that positive organizational outcomes will automatically be supported by individuals.

Table 6.3	Organizational and Individual Consequences and the Support for Change	
Perceived Impact of the Change on the Organization	**Perceived Impact of the Change on the Individual**	**Direction of Support of the Change**
Positive consequences for the organization	Positive outcome for the individual (e.g., less work, better work)	Strong support for change
Positive consequences for the organization	Negative outcome for the individual (e.g., more work, worse work)	Indeterminate support for change but very possibly resistance
Neutral consequences for the organization	Positive outcome for the individual (e.g., less work, better work)	Positive support for change
Neutral consequences for the organization	Negative outcome for the individual (e.g., more work, worse work)	Resistance to change
Negative consequences for the organization	Positive outcome for the individual (e.g., less work, better work)	Indeterminate support for change
Negative consequences for the organization	Negative outcome for the individual (e.g., more work, worse work)	Resistance to change

In addition to considering the direct impact of a change on a person, individuals will also think about and be influenced by the effects of the change on their coworkers and teammates. The strength of interpersonal bonds, including the shared values, goals, and norms within an organization, can have a significant impact on attitudes and actions. The traditions of how work is divided, how people and departments interact or do not, and simply the way of doing business create a culture within an organization. The desire to maintain the organization's traditions, even if there is a mutual understanding for a need to move on, can hinder the acceptance of changes. This challenge is greater if there are shifts in roles and responsibilities and therefore a shift in power. A change leader needs to understand and respect individuals' and organizational history and the individual members' perceptions of that history to effectively negotiate the change process and appropriately engage stakeholders.

Change agents need to think of the impact on individuals—particularly people critical to the change. When doing so, consider also the people who will actually have to change and how they will view the change equation and assess the benefits, costs, and risks. A general manager may decide that new systems are needed, but it is the individual who will be operating the systems who will have to learn how to work with them and change his or her behavior.

To consider the perceived impact of change see **Toolkit Exercise 6.3**.

Identifying the Organizational Dynamics at Play

Each of the organizational models introduced in Chapters 2 and 3 assumed that organizations consist of people, systems, and structures that interact according to different forces at play. In organizational change, the key is to understand the forces and how they respond to shifts in pressure. In system terms, the technical term is *homeostasis*, meaning a system has a tendency toward a relatively stable equilibrium among its interdependent factors. Organizations are as they are because the forces involved are in balance. If one force is changed, it could affect many things and may well be resisted. Alternatively, it may give rise to unanticipated support for the change.

Two tools are particularly useful in helping change leaders to understand such forces and why the organization changes or doesn't.

1. **Force field analysis**—a process of identifying and analyzing the driving and restraining forces impacting an organization's objectives

2. **Stakeholder analysis**—a process of identifying the key individuals or groups in the organization who can influence or who are impacted by the proposed change and then of working with those individuals or groups to make them more positive to notions of change

Once these tools have been deployed, it is important to integrate them. Stakeholders will show up in the force field analysis as forces that need to be considered, and an in-depth assessment of them in the stakeholder analysis will put the change agent in a stronger position to manage those forces in ways that will advance the change.

Force Field Analysis[13]

The force field analysis identifies the forces for and against change. In situations that are stable or in equilibrium, the forces for change (driving forces) and the forces opposing change (restraining forces) are balanced. To create change, the balance must be upset by adding new pressures for change; increasing the strength of some or all of the pressures for change; reducing or eliminating the pressures against change; or converting a restraining force into a driving force. Figure 6.2 depicts a force field analysis chart.

Figure 6.2   Force Field Analysis

Driving Forces   Restraining Forces

Pressures for change come in many shapes and include both internal and external sources. External factors often are the initial triggers that give rise to internal pressures. External driving forces could include benchmark data and various market forces that are putting pressure on senior management to improve their performance in the private sector. Politicians concerned about increased costs or declining service levels could generate driving forces in the public sector. Alternatively, external factors may involve opportunities for future growth or access to special incentives (e.g., tax relief) designed to promote certain activities. Internal pressures, such as the vision of a champion, work group attitudes and norms, and internal systems (e.g., the reward system) that are aligned with the change have the potential to act as driving forces.

Restraining forces for change might come from lack of access to sufficient resources, missing skills and abilities, power dynamics, cultural norms, and/or formal organizational systems that are incongruent with the change. They can also come from outside of the organization in the form of customer and supplier concerns, industry standards, rules, and regulations. For example, if innovation is part of the desired change, control systems that focus on efficiency and minimize experimentation or variance from standards to reduce costs will act as a restraining force. Changes that are seen as threats to individuals will lead to resistance. Habits or patterns of behavior that could impede the change might be difficult to alter, even when individuals are supportive. The longer those habits have been in place, the more difficulty individuals will have in extricating themselves from those patterns. Work group norms, informal leadership patterns, and workplace culture may act as either driving or restraining forces, depending on the situation.

To do a force field analysis,

1. Identify the forces acting in the situation and estimate their strength. Both the immediate and the long-term forces need to be considered. The immediate forces are the ones that are acting now and have an immediate impact (e.g., quarterly sales targets). The long-term forces

are those that may have less immediate effect but whose impact may linger longer, such as customer satisfaction or employee morale.

2. Understand how the forces might be altered to produce a more hospitable climate for the change and develop strategies that will maximize your leverage on the driving and restraining forces with the minimum effort. Conserving your energy and resources is important because change management is a marathon, not a 100-yard dash.

3. Look beyond the immediate impact and identify ways to increase support and reduce resistance. Consider unanticipated consequences that may result from what is implemented. For example, you may be able to reduce resistance by throwing financial rewards at individuals, but in doing so you may inadvertently promote unethical behavior, reduce organizational commitment, and destroy your compensation system.

In the 3M example mentioned earlier, the appointment of McNerney created a new force in the organization. The Six Sigma system he introduced from GE was data driven and thus appealed to the values of 3M employees. At the same time, he reduced defensiveness as a force by praising the 3M culture and showed how the employees could achieve more by focusing on the data and explicit goals. All of these things added to forces for change and reduced or eliminated forces against change. As positive outcomes began to ensue from these initiatives, the process provided sustaining reinforcement.

Strebel suggests looking at force field analysis graphically. That is, consider the forces for and against change separately—not necessarily opposing each other directly but operating orthogonally (at right angles).[14] Figure 6.3 shows this.

Strebel's view of the change arena allows us to plot where forces for and against change are in balance. The change arena helps us to identify four areas with which many change agents are familiar: areas of constant or **continuous change**, areas of high resistance, areas of "breakpoint" change, and areas of "sporadic" or "flip-flop" change. With **breakpoint change**, pressures are significant and the resistance will be strong. Under these circumstances, resistance will prevent change until the driving forces strengthen to the point that the system snaps to a new configuration. For example, World War II was seen by many Americans to be someone else's battle until the attack on Pearl Harbor dramatically altered the status quo. When breakpoint change occurs, it will be radical and create significant upheaval because of the strength of the changes involved. The situations faced by General Motors and the UAW in 2006 and 2009 are classic breakpoint situations. The market pressures on General Motors were very strong. The UAW faced equally strong resistance forces from both active and retired members, who wished to protect their health benefits and their pension plans.[15] In 2006, this led to significant concessions from the UAW, but these were a pale imitation of those obtained in 2009 after GM exercised breakpoint change through declaring bankruptcy and seeking court protection while it restructured.

In **flip-flop changes**, forces are weak and change events are not very important, and the situation could change only to reverse itself easily. Flip-flop changes tend to occur when participants have shifting preferences or are ambivalent concerning matters that are of only modest importance to them.

Figure 6.3   Forces for and Against Change

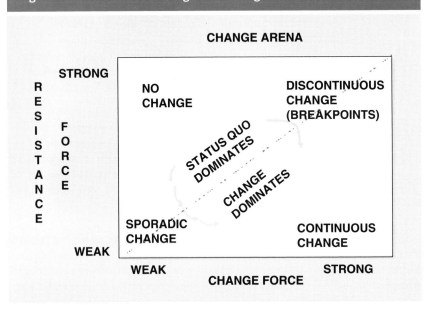

Source: Strebel, P. (1994, Winter). Choosing the right change path. *California Management Review*, 29–51.

Force field analysis requires careful thinking about the dynamics of the situation and organization, including how people, structures, and systems affect and are affected by what is happening. How will these factors assist or prevent change?

Toolkit Exercise 6.4 asks you to do a force field analysis in order to develop your skills in this area.

Such analysis does lead individuals to think in relatively linear ways—forces are either for or against change. Their influence is linear and direct. However, a different, more nonlinear perspective is often needed. A tool called stakeholder analysis is valuable in gaining insights into a nonlinear interactive view of organizations.

Stakeholder Analysis

Stakeholder analysis is the identification of those who can affect the change or who are affected by the change. Included in this is the analysis of the positions, the motives, and the power of all key stakeholders. Stakeholder management is the explicit influencing of critical participants in the change process. It is the identification of the "entanglements" in the organization, the formal and informal connections between people, structures, and systems.

The purpose of stakeholder analysis is to develop a clear understanding of the key individuals who can influence the outcome of a change and thus be in a better position to appreciate their positions and recognize how best to manage them and the context. A useful starting point is to think carefully about who will be affected and who has to change their behavior in order for the change to be successful. An obvious but often overlooked point is exactly that—someone or some people will be affected and some will have to change their behavior!* Once the key person or persons are identified, change leaders must focus on who influences those people and who has the resources and/or power to make the change happen or to prevent it from happening.

In doing a stakeholder analysis, the first step is to identify those people who need to be concentrated on. A change leader can identify those people by asking the following questions:

- Who has the authority to say "yes" or "no" to the change?

- Which areas or departments or people will be impacted by the change? How will they likely react, and who leads and has influence in those areas and departments? Note that the stakeholders relevant to a change do not always reside in the organization and can include customers, suppliers, communities, and government bodies.

- Who has to change their behavior or act differently for the change to be successful? This is a key question—the change ultimately rests on having these people doing things differently.

- Who has the potential to particularly ease the path to change, and who has the potential to be particularly disruptive?

Savage developed a model that plots stakeholders on two dimensions: their potential for threat and their potential for cooperation.[16] If a stakeholder has high potential for both threat and cooperation, Savage suggests that a collaborative approach should be developed. In this way, the stakeholder is brought onside and his or her support obtained. If the stakeholder is supportive, that is, has high potential for cooperation and low potential for threat, Savage argues for a strategy of involvement where the change agent maximizes support from the stakeholder. A stakeholder who is non-supportive, that is, has limited potential for cooperation but high potential for threat, should be defended against. Finally, a marginal stakeholder, one with limited potential for either cooperation or threat, should be monitored to ensure the assessment is correct.

Once these vested interests are mapped, the change leader can examine the effects of organizational systems and structures. Only with this deep understanding can change be managed well.

Change agents need to know who the key participants are, their motivations, and the relationships between them. Creating a visual picture of the key participants and their interrelationships can be helpful to understanding the dynamics of the situation. A stakeholder map lays out the positions of people pictorially and allows the change agent to quickly see the interdependencies. In drawing stakeholder maps, some add complexity: Members of the same groups can be encircled; different thickness of lines can be used to signify the strength of the relationship; different colors can be used to signify different things (e.g., level of support or resistance); or arrows can be used to point to influence patterns, with their thickness often used to characterize the strength of the relationship.

---

*We are reminded of the old definition of insanity: Doing the same thing over and over, but expecting a different result!

The only constraint on the construction of a stakeholder map is one's ability to translate data into a meaningful visual depiction of the key stakeholders and their interrelationships. As noted earlier, it is critical to not leave out stakeholders that are external to the organization. External stakeholders create and are a part of important dynamics, and understanding their connection to the organization as well as their power and influence will help the change agent in plotting the complete landscape.

Some of the factors that are useful to depict are

- their wants and needs,

- their likely responses to the change,

- how they are linked,

- their sources and level of power and influence,

- the actual influence patterns,

- how they currently benefit from the status quo,

- how they may benefit from the change, and

- how they may be worse off from the change.

Figure 6.4 shows a hypothetical stakeholder map.
Cross and Prusak classify organizational members as:

- **Central connectors**—people who link with one another. For example, Stakeholder #4 links Stakeholders #2, #3, and #6.

- **Boundary spanners**—people who connect the formal and/or informal networks to other parts of the organization. In the map, the change agent and Stakeholder #4 are both serving as boundary spanners.

- **Information brokers**—people who link various subgroups. In Figure 6.4, the change agent has the potential to play that role.

- **Peripheral specialists**—people who have specialized expertise in the network.[17] Once the stakeholder map is developed, change agents can visually see groupings and influence patterns, levels of support and resistance, and the strength of existing groupings and relationships. They can use this map to assess their assumptions concerning the stakeholders by soliciting input and feedback from others. Action plans can be reviewed relative to the map and to see if the strategies and tactics are likely to produce stakeholder responses that will contribute to the desired results. These are just a few of the ways these maps can be applied.

Once the stakeholder map is developed, change agents can visually see groupings and influence patterns, levels of support and resistance, and the strength of existing groupings and relationships. They can use this map to assess their assumptions concerning the stakeholders by soliciting additional input and feedback. Action plans can be reviewed relative to the map, to see if the strategies and approaches are likely to produce stakeholder responses that will contribute to the desired results. These are just a few of the ways that the map can be applied.

Figure 6.4   Hypothetical Stakeholder Map

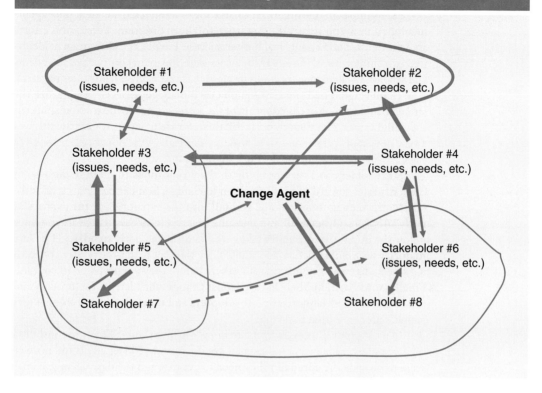

Understanding the positions of key players or stakeholders is essential if a change agent is to alter the forces that resist change and strengthen those that promote change. One can think about moving each stakeholder on **a change continuum** from an **awareness** of the issues to **interest** to a **desire for action** to **taking action** or supporting action on the change. One also wants to guard against unnecessarily driving them to actively resist the change.

Awareness → Interest → Desire for action → Take action

Classifying stakeholders according to this continuum is useful because it can guide what change tools you should use. For example, in the initial stages of a change process, the issue may be one of creating awareness of the need for change. Here, one-on-one communication to organization-wide publicity counts. Articles in an internal organizational newspaper can educate people. Forums or open sessions discussing the issues can play a role. Addresses by senior executives can both inform and generate interest in a topic. Benchmark data can convince skeptics that change is necessary, and a special budgetary allocation or a pilot project can pave the way for people to try out a change program. Which tactics are most appropriate to use at different points in time will depend on the situation; the people affected; the change agent's skills, abilities, reputation, and relationships; as well as on the organization's culture and previous experiences with change.

As a general rule, change leaders should shift from low-intensity forms of communication to high-intensity forms as individuals shift from awareness to interest and action. Impersonal but educational messages might inform, but persuasion often takes direct one-on-one action.

For example, in one organization, the CEO wanted independent sales agents to adopt a new and relatively expensive software program. Persuasion efforts about the costs and benefits had limited success. Finally, the change agent identified two things: First, the key influencers were the managers of the sales agents and second, these managers could be classed as supportive, neutral, or negative. The change agent had the CEO phone each manager directly, emphasize the strategic importance of the adoption of the software, query them about concerns they might have, and then directly ask them for their support. Clearly, this was a very powerful and persuasive technique, using all of the power and prestige of the CEO along with his considerable interpersonal skills.[18]

Stakeholders will vary not only in their **readiness to change** but also in their attitudes toward or predisposition to change. Some individuals tend to be inherently keener about change and fall into the categories of **innovators** or **early adopters**. Others will wait until the first results of the change are in—they follow the initial two groups of adopters and form the **early majority**. The **late majority** wait longer before adopting. They want more definitive data concerning the change and the reactions of others before they are prepared to commit. Finally, some will, by their nature, resist change until late in the process and can be classified as **laggards** or **late adopters** and **non-adopters**. Table 6.4 lists people's predisposition to change.

In most organizations, we tend to know the innovators. They are constantly trying something new, including new products and services. Risk and novelty seem to provide the adrenalin they need to get through the day! Change comes easily and is sought. In contrast, we also know those who tend to be uncomfortable with new things. These individuals have a strong preference for order and routine. Change is to be avoided and when it must happen, it happens only after most others have shown the way and the status quo is no longer viable.

Change agents need to identify and work first with innovators and early adopters. There is no sense trying to shift someone whose personality resists change until others have adopted. It may be useful to keep certain stakeholders informed of your activities even though they are typically later adopters so as to

Table 6.4 Individual Predispositions to Change	
Innovators or early adopters	Individuals who seek change and want variety
Early majority	Individuals who are receptive to change but are not first adopters
Late majority	Individuals who follow others once the change has been introduced and tried
Laggards or late adopters	Individuals who are reluctant to change and do so only after many others have adopted
Non-adopters	Individuals who will not change or adapt under most circumstances

avoid unnecessary backlash. However, the simple act of keeping people informed is not the same as working closely with innovators and early adopters to advance the initiative. Early in any change program, change agents must anticipate that they will lack support. Few people will know about the change, let alone support it. The process of adoption will often be gradual until a critical mass of support exists. This will be explored in greater detail in Chapter 9 when the topic of the tipping point is introduced.

While the willingness to change can be viewed, in part, as a personality variable, it is also dependent upon the degree to which someone understands the change and his or her commitment toward the change. Floyd and Wooldridge differentiated between understanding and commitment.[19] In their view, someone could have high or low understanding of the change and have high, low, or negative commitment to the change.* This provides a matrix of possibilities that helps us to think about stakeholders and their positions. Change agents need to consider those who actively oppose the change as well as those who are positive in their commitments. Being neutral or skeptical due to ambivalent feelings about the change is not the same as being an informed opponent of the change. See Table 6.5.

Floyd and Wooldridge stress that change agents need to understand people's perspectives of the initiative and that there is no one "right" position. Often we assume that it is best to have people who both understand the change and are committed to it. This is the "strong consensus" cell in Table 6.5. Floyd and Wooldridge argue that at different times, blind devotion, informed skepticism, or a weak consensus is desirable. That is, at times we may need people to be blind devotees—if the change is a strategic secret, people need to accept the change and be committed to act and not ask questions because the change leaders are not in a position to answer them. On the other hand, when beginning a project and testing out ideas for action, change leaders may well want informed skeptics—people who understand the situation well and who are not too committed. These people may well give valuable advice regarding change tactics and strategies as well as contribute to the actual design of the change.

Table 6.5 Stakeholder's Understanding and Commitment		
	High Understanding of the Change	**Low Understanding of the Change**
High, positive commitment to the change	Strong consensus	Blind devotion
Low, positive commitment to the change	Informed skeptics	Weak consensus
Negative commitment to the change	Informed opponents	Fanatical opponents

*Another way of looking at commitment is to categorize people as "make it happen," "help it happen," "let it happen," or "keep it from happening."

Table 6.6	Analysis of Stakeholder's Readiness to Take Action				
Stakeholder's Name	Predisposition to Change (innovator, early adopter, early majority, late majority, laggard)				
	Current Commitment Profile (resistant, ambivalent, neutral, supportive or committed)	Aware	Interested	Desiring Change	Taking Action
Jones					
Smith					
Douglas					

Table 6.6 provides a grid that allows each stakeholder's position and degree of resistance and awareness to be plotted. This form provides a systematic analysis of stakeholders. In the second column, each stakeholder's predisposition toward change can be noted. Is the person typically an innovator or an early adopter, or does that individual wait and see how others are reacting? If the person waits, is he or she normally a part of the early majority of adopters or the late majority group, or does he or she tend to lag further (i.e., the laggards and non-adopters)?

The second column can also be used to assess the stakeholder's current commitment profile. Is this person currently resistant, ambivalent, neutral, somewhat predisposed, or supportive of the change, or is he or she already committed to the initiative? The change agent can then consider power and influence patterns and develop strategies and tactics that will move the individual stakeholders along the adoption continuum (aware, interested, desiring the change, and taking action). The movement of the stakeholders can be plotted in the appropriate columns, with attention given to learning (e.g., what was the impact of the action undertaken?) and the refining of strategies and tactics in the future. In the end, the objective is to move key stakeholders along the adoption continuum, or at minimum, prevent them from becoming significant obstacles to the success of the change initiative.

SUMMARY

Change agents need to understand the power and informal dynamics in their organizations, including culture. They must recognize that resistance to change is likely and is not necessarily a bad thing—there is potential to use resistance in a positive way. It is important to know the forces impacting the organization and the individuals within them, as well as the internal and external stakeholders that will impact and will be impacted by the change process.

Two powerful tools to help us think through the organizational situation are force field analysis and stakeholder analysis. Force field analysis helps change agents to plot the major structural, systemic, and human forces at work in the situation and to anticipate ways to alter these forces. Stakeholder analysis helps us to understand the interactions between key individuals and the relationships and power dynamics that form the web of interactions between individuals. See **Toolkit Exercise 6.1** for critical thinking questions for this chapter.

KEY TERMS

Informal organization—represented by relationships and processes that emerge spontaneously from the interaction of people within the formal systems and structures that define the organizational context. They include informal leadership, communication, and influence patterns; norms and informal roles; and, at a macro level, the culture of the organization that emerges and influences behavior.

Power—the capacity to influence others to accept one's ideas or plans. The chapter set out a number of sources from which power can be derived.

Power tactics—strategies and tactics deployed to influence others to accept one's ideas or plans.

The change equation—says that change occurs when the perception of dissatisfaction with the status quo times the perceived benefits of the change times the perceived probability of success is greater than the perceived cost of the change.

Force field analysis—a process tool that identifies and analyzes the energies in an organization and then alters those forces to accomplish change. The force field is made up of driving and restraining forces.

Stakeholder analysis—the identification and assessment of those who can affect the change or who are affected by the change. Included in this is the analysis of the positions, motives, and power of all key stakeholders. It is the identification of the relationships in the organization, the formal and informal connections between people, structures, and systems. Stakeholder management is the explicit influencing of critical participants in the change process. As such, it is common to see stakeholders also reflected in the force field analysis.

Continuous change—occurs continuously because the forces for change are strong and the resistance forces are weak.

Breakpoint change—change that occurs in a context defined by strong forces for change and strong sources of resistance. When things occur that heighten the change forces and/or weaken the resistance forces, the system is snapped into a new configuration.

Flip-flop change (or sporadic change)—change that occurs within a context of weak change forces and resistance forces. Within this context, the change is not viewed as particularly important and as a result, change may occur, only to be easily reversed.

Stakeholder map—a visual representation of the key stakeholders, their interrelationships, influence patterns, wants, needs, issues, and predispositions toward the change.

Central connectors—people who link with one another.

Boundary spanners—people who connect the formal and/or informal networks to other parts of the organization.

Information brokers—people who link various subgroups.

Peripheral specialists—people who have specialized expertise in the network.

Change continuum—describes the four stages stakeholders may progress through during a change project. The stages are awareness, interest, desire for action, and taking action.

Awareness—the first stage in the change continuum and describes stakeholders who are only just aware of the change initiative.

Interest—the second stage in the change continuum and describes stakeholders move from general awareness to active interest in the initiative.

Desire for action—the third stage in the change continuum and describes stakeholders move from an interest to a desire to take action. It is important in this stage to make action steps clear for stakeholders.

Taking action—the final stage in the change continuum and describes stakeholders who are fully committed to the change and taking action for the change.

Readiness to change—a person's predisposition toward change in general. Is the individual generally an innovator, an early adopter, a member of the early majority, a member of the late majority, or a laggard?

Innovators or **early adopters**—individuals who seek change and want variety. They have a natural predisposition to change.

Early majority—individuals who are receptive to change, but are not the first adopters.

Late majority—individuals who follow others once the change has been introduced and tried

Laggards or **late adopters**—individuals who are reluctant to change and do so only after many others have adopted. They have a very low predisposition to change.

Non-adopters—individuals who will not change or adapt under most circumstances. These individuals will actively resist change efforts.

Commitment profile—a person's orientation toward the specific change in question. Is the individual resistant, ambivalent, neutral, supportive, or committed to the change?

Resistance to change—the desire to *not* pursue the change. Resistance can stem from a variety of sources, including differences in information, perceptions, needs, and beliefs. In addition, existing informal and formal systems and processes have the potential to act as impediments to change.

CHECKLIST: STAKEHOLDER ANALYSIS

1. Who are the key stakeholders in this decision or change effort?

2. Who is the formal decision maker with the formal authority to authorize or deny the change project? Who is that person (or persons)? What are his/her attitudes to the project?

3. What is the commitment profile of stakeholders? Are they against the change, neutral (let it happen), supportive (help it happen), or committed champions of the change (make it happen)? Do a commitment analysis for each stakeholder.

4. Who are the initiators, early adopters, early majority, late majority, or laggards when it comes to change?

5. Why do stakeholders respond as they do? Does the reward system drive them to support or oppose your proposal? What

consequences does your change have on each stakeholder? Do the stakeholders perceive these as positive, neutral, or negative?

6. What would change the stakeholders' views? Can the reward system be altered? Would information or education help?

7. Who influences the stakeholders? Can you influence the influencers? How might this help?

8. What coalitions might be formed among stakeholders? What alliances might you form? What alliances might form to prevent the change you wish?

9. By altering your position, can you keep the essentials of your change and yet satisfy some of the needs of those opposing change?

10. Can you appeal to higher-order values and/ or goals that will make others view their opposition to the change as petty or selfish?

END-OF-CHAPTER EXERCISES

TOOLKIT EXERCISE 6.1
Critical Thinking Questions

The URLs for the videos listed below can be found in two places. The first spot is next to the exercise and the second spot is on the website at study.sagepub.com/cawsey4e.

1. GM Edgar Schein on Corporate Culture—3:18 minutes

   https://www.youtube.com/watch?v=6ZB3jJlGWuk

   - How has Schein's thinking on culture evolved over time?

   - Schein says that change leaders need to learn how to create "cultural islands." What does he mean and why are cultural islands useful?

   - What do you think of Schein's advice on how to better prepare yourself for dealing with different subcultures, such as the professional subcultures of doctors and nurses?

2. Simon Sinek: If You Don't Understand People, You Don't Understand Business—30:40 minutes

   https://www.youtube.com/watch?v=8grVwcPZnuw

   - According to Sinek, how is trust built?

   - How does understanding people help us better understand business?

   - What is Sinek's case for authenticity?

*Please see **study.sagepub.com/cawsey4e** for a downloadable template of this exercise.*

TOOLKIT EXERCISE 6.2

Assessing Power

Personal:

1. What sources of power do you have?

    Your personal style and comfort zone will affect your choice of tactics. What power tactics have you used in the past?

2. Consider a particular context in which you regularly find yourself (e.g., work, school, church, community group). What could you do to increase the power you have available to you in that context?

    What types of power are involved?

3. As it is important to know exactly the sources and limits to your power, it is also very important to understand the key players, structures, and systems in your situation. How do these influence the types and amount of power available to you?

    What could you do to change this?

Organizational:

1. Pick an organization you are quite familiar with. What were the perceptions around power in the organization?

In particular, what factors led to the assumption of power?

Which departments carried more weight and influence? What behaviors were associated with having power?

2. Think of a change situation in the organization. What types of power were at play?

Who had position, knowledge, and personality power? What individuals and departments handled uncertainty, were central, and were not very substitutable?

3. In Hardy's terms, who controlled resources?

Who had process power—that is, set the agendas, managed the nomination or appointment process to key committees, and so on?

Who had meaning power—that is the power to define and influence people's perception of what things meant and how important they were.

4. Who had yea-saying power? On what issues?

Who had nay-saying power?

*Please see **study.sagepub.com/cawsey4e** for a downloadable template of this exercise.*

TOOLKIT EXERCISE 6.3

Understanding the Forces for and Against Change: The Force Field Analysis

Consider an organizational change situation you are familiar with. Use the following questions to guide you through the process of drawing a force field analysis.

1. What are the forces for change? Include external forces as well as a consideration of key individuals or groups. How strong and committed are these forces? (Who will let it happen; who will help it happen; who will make it happen?)

2. How could these forces be augmented or increased? What forces could be added to those that exist?

3. What are the forces that oppose change? Include structural forces such as reward systems or formal processes in the organization. Consider as well the effect of informal processes and groups or the culture of the organization.

4. How could these forces be weakened or removed? What things might create major resentment in these forces?

5. Can you identify any points of leverage that you could employ to advance the change? For example, might you deploy to the department or organization key well-respected individuals who support the change? Or might you or someone else provide low-cost guarantees related to serious concerns?

*Please see **study.sagepub.com/cawsey4e** for a downloadable template of this exercise.*

PATRICK'S PROBLEM

By Stacy Blake-Beard, Ph.D.

Deloitte Ellen Gabriel Chair of Women and Leadership

School of Business, Simmons University, Boston, MA

Patrick Jackson sat at the table, trying very hard to keep his mouth from dropping open. He and the other nine executive directors on John Pointer's leadership council were completing their annual talent reviews, discussing various individuals on their teams who would be good candidates for promotion to director. Of course, the logistics of this advancement opportunity would be handled through the Learning and Development Department. But Patrick was well aware that the conversations that he and his fellow executive directors were having in John Pointer's "closed room" meeting were going to be very influential in who was tapped and who wasn't. John, vice president of marketing, and his team sitting around the table, represented a powerful segment of the leadership at Millenial. [20]

The informal banter belied the seriousness of the discussion they were having. There were several candidates that were being considered for the two spots available. As names were raised, each executive director shared his experiences with that particular associate director. Some of the candidates generated enthusiasm. For example, Alan Witherspoon was especially well regarded. Steve Winter, Alan's executive director and another senior leader on John's team, had worked closely with Alan. Others had observed and heard enough about Alan that they felt comfortable speaking on his behalf. They spoke strongly in support of Alan, with Steve joking that they had attended the same school so of course he was a strong player. Alan's achievements were enumerated and the praise was being laid on thick and heavy. . . a little too much from Patrick's perspective.

Patrick worked in a cross-functional team with Alan. His own experiences with Alan had not been as positive. He saw Alan's performance as primarily self-serving. He also noticed that Alan was rather absent from the team, especially when they were in crunch time. Alan didn't seem particularly open to feedback either. When Patrick sent out congratulations to the team to acknowledge their strong work in finishing the project, he also offered an opportunity for each team member to meet for a post-mortem discussion. While the project had ended successfully, there were many learning opportunities along the way that Patrick wanted to discuss with his team members—learning that could be used to make their next project go more smoothly. Additionally, Patrick wanted to enhance his own learning, so he was interested in a discussion that drew from their insights. Alan had opted not to take up this invitation, curtly declining.

Patrick was waiting to hear how Alicia Conrad, another associate director, was going to be discussed by his colleagues. He breathed a slight sigh of relief when James Valencio, a fellow executive director, started the discussion with positive comments. He said that she was motivated, that she could be counted on to exceed her clients' expectations, and that she was quite strategic in her approach to problem solving. But James quickly qualified that statement. Yes, she could be counted on to exceed her clients' expectations. But did she need additional support from her coworkers to perform at that level? James also had some questions about Alicia's readiness to be promoted. "You know, she doesn't have that much experience.

I think we should give her a year or two more to get better prepared for the director role." Patrick felt himself tense up—these concerns were issues that had consistently been raised. . . but only in regards to their female candidates. Women, and some men, in the organization had noticed this troubling trend. Although the Learning and Development Department was monitoring the promotion cycle, the ultimate decisions rested with the leadership team. And. . . old habits die hard.

One of the initiatives that Learning and Development sponsored was the Male Ally Program. The Male Ally Program had been initiated to address the dearth of women in senior leadership positions. Alicia was his partner in this program. Because of their interactions, Patrick knew firsthand how Alicia was showing up and impacting the business. He wondered if Alicia's collaborative style was what James saw as "needing support." There was still an old-fashioned, outdated definition of leadership in Millenial; "leaders" were expected to ride in on a white horse and save the day. But Patrick was well aware that leadership was exemplified with many different behaviors. A primary aspect of a leader is that he—or she or they—achieved identified goals. Indeed, Alicia and her team had successfully managed a large portfolio of clients, winning high satisfaction scores and scoring repeat business despite the challenging nature of some of the clients. She had done everything from meeting goals, supporting a team, to satisfying customers. Was it still not enough?

Clearly Alicia was successful in her role, and Patrick felt certain that she was ready for this promotion now, not in a year or two. But as James continued to share his concerns about Alicia, doubts about her were spreading across the room. Patrick wondered if he should speak up. But he was running out of time—they had spent so much time talking about Alan that they couldn't give the same attention to Alicia. And anyway, what happened in that room would stay in that room. They agreed to one more quick meeting in a few days before sharing their candidates for promotion with Talent Management.

As Patrick left the room, he wondered again about the Male Ally Program—about his involvement and the organization's commitment. Was Millenial really committed to this "initiative?" All of the men around the table were signed up for the program; some of them even had partners who were also being considered for this director role. Interestingly, Patrick was the only Male Ally to speak on behalf of his partner. This lack of advocacy was not surprising; many of the women in Millenial shared their concerns that the program had been thrown together and launched as a tool to quiet their loud voices. With enough time, those voices would be quelled—isn't this what had happened in the past? Patrick believed that the program was an important initiative that held great promise for advancing women and increasing their presence in the senior ranks. "If anyone is going to take a stand, not just for Alicia but for the program as well, I believe I am going to have to be the one," thought Patrick. But he understood that taking a stand could result in some challenges for him. His colleagues were not going to be pleased if he spoke up more strongly on Alicia's behalf. So, he wanted to think carefully about the meeting next week.

DISCUSSION QUESTIONS

1. What are the reasons that Patrick might choose not to advocate for Alicia?

2. How should he go about advocating for Alicia?

3. What does Patrick risk if he speaks out on her behalf?

4. What will happen if he opts to say nothing?

5. What tensions has the launch of the Male Ally Program raised in Millenial?

CHAPTER SEVEN

MANAGING RECIPIENTS OF CHANGE AND INFLUENCING INTERNAL STAKEHOLDERS

Chapter Overview

- People respond to change in many ways. Some embrace it. Others are ambivalent. Some view change negatively. Reactions depend on the nature of the change, the situation, the individuals involved, and how it is approached. Change leaders need to understand why people react to change as they do, gathering data to understand individuals' situations and their responses.

- Change leaders need to rethink their assumptions about resistance to change. Employees often have good reasons for resisting the change leaders' proposals, and these reasons need to be understood and learned from.

- Change leaders can rethink the language that they use, seeing employees as "stakeholders and participants in the process." This new language implies a different stance toward power and the legitimacy of employees to voice their opinions during the change process.

- Change leaders need to be aware of the established psychological contract between the organization and its employees and to recognize that changes to the psychological contract need to be handled carefully.

- People usually respond emotionally to change directives, and leaders need to prepare themselves for the emotional upheaval, even though the need for change is often driven by rational factors.

- A present-day challenge is to make change the norm and encourage people to become change leaders or change implementers themselves. This capacity can be thought of as organizational agility and resilience.

It was 2003 and the women of Liberia changed their status and role from recipients of change to stakeholders in the national political process of their country. Charles Taylor, president of Liberia since 1997, controlled about one third of the country, and the Liberians United for Reconciliation and Democracy (LURD) and other rebel factions controlled the rest of the country. All groups were accused of a range of atrocities, from creating child soldiers and the raping of women and young girls to painful maiming of enemies. No one was safe, and many were starving and homeless. In these desperate circumstances, the women of Liberia united. Christian and Muslim women, rather than seeing their differences and continuing their exclusive affiliation with their own religious and ethnic rebels, recognized that a change in political party from Taylor's National Patriotic Front of Liberia (NPFL) to LURD would not change their lives since violence was the permanent and lasting legacy of all the fighting factions.

The women's political slogan became PEACE. They dressed in white and sat in the fields in the sun, the rain. At first, they were ignored. Then their persistent presence was finally noted and President Taylor recognized the women as individuals who could no longer be dismissed. However, he did too little, too late. By the fall of 2003, Taylor was forced to resign and go into exile in Nigeria. (It should be noted that there were multiple forces, including but not limited to the Economic Community of West African States [ECOWAS], the United Nations, and the United States of America's government, that demanded Taylor's exile.) In 2005, Ellen Johnson-Sirleaf was elected president of Liberia with the support of the women's peace movement, Women of Liberia Mass Action for Peace. She took office in January 2006, and was reelected in 2011. She was awarded the Nobel Peace Prize in 2011, jointly with Leymah Gbowee of Liberia and Tawakkol Karman of Yeman, for their nonviolent initiatives to advance women's rights to safe and full participation in the peace process. India honored her in 2013 by awarding her the Indira Gandhi Peace Prize, and in 2014 *Forbes* listed her as the 70th most powerful woman in the world.[1]

This remarkable story is told eloquently in *Pray the Devil Back to Hell*.[2] From the perspective of change leaders, it is important to note that these Liberian women upended their status as recipients of change and violence and established themselves as powerful stakeholders in the national political process. While most organizational change situations are not about physical violence, change leaders need to acknowledge that change can require people to modify their personal or professional identities, skill sets, and other deeply held beliefs and expectations. It is to legitimize these struggles of internal stakeholders that we use this language.

The reality of people's lives is that they are often on the receiving end of change, often called "the **recipients of change**." This chapter suggests how recipients of change may react and how change agents can incorporate this understanding to improve both their change plans and the outcomes for others. The chapter deals with the reality of those who find themselves on the receiving end of change. It will consider the range of different reactions to change: support or enthusiasm, mixed feelings or ambivalence, and opposition or **resistance to change**.

While positive responses toward change are fairly common, depending upon the nature of the change and how it is introduced, this chapter focuses on people who are mixed or negative toward change. The chapter helps managers understand the phases people as recipients of change go through. As well, the chapter considers the factors that influence how people respond to change: their personalities, their coworkers or teams, their leaders or managers, and their past experiences with change. It recognizes that both the content (the what) of change and the process (the how) of change matter. Change leaders need to ensure that what they do is based on sound analysis and that the process of change (the how), allows for and encourages the involvement and input of others in both the assessment and implementation phases. Finally, this chapter looks at how change leaders can reduce the negative effects of change initiatives on recipients. Figure 7.1 summarizes the change model and highlights the key issues in dealing with recipients of change and influencing internal stakeholders.

STAKEHOLDERS RESPOND VARIABLY TO CHANGE INITIATIVES

Not Everyone Sees Change as Negative

Many managers assume that resistance is inevitable in change situations. It is time to dispel this myth. Employees do not always react negatively and in many situations will react quite positively. Will they raise questions and experience a sense of uncertainty or ambivalence when change is introduced? Of course they will. They are thinking individuals, trying to make sense out of the change and its impact. This questioning often is perceived as resistance but is not necessarily change resistance. Questions and concerns can give rise to tense times for the change agent, but don't be afraid to engage others constructively about their perceptions and concerns. Nurturing support for the change is highly likely if they conclude: the benefits to them and their coworkers clearly outweigh the costs; have high personal, team and organizational relevance; and are consistent with their attitudes and values.[3] True resistance arises only after people have resolved their mixed feelings in ways that cause them to firmly conclude that the initiative should be opposed, either passively or actively. As was noted in Chapter 6, negative reactions to change increase in frequency and intensity when people believe that the potential costs and consequences to them and the things they value outweigh the benefits.

A second myth that needs dispelling is the belief that age and resistance to change go hand in hand. A person's predisposition to change was found to be a stronger influence than age when it came to resistance to information technology (IT) changes being undertaken.[4] Another research study found age to be negatively related to resistance. In other words, resistance decreased as age increased.[5] To understand people's reaction to change, look well beyond their chronological age. The causes likely lie elsewhere.

Some researchers have suggested that "resistance to change" is a term that has lost its usefulness because it oversimplifies the matter and becomes a self-fulfilling prophecy. We agree. That is, if change leaders assume resistance will occur, it becomes more likely. Change leaders should focus on trying to understand why people react to the change as they do and how those reactions are likely to evolve over time.[6] When changes are introduced, people will have their own immediate reactions and often find themselves pulled in different directions. Family, friends, relatives, coworkers, and subordinates may hold divergent views concerning the proposed change, and organizational leaders and managers may deliver ambiguous or conflicting messages concerning its rationale and implications. If things become polarized around the change, people who have come to a decision may view those who are of a different opinion with suspicion and disapproval. All of these pressures can lead stakeholders to feel ambivalent about the change.

These mixed feelings can be magnified by concerns about the impact of the change on (a) their relationships with others; (b) their ability to do what is being

Figure 7.1   The Change Path Model

Awakening
Chapter 4

1. Identify a need for change and confirm the problems or opportunities that incite the need for change through collection of data.
2. Articulate the gap in performance between the present and the envisioned future state, and spread awareness of the data and the gap throughout the organization.
3. Develop a powerful vision for change.
4. Disseminate the vision for the change and why it's needed through multiple communication channels.

Mobilization
Chapters 5 through 8

1. Make sense of the desired change through formal systems and structures, and leverage those systems to reach the change vision (Chapter 5).
2. Assess power and cultural dynamics at play, and put them to work to better understand the dynamics and build coalitions and support to realize the change (Chapter 6).
3. **Communicate the need for change organization-wide and manage change recipients and various stakeholders as they react to and move the change forward (Chapter 7).**
4. Leverage change agent personality, knowledge, skills and abilities, and related assets (e.g., reputation and relationships) for the benefit of the change vision and its implementation (Chapter 8).

Acceleration
Chapter 9

1. Continue to systematically reach out to engage and empower others in support, planning, and implementation of the change. Help them develop needed new knowledge, skills, abilities, and ways of thinking that will support the change.
2. Use appropriate tools and techniques to build momentum, accelerate and consolidate progress.
3. Manage the transition, celebrating small wins and the achievement of milestones along the larger, more difficult path of change.

Institutionalization
Chapter 10

1. Track the change periodically and through multiple balanced measures to help assess what is needed, gauge progress toward the goal, and to make modifications as needed and mitigate risk.
2. Develop and deploy new structures, systems, processes and knowledge, skills, and abilities, as needed, to bring life to the change and new stability to the transformed organization.

asked of them; (c) the fit with their needs and values; and (d) their job security and future career prospects. These concerns are further intensified when people lack confidence that the change will produce the intended results. When employees see themselves as relatively powerless, a variety of less constructive coping responses, including avoidance, alienation, passivity, absenteeism, turnover, and sabotage may result.[7]

Feelings of powerlessness can lead to **sedentary activation** (a term coined by Cory Booker). He described sedentary activation as what happens when you sit and yell at the TV or social media feeds but don't take concrete action.[8] Feelings of powerlessness are not good for your health!

The perceptions of costs and benefits of change depend on what people are concerned about, what they have experienced in the past, and what they think they know. Sometimes relatively small changes will produce strong responses in one group due to the perceived consequences. In another group, more significant changes might produce mild reactions because of perceptions that the impact on them will not be significant or they are simply more comfortable with change.[9] Consider the reactions of employees of Desjardins Group to the selection and subsequent actions of their new CEO in 2008.

MONIQUE LEROUX AND CHANGE AT DESJARDINS

If cultural change in for-profit, publicly traded organizations is difficult, consider the challenges inherent in doing so in a 100-plus-year-old financial services cooperative, made up of over 500 independent, affiliated member branches with strong rural roots, governed by over 6,000 elected officers in Quebec, Canada. Monique Leroux is a chartered accountant who was one of the first female partners at Ernst & Young and the senior Quebec VP for the Royal Bank of Canada before joining Desjardins in 2001. She became its CFO in 2004 and successfully ran for election as its CEO in 2008, being selected over several other candidates by the 256 voting members who represented the affiliated branches.

Her election surprised many. Desjardins was viewed as an "old boys club," and her earlier career experiences meant that she was still an outsider to many. However, her ability to articulate the challenges, constructively engage employees and members in conversations about what was needed, and her managerial and leadership skills resonated. A majority of those voting believed she represented the best leadership option, given her skills and her commitment to Desjardins, its members, and its heritage. Leroux took office just prior to the financial crisis of 2008. She successfully helped the organization navigate the crisis and then

undertake the significant changes needed to effectively compete in the financial services industry—one dominated by large, sophisticated, and successful firms in Canada.

Desjardins had a strong, customer-oriented culture and had been successful at attracting and retaining membership in its core rural communities, but the world of financial services was changing rapidly. Its Quebec membership was graying and the population was becoming more urban. Furthermore, the Quebec economy was not performing well and suffered from relatively high levels of unemployment. Leroux recognized that significant adaptations of their business model were needed if they were to continue to successfully serve their members, grow, and not become an anachronism. The organization operated in a fairly fragmented manner due to the independence of its member affiliates, and the lack of integration needed to be addressed if customers were to be served effectively and efficiently. This, in turn, required systems and processes to better integrate services, manage costs, and evolve their online presence and portfolio of services. Leroux based her campaign to be CEO on the need to develop the organization and its services in order to compete effectively, while staying true to their core values as a cooperative. She believed it was important to extend

(Continued)

(Continued)

Desjardins' reach outside of Quebec, but they would first have to deal with needed changes to their internal structure, system, processes, and service offerings.

Soon after her appointment as CEO, the autonomous and close-knit culture of the Desjardins' network of independent branches and associated divisions came face-to-face with Leroux's approach to change. It was one grounded in the active engagement of members and employees in consultative processes, often through the use of teams. Consultation was followed by decision making, and between 2008 and 2012 this led to a flattening of the hierarchy, the successful restructuring and realignment of services and processes, and a reduction in the number of VPs from 250 to 112 and the number of senior VPs from 40 to 12. It also led to 1,000 job cuts. These waves of consultation and engagement also gave rise to initiatives related to new lines of business, staff and managerial development, diversification of the managerial and executive group, the establishment of separate groups outside the cooperative structure (e.g., business units targeting commercial markets) but owned by the cooperative, and a more performance-driven and customer-oriented approach to service delivery. To support these initiatives, Leroux actively built her management team so that it contained the diversity of perspectives, skills, and values needed to respond effectively to the challenges. The combination of restructuring and issues of individual fit or alignment with the new organization led to turnover in the executive and managerial ranks.

Leroux was well aware of the fact that employees and members had valid concerns for what these changes might do to their cooperative culture. She believed in the value of the cooperative movement, was committed to it, and was very respectful of Desjardins' roots—as indicated by her approach to change which was characterized by the active engagement and involvement of others, rich communication of ideas and perspectives, and listening. However, once decisions were made and it was time to move to action, she actively promoted and reinforced the expected changes. Leroux is reported to have said, "I will not go for bitterness or backstabbing, and fights, and territorial management. You guys are responsible to make it happen and work as a team" (pg. 7, Harvard Business School case).

Leroux adopted an approach that allowed organizational members to see the need for change themselves and to actively participate in its development and implementation. Some had difficulty adjusting to the changes and the pace. Dissatisfaction, lower morale, and turnover were reported by managers in some divisions, particularly with those who had experienced title reductions or a disruption of work relationships they valued.

The changes pursued under Leroux's leadership were challenging for the recipients of change, but they have proven very successful. By 2012, Desjardins had moved into new markets and lines of business (e.g., payroll services, commercial and investment services, insurance), increased the number of employees from 17,000 to 45,000, increased their total assets from $152 billion to $190 billion, and increased their cash distributions or dividends to their 5.8 million members from $215 million in 2008 to $401 million to 5.6 million members by 2012. In terms of bank safety, they were rated number 3 in North America by Global Finance and were assessed as the 13th strongest bank in the world in 2013. They were rated highest in investor satisfaction for three years in a row when evaluated against other discount brokerage firms by J. D. Power, and were named one of Canada's 10 best companies to work for by the *Financial Post*.

By 2014, they were underway with the expansion of their services outside of Quebec, as seen in their acquisition of the largest network of insurance brokers in Western Canada in 2010, the acquisition of Vancouver-based Qtrade Financial Group in 2013, and their 2013 opening of an office in Canada's financial heartland in downtown Toronto, Ontario.[10] They were also actively engaged in conversations with other financial services cooperatives in Canada and internationally, to explore ways they might be able to leverage one another's strengths and capacities.[11]

Leroux was elected to a second term in 2012, and under her leadership Desjardins has continued to experience steady progress on all fronts, including being recognized as a best place to work for 5+ years in a row.[12] She has been an active and influential advocate and mentor, nurturing diversity and the advancement of female leaders and others. In addition to having been Desjardins' CEO and chair of its board, she has been a member of a number of other cooperative boards and advisory groups nationally and internationally, as well as several educational and not-for-profit advisory bodies.

Lemeux is a member of the Order of Canada and the recipient of many other national and international honors that recognize her expertise, contributions, and commitment to the betterment of society. She stepped down at the end of her term in 2016 but has not slowed. Leroux was president of the International Co-operative Alliance (2016-2017) and she is currently chair of the board of Investment Quebec and vice chair of Fiera Holdings, to name just two of the organizations that continue to benefit from her energy, intelligence, insight and leadership capacities. She was inducted into the Canadian Business Hall of Fame in 2018.[13]

How employees perceive change will depend upon their assessment of the situation. If they see themselves *and* the organization benefiting from the change, they are more likely to embrace the change. If they see themselves as involved and participating in the initiative, they are more likely to be supportive.[14] If the outcomes are viewed as likely to be negative for the organization and the individuals, they will be unsupportive of the change. If their views are mixed, they will experience **ambivalence to the change**.[15]

The successes achieved at Desjardins under Leroux's leadership were due, in part, to her engagement of people in the renewal of the organization's services, systems, processes, and structures. Leroux was transparent when she brought the challenges to the employees, and worked hard to create a shared understanding of the need for change and to think through what change could look like. She used change tools such as stakeholder engagement, environmental and organizational analyses, participative teams, active communication through diverse channels, goal setting, and change teams to bring needed changes to life and to help reinforce commitment to a renewed culture that was congruent with Desjardins' cooperative roots. Along the way, she succeeded in converting many skeptics and resistors into becoming partners in the change process.

The range of possible perceptions and responses is complex, as people assess the change against their interests, attitudes, and values. What Monique Leroux and her team were able to accomplish can be attributed to their engagement of both recipients of change and new recruits in helping to define the problem, design solutions, and implement them. This was aided by their use of hard data that all could understand; institutionalizing the change through projects, systems, and processes; and sustaining the change by creating a structure to promote collaboration and accountability. It was critical that the company's internal systems and processes catch up, and the proof of their success lies in the organization's improved financial performance and the growth of its capabilities and capacity to deliver.

However, even in the face of improved performance on multiple fronts, not all ambivalence concerning the changes disappeared, and pockets of resistance remained at Desjardins. A number of employees reported in 2011 that they were still concerned that the pace of change had been too fast and that too high a price had been paid in the form of the deterioration in employee morale and elevated levels of turnover in some areas.

Recipients' understanding and responses to the change will evolve over time as the change unfolds. As a result, the approaches used by change leaders will need to vary over the course of the change process. Whereas factual information delivered in a speech or a consultant's report may be useful when dealing with beliefs concerning the need for change and developing initial awareness, informal discussions and social support may be much more useful when ambivalence is stemming from conflicting emotions.[16] If downsizing or relocation is required, it will take more than the rational presentation of data or delivery of equitable relocation packages or early retirement provisions to alleviate distress. Often, executives have had months to consider the changes, and employees need time to adjust.

If resistance occurs, it may stem from those in middle and/or more senior roles, since they often have the most to lose, which happened at Desjardins. They may be seeking to maintain power and influence, sustain their capacity to perform, or avoid what they perceive to be a worsening of their position.[17] Change leaders need to be aware of this as they manage the situation. Finally, attribution errors may cause change leaders to fixate on individual resistance rather than probe more deeply for causal factors. For example, behavior that is being categorized as individual resistance may be due to misaligned structures and systems rather than individual opposition.[18] As well, many managers are predisposed to expect resistance in subordinates. Care needs to be taken that a self-fulfilling prophecy is not created.

Authentically engaging the hearts, as well as the heads and hands of those critical to the success of the change, is a key ongoing challenge change leaders need to be very attentive to.

RESPONDING TO VARIOUS FEELINGS IN STAKEHOLDERS

Positive Feelings in Stakeholders: Channeling Their Energy

In Chapter 6 approaches were discussed that help change agents anticipate the reactions of different stakeholders. Let's turn now to how best to respond to their feelings. As noted earlier, many individuals welcome change. A change initiative can represent a chance for personal growth or promotion. Some people enjoy variety and seek opportunities to create. Others want the challenge of new situations. Still others imagine a change is needed to improve the situation.

When people are feeling positive, engaged, informed, and hopeful, these emotions can be harnessed in support of the change.[19] It is important, however, to anticipate the risks that may accompany the positive feelings in some stakeholders while others remain uncertain. Blind acceptance by some employees may lead to a lack of reflection in both them and others. Strong positive support of organizational initiatives from respected individuals may cause others to censor their doubts and give rise to the risk of groupthink. This potential tyranny of the minority or majority may lead to a stereotyping of those ambivalent to or opposing the change as "the enemy." This can lead to infighting rather than thoughtful analysis and the productive pursuit of organizational benefits.

Change leaders need to

- channel the energy in positive ways, not letting the enthusiasm for change overwhelm legitimate concerns;

- "name" the problem of mixed feelings and the need to understand the different reactions to change;

- appoint highly respected, positively oriented stakeholders to chair significant committees or other change initiative structures, and ensure they have the skills and resources required to fill these roles in ways that don't stifle needed discussions and debate. Transparency, openness to learning, and the willingness to translate learning into practice will advance recipients' openness to change; and

- manage the pace and remember that going too slow can dampen support for change with enthusiasts, while going too fast will create anxiety in those who are doubtful and fatigued.

Ambivalent Feelings in Stakeholders: They Can Be Useful[20]

It comes as no surprise that employees are likely to have mixed feelings about change, as it often gives rise to perceptions of increased complexity, uncertainty, higher risk, and the disruption of agreed-to work responsibilities and relationships. People's beliefs about a change and its potential impact can be both positive and negative and can vary in intensity. To illustrate this, consider the example of an industrial paint manufacturer that changed how it handled its major customers by moving key technical service representatives from the head office to the customers' plants. The change provided staff with desired opportunities for increased responsibility, autonomy, and pay, but it required their relocation to a new workplace and the disruption of their cohesive work group. Naturally, their feelings were mixed. Some were excited and others anxious about their new responsibilities. Some were sad about leaving close friends behind.[21] This also created change in role definition, as the new duties required service representatives to play a much more active client-management role. These were activities that customer service representatives had viewed as belonging to sales personnel.

When ambivalence is prevalent, change leaders should create conditions that will increase the likelihood that people will voice concerns. They need to create an environment that welcomes feedback. Piderit states that people are more likely to speak up when the ambivalence stems from conflicting beliefs. When conflicting emotions are involved, though, she notes that individuals often have more difficulty giving voice to negative emotional responses. She hypothesizes that "they would be more likely to wrestle with their ambivalence alone or to avoid the subject entirely.[22]" Ambivalence generates discomfort for people, causing them to seek resolution of the feeling. Once this resolution occurs and people come to feel more certain about their position, subsequent changes to attitudes become more difficult.

A person's sense of certainty grows when there is a consensus of opinion about the matter among those whose opinions they value, when there is a repetition of messages that support that consensus view, when the path to take actions in support of the consensus view are easily accessed and we begin to invoke our attitudes and actions in defense of that consensus. People protect their attitudes by employing a variety of strategies:

- turn to habits and approaches that have served them well in the past;[23]

- engage in selective perception (actively seeking out confirming information and avoiding disconfirming data);[24]

- recall selectively (being more likely to remember attitude-consistent rather than inconsistent data);[25] and

- deny in the form of counterarguments geared to support and strengthen one's position.

- More extreme defensive responses can include sarcasm, anger, aggression, and withdrawal. Since attitudes become much more difficult to change once they solidify, there is all the more reason to invest the time needed at the front end of the change in order to effectively process people's reactions to change.

Rather than interpreting mixed feelings as resistance, change leaders are better served by

- focusing on helping people make sense of the proposed changes;

- listening for information that may be helpful in achieving the change;

- reconciling constructively people's ambivalence; and

- sorting out what actions are now needed.

- Injecting elements of uncertainty can prove helpful to change agents when dealing with ambivalence and also resistance. It assists in encouraging additional reflection on the matter. When change agents are seen as open to the perspectives of others by modeling such behavior, they will tend to find they are more successful in helping recipients come to an informed judgement and resolve their ambivalence (and even resistance) in ways congruent with the change initiative. Further, change agents may find that by modeling this behavior they increase their capacity to develop insights that inform the change and contribute to its success.[26]

It is almost always in the best interest of change agents to actively engage people in meaningful discussions early in the change process and help to align their interpretations with the process.[27] Employees' input can prove invaluable in identifying potential problems and risk points.[28] Their engagement and involvement can allow concerns to be addressed.[29] Meaningful engagement can increase the likelihood of the formation of supportive attitudes toward the change and perceptions of fairness as they attempt to make sense of what they are being asked to do.[30] Desjardins' organizational change was effective due to the adoption of approaches such as these, by highly skilled and respected change champions.

Balogun and Johnson note that once the blueprint for more complex change is set out, it is brought to life through the interpretations and responses of employees. As a result, these authors argue that "managing change is less about directing and controlling and more about facilitating recipients' sense-making processes to achieve an alignment of interpretation.[31]" As this evolves, so too does the change that subsequently unfolds. All this points to the importance of employee perceptions of organizational support for what lies ahead. When they feel this is present, perceptions of uncertainty are reduced because they have a greater sense that they know what is going on and that support will be available, if and when they need it. As a result, adaptability increases, and job satisfaction and performance rise relative to what is seen when such support is lacking. In essence, recipients have a clearer sense that they know what is going on; someone has their "back"; there is open, supportive communication to sort through matters as they arise; and that there are reasons for hope concerning what lies ahead.[32]

Negative Reactions to Change by Stakeholders: These Too Can Be Useful

Change leaders undertake an initiative because they believe the benefits outweigh the costs. However, anticipate that stakeholders may have a range of different perspectives, from feeling imposed upon and unprepared, to perceiving the change is ill advised and/or poorly designed and likely to fail, to feeling anger and rage. Table 7.1 outlines the causes of negative reactions to change.

Concerns and negative reactions toward change develop for a variety of reasons. Perception of negative consequences of the change may be a reality. The change may be fundamentally incongruent with things the people deeply value about their jobs (e.g., autonomy, significance, feedback, identity, and variety)[33] or the workplace (e.g., pay, job security). The loss of a job is likely the most extreme form of this. When significant job losses are involved, such as when the major employer in a town decides its plant needs to be closed for the good of the corporation, the costs are all too real for the recipients. In situations such as the above,

Table 7.1 Causes of Negative Reactions to Change
1. Negative consequences appear to outweigh the benefits.
2. The communication process is flawed, leading to confusion and doubt.
3. There is concern that the change has been ill conceived, insufficiently tested, or may have adverse consequences that are not anticipated.
4. The recipients lack experience with change and its implications or have habituated approaches that they rely upon and remain committed to (group and/or structural inertia).
5. The recipients have had prior negative experience with a similar change.
6. The recipients have had prior negative experience with those advocating the change.
7. The negative reactions of peers, subordinates, and/or supervisors whom you trust and respect and with whom you will have to work in the future influence your views.
8. The change process is seen to be lacking procedural justice and/or distributive justice and breaching the recipient's sense of their employment contract (threat to established power relationships).
9. The recipients fear that they don't have the necessary skills and competencies to perform well after the change has been implemented (threat to expertise).

it is difficult, if not impossible, for people to see positive consequences ensuing from the change. The closing of the Fishery Products International plant provides an example of employment loss.[34]

JOB LOSS AT FISHERY PRODUCTS INTERNATIONAL

The 2008 closing of the Fishery Products International (FPI) processing plant in Harbour Breton, Newfoundland, is "devastating," says Earle McCurdy, president of the Fish, Food and Allied Workers Union. "This closing has put 350 people out of work in a community of 2,100. You don't have to be a Ph.D. to determine the size of the impact," he says. "And it's not only Harbour Breton; it's the entire peninsula."

FPI officials blame the closing on an independent report that claims "the plant has major structural problems and is no longer safe for occupancy." However, FPI spokesman Russ Carrigan released a statement saying, "The entry of China into the market for headed and gutted cod has driven the commodity price up dramatically—well beyond the point of our commercial viability.[35]" In this example, recipients would have difficulty accepting the corporate perspective on the need for change.

In examples such as FPI, recipients would have difficulty accepting the corporate perspective on the need for change for a number of reasons:

- *Communication processes may be flawed*, and people may be left feeling ill informed or misled.[36] Support for management is less likely when people feel they lack the information they need to make an informed judgment or lack the supervisory support needed to successfully follow through on the proposed course of action. The prospects for support diminish further and faster when employees feel that information has been intentionally and arbitrarily withheld or manipulated. In our FPI example, there appears to be confusion over the reasons for the closure. Is it the structural problems, the entry of Chinese competition to the marketplace, or both?

- *People may have serious doubts about the impact and effectiveness of the change.* They may be concerned that the change initiative has not been sufficiently studied and tested, or they may believe that the change will have adverse consequences that have not been thought through.[37] For example, a move by a head office to consolidate warehouse operations and trim inventory levels may be seen as a sure fire way to increase efficiency, but it could cause serious concerns in sales and marketing about the firm's ability to effectively service its customers.

- *People may lack experience with change and be unsure about its implications or their capacity to adjust.* When conditions in an organization have been stable for long periods, even modest changes can seem threatening. During extended periods of stability, people tend to develop well-engrained habits, and the patterned behavior can result in negative reactions to change. Habituated approaches represent strategies that we believe have served us well in the past and that we are often not even conscious of.[38] The Desjardins example earlier in the chapter demonstrated this, as the culture of the independent branches prior to 2008 had resulted in issues of service fragmentation and inefficiency and insufficient awareness that this was a pressing issue that needed to be dealt with.

- *People may have had negative experiences with change initiatives or approaches that seem similar to the one being advocated.* To use an old adage, once burned, twice shy. If stakeholders have learned that change initiatives lead to layoffs or that the initiatives begin with great fanfare but are never completed, people will be more negative. They have learned that they should be skeptical about change and its consequences.[39]

- *They may have had a negative experience with those advocating the change.* They may mistrust the judgment of those promoting the change, their ability to deliver on promises, their access to resources, their implementation skills, or their integrity.

- *People may be influenced by the negative reactions of peers, subordinates, or supervisors* whom they trust and respect and/or whom they have to work with in the future. These opinion leaders can have a significant impact.

- *Last but not least, there may be justice-related concerns.* People may see the process as lacking in procedural justice (i.e., was the process fair; did people have an opportunity to question change leaders, voice opinions, and suggest options?). For example, an absence of participation and involvement may leave employees feeling ignored and relatively powerless.[40] In addition to concerns about procedural fairness and the trustworthiness of leaders,[41] they may also believe that distributive justice was lacking (i.e., the final decision was fundamentally unfair).[42] Matters related to this will be discussed in the section in this chapter dealing with the psychological contract the recipients feel they have, involving their working relationship with an organization.

When things do not unfold as planned, resistance is often flagged as the cause. Rather than assess the situation carefully and objectively, managers responsible for change are quick to lay the blame at the feet of those thought to be acting as obstacles.[43] The dynamics of this likely increases resistance as each blames the other and tensions rise. When managers and employees point fingers at each other as the cause of change difficulties, the focus is not on advancing the agenda for change. The key question is not who is to blame, but rather what is happening, why is it happening, and what does this tell us about what we should do now?

Kotter notes that impediments to change are much more likely to come from problems related to the misalignment of structures and systems than from individuals engaged in resistance.[44] For example, if existing systems continue to reward competitive behavior, why would you expect employees to behave in a cooperative manner?[45] Likewise, if critical information or resources are not available, how can individuals implement the change program? Change leaders need to be aware of the tendency to focus on individuals and not the roles that the existing structures, systems, and processes may be playing in impeding progress and influencing people's reaction to the initiative.

For successful change management and implementation, there needs to be engagement and open conversation, especially in the face of resistance. Such communications can create a shared understanding of different perspectives, and have the potential to be a valuable resource when approached constructively, by identifying new ways of thinking about the situation and possible paths forward.[46] Alignment also needs to exist between what is communicated and the systems and structures of the organization. When the change leader asks you to do "A," but other systems and structures tell you that "B" is what you should do, one should expect ambivalence and/or resistance until issues of alignment are addressed. If resistance is based on different definitions of the issues, then leaders need to return to the framing and analysis of the underlying problems and attempt to resolve the differences. If the resistance is based on differing views of the consequences, the reasons need to be understood and change plans modified if appropriate.

MAKE THE CHANGE OF THE PSYCHOLOGICAL CONTRACT EXPLICIT AND TRANSPARENT

People don't resist change. They resist being changed – Peter Senge

The organizational context plays a major role in determining reactions of people to change. People want some sense of agency or control and informed consent over what happens to them in their work lives. The **psychological contract** that people have with the organization can be a critical contextual variable in this regard.[47] The psychological contract represents the sum of the implicit and explicit agreements we believe we have with our organization. It defines our perceptions of the terms of our employment relationship and includes our expectations for ourselves and for the organization, including organizational norms, rights, rewards, and obligations. As such, they both influence and are influenced by the culture of the organization.[48] Much of the psychological contract is implicit. Because of this, change initiators may be unaware of it when they alter existing arrangements. In effect, leaders often don't recognize the impact such changes may have on the psychological contract. They fail to realize that employees may have a very different view than they do of what constitutes "their deal," their employment contract, including what they have a right to expect and what is fair and equitable. The perceptions of sudden and arbitrary changes to the psychological contract of employees can lead to trouble.

While most people recognize that their psychological contracts will have to adapt to changing conditions, they don't react well to surprises and unilateral actions that fail to consider their input or that of their representatives. Changes that threaten our sense of security and control will produce a loss of trust, fear, resentment, and/or anger.[49] People need to devote time and effort to absorbing the change and its implications. Even unilateral changes that will have a positive impact on employees may be resisted because of factors such as suspicion over the "real agenda" and concerns about a reduced sense of control or the capacity to perform.

When dealing with psychological contracts, remember that they do not exist in a vacuum. Changes to one person's contract can have an impact on the psychological contracts of others, including the managers involved and the change leaders themselves. Effectively managing the interpersonal as well as personal dynamics when dealing with changes to psychological contracts represent important work that change leaders need to address.[50]

Ideas related to supervisory support, communications, and issues of fairness that have been discussed earlier will assist change leaders in dealing with the impact of the change on the psychological contract. Dmitriy Nesterkin argues that negative emotions and resistance to changes in the contract are reduced "by implementing and sustaining socially supportive and interpersonally just organizational environment, led by an emotionally intelligent management staff (p. 573).[51] This includes following through and delivering on both the transactional commitments related to the change, as well as the relational elements of the contract.[52]

THE WASHINGTON SUBURBAN SANITARY COMMISSION

In 2002, Washington Suburban Sanitary Commissions (WSSC) new general manager, John Griffin, was brought in to implement change given the threat of privatization that the organization faced. As an outsider hired into this role, he engaged in open and honest communication immediately, asking questions and being transparent with all stakeholders. Griffin led the organizational change with structural reorganization. As a manager working closely with Griffin, Steve Gerwin told his employees, "Don't worry, when the change comes, there will be a job for you and even a better one than you have now. But if you think the job you used to have is going to be there, you're wrong."[53]

Gerwin explicitly communicated that there was going to be a significant change in the psychological contract. "If you want to come to work and read the newspaper, talk to your friends and fill up space and get your pay check, that job is gone. But if you want a challenge and something to do, there may be an opportunity there." He used language the people could understand and remember: They could not have their old jobs after the reorganization, but they could have a challenging job.[54]

Predictable Stages in the Reaction to Change

Change is inevitable—growth is optional

—from a bumper sticker

Reactions to changes that are viewed by recipients as very disruptive can be thought of as occurring in three phases: before the change, during the change, and at the end of the change. The **stages in the reaction to change** typically begin in advance of the actual change initiative as individuals worry about what will happen and what their personal consequences will be. The reaction can continue until long after the change initiative has been completed as people work through the feelings created by the change. When experiencing traumatic changes and transitions, people tend to go through a predictable sequence of stages similar to those outlined by Elizabeth Kübler-Ross in her work on grieving.[55] The model suggests that emotionally healthy people will work through issues until they accept the change. From a change agent's perspective, this is sometimes referred to as helping others work through the "valley of despair." Table 7.2 integrates her insights with those of Fink,[56] Jick,[57] and Perlman and Takacs.[58]

Before the change: People who are anticipating significant change may experience pre-change anxiety. At this stage, people think something is in the wind, but they don't know exactly what it is or how it will show itself. Uncertainty escalates and people often find themselves agonizing over the impact it could have on them as well as its impact on others. For many, the anticipation phase can be debilitating. In their desire to reduce uncertainty and anxiety, many will search for signs of what might be on the horizon. Rumors may abound. Others will deny the signs and signals of change, finding it too threatening to think about. During this phase, the organizational rumor mill often moves into high gear and increases anxiety levels. The confusion and uncertainty created often continue long after the change has been announced and may be coupled with fear, anger, alienation, defensiveness, and a variety of other responses that have strong attitudinal and performance implications. Ambivalent feelings described earlier are often generated at this point and are evident in comments and actions. As noted earlier in this chapter, people are more likely to speak up when the mixed emotions stem from conflicting beliefs. When conflicting emotions are involved, though, individuals often have more difficulty giving voice to negative emotional responses.[59]

Once change is announced and implementation is underway: Even though people know that change is coming, many still experience shock when it actually arrives. Individuals at this stage may feel overwhelmed by events to the point of immobilization. Some people will engage in defensive retreat, holding onto the past and experiencing anger over the changes. Insecurity and a sense of loss and unfairness are common reactions. People will often try to avoid dealing with the real issues and try to reduce their risk by lowering their exposure and relying on habituated responses that have worked in the past. The sense of betrayal will be strongest for those who placed their greatest trust in the firm and who feel their psychological contract with the organization has been violated. Their trust in the leadership will typically decline. Some individuals may agree outwardly, announcing their willingness to cooperate ("We're behind you all the way!"), only to act in a noncompliant manner when they are out of sight of those advocating the change. This behavior can sometimes extend to sabotage. Some people will engage in bargaining behavior, negotiating to make the change go away or to minimize its negative impact on them. Depression and guilt, stress and fatigue, and reduced risk taking and motivation have been regularly reported to follow such unsuccessful attempts to reverse the tide. Alienation can result.

At the end: Finally, people begin to accept the change and acknowledge what they have lost. They begin to let go of the past and start to behave in more constructive ways. At this point, they can again take risks—not those associated with getting even, but rather those associated with liberation from the past and moving on. As risks are rewarded with success, confidence builds in the change. During the adaptation and change stage, people become more comfortable with or accepting of the change, internalize it, and move on.

People need to work their way through their reactions to the change phases in a systematic fashion to avoid becoming stalled. To facilitate this, managers need to be in a position to help them do so, and more will be said about later in this chapter in the two-way communication section. The same is true for the change process itself, which needs to happen in the appropriate order, according

Table 7.2 Stages of Reactions to Change		
Before the Change	**During the Change**	**After the Change**
Anticipation and anxiety phase	Shock, denial, and retreat phase	Acceptance phase
Issues: Coping with uncertainty and rumors about what may or may not happen	Issues: Coping with the change announcement and associated fallout; coping with uncertainty and rumors; reacting to the new "reality"	Issues: Putting residual traumatic effects of change behind you, acknowledging the change, achieving closure, and moving on to new beginnings—adaptation and change
1. Pre-change anxiety—Worrying about what might happen, confusion, and perhaps significant denial of what change is needed or likely	2. Shock—Perceived threat, immobilization, no risk-taking 3. Defensive retreat—Anger, rejection and denial, compliance; sense of loss, risk-taking unsafe 4. Bargaining 5. Depression and guilt, alienation	6. Acknowledgment—Resignation, mourning, letting go, energy for risk-taking begins to build 7. Adaptation and change—Comfort with change, greater openness and readiness, growing potential for risk-taking

to Kotter. As the subtitle of his article *Leading Change: Why Transformation Efforts Fail* says, "Leaders who successfully transform businesses do eight things right (and they do them in the right order)." This order is as follows: establishing a sense of urgency, forming a change team, creating a vision for change, communicating the vision of change, empowering others to act, planning for and creating short-term wins, consolidating wins to reinvigorate the process, and institutionalizing the change. Skipping steps, Kotter says, only creates an illusion of speed and never produces a satisfying result.[60] Both what you do and how you do it are important.

Another often mentioned method for overcoming resistance to change is the **ADKAR** model. Its elements highlighted the importance of: creating **awareness** of the need for change; developing **desire** to participate in and support the change; developing **knowledge** of how to change and a clear sense of the vision for the change; developing people's ability to implement the change and put it to use; and reinforcement to ensure the change stays in place.[61] Concerns have been identified with both of the above approaches, including comments that they are too linear, simplistic and business process improvement focused and not attentive enough to the emotional dimensions of change management. However, they provide the change agent with useful food for thought concerning how to think about and respond to ambivalence and resistance, if they set in.

See **Toolkit Exercise 7.2** to think about the phases of change.

Even when people recognize the need for difficult decisions, they may have difficulty emotionally accepting and adapting to the consequences of change decisions.[62] This emotional distress can be true regardless of the consequences. For example, even those who are retained after organizational downsizing will experience emotional upset. The **survivor syndrome** is a term that refers to the reaction of those who survive a poorly handled, traumatic change such as a downsizing.[63] Survivor syndrome effects include lower levels of job satisfaction, motivation, and organizational loyalty; greater stress; greater ambiguity; vulnerability about one's future position; a sense of entrapment in a negative situation; and guilt about being retained while others have been let go.[64] To avoid some of the traps related to the survivor syndrome, individuals remaining with the organization need to understand the reasons for the decisions, feel people have been fairly dealt with, and that there are solid reasons for hope in the future of the organization and its positive implications for them. The actions and words of the change agents and the way the initiative is rolled out can help recipients constructively adjust to the new realities. More will be said of this later.

As Jick and Peiperl point out, the sequence described in Table 7.2 provides a prescriptive, optimistic, and simplistic view of how individuals adjust to disruptive change.[65] Some will move through the stages quickly, others will move more slowly, some will get stuck, and some will move more quickly than they should, taking unresolved issues with them. As an example, consider the actions of a senior executive we know who lost his job as the result of a merger. During the eight months it took him to find a new position, he focused on maintaining a very positive attitude. Friends marveled at his resilience, though some questioned whether he was living in denial. Upon joining a new firm as a vice president, he became increasingly critical and bitter about his new employer. His hostility had little to do with the organization he had joined or his new position. It was unresolved anger and other baggage related to his earlier dismissal. His inability to recognize and deal with this ultimately cost him the new position.[66] When individuals get "stuck" in the early and middle stages, extricating themselves can prove very difficult.

Individual reactions to organizational change will be related to perceptions of the potential outcomes, and most changes will not be as severe and disruptive as those envisioned above. In the next section, the chapter explores three specific factors that have an influence on how people adapt to change:

- personality and experience with the rate of change
- the reactions of coworkers and teammates
- experience with and trust in leaders

See **Toolkit Exercise 7.3** to consider your personal reactions to a change situation.

Stakeholders' Personalities Influence Their Reactions to Change

Some individuals (innovators, early adopters, or members of the early majority) are generally more predisposed to change (see our discussion in Chapter 6). Others tend to review carefully the experience of others and commit later in the process (the late majority and late adopters). Finally, there are those who resist adopting change until the bitter end.[67] These **predispositions to change** are influenced by individual factors such as susceptibility to the social influence of others, tolerance for risk and ambiguity, self-image (e.g., innovator versus cautious adopter), and (of course!) the nature of the actual change and its perceived impact on them and the things they value.[68] See **Toolkit Exercise 7.4** to think about your natural predisposition to change.

As the above suggests, individuals' perceptions of the change experience and the risk of change will be influenced by their personalities.[69] People who have a low **tolerance for turbulence and ambiguity** tend to be most comfortable in stable environments.[70] As the rate of change accelerates, they will experience increased stress as they attempt to cope and adjust. At low to moderate levels, though, this increased stress may also lead to increased job satisfaction if people experience success with change. However, when change comes to be seen as increasingly disruptive or radical, the resulting stress and strain will tend to produce increasingly elevated levels of anxiety and fear, defensiveness, fatigue, and ultimately hopelessness, alienation, and resignation. Levels of absenteeism and turnover, errors and accidents, and depressed levels of work satisfaction are commonly observed to escalate as such stressors rise.[71]

People who have a high tolerance for turbulence and uncertainty will find stable and unchanging environments unsatisfying after a period of time. When they find novelty and challenge lacking, concerns grow that their careers have stalled,[72] and they experience increasing levels of boredom, frustration, absenteeism, and turnover.[73] As the rate of change increases to moderate levels, so will their levels of satisfaction and interest, particularly if they become directly engaged with the change initiative. As the rate of change and the accompanying levels of turbulence and uncertainty intensifies to levels that are outside their comfort zones, effects similar to those seen in low-tolerance individuals are observed, although the effects occur later at higher rates of change (see Figure 7.2).

Take a few moments to revisit the question of how you react to change and reflect on your experience. What is your predisposition to accept change? You can also use this to help understand your stakeholders (see **Toolkit Exercise 7.5**).

Prior Experience Impacts a Person's and Organization's Perspective on Change

Previous experience with change will affect a person's view and behavior. Long periods of stability and minimal change will lead to people seeing change as more unsettling and risky than those with somewhat more frequent encounters with change.[74] Even those who are thinking "thank goodness, we're finally doing something!" may at first experience elevated levels of perceived risk and stress from exposure to even moderate levels of change.

A sustained period of continued success with a particular strategy can cause individuals and organizations to become trapped by those strategies and tactics that have served them well. The tendency to rely on competencies and strategies that have worked in the past is referred to as a **competency or a complacency trap**.[75] Faced with the need for change, they rely on those approaches that have served them well in the past, even though conditions have changed and the old strategies are no longer well aligned with their environment. Breaking out of these traps is not easy. Related to this is **confirmation bias**—our tendency to embrace information that supports our beliefs and reject contradictory information and a related tendency to think we know much more than we do about those things we have strong beliefs about. The more imbedded these are, the more work change agents have on their hands to help individuals (including themselves) break free of these traps so that they are more able to see, understand and adapt.[76]

If organizations and their employees have adapted successfully to ongoing experiences with moderate levels of change, then those employees are likely to be more open and flexible. The organization's change "muscles" are toned. Those who have regular, ongoing exposure to moderate amounts of positive change (e.g., through continuous improvement) tend to find change to be less unsettling and hence less risky because they become accustomed to believing that tomorrow will likely be different from today and that this is not something to be avoided.[77] However, when organizations and employees live in an environment with sustained periods of major upheavals and uncertainty, the sense of personal risk escalates and remains high. Under these conditions, employees may become exhausted and feel increasingly vulnerable to the next wave of change. They become jaded and alienated if earlier promises and hopes for improvement have gone unmet. Those who have not exited the firm may resign themselves to adopting a strategy of keeping their heads down to avoid personal risk. Under these extreme conditions, the perceived risk attached to a particular change initiative may actually diminish. Like those in danger of being swept overboard in a storm, individuals may be prepared to grasp onto any plausible change initiative that looks like it could serve as a lifeline, unless their alienation is such that they have effectively given up.

Figure 7.2 depicts a hypothetical connection between past rates of change experienced by people in an organization and the degree of perceived risk with an anticipated change. It illustrates the adaptability and resilience that individuals exhibit as a result of their experience with the previous rates and types of change within an organization. For example, if people have experienced long periods of minimal change, they will likely perceive higher risks with the proposed change. The perceived risk of the proposed change declines if there has been a moderate rate of change within the organization and a general normalization and level of comfort associated with past changes. As the normal rate of change increases in intensity and/or becomes drawn out, the perception of risk associated with the new change begins to rise again. When the rate and level of intensity of change reach a certain point, those involved will be ready to grasp at anything with the potential of offering a way out (see drop-off line in Figure 7.2). This pattern can be seen when participants recognize that the organization is in a crisis state, and they become unfrozen and ready to change. In a crisis situation, one can expect initial defensiveness followed by openness to change if a viable path forward can be offered.[78]

As has been discussed, both personality and past experiences with change affect how people view proposed changes. Table 7.3 outlines the hypothesized interactions between an individual's need for change, tolerance for ambiguity, and the frequency and magnitude of the change experience. Change agents who recognize why people are reacting to change as they are and who understand how to help them adapt possess a valuable skill set.

Coworkers Influence Stakeholders' Views

Our views of change are also influenced by the comments and actions of those around us—particularly those whose opinions and relationships we value (see Table 7.4). Trusted mentors, managers, and friends can be particularly influential. If those we trust are positively predisposed toward a change initiative, we may be influenced in that direction. Similarly, if they are experiencing serious

Figure 7.2   Degree of Perceived Risk Associated With a Particular Change

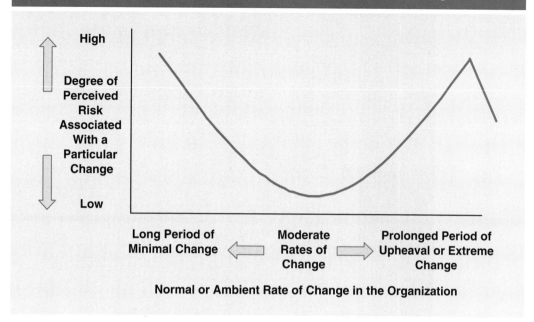

concerns about the change or are opposed to it, they will influence us to consider factors that may move us in the opposite direction.[79]

Consider, for example, the reactions of the immediate supervisor who is on the firing line when it comes to implementing change. Have they been involved in developing the change and/or do they feel fully informed about the need for and nature of the change, and its implications? Do they feel that they have been listened to? Research shows that supervisors/managers have a significant influence on how the change is perceived and reacted to by their direct reports. It comes as no surprise to find that managers who are more committed to the change are more likely to generate more positive responses to the change in those who report to them.[80] Yet all too often, frontline managers report that they found out about the change at the same time as their direct reports. They see themselves as being expected to explain and voice support for the change but feel ill-informed about it and excluded from the process until the very end. Ignoring them is a mistake to be avoided. Engaging them as valued contributors to the change process increases the likelihood that they will communicate support for the change with those they influence, and constructively participate in its implementation.[81]

Coworkers and work groups play a critical role in how people sort out their own reactions to change, because these individuals live in a similar organizational world and their relationships are bound together by norms, roles, and shared obligations and experiences. When coworkers are ambivalent on the desirability of a particular change, one can expect to see **skepticism** in others as they sort out their own feelings about the matter. The importance of coworkers' reactions increases as the strength of relational ties rises. The more coworkers see themselves as part of a cohesive team, the greater will be their influence.[82] Even groups that seem to

Table 7.3 The Interaction of Personality With the Experience of Change

Individual Difference	Change Experience			
	Low	**Some**	**Frequent**	**Chaotic**
	No change experience for an extended period, a belief that this job will last indefinitely	Some change experience that demonstrates both the difficulties and survivability of change	Frequent change experience, nothing static, major upheavals and uncertainty	Chaotic environment characterized by temporary systems, fluid environments, and constant change
Individuals who have higher tolerance for ambiguity, novelty, and change	Restlessness, boredom, attempts to create change or to disrupt routines	Grappling with change issues; feelings of invigoration and new meaning in the job, expectation of improvement	Stress showing, coping strategies being developed, energy still present but fatigue starting, voicing of concerns; the desire to exit increases	Stress effects, fear, and fatigue as they attempt to cope; voicing of concerns exists, but the likelihood of resignation, alienation rises; and/or a willingness to grasp onto a plausible course of action as a way to reduce the chaos
Individuals who have a lower tolerance for ambiguity, novelty, and change	Acceptance of the situation, buy-in to the steady state, no preparation or anticipation of change	Stress effects present, concerns voiced, but a willingness to adjust to moderate amount of change present	Significant coping difficulties; stress effects, including fear, fatigue, and alienation often present; increased willingness to grasp on to a plausible course of action to reduce the chaos	Severe coping difficulties and resultant stress and strain, alienation, resignation and/or exit at high levels and/or elevated willingness to grasp at plausible courses of action to reduce the chaos

Table 7.4   Impact of Trusted Peers on Recipients

Opinions of Those Trusted by Recipients	Recipients' Initial Attitude to the Change	Possible Implications on the Attitude of the Recipients
Positive toward the change	Positive toward the change	Very motivated to support and predisposed to get involved
	Negative toward the change	Opposed to the change but potentially open to other perspectives because of new information and peer pressure
Negative toward the change	Positive toward the change	Support of the change may become more tempered due to information and the perspectives offered by trusted peers. Will often experience pressure to reconsider their support or perhaps be silenced by peer pressure
	Negative toward the change	Opposed to the change and reinforced in those views by trusted peers and the peer group

be in conflict will often become cohesive and turn on the "outsider" who is seen to be threatening group members. Change leaders who ignore cohesion, norms, and varying levels of ambivalence do so at their own peril.

Feelings About Change Leaders Make a Difference

How employees view and react to change is influenced by their perceptions of the change leaders. If people believe their perspectives and interests are recognized and they trust these leaders, then they are likely to respond positively to the suggestions for change.

When change leaders talk about significant change, they often focus on the rationale, including the costs and benefits of changing. They may pay some attention to the costs of *not* changing, but usually little focus is given to the benefits of the status quo. Followers, on the other hand, assessing change at a personal level, will often reflect on the benefits of not changing and discount the costs of staying with the status quo. The followers may prefer the devil they know to the unknown one. They can estimate, and often inflate, the costs of changing but may feel far less certain about the benefits. As a result, change leaders and followers' estimates of the benefits and costs can differ dramatically.

If change leaders recognize and deal with the issues factually, constructively, and sensitively, they will help people interpret the context in a more predictable manner and concerns can be brought to the surface and addressed.[83] An approach that has been advocated by Cranston and Keller is to communicate the reasons for the change to recipients in five different ways. The first (1)1 is the traditional business case approach that we are very familiar with (e.g., we're losing market share, this is an opportunity to increase sales and profitability, lower costs will strengthen the bottom line). However, they also recommend discussing why the change is important to (2) society, (3) customers, (4) the working team, and (5) the individuals doing the work. In addition, they believe supervisory support, in conjunction with soliciting recipients' ideas and engaging them in target setting, will enhance engagement and commitment. They also recommend the use of small, unexpected rewards to recognize progress and motivate along the way.[84]

From a procedural justice and a personal efficacy point of view, people want their voices to be heard, even if it doesn't result in a change in the decision. In 1998, when the president of Continental Airways told employees that he was closing their airport's operations, his candor, combined with his positive reputation as a leader, resulted in an acceptance of the change.

CANDOR AT CONTINENTAL AIRWAYS

I met with the employees and their families—about 600 people in all. Along with explaining the details of the closing and relocation plans (the company had doubled the financial aspects of the relocation package over what was required by the contract), I also shared with them my vision for Continental and how far we had come. I then opened the floor to questions and answers.

For about five minutes, employees expressed appreciation that I had personally come to give them the news and had developed a financial package to meet their needs. But then the pilots walked in—in full uniform—with their families. They surrounded the room and refused to sit down. A pilot came to the microphone to express how incompetent he felt management was and how Continental was once again making the wrong decision. The rest of the pilots applauded.

Do you know what happened? The rest of the employees, led by a baggage handler who was also being relocated, stood up and defended me, one after another, for 20 minutes. They told the pilots that they should feel lucky that Continental finally had a senior management team that treated them with enough respect to deliver the bad news—as well as the good relocation package—in person. I left to a standing ovation.[85]

How change leaders handle the perceptions and the alterations to the psychological contract will matter to employees. The president of Continental was more successful in managing the shift in psychological contract with the ground employees than with the pilots. Perceptions of his promises may have been influenced by the employees' views that they were being treated reasonably under the circumstances—procedural and distributive justice was upheld.[86] The fact that he was personally present to deliver the news also mattered. People react positively to courage, empathy, honesty, and sound logic and these are better conveyed in person than when they are relegated to talking points or a report. When people feel steamrollered by the pressure exerted on them rather than reasonably engaged, resistance may go underground and resurface at a later date in the form of resentment for the change leader.[87]

INTEGRITY IS ONE ANTIDOTE
TO SKEPTICISM AND CYNICISM

Some people believe change leaders when they promise a bright future or state that there is no alternative except what is offered. However, others are more skeptical—often for good reasons. Followers may believe that the promises are suspect, particularly if the leader is relatively unknown or untested. If followers have received promises before and found them wanting, then people will be skeptical. Followers sometimes report that change leaders have said the right things but acted in ways that advanced their own self-interest, ignoring what was good for most employees and the organization. That was the concern about Thorsten Heins (CEO, BlackBerry) that was voiced quietly at first when people read about his compensation arrangements in required public disclosures. It was voiced much more loudly when he departed BlackBerry with a $22 million severance after less than two years of rapidly deteriorating performance and the unsuccessful sale of the firm.[88] Similar concerns were initially raised about his replacement, John Chen, but those doubts have now been replaced with hope. Chen has guided Blackberry through a long and difficult journey. A well-earned reputation for sound judgement, candor, a clear eye on the longer term and integrity have provided internal and external stakeholders with light at the end of the tunnel.[89]

Skepticism can shift to **cynicism** (a real loss of faith) and heightened pessimism when people whose opinions we value share a similar negative belief.[90] The consequences of such cynicism include reduced satisfaction, reduced organizational commitment, and less motivation to work hard. It results in an increase in accidents and errors, a lessened desire and will to engage in future change initiatives, and decreased leader credibility. As Reichers, Wanous, and Austin say, "People do not deliberately become cynical, pessimistic and blaming. Rather these attitudes result from experience, and are sustained because they serve useful purposes. Cynicism persists because it is selectively validated by the organization's mixed record of successful change, and by other people in the organization who hold and express similar views."[91]

The perceived trustworthiness and integrity of the change leader play important roles in the judgments made by the recipients. When change leaders are viewed as credible and trustworthy, their vision of the future reduces the sense of uncertainty and risk and increases the sense of hope in recipients as they put their faith in the leader's judgment. People often turn to credible leaders and colleagues to help them absorb uncertainty and make sense of confusion.[92] Leaders' efforts to actively involve recipients in the change initiative further reduce the chances of cynicism developing.[93]

Periods of transition represent a time when the ethical and reputational risks for leaders are particularly high. The "best course of action" is far from clear. Offering hope and direction without misleading or overstating the case is the narrow path that change leaders must navigate. As one CEO noted, the difference between a visionary leader and a huckster is the thin edge that is integrity.[94]

AVOIDING COERCION BUT PUSHING HARD: THE SWEET SPOT?

Change leaders may find that they have to resort to the use of coercion. Kramer argues that under certain circumstances, intimidating leaders apply their political intelligence to creatively push followers to higher levels of performance than would otherwise have been achieved.[95] Importantly, Kramer specifically notes that while such individuals are tough and demanding, they are not simply bullies. Their initial coercion is to unfreeze the situation and achieve initial shifts in position. However, leaders who rely primarily on the application of fear and force to gain commitment to change are taking significant risks.[96] While it may be true that "if you have them by their throats, their hearts and minds will follow,"[97] any release of the throat risks resistance and revolt. Effective change must be about more than the leader's power.

Monique Leroux at Desjardins challenged the employees, but she did so with a mix of encouragement, active engagement, occasional ultimatums around unacceptable behavior, staff changes and dismissals when necessary, and modeling the desired change through her own behavior. She used metrics and other information to make the business challenges visible to everyone in ways they could understand and relate back to their work and the company they were committed to. The use of such information was not only to help senior management understand the business, the underlying problems, the paths forward, and progress along the way; the metrics and related information and stories had a psychological effect with the broader organization as well, increasing employee awareness of what they were working toward and why it was important.

At times, employees respond to leaders out of fear of what will happen if they don't comply. While fear can motivate, leaders who rely primarily on fear or coercion are following a risky path—both ethically and pragmatically (i.e., will the support be there when the stick or threat is no longer present?).[98] In his book *From Good to Great*, Collins refers to this "doom loop" as the enemy of effective leadership.[99]

Leaders, frustrated by a lack of progress, are attracted to the use of punishment and fear, because these tools are available, are immediate in their short-term effects, and carry the illusion of control through obedience and compliant behavior.[100] However, we do *not recommend* the use of such strategies in most situations. Years ago, Deming noted that the move to total quality could not be achieved through fear and evidence in the intervening years continues to demonstrate the lack of effectiveness of fear.[101] While fear may produce compliance in the short run, they have proven to be ineffective over the intermediate to longer term.[102] Further, such techniques can create undesirable side effects (e.g., frustration, withdrawal in the form of absenteeism and turnover, aggression, and sabotage). A much more desirable and less risky course of action is through the positive engagement of people through initiatives that enhance the recipients' capabilities to deal effectively with the change.[103] At the same time, managers can use their power to make expectations and standards explicit in order to challenge employees.

CREATING CONSISTENT SIGNALS FROM SYSTEMS AND PROCESSES

While the leader's words and deeds are important, so too are other parts of the organizational context. A leader's credibility will be either enhanced or diminished by the extent to which organizational systems and processes send a consistent message or are themselves the focus of changes that will bring them into alignment with the change vision. This is enhanced further when social media and informal channels are also consistent in the messages they are carrying. However, this *should not* be interpreted as a call to wall people off from conflicting or contrary messages that are sent in good faith as people question what is occurring and why.

Change agents may be tempted to try to create a communication "echo chamber" in order to get everyone on the same page, but it is *highly recommended that this temptation be avoided*. Rather, use these channels as an opportunity to deal openly and candidly with concerns, so that the value of critical thinking and the honest voicing of concerns are reinforced and confidence is built in the honesty and integrity of what is being communicated by the change agent and organization. This open approach may take more time and energy in the short term but will pay dividends in reducing unsubstantiated rumors and helping to move changes forward in the intermediate to longer terms.[104]

Credibility and trust are diminished when the leader's words say one thing (e.g., quality is critical) but the systems and processes signal something else (e.g., ship now, fix later). In *Built to Last*, Collins and Porras found that firms with staying power possess resilient cultures that have the capacity to adjust and realign their systems and processes in response to changing conditions. This resilience was made functional by the underlying value set and supportive systems and processes that were installed by leaders.[105] As such, they provided continuity for organizational members while at the same time contributing to the adaptability and change of existing systems and processes. This reflects an interesting and important paradox for the change leader. The successful management of change is enhanced by giving voice to factors that develop the sense of continuity, the connection between the past and the future, as well as by giving voice to the need for and nature of the change.[106]

STEPS TO MINIMIZE THE NEGATIVE EFFECTS OF CHANGE

Those who have been involved in significant changes know that how people view the change will have a profound impact on the ultimate success or failure of a change initiative.[107] Success is aided when change recipients become willing implementers. Therefore, the effects of change on recipients need to be approached with care during the initial planning phases and throughout the change process, including the post-change period.

Engagement

Trust is increased and rumors are reduced when leaders share story after story about the problems that are driving the need for change, what is known and not known, process, action plans, and timelines.[108] When coupled with the personal involvement of engaged leaders and executives and a meaningful degree of employee involvement in decisions that affect them (at minimum, the ability to ask questions, voice concerns, and receive answers that reduce uncertainty), individual adaptation and acceptance are advanced.[109] People want to know where things are going, why, and what the implications are on the organization, their parts of the operation, and on them personally. When change leaders don't know the answers to questions that are raised, people should be given a timetable detailing when they can expect to hear and the commitments to follow up should be honored.

Timeliness

Employees often want to vent their concerns and frustrations, and, at times, grieve what has been lost. If this is to be handled constructively, they need to hear in a timely fashion and be given time to constructively process what they have heard. No one benefits when recipients first hear about a particular change on the evening news or in the local coffee shop. When this happens, the information needs to be quickly and credibly dealt with through internal communication channels. The more that critical messages can be communicated in a timely, face-to-face manner (backed up by appropriate documents and systems/processes, as needed, to handle complexity and retention), the better. Otherwise, the rumor mill will shift into overdrive as people attempt to make sense of new and potentially conflicting information.[110] Once the message is in their hands, they may need time and assistance to make sense of what they have heard and constructively react, both on their own and with their peers. Otherwise, they may well come to believe that they have not been fairly dealt with by the change leaders or organization.

Two-Way Communication

Change communication needs to be two-way, as change leaders need to be open to learning as much from exchanges as followers. A variety of communication channels are available to change leaders, and multiple channels are best. Redundancy is clearly preferable to gaps. Communicating through executive-staff briefings, teams, task forces, recipient representatives, advisory groups, video, newsletters, hotlines, social media and the creative use of the intranet (including bulletin boards, blogs, social media and e-mail to monitor concerns and expedite the delivery of answers) *all* have a role in helping people learn about and adapt to change. When coupled with transparency, authenticity, and minimal levels of executive defensiveness, these communication approaches advance recipient engagement and adaptation to change.

Exposure to employees' feedback and reactions allows change leaders to adapt strategies and approaches in an informed and sensitive manner. For example, tracking themes from e-mails, postings on bulletin boards, social media, and surveys results can provide insights into how followers are interpreting and responding to the change. The importance of such feedback proves the adage that leaders who think they know it all have a fool as their advisor. To quote the movie director Blake Edwards, "Every time I think I know 'where it's at,' it's usually somewhere else."

Bringselius provides interesting food for thought concerning what is driving employee objections to the organizational changes, the importance of managers testing their assumptions, and developing a deeper understanding of those employee reactions. This allows managers to alter their responses to different causes in ways that (a) test the legitimacy of concerns, (b) have a positive impact on the recipients' sense of how they are being treated, (c) allow new information to be factored into the unfolding of the change process, and (d) help employees work their way through the concerns they have.[111] The ability to have new information factored into the unfolding of the change process can create improvisational space that frees individuals (in the short term) from their traditional roles; allows them to explore; provides them with a greater sense of **self-efficacy and agency** (the strength of a person's belief that they have the ability to complete tasks, accomplish goals, and have some degree of influence over what happens to them); and makes possible the refinement of what is being pursued and how it is being pursued.[112]

Jick and Peiperl have identified a number of strategies that can assist both the recipients and their managers in coping with different stages of the change (see Table 7.5).

Change recipients can develop support networks to facilitate letting go and moving on if they know and understand the stages of change. Change leaders need to develop an understanding of the dynamics around change and recognize the need to work through the change-management process in a systematic and supportive fashion. Often, followers' understanding of the need for change lags behind that of change leaders. By definition, those leading change have diagnosed the need for change, mourned the loss of the old, understood and embraced the new vision, and moved to action. Those impacted by the change need to work through the same process—but are lagging behind their leaders and lack their

Table 7.5   Strategies for Coping With Change

Recipients	Change Leaders
Accepting Feelings as Natural	**Rethinking Resistance**
• Self-permission to feel and mourn	• As natural as self-protection
• Taking time to work through feelings	• As a positive step toward change
• Tolerating ambiguity	• As energy to work with
	• As information critical to the change process
Managing Stress	**Giving First Aid**
• Maintaining physical well-being	• Accepting emotions
• Seeking information about the change	• Listening
• Limiting extraneous stressors	• Providing safety
• Taking regular breaks	• Marking endings
• Seeking support	• Providing resources and support
Exercising Responsibility	**Creating Capability for Change**
• Identifying options and gains	• Making organizational support of risks clear
• Learning from losses	• Providing a continuing safety net
• Participating in the change	• Emphasizing continuities, gains of change
• Inventorying strengths	• Helping employees explore risks, options
• Learning new skills	• Suspending judgment
• Diversifying emotional investing	• Involving people in decision making
	• Teamwork
	• Providing opportunities for individual growth

Source: Adapted from Jick, T., & Peiperl, M. A. (2003). *Managing change, cases and concepts* (2nd ed.). New York: McGraw-Hill.

direct involvement. As change leaders, we need to give them time to adapt and catch up! See **Toolkit Exercise 7.6** to analyze a time when you were a change recipient and the quality and actions of change leadership during that period.

MAKE CONTINUOUS IMPROVEMENT THE NORM

One way that organizations can reduce the perceived threat of change is to adopt managerial approaches that challenge everyone to regularly question the status quo and seek to improve existing practices as part of their ongoing activities. If organizational members routinely question and initiate continuous improvement projects, then shifts in the environment will not be seen as threatening events. Leaders generate an atmosphere in which change is experienced as a naturally occurring condition by creating an organizational climate in which incremental changes are sought out and embraced. The fact that tomorrow is unlikely to be exactly the same as today becomes the expected norm as opposed to an unexpected shock.[113]

One benefit of continuous improvement approaches such as Six Sigma is the legitimization of ongoing changes in ways that provide continuity with the past. Rather than searching for the silver bullet that will produce the cure for current organizational ills, these approaches seek to advance less heroic, ongoing initiatives that will enhance organizational health in incremental ways.[114] In so doing, these approaches make revolutionary changes less likely and threatening because the real and perceived magnitude of the change is reduced.

If the organizational culture promotes an ongoing and constructive embrace of change, perceptions of the threat related to change are bound to be reduced. Abrahamson refers to this as dynamic stability. Firms like Pepsi and Apple appear to be exemplars of the approach.[115] The experience tells organizational members that changes are normal and tend to work out for the best.

When the news is bad (maybe more importantly than when the news is good), an approach of ongoing employee engagement with change can lead to lower levels of uncertainty, quicker response times (people know what they are facing), improved outcomes (e.g., less undesirable employee turnover), and higher levels of satisfaction than likely would otherwise have occurred. If people (or their representatives) have participated in the analysis, planning, and/or implementation efforts, this tends to further reduce the fear and uncertainty.[116]

Creating organizational agility and resiliency enables organizations to be more prepared for change. Agility allows an organization to be more open to change while resiliency strengthens the core—common purpose, shared beliefs, and identity—to thoughtfully and strategically guide a change process. This requires the establishment of a knowledge-sharing system, commitment from top leadership, and cross-training of employees. In addition, there needs to be a commitment to organization-wide reevaluation and the use of all successes and failures as learning opportunities.[117] Today's and future organizations need to be designed to institutionalize change. This can be done through the promotion of organizational modularity, quick anticipation and response to external forces, construction of conflict-management processes, and building of organizational coherence around values and culture rather than structure.[118]

A final approach to reducing the perceived threat of change is to use approaches that do not cause people to believe they have to bet the farm. One can do this through encouraging the use of experimentation and pilot programs and through ensuring that the perceived rewards and punishments associated with success and failure are not excessive. Again, experience has demonstrated that a series of smaller, interrelated changes by dedicated change agents over time can produce substantial, even revolutionary changes in the organization—sometimes without the organization even knowing they were underway.[119]

ENCOURAGE PEOPLE TO BE CHANGE AGENTS AND AVOID THE RECIPIENT TRAP

It is clear from this chapter that being a change recipient is not as energizing or exciting as being a change agent! Change agents are active and involved. Change recipients find themselves on the receiving end and may experience a lack of power and control. One way to reduce the negative effects of change is to take risks, get more involved, and become a change agent.

When people attempt to influence the events swirling about them, they are, in effect, acting as their own change agents. Since they are often in subordinate roles and dependent, to varying degrees, on the actions of others, recipients can manage the influence process by: recognizing whom they are dependent on;[120] engaging in appropriate stakeholder analysis; and taking actions that use the advantages of what they've learned. By demonstrating initiative, presenting ideas, taking actions, and attempting to make a difference, change recipients can shift their role and potentially can gain power in both real and perceived terms. It will enhance both their self-efficacy and agency and they will be viewed differently in the organization.

As you will have recognized by now, these notions of agency and active involvement in change by organizational members, from awareness creation to ideation and implementation, are themes upon which this book is built. The search for autonomy, mastery and purpose in one's life is advanced when one becomes an agent of change.[121]

SUMMARY

This chapter has dealt with how people react and why they respond positively, negatively, or with ambivalence to change initiatives. It suggests that change leaders use feelings of ambivalence as opportunities to learn and to influence stakeholders in constructive and informed ways. Change agents need to understand ambivalence and resistance to change and use the awareness of these emotions to develop a solid appreciation for the change environment.

The chapter outlines the prescriptive model of change phases that people go through when disruptive changes are involved. Knowing the model may provide useful insights as to how to act. The chapter deals with the factors that affect how people view change: their personalities, their experiences with change, their coworkers, the organization, and the change leaders themselves. Finally, the chapter ends by considering what change agents and leaders can do to manage the process and minimize the negative impact of change. See **Toolkit Exercise 7.1** for critical thinking questions for this chapter.

Recipients of change—find themselves on the receiving end of a change initiative and have little power to alter the direction or content of a change initiative.

Resistance to change—includes actions that are intended to slow or prevent change from happening. Resistance arises when an individual comes to believe that the costs outweigh the benefits and that opposition is warranted. Actions can vary from the expression of concern and "go slow" responses through to more active forms of resistance, including coalition building, formal protests, and even sabotage. Too often managers expect resistance and it becomes a self-fulfilling prophecy.

Ambivalence to change—the mixed emotions that a change initiative can trigger. Ambivalence arises from uncertainty and occurs when we are asked to act in ways that are inconsistent with our existing attitudes. These mixed emotions generate discomfort that we seek to resolve. There is evidence that suggests we have an easier time giving voice to mixed feelings involving conflicting beliefs than we do when negative emotional responses are involved. Once the individual has resolved his or her ambivalence, subsequent changes to those attitudes become much more difficult until a new sense of ambivalence arises.

The **psychological contract**—represents the sum of the implicit and explicit agreements we believe we have with key individuals and the organization concerning our employment relationship. These ground our expectations concerning ourselves and the organization, concerning terms and conditions, norms, rights, rewards, and obligations.

The **stages in the reaction to change**—typically must progress through when coping with a more traumatic change are the anticipation and anxiety phase, the shock, denial, and retreat phase, and the acceptance phase.

The **ADKAR model**—this model highlights the importance of: creating awareness of the need for change; developing desire to participate in and support the change; developing **knowledge** of how to change and a clear sense of the vision for the change; developing people's **ability** to implement the change and put it to use; and **reinforcement** to ensure the change stays in place.

Survivor syndrome—refers to the reaction of those who survive a poorly handled, traumatic change such as a downsizing.

Predisposition to change—relates to our general inclination toward change. Are we typically innovators, early adopters, members of the early majority of adopters, members of the late majority, or in the group of individuals who are very late adopters or non-adopters?

Tolerance for turbulence and ambiguity—involves our comfort level with these conditions. Individuals who have higher tolerance levels generally will be more comfortable and open to change, while those who have lower tolerance levels will prefer more stable and predictable environments.

Competency or a complacency trap—the tendency to rely on competencies and strategies that have worked in the past.

Confirmation Bias—our tendency to embrace information that supports our beliefs and reject contradictory information, and a related tendency to think we know more than we do about things we have strong beliefs about.

Skepticism—relates to doubts and concerns we may have concerning the capacity of the change to deliver the promised results. These may be rooted in the change itself, the adoption process, concerns about the change leadership, or unease about the organization's and other key stakeholders' responses to the change.

Cynicism—occurs when we fundamentally lose faith in the change, the adoption process, the key individuals involved, or the organization.

Self-Efficacy and Agency—the strength of a person's belief that they have the ability to complete tasks, accomplish goals, and have some degree of influence over what happens to them.

CHECKLIST: HOW TO MANAGE AND MINIMIZE CYNICISM ABOUT CHANGE[122]

1. Keep people involved in making decisions that affect them.

2. Emphasize and reward supervisors who foster two-way communication and good working relationships and show consideration and respect for employees.

3. Keep people informed about ongoing change—when, why, and how—and include honest appraisals of risks, costs, benefits, and consequences.

4. Keep surprises to a minimum through regular communication about changes, anticipating questions and concerns.

5. Enhance credibility by

   a. Using credible spokespersons who are liked and trusted.

   b. Using positive messages that appeal to logic and consistency.

   c. Using multiple channels and repetition.

6. Acknowledge mistakes, accept responsibility, apologize, and make amends.

7. Publicize successful changes and progress.

8. Use two-way communication in order to see change from the employees' perspectives and use this awareness to help with planning and future communications related to change.

9. Provide opportunities for employees to express feelings and receive validation and reassurance. Ensure you address the concerns raised.

10. Ensure existing structures, systems, and processes are not sending conflicting messages, obstructing the change, and creating cynicism in the process. If they are, recognize their impact, discuss them openly, and take steps to address the issue and either bring them into alignment with the change or minimize their negative impact.[123]

END-OF-CHAPTER EXERCISES

TOOLKIT EXERCISE 7.1
Critical Thinking Questions

The URLs for the videos listed below can be found in two places. The first spot is next to the exercise and the second spot is on the website at **study.sagepub.com/cawsey4e.**

1. The Power of Vision: Dreaming of Peace

    View *Pray the Devil Back to Hell* (Information about documentary available at http://www.pray thedevilbacktohell.com/).
    This is the story of how Liberian women who were recipients of a harsh political regime and leader became leaders of change within their country.

    - Why did the women dress in white and sit in the marketplace for days on end? What did they hope to accomplish? Why were they successful in reaching their goal of petitioning the dictator, Charles Taylor?

    - How did the Liberian women, who were not a formal part of the negotiating teams in Ghana, impact the negotiation processes? Who were the important allies of the Liberian women during the negotiations?

    - Would you agree that the Liberian women went from being recipients of change to being leaders of change? Which of their strategies and tactics do you think other powerless groups can use to become powerful and lead change?

2. The "X" Model of Employee Engagement: Maximum Satisfaction Meets Maximum Contribution—7:43 minutes

   https://www.youtube.com/watch?v=gZ3wxgog4nc

   Consider the following:

   - How can you engage employees in each area to increase their engagement to the organization and an organizational change effort?

   - Which group are your greatest allies within the change, and how can you use them?

   - Think about jobs in the past and describe your engagement using this model.

Please see **study.sagepub.com/cawsey4e** *for the above case and a downloadable template of this exercise.*

TOOLKIT EXERCISE 7.2

Working Through Emotional Responses to Change

1. Consider a significant and disruptive change situation that you know about (or talk to a friend or relative about such a change situation). Identify the different phases of change.

2. Can you identify strategies that people used or could have used to help them work their way through the different phases?

3. Can you identify strategies that change leaders used or could have used to help people work their way through the different phases?

	Are recipients aware of how they are reacting? Yes/No	Strategies recipients can use to work through an emotional response to a change initiative	Strategies change leaders can use to help recipients work through an emotional response to a change initiative
Pre-change anxiety			
Shock			
Defensive retreat			
Bargaining			
Depression, guilt, and alienation			
Acknowledgment			
Adaptation and change			

Does the model hold? Why or why not?

What other consequences of change can you identify?

*Please see **study.sagepub.com/cawsey4e** for a downloadable template of this exercise.*

TOOLKIT EXERCISE 7.3

Personal Reactions to Change

1. Think through your organizational experiences at school and at work when you have been a recipient of change. How have you typically responded to these changes? What were the factors that led to those responses?

    To help you think about these questions, ask yourself the following concerning three to four such changes:

    a. What was the change, and how was it introduced?

    b. What was the impact on you?

    c. What was your initial reaction? Enthusiasm? "Wait and see" attitude? Ambivalence, due to conflicting reactions? Cynicism?

    d. Did your attitudes change over time? Why or why not?

2. Was there a pattern to your response?

    a. Under what circumstances did you support the change? When did you resist? What can you generalize from these experiences?

    b. If you experienced ambivalence, how did you resolve it and what happened to your attitudes toward the change once the ambivalent feelings were resolved?

3. Overall, have your earlier experiences with change been largely positive, largely negative, or mixed?

    Have these experiences colored your expectations and feelings toward change in the future?

*Please see **study.sagepub.com/cawsey4e** for a downloadable template of this exercise.*

TOOLKIT EXERCISE 7.4

Your Normal Reaction to Innovation and Change

When you find yourself dealing with matters of innovation and change, how do you typically react?

1. Do you find that you fall into the category of innovator or early adopter, readily considering and often adopting new approaches, well in advance of most people?

2. Or do you generally fall into the category of the early majority? If the initial responses and experiences of the early adopters are generally positive, you are willing to take the risk and adopt the new approach.

3. Or are you generally in the category of the late majority? You wait until the innovation or new approach has been tried and tested by many people before you commit to adopt.

4. Or are you a person who typically does not adopt the innovation or new approach until the vast majority of people have done so? In other words, are you a late adopter or even a non-adopter until forced to do so?

5. What is your tolerance for change? What level of turbulence and ambiguity in a work situation do you find most stimulating and satisfying?

6. How do you react when the rate of change is quite low and is likely to remain there?

7. How do you react when the rate of change is at a moderate level? What constitutes a moderate level for you? Are your tolerance levels lower or higher than those of others you know?

8. What price do you find you pay personally when the rate of turbulence and ambiguity exceeds what you are comfortable with? When it is either too low or too high?

9. Have you had to cope with prolonged periods of serious upheaval or periods of extreme turbulence? Have these experiences affected your acceptance of change?

*Please see **study.sagepub.com/cawsey4e** for a downloadable template of this exercise.*

TOOLKIT EXERCISE 7.5

Disruption of the Psychological Contract

Think about a change initiative that you are aware of. What happened or will likely happen to the psychological contracts of recipients?

1. What is the existing psychological contract? (If in the past, what was the contract?)

2. What were the explicit and implicit pieces?

3. In what ways did the change disrupt the existing psychological contract? To what extent was this perception real? (If in the past, in what ways did the change actually disrupt the psychological contract?)

4. Given the individuals and the context, what reactions to these disruptions to the psychological contract do you anticipate? (If in the past, what were the reactions?)

5. Are there steps that could be taken to reduce the negative effects stemming from the disruption? (If in the past, could anything have been done?)

6. How should a new psychological contract be developed with affected individuals? (If this is in the past, how could this have been done?)

7. If you are the recipient of change, what steps could you take to better manage your way through the development of a new contract? (If this is in the past, what could you have done?)

*Please see **study.sagepub.com/cawsey4e** for a downloadable template of this exercise.*

TOOLKIT EXERCISE 7.6

Leadership and Change Recipients

Think more specifically about an example of change leadership that you know.

1. What was the nature of that leadership?

2. Was the leader trusted?

3. Did he or she deserve the trust given?

4. What kind of power did the leader use?

5. How were the messages about the change conveyed? Were they believable messages?

6. Did organizational systems and processes support, or at minimum, not impair the change leader's messages?

7. Was there a sense of continuity between the past and the anticipated future? How was that sense of continuity developed and communicated? What was the impact?

8. What can you learn about the impact of the leader on people and stakeholders as a result of your responses to the above questions?

9. What can you learn about the impact of organizational systems and processes on the people and stakeholders?

10. Talk to others about their experiences. Can you generalize? In what way? What cannot be generalized?

*Please see **study.sagepub.com/cawsey4e** for a downloadable template of this exercise.*

TRAVELINK SOLUTIONS*

By Noah Deszca, Teacher

Durham Board of Education

Gene Deszca, Professor Emeritus

*Lazaridis School of Business and Economics,
Wilfrid Laurier University, Waterloo, Ontario, CA*

Sixteen months had passed since Will had joined Travelink Solutions' Call Center. It had been both a fulfilling and frustrating employment experience. Now he was facing a decision concerning what to do next. Should he remain and try to make a difference or should he follow through on his plans to leave? Rather than let the experience simply fade, he had documented events, hoping it might be helpful to him and maybe even to the firm. He had submitted his resignation on Monday, but his call center manager had asked him to reconsider and Will was scheduled to meet with her on Friday.

On Wednesday of that week, Will met with Robert, his close friend and a marketing manager at Travelink. Robert had been with Travelink for three years. Will told him about his looming decision and he shared what he had documented. Robert's first job had been in the call center and he remained keenly interested in its operation, due to its impact on customer relations. He winced as he read. The writing captured what had been happening and left him pondering not only what Will should do, but what he ought to do with the concerns it raised. It was a topic he'd been thinking about for months but had yet to move on. Change was urgently needed if "the ship was to be righted" and it would not be easy. He turned to Will and shook his head. "Fascinating—let me read this once again."

WILL'S BACKGROUND

Will was enthusiastic when he started at Travelink Solutions Canada: a service company that provided travel assistance to global travellers on a 24/7 basis. Its core product had been emergency roadside automobile assistance, but over the years Travelink had expanded into other areas of travel help, such as medical coverage, legal assistance, and emergency travel arrangements. The company did this for both its own individual customers and for other firms that offered related services but who had outsourced the product design and/or post sale customer service function to Travelink.

Will had completed his final university course requirements while working full time as a baker on the midnight shift at a Tim Horton's franchise, a fast food outlet. After eight months of beginning his workday at 11 pm, he looked forward to more normal working hours. He knew that there would be occasional night and weekend shifts at the Call Center, but Will had been told that it would be no more than one week or weekend per month. That would be fine, reasoned Will. He was confident that the challenge of this new job would prove more satisfying than slinging dough at 4 a.m.

The application process had been an intensive experience. At the age of 23, Will had never applied for a position that demanded a lengthy series of interviews, references that were verified, and tests designed to document his computer literacy and interpersonal and problem-solving skills. He felt very positive about having made it through their rigorous selection system. It suggested to him that this firm must be serious about the quality of the people it hired.

CALL CENTERS: HOW THEY OPERATED

A number of call centers were located in Will's home region. The presence of three universities, a college, and the ethnic diversity of the area provided call centers with access to a literate and multilingual labor pool. Further, office rental costs and labor rates were moderate by provincial standards and there was an excellent telecommunications infrastructure. As a result, several of Will's friends had worked or were working for other call centers. Their experiences, however, had generally been negative—particularly for those working in outbound call centers, where employees made unrequested solicitations for everything from rug cleaning services to cell phones and charitable donations. Friends who had worked in this type of business told him that there were attractive sales-related performance bonuses but that the base pay of around $15 per hour was what most had to rely upon to pay the rent. In addition, his friends reported that there seemed to be few employment benefits (e.g., dental plans) available in these firms and that a number of the positions were essentially permanent part-time positions, in order to fit the need for labor in the late afternoon and early evening periods and reduce benefit obligations further. They were almost unanimous in their descriptions of their outward bound call center jobs as quite stressful, characterized by hang-ups, call recipient abuse, and performance pressure.

Travelink, however, was an inbound call center that responded to customer requests for help with services they had already purchased. Furthermore, the people Will knew who had worked for the firm spoke very positively about the work atmosphere. Robert, for example, had started on the phones but had been promoted three times over a two-year period, most

recently to a marketing management position. Robert was the person who had urged Will to apply. At that time, he had commented on the supportiveness of coworkers and his boss, the decent pay, and the satisfaction derived from helping a customer sort through a difficult situation.

Will's new position came with comprehensive health benefits, paid holidays that exceeded legislated standards, and special rates for things such as local gym memberships, theme park passes, and concerts—discounts that the human resources department had negotiated for Travelink employees. It seemed to Will that his new employer had thought about how to make the firm an appealing company to work for. "Wow! A living wage, combined with such benefits—what a pleasant change." (See Exhibit 1 for compensation and benefit details.)

BUILDING A BUSINESS

Travelink was founded in 1987, in Jackson, Mississippi, to provide roadside assistance to car owners. It had grown from a tiny office space of fifteen employees to a billion-dollar, global service firm with offices based in Europe, Asia, and Australia. In 2002, a Canadian office of 20 employees was established in Will's home town. Sixteen years later, Travelink Solutions Canada had grown. Two hundred of its employees and its Canadian call center were located in two stories of a ten-story office building. Travelink's offerings had been extended over the years to include insurance policies that provided emergency support for national and international travelers facing a variety of perils, including medical emergencies, the theft of personal property, automobile breakdowns, accidents, legal assistance, travel interruptions, and emergency travel related concierge services. Policies were modular in nature and were designed for the traveler who wanted to avoid unpleasant surprises.

Travelink's Canadian call center was located on the lower of the two floors it occupied and involved approximately 150 of the 200 employees located in the building. A reception area on the upper story led into office space for underwriting and marketing employees, the human resources and training department, IT, accounting, supervisory personnel, and senior administration (see Exhibit 2 for a partial organization chart of the Canadian Division). Call center activities were supported by a website that provided customers with valuable travel-related information, advice,and links to other relevant websites.

NEW EMPLOYEE ORIENTATION AND TRAINING

Training for Will commenced December 1st and lasted one month. On his first day, Will joined eleven other new employees, all of whom were university arts graduates. Some (Will included) had been referred to the company through friends that worked for the firm. As a recruitment incentive, a bonus of $500 dollars was offered to any employee who referred a potential employee who was hired and successfully completed the training. Travelink Solutions tried to coordinate its hiring so that a group of 6 to 12 began training at the same time.

Will's trainers, Luther and Marie, seemed approachable and knowledgeable. They worked diligently to accommodate any questions that were asked about work procedures, customer service, company policies, or the call center industry. Will found himself quickly integrated into a comfortable training environment where dialogue occurred openly and people seemed to be genuinely helpful. The training program was quite structured and occurred in a classroom environment. The first two weeks focused on industry and firm specific information that would be relevant to those who would be addressing customer questions and concerns. It included information related to specific products and services, what associates could expect from the customer and their employer, and what was expected of them. The second two weeks included additional content related to products, corporate policies, and workflow procedures, as well as call center simulations and role plays. These latter activities were designed to develop employee competence with the firm's customer service strategies and effective work practices.

At one of the first training sessions, Marie explained that the Travelink Solutions Call Center offered uniquely satisfying service opportunities. As Marie said, "You are not merely the voice on the end of the line. You are the help line. You are someone's lifeline during an experience that will vary from the simply inconvenient to situations that are frustrating and, at times, frightening. If a customer is involved in a serious accident in Mexico, has a medical emergency they need to deal with, or gets mugged or arrested in a foreign land, you are one of the first persons they turn to for help."

Luther told Will's training group that the average cost of recruiting and training a new call center employee was approximately $8,000. Will learned that Travelink Solutions employed approximately 200 people in the Canadian office, 75% of whom were directly involved with the phones in the call center. Direct sales of Travelink's services were done through brokers, agencies, and the internet. Travelink Solutions had a team of underwriters and marketers who crafted and promoted automobile, medical, and travel-related service policies throughout Canada, via its distribution systems. This group was also heavily involved in the design and delivery of similar services for other firms (e.g., banks and insurance companies), under their clients' brand names. This accounted for approximately 75% of Travelink's gross billings, profitability, and call center volumes. Trainees were told that Travelink was considered a leader in customer service quality. Industry benchmark data rated them in the top 10% in customer satisfaction and quality and it was reported that they had almost never lost a corporate account once the business was won. Business volumes and profitability had been growing by more than 20% per year since 2002.

At the end of the month-long training period, each new employee was required to write a three-hour comprehensive exam, dealing with the information that they had been exposed to. If a grade of 90% was not achieved, then an employee was required to retake the test before being permitted to field calls. Although he was nervous, Will believed that his training sessions had been effective in transferring the needed knowledge, and he passed the exam with flying colors. Out of his training group of 12, two people needed to retake the exam before receiving a desk within the call center one week later.

THE WORK BEGAN

When he graduated to the phones and live customers, Will was initially apprehensive. He often consulted online and paper manuals to ensure that he was providing callers with the proper information and advice. For the first few weeks, Luther and Marie were available on the floor to answer trainee questions that arose. Beyond the presence of the trainers, team leaders encouraged new employees to discuss any questions or concerns with experienced associates. Will was directed to Yolanda, a senior associate who said that she would be happy to help. She had been working at Travelink Solutions for over three years and the supervisors allowed Yolanda to log off her phone whenever new associates approached her with questions. Overall, it seemed to Will that the call center was a smooth and efficient operation. The friendly and helpful environment gave him confidence that he would be able to effectively assist callers. Initial supervisory checks and feedback during his first month on the phones further honed his competence and reinforced his confidence.

Marie's comments during the training session concerning the importance of the services that call center employees provided to customers proved true. Offering assistance to distressed travelers was quite satisfying. Will deepened his familiarity with policy details and advisory support materials to ensure that he was providing callers with the correct information, useful advice, and effective service. Of course, there were occasional complaints and angry callers who vented their unhappiness with the quality of service (e.g., tow truck operators who were slow to respond or rude) or the answers they received concerning whether or not they were eligible for the requested coverage. Will quickly learned that it was not helpful to dwell on such calls. Instead, through the guidance of the trainers and Yolanda, he developed techniques that calmed customers and helped to defuse difficult situations. By and large, Will received positive feedback from the callers and this increased in frequency over his first three months on the phones.

Will's experience within the call center was not an anomaly. Comments from fellow trainees echoed his reactions. He noticed that there was far less turnover and absenteeism than what friends at other call centers had led him to believe were the norms in the places they worked. Employees at Travelink voluntarily participated in and seemed to enjoy company events such as potluck lunches. Friends employed at other call centers told him that this was not the case within their firms. One person reported that her firm had made participation mandatory at its corporate social events, leading her to post a message stating that management had decided the floggings would continue until morale improved.

THE CHANGES

After about five months of employment, Will began to notice changes in his workplace. For example, senior managers were voicing concerns related to the need for greater efficiency and new business at the monthly company meetings and team leaders seemed more stressed than they had been earlier. Robert, the marketing manager and Will's friend, explained to him that Travelink had ramped up its staff levels within the call center in anticipation of obtaining new business that had not materialized. As a result, management was under pressure from the head office to improve its financial performance. Robert commented, "I've been working 60-hour weeks for the past several weeks, exploring new opportunities, and drafting proposals related to potential contract bids, and there are rumours that senior management is considering layoffs."

Will was shocked by Robert's candid comments. Sure, the phones had been less busy lately, but this was also May, a month in which clients were no longer faced with the winter elements that breed traffic accidents and mechanical breakdown. May was also a month in which vacation travel was typically down, resulting in fewer travel-related emergencies. Was this not a time when the phones were supposed to be quieter, allowing staff to follow up on the claims that had arisen earlier?

Within the next four weeks, four of the people who had trained with Will left the firm. In their places were empty cubicles. Every time an employee was laid off or quit, the human resources department would send an email to all employees, notifying them of the person's departure. For example, one day Will came into work to find that Linda, a friendly woman who sat in the cubicle next to him, was no longer there. Within two hours, he received a company message that read, "We regret to inform you that, as of today, Linda Jameson is leaving Travelink Solutions. Please join us in wishing Linda all of the best in her future endeavours." Within an hour, Will received a second email that read, "Please be advised that the door security codes have been changed to 25678. Thank you for your cooperation."

Over the following weeks the number of empty cubicles grew. He was surprised that the departures were almost never discussed on the floor. It was as if the employees who had once filled the space had never been there in the first place. The loss of people also seemed to be associated with declining morale. People's willingness to help one another decreased, as did the overall friendliness of the workplace. Will began to save his money to ensure that he would have something to carry him through in the event that he too "went missing."

A NEW ASSIGNMENT

But Will did not go missing. One afternoon in June, he was surprised to find that his employment situation was about to change for the better. He was invited by his team leader and the director of information technology to participate in the "Datasmart" project, as the individual who would be in charge of drafting and editing the standardized company correspondence forms that would be used by employees in Canada. He would be entering these documents into a new corporate database that was under development. He was excited about the opportunity to advance within the company and use some of the writing skills he'd developed at university. As part of his new assignment, Will was offered a pay increase that would kick in after his next performance review which he anticipated would be held within a few weeks. He was given a quiet workspace away from the call center where he could concentrate on his writing and editing tasks.

The company correspondence project was part of a larger organizational undertaking that involved the revamping of their information systems. In order to pave the way for a new work flow management system called Datasmart, all company information, standardized documents, reports, and work flows were to be charted, reviewed, and revised to reduce error rates and enhance operational efficiency and effectiveness. While working on the project, Will was to report to the Datasmart project manager and was involved in weekly meetings with the IT staff who were overseeing the implementation.

Shortly after moving into his new role, Will was sent on his first business trip to attend a training seminar at the parent company's U.S. headquarters. However, supervisory guidance in Canada was quite limited. His new supervisor was always very busy with more pressing tasks and had minimal time to discuss questions that Will had regarding the content of specific documents or due dates. "Sorry, but I can't meet with you this week. I'm drowning in work. Can we reschedule? Just use your judgment—you seem to be making good progress," was the usual response he received from his supervisor.

All members of the 10-person Datasmart project team seemed to be very busy with the components that they were individually responsible for. Will could not help but feel somewhat out on a limb as he revised company forms and documents that were to be housed in the Datasmart system. People were beginning to use some of his revisions, but had he understood the implications of the wording and made the right changes? He was concerned that one day, he would be terminated as the result of something he had written that opened the firm to unanticipated liabilities or created serious difficulties with one of the firms for whom Travelink supplied services. The processes related to approving document changes had been fairly informal over the years, with the individuals processing the claims handling these elements largely on their own.

A number of other events over the next three months caused Will additional concerns about his future prospects at Travelink. Will knew that the firm had invested a lot of time and money developing Datasmart. However, the launch date for this software solution had come and gone on two separate occasions. Each time that Datasmart appeared ready to go live with some of its modules, an email would come out advising that the launch would be postponed to a later time. The emails that Will received, as a member of the project team, suggested that both the U.S. and Canadian offices were having implementation problems. Eventually, no new emails concerning the release date were sent out.

By mid-September, Will was noticing that there was a new topic on the embargo list. No one in management was discussing the new software. In June, all employees had received two hours of training on the basic purpose and planned functions of the new software, and staff had been told that detailed training related to the use of the software would follow. In the beginning there had been some excitement generated concerning the benefits that the new system would bring and special T-shirts had been distributed to celebrate its anticipated benefits. Will wondered if others were wondering what had happened to Datasmart but were afraid to ask. Robert told him that it looked like the project was going to be halted and that the Americans were planning to bring in consultants to sort out the underlying problems. Will was not surprised by the rumors, but he took pride in the fact that a number of his rewritten documents were being put to use on a daily basis.

FRUSTRATIONS DEEPEN

Will had still not received his performance review and promised raise by the middle of September. The Travelink Solutions employee handbook stated that each call center associate would receive an appraisal review after six months of continuous employment. Once a successful review was completed, an employee would be entitled to a pay increase. He had checked with the remaining members of his training group and none had been approached yet, regarding their six-month reviews, despite the fact that they were now into their tenth month of employment.

The initial feelings of frustration that Will experienced concerning this were slowly turning into anger. After all, he believed that he had performed very well. He had taken the initiative to learn about the office structure, the policy and procedure intricacies underlying different types of services, and different service techniques that went well beyond the competence required of a phone operator. When asked to join the Datasmart team, he had willingly volunteered and worked hard to understand and improve standardized documentation templates and corporate correspondence and had done so under minimal guidance. Yet, ten months had passed and there had been no formal review and no increase in pay, despite his attempts to remind his supervisors that such a review was overdue. There had been consistent supervisory comments that he was doing a terrific job and that the performance review would be looked after soon. However, managers were very busy and nothing was ever scheduled.

By October, Will's correspondence and documents project was three quarters of the way to completion, but the phones in the call center were busy again—very busy! Robert had told him in mid-August that they had won a major new contract. While management was pleased to have obtained the new business, Robert was apprehensive. As a marketing manager, he was delighted that his hard work had contributed toward obtaining this new account. As a former employee in the call center, however, Robert was frightened that the additional call volume would greatly exceed the current resources available. Robert told Will that he had argued to have new employees hired and trained in advance of the start dates for the new contracts but senior management said no. Robert said "the word from upstairs was that they would scale their capacity to handle an increased volume of calls closer to when the new revenue began to flow. Even crazier, a number of senior managers seem to believe that fewer new employees would be required once the call center was organized to better respond to volume patterns and leverage existing technology. I don't see how this approach can work."

Robert's concerns became a nightmare for the employees within the call center over the next few months. The phones started ringing and there were simply not enough hands to pick them up (see Exhibit 3 for call center volumes). In addition to the spikes in call volume generated from the new contracts, Travelink was now entering its busier season. Just a few months ago, the phones had been relatively quiet—to the extent that employees found time in between calls to provide extra service steps for their clients, such as arranging billing for insured expenses or expediting alternative hotel and flight arrangements. Now, there was no time between calls. From his new workspace, Will overheard managers discussing that it was not uncommon for clients to be placed on hold for up to five minutes while waiting for an available agent. Travelink provided a contractual guarantee that clients would only be on hold for a maximum of three minutes, and Robert told Will that account managers were finding themselves having to explain to their contract representatives why individual customers were forced to hold for extended periods of time.

One day in early November, Will was asked to move back to the phones. The increase in call volume necessitated his reassignment to his old position, without even a formal "thank you" for the work he had been doing. With the lack of available trained employees to service the increasing volume of incoming calls, the customer service managers were scrambling to ensure that the hold time was eased as much as possible. The following Monday morning, Will entered the call center and noticed that Luther, the trainer, was sitting beside him in the cubicle Linda used to occupy. Marie was sitting directly behind him. As he looked around the office, Will realized that other staff members were also in the call center, answering calls. When asked why he was there, Luther simply shook his head and said, "I worked here and earned my way

to a training position. Now, I'm back where I started." Marie overheard the conversation and simply threw her arms up in frustration when Will nodded to her. All available hands were now busy answering calls rather than providing their usual support services.

Will noted that there were now almost no company events being organized by the human resources department. Social events and birthday celebrations were cut from the schedule due to work pressures and the monthly management-staff noon hour corporate update meetings were postponed. When an event did occur, added pressure was placed on employees to partake. It seemed to Will that managers desperately wanted to believe that employees were still enjoying their work and feeling good about the firm.

By mid-February, customers' hold times had increased from five minutes to, at times, thirty minutes or more. On one occasion, Will talked to a man who had been on hold for over an hour waiting for someone to arrange for a tow truck. Team leaders sent out emails that reminded agents to apologize to customers who were required to wait for periods of ten minutes or longer. "Please apologize profusely," the messages read. At this point, Will was so frustrated that he would often forget to apologize. After all, it was not his fault that the company he worked for had not made the proper arrangements to service their clients. Why should he apologize when he and his coworkers were suffering too? Will found himself making less use of some of the techniques that contributed to customer service excellence, such as empathy, friendliness, and attention to detail.

The lack of appropriate planning and implementation related to heightened call volumes was having a visible, negative impact on the performance of all call center associates. For example, anytime that an agent logged off the phone to document a call, they were required to go on "not ready" status. This status was employed in order to write the required case notes into the Travelink database. According to the employee manual, agents were allowed to go on "not ready" for an hour each day, in addition to scheduled break times. With so many calls flowing into the call center, however, acceptable "not ready" time had disappeared.

Team leaders were able to see agents who were not taking calls and they began sending out emails that read, "Please log in. Several calls are waiting." Out of frustration, Will began counting the number of emails he had received that were titled "Please log in." Within one week, the tallied amount was 32.

Eventually, team leaders stopped using emails to ask agents to log in and began phoning their direct extensions every time they were not prepared to take a call. On one occasion, Will received a call from his team leader asking him to log in while he was documenting a call that he had received from an elderly couple that had been in a serious automobile accident in Mexico. From that point on, he attempted to type his notes for one case while he was on the phone with the next client. He questioned the efficacy of the new shortcuts that he was employing, but there was nothing that could be done. Every time that Will or any of the other operators tried to log off of their phones to document a call, they were messaged to log back in. Scrambling to keep one's head above water had become the new normal. To make matters worse, the claims department, which was in charge of reviewing the documented cases, was growing increasingly frustrated with the customer service agents over the increasing number of mistakes. The workload related to correcting errors in claims that had been opened by operators had essentially quadrupled.

Travelink began to actively recruit new phone agents in January, with the first ones arriving in the call center on February 1st. Melanie, a new agent, moved into the empty desk in front of Will. She was friendly and a hard worker, but she noted that she was feeling overwhelmed and ill prepared. She explained that some of the new employees were being hired on a contractual basis and that her contract was for a period of three months. Will could not understand the rationale behind hiring new employees for short-term contracts. The volume and complexity of the work was not going to go away. Furthermore, the fact that the new hires had only received two weeks of training made them unaware of several elements, including workflows and basic policy terms and conditions that were essential to the proper decision making and documentation. Will believed that the impact in errors, added costs (e.g., authorizing services the customer was not entitled to), and service failures would become all too apparent. By this point, employee turnover and absenteeism had risen markedly (see Exhibit 4).

Robert was equally distressed by the fallout that was occurring due to growing call volumes and a lack of properly trained customer service agents. Some of the companies that had placed their customer service contracts with Travelink Solutions call center were now threatening to pull their contracts because Travelink was not honoring its service delivery promises. The operations department noted that 10% of all calls were now being lost due to the lengthy response time. In other words, 10% of all customers were not getting through to a representative, even though this might be a time of great need.

CONSIDERING HIS ALTERNATIVES

One evening in early April, Will sat down to consider his future with Travelink Solutions. He was thankful for the training and job experience that he had received—competencies that would undoubtedly be useful in many other positions—but he was unsure how much more turmoil he could endure. He had saved enough money to, at the very least, pull himself through until a better opportunity came along. One thing seemed certain: Travelink Solutions no longer fit well with his goals.

Will submitted his resignation on Monday of the second week of April, to take effect on April 30, sixteen months after he had commenced employment. On the day after he submitted his resignation, Will received an email, apologizing for his long overdue performance appraisal interview. In the email, his manager applauded his performance, rated his potential as excellent in all categories, and asked what it would take to get him to reconsider and stay. The manager requested that they meet Friday. As Will thought about the offer, the words that came to mind were these: Too little, too late.

Will, however, bit his tongue: Before confirming his decision to quit, should he meet and hear what his manager had to say? If he did meet, should he discuss his concerns about how the call center was operating, including possibly sharing his written comments and thoughts concerning possible solutions? As he sat discussing his options with Robert, his friend was pondering similar questions.

QUESTIONS TO CONSIDER

- What is your assessment of the situation at Travelink at the end of the case? What are the underlying problems in the organization?

- If you found yourself in Will or Robert's situation, what would you do? Why?

- If Will and Robert both decide to stay and try to advance needed changes, what changes would you recommend they focus on and how would you recommend they go about it? Would you, for example, share Will's documentation of the problems within the company? Why or why not?

- Have you ever been in a situation where you were a recipient of change and things went poorly? How did it affect you and others in the organization?

Exhibit 1	Travelink Solutions Compensation Package for Full-Time Customer Service Representatives
Salary	$17 per hour or $35,360 to start, progressing to $25 per hour or $52,000 after 2 years (performance reviewed every 6 months)
Performance Bonus	Up to a 5% bonus in available to individual representatives, on an annual basis, based upon individual and corporate performance
Salary Review	Every 6 months until staff reaches the maximum for their pay category. After that, salary is reviewed annually
Benefits	A comprehensive benefit package, including dental, eye care, drugs, extended health, and insurance
Pension	Firm contributes 3% of employee's annual salary, employee can elect to contribute up to an additional 5% of their salary, with the firm matching this at a 50% level
Vacation	2 weeks of vacation for the first year of employment; 3 weeks after 5 years, 4 weeks after 15 years
Sick Days	5 paid sick days per year
Personal Obligation Days	Up to 2 paid personal obligation days per year
Education and Development	100% reimbursement for courses preapproved by the manager

Exhibit 2   Partial Organization Chart for the Canadian Operations

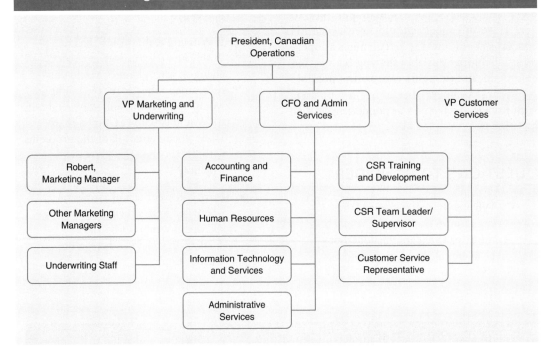

Assumptions:

- Call staff answering norms are 15 minutes per call or 26 calls per 8-hour shift (1 hour is allocated for post call documentation and follow-up work + two 15-minute breaks)

- It takes approximately 2 months (1 month of training and 1 month on the phones) before an operator is fully able to operate at capacity, handling both direct customer contact and call documentation with < 1% error rate

- One full-time, trained employee equates to approximately 18 availing working days per month. Absenteeism is estimated at 5%. Since all non-statutory holidays are taken in the July-August period, available days during the winter remains at 18 days

- Further capacity could be created by scheduling overtime and statutory holiday work.

- A maximum of 80 call cubicles are available, leading to a maximum shift capacity of 2,080 calls per 8-hour shift.

- At a staffing level of 140 full-time employees on the phones, total call volume capacity per month = 65,520.

Exhibit 3   Call Center Call Volumes by Month

	Jan	Feb	Mar	Apr	May	June	July	Aug	Sept	Oct	Nov	Dec	Jan	Feb	Mar
Call Volume	48,600	48,600	47,000	44,300	40,000	36,200	35,000	33,200	33,000	40,700	42,900	46,700	52,900	56,500	57,200
Wait Time Avg	<2 min	<3 min	<2 min	<1 min	<1 min	<1 min	<1 min	<1 min	<1 min	4 min	5 min	6 min	10 min	11 min	12 min
Lost Calls	<1%	<1%	<1%	<1%	<1%	<1%	<1%	<1%	<1%	2%	3%	6%	8%	10%	10%

Exhibit 4 Call Center Turnover Data by Quarter and With the Year-End Total

	Jan–Mar 04	Mar–May 04	June–Aug 04	Sept–Dec 04	Year 04 12-Month Summary	Jan–Mar 05
Absenteeism	3%	2%	3%	6%	3.6%	8.3%
a) Quits	0	2	5	10	17	19
b) Layoffs	0	0	16	0	16	0
c) Dismissals	0	1	1	2	4	0
Total (a+b+c)	0	3	22	12	37	19
New Hires	24	9	0	13	46	20 Full-Time + 19 Contract Employees
Total Call Center Staff (excluding trainers and team leaders)	140	146	124	125		145 Full-Time + Contract Employees

CHAPTER EIGHT

BECOMING A MASTER CHANGE AGENT

Chapter Overview

- The success of a change agent involves knowing your strengths and weaknesses and how these interplay among the team, the situation, and a vision.

- Successful change agents have a set of skills and personal characteristics: interpersonal, communication, and political skills; emotional resilience and tolerance for ambiguity and ethical conflicts; persistence, pragmatism, and dissatisfaction with the status quo; and openness to information, flexibility, and adaptability. They act in a manner likely to build trust. Change agents develop their skills with experiences in changing situations.

- This chapter describes four change agent types: Emotional Champion, Developmental Strategist, Intuitive Adapter, and Continuous Improver. Each has a different preference for his or her method of persuasion (vision versus analytical) and orientation to change (strategic versus incremental).

- This chapter considers different change roles: an internal change agent, an external consultant, and a member of a change team.

This chapter examines what makes a change agent. It looks at change agents' individual characteristics and how these interact with a situation and vision to determine change agent effectiveness. We contrast change managers from leaders and examine how change leaders develop. Four types of change leaders are identified: Emotional Champion, Developmental Strategist (particularly important for a transformational change), Intuitive Adapter, and Continuous Improver. We examine the skills of internal change agents, the roles of the external change agents, and the usefulness of change teams. The chapter ends with rules of thumb for change agents from the wisdom of organizational development and change agent experts. Figure 8.1 highlights this chapter's place in the Change Path.

The role of change agent is a double-edged sword. While it can prove exciting, educational, enriching, and career enhancing, it can also be hazardous to your career, frustrating, and demoralizing when risks escalate and failure looms. In general, people who become change agents will improve their understanding of organizations, develop special skills, and increase their networks of contacts and visibility in the organization.[1] Those who choose not to respond to the challenge of leading change, on the other hand, run the risk of becoming less central and relevant to the operation of their organizations.

When changes fail, there is the sense that the change agent's career has ended. However, this is seldom the case. While failure experiences are painful, change agents are resilient. For example, when Jacques Nasser left his CEO position at Ford in 2001, many thought he was a spent force. However, about a year after leaving Ford, he took over as chairman of Polaroid after it was acquired by One Equity Partners in a bankruptcy auction. In 2½ years, Nasser turned it around and its resale resulted in a $250 million gain for One Equity.[2] In August 2009, Nasser again hit the business press news when he was nominated chairman of BHP Billiton, the world's largest mining company; he took office in March, 2010.[3] Nasser served in that role until 2017. Although CEO Nasser instituted a number of controversial—some would even say unsuccessful—changes at Ford, he also acquired skills and personal attributes that have served him well since he left Ford in 2001.

Many individuals find it difficult to identify where and how they fit into the change process. They believe that they cannot ignite change with their low- or mid-level roles and titles, and minimal experiences in organizations. Years of autocratic or risk-averse bosses and top-down organizational cultures make it hard to believe that this time the organization wants change and innovation. Critics of present-day educational systems have suggested that schools encourage dependent rather than change-agent thinking. If teachers and professors see the students' role as absorbing and applying within prescribed boundaries rather than raising troubling questions, independent and innovative thinking will not be advanced.

In the turbulent years that have defined the first couple of decades of the 21st century, however, individuals find themselves living in organizations that challenge them to take up one of the roles of change agency: initiator, implementer, facilitator, and/or task force team member. Leaders in organizations are asking people to step forward and make a difference. While the specific role will vary over time and context, moving to a more active role is critical. Simply providing information or offering armchair solutions seldom produces meaningful change. To disrupt inertia and drift, some individuals must move from an observer status to active change agent. Those who want to advance their careers and add value to their organizations will challenge themselves to take on change leadership roles.

For many, their implicit model of change assumes that they must have the involvement and support of the CEO or some other senior sponsor before they can create meaningful change. There is no question that if a change initiative has the commitment and budget of a senior change champion, the job is immeasurably easier. However, for many individuals acting from subordinate organizational roles (e.g., technical professionals, first-line and middle managers, frontline staff), the changes they want to promote require them to question existing systems and processes, with little top-level, visible support when they begin.

In *Leading the Revolution*, Hamel argues that every "company needs a band of insurrectionists" who challenge and break the rules and take risks.[4] One teacher provides an example.

REFLECTIONS ON A TEACHER

The teacher that influenced me the most was concerned with our learning and not with the power and influence of the administration. For example, when *Catcher in the Rye* was deemed unfit for our youthful eyes, he informed the class that this book was classed as unsuitable. This teacher reported that the book by J. D. Salinger should be avoided and while it was recognizable because of its red cover with yellow print and found in most bookstores, libraries, and magazine stores, we should not seek it out. Later, the same teacher was instructed to black out certain risqué phrases from one of the assigned books for class. Of course, he marched into the class, described that the phrases on p. 138, lines 7 and 8, that were to be blacked out and that he was enlisting the class's help to do the work for him.

Anonymous caller,
CBC Radio, January 2004.

Testing orthodoxies will become critical in the drive to keep pace with environmental demands.[5] The individuals wanting to remove student exposure to the perceived immorality in the books likely thought they were change agents as well. However, by doing so, they were limiting student access to information and the opportunity to think about common realities. For the teacher in the example, this was viewed as violating the prime purposes of a school system—educating the students and instilling a desire for learning. It drove him to action.

With the ever-increasing need for innovation and change in organizations, there is the recognition that change management is an essential part of every good manager's skill set.[6] Change agency has shifted from notions of "lone ranger," top-down heroic leadership to ones involving leaders who enable change teams and empower workers to envision change and make it happen.[7] As Jick points out, "implementing their own changes as well as others."[8]

While we might think that change is led from the top, Jick and others dispute this. "Most well-known change initiatives (*that are*) perceived as being "top-down" or led by a senior executive or the CEO, probably started at the bottom or the middle, years earlier."[9] As Rosabeth Moss Kanter states, real change is for the long haul. It "requires people to adjust their behavior and that behavior is often beyond the direct control of top management."[10] Bold strokes taken by top management likely do not build the long-term capabilities of the organization unless they are buttressed by a concerted commitment to an underlying vision. Bold strokes can reduce, reorganize, and merge organizations, but each of these takes a toll on the organization. Unfortunately, the long-term benefits can prove to be illusory if the initiative fails to sustainably embrace the hearts as well as the heads of organizational members in ways that generate internal and external environmental congruence.

Figure 8.1 The Change Path Model

Awakening
Chapter 4
1. Identify a need for change and confirm the problems or opportunities that incite the need for change through collection of data.
2. Articulate the gap in performance between the present and the envisioned future state, and spread awareness of the data and the gap throughout the organization.
3. Develop a powerful vision for change.
4. Disseminate the vision for the change and why it's needed through multiple communication channels.

Mobilization
Chapters 5 through 8
1. Make sense of the desired change through formal systems and structures, and leverage those systems to reach the change vision (Chapter 5).
2. Assess power and cultural dynamics at play, and put them to work to better understand the dynamics and build coalitions and support to realize the change (Chapter 6).
3. Communicate the need for change organization-wide and manage change recipients and various stakeholders as they react to and move the change forward (Chapter 7).
4. **Leverage change agent personality, knowledge, skills and abilities, and related assets (e.g., reputation and relationships) for the benefit of the change vision and its implementation (Chapter 8).**

Acceleration
Chapter 9
1. Continue to systematically reach out to engage and empower others in support, planning, and implementation of the change. Help them develop needed new knowledge, skills, abilities, and ways of thinking that will support the change.
2. Use appropriate tools and techniques to build momentum, accelerate and consolidate progress.
3. Manage the transition, celebrating small wins and the achievement of milestones along the larger, more difficult path of change.

Institutionalization
Chapter 10
1. Track the change periodically and through multiple balanced measures to help assess what is needed, gauge progress toward the goal, and to make modifications as needed and mitigate risk.
2. Develop and deploy new structures, systems, processes and knowledge, skills, and abilities, as needed, to bring life to the change and new stability to the transformed organization.

FACTORS THAT INFLUENCE CHANGE AGENT SUCCESS

The Interplay of Personal Attributes, Situation, and Vision

Images of organizational change agents often revolve around personalities that appear to be bigger than life: Jack Welch, former CEO of GE; Bill Gates, former CEO of Microsoft; and Meg Whitman, former CEO of eBay and HP. If such grand standards are the benchmarks employed to assess personal qualities and potential as a change agent, most people will inevitably fall far short of the mark.

However, history suggests that leading change is about more than just the person. In the 1930s, Winston Churchill was a politician in decline. When World War II began, suddenly his skills and personality matched what was needed, and the British public believed he was uniquely qualified to be prime minister. Churchill did not change who he was, but the situation changed dramatically and, as prime minister, Churchill projected a vision of victory and took actions that changed history and his reputation. This match of person and situation is further highlighted by the fact that Churchill experienced electoral defeat in the postwar environment despite his enormous popularity during the war.

In other words, it was the person *and* it was more than the person. **Change agent effectiveness** was a function of the situation, the vision the person had, and the actions he took. A robust model for change considers the interaction between personality, vision, and situation. Michael J. Fox exemplifies a person who became a change agent extraordinaire in the fight against Parkinson's disease.

MICHAEL J. FOX BECOMES A CHANGE AGENT

Most people get Parkinson's disease late in life. Michael J. Fox, a television and movie star, contracted it when he was 29 years old. Before his disease, Fox was focused on his career, but he has since refocused his energies. By 2000, Fox was a major player in funding research into analyzing and curing Parkinson's. Fox created the Michael J. Fox Foundation (MJFF), which has become an exceptionally effective organization in fundraising and in shaping the research agenda for Parkinson's disease.[11] In August 2018, *Variety* magazine named Fox as their "Philanthropist of the Year" for his commitment to mobilizing patients and research to bring an end to Parkinson's disease.

Fox's basic personality didn't change with the onset of Parkinson's. But suddenly he was faced with a situation that generated a sense of purpose and vision that both transcended his self-interest and captured the attention and emotions of others. This powerful vision was crucial to Fox's transformation from movie star to change agent. He deployed his energy, interpersonal skills, creativity, and decision-making abilities to pursue this vision. His contacts, profile, and reputation gave him access to an influential board of directors. In record time, he recruited a key executive director and created a foundation that became a funding force. Most important, he chose to act. He articulated values that resonated with key stakeholders and raised awareness and interest through his strategies and tactics. The ability to create alignment among stakeholders on values has been shown to be valuable in reducing resistance and advancing change.[12] His is far from an isolated incident. From Paul Newman's social entrepreneurship and philanthropy with salad dressing[13] to Andrea Ivory's initiative to bring early breast cancer detection to uninsured women in Florida,* individuals from all walks of life are choosing not to accept the status quo and are making a difference.

---

*CNN's Heroes Project seeks to inspire people to take action by annually recognizing the change initiatives of everyday people in their communities and celebrating the impact they are having. Their initiatives are highlighted on http://www.cnn.com/SPECIALS/us/cnn-heroes.

In the above cases, the interaction of the person, situation, and powerful vision transformed a person into a change agent. This can be summarized in the following equation:

Being a Change Agent = Person × Vision × Situation

Situations play a crucial part in this three-way interchange. Some situations invigorate and energize the change agent. Enthusiasm builds as coalitions form and the proposed change gains momentum and seems likely to succeed. Other situations suck energy out of the change agent and seem to lead to a never-ending series of meetings, obstacles, and issues that prevent a sense of progress. Borrowing from the language of chemical reactions, Dickout calls the former situations exothermic change situations. Here energy is liberated by actions.[14] Conversely, the latter situations he calls endothermic. Here the change program consumes energy and arouses opposition—which in turn requires more energy from the change agent.

Change agents need exothermic situations that "liberate the energy to drive the change."[15] However, they will experience both exothermic and endothermic periods in a change process. Initial excitement and discovery are followed by snail-paced progress, setbacks, dead ends, and perhaps a small victory. The question is how do agents develop the staying power and the ability to manage their energy flows and reserves during this ultra-marathon? What type of team do they need and have to help replenish their energy and keep them going? Colleagues who serve as close confidantes can play an important role in sustaining energy. They can help to keep things in perspective, enabling the change leader to face challenges and pitfalls. While action taking is the defining visible characteristic of change, discussion and reflection play important and often undervalued roles in the development and maintenance of change leaders.[16] Reflection as a critical practice of change leaders is discussed later in this chapter.

Change Leaders and Their Essential Characteristics

An examination of the literature on the personal characteristics of change leaders yields a daunting list of personal attributes ranging from emotional intelligence to general intelligence, determination, openness to experience, and so forth.[17] Textbook treatments of leadership provide lists of the traits and behaviors that prove difficult to reconcile. While most of the literature is inconclusive about attributes that matter and can be generalized, six stand out as particularly relevant for change leaders.

1. Commitment to Improvement

The essential characteristic of change leaders is that they are people who seek opportunities to take action in order to bring about improvement. They possess restlessness with the way things are currently done, inquisitive minds as to what alternatives are possible, and the desire to take informed risks to make things better. Katzenbach argues that change leaders are significantly different in their orientation from traditional managers.[18] For Katzenbach, the basic mindset of a "real change leader" is someone who does it, fixes it, tries it, changes it, and does it again—*a trial-and-error approach* rather than an attempt to optimize and get it perfect the first time.

2. Communication and Interpersonal Skills

Doyle talks about potential change agents and argues that they need sophisticated levels of interpersonal and communication skills to be effective.[19] He describes change agents as requiring emotional resilience, tolerance for ethical conflicts and ambiguities, and they need to be politically savvy. Conflict goes with the territory when stakeholders believe the changes will negatively impact them, and researchers have noted the importance of conflict-facilitation skills in change agents, including skills related to constructive confrontation and the development of new agreements through dialogue and negotiation.[20] Barack Obama's soaring oratorical skills allowed him to speak directly to the American people and bypass much of the Washington establishment when he was pushing for changes to the American health system in 2009. This set the stage for the difficult discussions, negotiations, and tactical maneuvers that followed and resulted in new health care legislation in March 2010. By 2016–2018 the Affordable Care Act, or Obamacare, was back on the agenda for the U.S. Congress. Because of the diversity of perspectives about healthcare in the United States and because of the fragmentation of the U.S. healthcare system, it is likely that there will be continuing debates in Congress on this policy area.

Kramer maintains that political awareness about what needs to be done may lead, in certain situations, to abrasive, confronting, intimidating behavior (yes, Kramer said this before the national elections in the United States in 2016).[21] Such challenging behavior may be what is needed to "unfreeze" a complacent organization. Stories of Churchill's arrogant behavior, for example, which was appropriate in wartime, cost him the prime ministry in the postwar election.

The communication and interpersonal skills needed to navigate the political environment and awaken the organization to needed action receive a lot of attention. However, this more muscular image of the transformational communications skill of change leaders is but a subset of the range of approaches they may deploy. Not all change leaders have a gift for rhetoric, and many are not charismatic in the traditional sense of the term.* In his book *From Good to Great*, Jim Collins[22] explores the skill sets of change leaders who successfully transformed their average organizations into great ones. He highlights the quiet, humble, grounded, and committed way in which many of these change leaders interacted with others on a day-to-day basis and the influence this had on the outcomes their organizations were able to achieve. Their positive energy was clearly visible, and frustration didn't give rise to the communication of cynicism that can taint the perspectives of others and derail a change.[23]

McCall and Lombardo identified a number of other characteristics that derail change leaders when they are communicated to others: being cold and aloof, lacking in critical skills, displaying insensitivity to others, being arrogant, being burned out, lacking trustworthiness, and being overly ambitious from a personal perspective.[24] When Malcolm Higgs looked at the question of bad leadership, he

---

*Charisma is defined as a trait found in persons whose personalities are characterized by a personal charm and magnetism/attractiveness along with innate and powerfully sophisticated abilities of interpersonal communication and persuasion (http://en.wikipedia.org/wiki/Charisma).

identified four recurring themes: abuse of power, inflicting damage on others, over-exercise of control to satisfy personal needs, and rule breaking to serve the individual's own purposes. He saw these actions as caused by narcissism in the leader—a view of oneself as superior, entitled, and central to all that happens.[25]

3. Determination

Change agents need a dogged determination to succeed in the face of significant odds and the resilience to respond to setbacks in a reasoned and appropriate manner. After all, in the middle of change, everything can look like a failure. Change agents need to be able to persist when it looks like things have gone wrong and success appears unlikely.

4. Eyes on the Prize and Flexibility

Change agents also need to focus on the practical aspect of "getting it done." They must have a constant focus on the change vision, inspiring and keeping others aligned with the change goal. Change agents must keep their eyes on the prize to avoid getting bogged down in day-to-day stresses and abandoning the change vision. At the same time, they must be ready to take informed risks, modify their plans to pursue new options, or divert their energies to different avenues as the change landscape shifts—sometimes because of their actions, sometimes because of the actions of others, or sometimes because of shifts in the environment. Doggedness is balanced by flexibility and adaptability, and impatience is balanced by patience. Time for dialogue and reflection on the change process is needed to give perspective and make informed judgments.[26] Change agents must reflect this delicate balance of being driven by the change vision, but not so much that they are unwilling to make modifications to the process as the environment inevitably shifts along the way.

5. Experience and Networks

Given their desire to make things happen, it is not surprising to find that experience with change is an attribute common to many successful change agents. These individuals embrace change rather than avoiding it and seeing it as "the enemy." They are constantly scanning the environment, picking up cues that allow them to develop a rich understanding of their organization's situation and the need for change. As the situation shifts, they are aware of those shifts and respond appropriately to them. They make this easier for themselves by ensuring that they are part of networks that will tell them what they need to hear—not what they *want* to hear. They build these networks over time through their trustworthiness, credibility, and interpersonal skills and through the value other members of these networks derive from them. Networks don't work for long if others don't feel they are getting value from them. To ensure that members of the networks and others continue to communicate with them, change leaders are well advised to remember to never be seen as shooting the messenger. If messengers believe the act of communicating will put them at risk, they will alter their behavior accordingly.[27]

6. Intelligence

Intelligence is needed to engage in analysis, to assess possible courses of action, and to create confidence in a proposed plan.[28] In general, one has more confidence in a proposal developed by a bright individual than one brought forward by a dullard. However, traditionally defined intelligence is not enough. Interpersonal skills, empathy, self-regulation, a positive and yet realistic outlook, attention to detail, and the motivational drive to see things through are needed to frame proposals effectively and implement them. These factors make up what is called emotional intelligence and it is often highlighted in discussions of change agent characteristics.[29]

In his investigation of the characteristics of change leaders, Caldwell differentiates the attributes of **change leaders** from those he calls **change managers**.[30] Table 8.1 outlines his view of the differences. Caldwell argues that change leaders operate from a visionary, adaptable perspective while change managers are much more hands on and work with people. Of course, there is nothing that says a change agent cannot possess the attributes of both change leaders and change managers (as defined by Caldwell). In fact, they will need access to both, depending upon their role(s) and the change challenges they are addressing. Another way to think about the various attributes of change agents is to consider the sorts of behaviors they give rise to. The following three categories of change behaviors are a helpful way of grouping their actions:[31]

- *Framing behaviors:* behaviors oriented toward changing the sense of the situation, establishing starting points for change, designing the change journey, and communicating principles

- *Capacity-creating behaviors:* behaviors focused on creating the capacity for change by increasing individual and organizational capabilities and creating and communicating connections in the organization

- *Shaping behaviors:* actions that attempt to shape what people do by acting as a role model, holding others accountable, thinking about change, and focusing on individuals in the change process

Table 8.1 Attributes of Change Leaders and Change Managers

Attributes of Change Leaders	Attributes of Change Managers
• Is a visionary	• Empowers others
• Is an entrepreneur	• Builds teams
• Has integrity and honesty	• Learns from others
• Learns from others	• Is adaptable and flexible
• Is open to new ideas	• Is open to new ideas
• Takes risks	• Manages resistance
• Is adaptable and flexible	• Resolves conflict
• Nurtures creativity	• Networks
• Experiments	• Has in-depth knowledge of the business
• Uses power	• Solves problems

Source: Adapted from Caldwell, R. (2003). Change leaders and change managers: Different or complementary?" *Leadership & Organization Development Journal, 24*(5), 285–293.

Higgs and Rowland examined such behaviors and discovered that "framing change and building capacity are more successful than shaping behavior."[32] They suggested that change leaders should shift from a leader-centric, directive approach to a more facilitating, enabling style in today's organizations.

The attributes were ranked by experts. The most highly ranked are at the top of the list, with the others following in order. Note that Table 8.1 identifies attributes not specifically mentioned in the preceding pages.

Kouzes and Posner provide an important model of the behavioral characteristics of effective change leaders, based on answers from thousands of managers and executives to the fundamental question: When you were a leader at your best, what did you do? In the *Leadership Challenge*, the authors synthesize their extensive research and argue that leaders who are adept at getting extraordinary things done know how to do the following: (1) model the way; (2) inspire a shared sense of vision; (3) challenge the status quo; (4) enable others to act; and (5) encourage the heart of those involved with the change.[33] The authors do an excellent job setting out how to accomplish these things, and their book is recommended reading for those interested in pursuing these ideas further.[*]

See **Toolkit Exercise 8.2** to rate yourself as a change leader.

DEVELOPING INTO A CHANGE LEADER

Intention, Education, Self-Discipline, and Experience

Many change leadership skills can be learned, which means that they can be taught.[**] The acquisition of concepts and language establishes mental frameworks for want-to-be change leaders. Reading about best practices and landmines can alert novices to predictable success paths and mistakes. The Center for Creative Leadership[34] is one of a number of organizations that produce publications about relevant leadership challenges and practices. In a 2007 article, Corey Criswell and Andre Martin identified a number of trends that future leaders need to be aware of that are creating change to the way business is done. They include (a) more complex challenges, (b) a focus on innovation, (c) an increase in virtual communication and leadership, (d) the importance of authenticity, and (e) leading for long-term survival.[35] The awareness of these macro-level trends will help change agents better understand the environment and use and develop necessary skills to lead change internally.

Change leaders also need to understand and embrace the notion of experiential learning. It is rare that someone is a change agent only once. Change leadership capacities are a sought-out skill set. These skills are developed similarly to the way individuals strengthen their physical skills. Once you start toning a muscle set, it feels good and you strive to continue to maintain and develop that muscle. But performance typically is tied to our capacity to have our muscles act interdependently. When one set of muscles develops, you may find others that need strengthening to improve your overall capacity to perform. Similarly, within an organization,

---

[*] As you reflect on the material in this section, you may find it useful to review the story in Chapter 7 of Monique Leroux's change leadership at Desjardin.
[**] Like many fields, formal study and education play their role in developing change leaders—thus this book!

change agents seek opportunities to continuously improve both themselves and their organizations. They may have great interpersonal skills, but they need expertise in crafting financial arguments, or vice versa. Over time, this process of development becomes part of one's professional identity. The journey never ends.

As part of this process, self-discovery, discipline, and reflection are critical to ongoing success and growth. Jeanie Daniel Duck argues that an organization will not change if the individuals within that organization do not develop themselves. As a change leader, if you intentionally model reflective behavior, you will encourage others to do the same. The key questions to ask, according to Duck, are these:

Questions for oneself:	Behavior to modify:
Which of your behaviors will you stop, start, or change?	Identify this behavior and replace it with something else.
What, specifically, are you willing to do?	Brainstorm different actions and how you might measure them.
How will others know?	Help yourself by engaging others to hold you accountable.
How might you sabotage yourself?	Identify ways in which you might hold yourself back.
What's the payoff in this for you?	Construct an encouraging reward and motivate yourself.[36]

Bennis describes four rules that he believes change leaders should accept to enhance their self-development:

1. You are your own best teacher.
2. You accept responsibility and blame no one.
3. You can learn anything you want to learn.
4. True understanding comes from reflection on your experience.[37]

Bennis's fundamental message is to take responsibility for your own learning and development as a change leader. This requires reflection. Of course, reflection implies something to reflect on—thus, the role of experience. It is through reflection that a change leader hones existing skills and abilities, becomes open to new ideas, and begins to think broadly, widening the lens through which he or she looks at the situation at hand. In a disciplined manner, a would-be change leader needs to establish personal change goals and write them down. This calls for intentional reflection and continuous learning, which are important for both the individual level, as described by Duck, as well as the organizational level, in developing the ability to change.

What Does Reflection Mean?

Organizations are able to change more effectively when individuals and change leaders within the organization shift their mental maps and frameworks, and this requires openness and reflection. The skill of communication is essential here, as it is through conversation and open dialogue that change occurs. There is a need to think *with* others in a reflective way to see change happen. In order to do this, an individual needs to understand what the group thinks and why. The group then needs to identify its shared assumptions, seek information, and develop a mutual understanding of the current reality. This involves open and honest communication in a space where no one is wrong and there is a commitment to finding that common ground—for the present situation and the vision for the future. Change leaders are in the position to create safe spaces for reflection where members of the organization have a voice that is listened to and valued.

Appreciative inquiry (AI), a concept introduced by Dr. David L. Cooperrider at Case Western Reserve University, is critical in these conversations of reflection. AI is the engagement of individuals in an organizational system in its renewal. If you can find the best in the organization and individuals—that is, appreciate it—Cooperrider argues that growth will occur and renewal will result. Through AI, people seek to find and understand the best in people, organizations, and the world by reflecting on past positive experiences and performance. In doing so, the positive energy and commitment to improve is embraced.[38] By framing positively, a different type of energy is found within the organization to move forward in the direction of change.

AI provides an interesting approach for change agents to consider when thinking about how best to approach change, because it recognizes the value of ongoing individual and collective reflection to the enactment of effective change. In order for reflection to add value, there can't be a "wrong" understanding. Everyone must strive to fully understand people's perceptions, assumptions, and visions through discussing and challenging one another's views. In a global society with relationships developing and evolving at all levels, organizations operate in an ever-changing context, making the development of shared understanding and mutual respect all the more important.

DEVELOPMENTAL STAGES OF CHANGE LEADERS

Miller argues that there are **developmental stages of a change agent**. He believes that individuals progress through stages of beliefs about change, increasing in their complexity and sophistication.[39] (See Table 8.2 for an outline of his belief stages.) He believes that movement from Stage 1, Novice, to Stage 2, Junior, to Stage 3, Experienced, might be learned vicariously—by observing others or by studying change. However, movement to Stage 4, Expert, requires living with a change project and suffering the frustrations, surprises, and resistance that come with the territory.

There is evidence that these change agent skills and competencies can be acquired through the systematic use of developmental assignments.[40] See **Toolkit Exercise 8.3** to evaluate your development as a change agent.

FOUR TYPES OF CHANGE LEADERS

Regardless of their skill sets, change agents' ability to sense and interpret significant environmental shifts is of particular importance to their capacity to respond. Part of such an ability comes from the deep study of a field or industry. As well, some might have the intuition to understand significant changes in the environment by their ability to detect and interpret underlying patterns.[41] Take, for example, Glegg Industries of Glegg Water Treatment Services.

Table 8.2 Miller's Stages of Change Beliefs

Stage	Description
Stage 1 Novice	Beliefs: People will change once they understand the logic of the change. People can be told to change. As a result, clear communication is key. Underlying is the assumption that people are rational and will follow their self-interest once it is revealed to them. Alternately, power and sanctions will ensure compliance.
Stage 2 Junior	Beliefs: People change through powerful communication and symbolism. Change planning will include the use of symbols and group meetings. Underlying is the assumption that people will change if they are "sold" on the beliefs. Again, failing this, the organization can use power and/or sanctions.
Stage 3 Experienced	Beliefs: People may not be willing or able or ready to change. As a result, change leaders will enlist specialists to design a change plan and the leaders will work at change but resist modifying their own vision. Underlying is the assumption that the ideal state is where people will become committed to change. Otherwise, power and sanctions must be used.
Stage 4 Expert	Beliefs: People have a limited capacity to absorb change and may not be as willing, able, or ready to change as you wish. Thinking through how to change the people is central to the implementation of change. Underlying is the assumption that commitment for change must be built and that power or sanctions have major limitations in achieving change and building organizational capacity.

Source: Adapted from Miller, D. (2002). Successful change leaders: What makes them? What do they do that is different? *Journal of Change Management, 2*(4), 383.

GLEGG WATER SYSTEMS[42]

In 2000, GE bought Glegg Industries. Glegg Water Treatment Services had been an entrepreneurial organization that grew at a compound growth rate of 20% to 25% in the 1980s and 1990s. The executives had a clear and strong vision: "pure water for the world." They used this vision to pull the organization in the direction they wanted. They were tough, realistic analyzers of data that provided a sophisticated understanding of the company's market. Three times in their history, the leadership forecasted a decline in growth rates in the technology that the organization was using —so they shifted into completely new but related areas. For example, the organization delivered water treatment systems for power industries. As that market matured, the company shifted to produce high-quality water systems for computer makers. Later, it shifted to a new membrane technology, which permitted integrated systems to be sold.

When GE bought the company, it branded the products as GE Glegg Water Technologies. By 2002, however, GE rebranded the products again to GE Water Technologies.

At Glegg Water Treatment Services, change leaders understood the strategic shifts in the industry and what that implied for their organization. Between these major disruptions, they worked incrementally to improve operations and to change the organization for the better. To do this, they motivated people by reinforcing their belief in the importance of what they were doing—providing the purest water possible. However, they did not just use these visionary or emotional appeals, they also used data to persuade. Hard, calculated numbers pushed their perspectives forward and provided convincing evidence of the need for change and the value of the vision.

Much of the change literature differentiates between the types of change that Glegg experienced: strategic or episodic change followed by incremental or continuous change.[43] Episodic change is change that is "infrequent, discontinuous, and intentional." Continuous change is change that is "ongoing, evolving and cumulative." Weick and Quinn suggest that the appropriate model here is "freeze, rebalance and unfreeze." That is, change agents need to capture the underlying patterns and dynamics (freeze the conceptual understanding); reinterpret, relabel (reframe and rebalance those understandings); and resume improvisation and learning (unfreeze).[44] Further, Weick and Quinn suggest that the role of change agents shifts depending on the type of change. Episodic change needs a prime mover change agent—one who creates change. Continuous change needs a change agent who is a sense maker who is then able to refine and redirect the organization's actions.

The Glegg Water example also shows that change agents and their agendas can act in "pull" or "push" ways. *Pull actions* by change agents create goals that draw willing organizational members to change and are characterized by organizational visions of higher-order purposes and strategies. *Push actions*, on the other hand, are data based and factual and are communicated in ways that advance analytical thinking and reasoning and that push recipients' thinking in new directions. Change agents who rely on push actions can also use legitimate, positional, and reward-and-punishment power in ways that change the dynamics of situations.[45] At Glegg Water, markets were assessed and plans were created and implemented based on the best data available.

Table 8.3 outlines a model that relates the motivational approaches of the change agent (analytical push versus emotional pull) to the degree of change needed by the organization (strategic versus incremental). The model identifies four change agent types: Emotional Champion, Developmental Strategist, Intuitive Adapter, and Continuous Improver. Some change agents will tend to act true to their type due to the nature of their personalities, predispositions, and situations. Others will move beyond their preferences and develop greater flexibility in the range of approaches at their disposal. The latter will therefore adopt a more flexible approach to change, modifying their approach to reflect the specific situation and the people involved.

The **Emotional Champion** has a clear and powerful vision of what the organization needs and uses that vision to capture the hearts and motivations of the organization's members. An organization often needs an emotional champion when there is a dramatic shift in the environment and the organization's structures, systems, and sense of direction are inadequate. To be an emotional champion means that the change agent foresees a new future, understands the deep gap between the organization and its future, can articulate a powerful vision that gives hope that the gap can be overcome, and has a high order of persuasion skills. When Glegg Water Treatment Services was faced with declining growth and needed to find new growth markets, it needed the visionary who could picture the strategic shift and create an appealing vision of that future.

Table 8.3 Change Agent Types

Strategic Change and Incremental Change *versus* Vision Pull and Analytical Push

Strategic Change

Emotional Champion	*Developmental Strategist*

Vision Pull ———————————————————— Analytical Push

Intuitive Adapter	*Continuous Improver*

Incremental Change

An Emotional Champion

- is comfortable with ambiguity and risk;
- thinks tangentially and challenges accepted ways of doing things;
- has strong intuitive abilities; and
- relies on feelings and emotions to influence others.

The **Developmental Strategist** applies rational analysis to understanding the competitive logic of the organization and how it no longer fits with the organization's existing strategy. He or she sees how to alter structures and processes to shift the organization to the new alignment and eliminate the major gap between the organization and the environment's demands. Again, in Glegg Water, the strategic shifts resulted not only from the capturing of a new vision but also from market intelligence and analysis. Hard-nosed thinking enabled Glegg Water to see how to take its company to a new level by finding a new market focus.

A Developmental Strategist

- engages in big-picture thinking about strategic change and the fit between the environment and the organization;

- sees organizations in terms of systems and structures fitting into logical, integrated components that fit (or don't) with environmental demands; and

- is comfortable with assessing risk and taking significant chances based on a thorough assessment of the situation.

The **Intuitive Adapter** has the clear vision for the organization and uses that vision to reinforce a culture of learning and adaptation. Often the vision will seem less dramatic or powerful because the organization is aligned with its environment and the change agent's role is to ensure the organization stays on track. The change agent develops a culture of learning and continuous improvement where employees constantly test their actions against the vision. At Glegg Water, continuous improvement was a byword. Central to this were the people who understood the pure water vision and what it meant to customers. Efficiency was not allowed to overrule a focus on quality.

An Intuitive Adapter

- embraces moderate risks;

- engages in a limited search for solutions;

- is comfortable with the current direction that the vision offers; and

- relies on intuition and emotion to persuade others to propel the organization forward through incremental changes.

The **Continuous Improver** analyzes micro environments and seeks changes such as reengineering systems and processes. The organization in this category is reasonably well aligned with its environment and is in an industry where complex systems and processes provide for improvement opportunities. At Glegg Water, information systems captured data on productivity and processes. These data were used to improve efficiency and profits.

A Continuous Improver

- thinks logically and carefully about detailed processes and how they can be improved;

- aims for possible gains and small wins rather than great leaps; and

- is systematic in his or her thinking while making careful gains.

The purpose of this model is to marry types of change with methods of persuasion. Each change agent will have personal preferences. Some will craft visions that could sweep employees onto the change team. Others will carefully and deliberately build a data-based case that would convince the most rational finance expert. Change agents will have their preferred styles but, as noted earlier, some will be able to adapt their approach and credibly use other styles as the situation demands. By knowing your own level of flexibility, you can undertake initiatives that will develop your capacity to adapt your approach as a change agent in a given situation. Alternatively, if you're concerned about your own capacity to respond, you can ally with others who possess the style that a particular situation demands.

In Chapter 1, we briefly discussed the preferences of adaptors (those with an orientation toward incremental change) and innovators (those who prefer more radical or transformational change).[46] Kirton's work with these two orientations points out that individuals tend to have clear preferences in their orientation and sometimes fail to recognize the value present in the alternative approach to change as they focus on what they are most comfortable with. When this occurs, there may be an inappropriate fit of approach with the situation or the people involved. Alternatively, when individuals with both preferences are present, this can lead to disagreement and conflict concerning how best to proceed. While constructive disagreement and debate about alternatives is valuable, managers need to avoid dysfunctional personal attacks and defensive behavior. This points again to the importance of developing greater awareness of the different change styles and the benefits of personal flexibility. When managers lack the needed orientation and style, they need access to allies with the requisite skills.

Many organizations expect their managers to develop skills as change agents. As a result, managers need to improve their understanding of internal change agent roles and strategies. Internal organizational members need to learn the team-building, negotiating, influencing, and other change-management skills to become effective facilitators. They need to move beyond technical skills from being the person with the answer to being the person with process-management change skills: the person who helps the organization find the answers and handles the complex and multivariate nature of the reality it faces.[47]

Hunsaker identified four different internal roles a change agent can play: catalyst, solution giver, process helper, and resource linker.[48] The **catalyst** is needed to overcome inertia and focus the organization on the problems faced. The **solution giver** knows how to respond and can solve the problem. The key here, of course, is having your ideas accepted. The **process helper** facilitates the "how to" of change, playing the role of third-party intervener often. Finally, the **resource linker** brings people and resources together in ways that aid in the solution of issues. All four roles are important, and knowing them provides a checklist of optional strategies for the internal change agent. See **Toolkit Exercise 8.4** to find your change agent preference.

INTERNAL CONSULTANTS: SPECIALISTS IN CHANGE

Internal change agents involved with leading projects often have line responsibilities for the initiative. However, larger organizations also advance change through the use of individuals who are internal consultants. Organizational-development specialists, project-management specialists, lean or Six Sigma experts, and specialists from other staff functions such as accounting and IT are examples of this. When internal change agents are operating from a consulting role, Christopher Wright found that they manage the ambiguity and communicate the value associated with such roles by developing a professional persona that highlights their distinctive competencies as well as reinforces their internal knowledge and linkages.[49]

Internal change agents are critical to the process because they know the systems, norms, and subtleties of how things get done, and they have existing relationships that can prove helpful. However, they may not possess needed specialized knowledge or skills, lack objectivity or independence, have difficulty reframing existing relationships with organizational members, or lack an adequate power base. When there are concerns that these gaps cannot be sufficiently addressed by pulling in other organizational members to assist with the process, organizational leaders may believe that it is necessary to bring in external consultants to assist with the project. Sometimes the external consultants are sought out by the internal change agents, while at other times they are thrust upon them. Wise organizational leaders know that external consultants need strong credentials if they are to win over the skeptics about a change project. In fact, poorly performing external consultants can create resistance to a change initiative.

EXTERNAL CONSULTANTS: SPECIALIZED, PAID CHANGE AGENTS

Provide Subject-Matter Expertise

External change agents are often hired to promote change through the technical expertise and credibility they bring to an internal change program. This was the case at Simmons College.

USING AN EXTERNAL CONSULTANT AT SIMMONS UNIVERSITY[50]

In 2006, the School of Business, Simmons University, Boston, Massachusetts, turned to an external consultant when working to gain AACSB International accreditation. The faculty had floundered for several years about how to assess students' learning of the overall management curriculum. Required by the AACSB's Standards to illustrate that its graduating students have learned a program's curriculum, some schools institute standardized tests to assess students' learning. However, the School of Business wanted a customized approach to evaluate the unique aspects of its management curriculum. The faculty struggled to envision methodologies and content to reach its goals. Finally, Katherine Martell, an assessment guru, was hired, bringing with her knowledge of how 50 other business schools conducted their assessment processes. When she left the school after two days of working with the faculty, the assessment processes and plans were in place and readily implemented in the following months.

Katherine Martell, the external consultant, was able to help faculty solve the "assessment of learning" problem that had stalled their progress in attaining AACSB accreditation. She did so by helping them work their way through the issues and find a solution. In addition to her technical skills and professional credibility, she was also retained because she possessed well-developed team-process skills that were instrumental in helping them work their way through the problem. When internal change agents or their teams feel they lack the technical skills needed in these areas, they often turn to external expertise.

Bring Fresh Perspectives
From Ideas That Have Worked Elsewhere

Too often, insiders find themselves tied to their experiences, and outside consultants can help extricate them from these mental traps.[51] Much can be learned from the systems and procedures that others have used elsewhere. In the following example, the leadership team at Knox Presbyterian Church (Waterloo) recognized it had a problem with how to approach fundraising and turned to RSI Consulting, who had helped many other churches address similar challenges through the use of established procedures. Once it had examined RSI's approach, the church's leadership team retained Craig Miller's services and was able to successfully adopt the approach.

EXTERNAL CONSULTANTS AS PROCESS EXPERTS[52]

When Knox Presbyterian Church, Waterloo, Canada, was planning a new building, church leaders decided they needed a capital campaign to bring life to their change initiative. However, the coordinating team knew that their view of fundraising was tied to past approaches and they recognized that these would not be able to raise the funds required. They searched out and hired RSI Consulting, specialists in church campaigns, with more than 9,000 conducted in 38 years. Craig Miller of RSI brought standard templates, which he used to guide church volunteers in framing the campaign and organizing their fundraising work. The Knox Congregation had the vision and the manpower but lacked the expertise and structure in how to handle the fundraising. By hiring RSI, they did not have to design the structure for a capital campaign; they borrowed it. As a result, Knox church members raised more than $2.3 million in pledges, in the 90th percentile of results for that size of church, and they did so very economically.

Provide Independent, Trustworthy Support

To help them manage the change process, internal change agents may find they need access to outside consultants who are viewed as independent, credible, competent, and (most importantly) trustworthy by others in the organization. In addition to guidance, they may be able to lend external credibility and support for analyses that advance the change initiative. Such consultants can prove extremely helpful with internal and external data gathering and the communication of the findings and their implications. Organizational members may feel more comfortable sharing their thoughts and concerns with the consultants than they would with internal staff. Finally, the external validation their analyses and conclusions provide may be the nudge needed to generate high levels of internal support for the change and action.

Limitations of External Consultants

External consultants can be instrumental in helping foster an atmosphere conducive to change by leveraging their reputations and skill sets through the way they manage the process. However, they have their limitations. They lack the deep knowledge of the political environment and culture of the organization that the inside change agents should have, and in the end it is the organization that needs to take responsibility for the change, not the external consultant. As a result, external change consultants may be able to assist internal agents, but they cannot replace them. Final decision-making needs to reside with the internal change leader and the organization.

How an internal change leader selects, introduces, and uses external consultants will have a lot to do with the ultimate success or failure of a change initiative. Consultants come in many forms, with different backgrounds, expertise, price tags, and ambitions. They often come with prescribed methodologies and offer prepackaged solutions. As a result, some consultants are insensitive to the organization's culture. The provision of ready-made answers not based in specific organizational research can be frustrating, and prescription without diagnosis is arguably malpractice.[53] Responsibility for this failure will fall back on the manager who retained the consultant, since he or she is accountable for managing this relationship.

Another risk factor is that consultants may receive signals that they are expected to unquestioningly support the position of the leader of the organization that brought them in, even when the external consultants have serious concerns with the course of action being undertaken. When external consultants lose their ability to provide independent judgment, their value and credibility are seriously reduced and their reputations may suffer irreparable harm if they succumb to pressure and the change subsequently fails in a very public manner.[54] In spite of these and other risks, many organizations continue to use external consultants to advance their change agendas and mitigate the risks of failure. One study reports that 83% of organizations that used consultants said they would use them again.[55] To increase the chances of success, consider the following advice on how to select an external consultant.

HOW SHOULD YOU SELECT AN EXTERNAL CONSULTANT?[56]

Since the appropriate consultant or consulting team will either advance or detract from the success of your change initiative, selecting a suitable one is a critical step. The following process is recommended for complex organizational change situations:

1. Ensure that you have a clear understanding of what you want from the consultants. Too often organizations hire consultants without thinking through exactly what value they can and will bring. Know who they will report to, what roles they will play, and how much you are willing to pay for their services.

2. Talk with multiple (up to five) consultants and/or consulting organizations. Internal change leaders will learn a great deal about the organization's problems and how they might be solved by talking with multiple vendors. They will also be able to compare and contrast the consultants' working styles, allowing them to gauge the chemistry between the change leader and team and the consultant. The internal change leader needs to ask, Do we have complementary or similar skills and outlook? Does this consultant bring skills and knowledge that I lack internally? Does the organization have the budget that is needed to engage this consultant?

3. Issue a request for proposals (RFP). Only ask those consultants with whom you would like to work, since writing and responding to RFPs is a time-consuming and labor-intensive process. Ask the internal leaders of the change process to objectively review the RFPs and provide you with feedback.

4. Make your decision and communicate expectations. Indicate clearly to the internal change leaders, the consultant(s), and all stakeholders the time line, roles, expectations, deliverables, and reporting relationships

CHANGE TEAMS

To balance access to needed perspectives, organizational leaders are moving toward the use of **change teams** that embody both internal and external perspectives. Change initiatives that are large require the efforts of more than one change agent. Outside consultants may be helpful, but as was noted earlier, they may be too expensive, and lack credibility. As a result, change agents look to extend their reach by using change teams. Worren suggests that teams are important because "employees learn new behaviors and attitudes by participating in ad-hoc teams solving real business problems."[57] Further, as change agents become immersed in the change, the volume of work increases and the roles and skills required of them vary. A cross-functional change team can be used to bring different perspectives, expertise, and credibility to bear on the change challenge inherent in those different roles.[58]

Organizational downsizing and increasing interest in the use of self-managed teams as an organizing approach for flattened hierarchies and cross-functional change initiatives have spurred awareness of the value of such teams.[59] Involvement in self-managed teams gives people space and time to adjust their views and/or influence the change process. It moves them out of the role of recipient and makes them active and engaged stakeholders.

In a benchmarking study focused on the best practices in change management, Prosci describes a good change-management team member as follows:

- Being knowledgeable about the business and enthusiastic about the change

- Possessing excellent oral and written communications skills, and a willingness to listen and share

- Having total commitment to the project, the process, and the results

- Being able to remain open minded and visionary

- Being respected within the organization as an apolitical catalyst for strategic change.[60]

Some of these characteristics of a good change team member appear contradictory. For example, it is tricky to be simultaneously totally committed and open-minded. Nevertheless, skilled change leaders often exhibit paradoxical or apparently contradictory characteristics. For example, the need to both be joined with and yet separate from other members of the change team in order to maintain independence of perspective and judgment is a difficult balance to maintain.[61] See **Toolkit Exercise 8.5** to analyze your skills as a change team member.

Working with and in teams is a baseline skill for change leaders. They must not only work to achieve the change, but they must also bring the change team along so that it accepts, is enthusiastic about, and effectively contributes to the implementation of the change initiative. Many might believe that this requires individuals who are adept at reducing stress and strain in the team, but this is not always the case.

BILL GATES: TEAM LEADER

Gates rarely indulges in water-cooler bantering and social niceties that put people at ease. But while Microsoft's former CEO and chairman was not considered a warm, affable person, he was an effective hands-on manager, says one former employee. "Bill is an exceptional motivator. For as much as he does not like small talk, he loves working with people on matters of substance," says Scott Langmack, a former Microsoft marketing manager.[62]

The most effective response will depend upon the needs of the situation. Bill Gates, for example, developed high-performance change teams in spite of a dominating personality and awkward social skills because of his abilities in the areas of vision and his capacity to attract and motivate highly talented individuals.

In the summer of 2008, Gates announced that he would cease full-time work at Microsoft to focus on his charitable foundations.[63] With this announcement, change agents and teams within Microsoft faced a new set of challenges related to managing this transition. Teams were essential components in making change happen.

A SUCCESSFUL CHANGE TEAM AT CASE WESTERN RESERVE UNIVERSITY

Many years ago, a group of students at Case Western Reserve University decided that there had to be better ways of teaching organizational change and development. This small group dedicated itself to changing the system. In two years, they transformed parts of Case Western and created the first doctoral program in organizational development with themselves as potential graduates. They planned and plotted. They identified key stakeholders and assigned team members to each stakeholder with the responsibility of bringing that stakeholder onside—or at least neutralizing their opposition. It was the team that made the change happen. They put into practice what they were learning as students.[64]

Creating the conditions for successful change is more than having an excellent change project plan. Equally important is recognizing the different change roles that need to be played and then developing a strong change team. This section covers the different change roles that team members play and how you design an excellent change team.

Possible Roles Within Change Teams*

Many change examples point out the need for a **champion** within the team who will fight for the change under trying circumstances and will continue to persevere when others might have checked out and given up. These change champions represent the visionary, the immovable force for change who will continue to push for the change regardless of the opposition. Senior managers need to ensure that those to whom the change is delegated possess the energy, drive, skills, resilience, and credibility needed to make it happen. If these are lacking, steps need to be taken to ensure that they are either developed or appropriate team members pick up the slack.

Change champions should consider two further organizing roles that are often better operationalized through the use of two separate teams: a **steering team** and a **design and implementation team**. The steering team provides advice to the champion and the implementation team directs the change in light of other events and priorities in the organization. As suggested by the name, the steering team plays an advisory and navigational function for the change project. It provides direction to the team's mandate, helps secure needed resources, suggests higher-order policies, and participates in major go/no-go decisions.

The design and implementation team plans the details of the change, deals with the stakeholders, and has primary responsibility for the implementation. The responsibilities of the different team members will vary over time, depending upon what is needed and their skill sets. The team will often have a **change project manager** who will coordinate planning, manage logistics, track the team's progress toward change targets, and manage the adjustments needed along the way.

Senior executives who act as **sponsors** of change foster commitment to the change and assist those charged with making the change happen.[65] Sponsors can act visibly, can share information and knowledge, and can give protection. **Visible sponsorship** means the senior manager advocates for the change and shows support through actions (i.e., use of influence and time) as well as words. **Information sharing and knowledge development** has the sponsor providing useful information about change and working with the team to ensure that the plans are sound. Finally, sponsors can **provide protection** for those to whom the change has been delegated. Without such protection, the individuals in the organization will tend to become more risk averse and less willing to champion the change.[66]

Developing a Change Team

Developing the team is an important task for the change leaders because the ability to build teams, motivate, and communicate are all predictors of successful change implementation.[67] If **change teams** can be developed that are self-regulating, change can often be facilitated because teams leverage the change leader's reach. The engagement and involvement of team members tends to heighten their commitment and support for the initiative,[68] and because they operate independently, self-managed teams can reduce the amount of time senior

---

*In Chapter 1, we discussed the roles that an individual can play: change recipient, initiator, facilitator, and implementer. These same roles are looked at here in relation to change teams.

managers must commit to implementation-related activities. Self-managed teams share an understanding of the change goals and objectives, sort out the differentiation and execution of tasks, and have control over the decision process.

Wageman has identified the following seven factors as critical to team success with self-managed teams:

- clear, engaging direction;

- a real team task;

- rewards for team excellence;

- the availability of basic material resources to do the job;

- authority vested in the team to manage the work;

- team goals; and

- the development of team norms that promote strategic thinking.[69]

A similar list was developed by the Change Institute and is set out in Table 8.4[70]

The dedication and willingness to give it their "all" is the most obvious characteristic of highly committed change teams. The dogged determination to make changes regardless of personal consequences because of a deep-rooted belief in a vision creates both the conditions for victory and the possibilities of organizational suicide. In the earlier example at Case Western Reserve University, if the changes were not successful, the individuals involved would have sacrificed several years of their lives to no organizational effect. In the case of Lou Gerstner's turn-around at IBM,[71] there was a distinct possibility that the firm would not survive and members of his inner circle would be forever known as the individuals who oversaw the collapse of this American corporate icon. Instead, they are known as the inner circle who helped Gerstner turn around IBM from losing $8.1 billion in 1993 to renewal, profitability, and growth. At the time of his retirement in 2002, the value of a share of IBM's stock had risen from $13 to $80, adjusted for splits. Wanting to create one "Big Blue," Gerstner reorganized the corporation from individual fiefdoms to one integrated organization and tied the pay of his top

---

Table 8.4 Design Rules for Top Teams

1. Keep it small: 10 or fewer members.

2. Meet a minimum of biweekly and demand full attendance—less often breaks the rhythm of cooperation. How the team meets is less important—it may be face to face or through virtual means.

3. Everything is your business. That is, no information is off-limits.

4. Each of you is accountable for your business.

5. No secrets and no surprises within the team.

6. Straight talk, modeled by the leader.

7. Fast decisions, modeled by the leader.

8. Everyone's paid partly on the total results.

10 executives (his inner circle) to the overall company's performance. In reflecting upon his success in transforming IBM, Gerstner stressed "how imperative it was for a leader to love their business and to 'kill yourself to make it successful.' There is no substitute for hard work and the desire to win. CEOs face a multitude of choices, often peddled by a multitude of self-interested advisors, but they need to focus on exploiting competitive advantages in core businesses" (p. 2).[72]

In forming a change team, the personalities and skills of the members will play a significant role in the team's success. The change process demands a paradoxical set of skills: the ability to create a vision and the intuition to see the connections between that vision and all of the things that will need to be done. This includes identifying who will need to be influenced; thinking positively about stakeholders while recognizing what will influence them and why they may resist you; caring passionately for an initiative and yet not interpreting criticism as a personal attack; and translating strategy and vision into concrete change plans. Having the capacity to deal with these paradoxes requires comfort and skill in dealing with ambiguity and complexity.

DEVELOPING CHANGE TEAMS AT FEDERAL EXPRESS[73]

Federal Express has developed a checklist for using change teams.

1. Ensure that everybody who has a contribution to make is fully involved, and those who will have to make any change are identified and included.

2. Convince people that their involvement is serious and not a management ploy—present all ideas from management as "rough" ideas.

3. Ensure commitment to making any change work—the team members identify and develop "what is in it for them" when they move to make the idea work.

4. Increase the success rate for new ideas: identify problems in a problem-solving, rather than blame-fixing, approach.

5. Deliver the best solutions: problem-solving teams self-select to find answers to the barriers to successful implementation.

6. Maintain momentum and enthusiasm: the remainder of the team continues to work on refining the basic idea.

7. Present problem solutions, improve where necessary, approve, and implement immediately.

8. Refine ideas, agree upon them, and plan the implementation process.

Adapted from Lambert, T. (2006). Insight. MENAFN.com.

While the tasks around change demand the paradoxical expertise explained above, functional and technical competencies also play a very important role. It is difficult to imagine a team establishing credibility if it lacks such basics. However, the personalities present in the team will influence how the team interacts and performs, including its ability to manage the inherent paradoxes. While it is usually not necessary for the team to be highly cohesive, cohesion, rooted in a shared sense of purpose, will lend strength to the change effort and focus the team's activities. Implementing change requires considerable energy and can be frustrating and exhausting. At such times, having access to a cohesive and committed team can be invaluable in sustaining the team during difficult times.

The boxed insert below describes how Federal Express systematically develops a team approach to change.

Use to your advantage the Checklist: Structuring Work in a Change Team that follows the Key Terms section in this chapter.

CHANGE FROM THE MIDDLE: EVERYONE NEEDS TO BE A CHANGE AGENT

Increasingly, successful organizational members will find that they need to act as change agents in their organizations. As Katzenbach suggests, the real change leader will take action—do things, try them out, and then do it again while getting better.[74] While this book applauds this type of initiative, remember the first rule for change agents: *Stay alive.*

When managers find themselves involved with change, most will be operating from the middle of the organization. At times, they will have those above them attempting to direct or influence change while they are trying to influence those superiors about what needs to be initiated and how best to proceed. At other times, middle managers will need to deal with subordinates and peers who will be on the receiving end of the change or who are themselves trying to initiate activities.

Oshry recognized the feelings of **middle powerlessness** that many feel when operating in the "middle" and outlined strategies for increasing one's power in these situations.[75] Problem ownership is one of the key issues. Far too often, managers insert themselves in the middle of a dispute and take on others' issues as their own when, in fact, intervention is not helpful. As well, when the issue is the managers, they may refuse to use their power. They need to take responsibility, make a decision, and move on. Or, they need to refuse to accept unreasonable demands from above and attempt to work matters out rather than simply acquiesce and create greater problems below.

Oshry's advice to those in the middle is as follows:

1. "Be top when you can and take responsibility for being top."

2. "Be bottom when you should." Don't let problems just flow through you to subordinates.

3. "Be coach" to help others solve their own problems so they don't become yours.

4. "Facilitate" rather than simply carry messages when you find yourself running back and forth between two parties who are in conflict.

5. "Integrate with one another" so that you develop a strong peer group that you can turn to for advice, guidance, and support.

Whether a manager uses logic or participation to engage others in a change initiative, or acts on his or her own,[76] the message is clear: managers are increasingly being held accountable for taking action. Scanning the environment, figuring out what will make things better, and creating initiatives are the new responsibilities today's managers carry. This text argues that any change agent role—initiator, implementer, facilitator, or team member—is preferable to constantly finding yourself on the receiving end of change. A strategy of passively keeping one's head down and avoiding change increases a person's career risk because he or she will be less likely to be perceived as adding value.

FROM A CHANGE EXPERT

Greg Brenneman has made a career out of turning large companies around and encourages people to work with sick organizations. "If you have a chance of working for a healthy or a sick one, choose the sick one. The sickest ones need the best doctors and it's a lot easier to stand out in a company that needs help," he said to MBA students in 2008.[77] These companies are the ones where you really get into the work and help a company truly succeed. The successful ingredients in turnarounds, according to Brenneman, are the financials; developing and sticking to a clear strategy, especially in a time of crisis; identifying new leaders from the industry to lead the company; and plain hard work.

RULES OF THUMB FOR CHANGE AGENTS

How should managers act as change agents? Several authors have proposed useful insights and wisdom from their experiences and analysis of change leaders. These **rules of thumb for change agents** which have been integrated, combined, and added to, are listed below:[78]

Stay alive—"Dead" change agents are of no use to the organization. The notion that you should sacrifice yourself at the altar of change is absurd unless you truly wish it. At the same time, the invocation to "stay alive" says you need to be in touch with those things that energize you and give you purpose.

Start where the system is—Immature change agents start where they are. Experienced change agents diagnose the system, understand it, and begin with the system.

Work downhill—Work with people in the system in a collaborative fashion. Confront and challenge resisters in useful ways. Don't alienate people if at all possible. Work in promising areas and make progress.

Organize, but don't over-organize—Plans will change. If you are too organized, you risk becoming committed to your plan in ways that don't permit the inclusion and involvement of others.

Pick your battles carefully—Don't argue if you can't win. A win/lose strategy deepens conflict and should be avoided wherever possible. The maxim "If you strike a king, strike to kill" fits here. If you can't complete the job, you may not survive.

Load experiments for success—If you can, set up the situation and position it as positively as possible. Change is difficult at the best of times—if you can improve the odds, you should!

Light many fires—High-visibility projects often attract both attention and opposition. Work within the organizational subsystems to create opportunities for change in many places, not just a major initiative.

Just enough is good enough—Don't wait for perfection. Beta test your ideas. Get them out there to see how they work and how people react.

You can't make a difference without doing things differently—Remember that definition of insanity—"doing things the same way but expecting different results." You have to act and behave differently to have things change. Hope is not an action.

Reflect—As individuals, as change teams, and as organizations, a commitment to learning from each experience and creating space for reflection on both positive and challenging moments is essential to effective and productive change.

Want to change: focus on important results and get them—Not only does success breed success, but getting important results brings resources, influence, and credibility.

Think and act fast—Speed and flexibility are critical. Sensing the situation and reacting quickly will make a difference. Acting first means others will have to act second and will always be responding to your initiatives.

Create a coalition—Lone ranger operatives are easy to dismiss. As Gary Hamel says, an "army of like-minded activists cannot be ignored."

SUMMARY

This chapter describes how anyone, from any position in the organization, can potentially instigate and lead change, assuming a change agent role is a matter of personal attributes, a function of the situation, and the vision of the change agent. Four types of change leaders are described: the emotional champion, the intuitive adapter, the continuous improver, and the developmental strategist. Finally, the use of change teams was discussed. There was also advice to managers on how to handle the middle-manager role they might find themselves in when dealing with change.

The management of change is an essential part of the role of leaders. Leading change will tax your skills, energize and challenge, exhaust, depress, occasionally exhilarate, and leave you, at times, with a profound sense of accomplishment. What it will not do is leave you the same.

The demands of organizations are clear—managers are expected to play an increasingly significant role in the management of change. Earlier, this book advised managers to know themselves, assess the situation carefully, and then take action. The next chapter outlines action planning to assist leaders of change. See **Toolkit Exercise 8.1** for critical thinking questions for this chapter.

KEY TERMS

Change agent effectiveness—a function of the person, his or her vision, and the characteristics of the situation.

Exothermic—describes a change situation when energy is liberated by actions.

Endothermic—describes a change program that consumes energy and arouses opposition, which then requires more energy from the change agent.

Change leaders—pull people to change through the use of a powerful change vision.

Change managers—create change by working with others, overcoming resistance, and problem solving situations.

Developmental stages of a change agent—vary from a novice stage to an expert stage through successful experiences with increasingly complex, sophisticated change situations.

Types of Change Leaders

The Emotional Champion—has a clear and powerful vision of what the organization needs and uses that vision to capture the hearts and motivations of the organization's members.

The Developmental Strategist—applies rational analysis to understanding the competitive logic of the organization and how it no longer fits with the organization's existing strategy.

The Intuitive Adapter—has the clear vision for the organization and uses that vision to reinforce a culture of learning and adaptation.

The Continuous Improver—analyzes micro environments and seeks changes such as re-engineering systems and processes.

Hunsaker's Change Roles

The **catalyst**—needed to overcome inertia and focus the organization on the problems faced.

The **solution giver**—knows how to respond and can solve the problem as well as convince others to pursue their solutions.

The **process helper**—facilitates the "how to" of change, playing the role of third-party intervener often.

The **resource linker**—brings people and resources together in ways that aid in the solution of issues.

An **internal change agent**—an employee of the organization who knows the organization intimately and is attempting to create change.

An **external change agent**—a person from outside the organization trying to make changes. Often this person is an outside expert and consultant.

The **change team**—the group of employees, usually from a cross-section of the organization, that is charged with a change task.

The **champion**—the person within the change team who will fight for the change under trying circumstances and preserve throughout adversity.

The **steering team**—plays an advisory and guidance role to change leaders and design and implementation teams.

The **design and implementation team**—responsible for the actual design and implementation of the change initiatives.

The **change project manager**—coordinates planning, manages logistics, tracks the team's progress toward change targets, and manages the adjustments needed along the way.

A **sponsor** of change—senior executive who fosters commitment to the change and assists the change agents who are actively making the change happen.

Visible sponsorship—entails actions including leveraging of influence and time to advocate for the change.

Information sharing and knowledge development—when the sponsor provides useful information to the change team and ensures that the team's change plans are sound.

Sponsors may also **provide protection** for those who are delegated with change tasks, allowing change agents to be less risk averse and more willing to champion the change.

Middle powerlessness—the feeling of a lack of power and influence that those in middle-level organizational roles often experience when organizational changes are being implemented. Pressure comes from above and below and they see themselves as ill-equipped to respond.

Rules of thumb for change agents—things for change agents to keep in mind to ensure their survival and success over the long term.

CHECKLIST: STRUCTURING WORK IN A CHANGE TEAM

Once the nature of the change initiative has been set out, team members will need to sort out what needs to be done when and who will do it.

A shorthand designation, **BART**, is a useful way to structure tasks among a working group. Talking about BART in the context of a newly forming team can make the roles and responsibilities among people clear and decrease conflict among group members.

To be a useful tool, start with *Tasks* and end with *Boundaries*. It is wise to have a conversation about these issues, put what has been agreed-upon in writing, and then revisit the structure at a designated time.

1) **Tasks**: This is the work that needs to be completed in a particular situation. Make a comprehensive list of tasks; next, assign the tasks to specific roles; then decide how much authority an individual has in the role; and, finally, describe how one role interfaces with another.

2) **Authority**: This is the scope of decision making that a particular team member has in her or his role.

3) **Roles**: These are the parts that individual team members have been explicitly assigned

to be responsible for in the execution of specific tasks.

4) **Boundaries**: The edge where one person's responsibilities end and another's begins.

In addition to the above items, team members need to come to agreement on how they will operate as a team. This includes

(a) values the team shares and norms of behavior,

(b) performance expectations they have for themselves and for one another,

(c) how they will communicate with and support one another,

(d) how they will manage and resolve conflicts,

(e) how they will manage documents and reports,

(f) how they will track and measure progress, and

(g) how they will otherwise manage their team processes.

Once again, it is useful to put what has been agreed-upon in writing and then revisit it, as needed.

END-OF-CHAPTER EXERCISES

TOOLKIT EXERCISE 8.1
Critical Thinking Questions

The URL for the video listed below can be found in two places. The first spot is next to the exercise and the second spot is on the website at **study.sagepub.com/cawsey4e.**

1. LeadersAngle Gene Deszca Organisational Change—14:59 minutes

    https://www.youtube.com/watch?v=n9lzudH-uJI

    - Evaluate yourself on the core competencies mentioned in the video.

    - What do you think that you need to do to improve your skills or create a situation where you can be a successful change agent?

Please see **study.sagepub.com/cawsey4e** *for a downloadable template of this exercise.*

TOOLKIT EXERCISE 8.2

Myself as Change Agent

1. The following list of change agent attributes and skills represents an amalgam drawn from the previous section. Rate yourself on the following dimensions on the seven-point scale.

Attributes of Change Leaders from Caldwell

Low 1 2 3 4 5 6 7 High

- Inspiring vision   1 2 3 4 5 6 7
- Entrepreneurship   1 2 3 4 5 6 7
- Integrity and honesty   1 2 3 4 5 6 7
- Learning from others   1 2 3 4 5 6 7
- Openness to new ideas   1 2 3 4 5 6 7
- Risk taking   1 2 3 4 5 6 7
- Adaptability and flexibility   1 2 3 4 5 6 7
- Creativity   1 2 3 4 5 6 7
- Experimentation   1 2 3 4 5 6 7
- Using power   1 2 3 4 5 6 7

Attributes of Change Managers from Caldwell

- Empowering others   1 2 3 4 5 6 7
- Team building   1 2 3 4 5 6 7
- Learning from others   1 2 3 4 5 6 7
- Adaptability and flexibility   1 2 3 4 5 6 7
- Openness to new ideas   1 2 3 4 5 6 7
- Managing resistance   1 2 3 4 5 6 7
- Conflict resolution   1 2 3 4 5 6 7
- Networking skills   1 2 3 4 5 6 7
- Knowledge of the business   1 2 3 4 5 6 7
- Problem solving   1 2 3 4 5 6 7

Change Agent Attributes Suggested by Others

- Interpersonal skills   1 2 3 4 5 6 7
- Communication skills   1 2 3 4 5 6 7

- Emotional resilience   1 2 3 4 5 6 7
- Tolerance for ambiguity   1 2 3 4 5 6 7
- Tolerance for ethical conflict   1 2 3 4 5 6 7
- Political skill   1 2 3 4 5 6 7
- Persistence   1 2 3 4 5 6 7
- Determination   1 2 3 4 5 6 7
- Pragmatism   1 2 3 4 5 6 7
- Dissatisfaction with the status quo   1 2 3 4 5 6 7
- Openness to information   1 2 3 4 5 6 7
- Flexibility   1 2 3 4 5 6 7
- Capacity to build trust   1 2 3 4 5 6 7
- Intelligence   1 2 3 4 5 6 7
- Emotional intelligence   1 2 3 4 5 6 7

2. Do you see yourself as scoring high on some items compared to others? If so, you are more likely to be comfortable in a change agent role. Lack of these attributes and skills does not mean you could not be a change agent—it just means that it will be more difficult and it may suggest areas for development.

3. Are you more likely to be comfortable in a change leadership role at this time, or does the role of change manager or implementer seem more suited to who you are?

4. Ask a mentor or friend to provide you feedback on the same dimensions. Does the feedback confirm your self-assessment? If not, why not?

Please see **study.sagepub.com/cawsey4e** *for a downloadable template of this exercise.*

TOOLKIT EXERCISE 8.3

Your Development as a Change Agent

Novice change leaders often picture themselves as being in the right and those that oppose them as somehow wrong. This certainty gives them energy and the will to persist in the face of such opposition. It sets up a dynamic of opposition—the more they resist, the more I must try to change them, and so I persuade them more, put more pressure on them, and perhaps resort to whatever power I have to force change.

1. Think of a situation where someone held a different viewpoint than yours. What were your assumptions about that person? Did you believe they just didn't get it, were wrong headed, perhaps a bit stupid?

    Or did you ask yourself, why would they hold the position they have? If you assume they are as rational and as competent as you are, why would they think as they do? Think back to Table 8.2. Are you at Stage 1, 2, 3, or 4?

2. Are you able to put yourself into the shoes of the resister? Ask yourself: What forces play on that person? What beliefs does he or she have? What criteria is he or she using to evaluate the situation?

3. What are the implications of your self-assessment with respect to what you need to do to develop yourself as a change agent?

*Please see **study.sagepub.com/cawsey4e** for a downloadable template of this exercise.*

TOOLKIT EXERCISE 8.4

What Is Your Change Agent Preference?

1. How comfortable are you with risk and ambiguity?

   Do you seek order and stability or change and uncertainty?

   Describe your level of comfort in higher-risk situations.

   Describe your degree of restlessness with routine, predictable situations.

2. How intuitive are you?

   Do you use feelings and emotion to influence others? Or are you logical and systematic?

   Do you persuade through facts and arguments?

3. Ask someone who knows you well to reflect on your change preferences and style. Does that person's judgment agree or disagree with yours?

   Why? What data do each have?

4. Given your responses to the above, how would you classify yourself?

   - An Emotional Champion
   - An Intuitive Adapter
   - A Developmental Strategist
   - A Continuous Improver

5. How flexible or adaptive are you with respect to the approach you use?

(Continued)

(Continued)

Do you always adopt the same approach, or do you use other approaches, depending on the needs of the situation?

Which ones do you feel comfortable and competent in using?

Again, check out your self-assessment by asking a significant other for comments. Comment on their response.

*Please see **study.sagepub.com/cawsey4e** for a downloadable template of this exercise.*

TOOLKIT EXERCISE 8.5

Your Skills as a Change Team Member

1. Think of a time when you participated in a team. What was the team's goal?

    How well did the team perform? Were the results positive?

    Why or why not?

2. Did the team members exhibit the characteristics listed by Prosci, below? Rate your team members' performance on these characteristics.

    *   Being knowledgeable about the business and enthusiastic about the change

    *   Possessing excellent oral and written communications skills and a willingness to listen and share

    *   Having total commitment to the project, the process, and the results

    *   Being able to remain open-minded and visionary

    *   Being respected within the organization as an apolitical catalyst for strategic change[79]

3. What personal focus do you have? Do you tend to concentrate on getting the job done—a task focus? Or do you worry about bringing people along—a process focus?

4. How would you improve your skills in this area? Who might help you develop such skills?

Please see **study.sagepub.com/cawsey4e** *for a downloadable template of this exercise.*

MASTER CHANGE AGENT: KATHERINE GOTTLIEB, SOUTHCENTRAL FOUNDATION

By Erin E. Sullivan, Research Director, PhD

Center for Primary Care, Harvard Medical School, Boston, MA

Katherine Gottlieb, president and chief executive officer (CEO) of Southcentral Foundation (SCF) in Anchorage, Alaska, was up at 4 a.m. She thought about how much SCF had changed since she started as a receptionist in 1987. In June 2014, Gottlieb was leading 1,750 staff members, and had grown the organization to include the robust Anchorage Native Primary Care Center, and other community health centers across Southern Alaska. These centers provided services that supported the wellness of the American Indian and Alaska Native (AIAN) population. With all her accomplishments at SCF, Gottlieb still maintained an endless list of ideas for SCF. At the same time, Gottlieb had been at the helm of SCF for more than two decades and was approaching retirement. She had worked hard to develop a cadre of leaders within the organization and a culture that could be sustained while managing the 21st-century challenges of leading a large health system.

KATHERINE GOTTLIEB: LEADER

Gottlieb, who belonged to three tribes in the AIAN community, grew up in the remote fishing village of Seldovia, Alaska. The village had no electricity and a population of about 100 people. In 1987, Gottlieb walked into SCF with a grin on her face, in search of a job and proclaimed she wanted to be CEO. Although the organization responded by making her a receptionist, Gottlieb defied circumstances by finding ways to serve as a leader in every role she held. She understood that leadership was not exclusive to those with the title of "CEO."

Shortly after joining SCF, Gottlieb requested funds and purchased a new sturdy, oak desk to replace the metal one that clanged and rattled as she sat welcoming patients all day. Gottlieb intentionally replaced the desk because she recognized that she was the face of SCF. Her goal, in serving the AIAN people, was to immediately raise their self-esteem by welcoming them into an environment that was inviting and safe as opposed to sterile or run-down. Gottlieb's own experience with the health system inspired her departure from the status quo:

> I began my experience in the healthcare field as patient number 32041 in a hospital system that was managed by a very bureaucratic government system. No matter what I needed, if it was dental care, strep throat, pregnancy, or eye care, I went through the emergency room, and that was our entry level. No one was happy, the waiting room was filled with sick babies, and everybody was sick. . . .Our wait time could be up to 7–9 hours. If I went with babies, I would just bring a blanket and food and we would picnic over off in the corner because we knew we were going to be stuck. . . .So as a patient, everybody was grumpy. . . .Our lines were really, really long and I felt like cattle, like cattle being prodded through the system—that is the feeling that I had.

Over the next four years at SCF, Gottlieb proceeded to create new positions for herself. They included administrative assistant, corporate compliance director, and associate director. Gottlieb was appointed deputy director of SCF in 1989 and executive director in 1991 (see Exhibit 1 for a timeline of Gottlieb's accomplishments). In 1996, Gottlieb changed her title from executive director to president and CEO of SCF, and worked to build partnerships across Alaska. One of those seminal relationships was with former U.S. Senator Ted Stevens, an avid supporter of the AIAN people. Gottlieb routinely cultivated relationships with both local and Washington politicians. Furthermore, Gottlieb and her VPs spent approximately 25% of their time engaging constituents and stakeholders in dialogue.

During her tenure as president and CEO, Gottlieb demonstrated that it was possible to be both family oriented and to serve as an organizational leader. Gottlieb was not only devoted to her large family, but also established herself as a visionary leader. SCF's VP of medical services asserted, "One of the most powerful things is that she [Gottlieb] has almost a vision of limitless possibility. Most human beings are limited in their ability to dream about what's possible. Gottlieb has practically no limits, especially considering where we started from."

Gottlieb's leadership was nationally recognized, earning her a MacArthur Fellowship in 2004 and the Harry S. Hertz Leadership Award from the Foundation for the Malcolm Baldrige National Quality Award in 2015.

SCF: ORGANIZATIONAL CULTURE

In 1998, the Alaska Area Indian Health Service (IHS) transferred ownership of the Alaska Native Medical Center to SCF and the Alaska Native Tribal Health Consortium (ANTHC). This transfer of ownership to SCF and the ANTHC marked the beginning of SCF's implementation of their "customer-owner" approach, the bedrock of its health care delivery model. This approach centered on renaming and reframing patients as customer-owners based on the premise that Alaska Native people owned their health system and should therefore fully engage with their health care.[1] Focus groups,

interviews, tribal leadership meetings, and surveys were used to engage customer-owners. Through this process, SCF created its current mission and vision statements. SCF's vision statement described "a Native Community that enjoys physical, mental, emotional and spiritual wellness." SCF's mission statement emphasized "working together with the Native Community to achieve wellness through health and related services" (see Exhibit 2 for SCF's operational principles).

SCF's mission and vision worked to support the Nuka System of Care (Nuka), which was the name SCF used to describe its approach to working together with the Native Community to achieve health and wellness in Alaska. The word Nuka represented "big living things" in many indigenous cultures. Named by Gottlieb, Nuka "addresses the challenges that health care systems around the world face—how to improve health care outcomes and customer satisfaction without skyrocketing costs."[2] In other words, it was about customer-ownership, relationships, and system transformation. According to SCF leadership, trust and accountability, maintained over time, were central to Nuka and formed the basis for the relationships between employees and between the customer-owner and the health care provider.[3] To understand and then implement Nuka, SCF required its employees to attend mandatory Core Concepts training.

Core Concepts

SCF leadership developed a three-day program called Core Concepts as a way to teach the story of SCF and Nuka. This training also provided employees with the tools of empathy, compassion and relationship-building. Core Concepts explored how individual narratives and stories affected and shaped relationships people had with themselves and with others. SCF developed a pilot training program focused on setting goals, managing conflict, understanding personal motivations and assumptions about the world, and building relationships through sharing personal narratives. This program was piloted with 100 managers and program directors. "Putting the managers and directors through the program was essential to achieve buy-in for the concept," remembered Gottlieb.

Core Concepts officially started in 2008. Once the majority of the workforce was trained, SCF offered Core Concepts three to four times annually. Gottlieb also conducted mini-sessions to refresh Core Concepts principles for SCF division and department leaders. Additionally, SCF put their operations on hold for an Annual Learning Event for all staff. One SCF staff member noted that she applied Core Concepts outside of the workplace. Applying Core Concepts tools at home added to the holistic wellness of the AIAN community, and provided a common language for healthy communication in families and relationships.

A Culture of Improvement

Gottlieb, along with her executive team, developed a cultural and operational structure to support continuous change and improvement. SCF leadership had looked to corporations like Disney and Ritz Carleton for best practices in customer service, and created multiple ways of soliciting and responding to feedback from customer-owners. SCF received customer-owner feedback via multiple channels, including iPads placed in primary care clinics, social media platforms, direct emails to Gottlieb, the Gathering (an annual SCF community event attended by more than 2,000 people each year), satisfaction surveys, comment cards, and a 24-hour phone hotline. Customer-owners were also present in SCF's workforce (50 –60%) and were another valuable source of feedback. SCF's joint operating boards and advisory committees, entirely comprised of customer-owners, periodically met with SCF's senior leadership team.

According to an SCF improvement advisor, this constant feedback loop within SCF empowered staff to think constantly about improvement and a culture of change. Improvement work was an essential part of every job function at SCF, and the organization provided ongoing training opportunities so that every employee could meet that expectation. SCF received and responded to

an average of 10 customer-owner comments per day. Gottlieb explained that SCF's practice was to act directly on the feedback and then close the loop with customer-owners. Gottlieb elaborated: "We say we changed this because you asked for it. We built this because you said to. Pretty soon you own the change, not us, not we who are working on the job." SCF's customer-owner satisfaction rate consistently exceeded 90%.

SCF: GOVERNANCE STRUCTURE

As Gottlieb expanded SCF, she reflected on its governance structure and noted, "to be successful at working with a governance body, building relationships is essential." Gottlieb worked to build high trust and transparency throughout all levels of the organization. She explained that trust and transparency were important not only between executive leadership and the board, but also between the board and employees. To demonstrate her commitment to trust and transparency, Gottlieb removed the walls of the SCF boardroom and replaced them with glass— earning it the nickname "the fishbowl." Gottlieb made sure that the SCF Board remained involved in SCF events, from special visits from external organizations to celebrations. Gottlieb reported, "There's a relationship between the governance and community of employees we have. And they're customer-owners—they're Alaska Native people so they have a stake in the community and that's a pretty big deal."

SCF's Vice Presidents

Gottlieb's executive team had all "grown up" in the organization together. Joining SCF between 1980 and 1996, the VPs had extensive knowledge of the organization having served in various administrative and clinical roles before assuming leadership positions as VPs. All six VPs reported to Gottlieb and were housed in the same location. She stated, "SCF's VPs are all located in the same area so they interact as a team and have easy access to one another." She met with SCF's VPs frequently, and the group made many of the high priority decisions. If consensus could not be reached, Gottlieb made the final decision. Gottlieb explained, "We work as a team, encourage each other to voice opinions, oppose ideas and are willing to struggle through long, hard discussions in order to reach consensus. . . .We've never brought an idea or concept to the Board without us [the VPs and Gottlieb] all in 100% agreement."

Annual Strategic Planning Process

SCF's annual strategic planning process engaged the entire organization, from individual employees to the board. This process was grounded in SCF's mission, vision, and corporate goals (shared responsibility, commitment to quality, family wellness, and operational excellence). The process involved implementing new initiatives and evaluating ongoing initiatives generated through the organization's improvement processes. Starting in January, SCF leadership generated a strategic input document that assessed both external (e.g., customer-owner feedback) and internal (e.g., staffing needs) factors, including strategic challenges and advantages, that might affect the organization.

After reviewing the strategic input document, SCF's board assessed how SCF's corporate objectives would be impacted. With a set of corporate initiatives, linked to the corporate objectives, SCF divisions, committees, and departments completed their annual work plans every summer to address any new or ongoing initiatives in the strategic plan. SCF employees then met with their managers in November to create Personal Development Plans (PDPs) that outlined how they would support the annual work plans in the year ahead. SCF's board also approved the budget in August/September. To keep the entire organization uptodate, any employee could log in to the corporate intranet to view all documents developed during the strategic planning process.

PLANNING FOR SCF'S FUTURE

Gottlieb partnered with SCF leadership to build the infrastructure and services required to meet the community's needs. In order to ensure the continuity of those resources after she retired, Gottlieb explained that she "put systems in place that are flexible, but very hard to change." In particular, Gottlieb implemented structures to ensure SCF's growth, which included creating several leadership development programs to ensure a pipeline of talent within the organization (see Exhibit 3 for the five leadership training programs launched with Gottlieb's support). SCF also worked to retain as many employees as possible once they were hired. The only person who could officially fire an employee at SCF was Gottlieb, and she believed in "first, second, third, and fourth chances."

As she contemplated retirement, Gottlieb recognized that a new CEO would inherit all of the challenges associated with running a health care organization in Anchorage, Alaska. The increasing number of older Alaska Native people with chronic diseases and a demand for specialty care would stretch the services SCF needed to provide. SCF would need to consider strategies for increasing preventive services and health education for the younger Alaska Native community. As the AIAN community moved from rural areas to Anchorage, this in turn increased the number of customer-owners that SCF served. However, despite SCF's growing customer-owner population, IHS funding remained constant and did not increase accordingly. Recruiting physicians to Alaska was never easy. The political climate in the United States and health care reform also had the potential to affect the Alaska Native community.

Gottlieb believed that what mattered most was that a new CEO would continue the commitment she had made to all SCF employees and the 60,000+ AIAN people that SCF served. Gottlieb had nurtured a specific culture over the last twenty-five years, and it was important that a new CEO embody and sustain it. However, she wanted a new CEO to have his or her own dreams for SCF, and thought to herself, "If you get a new leader and nothing changes, what did you hire that person for?"

Exhibit 1   Timeline of Accomplishments During Katherine Gottlieb's Tenure at SCF

| 1993 | 1994 | 1997 | 2001 | 2003 | 2004 | 2006 | 2011 | 2015 |

SCF grew to include five clinics and some 50 employees

The first family medicine clinic at SCF opened

Congress passed Sections 325 and 326 of Public Law 105–83 to address tribal management and control of the health care services

New Alaska Native Medical Center opened

Gottlieb added a wing that provided family physicians the opportunity to refer patients to a complementary medicine practice as well as a traditional healing service staffed by tribal doctors

SCF opened its Fireweed Building in 2003, which housed dentistry, optometry, and behavioral health services

SCF launched its Health Education and Wellness Center, staffed with dieticians, exercise physiologists, behavioral health practitioners, health educators, and programs designed to support customer-owner and employee wellness

Gottlieb became a MacArthur Fellow in 2004 as a result of her health care work with Alaska Native people

SCF received the Malcolm Baldrige National Quality Award (Baldrige) from the US Department of Commerce's National Institutes of Standards and Technology in 2011 for work around improvement and organizational performance

Gottlieb received the Harry S. Hertz Leadership Award from the Foundation for the Malcolm Baldrige National Quality Award

Source: Compiled by case writer based on biographical information available

Exhibit 2   Operational Principles of Southcentral Foundation

Relationships between customer-owner, family and provider must be fostered and supported

Emphasis on wellness of the whole person, family and community (physical, mental, emotional, and spiritual wellness)

Locations convenient for customer-owners with minimal stops to get all their needs addressed

Access optimized and waiting times limited

Together with the customer-owner as an active partner

Intentional whole-system design to maximize coordination and minimize duplication

Outcome and process measures continuously evaluated and improved

Not complicated but simple and easy to use

Services financially sustainable and viable

Hub of the system is the family

Interests of customer-owners drive the system to determine what we do and how we do it

Population-based systems and services

Services and systems build on the strengths of Alaska Native cultures

Source: Southcentral Foundation

Exhibit 3   Five Leadership Programs Developed Through Gottlieb's Support

Executive Leadership Experience (ELE): In order to prepare future AIAN VPs, Gottlieb launched the ELE in 2012. In the inaugural year, two staff members spent six months shadowing her. Gottlieb developed and coached the staff as they worked with her on projects. In 2015, eight staff members will enter into a full curriculum designed to prepare ELE participants for VP roles.

Special Assistant Program: This program provided executive level experience, connection across the organization, and leadership skills for an entry-level SCF staff member aspiring to work at the VP level. In this program, staff worked with Kevin Gottlieb, or other SCF VPs, on projects for the board and traveled on behalf of SCF.

Foundations: This program served as the long-term, on-the-job, core leadership training for entry-level staff climbing the career ladder and moving into positions requiring more leadership skills. The classroom portion of the course met once a month for eight hours, and covered two to three topics during each session; at Gottlieb's request, this program covered relationship building and leadership tools. Staff could begin at any point and cycled through 12 months of classes.

(Continued)

Exhibit 3   (Continued)

Administrative Support Training Program (ASTP): In 2002, ASTP was created in response to retention rates of under 50% for front line staff (i.e. receptionists and schedulers). Before the eight-week ASTP training period, administrative support staff candidates first completed a one-week new hire orientation. During training, SCF classified these candidates as temporary, non-benefited employees. Candidates spent the first three weeks at the center on SCF's campus in Anchorage learning technical skills specific to their jobs, relationship building, and communication and conflict resolution skills.

Then the center, in consultation with division managers, placed trainees in available support positions throughout SCF for a five-week in-clinic training period. Candidates worked closely with a manager/supervisor to apply the skills learned in ASTP and to receive on-the-job training. At the end, the center staff met with managers to hire the candidates that were a good fit for the divisions for benefited positions. In 2014, SCF's ASTP retention rate was 90%.

Responsible Adolescents in Successful Employment (RAISE) Program: RAISE was SCF's summer internship program for AIAN youth between the ages of 14 and 19. This program, led by Ileen Sylvester, VP of tribal affairs, focused on providing training and leadership development for ~60 AIAN summer interns in addition to smaller numbers of winter and graduate interns. Gottlieb felt that this was one of her proudest accomplishments because it worked to build self-esteem and a culture of wellness among Alaska Native youth. As of 2014, 46 RAISE internship alumni were hired in full-time positions.

Source: Southcentral Foundation

REFERENCES

1. Gottlieb, K. (2013). "The Nuka System of Care: improving health through ownership and relationships." *International Journal of Circumpolar Health*, 72.
2. Ibid.

CHAPTER NINE

ACTION PLANNING AND IMPLEMENTATION

Chapter Overview

- Change leaders recognize the usefulness of plans and the imperative of action. Prepare, take action, and learn from the results. Change initiators have a "do it" attitude.

- Action planning and implementation involves planning the work and working the plan. "Right" decisions mean approximately "right" as change agents obtain feedback from action and make adjustments as they act.

- Change agents learn to specify who does what, when, and how to monitor and track their change initiatives. Agents use a variety of management tools, such as responsibility and project planning charts, surveys and survey feedback, and critical path methods to successfully plan and implement their change programs.

- Successful change agents develop detailed communications plans and understand how to manage transitions from the present to a future desired state.

This book has a philosophical bias for taking action. Rather than passively waiting or complaining from the sidelines, change agents get engaged. However, the goal is not action simply for novelty and excitement. Action must increase the likelihood of positive change. Great ideas don't generate value until they are effectively executed. One of the ways to improve the quality of action is to use proven tools to execute a change agenda.

Tools in Chapter 9 translate plans to action. If this were a political campaign, these tools would be steps that are deployed after the candidate has been selected, the platform finalized, and the election called. The chapter provides advice on implementation tactics and project management tools. It addresses communication and influence tactics during the change process. And finally, the management of transition, or the process of keeping the organization operating while implementing the change, is detailed. In terms of the model in Figure 9.1, these are the implementation issues of "getting from here to there"—assessing the present in terms of the future, determining the work that needs to be done, and implementing the change.

WITHOUT A "DO IT" ORIENTATION, THINGS WON'T HAPPEN

Many major change initiatives start in the C-suite. Boards of directors and executives at the top of organizations have access to all of the data that an organization generates, and from this perspective and input they can observe a myriad of

Figure 9.1   The Change Path Model

Awakening
Chapter 4
1. Identify a need for change and confirm the problems or opportunities that incite the need for change through collection of data.
2. Articulate the gap in performance between the present and the envisioned future state, and spread awareness of the data and the gap throughout the organization.
3. Develop a powerful vision for change.
4. Disseminate the vision for the change and why it's needed through multiple communication channels.

Mobilization
Chapters 5 through 8
1. Make sense of the desired change through formal systems and structures, and leverage those systems to reach the change vision (Chapter 5).
2. Assess power and cultural dynamics at play, and put them to work to better understand the dynamics and build coalitions and support to realize the change (Chapter 6).
3. Communicate the need for change organization-wide and manage change recipients and various stakeholders as they react to and move the change forward (Chapter 7).
4. Leverage change agent personality, knowledge, skills and abilities, and related assets (e.g., reputation and relationships) for the benefit of the change vision and its implementation (Chapter 8).

Acceleration
Chapter 9
1. Continue to systematically reach out to engage and empower others in support, planning, and implementation of the change. Help them develop needed new knowledge, skills, abilities, and ways of thinking that will support the change.
2. Use appropriate tools and techniques to build momentum, accelerate, and consolidate progress.
3. Manage the transition, celebrating small wins and the achievement of milestones along the larger, more difficult path of change.

Institutionalization
Chapter 10
1. Track the change periodically and through multiple balanced measures to help assess what is needed, gauge progress toward the goal, and to make modifications as needed and mitigate risk.
2. Develop and deploy new structures, systems, processes and knowledge, skills, and abilities, as needed, to bring life to the change and new stability to the transformed organization.

organizational problems and envision viable solutions. Two examples of boards who hired strong, change agent CEOs are IBM's board when they brought in Lou Gerstner in 1993 and the board of New England Medical Center, Boston (now called Tufts Medical Center) when they hired Ellen Zane in 2002 to lead the transformation of the then-foundering nonprofit hospital (see cases on the website for the story about Zane's turnaround of the medical center).

Gerstner and Zane were seasoned executives when they took on the extremely difficult task of pushing change from the top down into the basements of their organizations. Both had a **"do it" orientation** and both were authorized by their boards and by their titles, jobs, and positions to lead change within their institutions. Having the authority to act makes certain aspects of the job of change agent easier than working from the middle. Gerstner, for instance, when he claimed the title of CEO, quickly changed the reward system for his top executives, focusing their attention on the performance of IBM as a whole, rather than just their divisions or areas. Such quick structural change is unlikely in a mid-level role.

In an ideal world, change leaders located in the middle of the organization will also find support for their projects. They need ready access to supportive executives who provide directional clarity, ensure their organizations are ready for change, approve needed resources, provide other modes of support and oversight, and cultivate broad employee commitment for the change. In some instances, this is not the case. Many executives will have little or no knowledge of the initiative or its value and implications. If they have heard of the idea, they may lack interest because of other priorities and political realities; some may have heard of it and have concerns, while others will simply want to distance themselves from the change in the event it doesn't work out. Some will fail to understand the important role they have to play in nurturing innovation from within the organization; others will not see it as their role.

Organizations are complex systems, and their prospects for successful adaptation are advanced when they can also learn and grow from the bottom up. This is one of the reasons that firms such as 3M, Procter & Gamble, and Deloitte have demonstrated such staying power: They grow from within and from the bottom up. Wise senior managers know how to nurture and leverage employees' adaptive energy.

Wise change agents know how to save short-sighted senior managers from themselves. If you work in an organization such as 3M, then "lucky you!" If you do not, an early task is to seek—and hopefully acquire—senior-level support for your initiative. An e-mail from the CEO or SVP announcing her support for your project will help garner support from other organizational members.

INNOVATION AND CHANGE AT 3M

Front-line freedom to innovate and senior-level support have been critical ingredients to 3M's success. Technical and marketing employees commit 15% of their time to work on projects of their own choosing, without supervision. The environment is open and informal, input from customers and lead users is sought, and collaboration and inquisitiveness are valued.

(Continued)

Social media facilitates front-line collaboration and helps to overcome the communication barriers that organizational size and complexity bring. At the same time, 3M's culture is demanding, and the process for funding new ideas is highly structured.

The degree of management scrutiny and oversight increases as new ideas evolve to require significant resources. Products that are eventually successful in the marketplace are typically rejected several times in management's funding process before receiving funds, requiring persistence from innovators. Management and employees embrace and learn from failures because innovation won't happen otherwise. George Buckley, 3M's CEO from 2005 to 2012, a PhD in engineering, was deeply interested in innovation. He regularly visited the labs to find out what people were exploring, believing that "creativity comes from freedom, not control."[1]

As it had in the past, this commitment to innovation has allowed new products and services to percolate and develop from the ground up throughout the years.[2] Inge Thulin (2012-18) and Michael Roman (the current CEO) have demonstrated their commitment to sustaining this commitment in more recent years. This spirit is captured in the following statement of 3M's purpose:

"3M captures the spark of new ideas and transforms them into thousands of ingenious products. Our culture of creative collaboration inspires a never-ending stream of powerful technologies that make life better. 3M is the innovation company that never stops inventing."[3]

If senior-level support for change is unlikely to develop in the near future, change initiators may feel that abiding by formal organizational protocols and waiting for official support will slow progress unduly. Faced with this situation, change agents may choose to follow the advice of Rear Admiral Grace Hopper, a pioneering female software engineer in the U.S. Navy, who said, "It is easier to seek forgiveness than permission."[4]

Pfeffer and Sutton state "actions count more than elegant plans or concepts" and that "there is no doing without mistakes." They ask, however, a crucial question: "What is the company's response?"[5] If the organization's response to reasoned initiatives and honest mistakes is to scapegoat and blame, people quickly learn not to take risks that might lead to mistakes. Or, they learn to cover up mistakes. Either way, the organization suffers.* However, beliefs about likely organizational responses can also become a convenient excuse for inaction and the avoidance of risk taking (e.g., What if my idea really won't work or what will I do if it does work?). If such beliefs are never challenged, their stability will produce self-fulfilling prophecies.

Effective executives and managers of change are aware of the consequences of their actions and intuitively test their organizational assumptions by engaging in an action–learning–reaction cycle.[6] Sayles recognized this when he wrote, "Working leaders instead of simply waiting for and evaluating results seek to intervene. And the interventions they undertake require a more intimate knowledge of operations, and more involvement in the work than those of traditional middle managers."[7]

---

* This does lead to an accountability paradox. Accountability is a needed and useful attribute. However, there needs to be a fine balance between holding change leaders accountable for what they do and encouraging the risk-taking behavior that leads to needed learning and change.

For employees lower in the hierarchy, action is also key. Instead of being discouraged by lack of authority or reach, one must fully understand the resources and tools they have at their disposal. Dr. Ross Wirth, retired dean of the College of Business, Franklin University, reflected on his 32-year career at Citgo Petroleum with the following wisdom:[8] "Traditional thought says that nothing happens without top management's approval (but) change need not be something that is 'done to you.' Here is another way to think of it: empowerment is something you grasp until you find its limits. I tell people that they can constantly test the limits of their empowerment, carefully reading internal politics to see when they are pushing up against a boundary. Too many people think they are not empowered, but actually they have failed to test their limits."

The reality of much organizational life is somewhere between an environment that punishes those who dare to challenge the status quo and one in which all such initiatives are unconditionally embraced and rewarded. When the latter is the case, disciplined development and governance processes help organizations and their members to sort through those ideas, nurture their development, and bring the most viable to life. If such processes are absent, it can lead to the organization running off in all directions.

Organizational members who choose not to wait on formal permission and undertake reasonable self-initiated change initiatives may experience some chastisement for not first seeking approval, particularly if the initiative runs into difficulty. However, in many organizations, they are also commended for showing initiative and having a positive impact. The organization's culture and the personality of a boss (e.g., managerial style and tolerance for ambiguity) will obviously influence what response the initiator receives, but most managers value initiative.

What can be done to increase the likelihood that taking action will produce desired results? The following sections address this question by exploring a variety of planning and implementing tools. The purpose of these tools is to assist change leaders in designing and then managing their initiatives in ways that increase their prospects for success.

PRELUDE TO ACTION: SELECTING THE CORRECT PATH

Any action plan for change needs to be rooted in a sophisticated understanding of how the organization works and what needs to be achieved. Since there are a variety of action paths available, how do you decide which to take? Mintzberg and Westley provide guidance in this matter by setting out three generic approaches: thinking first, seeing first, and doing first.[9]

- **Thinking first strategy** works best when the issue is clear, data are reliable, context is structured, thoughts can be pinned down, and discipline can be established as in many routine production processes. The introduction of an initiative such as Six Sigma is an example where management needs to think first.

- **Seeing first strategy** works best when many elements have to be combined into creative solutions, commitment to those solutions is key, and communication across boundaries is essential. New product development is an example of the need to see first.

- **Doing first strategy** works best when the situation is novel and confusing, complicated specifications would get in the way, and a few simple relationship rules can help people move forward. For example, if a manager is testing a variety of approaches to customer service and wants feedback about what works best under what conditions, then doing first is appropriate. At the macro level, this approach often makes sense for organizations attempting to figure out how to deal with disruptions to their business models—something firms are experiencing with increasing frequency.

As complexity and ambiguity rise, Mintzberg and Westley argue that the preferred approach to action shifts. Thinking first fits when the situation is well structured, a manager has the needed data, and there is not much confusion about how to proceed. As ambiguity and complexity rise, though, certainty over how best to proceed becomes less clear. Seeing first approaches the challenge by experimentation, prototyping, and pilot programs so that commitment can be gained by having others see and experience an initiative. Doing first is a response to even more ambiguous situations and takes the process of exploration further in the search for new paths forward. As these paths begin to emerge, the approach can then be altered to seeing first or doing first, depending on what is suitable for the next stage.

Nitin Nohria offers a slightly different assessment of the generic change strategies available.[10] He identified three strategies, defined their characteristics, explained the typical implementation, and highlighted their risk points. **Programmatic change** (similar to Mintzberg and Westley's thinking first change) involves the implementation of straightforward, well-structured solutions. It is best suited to contexts that are clear and well defined and where the magnitude of the change is incremental in nature. Risks with this approach lie in potential problems with inflexibility, overreliance on a "one-size-fits-all" solution, and a lack of focus on behavior.

Discontinuous change involves a major break from the past. If the environment is shifting dramatically and a continuation of activities based on existing assumptions will not work, then discontinuous, top-down change may be fitting. Organizational restructuring due to downsizing, rapid growth, or the realignment of markets is an example of this category. Risks with this approach come from political coalitions that may form and derail the change, a lack of sufficient resources and control to support sustain and enforce (if needed) the changes, and the loss of talented people who become frustrated and quit.

Emergent change (similar to Mintzberg and Westley's doing first change) grows out of incremental initiatives and can create ambiguity and challenge for staff members. An employee-centered change initiative to modify the culture of the organization that emerges from customers' and staff's feedback would be an example. If the organization has a talented, knowledgeable workforce that understands the risks and possibilities, utilizing an emergent change approach may be appropriate. Risks with this approach come in the form of confusion over direction, uncertainty as to the impact of the change, and slow progress (see Table 9.1).

To counteract the pitfalls of programmatic or "thinking first" change, consider using employee engagement and feedback to connect with those on the

Table 9.1 Three Generic Change Strategies

Change Type	Characteristic	Implementation	Issues or Concerns
Programmatic change	Missions, plans, objectives	Training, timelines, steering committees	Lack of focus on behavior, one solution for all, inflexible solutions
Discontinuous change	Initiated from top, clear break, reorientation	Decrees, structural change, concurrent implementation	Political coalitions derail change, weak controls, stress from the loss of people
Emergent change	Ambiguous, incremental, challenging	Use of metaphors, experimentation, and risk-taking	Confusion over direction, uncertainty and possible slow results

Source: Adapted from Nohria, N., & Khurana, R. (1993, August 24). Executing change: Three generic strategies. *Harvard Business School* Note. #494–039.

receiving end, learn from their experiences, and decentralize decision making to allow for adaptation to local conditions. The pitfalls (including unintended consequences) from change will be lessened by processes that reduce ambiguity, promote feedback and learning, and build support by enhancing member understanding of the change and why it was undertaken.

The issues related to emergent or "doing first" change may be managed through the use of field experiments, evaluation tools and task forces to provide engagement and feedback on an ongoing basis. These can be used to enhance awareness of what is going on and why, create greater clarity concerning the implications of what is emerging and build understanding and support for the next steps in the change process. In metaphorical terms, this points to a move from "ready—aim—fire" to "ready—fire—aim—re-fire—re-aim"[†] for an emergent approach to planning. In fast-moving contexts, it is likely that a traditional planning process will be too lengthy and that by the time the planning is finished, the opportunity may have been missed. This metaphor recognizes that significant information can be obtained from action feedback. When a change leader initiates action, reactions will occur that can provide insight into how to respond and take corrective actions.

A third approach to thinking about change strategies is found in the unilateral versus participative approaches to change. Advocates of a **unilateral approach** to change believe that if one first changes systems and structures, forcing behavioral changes, that action will in turn produce changes in attitudes and beliefs over time.

[†] The managerial use of this metaphor is usually credited to T. Peters and R. H. Waterman Jr., *In Search of Excellence* (New York: Harper & Row, 1982). Our understanding is that its presence in its modified form has its roots in missile defense. If you are defending against incoming missiles, you don't have time to wait and plan a response. You do need to fire before you aim your missile. Then once you have things in motion, you can re-aim your missile based on new, current information.

Those who promote a **participative approach** believe the opposite. They argue that you first need to engage and change attitudes and gain acceptance of an initiative before restructuring systems and organizational structures.

Waldersee and Griffiths note that change initiatives have been traditionally grouped into two broad categories. **Techno–structural change** refers to change that is based in structures, systems, and technology. **Behavioral–social change** is focused on altering established social relationships. After investigating 408 change episodes, they concluded that the unilateral approach was perceived to be more appropriate for techno–structural change, while participative approaches were seen as more appropriate when behavioral–social changes such as cultural change were involved.[11] When Australian managers were asked about the perceived effectiveness of these two change approaches, they saw unilateral methods as more effective in bringing about successful change, regardless of the type of change. What does all of this mean for action planning? Waldersee and Griffiths concluded the following:

> Concrete actions taken by change managers are often superior to the traditional prescriptions of participation.[12] Forcing change through top-down actions such as redeploying staff or redesigning jobs may effectively shift employee behavior. With the context and behavior changed, interventions targeting attitudes may then follow. (p. 432)

While a unilateral approach may have appeal for those who want to ensure that things are done, such an approach can be risky and needs to be managed with care. When implementation lacks sensitivity, stakeholders may feel that their perspectives and concerns have been ignored. This can result in fallout and resistance that could have been avoided, and missed opportunities for valuable input.

What conclusions can be drawn from this material on a "do it" orientation and change strategies? Start a change process rather than waiting to get things perfect. Be willing to take informed risks and learn as you go. Finally, pick your change strategy with care and remember to take steps to manage the risks associated with the adopted approach. Regardless of how difficult change appears to be, Confucius was right—"a journey of a thousand miles begins with a single step."[13] You need to plan your work, work the plan and be prepared to adapt as you go.

PLAN THE WORK

If the change leader's approach to planned change has followed what this book suggests, then much planning will have already been done. In addition, Beer, Eisenstat, and Spector[14] offer a prescriptive list of "steps to effective change." Here are Beer et al.'s steps:

1. Mobilize commitment to change through joint diagnosis of business problems.

2. Develop a shared vision of how to organize and manage for competitiveness.

3. Foster consensus for the new vision, competence to enact it, and cohesion to move it along.

4. Spread revitalization to all departments without pushing it from the top.

5. Institutionalize revitalization through formal policies, systems, and structures.

6. Monitor and adjust strategies in response to problems in the revitalization process.

For many change situations, this checklist provides valuable guidance in the development of an action plan. However, assuming a "one-size-fits-all" approach to change is risky. For example, the above list assumes a fundamental cooperative orientation. That is, there is sufficient commonality of goals that a shared vision is possible. The list also suggests that change should evolve and not be pushed down by top management. However, change agents will need approaches that allow them to face situations in which cooperation and commonality of goals is weak or absent and where changes are being pushed from the top. Table 9.2 below compares Beer et al.'s steps with the prescriptions of others, which may be helpful in thinking about planning through multiple perspectives.[15]

As well, the need for contingent thinking needs to be addressed. That is, an action plan depends significantly upon the action-planning context. In complex and ambiguous situations, plans and tactics must be able to adapt as events unfold. As such, it is useful to remember the old saying: "No plan survives first contact."[16]

In summary, while careful planning is critical, change leaders must also recognize that planning is a means—not an end in itself. Don't ignore vital emerging information just because it does not fit with carefully conceived plans. The abilities to think contingently, consider alternative paths forward, and adapt are important contributors to enhanced adaptive capacity.[17]

Table 9.2   A Comparison of Four Models of Change

Beer et al.'s Six Steps for Change (1990)	Jick's Ten Commandments (1997)	Kotter's Eight-Stage Process for Successful Organizational Transformation (1996)	Lueck's Seven Steps for Change (2003)
Mobilize commitment to change through joint diagnosis of problems.	Analyze the organization and its need for change.	Establish a sense of urgency.	Mobilize energy, commitment through joint identification of business problems and their solutions.
Develop a shared vision of how to organize and manage for competitiveness.	Create a vision and a common direction.	Create a guiding coalition.	Develop a shared vision of how to organize and manage for competitiveness.

(Continued)

Table 9.2   (Continued)

Beer et al.'s Six Steps for Change (1990)	Jick's Ten Commandments (1997)	Kotter's Eight- Stage Process for Successful Organizational Transformation (1996)	Lueck's Seven Steps for Change (2003)
Foster consensus for the new vision, competence to enact it, and cohesion to move it along.	Separate from the past.	Develop a vision and strategy.	Identify the leadership.
Spread revitalization to all departments without pushing it from the top.	Create a sense of urgency.	Empower broad-based action.	Focus on results, not activities.
Institutionalize revitalization through formal policies, systems, and structures.	Support a strong leader role.	Communicate the change vision.	Start change at the periphery, then let it spread to other units, pushing it from the top.
Monitor and adjust strategies in response to problems in the revitalization process.	Line up political sponsorship.	Generate short-term wins.	Institutionalize success through formal policies, systems, and structures.
	Craft an implementation plan.	Consolidate gains and produce more change.	Monitor and adjust strategies in response to problems in the change process.
	Develop enabling structures.	Anchor new approaches in the culture.	
	Communicate, involve people, and be honest.		
	Reinforce and institutionalize change.		

Source: Based on Todnem, R. (2005). Organisational change management: A critical review. *Journal of Change Management,* 5(4), 369–381; and Beer, M., Eisenstat, R., & Spector, B. (1990, November-December). Why change programs don't produce change. *Harvard Business Review,* 1000, 158–166.

Engage Others in Action Planning

Occasionally, change planning must be undertaken under a cloak of secrecy, such as when a merger is in the works and the premature release of information would significantly affect the price and the level of competitive risk. In general, though, the active involvement of others and information sharing enhances the quality of action planning for most change strategies. Consider one of the experiences of Barbara Waugh, who spent 25 years as a change agent at Hewlett-Packard:

CHANGE AT HP LABS

Barbara Waugh's campaign for change at HP Labs began when its director asked her, "Why does no one out there consider HP Labs to be the best industrial research lab in the world?" Rather than propose answers, she and the director began by asking questions through a survey. The inquiry generated 800 single-spaced pages of feedback related to programs (e.g., too many projects and too few priorities), people (e.g., poor performers are not removed quickly enough and researchers lack sufficient freedom to do their jobs well), and processes (e.g., the information infrastructure is inadequate).

The feedback, says Waugh, was "800 pages of frustrations, dreams, and insights." But how could she capture and communicate what she learned? She drew on her experience with street theater and created a play about HP Labs. She worked passages from the surveys into dialogue and then recruited executives to act as staff members and junior people to act as executives. The troupe performed for 30 senior managers. "At the end of the play, the managers were very quiet," Waugh remembers. "Then they started clapping. It was exciting. They really got it."[18]

Waugh's approach is instructive because it illustrates the power of presenting potentially boring data in an engaging and compelling manner. This was not the first time she nurtured change in an emergent, grassroots fashion. Her approach leveraged listening and questioning, built networks with individuals with complementary ideas, and when needed, arranged for access to financial resources for worthy endeavors.[†]

Underlying planning-through-engagement strategies are assumptions regarding top-down (unilateral) versus bottom-up (participative) methods of change. Although Waldersee and Griffiths's study[19] showed that unilateral implementation methods have much to offer, the success of a change is enhanced when people understand what it entails, why it is being undertaken, what the consequences of success and failure are, and why their help is needed and valued. All too often, techno–structural changes have floundered because

---

[†] In planning the work, interviews, surveys, survey feedback, and appreciative inquiry (a rigorous commitment to active listening, feedback, mutual development, and renewal) are powerful action planning tools. They come from the Organizational Development (OD) approach to change. For more information, two good sources are D. L. Cooperrider, D. Whitney, and J. M. Stavros, *Appreciative Inquiry Handbook: For Leaders of Change* (Brunswick, OH: Crown, 2008); and T. G. Cummings and C. G. Worley, *Organization Development and Change* (Mason, OH: South-Western, 2009).

of design problems getting tangled up with acceptance and implementation issues that never get sorted out.

Regardless of the change strategy preferred, the plan needs to be examined carefully for logic and consistency. The next section highlights a series of questions (contained in Table 9.6) that can help change agents enhance their performance in this area.

Ensure Alignment in Your Action Planning

Change agents often understand what needs to be done but get the sequence of activities wrong. They might leave a meeting after a productive discussion but fail to sort out who is responsible for what. Sometimes critical steps in the plan are risky and alternative strategies need to be considered in case things do not go as planned. At other times, change agents may over- or underestimate the available resources and constraints, the time and energy required by various steps, or their own power and competence. Table 9.8 (later in this chapter) provides a checklist of questions to use when reviewing an action plan. This checklist tests the viability of the plan and asks for a rethinking of the connections between the analysis of the situation and the plan itself. Tough-minded thinking can improve the coherence and thoughtfulness of action plans.

ACTION PLANNING TOOLS

After all is said and done, more is often said than done! – Aesop or Lou Holz

This section explores a selection of action planning tools that change agents find particularly useful (see Table 9.3). Selecting the appropriate tool is both an art and science: An art as the story of Waugh at HP illustrated (see above), and a science as one analyzes data carefully and makes appropriate selections. In addition to the tools listed here, remember to reflect on action planning tools discussed in other chapters such as tools for assessing and/or handling: the need for change (Chapter 3); gap analyses, readiness for change and the framing of the vision for the change (Chapter 4); formal systems and processes (Chapter 5); the political and cultural dimension of change, including stakeholder and force field analyses (Chapter 6); recipients of change (Chapter 7), your own skills and competencies as a change agent (Chapter 8); and the use of measurement in the advancement of change (Chapter 10).

Table 9.3 Tools for Action Planning
1. To-do list—a checklist of things to do
2. Responsibility charting—who will do what, when, where, why, and how
3. Contingency planning—consideration of what should be done when things do not work as planned on critical issues
4. Flow charting—a way of diagramming the nature of the existing process you wish to examine and set out how you propose to change it

5. Design thinking—an approach used to engage others collectively in creative problem solving around what needs to change and the design of the change itself—a tool that can be used in conjunction with visioning initiatives

6. Surveys, survey feedback, and appreciative inquiry—capturing people's opinions and tracking their responses, observations, and insights over time, to assist in identifying what needs changing, nurturing engagement and support, and in tracking progress

7. Project planning and critical path methods—operations research techniques for scheduling work. These methods provide deadlines and insight as to which activities cannot be delayed to meet those deadlines.

8. Tools that assess forces that affect outcomes and stakeholders—these tools are closely related to force field and stakeholder analysis discussed in Chapter 6:

   a. Commitment charts—an evaluation of the level of commitment of major players (against, neutral, let it happen, help it happen, make it happen)

   b. The adoption continuum or awareness, interest, desire, adoption (AIDA) analysis—examination of major players and their position on the AIDA continuum related to the proposed changes

   c. Cultural mapping—an approach that provides for a more detailed assessment of the cultural context the change is occurring in; particularly useful when the goal is cultural change

9. Leverage analysis—determination of methods of influencing major groups or players regarding the proposed changes

10. Training and development tools—tools related to the design and delivery of educational initiatives that advance employee knowledge and ability to perform effectively, given the changes

11. Diverse change approaches—a variety of techniques and tools that brings about change and that continues to grow

1. To-Do Lists

When managers engage in action planning, they often begin by outlining in detail the sequence of steps they will take initially to achieve their goals. That is, they make a list. A **to-do list**, a checklist of things to do, is the simplest and most common planning tool. Sometimes this is all the situation requires. As the action planning becomes more sophisticated, simple to-do lists will not suffice and responsibility charting provides more control.

2. Responsibility Charting

Responsibility charting can be a valuable tool to detail who should do what, when, and how. As well, it can be used to help keep projects on track and provide a basis for record keeping and accountability. Table 9.4 provides an example responsibility chart. The process begins by defining the list of decisions or actions to be taken. Then individuals are assigned responsibility for achieving specific actions at specified deadlines.

Table 9.4   Example Responsibility Chart

Decisions or Actions to Be Taken	Responsibilities			
	Susan	Ted	Sonja	Relevant Dates
Action 1	R	A	I	For meeting on Jan. 14
Action 2		R	I	May 24
Action 3	S	A	A	Draft Plan by Feb. 17; action by July 22
Etc.				

Coding:

R = Responsibility (not necessarily authority)

A = Approval (right to veto)

S = Support (put resources toward)

I = Inform (to be consulted before action)

Note that if there are a large number of *As* on your chart, implementation will be difficult. Care must be taken to assign *As* only when appropriate. Likewise, if there are not enough *Rs* and *Ss*, you will need to think about changes needed here and how to bring them about.

Source: For a further discussion on responsibility charting, see Beckhard, R., & Harris, R. (1987). *Organizational transitions* (p. 104). Reading, MA: Addison-Wesley.

3. Contingency Planning

Contingency planning is the importance of thinking through what should be done should events not go as planned. Two tools that aid in contingency planning are decision tree analysis and scenario planning.[§]

Decision tree analysis asks change agents to consider the major choices and the possible consequences of those alternatives. Analysts are then asked to plan for the possible next actions and consider what the consequences of those actions might be. Such alternating action–consequence sequences can be extended as far as reasonable. As well, probabilities can be assigned as to the likelihood of each consequence. For many applications, a simple scale (*very likely, likely, possible, unlikely,* or *very unlikely*) is sufficient. This approach helps model the possible consequences to change decisions and assess the benefits and risks associated with the different pathways (see Figure 9.2).

A second tool that helps managers with contingency planning is **scenario planning**. Here a change strategy is formed by first developing a limited number of scenarios about how the future may unfold and then assessing what the implications of each of these would be to the organization.[20] Change leaders typically

---

[§] Readers are encouraged to consult standard operations research texts for further information on these tools.

Figure 9.2   Example Decision Tree

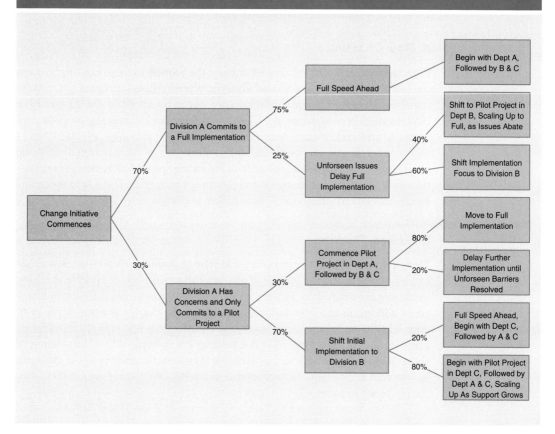

frame these around an issue of strategic and/or tactical importance. For example, if a firm producing paper forms is concerned about the long-term viability of its business model, then management could develop scenarios of what a paperless form producer would look like. Once the scenarios were developed, managers would ask themselves, How likely is this scenario? What would need to happen to make the scenario a reality? And what contingencies might arise that would need to be addressed? If one or more of these future scenarios seemed worth investing in, then management would develop its plans accordingly. To open people's minds to possibilities and avoid blind spots, external parties are often brought into the process to offer data and insights, challenge assumptions, and stimulate thinking and discussion.

Scenario planning is different from forecasting. Forecasting starts in the present and uses trend lines and probability estimates to make projections about the future. Scenario planning starts by painting a picture of the future and works backward, asking what would have to happen to make this future scenario a reality and what could be done.[21]

While most uses of scenario planning are at a strategy level, the principles can be applied to frame possible visions for change and develop the action pathways that will increase the likelihood that the vision will be achieved. Royal Dutch Shell[22] was one of the first users of scenario planning. The firm used it as a way to link future uncertainties to today's decisions.

4. Flow Charting

Flow charting is a technique used to track the sequences in an existing process (including key decision points and who is involved in those decisions) and to assist in the design of the change through setting out an improved or new approach for implementation consideration.[*] Visual representations of existing processes are typically undertaken early in the change process when change agents are seeking to understand what needs to change. While the visual representation of the future process is also developed early in the change process, it is used in conjunction with the vision for change throughout the change process to help recipients better understand what is being undertaken and why.

5. Design Thinking

Design thinking has its roots in multiple areas including architecture, new product development and the pursuit of processes that will advance creative thinking in the organization. It is used with matters that have proven difficult to effectively address in the past and is used early in the change process. It seeks to engage individuals collectively in context assessment; problem finding and framing; ideation; prototyping and pilot testing; evaluation; and the translation of those designs into actionable initiatives. It is an iterative process so the cycle can be repeated and designs refined several times until the parties are satisfied with the proposed solution.

Design thinking seeks to address matters in a less linear and more creative manner. Rather than approach matters through deductive or inductive reasoning (the traditional approaches), it seeks to do so through abductive reasoning. Abductive reasoning is solution rather than problem focused and involves looking for and exploring plausible solutions, trialing and refining different options, and so on until the desired path forward is selected and committed to. The more traditional deductive approach in organizations typically involves situational analyses, the development of decision criteria, the development and assessment of three to five alternatives, and the selection of the recommended path forward. Because design thinking is based on plausible solutions that have more uncertainty attached to them, they form the basis for the iterative exploration of options in the search for new approaches that can effectively address difficult problems and challenges that have resisted resolution.[23]

This human-centered, collaborative approach has at its core the interests and perspectives of the users that one is trying to design for. Users are engaged in the process to make sure that their interests and concerns are recognized and

---

[*] For introductory information on flowcharting, see Lucidchart's website: https://www.lucidchart.com/pages/what-is-a-flowchart-tutorial; or MindTool's website: https://www.mindtools.com/pages/article/newTMC_97.htm.

attended to. The goal of design thinking is to identify and address problems with creative solutions and create new opportunities. The nature of the process enhances the prospects for buy-in by the recipients of change due to their involvement in the design process.

6. Surveys and Survey Feedback

Change agents may find it is helpful to use surveys to capture people's attitudes, opinions, and experiences at particular points in time and then track those attitudes over time, including their readiness for change that was discussed in Chapter 4. Tools in this area can provide anonymity to the respondents and make it possible to capture the opinions of a larger proportion of the participants than might otherwise be possible. Political agendas don't disappear with the use of a survey, but they may make it possible for people to say things that they would not feel comfortable stating publicly. Services such as SurveyMonkey.com and EmployeeSurveys.com have made the design, delivery, and analysis easy to manage.

Surveys are used to access the opinions of internal and external stakeholders and assess attitudes and beliefs of relevance to the change. For example, how do customers view the firm's and its competitor's service levels, innovativeness, and product performance? What ideas do they have concerning new product offerings or service improvements? Employees can be sampled to assess the organization's readiness for change, the culture or work climate, their satisfaction and commitment levels, or what is helping or hindering their ability to do their jobs. Sometimes surveys are deployed to develop options and assess opinions on their viability. Later in the change process, surveys may sample understanding and knowledge levels, emerging attitudes and issues, and levels of acceptance and satisfaction with the change.

Some organizations go further in this area and adopt approaches to directly and systematically assess actual customer and employee actions in response to change (directly or via software monitoring tools) in order to recognize issues and address them in a timely manner.

The possible approaches in this area are restricted only by imagination, people's willingness to respond, and legal and ethical considerations. Privacy/anonymity considerations, transparency (people know what you are doing and why), and related ethical matters need to be carefully thought through. When this is not the case, the repercussions and potential for reputational damage can be serious, as seen in public reactions to Facebook's sharing of private user data.[24]

Ready-made surveys are available on virtually any topic. Some are publicly available at no cost, while others are proprietary and have charges attached to their use. Costs can vary from a few dollars per survey to thousands of dollars when outside consultants are used to design, administer, assess, and report the findings. When it comes to scoring and interpretation, some are straightforward and easy to interpret, while others require the assistance of a skilled practitioner. Some of these instruments have been carefully assessed for reliability and validity, while others have nothing more than face validity.

The bottom line with respect to surveys is that they can prove very helpful to change agents but need to be approached with care. Their design, administration, and analysis require the assistance of someone well trained in survey research. Even when a change agent is sampling opinions, the ability to frame good questions is a prerequisite to getting useful information. The same holds true for analysis and interpretation.[††]

A powerful use of surveys is an approach called **survey feedback**.[25] It is an action research method developed by organizational development (OD) practitioners as a way to stimulate and advance conversations concerning what is going on in the organization, how members are feeling, and how things could be improved. As the name suggests, it involves the sharing of survey results with the individuals affected by the findings. Those involved in the discussion will have responded to the survey.

Skilled facilitators guide work groups through the discussion of the findings. They use this as an opportunity to enrich their interpretation of what the data means, and to more fully explore the implications for action. The process is used to raise awareness and understanding, advance the analysis, and build support and commitment for actions that will benefit both the individuals and the organization. Appreciative inquiry approaches discussed earlier in this chapter and in Chapter 8 can be married effectively with survey feedback to engage and energize participants, learn from them, and set the stage for future actions.

7. Project Planning and Critical Path Methods

Project planning and critical path methods can provide valuable assistance to change managers as they think about what action steps to take.[‡‡] These methods have been developed into sophisticated operations research techniques to aid the planning of major projects. Critical path methods ask planners to identify when the project should be completed and to work backward from that point, scheduling all tasks that will require time, effort, and resources. These are arranged in time sequence such that tasks that can occur simultaneously can be identified. These tasks are then plotted on a timeline. Sequential tasks are plotted to determine the needed time to complete the project.

With this done, managers can assess potential bottlenecks, resource requirements, points in the process where there appears to be excess resources or idle time (referred to a slack resources) that could be deployed elsewhere, and progression paths. The critical path, the path with the least slack time, can be identified and special attention can be paid to it. If there are concerns about the time to completion, the project manager can add resources to speed up the project, revisit the specifications, look for viable alterations to the implementation path, or increase the amount of time required to complete the project. Likewise, if there are concerns over the cost of the project, the project manager can explore alternatives on this front.

The critical path method introduces the notion of parallel initiatives. That is, it recognizes that different things may be able to be worked on simultaneously

---

[††] For further information on survey research, see L. M. Rea and R. A. Parker, *Designing and Conducting Survey Research* (San Francisco: Jossey-Bass, 2005).

[‡‡] Software packages are available in this area. A commonly used one, Microsoft Office Project (http://www.microsoft.com/project/en/us/default.aspx), allows you to track steps, resource requirements, and costs; see the impact of possible changes; trace the source of issues; visually communicate project information to others; and collaborate with them on the plans.

if the work is properly organized. Phase 1 tasks don't have to be totally completed before beginning work on Phase 2 tasks. Care and sophistication are required with this approach because it carries the risk of increasing confusion and redundant effort. When properly applied, though, it can shrink the time required to complete the change. This is readily visible in areas such as new product development. Figure 9.3 gives an example of a sequential and a parallel plan for new product development. In the upper half of the figure, the tasks are plotted sequentially. In the lower half of the figure, the tasks overlap. Concept development begins before opportunity identification ends and the cycle time to completion is reduced.

In summary, change leaders involved with implementation will find it useful to review the advice found in the project management literature before undertaking major changes as it contains information related to tools and techniques that may prove helpful.[§§]

8. Tools to Assess Forces That Affect Outcomes and Stakeholders

Force field analysis asks change agents to specify the forces for and against change. **Stakeholder analysis** and related maps ask that the key players be identified and the relationships among players and the change initiative be

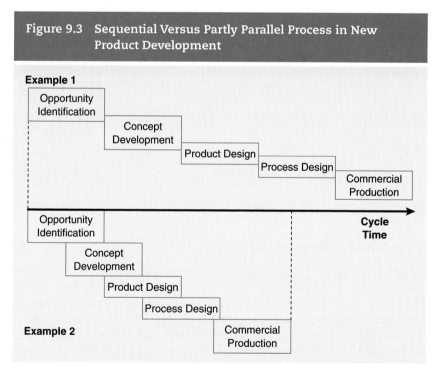

Figure 9.3 Sequential Versus Partly Parallel Process in New Product Development

Source: Shilling, M. A., & Hill, W. L. (1998). Managing the new product development process: Strategic imperatives. *Academy of Management Executive,* 12(3), 67–81.

[§§] Colleges, universities, and organizations such as the Project Management Institute (http://www .pmi.org/Pages/default.aspx) offer professional training in project management.

examined. (See Chapter 6 for discussion of these topics.) Three additional tools that are helpful when planning actions related to stakeholders are commitment analysis charts, AIDA (awareness, interest, desiring, action) charts, and cultural mapping tools.

A. Commitment Analysis Charts

Managers can use **commitment charts** to analyze the engagement of each stakeholder. Stakeholders can be thought of as being weakly to strongly opposed (against) to your change project, "neutral" (let it happen), slightly positive (help it happen), or strongly positive (make it happen). Change leaders also need to consider the level of understanding that underpins stakeholders' commitment level and the reasons that underpin their levels of support at the present time. Identifying the existing level of commitment is the first step in planning tactics designed to alter those preexisting patterns. Table 9.5 provides an example commitment chart. (Note that the "X" in the table shows where the person is and the "O" shows where a change agent wants them to be.)

Table 9.5 An Example Commitment Chart[26]

| Key Players | Level of Commitment | | | | | Level of Understanding (high, med, low) |
	Opposed Strongly to Weakly	Neutral	Let It Happen	Help It Happen	Make It Happen	
Person 1		X	→O			Med
Person 2				X	→O	High
Person 3		X		→O		Low
Etc.						

Source: Beckhard, R., & Harris, R. (1987). *Organizational transitions* (p. 95). Reading, MA: Addison-Wesley.

B. The Adoption Continuum or AIDA

Stakeholder analysis will have identified the people who are critical to the change process. With this information in hand, change agents need to consider how they propose to encourage those individuals to move along the **adoption continuum** until the needed stakeholders are aligned with the change, or at least their opposition and/or potential to disrupt the change initiative has been minimized.

As noted in Chapter 6, change agents can think of the process of getting people onside with change as one of first creating awareness and then encouraging them to move from awareness of the issues to interest in the change to desiring action and, finally, to taking actions related to adopting the change. This is called the AIDA or adoption continuum. Table 9.6 provides an example of how a change agent might map people on to the adoption continuum as a method of tracking their change attitudes.

Different individuals will be at different points on the AIDA continuum, which makes change strategies complex. For each stage, change agents need to use different tactics. For example, to raise initial awareness, well-designed general communication vehicles such as e-mails, newsletters, reports, and videos can be used. The messages should raise awareness of the need for change, set out the vision for the change, and provide access to thought-provoking information and images that support the initiative.

To move people to the interest phase, managers need to outline how the change will affect stakeholders personally and/or why this change should be of interest to them. Discussion groups on the issue, benchmark data, simulations, and test runs showing results can be effective in stimulating interest. Once interest is aroused, specific tactics to demonstrate and reinforce the benefits and build commitment are needed. Change agents might use one-on-one meetings to influence stakeholders, to persuade them to get directly involved with the change, or to connect them with influential supporters of the change. Change agents might reallocate resources or designate rewards in ways that reinforce adoption. Influencing people one at a time or in small groups can be valuable if influential individuals are identified and the right message is communicated to them.

Table 9.6   Mapping People on the Adoption Continuum

Persons or Stakeholder Groups	Awareness	Interest	Desiring Action	Moving to Action or Adopting the Change
Person 1				
Person 2				
Person 3				
. . .				

C. Cultural Mapping Tools

Cultural mapping tools are used to conduct deeper dives into understanding the nature of the cultural context, including subcultures, which influence how and why the organization operates as it does. These tools are also used to help set out the desired culture and assess what needs to change in order to bring it to fruition. Scholars such as Schein, Cameron and Quinn[27] have provided change agents with cultural categorization frameworks that can be used to assist them in the above tasks.

Cultural mapping approaches seek to understand subcultures (e.g., ones present in marketing, production, quality control, finance, etc.) as well as the dominant culture. It seeks to understand the outcomes achieved, the knowledge and beliefs nested in cultural norms and artifacts, the behaviors observed and the enablers and blockers that promote those behaviors and outcomes. Given that change typically involves the goal of moving away from certain behaviors and outcomes in order to move toward different behaviors and outcomes, the approach shares similarities with force field analyses. A key question revolves around how enablers and blockers can be worked with in order to help parties to move away from certain cultural practices and move toward those desired practices. Cultural mapping tools can be used at the team level or extended to assess departmental, divisional or the organization level cultural challenges and conflicts.

Practices in this area have become increasingly interdisciplinary in nature. Their applications have extended to areas such as the development of products and services, the development of marketing campaigns, urban planning and community development, and a full treatment on this topic is beyond the scope of this book.[28]

9. Leverage Analysis

People's position on the adoption continuum is influenced by their general orientation to change—whether they tend to be an innovator, early adopter, early majority, late majority, or laggard in matters related to change. One of the action planning challenges for the change leaders is to sort out people's overall predisposition to change in general and the proposed change in particular.

Moving individuals on the adoption continuum is aided by engaging in leverage analysis. Leverage analysis seeks to identify those actions that will create the greatest change with the least effort. For example, if opinion leaders of a key group of individuals can be identified and persuaded to back the proposed organizational change, the job of the change leader is easier. Likewise, if the task is to persuade senior management, one needs to identify influential individuals in this group who support the change. Identifying high-leverage methods will depend on the quality of your knowledge of the participants and your analysis of the organization and its environment. For example, one successful change agent ensured the adoption of a new software system by persuading the CEO to personally call every regional manager as they were key stakeholders in the change, and ask for their support.[29]

Gladwell presents an excellent example of the notion of leverage in his book *The Tipping Point*.[30] Gladwell points out how little things can have large consequences if they occur at the right moment and are contagious. If things catch on and momentum builds, eventually a tipping point is reached. This is the point where a critical level of support is reached, the change becomes more firmly rooted, and the rate of acceptance accelerates. As Burke puts it, change agents need to find the critical few individuals that can connect with others in ways that change the context and tip things into a new reality. The vision needs to be sticky (i.e., cast as a story so that it will stay in people's minds), and change agents need to understand the connectors in the organization who can get the message out.[31]

Moore notes that one of the biggest challenges to reaching the tipping point is to build sufficient support to allow the acceptance of the change to cross the "chasm" between the early adopters and visionaries and the early majority.[32] Once this gap has been bridged, the rate of progress accelerates. As things accelerate, new challenges emerge, such as how to scale your efforts so that momentum is maintained and enthusiasm is not soured due to implementation failures or stalled progress.

TIPPING POINTS AND THE MOMENTUM FOR CHANGE IN THE OBAMA ELECTION

Barack Obama's path to the presidency was dotted with several tipping points during the state primaries and the federal campaign. Some were related to specific things done by the candidate; some related to the actions of others; and some tied to specific situations (e.g., the mortgage/banking crisis). His creative use of social media (e.g., Facebook) is particularly noteworthy. It allowed him to reach out virally to groups of electors and move them along the commitment continuum at speeds not seen before. This generated grassroots financial support and media buzz that legitimized his candidacy very early on.

During the primaries, Representative James E. Clyburn, a prominent uncommitted South Carolina Democrat, felt the tipping point occurred around midnight on Tuesday, May 6, 2008. "I could tell the next day, when I got up to the Capitol that this thing was going to start a slide toward Obama. I don't believe that there is any way that she (Hillary Clinton) can win the nomination." Contentious remarks by former President Bill Clinton created a rift with African Americans, Obama's 14-point North Carolina victory exceeded expectations, and Hillary Clinton's weaker-than-expected win in the Indiana primary all conspired to take the wind out of her campaign while energizing Obama's.

Superdelegates were still not committing in large numbers to Obama in early May. Clyburn saw this as "the long shadow of the Clintons in the Democratic Party stretching back more than a decade and the reservoir of goodwill." However, he expected to see a steady and significant movement in the days ahead. "That's pretty much where everybody knows it's going to end up." Representative Rahm Emanuel, the Democratic conference chairman, went further and labeled Obama the presumptive nominee.[33]

10. Employee Training and Development

Training and development play critical roles in any change initiative that requires individuals to assess and respond differently to things they are accountable for. Changes in reporting structures, task designs, work flow, team structures, and the technologies deployed will often require the acquisition of new skills, abilities and attitudes to support the initiative. Even supportive individuals will become frustrated if they don't understand what they are being asked to do, or if they don't have the skills to perform the new tasks.

Well thought through and effectively delivered training initiatives will facilitate change by providing individuals with an opportunity to raise concerns, and develop their competences and confidence with the new work. Change agents would be well advised to explore the training and development literature when considering which initiatives to pursue in this area and how best to structure them.***

11. Diverse Change Approaches

The variety of techniques and tools to bring about change continues to grow. Over the years, Darrell Rigby and Barbara Bilodeau have tracked management's use of different change tools on a global basis and assessed managerial satisfaction with them (see Table 9.7 and Figure 9.4).[34] By tracking usage patterns by region and types of firms, differences in the sorts of change issues seen as most needing attention become apparent. This generic listing of change approaches provides a useful touch point for change leaders when they are considering how to proceed given the needs for change that they have identified.

In summary, planning the work asks change leaders to translate the change vision into specific actions that people can take. The plan outlines targets and dates and considers contingencies—what might go wrong (or right), how managers can anticipate those things, and how they can respond. Further, it examines how realistic the chances are for success and how a change agent increases the probabilities for success.

Table 9.8 provides you with a checklist of things to think about when developing and assessing your action plan.

Figure 9.4 Management Tool Usage Rate and Satisfaction Level

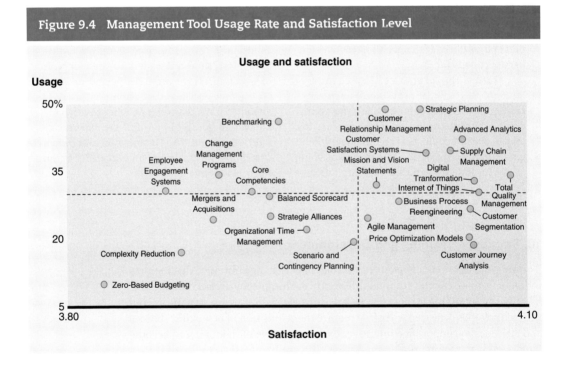

*** The following provide a good overview: Saks, A., & Haccoun, R. (2015). *Managing performance through training and development (5th ed.).* Toronto: Nelson; Biech, E. (Editor). (2014). *ASTD handbook: The definitive reference for training and development.* Danvers, MA: American Society for Training and Development.

Table 9.7   Usage Patterns of Change Approaches From 1993 to 2017

1993	2000	2014	2017
Mission and Vision Statements (88%)	Strategic Planning (76%)	Customer Relationship Management (46%)	Strategic Planning (48%)
Customer Satisfaction (86%)	**Mission and Vision Statements (70%)**	**Benchmarking (44%)**	Customer Relationship Management (48%)
Total Quality Management (72%)	**Benchmarking (69%)**	Employee Engagement Surveys (44%)	**Benchmarking (46%)**
Competitor Profiling (71%)	Outsourcing (63%)	Strategic Planning (44%)	Advanced Analytics (42%)
Benchmarking (70%)	**Customer Satisfaction (60%)**	Outsourcing (41%)	Supply Chain Management (40%)
Pay-for-Performance (70%)	Growth Strategies (55%)	Balanced Scorecard (38%)	**Customer Satisfaction (38%)**
Reengineering (67%)	Strategic Alliances (53%)	**Mission and Vision Statements (38%)**	Change Management Programs (34%)
Strategic Alliances (62%)	Pay-for-Performance (52%)	Supply Chain Management (36%)	**Total Quality Management (34%)**
Cycle Time Reduction (55%)	Customer Segmentation (51%)	Change Management Programs (34%)	Digital Transformation (32%)
Self-Directed Teams (55%)	Core Competencies (48%)	Customer Segmentation (30%)	**Mission and Vision Statements (32%)**

Source: Bain Management Tools & Trends survey, 2017
Note: Tool rankings based on usage

Table 9.8 Action Planning Checklist

1. Given your vision statement, what is your overall objective? When must it be accomplished?

2. Is your action plan realistic given the level of organizational support, your influence, both formal and informal, and the resources likely to be available to you? What can you do to address shortfalls?

3. Are you and your team committed to implementing the change and does it have the competences and credibility needed to implement the action steps? If not, how will you address the shortfall?

4. Is your action plan time-sequenced and in a logical order? What would be the first steps in accomplishing your goal?

5. What is your action plan? Who will do what, when, where, why, and how? Can you do a responsibility chart?

6. What would be milestones along the way that will allow you to determine if you are making progress? What is the probability of success at each step?

7. Have you anticipated possible secondary consequences and lagging effects that your plans may give rise to and adjusted your plans accordingly?

8. Do you have contingency plans for major possible but undesirable occurrences? What things are most likely to go wrong? What things can you not afford to have go wrong? How can you prevent such things from happening?

9. Do you have contingency plans in the event that things go better than anticipated and you need to move more quickly or in somewhat different directions than initially planned, to take advantage of the opportunities?

10. Who does your plan rely on? Are they onside? What would it take to bring them onside?

11. Does your action plan take into account the concerns of stakeholders and the possible coalitions they might form?

12. Who (and what) could seriously obstruct the change? How will you manage them?

WORKING THE PLAN ETHICALLY AND ADAPTIVELY

Working the plan requires change agents to focus, develop support and delivery capacity, test their thinking, see things as opportunities, adapt to changes in the environment, and take appropriate risks. At the same time, change agents need to proceed ethically. Otherwise they risk destroying credibility and the trust others have in them. Relationships can and do recover from strong disagreements, but recovery is less likely if people feel they have been lied to. A permanent sense of betrayal tends to ensue when you have been dealt with unethically.

Working the plan recognizes the importance of being able to roll with the punches and learn as you go. Chris Argyris warns, "People who rarely experience (and learn from) failure end up not knowing how to deal with it."[35] De Bono echoes this sentiment, saying, "Success is an affirmation but not a learning process."[36] Post-hoc memories of what led to success (or failure) tend to be selective; valuable learning will be lost if steps aren't taken to actively and objectively reflect on the process as you go. There will be missteps and failures along the way, and a key attribute of a "do it" orientation to working the plan is the capacity to learn and adapt the paths to change along the way.

When working the plan, generating stakeholder and decision-maker confidence in the viability of the initiative is critical. However, it is also important not to be deluded by your own rhetoric. Russo and Shoemaker provide us with guidelines for managing under- and overconfidence; in particular, they differentiate the need for confidence when one is an implementer as opposed to a decision maker. Decision makers need to be realistic; implementers can afford to be somewhat overconfident if it provides others with the courage to change.[37]

Developing a Communication Plan

When implementing a change program, change leaders often find that misinformation and rumors are rampant in their organization. The reasons for change are not clear to employees, and the impact on employees is frequently exaggerated, both positively and negatively. In all organizations, the challenge is to persuade employees to move in a common direction. Good communication programs are essential to minimize the effects of rumors, to mobilize support for the change, and to sustain enthusiasm and commitment.[38]

In a study on the effectiveness of communications in organizations, Goodman and Truss found that only 27% of employees felt that management was in touch with employees' concerns, regardless of the fact that the company had a carefully crafted communications strategy.[39] Often, much of the confusion over change can be attributed to the different levels of understanding held by different parties. Change agents and senior management may have been considering the change issues for months and have developed a shared understanding of the need for change and what must happen. However, frontline staff and middle managers may not have been focused on the matter. Even if they have been considering these issues, their vantage points will be quite different from those leading the change.

RUMORS AND REALITY IN ORGANIZATIONAL CHANGE

In an inbound call center of an insurance firm, employees became convinced that the real purpose of an organizational change initiative was to get rid of staff. Management made public announcements and assurances that the reorganization was designed to align processes and improve service levels, not reduce headcount. However, staff turnover escalated to more than 20% before leaders convinced employees that the rumor was false.

The **purpose of the communication plan for change** centers on four major goals: (1) to infuse the need for change throughout (in particular) the affected portions of the organization; (2) to enable individuals to understand the impact that the change will have on them; (3) to communicate any structural and job changes that will influence how things are done; and (4) to keep people informed about progress along the way. As the change unfolds, the focus of the communication plan shifts.

Timing and Focus of Communications

A communication plan has four phases: (a) pre-change approval, (b) developing the need for change, (c) midstream change and milestone communication, and

Table 9.9 Communication Needs for Different Phases in the Change Process

Pre-change Approval Phase	Developing the Need for Change Phase	Midstream Change and Milestone Communication Phase	Confirming and Celebrating the Change Phase
Communication plans to sell top management	Communication plans to explain the need for change, provide a rationale, reassure employees, clarify the steps in the change process, and generating enthusiasm and a sense of urgency	Communication plans to inform people of progress, to obtain and listen to feedback on attitudes and issues; to address any misconceptions; to clarify new organizational roles, structures, and systems; and to continue to nurture enthusiasm and support	Communication plans to inform employees of the success, to celebrate the change, to capture learning from the change process, and to prepare the organization for the next changes

Source: Based on Klein, S. M. (1996). A management communications strategy for change. *Journal of Organizational Change, 9*(2).

(d) confirming and celebrating the change success. The messages and methods of communication will vary depending upon which phase your change is in. Table 9.9 outlines the communication needs of each phase.

A. Pre-change phase: Change agents need to convince top management that the change is needed. They will target individuals with influence and/or authority to approve a needed change. Dutton and her colleagues suggest that packaging the change proposal into smaller change steps helps success. She found that timing was crucial in that persistence, opportunism, and involvement of others at the right time were positively related to the successful selling of projects. Finally, linking the change to the organization's goals, plans, and priorities was critical.[40]

B. Developing the need for the change phase: When creating awareness of the need for change, communication programs need to explain the issues and provide a clear, compelling rationale for the change. If a strong and credible sense of urgency and enthusiasm for the initiative isn't conveyed, the initiative will not move forward. There are simply too many other priorities available to capture people's attention.[41] Increasing awareness of the need for change can also be aided by the communication of comparative data. For example, concrete benchmark data that demonstrate how competitors are moving ahead can shake up complacent perspectives. Spector demonstrates how sharing of competitive information can overcome potential conflicting views between senior management and other employees.[42]

The vision for the change needs to be articulated and the specific steps of the plan that will be undertaken need to be clarified. People need to be reassured that they will be treated fairly and with respect.[43] The vision for change can be used to underpin your elevator pitch—that succinct message that helps others to capture the essence of what you have in mind and why it is worth pursuing.

Birshin and Kar use the term "sticky messages" to convey the notion that recipients will be more likely to remember messages if they share the following characteristics: simple, unexpected, concrete, credible, emotional, and tell a story. When it comes to telling the story, they recommend not being constrained by solely the business rationale for the change. In addition, they recommend the stories include why it is important to the individual doing the work, the working team, customers, and society—aspects that are likely to heighten the sense of purpose and meaning surrounding the change.[44]

C. Midstream change phase and Milestone Communication Phase: As the change unfolds, people will want to have specific information communicated to them about future plans and how things will operate. If the organization is being reorganized, employees will want to understand how this reorganization will affect their jobs. If new systems are being put into place, training needs to happen in order to help employees understand and use the systems properly. If reporting relationships are altered, employees need to know who will do what in the organization. Thus, intentional strategies are needed to communicate this information.

In the middle phases of change, people need to understand the progress made in the change program. Management needs to obtain feedback regarding the acceptance of the changes and the attitudes of employees and others (e.g., customers, suppliers) affected by the initiative. Change leaders need to understand any misconceptions that are developing and have the means to combat such misconceptions. During this phase, extensive communications on the content of the change will be important as management and employees begin to understand new roles, structures, and systems.[45]

As the newness of the initiative wears off, sustaining interest and enthusiasm and remaining sensitive to the personal impact of the change continue to be important. Change leaders need to remain excited about the change and communicate that enthusiasm often. Recognizing and celebrating progress, and milestones all help in this regard.[46] The power of small, unexpected rewards to recognize progress should not be underestimated, if they are offered forward with sincerity. In addition, communication approaches that offer individuals the opportunity to participate in exploring ideas, identifying paths forward, and setting targets will enhance the sense of engagement and commitment.

The Power of Apple Fritters: The launch of a new MBA class requires the concerted efforts of many people and the day following the launch coincided with one of the days when the local farmers' market is open in our community and one of the vendors sells freshly made, hot apple fritters. I was relatively new to the MBA director's role and by chance, while driving into the university, I stopped and picked up two dozen apple fritters, plus coffee and tea for the team. The positive impact was immediate and sustained and instantly reinforced for me the importance of such acts to communicate thanks (personal experience of one of the authors).

Unrelated messages, rumors, and gossip will compete with the messages from the change leaders, and the frequency of the latter two rises when the change leader's credibility declines, ambiguity increases, and setbacks are encountered. Employees tend to believe friends more than they do supervisors and tend to turn to supervisors before relying on the comments of senior executives and outsiders. Change agents have a choice: they can communicate clear, timely, and candid messages about the nature and impact of the change or they can let the rumors fill the void. An effective communications campaign can reduce the number of rumors by lowering uncertainty, lessening ambivalence and resistance to change, and increasing the involvement and commitment of employees.[47]

Change websites, electronic bulletin boards, online surveys to sample awareness and opinions, change blogs, and other types of social media can all play useful roles in the communications strategy. The earlier discussion in this chapter of Obama's campaign points to the value that social media can play in raising awareness and advancing commitment levels. Political parties of all stripes have recognized this and are become increasingly sophisticated in its use. Trump's sustained use of Twitter to shift the conversations dominating the media on a given day, focus news cycles in directions more favorable to him, and otherwise advance his presidential prospects was readily apparent in 2016.

Blogs, Facebook pages, Twitter, Instagram, Pinterest—the terrain continues to evolve, and change agents need to pay attention to how these technologies can be used to leverage their plans. In their global survey of the corporate deployment of social media tools in change initiatives, McKinsey and Company reports their use has become mainstream and that they are playing significant roles in the success of change initiatives. They are being used to communicate with and inform staff; seek feedback; and engage, energize, and otherwise enhance the sense of front-line ownership in change initiatives.[48]

However, when uncertainty rises on things of importance, don't forget the power of face-to-face communications. Positive reactions tend to increase and negative reactions are lessened when people have an opportunity to hear directly from those in authority and ask them questions about the change and its impact.[49]

D. Confirming and Celebrating the Change Phase: The final phase of a change program needs to communicate and celebrate the success of the program. Celebration is an undervalued activity. Celebrations are needed along the way to mark progress, reinforce commitment, and reduce stress. They are certainly warranted at the conclusion! The final phase also marks the point at which the change experience as a whole should be discussed (more will be said about this in the next section on transition management) and unfinished tasks identified. The organization needs to be positioned for the next change. Change is not over—only this particular phase is.

As change agents attend to the different phases in the change process, they need to align the communications challenge with the communications channel selected.[50] Channel richness ranges from standard reports and general information e-mails at one end through to personalized letters and e-mails, telephone conversations, videoconferencing, and face-to-face communications at the other end. When the information is routine, memos and blanket e-mails can work well. However, when things become more complex and personally relevant to the recipient, the **richness of the communication channel** needs to increase. A change agent can follow up with a document that provides detailed information, but face-to-face approaches are valuable when matters are emotionally loaded for stakeholders or when you want to get the recipients' attention.

Goodman and Truss suggest using line managers and opinion leaders as lynchpins in the communications strategy, but this requires that they be properly briefed and engaged in the change process. They also stress that change agents need to recognize communication as a two-way strategy.[51] That is, the gathering of information from people down the organizational ladder is as important as delivering the message.

Key Principles in Communicating for Change

Klein[52] suggests six principles that should underlie a communications strategy:

1. **Message and media redundancy are key for message retention**. That is, multiple messages using multiple media will increase the chance of people obtaining and retaining the message. Too often, management believes that since the message was sent, their work is done. It is the employee's fault for not getting the message! As one author pointed out, it takes time for people to hear, understand, and believe a message, especially when they don't like what they hear.[53] Some change agents believe that it takes 15 to 20 repetitions before a message gets communicated effectively. The value of communicating messages in multiple ways to increase retention and meaningfulness that was discussed in Chapter 7 and the use of appropriate social media channels advance change initiatives speak to this.[54]

2. **Face-to-face communication is most effective**. While the impact of face-to-face is highest, the cost is also higher. Face-to-face permits two-way communication, which increases the chance of involvement of both parties and decreases the probability of miscommunication. When undertaking change in a larger organization and direct communication is not possible, video conferencing and related technologies can be used to approximate face-to-face.

3. **Line authority is effective in communications**. Regardless of the level of participative involvement, most employees look to their managers for direction and guidance. If the CEO says it, the message packs a punch and gets attention.

4. **The immediate supervisor is key**. The level of trust and understanding between an employee and his or her supervisor can make the supervisor a valuable part of a communications strategy. People expect to hear important organizational messages from their bosses.

5. **Opinion leaders need to be identified and used**. These individuals can be critical in persuading employees to a particular view.

6. **Employees pick up and retain personally relevant information more easily than general information**. Thus, communication plans should take care to relate general information in terms that resonate with particular employees.

The importance of communications in helping recipients deal with change was discussed in Chapter 7. Creating a sense of fairness, trust, and confidence in the leadership, and interest and enthusiasm for the initiative is important to the success of change initiatives. Well-executed communications strategies play an important role here.[55] However, change leaders seldom give enough attention to this topic. They intuitively understand the importance of the timely communication of candid, credible change-related information through multiple channels, but they get busy with other matters. As communication shortcomings escalate, so too do downstream implementation difficulties.[56]

Influence Strategies

Influencing others is a key concern for change leaders when working the plan. It involves consideration of how they can bring various stakeholders onside with the change. The sooner this is addressed, the better. When implementing change, there is a tendency to give insufficient attention to the constructive steps needed to foster employee support and alleviate dysfunctional resistance. When considering your communication plan and use of influence strategies, think about who you are communicating with and never underestimate the importance of the reputation (including their competence and trustworthiness) of those who are the face and voice of the change initiative.

Below are seven change strategies for influencing individuals and groups in the organization:[57]

1. Education and communication: This strategy involves using education and communication to help others develop an understanding of the change initiative, what is required of them, and why it is important. Often people need to see the need for and the logic of the change. Change leaders may fail to adequately communicate their message through the organization because they are under significant time pressure and the rationale "is so obvious" to them they don't understand why others don't get it.

2. Participation and involvement: Getting others involved can bring new energy and ideas, and cause people to believe they can be part of the change. This strategy works best when the change agent has time and needs voluntary compliance and active support to bring about the change. Participation fits with many of the norms of today's flattened organizations, but some managers often feel that it just slows everything down, compromising what needs to be done quickly.

3. Facilitation and support: Here change agents provide access to guidance and other forms of support to aid in adaptation to change. This strategy works best when the issues are related to anxiety and fear of change, or where there are concerns over insufficient access to needed resources.

4. Negotiation and agreement: At times, change leaders can make explicit deals with individuals and groups affected by the change. This strategy can help deal with contexts where the resistance is organized, "what's in it for me" is unclear, and power is at play. The problem with this strategy is that it may lead to compliance rather than wholehearted support of the change.

5. Manipulation and co-optation: While managers don't like to admit to applying this tactic, covert attempts to influence others are very common. Engaging those who are neutral or opposed to the change in discussions and engaging in ingratiating behavior will sometimes alter perspectives and cause resistors to change their position on the change. However, trust levels will drop and resistance will increase if people believe they are being manipulated in ways not consistent with their best interests.

6. Explicit and implicit coercion: With this strategy, as with the previous one, there is a negative image associated with it. Nevertheless, managers often have the legitimate right and responsibility to insist that changes be done. This strategy tends to be used when time is of the essence, compliant actions are not forthcoming, and change agents believe other options have been exhausted. Change leaders need to recognize the potential for residual negative feelings and consider how to manage these.

7. **Systemic or system adjustments:** Open systems analysis argues that adjustments can be made to formal structures, systems, and processes that reduce resistance while advancing the desired changes. For example, if employee resistance has coalesced in a group of employees who are employed in a particular function, organizational restructuring or the reassignment of group members to other areas may reduce resistance markedly. However, if it is mishandled, it can mobilize and escalate resistance in others.

SYSTEM ADJUSTMENTS (I.E., CLOSING STORES AND ELIMINATING JOBS) AT WALMART

Walmart has used systemic adjustments over the years as a change tool to assist in maintaining managerial discretion in employment practices by retaining their non-union status. In 2005, 200 employees at the store in Jonquière, Quebec, Canada, were attempting to negotiate the first-ever union contract with the firm. However, after nine days of meetings, over three months, Walmart announced it was closing the store because of concerns over its profitability. In 2008, the same approach was adopted when six employees in Gatineau, Quebec, won the right to unionize their small operation within Walmart. Walmart employees in Weyburn, Saskatchewan, voted to unionize, but quickly reversed field and voted to decertify in 2010.

The unions in both Quebec and Saskatchewan sued the employer for unfair labor practices and took their respective cases all the way to the Supreme Court of Canada. After years of litigation, the Quebec suit against Walmart's store closure met with limited success (some financial restitution was ordered), but the Saskatchewan case was unsuccessful. Currently no Walmart operation in Canada is unionized. The only other time a unionization drive had been close to succeeding was in 2000. Eleven meat cutters in their Jacksonville, Texas, store voted to join the UFCW. Walmart responded by eliminating the meat cutting job companywide.[58]

See **Toolkit Exercise 9.2** to think about influence strategies you've experienced.

Another way to think about influence strategies is to consider whether they attempt to push people in the desired direction or pull them. **Push tactics** attempt to move people toward acceptance of change through rational persuasion (the use of facts and logic in a non-emotional way) and/or pressure (the use of guilt or threats). The risk with the use of push tactics is that they can lead to resistance and defensiveness. Recipients may oppose the pressure simply because it is pressure and they feel a need to defend their positions.

Alternatively, change leaders can rely on **pull tactics**: inspirational appeals and consultation. Inspirational appeals can arouse enthusiasm based on shared values or ideals. *Consultation* (as it is used here) refers to when you seek the participation of others through appeals to the individuals' self-worth and positive self-concept. Both these approaches are designed to pull individuals in the desired direction.†††

Falbe and Yukl examined the effectiveness of nine different influence tactics. The most effective strategies were two pull tactics: (1) inspirational appeals and (2) consultation (seeking the participation of others). When considering these, never underestimate the importance of the credibility of the change leader.

The strategies of intermediate effectiveness were a combination of push and pull strategies: (3) rationale persuasion (facts, data, logic); (4) ingratiation (praise, flattery, friendliness); (5) personal appeals (friendship and loyalty); and (6) exchange tactics (negotiation and other forms of reciprocity).

The three strategies that were least effective were push strategies: (7) direct pressure, (8) legitimating tactics (framing of the request as consistent with policy and/or the influencer's authority), and (9) coalition building (creation of subgroups or linkages with other groups to exert pressure).[59]

Nutt categorizes four influence tactics used during implementation: (1) intervention, (2) participation, (3) persuasion, and (4) edict. **Intervention** is where key executives justify the need for change (often through the use of data) and provide new norms to judge performance. **Participation** involves engaging stakeholders in the change process. **Persuasion** is the use of experts to sell a change. And **edict** is the issuing of directives. Table 9.10 summarizes Nutt's data on the frequency of use, initial and ultimate adoption rate, and the time to install for each of these tactics.

This table demonstrates the value of a well-respected sponsor who acts as a lightning rod and energizes and justifies the need for change. The frequency of the use of participation as a strategy is somewhat higher than intervention and may reflect the challenge of managing change from the middle of the organization. Adoption takes longer, but it has the second-best success rate. Persuasion is attempted more frequently than the other three tactics, but its success rate is significantly lower than participation and the time to adoption slightly longer. Finally, it is difficult to understand the frequency of use of edict as a tactic, given its poor adoption rate and length of time to install.

When considering these four strategies, think about the value that a blended approach could bring to advancing change. In many cases a combination of both intervention and participation may make a great deal of sense, with edict only used as a last-ditch strategy with those who continue to resist.

When individuals actively resist change, it's useful to remember that some of them may see themselves as committed change agents who are acting to oppose what they believe is a problematic initiative. Keep that perspective in mind when considering how best to approach and engage them. However, there comes a time in a change initiative when the analysis of alternatives and the assessment of paths forward have been fully vetted and decisions made. At this point, individuals must decide if they are on the bus or off of it. At such times edict (including the option of transferring or removing such individuals) may need to come into play, to prevent resisting individuals from passively or actively obstructing and even sabotaging a change initiative.

Enact edict-like approaches only after giving the matter careful consideration. It is tempting to strike out at others, in the face of their opposition,

---

††† These styles are described more fully in Chapter 8.

Table 9.10 Implementation Tactics and Success[60]

Tactic	Percentage Use	Initial Adoption Rate	Ultimate Adoption Rate	Time to Adopt (Months)
Intervention	16%	100%	82%	11.2
Participation	20%	80.6%	71%	19.0
Persuasion	35%	65%	49%	20.0
Edict	29%	51%	35%	21.5

and such temptations may include undertaking a preemptive strike. However, acting on these impulses brings significant risks and often unanticipated consequences that can derail the change and ruin your reputation and relationship with others, so approach with extreme care and careful consideration before taking such action.

This section has outlined a variety of influence tactics that can be used to build awareness, reduce ambivalence and resistance, and move people to acceptance and adoption of the initiative. In general, it is wise to move as slowly as is practical. This permits people to become accustomed to the idea of the change, adopt the change program, learn new skills, and see the positive sides. It also permits change leaders to adjust their processes, refine the change, improve congruence, and learn as they go. However, if time is of the essence or if going slowly means that resisters will be able to organize in ways that will make change highly unlikely, then change leaders should plan carefully, move quickly, and overwhelm resistance where possible. Just remember, though, that it is far easier to get into a war than it is to build a lasting peace after the fighting ends. Don't let your impatience and commitment to moving the change forward get the better of your judgment concerning how best to proceed.[‡‡‡] See **Toolkit Exercise 9.3** to think about push and pull tactics.

TRANSITION MANAGEMENT

Change management is about keeping the plane flying while you rebuild it.[61]

When dealing with an ongoing operation, you typically don't have the luxury to put everything on hold while making a major change happen. You can't say, "Sorry, we aren't able to deliver the product we promised because we are making improvements." Most organizations have many change projects underway simultaneously. One part of the organization may be reengineering itself. Another might be introducing a quality program while another part focuses on employee empowerment. All of these must be managed concurrently while continuing to produce products and services.

[‡‡‡] These styles are described more fully in Chapter 8.

Morris and Raben argue for a transition manager (a change agent or implementer in the language of this book) who has resources, structures, and plans.[62] The transition manager has the power and authority to facilitate the change and is linked to the CEO or other senior executive. Resources are the people, money, training, and consulting expertise needed to be successful. Transition structures are outside the regular ones—temporary structures that allow normal activities to take place as well as change activities. The transition plan sets out how the organization will operate (including the delivery of goods and services) while undertaking the change and includes clear benchmarks, standards, and responsibilities for the change. Table 9.11 outlines a checklist for transition management.

Transition management is making certain that both the change project *and* the continuing operations are successful. The change leader and the transition manager are responsible for making sure that both occur. The change leader is visibly involved in articulating both the need for change and the new vision, while others involved in implementing the change manage the organization's structural and system changes and the individuals' emotional and behavioral issues so that neither is compromised to a danger point.[63] Ackerman described the application of a transition management model at Sun Petroleum.[64] She addressed the question, "How can these changes be put into place without seriously straining the organization?" Her solution was to create a transition manager who handled the social system requirements. Ackerman also argued for the use of a transition team to create a transition structure that would enable the organization to carry on operating effectively while the major changes take place.

Beckhard and Harris focus on the transition details in organizational change.[65] They reinforce the importance of specifying midpoint goals and milestones, which help motivate the members of the organization. The longer the span of time required for a change initiative, the more important these midcourse goals become. The goals need to be far enough away to provide direction but close enough to provide a sense of progress *and* an opportunity for midcourse changes in plans.

A second component of transition management is keeping people informed to reduce anxiety. During major reorganizations, many employees are assigned to new roles, new bosses, new departments, or new tasks. Those individuals have a right to know their new work terms and conditions. Transition managers will put systems in place to ensure that answers to questions (such as "how will I, my co-workers, and my customers be affected?" "Who is my new boss?" "Who will I be working with and where will I be located?" or "What is my new job description?") can be provided in a timely manner. An example of this need occurred in the Ontario (Canada) Ministry of Agriculture, Food and Rural Development. As the designer of a major change in that organization, Bill Allen commented that the ministry "underestimated the importance of a well thought out transition structure and plan. Employees of the Ministry had hundreds of questions about the organizational change and there was no formal structure to handle these in a consistent and professional manner."[66] The transition manager needs to be authorized and given the capacity to address such matters.

The final phase in transition management occurs in and around the same time as the celebrations are occurring in recognition of what has been accomplished. Project completion can be a bittersweet time for participants because

Table 9.11   A Checklist for Change: Transition Management
The following questions can be useful when planning transition management systems and structures.
1. How will the organization continue to operate as it shifts from one state to the next?
2. Who will answer questions about the proposed change? What decision power will this person or team have? Will they provide information only or will they be able to make decisions (such as individual pay levels after the change)?
3. Do the people in charge of the transition have the appropriate amount of authority to make decisions necessary to ease the change?
4. Have people developed ways to reduce the anxiety created by the change and increase the positive excitement over it?
5. Have people worked on developing a problem-solving climate around the change process?
6. Have people thought through the need to communicate the change? Who needs to be seen individually? Which groups need to be seen together? What formal announcement should be made?
7. Have the people handling the transition thought about how they will capture learning throughout the change process and share it?
8. Have they thought about how they will measure and celebrate progress along the way and how they will bring about closure to the project at its end and capture the learning so it is not lost (after-action review)?

they may not be working directly with one another in the future. They've worked hard, developed close friendships, and shared emotional highs and lows along the way. The experience can be extremely influential to their future development, and it needs to be processed and brought to closure in ways that do it justice.

One way to approach closure (in addition to the celebration) and maximize the learning for all is to conduct an **after-action review**.[67] An after-action review involves reviewing the change experience as a whole and learning from what transpired along the way. There needs to be a candid assessment from multiple perspectives of the change process and the strengths and weaknesses of the various approaches used along the way. It asks, (a) what were the intended results, (b) what were the actual results, (c) why did the actual results happen, and (d) what can be done better next time? As the participants explore these questions, the approaches, tools, sources of information, and insights that have the potential to improve performance in the future need to be identified, and the knowledge must be codified in ways that will allow others to access and learn from it. This knowledge is potentially the most significant legacy that those involved with the change can leave for themselves and others who will follow.

SUMMARY

"Doing it" demands a good plan and a willingness to work that plan. To advance a "do it" orientation, the chapter assesses several strategies for approaching the change and planning the work. The chapter examines various action planning tools and considers how to handle the communications challenges that arise during a change initiative. Finally, transition management is considered, because the delivery of services and products typically needs to continue while the change initiative is underway. See the **Toolkit Exercises** for critical thinking questions for this chapter.

KEY TERMS

"Do it" orientation—a willingness to engage in organizational analysis, see what needs to be done, and take the initiative to move the change forward:

Thinking first strategy—an approach used when the issue is clear, data are reliable, the context is well structured, thoughts can be pinned down, and discipline can be established, as in many production processes.

Seeing first strategy—an approach that works best when many elements have to be combined into creative solutions, commitment to those solutions is key, and communication across boundaries is essential, as in new product development. People need to see the whole before becoming committed.

Doing first strategy—an approach that works best when the situation is novel and confusing, complicated specifications would get in the way, and a few simple relationship rules can help people move forward. An example would be when a manager is testing an approach and wants feedback about what works.

Programmatic change—a traditional approach to planned change; starts with mission, plans, and objectives; sets out specific implementation steps, responsibilities, and timelines.

Discontinuous change—an approach adopted for a major change that represents a clear break from the previous approach, often involving revolutionary ideas.

Emergent change—a change that grows out of incremental change initiatives. It often evolves through the active involvement of internal participants. As it emerges, it can come to challenge existing organizational beliefs about what should be done.

Unilateral approach—top-down change. Change requirements are specified and implemented—required behavioral changes are spelled out, and it is anticipated that attitude changes will follow once people acclimatize themselves to the change.

Participative approach—bottom-up participation in the change initiative focuses on attitudinal changes that will support the needed behavioral changes required by the organizational change.

Techno–structural change—includes change initiatives focused on the formal structures, systems, and technologies employed by the organization.

Behavioral–social change—includes change initiatives focused on altering established social relationships within the organization.

Action Planning Tools

To-do list is a checklist of things to do.

Responsibility charting is who will do what, when, where, why, and how.

Contingency planning is consideration of what should be done when things do not work as planned on critical issues.

Decision tree analysis asks change agents to consider the major choices and the possible consequences of those alternatives.

Scenario planning is a change strategy formed by first developing a limited number of scenarios or stories about how the future may unfold and then assessing what the implications of each of these would be to the organization.

Surveys involve the use of structured questions to collect information from individuals and groups in systematic fashion.

Survey feedback is an organizational development technique that involves participants in the review and discussion of survey results. The goal is to actively engage them in the interpretation of the findings, the discussion of their implication, and the identification of how best to proceed.

Project planning and critical path methods are operations research techniques for scheduling work. These methods provide deadlines and insight as to which activities cannot be delayed to meet those deadlines.

Force field analysis examines the forces for and against change.

Stakeholder analysis is the position of the major players and why they behave as they do.

Commitment charts is an evaluation of the level of commitment of major players (against, neutral, let it happen, help it happen, make it happen).

The **adoption continuum** is an examination of major players and their position on the awareness, interest, desire, and adoption continuum related to the proposed changes.

Leverage analysis determination of methods of influencing major groups or players regarding the proposed changes

Purpose of the communication plan for change: (1) to infuse the need for change throughout the organization; (2) to enable individuals to understand the impact that the change will have on them; (3) to communicate any structural and job changes that will influence how things are done; and (4) to keep people informed about progress along the way.

Four phases in the communications process during change are outlined:

Pre-change phase centers on communicating need and gaining approval for the change;

Developing the need for change phase focuses on communicating the need for change more broadly, reassuring recipients, clarifying steps, and generating enthusiasm and a sense of urgency for the change;

Midstream phase involves disseminating details of the change and should include obtaining and listening to feedback from employees, addressing any misconceptions and nurturing enthusiasm and support;

Confirming the change phase focuses on communicating about and celebrating success, capturing learning from the process and preparing the organization to the next changes.

Richness of the communication channel different channels vary in the richness of the information they can carry. Standard reports and general-information e-mails represent the lean end of the continuum. Richness increases as one moves to personalized letters and e-mails, telephone conversations, video conferencing, and face-to-face communications (the richest channel).

Alternatives to reducing negative reactions to change and building support developed by Kotter and Schlesinger:

Education and communication is a strategy that helps others develop an understanding of the change initiative, what is required of them, and why it is important;

Participation and involvement get others involved and can bring new energy and ideas, and cause people to believe they can be part of the change;

Facilitation and support is a strategy that provides access to guidance and other forms of support to aid in adaptation to change;

Negotiation and agreement is when change leaders can make explicit deals with individuals and groups affected by the change;

Manipulation and co-optation include covert attempts to influence others;

Explicit and implicit coercion rests on change leaders' legitimate right and responsibility to insist that changes be done; and

Systemic adjustments are those made to formal systems and processes that reduce resistance while advancing the desired changes.

Push tactics attempt to move people in the desired direction through rational persuasion (e.g., the use of facts and logic) and/or direct or indirect pressure (e.g., guilt, threats).

Pull tactics attempt to draw people in the desired direction through arousing interests and enthusiasm through inspirational appeals, consultation, and their active participation.

Intervention is a strategy of influence identified by Nutt, which involves key executives justifying the need for change and providing new norms to judge performance.

Participation is a strategy of influence identified by Nutt, which involves engaging stakeholders in the change process.

Persuasion is a strategy of influence identified by Nutt, which involves the use of experts to sell a change.

Edict is a strategy of influence identified by Nutt, which is the issuing of directives.

Transition management is the process of ensuring that the organization continues to operate effectively while undergoing change

After-action review is a final phase of the transition-management process. It seeks to bring closure to the experience and engage participants in a process that will allow the learning gained through the change process to be extracted and codified in some manner for future use.

END-OF-CHAPTER EXERCISES

TOOLKIT EXERCISE 9.1
Critical Thinking Questions

The URLs for the videos listed below can be found in two places. The first spot is next to the exercise and the second spot is on the website at **study.sagepub.com/cawsey4e.**
Consider the questions that follow.

1. Terms of Engagement—3:32 minutes

    https://www.youtube.com/watch?v=O5-kI67mSAE

    Berrett-Koehler Publishers's "Change Authors" series focuses on four principles: widening the circle of involvement, connecting people to each other and to ideas, creating communities for action, and embracing democracy. *Terms of Engagement: Changing the Ways We Change Organizations* is a B-K Business Book by Richard H. Axelrod.

    *   Explain the four principles using examples from your own change experience.

    *   Brainstorm how you might begin to instill one of these principles in an organization you are familiar with.

2. It Starts With One: Changing Individuals Changes Organizations—26:25 minutes

    https://www.youtube.com/watch?v=1klZD0nKOF4

    Two professors from INSEAD (Hal Gregersen and Stewart Black) discuss the idea that you can't change organizations if you don't focus on change with individuals first. Investigate three barriers: the failure to see, failure to move (developing the capacity of individuals to do something new), and failure to finish (following through with support until capacities are where they need to be; need champions at the front line as well as elsewhere in the organization, as well as signposts that help people understand where they are in terms of implementing the change initiative). This includes helping leaders to understand the changes required within themselves.

    *   Which barrier resonated with your experience the most?

    *   How do you think these principles might facilitate a successful change project?

    (Continued)

(Continued)

3. Appreciative Inquiry—3:53 minutes, **https://www.bing.com/videos/search?q=appreciative+inq uiry+4%3a50+minutes&&view=detail&mid=C831E9F54B9B6ADF7EF5C831E9F54B9B6ADF7EF 5&&FORM=VDRVRV**

  - What is the basic idea of appreciative inquiry?

  - What emotions does this strategy center on?

  - How does an appreciative approach change process?

Please see **study.sagepub.com/cawsey4e** *for access to videos and a downloadable template of this exercise.*

TOOLKIT EXERCISE 9.2

Action Plans for Influencing Reactions to Change

1. What methods have you seen used in organizations to influence people's reactions to a specific change? Think specifically about a change instance and what was done:

   a. Education and communication

   b. Participation and involvement

   c. Facilitation and support

   d. Negotiation and agreement

   e. Manipulation and co-optation

   f. Explicit and implicit coercion

   g. Systemic adjustments

2. What were the consequences of each of the methods used? What worked and what did not work? Why?

3. What personal preferences do you have regarding these techniques? That is, which ones do you have the skills to manage and the personality to match?

*Please see **study.sagepub.com/cawsey4e** for a downloadable template of this exercise.*

TOOLKIT EXERCISE 9.3

An Additional Lens on Influence Tactics

1. Think specifically of change situations in an organization you are familiar with. What influence tactics did people use? Describe three situations in which three different tactics were used.

   a. Inspirational appeals
   b. Consultation (seeking the participation of others)
   c. Relying on the informal system (existing norms and relationships)
   d. Personal appeals (appeals to friendship and loyalty)
   e. Ingratiation
   f. Rational persuasion (use of facts, data, logic)
   g. Exchange or reciprocity
   h. Coalition building (creation of subgroups or links with other groups to exert pressure)
   i. Using organizational rules or legitimating tactics (framing of the request as consistent with policy and/or your authority)
   j. Direct pressure
   k. Appeals to higher authority and dealing directly with decision makers

2. Which of these would you classify as pull tactics and which would you classify as push tactics? Push tactics attempt to move people toward change through rational persuasion. Pull tactics attempt to move people toward change through inspirational appeals to shared values or ideals that arouse enthusiasm.

3. How successful were each of the tactics? Why did they work or not work?

4. How comfortable are you with each tactic? Which could you use?

*Please see **study.sagepub.com/cawsey4e** for a downloadable template of this exercise.*

TURNING AROUND COTE CONSTRUCTION COMPANY

By Cynthia Ingols, Professor of Practice

School of Business, Simmons University, Boston, MA

Tupper F. Cawsey, Professor Emeritus

Wilfrid Laurier University, Waterloo, Ontario, CA

Gene Deszca, Professor Emeritus

Lazaridis School of Business and Economics, Wilfrid Laurier University, Waterloo, Ontario, CA

INTRODUCTION

When Liam Cote decided to help his cousin Felix Cote turn around his business, he had no idea that things were as bad as they were. Liam knew that the bank's loan was coming due and the company could not pay it. However, Liam was shocked at the number of other problematic issues there were at Cote Construction. In his mind, the company's business model was straightforward: renting out specialized heavy construction equipment, either with or without operators, to a relatively easily defined set of customers, that is contractors who needed such equipment. Liam believed that the business had solid prospects that could sustain a solid return on investment. However, it certainly was not doing so now. Perhaps the strategy was clear, mused Liam, but things were a mess!

Nevertheless, three weeks earlier, Liam and Felix had signed papers at their local bank and at their lawyer's office. Based on Liam's reputation as a successful entrepreneur and his willingness to make a significant investment to improve liquidity, the bank agreed to renegotiate the operating loan and line of credit. This would provide the company with the breathing space needed to execute a turnaround. At their lawyer's office Felix authorized Liam to take on the role of CEO, while Felix became Head of Equipment and Operations.

After they signed the various papers, Liam and Felix enjoyed lunch together and then returned to the workplace to set up Liam's office. Since Liam was optimistic—and wanted—Felix to be an active partner with him in the areas that Felix found compelling, Liam took the office down the hall from Felix. While the office was slightly smaller, Liam wanted to send a signal that Felix was still an important partner in Cote Construction. About 4 p.m., Liam went to look for Felix and learned that he had left the offices an hour earlier with no word about where he was going or if he would return for the day. Alice Williams, the bookkeeper, said that Felix had stayed in the office later than he usually did and she did not expect that he would return that afternoon.

Liam found the supply room and searched for wall-sized flip chart paper to put up on his office wall. At the top of the paper, he wrote, "Problems at Cote Construction." His first entry was "Felix left the office about 3 pm without communicating to anyone where he was going or what he intended to do." Liam decided that he would give himself three weeks to diagnose what was wrong at Cote Construction and that he would write down every problem on the flip-chart paper in his office. He debated with himself about how he should manage the flip-chart papers: keep them up for all who entered his office to see;

or, take them out each night in private as he added to the list. Liam was still ambivalent as he closed and locked his door at 7 p.m.

BACKGROUND

Felix founded the company in 2003. He had grown it steadily through the first five years, but the Great Recession of 2008 had dramatically slowed construction in the area and Felix's business had been hit hard. In fact, a key competitor went bankrupt. By 2011-2012 the economy and area businesses had largely recovered, and business at Cote Construction began to boom. From 2013 to 2016 there was unprecedented growth in the area and Cote Construction grew dramatically, too. Staff levels more than doubled during the three years to 57 employees. Fifteen employees worked in the office area, handling administrative, sales, and accounting/finance functions. The remainder were in the repair shop, in the yard, or on the road, dealing with maintenance and delivery of equipment.

In the past year, however, sales had begun a modest decline. Other financial indicators showed worrying trends. Margins had gone down by almost 30%, and cash flow was negative. For two years, operating expenses had risen significantly. While Liam wasn't sure why, he thought that equipment purchases had led to higher interest charges and that labor costs had risen dramatically. It was as if Felix and his fellow managers had lost their capacity to manage the company's business and its cycles.

For the previous six months things had gone from difficult to worse. The company's bank loan was coming due. Felix had varied his management approach from requesting to pleading and finally to avoiding issues at work. Because Felix was impossible to find to make decisions or ask questions, employees referred to him as Waldo, after the character in the children's book, *Where's Waldo?*

When Felix turned over decision-making authority and power to Liam, he agreed to focus on what he knew best: the equipment and operations. He had grown up with a love for heavy equipment, and family members said that the only reason that he was in business was so that

he had newer and bigger toys to play with. He had specialized knowledge about which equipment was suitable for which jobs and, prior to the past couple of years, had been adept at developing relationships with customers that generated repeat business. However, the agreement and Liam's arrival did not reverse Felix's disappearing act. To his direct reports he seemed depressed and distant, with little appetite for assuming a more active operational role in the business.

DIAGNOSING AND ARTICULATING THE PROBLEMS

As Liam began to investigate the problems at Cote Construction, he was shaken to find a culture of permissiveness and waste. As he walked through the parts and maintenance areas, he found parts, tools, and equipment scattered about. Grease on the floor made walking a risky proposition. Pizza boxes, pop cans, and bottles were littered around. He thought he smelled liquor on some employees. He observed lateness and absenteeism were problems. No one seemed to be doing anything about these matters. Part of the problem was a tight labor market: supervisors were afraid if they reprimanded employees that they would walk.

The housekeeping within the administrative office area was somewhat better than in other parts of the operation, but it still left much to be desired. Some employees smoked in work areas despite no-smoking rules. Dishes often sat in the sink of the small kitchen area and it was only when left-over foods began to smell did someone in the office begin the task of throwing away old foods.

While Liam noted problems to address on the flip-chart papers in his office, he took immediate action when necessary. One day, for example, Liam smelled alcohol on the breath of an employee who appeared to be under the influence. He fired him on the spot. On another day Liam entered the workspace of people with dogs and asked, "Are these employees or pets?" The next day the employees—but not the dogs—came to work.

After reviewing sales information, Liam also found himself wondering about the source of orders. Most came from brokers rather than directly from customers. Taking into account their fee, he determined that Cote Construction was losing money by relying on brokers. Liam phoned one of their customers who regularly leased their equipment through a broker. After chatting and thanking the customer for doing business with Cote, Liam asked the customer why they did not place orders directly. The customer responded, "Because you never called us before!" Before he ended the conversation, he had a $50,000 work order placed directly. When Liam relayed this conversation and its results to the sales staff, they were at first defensive. Further conversation assured Liam that the sales staff wanted to make money, but they seemed unsure as to how they should change their sales approach.

During his third week, Liam noticed that certain pieces of equipment that had been in for repair in week one were still inoperable. He asked, "Why?" He was told that the maintenance supervisor was in a dispute with the field service foreman and sales staff over the allocation of repair and maintenance charges, and as a result, needed repairs had not been undertaken. The argument had been going on for more than a month, and he was told this was not the first time. This resulted, Liam noted, in lost rental sales. He blew up and called an urgent meeting of those involved. He ordered the equipment to be repaired immediately and stated that this was no way to resolve conflict. When Liam went back to his office, he added "unclear lines of authority" to his list of issues on the flip charts.

The accounting and finance area had difficulty providing the performance data that Liam requested. When he asked them to calculate the profit margin for each piece of equipment, the initial response was "Why do you want that?" After he explained his rationale to them, they began pulling together the information. But, employees in other departments saw the new cost reporting requirements as more paperwork that might get in the way of sales and servicing.

When Liam began to explore equipment repair invoices, he noted that many expensive repairs had been done on-site at their clients' premises. Much of the work looked routine but was made much more expensive because of the location and because the company had to negotiate

with clients over operational losses incurred while the machine was down. Liam wondered why the equipment hadn't been serviced prior to leaving the shop. When he inquired, he learned that there was no formal preventive maintenance program in place. Back in his office Liam added more problems to his flip chart list:

1. No formal preventive maintenance system

2. Questionable inventory management system; missing parts in some areas and excess inventory in others; and a significant volume of obsolete parts that were held in inventory

3. Missing tools and equipment, including some big-ticket items, such as a $35,000 loader and a $25,000 compressor

4. Sales relationships not actively managed; clients not phoned in a timely manner; customer complaints not acted upon until threats were invoked

5. Logistics, scheduling, customer delivery and pickups, and on-site servicing of equipment not handled well. Customers complained about downtime and their inability to predict when tasks would be accomplished

6. Lags between order fulfillment and client billing; slow payment of accounts payable

7. Poor relations with suppliers of parts and equipment, due in part to slow payment; disagreements over terms and conditions; and lack of supplier responsiveness to emergency requests

In an inspection of the operations Liam found seven new tires and rims stashed behind a building. When he checked purchasing invoices, he learned that nine had been bought the week before. On further investigation, he was told that no new tires had been counted on any equipment. Liam could not locate the missing two tires and rims, worth more than $2,000 each. It was a low point for Liam as he concluded that employees might be stealing from Cote Construction.

However, Liam thought that many members of the firm wanted to do a good job. That was the sense that he got as he visited departments, talked with individuals one-on-one, and heard about their frustrations. Still, he did have a few concerns. Some employees resented that others seemed to come and go as they wished. He had listened to one customer complaint about late delivery of equipment and learned that the person delivering the machinery had stopped for three hours on route. The driver's excuse was lunch and engine problems that had miraculously resolved themselves. Employees' morale was in the toilet, but turnover had yet to become a problem.

HOW TO BEGIN
THE TURNAROUND

As Liam sat in his office, he stared at the flip-chart sheets on his walls. During his first week, he had put up the sheets and began listing every issue or problem that he or others identified. After three weeks, there were now more than two dozen items. With this substantial list, Liam thought that he had a handle on the magnitude of the problems at Cote Construction. What he needed to do now was come up with a plan to address them. To begin, he had a number of decisions to make:

- What problems should he tackle first? Which were operational and which were organizational? What timeline should he establish?

- How should he consider the people in the company? What should he ask them? How should he approach them to solicit their ideas for the turnaround?

- How should he deal with Felix? Should he allow him to continue as head of Equipment and Operations? Should he sideline Felix and formally reduce his authority at Cote Construction? Would it, in fact, be a relief to employees to know that Felix no longer played a role in the company?

GET AND USE DATA
THROUGHOUT THE CHANGE PROCESS

Chapter Overview

- Measurement and control processes play a critical role in guiding change and integrating the initiatives and efforts of various parties.

- Though measurement is specifically included in the institutionalization phase of the Change Path Model, it plays an important role throughout the change process.

- Four types of management control processes are identified: Interactive controls, Boundary systems, Belief systems, and Diagnostic/steering controls. Different types of controls are needed as the change project shifts along the Change Path from Acceleration to Institutionalization.

- The use of strategy maps as an alignment tool is explored.

- Three measurement tools are presented: the Balanced Scorecard, the risk exposure calculator, and the DICE model: duration, integrity, commitment, and effort.

When British Columbia implemented its carbon tax in 2008, a key element in its climate strategy, there was significant anxiety and commentary in the press that it would kill economic development in this resource-rich province of Canada. However, that has not been the experience. This change initiative, designed to be revenue neutral, has resulted in this province having the lowest personal income tax rate in Canada. Fossil fuel use has been reduced by 16%, while consumption in the rest of Canada has risen by 3%, and BC's economy has performed slightly better, on average, than the rest of Canada. These results suggest that carefully designed programs such as this can reduce our appetite for fossil fuels while playing a positive role in economic growth. Challenges remain in achieving their carbon reduction targets but progress is being made in BC.[1] THis example also shows the importance of measurement and the power it has to dispel commonly held, though inaccurate, beliefs. For British Columbia, despite the fact that the carbon tax worked to improve not only the economy but also sustainability in the province, it took hard measurements to legitimize the change.

Measurements matter. What gets measured affects the direction, content, and outcomes achieved by a change initiative. Measurements influence what people pay attention to and what they do.[2] When organizational members see particular quantifications as legitimate, believe their actions will affect the outcomes achieved, and think those actions will positively affect them personally, the motivational impact increases. But when the legitimacy or impact of the measures is questioned or when people believe they can't affect the outcomes, the measurements are seen as interference and can result in cynicism and alienation.

Figure 10.1 The Change Path Model

Awakening
Chapter 4
1. Identify a need for change and confirm the problems or opportunities that incite the need for change through collection of data.
2. Articulate the gap in performance between the present and the envisioned future state, and spread awareness of the data and the gap throughout the organization.
3. Develop a powerful vision for change.
4. Disseminate the vision for the change and why it's needed through multiple communication channels.

Mobilization
Chapters 5 through 8
1. Make sense of the desired change through formal systems and structures, and leverage those systems to reach the change vision (Chapter 5).
2. Assess power and cultural dynamics at play, and put them to work to better understand the dynamics and build coalitions and support to realize the change (Chapter 6).
3. Communicate the need for change organization-wide and manage change recipients and various stakeholders as they react to and move the change forward (Chapter 7).
4. Leverage change agent personality, knowledge, skills and abilities, and related assets (e.g., reputation and relationships) for the benefit of the change vision and its implementation (Chapter 8).

Acceleration
Chapter 9
1. Continue to systematically reach out to engage and empower others in support, planning, and implementation of the change. Help them develop needed new knowledge, skills, abilities, and ways of thinking that will support the change.
2. Use appropriate tools and techniques to build momentum, accelerate and consolidate progress.
3. Manage the transition, celebrating small wins and the achievement of milestones along the larger, more difficult path of change.

Institutionalization
Chapter 10
1. Track the change periodically and through multiple balanced measures to help assess what is needed, gauge progress toward the goal, and to make modifications as needed and mitigate risk.
2. Develop and deploy new structures, systems, processes and knowledge, skills, and abilities, as needed, to bring life to the change and new stability to the transformed organization.

Change agents know that measurement is important, but sometimes they need to understand more fully how measures can be used to help frame and guide the change.[3]

For a variety of reasons, data collection and measurement are often given less attention than they deserve during change initiatives. The change is seen as complex, requiring multidimensional measurements tools that seem too complex and difficult to track; measures are not viewed as focusing on what is important; the evolution of change initiatives makes end-point measures difficult to quantify; or end-point measures suggest commitment to a line in the sand that is then difficult to modify to match changing conditions.[4] In addition, change leaders often explain that they lack time to assess outcomes, that they are too busy making the change happen, and/or that they did not get around to thinking fully about measurement of outcomes.

The reality is that **measurement and control systems** incorporated into change initiatives can clarify expected outcomes and enhance accountability. This leaves some change agents feeling vulnerable. They worry that critics will use the measures to second-guess an initiative and even undermine both the change and the change agent.

In spite of these concerns, well-thought-out measurement and control processes provide change leaders with valuable tools. Information from these measurement systems enables change managers to (1) frame the need for change and the implications of the change vision in terms of expected outcomes; (2) monitor the environment; (3) make monitoring and decision criteria more explicit and testable; (4) help protect against biases when measures are wisely selected; (5) help others involved and/or affected by the change to better understand what is expected of them; (6) guide the change, gauge progress, and make midcourse corrections; and (7) bring the change to a successful conclusion.[5] Key change leadership skills include identifying assessment measures, building them into the change process, adapting them as needed, and using them as tools to aid in decision making, communication, and action taking.[6] At RE/MAX (described below), the measurement system supported a change to the employment relationship that allowed the firm to attract and retain superior agents.

MEASUREMENT SYSTEMS AT RE/MAX

For RE/MAX, the Denver, Colorado–based real estate franchise network, a redefinition of customers away from industry norms was crucial. Cofounder and chairman David Liniger noted that the firm's success came from the simple idea that RE/MAX customers were the real estate agents themselves, not the buyers and sellers of real estate. More specifically, RE/MAX targeted high-performing agents who represented just 20% of the entire pool of real estate agents but accounted for approximately 80% of all sales.

RE/MAX's focus on high-performing agents originally consisted of changing the industry's traditional 50–50 fee split between broker and agent to a franchise system in which agents kept all commissions after payment of a management fee and expenses. In some cases, that shift changed retention rates of real estate agents

(Continued)

as much as 85%. RE/MAX followed the change in the reward system with additional services, including national marketing campaigns, training of agents in sales techniques by satellite, and coordinated administrative support.

The results have been impressive: According to CEO Liniger, in 2003, the average RE/MAX agent earned $120,000 per year on 24 transactions versus an industry average of $25,000 on seven transactions. "The customer comes second," he says, but hastens to add, "If our emphasis is on having the best employees, we're going to have the best customer service."[7]

The real estate sales meltdown in 2007–2008 and the subsequent slow recovery proved very challenging for the industry, but RE/MAX has rebounded. In North America it was recognized as one of the top 50 franchises for minorities in both 2012 and 2014, where it was the only real estate firm on the list.[8] It has been named the best real estate franchiser 15 times in the past 19 years and was ranked #10 in the Entrepreneur's Franchise 500 ranking in 2018. It has been named the highest ranked real estate franchise globally for four years in a row in the Franchise Times Top 200 survey.

A 2018 assessment of the top brokerages in the industry found that RE/MAX agents averaged almost twice as many transactions when compared with their major competitors, resulting in an average of $4.6 million in sales, or 78% more than that achieved by the average of all other agents in the survey. With over 120,000 agents and 6,000 offices in more than 100 countries and territories in 2018, it is arguably the number one brand in its industry.[9]

At RE/MAX, management's strategic realignment was anchored in a change to the reward system from fee-splitting the sales commission to one based on a franchise model. This example demonstrates that what is measured and rewarded will have a major impact on what outcomes are achieved. Sometimes measures are a matter of personal goal setting, as in the case of an athlete who links training metrics to performance goals and then celebrates small steps that lead to the accomplishment of a major milestone. In other situations, assessment grows out of expectations and/or requirements established by others, such as just-in-time measurement and cost reduction systems imposed on suppliers by automobile firms.

Employees' acceptance or rejection of measurements of a change initiative is important. When employees' acceptance of such measures increase, people experience less work stress, more job satisfaction, improved job performance, better work/family balance, less absenteeism, less job burnout, and more organizational commitment.[10] Because RE/MAX's executives structured a win–win strategy for the firm and for higher-performing agents, agents accepted the firm's measures and, in turn, the firm attracted and retained above-average real estate agents.[11] RE/MAX believes that the alignment of its strategy with its measurement system, innovative technology and sales approaches, and an ongoing commitment to agent education has been instrumental to its success.

This chapter looks at the role of measurement in change management and how assessment influences people's behavior. Issues over the development, use, and impact of measures are examined. The role of measurement and control in risk management is discussed, as is the question of what to measure at different stages in the life cycle of the change. Finally, strategy maps and balanced scorecards are introduced to demonstrate how to address the alignment of action with the change vision and strategy. Throughout this chapter, the goal remains the same: to learn how to use measurement and control mechanisms to increase the prospects for successful change.

Figure 10.1 suggests that measurement and control occur at the end of the change process, but in fact measurement and control aspects of a change need to begin at its inception. Change leaders should use these analytic tools throughout the life of the process. They can assist in helping to define the need for change, quantify what is expected from a change initiative, assess progress at specified intervals, and, at the end of the process, evaluate the change initiative's impact. Measures can help change agents in five ways:

a) clarify expectations,

b) assess progress and make mid-course corrections,

c) assess the extent to which initiatives are being internalized and institutionalized,

d) assess what has been ultimately achieved, and

e) set the stage for future change initiatives.[12]

Many managerial discussions of measurement systems and control processes focus on how they impede progress.[13] Though measurement systems can get in the way, well-designed and effectively deployed systems have the potential to overcome organizational barriers and contribute to successful change.

The following case example outlines how change agents at Control Production Systems (CPS) approached their deteriorating market position. The example shows how change agents benefited from consultation with key participants[14] and collaboration with diverse groups[15] and how they used measurement and control processes to frame and reinforce the needed changes.

A CASE STUDY IN THE VALUE OF REALIGNING MEASURES

Control Production Systems (CPS), a midsized firm that designs, manufactures, sells, and services customized production control systems, had noticed an erosion of its market share to competitors. Declining customer loyalty, greater difficulty selling product and service updates, and an increased reliance on price to win the business were shrinking margins and making competitive life difficult, even though product and service offerings were innovative and of a high quality. The firm possessed a strong, positive culture that reflected the values of innovation, quality, and open communications, but recent setbacks had shaken people's confidence.

As a result of a town hall meeting called to discuss the corporation's situation, the CEO acted on a suggestion to form a cross-functional change team to assess the firm's circumstances and recommend a course of action. The team included sales agents and customer support staff and was led by the director of sales and service. The director reported to the senior management team on a monthly basis, and the team was expected to diagnose and analyze the problem and frame

(Continued)

(Continued)

recommendations for change within two months, which would be followed by implementation activities. An intranet website facilitated communications about the change, and transparency, candor, and no reprisals were the watchwords for the change team's approach. As well, the team received sufficient resources to allow it to get on with its task.

Prior to the change, sales agents were organized geographically and paid on a salary-plus-commission basis. After a sale, agents handed off responsibility to customer support staff to address order fulfillment and post-sales servicing. The customer support staff was rewarded on the basis of cost control and throughput. If customers never contacted the firm for help, that was considered good because no contact generated no cost and suggested customer satisfaction. Short calls were seen as better than long ones due to cost implications, and standardized responses and online help were preferred over trouble-shooting phone calls for the same cost reasons. The firm kept no systematic record of customer calls and responded to customers on a first-come, first-served basis.

Analysis by the change team showed that customers who had minimal contact with the customer support staff were less likely to develop a relationship with the firm, were likely deriving less value from their purchases, and were less likely to be aware of product and service innovations and applications that could benefit them. In other words, the activities that kept short-term costs low hurt customer loyalty and long-term profitability. Benchmark data concerning service models, customer satisfaction, and purchase decisions confirmed that CPS was falling behind key competitors.

After the diagnosis, the team concluded that there was a need to change the way the firm dealt with and serviced its major customers. The team determined that the way to increase sales and profitability was to ensure that customers saw CPS as a trusted partner who could find ways to enhance customers'

productivity and quality through improvements in CPS's control systems.

The company realigned how it managed its relationships with customers. The firm integrated sales and customer support services, created sub-teams with portfolios of customer accounts by industry, and assigned the sub-teams to manage customers as ongoing relationships. The vision was a customer-focused partnership in which one-stop shopping, customer intimacy, service excellence, and solution finding would frame the relationship rather than simply selling and servicing in the traditional manner.

During the change, the change team measured employees' understanding and commitment to the new service model, employees' skill acquisition, and results of pilot projects. Further, the team measured service failures in areas of delivery, response time, quality, and relationship management to identify and deal with problems quickly if they occurred during the transition period. The team searched for systemic problems, developed remedies, encouraged openness and experimentation, and avoided finger pointing. Milestones for the change were established and small victories along the transition path were identified, monitored, and celebrated.

Once the team initiated the changes, it aligned performance measures by focusing on customers' satisfaction with the breadth and depth of services, response time, customers' referrals, repeat sales, and margins. The reward system shifted from a commission base for sales personnel and salary plus small bonus for customer service staff to a salary-plus-team-based performance incentive that included customers' satisfaction and retention, share of the customers' business in their product and service area, and customers' profitability over time. In the three years since implementation, there have been significant improvements in all the targeted measures, and feedback from customer service has become an important influencer of product refinement and development.

The case above demonstrates how measurements can support a change initiative at each stage of the process. At the beginning, change leaders used measurements in problem identification, in root cause analysis, and in the development of awareness for a new vision and structure. The leaders recognized the misalignment between measures that reinforced cost reductions in servicing clients (first-order effects) and the desired but unrealized long-term outcome of customer loyalty and profitability (second-order or lag effects). As the change leaders and team continued to diagnose their organization's structure and systems, at each step data were collected, analyzed, and used to fine-tune plans. Employees came to trust using data to make savvy decisions. In the end, clients' satisfaction with CPS's products and services (first-order effects) gave rise to customer loyalty and follow-up purchases and profitability (second-order effects) that management had not previously measured or really paid attention to.

To make the question of the impact of measures and control processes all the more real, consider a change you are familiar with and complete **Toolkit Exercise 10.2**.

SELECTING AND DEPLOYING MEASURES

There is no shortage of possible measurement indicators: cycle time, machine efficiency, waste, sales per call, employee satisfaction, waiting time, market share, profitability per sale, cost of sale, and customer retention, to name a few. If change agents try to measure everything concurrently, they are likely to lose focus. To focus attention, agents need to be clear about the stage of the change process and what dimensions are most important to monitor at a particular stage given the desired end results. Here is a list of six criteria to help change leaders determine which measures to adopt.

1. Focus on Key Factors

An accurate analysis of the change challenges will mean that change leaders will know which factors are key and what levers will move people in the direction of the desired change. Measures influence what people pay attention to and how they act, even when they believe those actions are ill advised.[16] Consider the all-too-common practice of trade loading, the inefficient and expensive practice of pushing excess inventory onto distributors and retailers in order to make the manufacturer's numbers look better in the short term.[17] For years, staff at Gillette knew that the practice of trade loading was having a negative effect on pricing, production efficiencies, customer relationships, and profitability. Trade loading meant unsold inventory was hidden from Gillette's eyes in the distribution channels and price discounting was eroding margins (distributors quickly learned how to time purchases to take advantage of such discounts). In spite of the widespread awareness that this practice was ill advised, it continued until new leadership realigned key measures and practices to support the desired changes and finally brought an end to an unhealthy practice.[18]

Knowing the critical measures to develop, deploy, and monitor at the different stages of the change process is a complex issue. In the Gillette case, this involved measures that demonstrated the negative consequences of trade loading, showed the positive consequences of the change vision, and assessed progress with the change and performance in ways that aligned with the change vision and targeted outcomes.

When considering what to focus on assessing, be cognizant of the role bias can play in your assessment, as noted in Chapter 3. Factors such as confirmation bias (seeking out supportive data), recency bias (expectation that previous events will repeat themselves, loss aversion (losses have a larger psychological affect than gains), herding (we should do it because it's worked for others), and outcome bias (belief that a successful outcome means our analysis was correct) will cloud your judgement and potentially put you on a risky path. Take steps to buffer the effects of such biases so that you are able to approach the change challenge with your eyes wide open. Daniel Kahneman's work on decision making provides excellent advice concerning how to avoid these pitfalls.[19]

2. Use Measures That Lead to Challenging but Achievable Goals

Employees need to believe that they can achieve challenging goals. Measurements that note small steps to the larger goal and measures within an individual's control will tap into desired motivations.

3. Use Measures and Controls That Are Perceived as Fair and Appropriate

Employees' perception of the appropriateness and fairness of the measures and control processes is driven as much by the process used to develop and legitimize them as by the outcomes they deliver.[20] Even reasonable measures may not be acceptable if people feel the measures were forced on them. Good processes will reduce resistance through communication, as communication provides opportunities for input and feedback while building trust and support. Avoid applying measures in ways that punish people who take reasonable actions based on their understanding of the change goals and what is expected of them.

Measurement and control processes are more likely to be accepted if the process used in developing them is seen as reasonable and fair, even if those measures lead to negative outcomes for those being measured (this matter of fair process was discussed earlier and in more detail in Chapter 7). It is very beneficial if individuals who are responsible for delivering on measures see them as relevant and fair.

Participation in the development of goals and how they will be measured is well worth considering because it has been shown to have the potential to increase the level of understanding of what the organization is attempting to do, heighten legitimacy of the targets, and increase commitment to them.[21] Be careful when you are assigning incentives to the accomplishment of goals, because excessively high rewards for success or severe sanctions for failure can lead to dysfunctional and unethical behavior (e.g., game playing, falsification of data). Approach financial incentives with care, because, mishandled, they can impair progress and get in the way of the positive role the participants' sense of autonomy, mastery, and a purpose can play in motivating desired actions.[22]

4. Avoid Sending Mixed Signals

Measurement systems related to change often send conflicting signals, and it is not unusual for change leaders to say one thing but signal another through what they measure and reward. For example, an organization may initiate changes aimed at enhancing quality and customer satisfaction but then "wink at" the shipment of flawed products to meet just-in-time delivery metrics and avoid exceeding its internal scrap and rework targets. Managers do this even though they know that substandard products will increase warranty work, require customers to do rework, and put the firm's reputation with the customer at risk. The fundamental problem in this example is that measures are not aligned with goals.

Aligning measurements and avoiding mixed signals is tricky because there are always trade-offs. For example, employees' acceptance of a particular step (as measured by survey results) and the achievement of a particular performance milestone (e.g., going "live" with a new customer service module) may end up conflicting. The firm may have succeeded in going "live" with the new module, but employees and customers may be unaware of or confused about the advantages associated with the new module versus the costs and benefits of remaining with the existing approach. Change leaders need to address such matters by providing advice on how these trade-offs associated with the change and the potentially conflicting signals generated by different measures should be handled. If this isn't done, change initiatives may flounder in the subsequent confusion and create cynicism and game playing.

The Canadian division of a U.S. auto parts firm initiated a change initiative in the form of a new quality program and reinforced it with a gigantic display board preaching, "Quality is important because General Motors demands it!" However, next to this sign sat pallets of completed parts with supervisory tags that approved shipment, overriding quality control inspection reports that had ordered rework prior to shipment. The firm's management had not addressed how to resolve conflicts between the new quality initiative and their just-in-time obligations. Supervisors looked at how they were measured and concluded that delivery trumped quality. Employees looked at how their supervisors reversed decisions on substandard quality and concluded the new quality program was a joke and a waste of money. The inability to reconcile the handling of the quality problems with their delivery obligations led to the loss of the GM contract and the closure of the plant approximately 18 months after the display board was first unveiled.[23]

Employees are aware of such conflicting messages. Confusion, frustration, sarcasm, and eventually alienation are the natural consequences. When such inconsistencies are built into a change initiative and go undetected or unaddressed by the change leader, cynicism about the change increases, and the change process falters. Kerr's well-known paper, "On the Folly of Rewarding A, While Hoping for B," explores many of the issues around measurement and the production of unintended consequences.[24]

When establishing such measures, remember to keep your eye on the end goal. If the end goal is cooperation and collaboration, avoid rewarding "A" (incentives for individually oriented, competitive behavior) if you are hoping to motivate "B" (incentives to promote collaborate, cooperate behavior). One common cause of such disconnects is related to what is rewarded by the legacy systems versus what is being promoted by the change initiative. Make sure the actions being nurtured through challenging but achievable goals in the short term will help you to get to your intermediate and long-term objectives.

5. Ensure Accurate Data

Employees, customers, and others are likely to supply accurate and timely data when they trust the measurement system and believe that data will not be used to harm them. Excessive rewards for success, undue sanctions for missed targets, or a very stressful work environment can lead to flawed information from carefully designed sets of measures.[25] These pressures create incentives for individuals to report inaccurately or to shade the reality of the situation. To ensure accurate and timely data from the measurement system, those supplying the data need to trust who it is going to and believe that it is their responsibility to comply fully and honestly. Keep pressure at reasonable levels and avoid excessive rewards for success or excessive consequences for not achieving targets.

6. Match the Precision of the Measure With the Ability to Measure

A measurement motto might read, "Better to be approximately right than precisely wrong!" Change leaders need to match the measures to the environment. If the change is significant, clearly structured, and predictable, leaders can devote time and resources to developing precise, sophisticated measures. However, if the change environment is turbulent and ambiguous, approximate measures are more appropriate.[26] Change agents need to make their choices based upon (a) how quickly they need the information, (b) how accurate the information needs to be, and (c) how much it will cost. Information economics point to the fact that designing the needed information for a change initiative inevitably involves trade-offs among these three components.[27]

The general rule of thumb is to keep the measures as simple and understandable as possible, and make sure that they attend to the important elements of the change in a balanced way. Table 10.1 looks at the nature of the change context and considers what types of measures will be appropriate.

Regardless of the measures chosen, change leaders need to be seen as "walking the talk." When leaders treat the measures as relevant and appropriate, employees will see that they are serious about what they are espousing. Use sound communication practices when dealing with questions related to what to measure, who to engage in discussions about measurement and control, how to

Table 10.1 The Change Context and the Choice of Measures		
Change Context	**Choose More Precise, Explicit, Goal-Focused Measures**	**Choose More Approximate Measures, Focus on Vision and Milestones, and Learn as You Go**
When complexity and ambiguity are:	Low	High
When time to completion is:	Short	Long

deploy the measures, and how to interpret and use the data effectively to manage the change. Change leaders' behaviors that reinforce perceptions of the fairness and appropriateness of the measures and instill confidence in their proper application are very important in legitimizing measurement as a powerful tool in the change process.[28]

MEASUREMENT SYSTEMS AND CHANGE MANAGEMENT

Robert Simon, an expert in the area of managerial measurement systems (also called management control systems), believes that managers focus too much on traditional diagnostic control systems developed from management accounting. He argues that managers need to think about four types of control levers as constituting the internal control systems when considering change. That is why strategy lies at the center of his model, because what one attempts to do needs to consider the influence of all four of these levers.[29]

- **Interactive controls systems**—the systems that sense environmental changes crucial to the organization's strategic concerns. For example, this would be market intelligence data that helps firms better understand and anticipate competitor actions.

- **Boundary systems**—the systems that set the limits of authority and action and determine acceptable and unacceptable behavior. For example, these would be limits to spending authority placed on managerial levels. These focus on what is unacceptable and identify both what is prohibited and what is sanctioned.

- **Belief systems**—the fundamental values and beliefs of organizational employees that underpin the culture and influence organizational decisions. For example, these are the stated organizational values that often accompany the vision and mission.

- **Diagnostic and steering controls systems**—the traditional managerial control systems that focus on key performance variables. For example, these would be sales data based on changed selling efforts.

Each of these systems can help in implementing change, but they serve different purposes depending upon where you are in the change process. *Interactive control systems* help sensitize change leaders to environmental shifts and strategic uncertainties and the relevance of these on the framing of the change initiative. This will allow them to modify change plans in the face of environmental factors and tend to play the biggest role when dealing with issues related to assessing the need for change and vision for the change.

Understanding the organization's *boundary system* means change leaders know what sorts of actions are appropriate and which are viewed as inappropriate or off limits. The firm's rules or boundaries need be respected and place limits on what actions are appropriate. If it is believed that such boundaries need to be questioned, change leaders can discuss and debate them explicitly, but they need to do so in an ethical and transparent manner.

An understanding of the *organization's belief system* informs leaders about the culture and how beliefs and values influence action. This allows change leaders to frame initiatives in ways that are aligned with the core beliefs and the organizations, and the higher-order values of individuals, and use this alignment to help motivate desired actions and overcome resistance to change. Data in this area comes from direct experience with others in the organization, employee surveys, and a systematic evaluation of past decisions, practices, and behaviors. As in the case of boundary systems, change leaders may wish to address the need to modify those beliefs as part of the change, but should again approach the matter in an ethical and transparent manner. Otherwise they risk being accused of misleading people and acting inappropriately. This will destroy trust in them and the initiative.

Finally, a well-developed *diagnostic and steering control system* helps change agents understand and track critical performance variables and milestones, and modify their approach to encourage desired behaviors and outcomes while discouraging dysfunctional ones. These are the steering controls and metrics they use to help them navigate their way on the change journey. As you can see, these controls and their related measures address the determination of the nature of the desired change, how it will be framed, and how progress will be monitored and assessed along the way (see Figure 10.2).

Table 10.2 sets out the different elements of the control system and relates them to the measures used at different stages of the change process. As the change progresses from initial planning to wrap-up and review, the control challenges and measurement issues also shift. The key is to align the controls and measures to the challenges posed at each stage of the change and prepare for the next. This helps to ensure that change leaders have the information and guidance they need to assess matters, make decisions, and manage their way forward.[30]

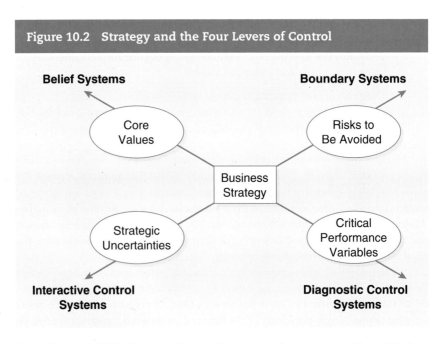

Figure 10.2   Strategy and the Four Levels of Control

Belief Systems

Core Values

Boundary Systems

Risks to Be Avoided

Business Strategy

Strategic Uncertainties

Critical Performance Variables

Interactive Control Systems

Diagnostic Control Systems

Source: Simons, R. (1995, March-April). Control in the age of empowerment. *Harvard Business Review,* 85.

Table 10.2 Control Systems, Measures, and the Stage of the Change

	Controls When Designing and Planning the Change	Controls in Beginning Stages of the Change Project	Controls in Middle Stages of the Change Project	Controls Toward the End of the Change Project
Interactive Controls (Environmental scanning; assessing possible paths and targets)	Environmental assessment; assess strengths, weaknesses, opportunities, and threats (SWOT); consider possibilities. Test the viability of existing vision, mission, and strategy given the environmental situation, and assess the need for change.	Affirm that the change project is aligned with environmental trends. Assess how to align the organization to increase the chances of the change's success and assess what specifically needs to change.	Ongoing monitoring. Confirm that environmental assessment continues to support the change.	Obtain feedback regarding the success of change initiative relative to the environmental factors. Ongoing environmental scanning and assessment of organizational strengths, weaknesses, opportunities, and threats (SWOT).
Boundary System (What behaviors are *not* OK?)	Limit the change options to those within the boundary conditions. Test the limits of what is acceptable. If boundary conditions represent issues or challenges that need discussing, bring them forward and assess need for new boundaries.	Go/no go guidance as to appropriateness of actions.	Go/no-go guidance as to appropriateness of actions. Reassess risks. Reestablish boundaries if needed. Test new boundaries where appropriate.	Reevaluate the boundary limits.
Belief System (What are our beliefs and values? What is our purpose?)	Assess congruence between core values of the firm, its mission, and the purpose of the change project. Communicate how the change relates to the core values and mission. Consider implications if change involves modifications of the belief system and how to facilitate the change.	Congruence assessment. Appeal to fundamental beliefs to overcome resistance or address need for change in those beliefs.	Congruence assessment. Reaffirm core values throughout the change project and/or assess progress in the needed modifications to the belief system.	Congruence assessment. Reassess and potentially reaffirm the core values and mission based on learning during the change project.
Diagnostic and Steering Controls (Focusing resources on targets; measuring progress; taking corrective action and learning as we go)	Assess the impact of existing controls on the change project. Consider what diagnostic systems will need to be developed and/or altered to provide guidance for the change.	Develop milestones, diagnostic measures, and steering controls for the change initiative. Develop tactics to alter control systems as needed.	Monitor progress on an ongoing basis and celebrate the achievement of milestones. Assess whether systems and processes are working as they should. Modify milestones and measures as needed.	Determine when the project has been completed. Confirm that new systems, processes, and behaviors established by the change are working appropriately. Evaluate project and pursue learning on how to improve the change process.

Data Used as Guides During Design and Early Stages of the Change Project

At the beginning of a major change, mission, and vision (i.e., belief systems), interactive control systems (e.g., environmental assessments), and boundary systems (risks to be avoided) play particularly important roles in clarifying the overall direction, as options and potential courses of action are explored. Data from primary and secondary research, exploratory discussions, internal organizational assessments, and initial experimentation are helpful at this stage because they allow projects and alternatives to be considered in a grounded manner. The organization's readiness for change (discussed in Chapter 4) can be assessed and steps taken to enhance readiness. Information from multiple sources is used to sort out options, assess what should be done next, and make an initial go/no-go decision on whether to proceed in the development of the initiative.

In the early stages, change leaders need to have systems that will identify who to talk to and who will tell them what they need to hear, not what they want to hear. Enthusiasm and commitment on the part of change leaders are beneficial to the change but can create serious blind spots if not tempered by the reality checks that control systems can provide. As go/no-go decisions are made, change agents need to develop and refine the directional and steering control measures and specify important milestones. Project planning tools, such as the critical path method, can play a useful role (see Chapter 9).

Data Used as Guides in the Middle of the Change Project

Indicators that define the overall purpose, direction, boundary conditions (what actions are acceptable and unacceptable) for the change, and core values and beliefs are still important in clarifying and framing what change is intended. However, diagnostic and steering controls (e.g., budgets and variance reports, project and activity schedules, and tracking of content from e-mails, phone conversations, and tracking of social media feed, if its use and content are relevant to the change) play an increasingly important role in the middle of the change project. At this point, change leaders want to be able to track and receive timely and accurate feedback on progress and people's reactions to what is going on. Change leaders need to recognize whether the people's reactions are leading or lagging the desired outcomes at that stage of the change process. As in the example of CPS discussed earlier in this chapter, customer satisfaction was a lead indicator of an improved sales climate, while repeat sales and profitability were lag indicators of the improved situation. If this had not been recognized, initiatives undertaken to improve customer satisfaction may have been discontinued because there was no immediate improvement in sales.

Milestones and road markers need to be developed through project planning and goal- and objective-setting activities. These markers can then be used to track progress and reinforce the initiative of others by recognizing their achievement. For example, if a firm were implementing a new performance management system, the completion and sign off on the design of the system, the completion of a training schedule, the achievement of needed levels of understanding and acceptance of the system (as assessed by measures of comprehension and satisfaction with the system), and the completion of the first cycle of performance reviews (with system evaluation data from those using the system) are possible road markers.

At important milestones, go/no-go controls once again enter the picture, with conscious decisions made about refinements to the change initiative.

Change leaders need to make decisions about the appropriateness and desirability of proceeding to the next stage. If milestones are not being achieved, change leaders need to consider what sorts of actions, if any, should be undertaken or they may need to revisit the timeline or refine the measures used to track progress. In that respect, change leaders also need to consider how measures can help them think about contingencies and adapt to unforeseen situations.

Data Used as Guides Toward the End of the Change Project

As the end of a planned change approaches, diagnostic and steering measures are replaced by concrete outcome measures. What was accomplished and what has been the impact? How do the results compare with what change agents expected at the beginning? What can be learned from the change experience? Change leaders need to capture the observations and insights from those who have been involved in the change, as it will help them prepare for future initiatives.

Toolkit Exercise 10.3 asks you to apply Simon's four levers of control model to a change initiative.

OTHER MEASUREMENT TOOLS

Four tools that can assist in planning, deploying, and managing change are discussed in the next section. These are the strategy map, the balanced scorecard, the risk exposure calculator, and the DICE model. They can enhance internal consistency and alignment and aid in assessing risk.

Strategy Maps

Once change leaders have framed their vision and strategy for the change, they will need to be able to communicate the end state and the action paths that will get them there. When complex changes are being pursued, change agents may find a visual representation of those end states and the action paths to be useful. This can be undertaken to help others understand what the change is attempting to accomplish and how actions in one area will influence outcomes in another. Further, in can be used to help change agents set out and test their assumptions concerning what they believe needs to be undertaken and aligned, in order to achieve the desired ends.

The tool developed by Robert Kaplan and David Norton called a **strategy map** can assist change agents in this regard.[31] As can be seen from Figure 10.3, financial outcomes are viewed as driven by customer results, and by contributions that come directly from internal systems and processes in the form of efficiencies. The customer results are viewed as coming from the performance of internal systems and processes, which in turn rest on the nature and quality of the organization's resources (human, informational, and capital).[32]

Once the change vision and strategy are defined in a for-profit organization, Kaplan and Norton recommend starting with financial goals and objectives of the change (the **financial perspective**) and then setting out the objectives, initiatives, and paths needed throughout the organization to generate those outcomes.

- If the vision for change is achieved, how will it look from the perspective of the *financial* results achieved?
- To accomplish these financial outcomes, what initiatives have to be undertaken from a **customer perspective** to deliver on the value

proposition in ways that generate the desired financial results? In addition, will the change produce direct contributions to the bottom line from the internal business processes, in the form of efficiency improvements?

- To accomplish these customer outcomes and/or generate contributions directly to the financial outcomes through efficiencies, what changes must be tackled from an **internal business process perspective**?

- Finally, to attain those internal process goals and objectives, what changes must be undertaken from a **learning and growth** perspective to increase the organization's capacity to do what is needed with the internal processes and customers? The learning and growth perspective embodies people, information, and organizational capital (e.g., culture, intellectual property, leadership, internal alignment, and teamwork).

For not-for-profit organizations, many advocates for the strategy map recommend placing the *customer perspective* at the top of the model (some have relabeled it as the stakeholder perspective) since this is the reason for the organization's existence. Some place the financial perspective parallel with the customer or stakeholder perspective, while others place it below learning and growth or elsewhere. Others have added levels or changed labels on the strategy map.[33] However, the goal remains the same: develop a coherent picture that helps people understand how you've aligned your change strategy with the organization's purpose so it generates the desired outcomes. It is all about translating the change vision into a visual representation of the action plan that is designed to support that change vision; communicating those actions and the change vision to key constituents so that they will better understand the change initiative and the underlying assumptions; testing assumptions so that modifications can be made in a timely manner; and implementing, learning and refining as you go.

The assumption underlying strategy maps in for-profit organizations is that financial outcomes are the end goals that they are striving for and that other objectives within the change program should be aligned to produce and support those desired outcomes. If particular activities and the objectives don't support the changes, they should be seriously questioned and either dropped or reduced in importance. Each of the change initiatives identified by the strategy map will need to be managed as to goals and objectives, success measures, timelines, resource requirements, and an action plan. These, in turn, need to be integrated with the other change initiatives that are embodied in the strategy map.

When properly deployed, strategy maps provide change leaders with a powerful organizing and communication tool.[34] This visualization helps people understand what is being proposed and why. It clarifies why certain actions are important and how they contribute to other outcomes that are critical to achieving the end goals of the change (i.e., cause–effect relationships). It helps people focus and align their efforts and appropriately measure and report progress. It can assist change leaders to identify gaps in their logic, including missing objectives and measures. When Mobil used strategy maps, it helped them to identify gaps in the plans that had been developed for one of their business units. Objectives and metrics were missing for dealers—a critical component for a strategy map focused on selling more gasoline.[35]

To give you a concrete example of how a strategy map can be used to help, one is set out in Figure 10.4. It shows the vision and mission for Control

Figure 10.3   Generic Strategy Map

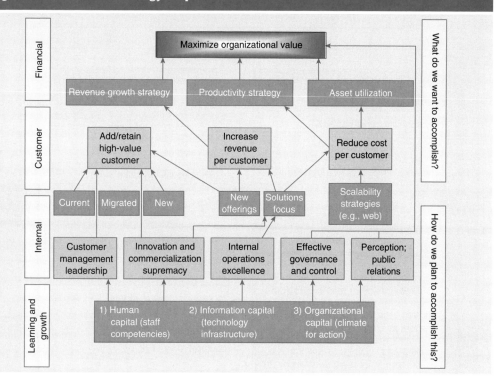

Source: From Armitage, H. M., & Scholey, C. (2007). Using strategy maps to drive performance. CMA *Management, 80*(9), 24. The figure sets out Kaplan and Norton's model discussed earlier in the chapter.

Figure 10.4   Strategy Map for Control Production Systems

Mission for CPS:

Design, manufacture, service, and support industry-leading production control systems that enable CPS to enhance the efficiency and effectiveness of its production processes beyond what is possible through other means. Customer loyalty and long-term profitability are built on a foundation of excellence in these areas.

Vision for the Change in Customer Orientation:

Our valued industrial partners will experience service and performance that delight. We will exceed all our competitors' standards through superbly designed and expertly installed and supported control equipment and software.

We will support our customers through technically competent account representatives who are focused on the challenges and needs of specific industries and customers and committed to ensuring that their success is significantly enhanced through the value derived from the production control systems. Our product leadership combined with superb customer care and excellent technical support will result in highly loyal and committed customers who look to CPS for all their more sophisticated control system needs.

(Continued)

Figure 10.4 (Continued)

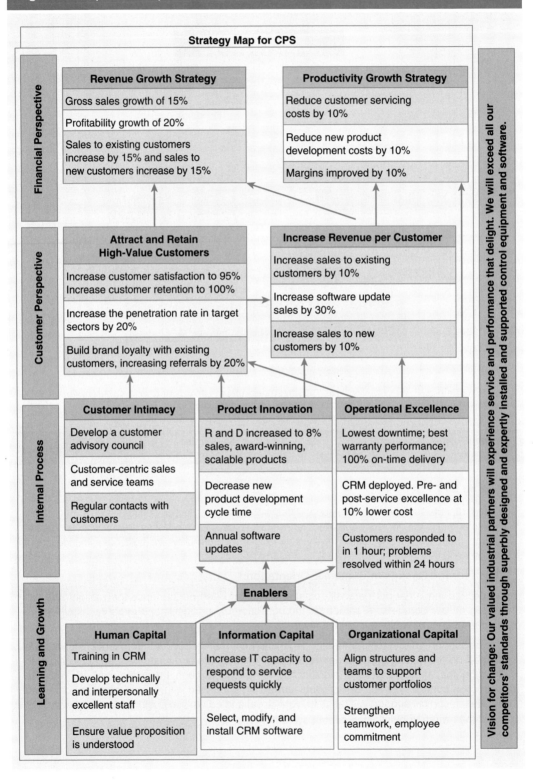

Strategy Map for CPS

Financial Perspective

Revenue Growth Strategy

Gross sales growth of 15%

Profitability growth of 20%

Sales to existing customers increase by 15% and sales to new customers increase by 15%

Productivity Growth Strategy

Reduce customer servicing costs by 10%

Reduce new product development costs by 10%

Margins improved by 10%

Customer Perspective

Attract and Retain High-Value Customers

Increase customer satisfaction to 95% Increase customer retention to 100%

Increase the penetration rate in target sectors by 20%

Build brand loyalty with existing customers, increasing referrals by 20%

Increase Revenue per Customer

Increase sales to existing customers by 10%

Increase software update sales by 30%

Increase sales to new customers by 10%

Internal Process

Customer Intimacy

Develop a customer advisory council

Customer-centric sales and service teams

Regular contacts with customers

Product Innovation

R and D increased to 8% sales, award-winning, scalable products

Decrease new product development cycle time

Annual software updates

Operational Excellence

Lowest downtime; best warranty performance; 100% on-time delivery

CRM deployed. Pre- and post-service excellence at 10% lower cost

Customers responded to in 1 hour; problems resolved within 24 hours

Enablers

Learning and Growth

Human Capital

Training in CRM

Develop technically and interpersonally excellent staff

Ensure value proposition is understood

Information Capital

Increase IT capacity to respond to service requests quickly

Select, modify, and install CRM software

Organizational Capital

Align structures and teams to support customer portfolios

Strengthen teamwork, employee commitment

Vision for change: Our valued industrial partners will experience service and performance that delight. We will exceed all our competitors' standards through superbly designed and expertly installed and supported control equipment and software.

Production Systems, Inc. (discussed earlier in this chapter). Then it shows the specific measures used in each category.

The Balanced Scorecard

While the strategy map links capabilities, change strategies, and outcomes, the **balanced scorecard** integrates measures into a relatively simple way of tracking the critical success factors. Kaplan and Norton argue that four categories of goals and measurement data need to be highlighted in a balanced scorecard: financial, a company's relationship with its customers, its *internal business process*, and its *learning and growth*. In doing so, management can achieve a balanced, integrated, and aligned perspective concerning what needs to be done to produce the desired strategic outcomes.[36]

Among these four indicators, some will lead while others will lag. For example, improvements in service levels, such as the response time to a customer's inquiry, could be a lead indicator of improvements in customer satisfaction. However, this may not immediately translate into new sales and increased profitability.

Figure 10.5 Generic Balanced Scorecard for Change

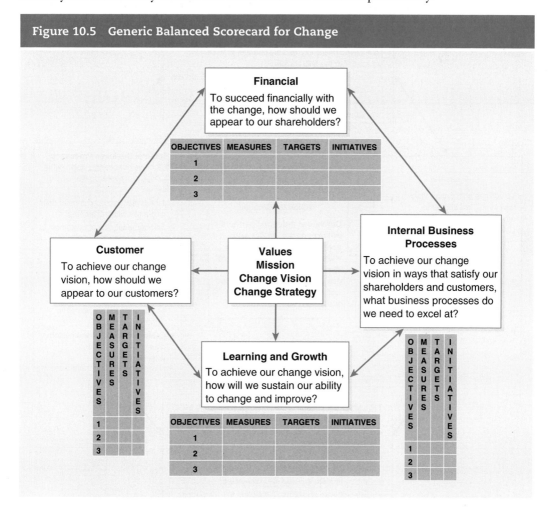

Source: Adapted from Kaplan, R. S., & Norton, D. P. (1996). Using the balanced scorecard as a strategic management system. *Harvard Business Review, 74*(1), 76.

Improvements in such measures will often be lag indicators of improvements in service levels because of the length of the purchase cycle. The balanced scorecard recognizes that not all effects are immediate. By setting out assumptions concerning what leads to what, it makes it easier for the change leader to test assumptions, track progress, and make appropriate alternations as necessary.

When developing a balanced scorecard for an internal change initiative, remember that the relevant customers may be employees in other departments of the organization, rather than the external customers of the firm. Kaplan and Norton argue that the use of multiple measures ensure a more balanced perspective on what a successful change will require. The likelihood that multiple measures will inadvertently mislead change leaders about what a successful change will require is much less than if they rely on a single indicator. Figure 10.5 outlines a generic balanced scorecard for a change project. Figure 10.6 outlines the balanced scorecard for Control Production Systems.

Figure 10.6   Balanced Scorecard for CPS

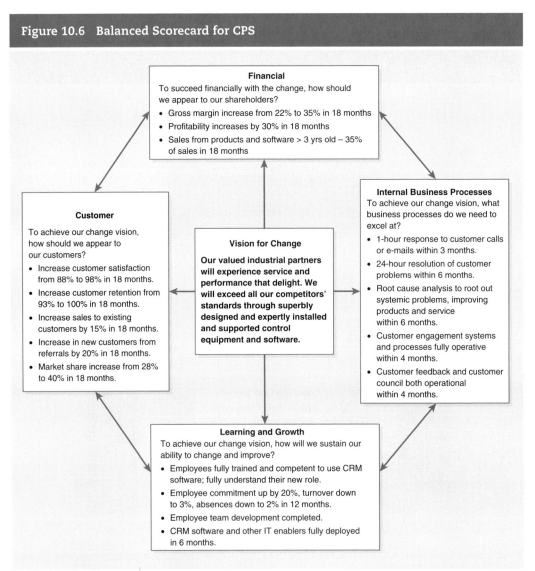

Financial
To succeed financially with the change, how should we appear to our shareholders?
- Gross margin increase from 22% to 35% in 18 months
- Profitability increases by 30% in 18 months
- Sales from products and software > 3 yrs old – 35% of sales in 18 months

Customer
To achieve our change vision, how should we appear to our customers?
- Increase customer satisfaction from 88% to 98% in 18 months.
- Increase customer retention from 93% to 100% in 18 months.
- Increase sales to existing customers by 15% in 18 months.
- Increase in new customers from referrals by 20% in 18 months.
- Market share increase from 28% to 40% in 18 months.

Vision for Change
Our valued industrial partners will experience service and performance that delight. We will exceed all our competitors' standards through superbly designed and expertly installed and supported control equipment and software.

Internal Business Processes
To achieve our change vision, what business processes do we need to excel at?
- 1-hour response to customer calls or e-mails within 3 months.
- 24-hour resolution of customer problems within 6 months.
- Root cause analysis to root out systemic problems, improving products and service within 6 months.
- Customer engagement systems and processes fully operative within 4 months.
- Customer feedback and customer council both operational within 4 months.

Learning and Growth
To achieve our change vision, how will we sustain our ability to change and improve?
- Employees fully trained and competent to use CRM software; fully understand their new role.
- Employee commitment up by 20%, turnover down to 3%, absences down to 2% in 12 months.
- Employee team development completed.
- CRM software and other IT enablers fully deployed in 6 months.

Toolkit Exercise 10.4 asks you to construct a strategy map and balanced scorecard for an organization that you know and a change you have some knowledge of. Remember that customers can be internal or external to the firm.

Risk Exposure Calculator

Robert Simon has developed a **risk exposure calculator** for use in assessing the level of risk associated with a company's actions.[37] Simon argues that risk is related to the rate of growth of the company, its culture, and how information and data are managed. The tool focuses primarily on internal rather than external environmental risks. Although it was designed for use on the overall organization, it has been modified to assess the risk exposure related to a particular change initiative as well as maintaining the status quo.

The first three risk drivers are grouped under **change pressure**. When the change leader is (a) under significant pressure to produce, (b) there is a great deal of ambiguity, or (c) employees are inexperienced in change, then the risks associated with the change initiative will be higher than if the pressures being experienced were lower for one or more of these three factors.

Change culture identifies the second set of risk drivers. If (a) the culture pushes risk-taking, (b) executives resist hearing bad news, or (c) there is internal competition, then risks will be further elevated.

The final set of risk drivers is grouped under **information management**. When (a) the change situation is complex and fast changing, (b) there are gaps in the diagnostic data that change measures, and (c) decision making regarding change is decentralized, then risks will rise once again. These nine risk factors are cumulative in nature. The overall level of change risk rises as the total number of significant risk factors rises.

If Simon's risk calculator had been applied to AIG's mortgage arm prior to the economic meltdown in 2007–2008, or Lehman Brothers by those knowledgeable about their internal operations, then scores indicating extreme risk in virtually all nine areas would have been recorded. The environments these organizations were operating in were complex, fast moving, and highly ambiguous. Many senior managers lacked knowledge and experience with the high-risk products and services they were responsible for: risk-taking and competition were pushed to the extreme by subordinates, and the bearers of concern and bad news put themselves at risk of being fired.

There are also dangers for the organization when risk levels get too low. Little positive change will occur if there is no pressure for change, little cultural support for risk taking, and if people perceive a very stable and predictable environment. If perceptions of low risk are sustained for a long periods of time, the capacity of the organization to be flexible and adapt will tend to atrophy. When low-risk organizational members are then faced with change that can no longer be ignored, their ability to respond will be compromised.

There is no optimal risk score that fits all organizations. Optimal risk scores vary, depending on the nature of the environment, the upside and downside consequences of risk-taking, and the ability to take steps to alleviate risks. The risk appetites of change leaders should prudently reflect the needs and opportunities for innovation and change balanced by the needs for appropriate levels of caution and oversight. Of course, the organization's resources and capabilities will also determine the degree of risk that is sustainable and desirable.

Change leaders can take advantage of the risk calculator by using the information from it to make the risks manageable during the planning and deployment stages. For example, ambiguity can be reduced by emphasizing the change vision or by creating explicit milestones. Risks related to inexperience can be moderated by adding experienced managers to the change team. Further, it can be used to monitor risk levels as the change proceeds, with steps taken along the way to moderate levels up or down, depending on the situation.

Toolkit Exercise 10.5 sets out a risk calculator based on Simon's work and allows you to calculate a risk score indicating whether a project is in a safety zone or not.

The DICE Model

A process-oriented approach to assessing and managing the risks associated with change projects is offered by Sirkin, Keenan, and Jackson. Based upon empirical data, they have developed a four-factor model for predicting the success of a change initiative. They refer to this as the **DICE framework**.[38]

Duration asks about how frequently the change project is formally reviewed. If the frequency of formal review is less than every two months, it receives a score of 1. A score of 2 is awarded when the frequency is from two to four months; a 3 for a frequency of between four and eight months; and a 4 for time intervals in excess of eight months. The message is that the risk of failure increases as the time between formal reviews rises. In other words, "out of sight, out of mind" is a bad idea when it comes to assessing and guiding major changes. Providing timely guidance and assistance requires a rigorous and systematic approach to managing the change—something that won't happen with a "how's it going → just fine" form of cursory assessment.

Integrity asks about the team leader's skills and credibility, and the skills, motivation, and focus of members of the change team. A score of 1 is recorded if the team leader has the skills needed and the respect of coworkers, if the team members have the skills and motivation to complete the project on time, and if at least 50% of the team members' time has been assigned to the initiative. If the change team and leader are lacking on all dimensions, a score of 4 is recorded. If the factors lie somewhere in between, scores of 2 or 3 are allocated.

Commitment *is a two-stage measure.* The first part assesses the commitment of senior management. If the words and deeds of senior managers regularly reinforce the need for change and the importance of the initiative, a score of 1 is given. If senior managers are fairly neutral, scores of 2 or 3 are recorded. When senior managers are perceived to be less than supportive, a score of 4 is applied.

Second, the employee or "local level" commitment is evaluated. If employees are very supportive, a score of 1 is given. If they are willing but not overly eager, the score shifts to 2. As reluctance builds, scores shift to 3 and 4.

Effort is the final factor in the DICE model and refers to the level of increased effort that employees must make to implement the change. If the incremental effort is less than 10%, it is given a score of 1. Incremental effort of 10% to 20% raises the score to 2. At 20% to 40%, the score moves to 3, while additional effort in excess of 40% raises the score to 4.

The overall DICE score is calculated in the following fashion: The Integrity and Senior Management Commitment scores are weighted more heavily in the model, with each being multiplied by 2. This is because the scores on these factors have been found to be more significant drivers of risk. Then the scores of all factors are added together.

Overall Dice Score = Duration + (2 X Integrity of Performance) + (2 X Senior Management Commitment) + Local Level Commitment + Effort	7–14: high likelihood of success
	15–17: worry zone
The research shows the following about scores:	17+: extremely risky, woe zone, with higher than 19 very unlikely to succeed

This model is useful in assessing risk and also in pointing to concrete things that can be done to make the risks manageable during the planning and deployment phases. For example, risks can be reduced by having more frequent formal project reviews and by the staffing of change initiatives with competent and credible team leaders and members. Likewise, increasing local and senior-level commitment and allocating sufficient time to change leaders and others working on the initiative will also help in reducing risks.

Toolkit Exercise 10.6 asks you to apply the DICE model to a change you are familiar with.

SUMMARY

Care taken in the selection of measures and control processes helps clarify what the change is about and focuses energy and effort. It also saves change agents a great deal of time later on because it enhances the efficiency and effectiveness of the change process, provides an early warning system of problems, and thus leads to faster attention to appropriate midcourse corrections. It also forces change leaders to be honest with themselves and others about what will be accomplished and what it will take to bring these things to reality. There is an old management adage that makes a lot of sense: It is far better to under promise and over deliver than to overpromise and under deliver.

The careful selection and use of data can be used to enhance ownership of the change through how the measures are selected (i.e., who participates in their selection) and through ensuring that those involved receive the credit for what is accomplished. See **Toolkit Exercise 10.1** for critical thinking questions for this chapter.

KEY TERMS

Measurement and control systems—developed to focus, monitor, and manage what is going on in the organization.

Simon's Four Management Control Systems

Interactive control—the systems that sense environmental changes crucial to the organization's strategic concerns, for example, market intelligence that will determine competitor actions.

Boundary systems—the systems that set the limits of authority and action and determine acceptable and unacceptable behavior, for example, limits to spending authority placed on managerial levels. These tend to focus on what is unacceptable and identify not only what is prohibited but also the sanction.

Belief systems—the structure of fundamental values that underpin organizational decisions, for example, the stated organizational values that often accompany the vision and mission.

Diagnostic and steering controls—the traditional managerial control systems that focus on key performance variables, for example, sales data responding to changed selling efforts.

Strategy map—the visualization of how the vision and strategy can be systematically brought to fruition. Strategy Maps begin by defining the vision and strategy for change.

Financial perspective—identifies the financial outcomes that the change will give rise to and define the paths that will produce those outcomes.

Customer perspective—focuses on service and customer-oriented goals to achieve financial objectives

Internal business process perspective—focuses on operational and process efficiencies that help accomplish financial goals and objectives.

Learning and growth perspectives—focuses on the internal staffing, training and development needed to allow staff to reach objectives across the map. This is defined as the human capital component. It also addresses the information capital component (the information systems related elements) and organizational capital components (e.g., structures).

Balanced scorecard—an integrated set of measures built around the mission, vision, and strategy. There are four measures: the financial perspective, customer perspective, internal business process perspective, and learning and growth perspective. As such, they provide a balanced perspective on what is required to enact the strategy.

Risk exposure calculator—an assessment tool developed by Robert Simon that considers the

impact that nine specific factors, noted below, may have on the risk levels faced by a firm.

    A. Change pressure—when change leaders feel significant pressure to produce and accomplish the change, when there are high levels of ambiguity, and the leaders have little experience with change, risk is increased.

    B. Change culture—when the rewards for risk taking are high, when senior executives resist hearing bad news, and when there is internal competition between units, risk is increased.

    C. Information management—necessary when the situation is complex and fast changing, when gaps in diagnosis exist, and if decision making is decentralized, risk is increased.

DICE framework—a process-oriented approach to assessing and managing the risks associated with change projects.

    A. Duration—measures how frequently the change project is formally reviewed. As duration increases, risk increases.

    B. Integrity—of performance is a two-part measure. The first part asks about the team leader's skills and credibility and the second part asks about the skills, motivation, and focus of members of the change team. As skills, credibility, and motivation decrease, risk levels increase.

    C. Commitment is a two-stage measure—The first part assesses senior management commitment. The second part evaluates employee or "local level" commitment. As commitment decreases, risk levels increase.

    D. Effort—measures the level of increased exertion that employees must make to implement the change. As the amount of incremental effort increases beyond 10%, risk levels increase.

CHECKLIST: CREATING A BALANCED SCORECARD

1. State the mission, vision, and strategy for the change.

2. Consider the mission, vision, and strategy of the organization:

   - Is the proposed change consistent with these?
   - If not, what needs to be done with the change or the existing mission, vision, and strategy to bring them into line?

3. Complete the financial component of the scorecard by answering the following questions:

   - If you succeed with the change vision, how will it appear to the shareholders or those responsible for funding the change?
   - How will you know (objectives and metrics)?
   - Which are leading indicators and which are lagging indicators?

4. Complete the customer component of the scorecard by answering the following questions:

   - If you succeed with the change, how will it appear to your customers?
   - How will you know (objectives and metrics)?
   - What are the leading and lagging indicators?

5. Complete the internal business processes component of the scorecard by answering the following questions:

   - If you succeed with the change, how will it appear in your business processes?
   - How will you know (objectives and metrics)?
   - What are the leading and lagging indicators here?

6. Complete the learning and growth component of the scorecard by answering the following questions:

   - If you succeed with the change, how will it appear to your employees and demonstrate itself in their actions?
   - What about the information and organizational capital?
   - How will you and they know (objectives and metrics)?
   - What are the leading and lagging indicators here?

7. Seek feedback from trusted colleagues on the scorecard you've developed. Does it help them to understand the change initiative you have in mind, key data that will indicate progress, and what will need to be done to achieve the desired outcomes?

END-OF-CHAPTER EXERCISES

TOOLKIT EXERCISE 10.1

Critical Thinking Questions

The URLs for the videos listed below can be found in two places. The first spot is next to the exercise and the second spot is on the website at **study.sagepub.com/cawsey4e.**

1. The Beauty of Data Visualization—18:17 minutes

    https://www.bing.com/videos/search?q=the+beauty+of+data+visualization&docid=608019685 193287796&mid=FA748A7A9F54F6F67357FA748A7A9F54F6F67357&view=detail&FORM=VIRE

    This is a TED Talk by David McCandless on the value of visualizing data in order to draw new meaning and insights from complex data in order to better design, innovate, make better decisions, and so on. Can be a useful video prior to discussing the development of information and metrics to help frame change, change views, and guide change initiatives.

    *   Give an example of how the reframing of data might bolster the change process in each of the four stages.

    *   How might the data presented in the video prompt change? Explain.

2. Susan Colantuono: The Career Advice You Probably Didn't Get—13:57 minutes

    https://www.youtube.com/watch?v=JFQLvbVJVMg

    *   How do the skills Colantuono talks about matter to measuring and implementing change?

    *   How should organizational leaders imbed the skills that Colantuono talks about into the organization in order to create continuous change?

*Please see **study.sagepub.com/cawsey4e** for access to video and a downloadable template of this exercise.*

TOOLKIT EXERCISE 10.2

Reflecting on the Impact of Measures and Control Processes on Change

Think of a change initiative that you are familiar with.

1. What measures and control processes were employed in tracking and guiding the change initiative? Were they consistent with the vision and strategy of the change? Were they viewed as legitimate by those who would be using them?

2. How was the measurement information captured and fed back to those who needed to use it? Was it a user-friendly process, and did the information arrive in a useful and timely form?

3. Did the change managers consider how the measures might need to evolve over the life of the change initiative? How was this evolution managed? By whom?

4. Were steps taken to ensure that the measures used during the change would be put to proper use? Were there risks and potential consequences arising from their use that would need to be managed?

5. Were goals and milestones established to plot progress along the way and used to make midcourse corrections if needed? Were the smaller victories celebrated to reinforce the efforts of others when milestones were achieved?

6. What were the end-state measures that were developed for the change? Were they consistent with the vision and strategy? Were they viewed as legitimate by those who would be using them?

7. How was the end-state measurement information captured and fed back to those who would need to use it? Was it a user-friendly process?

8. Were steps taken to ensure that the measures would be put to proper use? Were there risks and potential consequences arising from their use that would need to be managed?

*Please see **study.sagepub.com/cawsey4e** for a downloadable template of this exercise.*

TOOLKIT EXERCISE 10.3

Application of Simon's Four Levers of Control Model

Consider a change you are familiar with.

1. Describe the control processes and measures that were used with the change (i.e., the belief, interactive, boundary, and diagnostic controls). When and how were they used, and what was their impact?

    a. During the earlier stages of the change initiative

    b. During the middle stages of the change initiative

    c. During the latter stages of the change initiative

2. Were there forbidden topics in the organization, such as questions related to strategy or core values? Were those limits appropriate and did anyone test those limits by raising controversial questions or concerns? Were small successes celebrated along the way?

3. What changes could have been made with the control processes and measures that would have assisted in advancing the interests of the change?

Please see **study.sagepub.com/cawsey4e** *for a downloadable template of this exercise.*

TOOLKIT EXERCISE 10.4

Aligning the Change With Systems and
Building the Balanced Scorecard for the Change

Think about a change you are familiar with.

1. State the mission, vision, and strategy for the change.

2. Consider the mission, vision, and strategy of the organization:

   - Is the proposed change consistent with these?

   - If not, what needs to be done with the change or the existing mission, vision, and strategy to bring them into line?

3. Financial component of scorecard: If you succeed with the change vision, how will it appear to the shareholders or those responsible for funding the change?

   How will you know (objectives and metrics)? Are some of these leading indicators while others are lagging indicators?

4. Customer component of scorecard: If you succeed with the change, how will it appear to your customers?

   How will you know (objectives and metrics)? Are there leading and lagging indicators here?

5. Internal business processes component of scorecard: If you succeed with the change, how will it appear in your business processes?

   How will you know (objectives and metrics)? Are there leading and lagging indicators here?

6. Learning and growth component of scorecard: If you succeed with the change, how will it appear to your employees and demonstrate itself in their actions?

   What about the information and organizational capital? How will you and they know (objectives and metrics)? Are there leading and lagging indicators here?

7. Lay out the scorecard you've designed for your change and seek feedback.

8. Show how the different components are connected to each other by developing a strategy map for the change in the space below.

Please see **study.sagepub.com/cawsey4e** for a downloadable template of this exercise.

TOOLKIT EXERCISE 10.5

Using the Risk Exposure Calculator

Consider a change initiative that you know is currently being considered for adoption and apply the risk exposure calculator to it.

				Score
Change Pressure	Pressure to produce Low　　　　High 1　2　3　4　5 Score:	Level of ambiguity Low　　　　High 1　2　3　4　5 Score:	Experience with change High*　　　Low 1　2　3　4　5 Score: *Note: High and Low anchors are reversed for this item.	Out of 15 ___
Change Culture	Degree to which individuals are rewarded for risk taking Low　　　　High 1　2　3　4　5 Score:	Degree to which executives resist hearing bad news Low　　　　High 1　2　3　4　5 Score:	Level of internal competition Low　　　　High 1　2　3　4　5 Score:	Out of 15 ___
Information Situation	Degree to which situation is complex and fast changing Low　　　　High 1　2　3　4　5 Score:	Level of gaps that exist in diagnostic measures Low　　　　High 1　2　3　4　5 Score:	Degree to which change decision making is decentralized Low　　　　High 1　2　3　4　5 Score:	Out of 15 ___
Total Score =				

Using scoring criteria consistent with that developed by Simon:

- If your score is between 9 and 20, you are in the safety zone.

- Between 21 and 34, you are in the cautionary zone.

- Between 35 to 45, you are in a danger zone.

1. Does the organization have an appropriate level of risk taking given the nature of the business it is in? Does it play it too safe, about right, or does it take excessive risks?

2. Does the approach help you in thinking about risk and what factors may be contributing to the overall risk levels?

3. Do the findings help you to think about what can be done to make the levels of risk more manageable?

Source: Adapted from Simon, R. (1999). How risky is your company? *Harvard Business Review, 77*(3), 85–94.

*Please see **study.sagepub.com/cawsey4e** for a downloadable template of this exercise.*

TOOLKIT EXERCISE 10.6

Applying the DICE Model

Consider a change initiative that you know is currently being considered for adoption and apply the DICE model to it.

- Duration: How frequently is the project formally reviewed?

    a. Time between project reviews is less than 2 months—1 point

    b. Time between project reviews is 2–4 months—2 points

    c. Time between project reviews is 4–8 months—3 points

    d. Time between project reviews is more than 8 months—4 points

    Duration Score = _____

- Integrity: How capable is the project team leader? How capable and motivated are team members? Do they have the sufficient time to devote to the change?

    a. Leader is respected, team is capable and motivated, and members have sufficient time to commit to the project—1 point

    b. If leader or team is lacking on all these dimensions—4 points

    c. If leader and team are partially lacking on these dimensions—2 to 3 points

    Integrity of Performance Score: (Your Initial Score × 2) = _____

- Commitment of Senior Management: How committed is senior management to the project? Do they regularly communicate the reasons for the initiative and its importance? Do they convincingly communicate the message and their commitment? Is the commitment to the project shared by senior management? Have they committed sufficient resources to the project?

    a. If senior management clearly and consistently communicated the need for change and their support—1 point

    b. If senior management appears neutral—2 to 3 points

    c. If senior management is reluctant to support the change—4 points

    Senior Management Commitment Score: (Your Initial Score × 2) = _____

- Local Level Commitment: Do those employees most affected by the change understand the need and believe the change is needed? Are they enthusiastic and eager to get involved or concerned and resistant?

    a. If employees are eager to be engaged in the change initiative—1 point

    b. If they are willing but not overly keen—2 points

    c. If they are moderately to strongly reluctant to be engaged in the change—3 to 4 points

    Local Level Commitment Score = _____

- Effort: What incremental effort is required of employees to implement the change? Will it be added on to an already heavy workload? Have employees expressed strong resistance to additional demands on them in the past?

    a. If incremental effort is less than 10%—1 point

    b. If incremental effort is 10% to 20%—2 points

c. If incremental effort is 20% to 40%—3 points

d. If incremental effort is greater than 40%—4 points

Effort Score = _____

To calculate your overall DICE score: Add the scores from the above: _____

1. What score did the change project receive? Was it in the low-risk category (7 to 14), the worry zone (between 14 and 17), or the high-risk area (over 17)?

2. Do the findings help you to think about important sources of risk to the success of the project?

3. Do the findings help you to think about what can be done to make the levels of risk more manageable?

Source: Adapted from Sirkin, H. L., Keenan, P., & Jackson A. (2005, October). The hard side of change management. *Harvard Business Review, 91*(9), 108–118.

Please see **study.sagepub.com/cawsey4e** *for a downloadable template of this exercise.*

OMADA HEALTH: MAKING THE CASE FOR DIGITAL HEALTH

By Erin E. Sullivan, Research Director, PhD, and
Jessica L. Alpert, Researcher

Center for Primary Care, Harvard Medical School, Boston, MA

Adrian James and Sean Duffy's founded Omada Health (Omada) in 2011 with the initial goal of using digital therapeutics and behavioral health interventions for patients with prediabetes. The data supporting this approach was strong: in 2002, the Diabetes Prevention Program (DPP) randomized control study concluded that the most effective treatment for prediabetes is prevention and behavioral intervention. However, James and Duffy observed a problematic gap between a surplus of data that confirmed the efficacy of intensive behavioral health counseling in diabetes, and the 86 million individuals with prediabetes who have not yet completed a DPP type program. James and Duffy believed that Omada's digital approach to scaling a validated DPP program could resolve a critical need and increase access to DPP for patients with prediabetes.

PIONEERING DIGITAL THERAPEUTICS AND DIGITAL BEHAVIOR CHANGE

Although digital health often refers to health apps and products, James and Duffy were determined to design a service to guide participants through an interactive journey that was integrated into their everyday lives. As James asserted,

> The day that our participants see us as a health app is the day of obsolescence. In my smartphone I've got like 10 different health apps, many of which I never click on. We're saturated in this world of tracking. If you go out and ask someone, "How meaningful are these apps to you?," I think many would say that they are something they're curious about and will try, but that they are not really baked into their lives.

Above all, the core mission of the company was to empower people to take ownership over their health and to reduce their risk of disease. In keeping with this philosophy, they named their company, "Omada," the Greek word for "group," which was reflective of their desire to bring people together in a journey toward diabetes prevention.

Some of the access barriers associated with in-person DPP were the time and expense required to travel to and attend these sessions. James and Duffy sought to mitigate these challenges and also asked themselves how they could engage individuals in a way that was scalable. The Omada DPP approach was a 16-week digital behavioral intervention that featured four core elements: educational modules and an evidence-based curriculum; health coaches; peer support and networking groups; and tools and food and activity trackers, which included a cell-chip enabled scale that automatically transmitted daily weigh-in data to Omada's health coaches and data scientists.

When individuals qualified for and joined the program, they accessed Omada's platform using either its online web, or a smartphone interface. Omada's DPP was split into two distinct phases: Foundations and Focus.

- *Foundations*: For the first 16 weeks, participants participated in the

Foundations Phase. In this stage, participants completed weekly lessons designed to reinforce habits, communicated with their virtual group, led by a professional, full-time health coach. Additionally, participants privately worked with their coach to address individual challenges. In this phase, there were four four-week chapters covering nutrition and healthy eating, physical activity, managing environmental stressors and sleep. These chapters were aimed at reinforcing lifelong habits.

- *Focus*: After the Foundations Phase, participants entered the eight-month Focus Phase, during which they had continued access to their health coach, initial cohort, and weekly lessons. Participant groups were then merged into larger cohorts so that individuals could have access to a wider range of support and experiences.

USING DATA TO DRIVE HEALTHY OUTCOMES

Omada aimed to collect measures in a way that was simplistic and effortless for participants, but also maintained clinical integrity and monitored clinically meaningful outcomes while doing so. The digital scale was easy for patients to use and served as a program integrity safeguard given that health coaches and data scientists instantly knew whether or not participants were weighing in. Consequently, Omada data scientists and health coaches were able to closely monitor any spikes in weight and then determine if the observed weight gain was an outlier or a sign that further intervention and health coaching was required. The health coach served as the "human touch" between the data scientists and participants, helping the scientists better understand user patterns and the nuances of the large data set they collected.

To symbolically capture the dedication to outcomes and data, the Omada office featured a live map of patient weigh-ins from across the country. As of June 2017, the map amassed a cumulative total of 18 million weigh-ins. By thoughtfully collecting these measurements, the company increased compliance and therefore facilitated a more effective data collection process.

Consistent with their evidence-driven beginnings, Omada was paid by their clients based on their outcomes. James and Duffy believed that this outcomes-based pricing model demonstrated their commitment to delivering results for participants and a return on investment for their clients, namely self-insured employers and a small number of health plans. As part of the program, Omada kept clients up to date on process via real-time, de-identified, aggregate reports. Furthermore, Omada published outcomes data to demonstrate program replicability. One study indicated that after 16 weeks, Omada participants lost 4–5% of their body weight and kept most of the weight off years after completing the program, thereby preventing the progression from prediabetes to diabetes over time.

THE CHALLENGE IN GOING TO SCALE

In the summer of 2017, Omada was eagerly waiting for the Center for Medicare & Medicaid Services (CMS) to release the Medicare Physician Fee Schedule which would include the final rules for the Medicare Diabetes Prevention benefit. James and Duffy were hopeful for a favorable outcome, which would include telehealth and digital delivery of DPP programs. If CMS added these programs to the fee schedule, Omada planned to deliver their program to Medicare beneficiaries starting January 1, 2018. Ruminating on the possibilities, Duffy added that "it was an amazing moment because Medicare had the potential to influence private medical policies," which would provoke others to say, "If Medicare is doing it, why don't we?" Essentially, if Medicare started to pay for diabetes prevention, it would help catalyze activity and growth for Omada.

In November 2017 the CMS revealed that it would reimburse for in-person DPP programs, but that it would not yet reimburse for telehealth and digital delivery of DPP programs. CMS asserted the reason was a lack of compelling evidence regarding clinical efficacy. This was not the decision that James and Duffy were hoping for and they had to quickly decide how to move the company forward.

If you were James and Duffy, what are your next steps following CMS's decision not to reimburse? What are the viable options or strategies for addressing CMS's concerns regarding clinical efficacy?

CHAPTER ELEVEN

THE FUTURE OF ORGANIZATIONS AND THE FUTURE OF CHANGE

Chapter Overview

- Individuals wishing to become organizational change agents need to recognize that two main routes exist: sophisticated technical specialists and strategic generalists with the former often leading to the latter.
- Several paradoxes in the field of organizational change are summarized.
- The chapter ends with a summary checklist of lessons in organizational change.

Change is both normal and pervasive, and the capacity to lead and implement organizational change, denotes a skill set all managers need to possess. In summarizing the practical and theoretical approaches to organizational change, it is important to reiterate that the change process is rarely a straight path. You may begin the process of organizational change aiming at a particular vision and end up at some variation of the original goal. Change processes require adapting, compromising, reevaluating, and having an open mind, while at the same time remaining committed to the vision and persevering to see the change through.

The process contains inherent paradoxes that must be managed, and the journey can be confusing and frustrating for both those trying to implement changes and those whose lives are affected by the changes. However, it also has the potential to energize and excite, provide focus and hope. It represents the path through which revitalization and renewal occurs, from smaller incremental modifications to those larger-scale transformational changes that need to be undertaken from time to time.

Change management is not something you simply deal with, then can ignore. Rather, it is a continuing process of seeking to understand what is going on and what is needed, undertaking initiatives with others, and learning from the experiences and outcomes achieved. The completion of one change sets the stage for the changes that lie ahead. In essence, change is the normal state and if an organization is not attempting to challenge the status quo, adapt, and improve, it's likely undergoing less desirable forms of change—stagnation, atrophy, and decline. Developing your capacities to lead and manage this process increases your ability to add value and will enhance your career prospects. The search for talented individuals who can help make positive things happen will only intensify in the years ahead.

The paces of change and rates of disruption are accelerating across virtually every sector. Bricks and mortar (i.e., retail) businesses such as Sears, Radio Shack, and Toys "R" Us provide vivid examples of what happens when you do not effectively adapt. However, no one is immune. That is why firms as successful as Unilever, IBM, GM, Walmart, McDonald's, Scotiabank, and Facebook are aggressively pursuing initiatives that they hope will allow them to rapidly adapt, innovate, and scale successful new initiatives. They do not want to find themselves left behind, watching others eat their lunch. No organization—public, private or not-for-profit—that hopes to remain relevant and viable in the intermediate to long term can turn a blind eye to their emerging challenges and opportunities. Hospitals, government departments and agencies, school boards, universities, and charities are all grappling with these realities.

PUTTING THE CHANGE PATH MODEL INTO PRACTICE

The Change Path Model has provided an organizing framework for this book, and it is presented in its summary form in Figure 11.1. This model argues that change agents move systematically from analyses that stimulate interest in change and awaken the organization, through to mobilization, acceleration, and institutionalization of the change. A summary checklist for change is presented at the end of this chapter.

An important modification has been made to this final presentation of the model. An arrow has been added that links the fourth phase back to the first to reflect that the enactment of one set of changes sets the stage for the next ones. It's an ongoing process whose intensity will vary, depending upon the situation, the people, and the magnitude of what is being undertaken. There is no question that we need to rest and reenergize from time to time, celebrate what we've accomplished, and become fully competent in extracting the benefits the changes make possible. But then it's on to the next challenges. We can't change the past, but what we choose to do (or not do) now can change the future. If we choose to do nothing but more of the same—you get the picture!

FUTURE ORGANIZATIONS AND THEIR IMPACT

Barkema argues that in the future all organizations will need to be global in orientation.[1] Small- and medium-sized firms will access global markets through the Internet in low-cost/high-information-transmission ways. Others will form organizational networks, partnering with others to complete the value chain. Some will be large, focused global firms with worldwide activities.

Barkema states that organizations will have autonomous, dislocated teams. That is, organizations, large or small, will require motivated teams to coordinate their activities across borders and cultures. At the same time, structures will be "digitally enabled." They will have the electronic systems to facilitate coordination. Scanning systems will transmit sales data from stores and warehouses

Figure 11.1 The Change Path Model

Awakening
Chapter 4

1. Identify a need for change and confirm the problems or opportunities that incite the need for change through collection of data.
2. Articulate the gap in performance between the present and the envisioned future state, and spread awareness of the data and the gap throughout the organization.
3. Develop a powerful vision for change.
4. Disseminate the vision for the change and why it's needed through multiple communication channels.

Mobilization
Chapters 5 through 8

1. Make sense of the desired change through formal systems and structures, and leverage those systems to reach the change vision (Chapter 5).
2. Assess power and cultural dynamics at play, and put them to work to better understand the dynamics and build coalitions and support to realize the change (Chapter 6).
3. Communicate the need for change organization-wide and manage change recipients and various stakeholders as they react to and move the change forward (Chapter 7).
4. Leverage change agent personality, knowledge, skills and abilities, and related assets (e.g., reputation and relationships) for the benefit of the change vision and its implementation (Chapter 8).

Acceleration
Chapter 9

1. Continue to systematically reach out to engage and empower others in support, planning, and implementation of the change. Help them develop needed new knowledge, skills, abilities, and ways of thinking that will support the change.
2. Use appropriate tools and techniques to build momentum, accelerate and consolidate progress.
3. Manage the transition, celebrating small wins and the achievement of milestones along the larger, more difficult path of change.

Institutionalization
Chapter 10

1. Track the change periodically and through multiple balanced measures to help assess what is needed, gauge progress toward the goal, and to make modifications as needed and mitigate risk.
2. Develop and deploy new structures, systems, processes and knowledge, skills, and abilities, as needed, to bring life to the change and new stability to the transformed organization.

anywhere to manufacturing facilities in real time and will be used to determine future production levels. Personal communications devices such as the iPhone and other smartphones will mean that people can communicate any time, all the time. Such dispersed systems facilitated by almost instantaneous communications will make it easy for competitors to respond to each other's actions. The world will move fast. We can readily see signs of this increased speed.

Such changes will mean that organizations will need loose/tight controls both within and between firms. Inside organizations, critical strategic variables should be closely monitored and controlled. Visions will be articulated and adhered to. At the same time, rapid environmental shifts will demand local responses that will vary by region as well as responses that are broad in their geographic reach. What works in one country won't necessarily work in another. Think of the regional differences in the formulation of branded products such as Coke and McDonald's and this reality becomes clear. Maharaja burgers and separate vegetarian and non-vegetarian kitchens are found in McDonald's restaurants in India, but not the U.S. Managers will need to have the autonomy and the capacity (skills, abilities, and resources) to effectively recognize and respond to local needs and conditions, but they will need to do so within the boundaries that are acceptable to the firm.

Between organizations, networks of firms will be linked to allow for needed information exchange. What is shared will vary from the purely transactional to the strategic, depending on the levels of trust and intimacy existing between firms. At the same time, these firms will maintain their independence on key strategic dimensions viewed as proprietary and/or sources of competitive advantage critical to their long-term success.

Galbraith suggests that strategy and structure of organizations will continue to be closely tied.[2] Organizations will come in an enormous variety of forms and complexities. AI (artificial intelligence systems) and robots are taking over straightforward work that is repetitive and easily understood and these systems will become more sophisticated and capable over time. The key management tasks will involve innovation and the mastering of complexity. Galbraith classifies potential strategies and suggests matching structures.

According to Galbraith, organizations in the 21st century will become increasingly customer oriented and focused. In the customer-oriented organization, organizations will have three major organizational parts: business units, international regions, and customer accounts. These parts will be linked with lateral processes: teams and networks. Focused organizations will have subunits focused on different key criteria: costs, products, or customers.

Malone argues that tomorrow's organizations will have the benefits of both large and small organizations.[3] Digital technologies will enable economics of scale and knowledge creation while preserving the freedom, creativity, motivation, and flexibility of small organizations. There will be a shift from traditional centralized hierarchies to organizations of loose hierarchies, democracies, and markets—like organizations.

- *Loose hierarchy example:* Wikipedia, the free online encyclopedia that anybody can edit and when errors occur, others will spot and correct them

- *Democracy examples:* W. L. Gore, where you become a manager by finding people who want to work for you, or Mondragon, where employees elect a board of directors to make decisions

- *Market example:* An Intel proposal where plant managers propose to sell futures on what they produce and salespeople buy futures for products they want to sell. Prices fluctuate and will determine what products get produced at what plants and who gets to sell the products.

The above is suggestive of how organizations will evolve in the future. As a result of these and other trends, organizational change and change agents will need to shift as well. Table 11.1 summarizes these potential changes. The table suggests that change agents will need both a set of generalist capabilities providing basic competencies as well as change skills oriented around critical technical competencies.

Table 11.1	The Impact of Organizational Trends on Organizational Change and Change Agents	
Organizational Trends	**Organizational Change**	**Change Agent**
Globalization—be big, or specialized, otherwise be acquired, squeezed, or eliminated	Strategic global perspective for both large firms and niche SMEs	Pattern finder
Virtual and networked organizations	Knowledge of networks and emergent organizational forms increasingly important	Vision developer and framer
Loose/tight controls		Organizational analyst and aligner
24/7 response requirement	Knowledge and risk management: ability to use crowd sourcing, online communities, and big data to enhance knowledge creation, innovation, and risk management	Mobilizer, empowerment specialist, enabler, enactor
Cost and quality focus, outsourcing and supply chain rationalization		Disintegrator and integrator
Crowd sourcing for capital, innovation, and talent		Corporate gadfly and trend surfer
Use of big data, algorithms, and artificial intelligence (AI) to inform decision making	Web-enabled communication, change-related blogs, fast response capacity with a human face	Generalist capacities: facilitation, influencing, negotiating and visioning skills; project management expertise
Shorten product life cycles and increase in customer expectations	Negotiation and the development and leveraging of networks to enhance quality, cost leadership, and/or customer focus	Specialist roles, related to expertise needed for specific change initiatives. For example, software system integration, customer relationship management, flexible manufacturing, organizational integration following acquisition
Influential online communities spreading information access		
Increasing focus on integrated customer services and knowledge management	Creativity, innovation, and rapid deployment capacity	
Rapid technological change fundamentally alters industry structures, in terms of both the "what" and the "how"	Increased importance of agility, empowerment, teams, community engagement, and a strong process focus	Capacity to develop and sustain the trust and confidence of multiple stakeholders
Changing demographic, social, and cultural environment	Increased importance of AI, robotics, new materials, new processes and the internet of things (IOT) in the creation of goods and services.	
Political changes realign international alliances and the competitive environment		

In summary, those involved with organizational change need to develop

- a strong strategic and global perspective;
- knowledge of networks and emergent organizational forms and how they work;
- skills in risk management and knowledge management;
- understanding of the impact of Web-enabled communication, the use of social media in advancing external and internal change, and fast response capacity;
- the ability to communicate worldwide while maintaining a human face;
- perceptiveness of different cultures and norms, and how these factors affect organizational change; and
- the capacity to create, deploy, and work with empowered teams with the right mix of skills and abilities, operating with a focused vision. The teams' boundaries come from the vision and agreed-to expectations concerning performance, modes of operation, and other predefined standards and shared commitments. These capacities will apply to both co-located and virtual teams.

BECOMING AN ORGANIZATIONAL CHANGE AGENT: SPECIALISTS AND GENERALISTS

For many change agents, their initial involvement begins when they are asked to participate in a change initiative—often as a member of a team—due to their particular technical skills, past performance, and interest they have demonstrated in change initiatives. If the change involves the deployment of new sales support software, for example, individuals with appropriate technical competencies concerning both the software's implementation and the nature of the sales process will need to be involved with the project.

Over time, though, the careers of change agents tend to evolve in two different ways: those who are technically oriented in their change skills, and those who possess more generalist change agent skills.

The careers of *technically oriented change agents* will be characterized by projects of increasing size and complexity in their areas of technical expertise. For instance, if their educational background was in computer programming, their initial involvement could be the provision of training for corporate users of a system upgrade. Over time, as their expertise grows, these change agents will find themselves taking on bigger and more sophisticated technical change challenges. At their peak, individuals who began their careers providing computer training will have become respected change experts in large-scale software system integration projects.

Technically oriented change specialists will require some competence in more general change-management skills, such as gap analysis, communication of vision, and interpersonal skills; however, it will be their technical change-management expertise that will be sought after when an initiative lies within their domain—be it software, merger integration, or foreign market development.

Individuals pursuing this career path will often be found in consulting firms that specialize in their areas of expertise.

The careers of more *general management-oriented change agents* are characterized by a shift away from a technically focused path, as they work to develop change-management skills that are appropriate for a wider variety of situations. Those who choose to orient their development around general change-management skills may initially start their careers in technical and functional change management. However, over time, these individuals will develop increasingly sophisticated general change-management competencies associated with the Change Path Model. As a result, they will find themselves undertaking diverse challenges of increasing complexity, from turning around a poorly performing division to ramping up an operation to cope with growth, restructuring and integrating merged operations, or tackling cultural changes needed to increase organizational effectiveness in emerging markets.

To be successful, organizations need access to individuals with both technical and more general change-management competencies. At times, certain change skills will be more important than others for obvious reasons, but the management of complex change initiatives benefit from having access to both perspectives and is further aided when the change agents involved respect this need, recognize each other's skills and abilities, and understand what each of them is able to contribute to the initiative. Figure 11.2 outlines these two broad career paths.

An additional complexity to consider in the area of change management was noted in Chapters 1 and 8. Some change agents orient their careers around incremental change initiatives while others orient themselves around the management of more disruptive changes. Once again, it is not a matter of either/or as to which orientation is best. At different points in time, organizations will need access to both of these skill sets. When change agents with different orientations respect and value these differences in approach and recognize what each can contribute, the interests of change are advanced.

PARADOXES IN ORGANIZATIONAL CHANGE

The field of organizational change has a set of underlying paradoxes that change agents struggle with. Just as quantum physics considers an electron as both a particle and a wave,* some aspects of organizational change have two perspectives. Both aspects are important and neither should be rejected.

First, the management of organizations will become more complex as the strategic focus of organizations develops a global perspective. Organizational change will need tools and processes that encourage the systematic management of a wide number of elements (organizational systems, structures, cultures, leadership, technology, etc.) while maintaining the speed of change. Clearly a challenge will be to handle complexity without being overwhelmed and frozen by it. Organizational change as a field needs to handle the paradox of how to maintain the momentum of change (something that may require simplification) while not dismissing the complexity of an organization's environment.

---

*Under certain circumstances, the electron looks like a particle and has the characteristics of a particle (mass, solidity, etc.). Under other circumstances, the electron seems to be a wave. It has a frequency and other wave characteristics. This paradox is only resolved by accepting an electron as both.

Figure 11.2 Organizational Change Agents' Skills

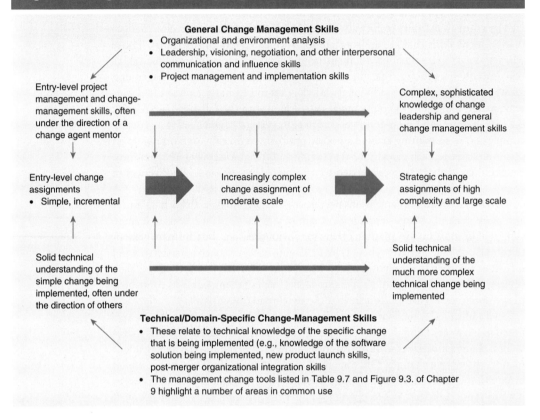

General Change Management Skills
- Organizational and environment analysis
- Leadership, visioning, negotiation, and other interpersonal communication and influence skills
- Project management and implementation skills

Entry-level project management and change-management skills, often under the direction of a change agent mentor

Complex, sophisticated knowledge of change leadership and general change management skills

Entry-level change assignments
- Simple, incremental

Increasingly complex change assignment of moderate scale

Strategic change assignments of high complexity and large scale

Solid technical understanding of the simple change being implemented, often under the direction of others

Solid technical understanding of the much more complex technical change being implemented

Technical/Domain-Specific Change-Management Skills
- These relate to technical knowledge of the specific change that is being implemented (e.g., knowledge of the software solution being implemented, new product launch skills, post-merger organizational integration skills
- The management change tools listed in Table 9.7 and Figure 9.3. of Chapter 9 highlight a number of areas in common use

A second paradox involves an organization's need to be simultaneously centralized and decentralized. Organizations must be centralized to have singularity of strategy, yet also decentralized so that they can remain competitive by responding agilely to changes in the environment. Organizational change agents need to learn how to help organizations understand this paradox and to evolve mechanisms to handle this tension.

As organizational leaders become skilled in promoting decentralized initiatives, they will face the challenge of handling multiple change initiatives simultaneously. Change agents need to consider which change initiatives will block or run counter to others and which ones will support and facilitate others. Interaction effects are not always self-apparent, and sometimes initiatives that look like they are supportive of other activities in the short run may have adverse consequences over the long term. How can change leaders help an organization institutionalize one project while continuing multiple other ones, and how can they assist in identifying and managing unintended side effects?

Organizational change involves both incremental/continuous and radical/discontinuous change. Depending on how rapidly the environment is changing, organizations may need to engage in both kinds of change. The challenge for change agents will be to develop adaptive, flexible organizations while simultaneously engaging in radical organizational change when it is needed. Organizational change agents need to develop insights into this paradox.

Finally, the digital world and the rise of the knowledge worker *may* shift the territory of organizational change from a hierarchical frame to a democratic, participative one. But the essence of many change projects is a new direction that, in the end, is mandated, non-democratically, from above. Most change projects need input from rank-and-file employees but also need some degree of central direction and management. The tension between participative involvement of many and the pressure to drive change from the top of an organization creates potential paradoxes.[†]

Given these paradoxes, change agents must develop a positive orientation to change that permits them to deal with inherent contradictions.

ORIENTING YOURSELF TO ORGANIZATIONAL CHANGE

Everyone who is a member of an organization will participate in organizational change. Change is a part of living, and opportunities will emerge that involve you in various roles. Sometimes your involvement will be mandated, whereas at other times you may choose to seek it out, or your change roles may evolve naturally over time. Sometimes you will be asked to take on the role of change leader; become a member of a team implementing the change; take on an advisory role; or, you may find yourself a recipient of a change initiative. Sometimes you will be able to exercise choice as to what roles you play in the change initiative, whereas at other times this will not be the case. As you experience organizational change from whatever role you find yourself in, the following advice will help you deal with it more effectively.

1. Gain perspective and insight by recognizing the dynamism and complexity of your organization. What connections exist between parts and how do they work?

2. Recognize that people's perceptions are critical. The perception of benefits and costs determines a person's reaction to a change proposal.

3. Understand that your perception is only one of many. Your view is neither right nor wrong. It is just your point of view of how things are.

4. Gather people as you go. There are multiple ways to achieve your change (even when you are starting as a recipient), but the ways that bring others with you are easier and more fun. And remember, people can't rock the boat when they are busy rowing.

5. Pull people toward you with a powerful change vision. Push people through argument and rewards when you need to, but gain support through their hearts.

[†] Organizational change will need to be prepared to use and respond to various social media platforms that discuss openly the issues surrounding change initiatives. Can change leaders accept and deal positively with open criticism that may show up on such media?

6. Get active in pursuit of your vision. If you do something, you will get responses, and you can learn from those. Not doing anything cuts you off from learning.

7. Have a plan oriented around your vision. Having an explicit plan means your thinking can be discussed and challenged. Know that your plan won't last and will require modification when you start implementing it, but it will be useful in starting a discussion and gaining commitment.

8. Do things that are positive. Actions that suck energy from you and the system are difficult to sustain. Growing your energy as a change agent is important.

9. To start meaningful change, you need only a few believers. To continue, you need to develop momentum until a critical mass of key participants is onside. Some will never join in, and that's OK, unless they attempt to sabotage or otherwise disrupt agreed to initiatives.

10. There are many routes to your goal. Find the ones with the least resistance that still allow you to proceed with integrity.

SUMMARY

That's it. It's an evolving list and its further development is up to you. You've been reading and thinking about how to develop your skills as an agent of change. It's time to deploy those ideas; see what works when, where, why, and how; and learn as you go. No excuses.

If you want to make things happen, you will have to learn to live with the frustration, excitement, uncertainty, loneliness, and personal development that come with being a change agent. The learning lies in the journey, while joy, a sense of accomplishment, and feelings of fulfillment accompany the completion of milestones and the realization of changes that have a positive impact on the lives of others. See **Toolkit Exercise 11.1** for critical thinking questions on this chapter.

And the day came when the risk it took to remain tight in a bud was more painful than the risk it took to blossom.

—Anaïs Nin

END-OF-CHAPTER EXERCISES

TOOLKIT EXERCISE 11.1

1. Choose a recent CNN Hero: think about how they managed to create change.

    https://www.cnn.com/specials/cnn-heroes

    - How did the person you chose create successful change?

    - What inspired them to take on the change?

    - Imagine in 10 years you become a CNN Hero. What story will they tell about you?

2. Look also at the We Day website. Consider the vision and success of Craig and Marc Kielburger in their various endeavors.

    - How were the Kielburgers able to create such sweeping change at such a young age?

    - What challenges do you think they may have faced, and how did they overcome them?

    - How are the youth involved in "We Day" working to create change?

    - What is it that you want to change?

*Please see **study.sagepub.com/cawsey4e** for a downloadable template of this exercise.*

TOOLKIT EXERCISE 11.2

Developing Your Change Plan

This toolkit exercise applies the tools from all chapters and asks you to develop a complete change plan for a change you want to make happen.

As a first step, develop your statement of the need for change and your vision for the change.

Once the need for change and vision has been articulated, your assignment is to begin the development of an action plan for the change. This will be broken into four parts:

a. The development of a sequence of action steps and the arrangement of them into a critical path with a clearly defined end goal, intermediate targets, and specific first step.

b. The consideration of contingencies—what might go wrong? How will these things be handled?

c. A responsibility chart, that is, who will do what, where, when, and how?

d. A transition plan including a communications plan. How will the transition be managed? Who will make the innumerable decisions required to handle the details? Who will provide information to those affected? As well, how will the change be communicated to organizational members?

The Action Plan

Begin the development of an action plan. What are the critical steps that must be accomplished? Arrange your action steps in sequence. Can some be done simultaneously? What activities cannot begin or should not start until others are completed? What timelines should you observe? Often it is useful to begin at the end of the project and work backward to now.

Who needs to become committed to the project?

Where are key players at on the adoption continuum? Are they even aware of the change? If aware, are they interested or have they moved beyond that stage to either desiring action or having already adopted?

What will it take to move them along the continuum in the direction of adoption?

The AIDA Continuum

Key Player Name	Aware?	Interested?	Desires Action?	Adopter?

What is the commitment to the adoption of those who have reached the adopter stage? That is, are they at the "let it happen" stage, the "help it happen" stage, or the "make it happen" stage?

How can the commitment levels of key stakeholders be increased?

Responsibility Charting[4]

Actions or Decisions	Person #1	Person #2	Person #3	Person #?
Action #1				
Action #2				
Decision #1				
Action #3				
. . . . .				

Who will do what, where, when, and how? Often a responsibility chart can be useful to track these things.

(Continued)

(Continued)

Coding:

R = Responsibility (not necessarily authority)

A = Approval (right to veto)

S = Support (put resources toward)

I = Inform (to be consulted before action)

Note that if there are a great number of As on your chart, implementation will be difficult. Care must be taken to assign As only when appropriate. Likewise, if there are not enough Rs and Ss, you will need to think about changes needed here and how to bring them about.

Formulate a transition plan including a communications plan. How will the transition be managed? Who will make the innumerable decisions required to handle the details? Who will provide information to those affected? As well, how will the change be communicated to organizational members?

The Measurement of Change

How will you know that your goal or change project is successfully implemented? (At times, success will be obvious—e.g., a new system in place. At other times, success will be more difficult to measure—e.g., attitudes toward the adoption and acceptance of a new system.)

What intermediate signals will indicate that you are making progress? What is the first step or sequence of steps?

Your end goal is:

You can measure it by:

Intermediate measures and milestones are:

The first step is:

Contingency Planning

Remember O'Brien's Law[‡]? Well, it holds, and things will not go as planned. But you can plan for the unexpected.

What are the critical decision points? Who makes those decisions?

What will you do if the decision or event does not go as planned?

What plans can you make to account for these contingencies? If you can, draw a decision tree of the action plan and lay out the decision–event sequence.

Please see **study.sagepub.com/cawsey4e** for a downloadable template of this exercise.

_____

[‡] O'Brien's Law states Murphy was an optimist.

NOTES

CHAPTER 1

1. Ebner, D. (2018, July 11). Tim Hortons plans 1,500-store China expansion. *The Globe and Mail*, Retrieved from https://www.theglobeandmail.com/business/article-tim-hortons-plans-1500-store-china-expansion/.

2. Strauss, M. (2014, February 25). Tim Hortons brewing "bold" changes. *Globe Investor*, Retrieved from http://www.globeinvestor.com/servlet/WireFeedRedirect?cf=GlobeInvestor/config&vg=BigAdVariableGenerator&date=20140225&archive=rtgam&slug=escenic_17078297. Press releases from Tim Hortons' website, retrieved from http://www.timhortons.com/ca/en/about/news_archives.html; Dunkin' brands announces strong global growth in 2013. Corporate press release, January 13, 2014. Retrieved from http://investor.dunkinbrands.com/releasedetail.cfm?ReleaseID=818737. Team, T. Examining Dunkin' Brands growth strategy. (2017, June 22). Forbes. Sourced from https://www.forbes.com/sites/greatspeculations/2017/06/22/examining-duncan-brands-growth-strategy/#55ddb5081c95.

3. A version of this quote can be found on p. 55 in Wheatley, M. J. (1994). *Leadership and the new science.* San Francisco: Berrett-Koehler.

4. Miles, R. H. (1997). *Leading corporate transformation.* San Francisco: Jossey-Bass.

5. Personal experience of the authors.

6. Appelbaum, S. H., Henson, D., & Knee, K. (1999). Downsizing failures: An examination of convergence/reorientation and antecedents—processes—outcomes. *Management Decision, 37*(6), 473–490.

7. Sourced from http://www.ziglar.com/quotes/its-how-you-handle-it.

8. The Conference Board of Canada. (2000, November). 2000 change management conference: Increasing change capability. See also Higgs, M., & Rowland, D. (2005). All changes great and small: Exploring approaches to change and its leadership. *Journal of Change Management, 5*(2), 121–151. Porter O'Grady, T. (2015, June). Through the looking glass: Predictive and adaptive capacity in a time of great change. *Nursing Management, 46*(6), 22.

9. The 100 best places to work for 2017. *Fortune.* Retrieved from http://fortune.com/best-companies/2017.

10. Pfeffer, J., & Sutton, R. (1999). Knowing "what" to do is not enough: Turning knowledge into action. *California Management Review, 42*(1), 83–108.

11. Maynard, M. (2010, April 5). U.S. is seeking a fine of $16.4 million against Toyota. *New York Times.*

12. GM ignition switch recall lawsuits. (2014, April 1). *About Lawsuits.com.* Retrieved from http://www.aboutlawsuits.com/gm-recall/; GM seeks immunity for ignition lawsuits before 2009. (2014, April 22). Associated Press. Retrieved from http://www.cbc.ca/news/business/gm-seeks-immunity-for-ignition-lawsuits-before-2009–1.2617417; Bellon, T. (January 19, 2018). GM ignition switch lawsuit. Judge throws out $1 billion settlement. Reuters. Retrieved from https://www.autoblog.com/2018/01/19/gm-ignition-switch-lawsuit-judge-settlement/

13. How to play chicken and lose. (2009, January 22). *The Economist.*

14. Meltdown warnings ignored, analysis shows. (2008, December 1). *CBS News.* Retrieved from http://www.cbsnews.com/news/meltdown-warnings-ignored-analysis-shows/.

15. Demography: China's Achilles heel. (2012, April 12). *The Economist;* Germany's demographic challenge. (2013, May 28). *The Economist;* Demography, growth and inequality: Age invaders. (2014, April 26). *The Economist;* Japan's economy: The incredible shrinking country. (2014, May 31). *The Economist;* Age invaders. (2014, April 26). *The Economist.*

16. Sovereign creditworthiness could be undermined by age-related spending trends. (2006, June 5). *Standard & Poor's.* Retrieved from http://www.standardandpoors.com.

17. Global Aging 2016: 58 Shades of Gray.(2016, April 28). *Standard and Poor's.* Retrieved from http://www.agefactifs.com/sites/agefactifs.com/file/fichiers/2016_-_58_shades_of_grey_28_april_16.pdf.

18. Chapter 2, Aging in the U.S. and other countries, 2010 to 2050. (2014, January 30). *Pew Research Center.*

Bloomberg, J. (2016, June 16). Change as core competency: Transforming the role of enterprise architect. Forbes. Sources from https://www.forbes.com/sites/jasonbloomberg/2016/06/16/change-as-core-competency-transforming-the-role-of-the-enterprise-architect/#33d23ff2164a.

Retrieved from http://ww.pewglobal.org/2014/01/30/chapter-2-aging-in-the-u-s-and-other-countries-2010-to-2050/. Half a billion Americans? (2002, August 22). *The Economist.*

19. Mounting medical care spending could be harmful to the G-20's credit health. (2012, January 26). *Standard & Poor's.* Retrieved from http://www.standardandpoors.com/ratings/articles/en/eu/?articleType=HTML&assetID=1245328578642; Sovereign credit worthiness could be undermined by age-related spending trends. (2006, June 5). *Standard & Poor's.* Retrieved from http://www.standardandpoors.com.

20. Falling fertility. (2009, October 31). *The Economist*, pp. 29–32.

21. The gain before the pain: Mexico's demographic dividend will be short-lived. (2012, November 24). *The Economist*; China's concern over population aging and health. (2006, June). *Population Reference Bureau.* Retrieved from http://www.prb.org/Publications/Articles/2006/ChinasConcernOverPopulationAgingandHealth.aspx; Ranasinghe, D. (2013, September 22). The aging in Asia face a new decade like no other. *CNBC.* Retrieved from http://www.cnbc.com/id/101045746.

22. The dividend delayed: Hopes that Africa's dramatic population bulge may create prosperity seem to have been overdone. (2014, March 8). *The Economist.* Falling fertility. (2009, October 31). *The Economist*, pp. 29–32.

23. Everyday essentials, or emerging consumer? (2018, June 300. *BMO Global Asset Management.* Retrieved from http://www.bmo.com/gam/us/capaigns/emerging-consumer.

24. Supporting aging populations as demographics shift. (2011, June 10). *International Monetary Fund.* Retrieved from http://www.imf.org/external/pubs/ft/survey/so/2011/NEW061011A.htm; Davis, I., &Stephenson, E. (2006). Ten trends to watch in 2006. *McKinsey Quarterly; The Online Journal.* Retrieved from http://www.mckinseyquarterly.com/article_print.aspx?12=18&L3=30&ar=1734; Drouin, J., Hediger, V., & Henke, N. (2008, June). Health care costs: A market-based view. *McKinsey Quarterly.*

25. Revell, J. (2002). GM's slow leak. *Fortune, 146*(8), 105; Why GM's plan won't work—and the ugly road ahead. (2005, May 9). *Business Week Online.* Retrieved December 2010 from http://www.businessweek.com/magazine/content/05_19/b3932001_mz001.htm; Maynard, M. (2008, March 7). GM to freeze pension plan for salaried workers. *New York Times.* Retrieved from http://www.nytimes.com/2006/03/08/automobiles/08auto.html.

26. Keenam, G. (2018, May 3). GM still facing huge pension shortfall. *The Globe and Mail.* Retrieved from http://www.globeandmail.com/report-on-business-/gm-still-faces-hugepension-shortfall/article547942/. Number of GM employeesbetween FY2010 and FY2017.Statistica. Retrieved from http://www.statistia.com/statistics/239843/employees-of-general-motors/.

27. The silver tsunami. (2010, February 4). *The Economist.*

28. A billion shades of grey: An ageing economy will be a slower and more unequal one—unless policy starts changing now. (2014, April 26). *The Economist.*

29. Kelleher, J. B. (2013, June 21). Analysis: As boomers age, Harley hunts for younger riders. Reuters. Retrieved from http://www.reuters.com/article/2013/06/21/us-harley davidson-boomers-analysis-idUSBRE95K0GU20130621; Marketing to the old. (2002, August 8). *The Economist.*

30. Haserot, P.W. (2017, April 5). The cost of ignoring older workers. *Forbes.* Retrieved from http://www.forbes.com/sites/nextavenue/2017/04/05/the-cost-of-ignoring-p;der-workers/#35d3a1d614e5. Hannon, K. (2013, January 25). Why older workers can't be ignored. *Forbes.* Retrieved from http://www.forbes.com/sites/kerryhannon/2013/01/25/why-older-workers-cant-be-ignored/.

31. Sedensky, M. (2013, September 13). Some employers see perks in hiring older workers, *AP.* Retrieved from Yahoo! News: http://news.yahoo.com/employers-see-perks-hiring-older-workers-144536527—finance.html.

32. Krogstad, J.M., & Lopez, M.H. (2015, June 25). Hispanic population reaches record 55 million but growth has cooled. *Pew Research Center.* Retrieved from http://pewresearch.org/fact-tank/2015/06/25/u-s-hispanic-popuation-growth-surge-cools/. Ennis, S. R., Rios-Vargs, M., & Albert, N. G. (2011, May). The Hispanic population in 2010, 2010 census brief. *United States Census Bureau,* Publication C2010BR-04; Suro, R., & Singer, A. (2002). *Latino growth in metropolitan America.* Center on Urban & Metropolitan Policy and The Pew Hispanic Center, The Brookings Institution; Saenz, R. (2010, December). Population bulletin update: Latinos in the United States 2010. *Population Reference Bureau,* Update 2010.

33. Suro, R., & Singer, A. (2002). *Latino growth in metropolitan America* (Table 4, p. 9). Center on Urban and Metropolitan Policy and the Pew Hispanic Center, The Brookings Institution.

34. Haparanda. (2018, June 30). Panic Attack: Confusion over immigration and crime is roiling European politics. *The Economist*. Retrieved from https://www.economist.com/europe/2018/06/30/confusion-over-immigration-and-crime-is-roiling-european-politics.

35. Erlanger, S. (2011, April 11). France enforces ban on full-face veils in public. *New York Times*; Seguin, R. (2014, January 21). Quebec Liberals stake out new position on PQ's secular charter. *Globe and Mail*.

36. Sam becomes first openly gay player to the drafted. (2014, May 10). *Reuters*. Retrieved from https://ca.news.yahoo.com/sam-becomes-leagues-first-openly-gay-player-ever-225731321—nfl.html?.tsrc=yahoo.

37. Bauder, D. (2018, September 29). More than 20 million people watched Kavanaugh Hearing. *Associated Press*. Retrieved from https://www.yahoo.com/news/more-20-million-people-watched-212701544.html.

38. Florida, R. (2012, June 27). Race, gender, and the creative class. Retrieved from http://www.citylab.com/work/2012/06/race-gender-and-creative-class/2225/; Race, gender and careers: Why "stuffing the pipeline" is not enough. (2012, September 7). *Knowledge@Wharton*. Retrieved from http://business.time.com/2012/09/07/race-gender-and-careers-why-stuffing-the-pipeline-is-not-enough/.

39. Almasy, S. (2014, May 20). NBA charges Donald Sterling, schedules June 3 vote. *CNN U.S.* Retrieved from http://www.cnn.com/2014/05/19/us/donald-sterling-nba/index.html.

40. Meyersohn, N. (2018. July 27). Disneyland agrees to pay its workers $15 an hour. *CNN Money*. Retrieved from https://money.cnn.com/2018/07/27/news/companies/disneyland-workers-pay-15-an-hour/index.html; Glatter, H. (2018, June 21). Massachusetts Legislature Passes Bill for $15 Minimum Wage. *Boston Magazine*. Retrieved from https://www.bostonmagazine.com/news/2018/06/21/massachusetts-15-minimum-wage/.

41. Rubin, C. (2010, November 8). Labor board backs workers' right to bad-mouth bosses online. *Inc.* Retrieved from http://www.inc.com/news/articles/2010/11/NLRB-backs-employees-right-to-gripe-about-bosses-online.html; Bacon, J. (2013, December 5). Fast-food worker strike, protest for higher pay. *USA Today*. Retrieved from http://www.usatoday.com/story/money/business/2013/12/05/fast-food-strike-wages/3877023/.

42. Young, C. (2014, March 27). Food firm disgusted by employee's racist posting. *Bradford News*. Retrieved from http://m.thetelegraphandargus.co.uk/news/11107456.Police_probe_racist_Facebook_posting_after_mum_s_suicide_at_Shipley_super market/.

43. See TD's corporate responsibility section of their website: http://www.td.com/corporate-responsibility/diversity/diversity.jsp.

44. Thomas, D. A. (2004). Diversity as strategy. *Harvard Business Review*, *82*(9), 98–109.

45. Mendoza, M. (2014, May 29). Google admits its work force is mostly white, male and must change. *Associated Press via the Globe and Mail*. Retrieved from http://www.the globeandmail.com/report-on-business/international-business/us-business/google-says-work-force-must-diversify-as-tally-shows-most-are-white-male/article18903708/#dashboard/follows/. McGirt, E. (2017, February 1, 2017). *Fortune*. Retrieved from http://fortune.com/google-diversity/.

46. Gabrielsson, M., & Manek Kirpalani, V. H. (2014). *Handbook of research on born globals*. Edward Elgar Pub.; Friedrich, J., Noam, A., & Ofek, E. (2014, May). Right up the middle: How Israeli firms go global. *Harvard Business Review*.

47. Savitz, A. W., & Weber, K. (2006). *The triple bottom line: How today's best-run companies are achieving economic, social and environmental success—and how you can too*. San Francisco: Jossey-Bass.

48. Flavelle, C. (2018, October 6). Miami will be underwater soon. Its drinking water could go first. Bloomberg. Retrieved from https://www.msn.com/en-ca/news/world/miami-will-be-underwater-soon-its-drinking-water-could-go-first/ar-BBO16VR?ocid=spartandhp.

49. Kurucz, E., Colbert, B., & Wheeler, D. (2013). *Reconstructing value: Leadership skills for a sustainable world*. Rotman-Utp Publishing; Rea, M. H. (2013). Kim, B-J., Nurunnabi, M., Kim, T-H.& Jung, S-J. (2018, 10) 2208. The influence of corporate social responsibility on organizational commitment: The sequential mediating effect of meaningfulness of work and perceived organizational support. *Sustainability*. Retrieved from https://www.mdpi.com/2071-1050/10/7/2208. *Review of sustainability reporting in South Africa 2013*. IRAS Integrated Reporting and Assurance Services; Deszca, G. (2014, May 2). Lessons from South Africa on sustainability, corporate social responsibility, and strategy. *LeadingIndicator*. Retrieved from http://www.leadingindicator.ca/article/478074/lessons-from-south-africa-on-sustainability-corporate-social-responsibility-and.

50. Volkswagen emissions scandal. *Wikipedia*. Retrieved from https://en.wikipedia.org/wiki/Volkswagen_emissions_scandal.

51. The data deluge. (2010, February 25). *The Economist*; Gantz, J., & Reinsel, D. (2012, December). The digital universe in 2020: Big data, bigger digital shadows, and biggest growth in the far east. *IDC IVEW*. Retrieved from http://www.emc.com/collateral/analyst-reports/idc-the-digital-universe-in-2020.pdf.

52. Tynan, D. (2012, March 19). How to get a hot job in big data. *InfoWorld*. Retrieved from http://www.infoworld.com/t/it-jobs/how-get-hot-job-in-big-data-188629?page=0,0.

53. The next disrupters. (2007, September). *Business 2.0.*

54. Manyika, J., Chui, M., Bughin, J., Dobbs, R., Bisson, P., & Marrs, A. (2013, May). Disruptive technologies: Advances that will transform life, business and the global economy. *McKinsey Global Institute*. Retrieved from http://www.mckinsey.com/insights/business_technology/disruptive_technologies.

55. 2016 international air travel soared to 3.7 billion passengers, a new record. (2012, December 18). *US Global ETFs*. Retrieved from http://www.usglobaletfs.com/insights/2016-international-air-travel-soared-to-3-7billion-passengersa-new-record.

56. Yergin, D., & Stanislaw, J. (2002). *The commanding heights: The battle for the world economy.* New York: Touchstone, 405.

57. List of countries by number of mobile phones in use. Retrieved from http://en.wikipedia.org/wiki/List_of_countries_by_number_of_mobile_phones_in_use.

58. Number of smart phone users worldwide from 2014–2020. *Statista*. Retrieved from http://www.statista.com.330695/number-of-smartphone-users-worldwide/. Lomas, N. (2014, February 13). Gartner: Smartphones sales finally beat out dumb phone sales globally in 2013. *TC (TechCrunch).* Retrieved from http://techcrunch.com/2014/02/13/smartphones-outsell-dumb-phones-globally/.

59. Morse, J. (2018, September 28). Facebook: 50 million accounts "directly affected" by hack. Yahoo! News. Retrieved from https://ca.news.yahoo.com/facebook-50-milion-accounts-could-172938933.html.

60. (2017, June 30). Online fraudcosts public billions but is still not a police priority, says watchdog. *The Guardian*. Retrieved from http://theguardian.com/uk-news/2017/june/30/online-costs-public-billions-but-is-still-not-a-police-priority-says-watchdog. Pagliery, J. (2014, May 28). Half of American adults hacked this year. *CNN Money*. Retrieved from http://money.cnn.com/2014/05/28/technology/security/hack-data-breach/index.html?hpt=hp_t3; Ponemon Institute

releases 2014 cost of data breach: Global analysis (2014, May 5). Retrieved from http://www.ponemon.org/blog/ponemon-institute-releases-2014-cost-of-data-breach-global-analysis; Skimming off the top. (2014, February 15). *The Economist*. Retrieved from http://www.economist.com/news/finance-and-economics/21596547-why-america-has-such-high-rate-payment-card-fraud-skimming-top.

61. Finkle, J. (2014, May 22). Hackers raid eBay in historic breach, access 145 million records. *Reuters*. Retrieved from http://uk.reuters.com/article/2014/05/22/uk-ebay-password-idUKKBN0E10ZL20140522; Isadore, C. (2014, January 11).Target: Hacking hit up to 110 million customers.*CNNMoney.* Retrieved from http://money.cnn.com/2014/01/10/news/companies/target-hacking/index.html; Mullen, R. (2005, March 11). Security issues lurking beyond VOIP's cost saving promise. *Silicon Valley/San Jose Business Journal*. Retrieved from http://www.sanjose.bizjournals.com/sanjose/stories/2005/03/14/smallb3.html; Foster, P., & Moore, M. (2014, May 19). US charges Chinese officers with hacking and opens new front in cyber-espionage war. *The Telegraph*. Retrieved from http://www.telegraph.co.uk/news/worldnews/asia/china/10842484/US-charges-Chinese-officers-with-hacking-and-opens-new-front-in-cyber-espionage-war.html.

62. Violino, B. (2004, July). Fortifying supply chains. *Optimize*, pp. 73–75. Retrieved from http://www.optimizemag.com/article/showArticle.jhtml?articleID=22101759.

63. Daigle, K. (2011, October 6). India unveils $35 tablet computer for the rural poor. *The Sydney Morning Herald*. Retrieved from http://www.smh.com.au/digital-life/digital-life-news/india-unveils-35-tablet-computer-for-rural-poor-20111005-11aao.html.

64. Melore,.C. (2017, November 15). Online dating the most common way newlyweds met in 2017, survey says. CBS Pittsburg. Retrieved from http://pittsburgh.cbslocal.com/2017/11/15/online-dating-newlyweds.2017/. Sleep texting is on the rise, experts suggest. *Huffington Post*. Retrieved from http://www.huffingtonpost.com/2013/02/14/sleep-texting-on-the-rise_n_2677739.html.

65. La Monica, P.R. (2018, September 28). Blackberry's comeback continues. *CNN Tech*. Retrieved from http://money.cnn.com/2018/09/28/technology/blackberry-earnings-john-chen/index.html. Silcoff, S., McNish, J., & Ladurantaye, S. (2013, September 27). How BlackBerry blew it: The inside story. *Globe and Mail*. Retrieved from

http://www.theglobeandmail.com/report-on
-business/the-inside-story-of-why-blackberry-is
-failing/article14563602/#dashboard/follows/.

66. (2016, June 15). 10 million self-driving cars will be on the road by 2020. Business Insider Intelligence, BI Intelligence. Retrieved from http://business insider.com/report-10-million-self-driving -cars-will-be-on-the-road-by-2020-2015-5-6. Markoff, J. (2014, May 27). Google's next phase in driverless cars: No steering wheel or brake pedals. *New York Times*. Retrieved from http://www .nytimes.com/2014/05/28/technology/googles -next-phase-in-driverless-cars-no-brakes-or -steering-wheel.html?ref=technology&_r=0.

67. Others believe otherwise. Note the protests whenever the WTO meets, for example.

68. False heaven. (1999, July 29). *The Economist*.

69. Farrell, D., Khanna, T., Sinha, J., & Woetzel, J. R. (2004). China and India: The race to growth. *McKinsey Quarterly, Special Edition*, 110–119.

70. (2017) Chapter III: World trade and GDP growth in 2016 and early 2017. World Trade Organization. Retrieved from http://www .wto.org/english/res_e/stats_e/wts2017_e/ WTO_03_e.pdf.

71. Speed is not everything. (2013, January 2). *The Economist*. Retrieved from http://www.economist .com/blogs/theworldin2013/2013/01/fastest -growing-economies-2013.

72. Transparency International Secretariat. (2002). Transparency international corruption perceptions index 2002. 10585 Berlin, Germany: Ott-Suhr-Allee, 97–99.

73. Transparency International Secretariat. (2002). Bribe payers' index. 10585 Berlin, Germany: Otto-Suhr-Allee, 97–99; Wawro, L. (2014, March 31). Arms deals in the dark: Secret contracts in the defense sector. *Transparency International*. Retrieved from http://blog. transparency.org/2014/03/31/arms-deals-in -the-dark-secret-contracts-in-the-defence -sector/; Corruption perceptions index 2013. (2013, December 3). *Transparency International*. Retrieved from http://www.transparency.org/ whatwedo/pub/cpi_2013.

74. Lawrence, A. (2007, Winter). Hewlett-Packard and a common supplier code of conduct. *Case Research Journal*; Siegle, L. (2013, October 6). How ethical are high-street clothes? *The Guardian*. Retrieved from http://www.theguard ian.com/environment/2013/oct/06/ethical -high-street-clothes-supply-chain-bangladesh; Strauss, M. (2013, April 25). Loblaw moves to improve safety at Bangladeshi factories. *Globe and Mail*. Retrieved from http://www.theglobean dmail.com/report-on-business/loblaw-moves -to-improve-safety-at-bangladeshi-factories/ article11563889/#dashboard/follows/.

75. Siemens sees green tech driving economic growth. (2009, August). *Industry Week*.

76. Senge, P., Smith, B., Kruschwitz, N., Laur, J., & Schley, S. (2010). *The necessary revolution: How individuals and organizations are working together to create a sustainable world*. New York: Crown (a division of Random House); Senge, P., & Carstedt, G. (2001). Innovating our way to the next industrial revolution. *Sloan Management Review, 42*(2), 24–38.

77. For an example of these arguments, see Wooldridge, A. A future imperfect: Why globalization went wrong. (2017, June 30). *TEDx LondonBusinssSchool*. Retrieved from https:// www.youtube.com/watch?v=agjGFwpTFaM.

78. Where have all your savings gone? (2008, December 4). *The Economist*.

79. Personal communication with one author.

80. Amadeo, K. National debt by year, compared to GDP and major events. (2019, April 6). The Balance. Retrieved from https://www.thebalance .com/national-debt-by-year-compared-to-gdp -and-major-events-3306287.

81. When giants slow down. (2013, July 27). *The Economist*. Retrieved from http://www.economist .com/news/briefing/21582257-most-dramatic -and-disruptive-period-emerging-market -growth-world-has-ever-seen; The hard slog ahead. The world in 2010. (2009, December). *The Economist*.

82. What is Cbina's one belt and one road initiative? (2017, May 15) *The Economist*. Retrieved from https://www.economist.com/the-economist -explains/2017/05/14/what-is-chinas-belt-and -road-initiative. China goes to Africa. (2017, July 20). *The Economist*. Retrieved from https://www.econo mist.com/middle-east-and-africa/2017/07/20/ china-goes-to-africa. China has designs on Europe. Here is how Europe should respond. (2018, October 4). *The Economist*. Retrieved from https://www.economist.com/leaders/2018/10/04/ china-has-designs-on-europe-here-is-how -europe-should-respond. Not so fast. The world in 2010. (2009, December). *The Economist*.

83. Inman, P. (2018, October 3). World economy at risk of another financial crash, says IMF. The Guardian. Retrieved from https://www.theguard ian.com/business/2018/oct/03/world-economy -at-risk-of-another-financial-crash-says-imf.

84. Stein, J. (2018, June 26). The federal debt is headed for the highest levels since World War II,

CBO says. *The Washington Post*. Retrieved from https://www.washingtonpost.com/news/wonk/ wp/2018/06/26/the-federal-debt-is-headed-for -the-highest-levels-since-world-war-ii-cbo -says/?utm_term=.3d5de9641a64.

85. Are Airbnb and Uber changing the world? (2014, July 5) *The Globe and Mail online*. Retrieved from http://www.theglobeandmail.com/globe-debate/ are-airbnb-and-uber-changing-the-world/ article19453855/?utm_source=Shared+Article+Sent +to+User&utm_medium-E-mail:+Newsletters+/+E -Blasts+/+etc.&utm_campaign=Shared+Web+Article +Links.

86. Barkema, H. G., Baum, J. A. C., & Mannix, E. A. (2002). Management challenges in a new time. *Academy of Management Journal, 45*(5), 916–930.

87. Abbosh, O., Savic, V. & Moore, M. (2018, January 28). How likely is your industry to be disrupted? *Harvard Business Review Webinar*. Retrieved from https:// hbr.org/2018/01/how-likely-is-your-industry -to-be-disrupted-this-2x2-matrix-will-tell-you.

88. Weick, K. E., & Quinn, R. E. (1999). Organizational change and development. *Annual Review of Psychology, 50*, 361–386.

89. Thomas, D. (2008, September). The digital company 2013: Freedom to collaborate. *Economist Intelligence Unit, The Economist*. Retrieved from http://graphics.eiu.com/upload/portal/Digital_ company_2013_WP2_WEB.pdf.

90. Savyas, A. (2005, March 8). Intel points to convergence. *Computer Weekly*, p. 12.

91. Lam, J. (2005, March 1). Continental sets tentative accords for cutting costs. *Wall Street Journal* (Eastern edition), p. A2.

92. Eastburn, R.W. & Sharland, A. (2017). Risk management and managerial mindset. *Journal of Risk Finance*, Vol. 18, 1, 21-47. Aggarwal, V.A., Hart, E., & Workiewicz, H.E. (2017). Adaptive capacity to technological change: A microfoundational approach. *Strategic Management Journal*, 38, 6, 1212-1231.

93. Jick, T., & Peiperl, M. (2003). *Changing the culture at British Airways and British Airways Update, 1991– 2000*. In T. Jick & M. Peiperl, *Managing change* (pp. 26–44). New York: McGraw-Hill Higher Education.

94. One strike and you're out: British Airways. (2003, August 2). *The Economist*, p. 64.

95. Flight plans: BA and Iberia take a step closer to becoming one of the world's biggest airlines. (2010, April 8). *The Economist online*. Retrieved from http://www.economist.com/node/15872745; and Maintaining altitude: BA's cabin staff appear to be fighting a losing battle. (2010, March 25). *The

Economist;* BA united (2011, May 12). *The Economist*. Retrieved from http://www.economist.com/blogs/ gulliver/2011/05/british_airways; British Airways: One giant step for BA. (2013, July 5). *The Economist*. Retrieved from http://www.economist.com/blogs/ gulliver/2013/07/british-airways?zid=303&ah=270 90cf03414b8c5065d64ed0dad813d.

96. Kirka, D. (2017, May 30). British Airways IT debacle puts spotlight on technological systems. *Star Business Journal*. Retrieved from http:// thestar.com/business/2017/05/30/shares-in -british-airways-parent-company-fall-after-it -failure-strands-passengers.html. Haines, G. (2017, November 7). British Airways to "bring back the glory days" with more free meals, better WiFi and 72 new planes. *The Telegraph*. Retrieved from http:// www.telegraph.co.uk/travel/news/british-airways -announces-bold-new-vision-for-future/.

97. An interesting comparison of TQM and employee involvement is contained in Lawler, E. E. III. (1994). Total quality management and employee involvement: Are they compatible? *Academy of Management Executive, 8*(1), 68–76.

98. Drawn from Morgan, G. (1994, June 28). Quantum leaps, step by step. *Globe and Mail*, B22.

99. Kirton, M. J. (1984). Adaptors and innovators— Why new initiatives get blocked. *Long Range Planning, 17*(2), 137–143; Tushman, M. L., & O'Reilly, C. A. III. (1996). Ambidextrous organizations: Managing evolutionary and revolutionary change. *California Management Review, 38*(4), 8–30.

100. Girod, S.J.G., & Whittington. R. (2015). Change escalation processes and complex adaptive systems: From incremental reconfigurations to discontinuous restructuring. *Organizational Science*, 26(5), 1520.

101. The life cycle of interventions is readily apparent in the management literature. First comes the concept, accompanied or followed closely by examples of successful implementation. Next are cautionary notes, examples of failure, and remedies. As the luster fades, new approaches emerge in the literature and the process recurs, hopefully building upon earlier learning. For example, see Miles, R. E., & Snow, C. C. (1992). Causes of failure in network organizations. *California Management Review, 34*(4), 53–72.

102. Helyar, J. (1998, August 10). Solo flight. *Wall Street Journal*. Quoted in T. Jick, *Managing change* (p. 503). New York: McGraw-Hill Higher Education.

103. Hamel, G., & Prahalad, D. K. (1994, October). Lean, mean and muddled. *Globe and Mail Report on Business Magazine*, 54–58.

104. Voelpel, S. C., Leibold, M., & Streb, C. (n.d.). The innovation meme: Managing innovation replicators for organizational fitness. *Journal of Change Management, 5*(1), 57–69.

105. Hamel, G., & Prahalad, D. K. (1994, October). Lean, mean and muddled. *Globe and Mail Report on Business Magazine*, 54–58.

106. McComb, W. L. (2014, April 1). Transformation is an era, not an event. *Harvard Business Review*; White, M. (2013, November 1). The reinvention imperative. *Harvard Business Review*.

107. An American revival: A Canadian manufacturer's quest to rebuild itself. (2014, July 7). *The Globe and Mail online*. Retrieved from http://www.theglobeandmail.com/report-on-business/an-american-revival-a-canadian-manufacturers-quest-to-rebuild-itself/article19476053/?utm_source=Shared+Article+Sent+to+User&utm_medium=E-mail:+Newsletters+/+E-Blasts+/+etc.&utm_campaign=Shared+Web+Article+Links.

108. The future of jobs: The onrushing wave. (2014, January 18). *The Economist*. Retrieved from http://www.economist.com/news/briefing/21594264-previous-technological-innovation-has-always-delivered-more-long-run-employment-not-less; The New "New Economy." (2003, September 13). *The Economist*, p. 62. Eastburn, R.W. & Sharland, A. (2017). Risk management and managerial mindset. *Journal of Risk Finance*, Vol. 18, 1, 21-47. Aggarwal, V.A., Hart, E., & Workiewicz, H.E. (2017). Adaptive capacity to technological change: A microfoundational approach. *Strategic Management Journal*, 38, 6, 1212–1231.

109. Aghina, W., De Smet, A., Lackey, G, Lurie, M., & Murarka, M. (Report, January, 2018). The five trademarks of agile organizations. *McKinsey and Company*.

110. Van Yperen, N. W. (1998). Informational support, equity and burnout: The moderating effect of self-efficacy. *Journal of Occupational and Organizational Psychology, 71*, 29–33.

111. Gordon, J. (1989, February 13). Employee alignment? Maybe just a brake job would do. *Wall Street Journal*. As reported in T. Jick. (1993). *Managing change*. Homewood, IL: Irwin.

112. Pfeffer, J. (1995). Managing with power: *Politics and influence* [video]. Executive Briefings. Stanford, CA: Stanford Videos.

113. Ricc, R., & Guerci, M. (2014, March 15). Diversity challenge: An integrated process to bridge the "implementation gap." *Business Horizons, 57*, 235–245.

114. Oshry, B. (1990). Finding and using a manager's power to improve productivity. *National Productivity Review, 10*(1), 19–33.

115. Russo, J. E., & Shoemaker, P. J. H. (1992). Managing overconfidence. *Sloan Management Review, 33*(2), 7–18.

116. Mishra, K. E., Spreitzer, G. M., & Mishra, A. K. (1998). Preserving employee morale during downsizing. *Sloan Management Review, 39*(2), 83–95.

117. Hamel, G. (2000). *Leading the revolution*. Boston: Harvard Business School Press.

118. CNNHEROES. Retrieved from https://www.cnn.com/specials/cnn-heroes.

119. Vogelgesang, G., Clapp-Smith, R., & Sland, J. (2014, May). The relationship between positive psychological capital and global mindset in the context of global leadership. *Journal of Leadership and Organizational Studies, 21*(2); Caligiuri, P., & Tarique, I. (2012, October). *Journal of World Business, 47*(4), 612; Rajah, R., Song, Z., & Richard, D. (2011, December). Taking stock of the past decade of research. *Leadership Quarterly, 22*(6), 1107; Shapiro, E. C. (1996). *Fad surfing in the boardroom: Managing in the age of instant answers*. Cambridge, MA: Perseus.

120. Higgs, M., & Rowland, D. (2005). All changes great and small: Exploring approaches to change and its leadership. *Journal of Change Management, 5*(2), 121–151.

121. Zander, L., Mockaitis, A. I., & Butler, C. L. (2012, October). Leading global teams. *Journal of World Business, 47*(4), 572.

122. Holt, K., & Kyoko, S. (2012, June). Global leadership: A developmental shift for everyone. *Industrial and Organizational Psychology: Perspectives on Science and Practice, 5*(2), 196–215; Smith, W. K., & Lewis, M. W. (2012, June). Leadership skills for managing paradoxes. *Industrial and Organizational Psychology: Perspectives on Science and Practice, 5*(2), 227–231.

CHAPTER 2

1. Arnoff, M. (2009, September 14). The challenges for McDonald's top chef. *Business Week*.

2. McDonald's corporate social responsibility and sustainability report 2012–2013. Retrieved from http://www.aboutmcdonalds.com/content/dam/AboutMcDonalds/2.0/pdfs/2012_2013_csr_report.pdf; Schwartz, A. (2009, July 6). First "green" McDonald's to offer ChargePoint EV charging stations. *Fast Company*; California McDonald's adds electric vehicle fast charge station. (2013, April 24). *QSR Web.com*. Retrieved from http://www.qsrweb.com/news/california-mcdonalds-adds-electric-vehicle-fast-charge-station/.

3. Retrieved from http://www.aboutmcdonalds.com/mcd/our_company/amazing_stories/food/catering_to_local_tastes.html.

4. Cullers, R. (2010, July 23). McDonald's goes local. *AdWeek.*

5. Bayley, R. (April 12, 2017). How has McDonald's been so successful for so long. *Franchise Direct.* Retrieved from http://corporate.mcdonalds.com/corpmcd/about-us/our-business-model.html

6. Schull, D. (1999). Why good companies go bad. *Harvard Business Review, 77*(4), 42–52.

7. Handy, C. (1994). *The age of paradox.* Boston: Harvard Business School Press.

8. Lewin, K. (1951). *Field theory in social science.* New York: Harper and Row.

9. A recent discussion of Lewin's contribution can be found in Rosch, E. (2002). Lewin's field theory as situated action in organizational change. *Organization Development Journal, 20*(2), 8–14.

10. Kotter, J. P. (1996). *Leading change.* Boston: Harvard Business School.

11. Kotter, J.P. (November 2012). Accelerate! *Harvard Business Review.*

12. Gentile, M. C. (2010). *Giving voice to values: How to speak your mind when you know what's right.* New Haven, CT & London: Yale University Press. To receive the B case and the Faculty-Only Teaching Notes, please contact Mary Gentile at Mgentile3@babson.edu

13. Shapiro, M., Ingols, C., & Gentile, M. (2011). Helen Drinan: Giving voice to her values. *Case Research Journal, 31*(2).

14. Duck, J. D. (2001). *The change monster: The human forces that fuel or foil corporate transformation and change.* New York: Crown Business.

15. Beckhard, R., & Harris, R. T. (1987). *Organizational transitions: Managing complex change.* Reading, MA: Addison-Wesley.

16. Beckhard and Harris, *Organizational transitions.*

17. Kotter, J. P. (1996). *Leading change.* Boston: Harvard Business School Press.

18. Duck, *The change monster.*

CHAPTER 3

1. Seigworth, G. (n.d.). A brief history of bloodletting. Retrieved from http://www.pbs.org/wnet/redgold/basics/bloodlettinghistory.html.

2. Bruch, H., & Gerber, P. (2005). Strategic change decisions: Doing the right change right. *Journal of Change Management, 5*(1), 99.

3. Bruch, H., & Gerber, P. (2005). Strategic change decisions: Doing the right change right. *Journal of Change Management, 5*(1), 98.

4. Ho, S. (2016, January 15). In surprise move, Target exits Canada and takes a $5.4 billion loss.

Reuters Business News. Retrieved from https://www.reuters.com/article/us-target-canada/in-surprise-move-target-exits-canada-and-takes-5-4-billion-loss-idUSKBN0KO1HR20150115.

5. Stacey, R. D. (2003). *Strategic management of organisational dynamics: The challenge of complexity.* Englewood Cliffs, NJ: Prentice Hall.

6. See Holling, C. S. (1987). Simplifying the complex: The paradigms of ecological function and structure. *European Journal of Operations Research, 30,* 139–146; Hurst, D. K. (1995). *Crisis and renewal: Meeting the challenge of organizational change.* Boston: Harvard Business Review Press.

7. Schumpeter, J. (1942). *Capitalism, socialism and democracy.* New York: Harper & Row.

8. Nadler, D. A., & Tushman, M. L. (1977). A diagnostic model for organizational behavior. In J. R. Hackman, E. E. Lawler, & L. W. Porter (Eds.), *Perspectives in behavior in organizations* (pp. 85–100). New York: McGraw-Hill.

9. Nadler, D. (1987). The effective management of organizational change. In J. W. Lorsch (Ed.), *Handbook of organizational behavior* (pp. 358–369). Englewood Cliffs, NJ: Prentice Hall.

10. Nadler, D. A., & Tushman, M. L. (Summer, 1999). The organization of the future: Strategic imperatives and core competencies for the 21st century. *Organizational Dynamics, 28*(1), 45–60.

11. McManamy, R. (1995). Fourth quarterly cost report: South America—Hyperinflation dying off. *ENR, 235*(26), 43–45.

12. Nadler, D. A., & Tushman, M. L. (1980). A model for diagnosing organizational behavior. *Organizational Dynamics, 9*(12), 35–51.

13. Peters, T., & Waterman, R. H. (1982). *In search of excellence.* New York: Harper & Row.

14. Material for the Dell story was drawn from Dell's do-over. (2009, October 26). *Business Week, 4152,* 36; and from Take two: Michael Dell pioneered a new business model at the firm that bears his name. Now he wants to overhaul it. (2008, May 1). *The Economist.* Retrieved February 2010 from the Dell website, http://content.dell.com/ca/en/corp/about-dell-investor-info.aspx.

15. Edwards, C. (October 15, 2009). Dell's extreme makeover. *Bloomberg Businessweek.* Retrieved from https://www.bloomberg.com/news/articles/2009-10-15/dells-extreme-makeover.

16. Datamonitor. (2011, June). *Computer & Peripherals Industry Profile: Global,* p. 18.

17. Madway, G. (2009, October 15). Dell CEO forecasts "powerful" computer hardware refresh.

18. Guglielmo, C. (2013, November 18). You won't have Michael Dell to kick around anymore. *Forbes*, *192*(7), p. 1.

19. Dell captures top position in worldwide PC monitors in the second quarter, moves ahead of Samsung for the first time since 2007. (2013, September 19). *IDC*. Retrieved from https://web.archive.org/web/20131019112049/http://www.idc.com/getdoc.jsp?containerId=prUS24322313. Gartner says worldwide PC shipments declines 8.3% in fourth quarter of 2015 (2016, January 12). *Gartner* Retrieved from https://www.gartner.com/newsroom/id/3185224.

20. Braithwaite, T. (2015, October 13). Dell-EMC deal: why VMware is falling. *Financial Times*. Retrieved from https://www.ft.com/content/1ca62047-4ca7-35cb-9fcc-c74b0b317fde.

21. O'Donnell, C., & Vengattil, M. (2018, July 2). Dell moves to go public, spurns IPO. Reuters. Retrieved from https://www.reuters.com/article/us-dell-vmware/dell-moves-to-go-public-spurns-ipo-idUSKBN1JS11X.

22. Grant, R. M., Shani, R., & Krishnan, R. (1994). TQM's challenge to management theory and practice. *Sloan Management Review*, *35*(2), 25–36.

23. Gates, R. (2003, September 3). How not to reform intelligence. *Wall Street Journal*, p. A16. See also Flynn, S., & Kirkpatrick, J. J. (2005). *The Department of Homeland Security: The way ahead after a rocky start*. Written testimony before a hearing of the Committee on Homeland Security and Governmental Affairs, U.S. Senate, Washington, DC.

24. Milstead, D. (2014, June 27). GM's bad news hangs over everything but its stock. *Globe and Mail*; GM fires 15 executives over deadly ignition switch. (2014, June 6). *ABC News*. Retrieved from http://www.abc.net.au/news/2014-06-06/general-motors-fires-15-exeutives-over-deadly-ignition-scandal/5504320.

25. Sahadi, J. (2018, October 11). What GM's Mary Bara learned early on: Speak up and stop saying sorry. *CNN Business*. Retrieved from https://www.cnn.com/2018/10/11/success/mary-barra-gm/index.html.

26. Burke, W. W. (2002). *Organization change: Theory and practice* (p. 191). Thousand Oaks, CA: Sage.

27. Sterman, J. (2001). System dynamics modeling: Tools for learning in a complex world. *California Management Review*, *43*(4), 8–25.

28. Shane, D. (October 4, 2018). How the trade war could make China even stronger. CNN Business. Retrieved from https://www.cnn.com/2018/10/04/business/us-trade-war-impact-china-economy/index.html.

29. Adapted from Sterman, J. (2001). System dynamics modeling: Tools for learning in a complex world. *California Management Review*, *43*(4), 13.

30. Argyris, C., & Schön, D. (1996). *Organizational learning II: Theory, method and practice*. Reading, MA: Addison-Wesley.

31. Senge, P. (1990). *The strategy*. London: Doubleday/Century Business.

32. Adapted from Gogoi, P., & Arndt, M. (2003, March 3). McDonald's hamburger hell. *Business Week*.

33. Rao, A. R., Bergen, M. E., & Davis, S. (2000). How to fight a price war. *Harvard Business Review*, *78*(2), 107–116.

34. Boosting productivity on the shop floor. (2003, September 12). *The Economist*, p. 62.

35. Quinn, R. E. (1991). *Beyond rational management*. San Francisco: Jossey-Bass.

36. See Quinn, R. E., et al. (1990). *Becoming a master manager*. New York: Wiley.

37. Rhodes, D. (March 23, 2018). Why are so many ICOs failing. *Coincentral*. Retrieved from https://coincentral.com/why-are-so-many-icos-failing/. Marr, B. (December 10, 2018). Is this the end of blockchain? *Forbes*. Retrieved from https://forbes.com/sites/bernardmarr/2018/12/10/is-this-the-end-of-blockchain/#5ab82aa83ede.

38. For a detailed treatment of this topic, see Weick, K. (1999). Organizational change and development. *Annual Review of Psychology*; Romanelli, E., & Tushman, M. L. (1994). Organizational transformation as punctuated equilibrium: An empirical test. *Academy of Management Journal*, *34*, 1141–1166; Gersick, C. G. G. (1991). Revolutionary change theories: A multilevel exploration of the punctuated equilibrium. *Academy of Management Review*, *16*, 10–36.

39. Strebel, L. (1994, Winter). Choosing the right change path. *California Management Review*, 29–51.

40. Greiner, L. (1998, May–June). Evolution and revolution as organizations grow. *Harvard Business Review*, 55–67.

41. Beckhard, R., & Harris, R. T. (1987). *Organizational transitions: Managing complex change*. Reading, MA: Addison-Wesley.

42. Mitleton-Kelly, E. (2003). The principles of complexity and enabling infrastructures. In E. Mitleton-Kelly, *Complex systems and evolutionary perspectives of organisations: The application of Stacey's Complexity Theory to organisations*. London: London School of Economics Complexity and Organisational Learning Research Programme, Elsevier.

43. Stacey, R. D. (1996). *Strategic management and organizational dynamics* (2nd ed.). London: Pittman.
44. Noori, H., Deszca, G., Munro, H., & McWilliams, B. (1999). Developing the right breakthrough product/service: An application of the umbrella methodology, Parts A & B. *International Journal of Technology Management, 17,* 544–579.
45. Letterman, E. (n.d.). Retrieved December 2010 from http://thinkexist.com/quotation/luck_is_what_happens_when_preparation_meets/11990.html.

CHAPTER 4

1. Ten people who predicted the financial meltdown. (2008, October 12). *Times Online, Money.* Retrieved May 2010 from http://timesbusiness.typepad.com/money_weblog/2008/10/10-people-who-p/comments/page/2/.
2. Schmitt, R. B. (2008, August 25). FBI saw threat of loan crisis: A top official warned of widening mortgage fraud in 2004, but the agency focused its resources elsewhere. *Los Angeles Times.*
3. The new role of risk management: Rebuilding the model. (2009, June 24). Knowledge@Wharton. Retrieved from http://knowledge.wharton.upenn.edu/article/the-new-role-of-risk-management-rebuilding-the-model/; How to play chicken and lose. (2009, January 22). *The Economist.*
4. Critics say WHO overstated H1N1 threat. (2010, January 14). *China Daily Science and Health.*
5. Ebola virus disease, West Africa–update. (2014, May 30). *World Health Organization.* Retrieved from http://www.who.int/csr/don/2014_05_30_ebola/en/; WHO/MERS update from WHO. (2014, May 14). *Unifeed.* Retrieved from http://www.unmultimedia.org/tv/unifeed/2014/05/who-mers/.
6. Stoll, J. D., & Terlep, S. G. M. (2009, May 22). UAW reach crucial cost-cutting pact—agreement to modify work rules, trim cash obligation helps ease way for quick bankruptcy filing. *Wall Street Journal,* p. B1.
7. Lanes, W. J. III, & Logan, J. W. (2004, November). A technique for assessing an organization's ability to change. *IEEE Transactions in Engineering Management, 51*(4), 483.
8. Keeton, K. B., & Mengistu, B. (1992, Winter). The perception of organizational culture by management level: Implications for training and development. *Public Productivity & Management Review, 16*(2), 205–213.
9. Darley, J. M., & Latane, B. (1968). Bystander intervention in emergencies: Diffusion of responsibility. *Journal of Personality and Social Psychology, 8,* 377–383.
10. Senge, P. M. (1994). *The fifth discipline: The art and practice of the learning organization.* New York: Currency Doubleday.
11. Sull, D. N. (1999, July–August). Why good companies go bad. *Harvard Business Review,* 42–52; Charan, R., & Useem, J. (2002). Why companies fail. *Fortune, 145*(11), 50–62; Schreiber, E. (2002). Why do many otherwise smart CEOs mismanage the reputation asset of their company? *Journal of Communication Management, 6*(3), 209–219.
12. Hamel, G. (2002). *Leading the revolution.* New York: Penguin.
13. Kotter, J. P. (2002). *The heart of change.* Boston: Harvard Business School Press.
14. Mintzberg, H., & Westley, F. (1992). Cycles of organizational change. *Strategic Management Journal, 13,* 39–59.
15. Stapenhurst, T. (2009). The benchmarking book: A how-to guide to best practice for managers and practitioners. Oxford, UK: Elsevier.
16. Sull, D. N. (1999, July). Why good companies go bad. *Harvard Business Review,* 42–52.
17. Vakola, M. (2014). What's in there for me? Individual readiness to change and the perceived impact of organizational change. *Leadership and Organizational Development Journal, 35*(3), 195–209.
18. Weisbord, M., & Janoff, S. (2005). Faster, shorter, cheaper may be simple; it's never easy. *Journal of Applied Behavioral Science, 41*(1), 70–82.
19. Gene Deszca, personal communication.
20. Sirkin, H., Keenan, P., & Jackson, A. (2005, October). The hard side of change management. *Harvard Business Review,* 4.
21. T. Cawsey, personal communication.
22. Collins, J. (2001). *Good to great.* New York: HarperCollins; Jennings, J. (2005). *Think big, act small.* New York: Penguin.
23. Corner office—Tony Hsieh of Zappos.com. (2010, January 10). *New York Times.*
24. Collins, J., & Porras, J. I. (1994). *Built to last* (p. 94). New York: HarperCollins.
25. Confidence trumps accuracy in pundit popularity. (2013, May 28). *Washington State University News.* Retrieved from https://news.wsu.edu/2013/05/28/confidence-trumps-accuracy-in-pundit-popularity/#.U44wT2dOWUk; Ariely, D. (2008).

Predictable irrationality. New York: HarperCollins; Kahneman, D. (2011). *Thinking fast and slow.* New York: Farrar, Strauss and Giroux.

26. Kahneman, D., Lovallo, D., & Sibony, O. (2011, June). Before you make the big decision. *Harvard Business Review,* 51–60.

27. Barsh, J., & Lavoie, J. (2014, April). Lead at your best. *McKinsey Quarterly*; Anderson, D., & Ackerman Anderson, L. (2011, Fall). Conscious change leadership: Achieving breakthrough results. *Executive Forum.*

28. Anders, G. (2014, May 26). Nadella's bid to fix Microsoft: What Ballmer didn't dare. *Forbes.* Retrieved from http://www.forbes.com/sites/georgeanders/2014/05/07/nadellas-bid-to-fix-microsoft-what-ballmer-didnt-dare/; Metz, C. (2014, April 4). Why Microsoft got it right with new CEO Satya Nadella. *Wired.* Retrieved from http://www.wired.com/2014/02/microsoft-ceo-satya-nadella/.

29. Cited in Tunzelmann, A. V. (2007). *Indian summer* (p. 105). London: Simon and Schuster.

30. Beckhard, R., & Harris, R. T. (1987). *Organizational transitions: Managing complex change.* Reading, MA: Addison-Wesley.

31. Spector, B. (1993). From bogged down to fired up. In T. D. Jick (Ed.), *Managing change: Cases and concepts* (pp. 121–128). Boston: Irwin/McGraw-Hill.

32. Wallace, E. (2009, May 5). Why Chrysler failed. *Bloomberg Businessweek.* Retrieved May 2010 from http://www.businessweek.com/lifestyle/content/may2009/bw2009055_922626.htm.

33. Target launch leaves retailers wary of coming to Canada. (2014, June 2). *CBC News.* Retrieved from http://www.cbc.ca/news/business/target-launch-leaves-retailers-wary-of-coming-to-canada-1.2662155; Lewis, K. (2003, November 10). Kmart's ten deadly sins. Book review in *Forbes.com.* Retrieved May 2010 from http://www.forbes.com/2003/10/10/1010kmartreview.html.

34. Wessel, M. (2011, September 7). The failure of Yahoo's board. *Hbr Blog Network.* Retrieved from http://blogs.hbr.org/2011/09/failure-yahoo-board/; Silcoff, S., McNish, J., & Ladurantaye, S. (2013, September 27). How BlackBerry blew it: The inside story. *Globe and Mail.* Retrieved from http://www.theglobeandmail.com/report-on-business/the-inside-story-of-why-blackberry-is-failing/article14563602/#dashboard/follows/.

35. Thornhill, S., & Amit, R. (2003). *Learning from failure: Organizational mortality and the resource-based view.* Research Paper, Statistics Canada. Retrieved May 2010 from http://www.statcan.gc.ca/pub/11f0019m/11f0019m2003202-eng.pdf.

36. Verdú, A. J., & Gómez-Gras, J. M. (2009). Measuring the organizational responsiveness through managerial flexibility. *Journal of Organizational Change,* 22(6), 668–690; Santos, V., & García, T. (2007). The complexity of the organizational renewal decision: The managerial role. *Leadership and Organizational Development Journal,* 28(4), 336–355.

37. Trahant, B., & Burke, W. W. (1996). Creating a change reaction: How understanding organizational dynamics can ease reengineering. *National Productivity Review,* 15(4), 37–46; Lannes, W. J. III, & Logan, J. W. (2004). A technique for assessing an organization's ability to change. *IEEE Transactions in Engineering Management,* 51(4), 483.

38. Ratterty, A., & Simons, R. (2002). The influence of attitudes to change on adoption of an integrated IT system. *Organization Development Abstracts,* Academy of Management Proceedings; Mitchell, N., et al. Program commitment in the implementation of strategic change. *Organization Development Abstracts,* Academy of Management Proceedings.

39. Hyde, A., & Paterson, J. (2002). Leadership development as a vehicle for change during merger. *Journal of Change Management,* 2(3), 266–271.

40. Nevis, E. C., DiBella, A. J., & Gould, J. M. (1995). Understanding organizations as learning systems. *Sloan Management Review,* 36(2), 73–85.

41. Armenakis, A. A., Harris, S. G., & Field, H. S. (1999). Making change permanent: A model for institutionalizing change interventions. In W. Passmore & R. Woodman (Eds.), *Research in organizational change and development* (Vol. 12, pp. 289–319). Greenwich, CT: JAI Press.

42. Holt, D. (2002). Readiness for change: The development of a scale. *Organization Development Abstracts,* Academy of Management Proceedings.

43. Judge, W., & Douglas, T. (2009). Organizational change capacity: The systematic development of a scale. *Journal of Organizational Change Management,* 22(6), 635–649.

44. Stewart, T. A. (1994, February 7). Rate your readiness to change. *Fortune,* 106–110.

45. Castellano, J. F., Rosenzweig, K., & Roehm, H. A. (2004, Summer). How corporate culture impacts unethical distortion of financial numbers. *Management Accounting Quarterly*; Gellerman, S. W. (1989, Winter). Managing ethics from the top down. *Sloan Management Review.*

46. Lazaric, N., & Raybaut, A. (2014, January). Do incentive systems spur work motivation of inventors in high tech firms? A group based perspective. *Journal of Evolutionary Economics,* 24(1), 135–157; Proenca, E. J. (2007, December). Team dynamics

and team empowerment in health care organizations. *Health Care Management Review*; Bartol, K. M., & Srivastava, A. (2002, Summer). Encouraging knowledge sharing: The role of organizational reward systems. *Journal of Leadership and Organizational Studies, 9*(1), 64–76.

47. Klarner, P., Probst, G., & Soparnot, R. (2005). Organizational change capacity in the public service: The case of the World Health Organization. *Journal of Change Management, 8*(1), 57–72.

48. Willey, D. (2008, February 28). Naples battles with rubbish mountain. *BBC News*. Retrieved May 2010 from http://news.bbc.co.uk/2/hi/europe/7266755.stm; Quattrone, A. M. (2009, November 20). Garbage crisis and organized crime. *Naples Politics*. Retrieved May 2010 from http://naplespolitics.com/2009/11/20/garbage-crisis-and-organized-crime/; Italy slammed by EU court over Naples garbage. (2010, March 4). *EUbusiness*. Retrieved May 2010 from http://www.eubusiness.com/news-eu/court-italy-waste.3h2/; Harrell, E. (2011, May 9). This stinks: Italy sends troops to handle trash crisis. *Time*. Retrieved from http://science.time.com/2011/05/09/this-stinks-italy-sends-troops-to-handle-trash-crisis/.

49. Mesco, M. (2013, November 25). Naples's garbage crisis piles up on city outskirts. *Wall Street Journal*. Retrieved from http://online.wsj.com/news/articles/SB10001424052702304465604579218014071052296.

50. Havman, H. A. (1992). Between a rock and a hard place: Organizational change and performance under conditions of fundamental environmental transformation. *Administrative Science Quarterly, 37*(1), 48–75.

51. Barnett, C. K., & Pratt, M. G. (2000). From threat-rigidity to flexibility: Toward a learning model of autogenic crisis in organizations. *Journal of Organizational Change Management, 13*(1), 74–88.

52. Simons, T. L. (1999). Behavioral integrity as a critical ingredient for transformational leadership. *Journal of Organizational Change Management, 12*(2), 89.

53. Hosmer, L. T., & Kiewitz, C. (2005). Organizational justice: A behavioral science concept with critical implications for business ethics and stakeholder theory. *Business Ethics Quarterly, 15*(1), 67.

54. Leadership tips, New York style: Lessons from the NYC MTA. (2012, November 14). *Forbes*. Retrieved from http://www.forbes.com/sites/johnkotter/2012/11/14/leadership-tips-new-york-style-lessons-from-the-nyc-mta/; Tucker, B. A., & Russell, R. F. (2004). The influence of the transformational leader. *Journal of Leadership and Organizational Studies, 10*(4), 103–111.

55. Lee, C. C., & Rodgers, R. A. (2009, Summer). Counselor advocacy: Affecting systemic change in the public arena. *Journal of Counseling and Development, 87*(3), 284–287.

56. Akgun, A. E., Lynn, G. S., & Bryne, J. C. (2006, January). Antecedents and consequences of unlearning in new product development teams. *The Journal of Product Innovation Management, 23*(1), 73–88.

57. Tucker, B. A., & Russell, R. F. (2004). The influence of the transformational leader. *Journal of Leadership and Organizational Studies, 10*(4), 103–111.

58. Naughton, K. (2002). The perk wars. *Newsweek, 140*(14), 44.

59. Mintzberg, H., Simons, R., & Basu, K. (2002, Fall). Beyond selfishness. *Sloan Management Review*, 67–74; Collins, J. (2001). *From good to great: Why some companies make the leap . . . and others don't*. New York: HarperBusiness; De Geus, A. (1997). The living company. *Harvard Business Review, 75*(2), 51–59

60. Wall, S. J. (2005). The protean organization: Learning to love change. *Organizational Dynamics, 34*(1), 37.

61. Enderle, R. (2014, March 5). Meg Whitman's amazing turnaround at HP. *IT Business Edge*. Retrieved from http://www.itbusinessedge.com/blogs/unfiltered-opinion/meg-whitmans-amazing-turnaround-of-hp.html; Hough, J. (2014, April 5). Meg Whitman's turnaround at HP. *Barron's*. Retrieved from http://online.barrons.com/news/articles/SB50001424053111903698104579473470353264720; Coyle, E. (2013, October 10). Meg Whitman's 6 steps to an HP turnaround. *Wall St, CheatSheet*. Retrieved from http://wallstcheatsheet.com/stocks/meg-whitmans-6-steps-to-an-hp-turnaround.html/?a=viewall; Canada's top 100 employers. (n.d.). Retrieved from http://www.canadastop100.com/national/.

62. Enderle, R. (November, 2018). The secret of HP's success: A new standard emerges. IT Business Edge. Retrieved from https://www.itbusinessedge.com/blogs/unfiltered-opinion/the-secrets-of-hps-success-a-new-standard-emerges.html. HP share price retrieved from Yahoo Finance at https://finance.yahoo.com/quote/HPQ.

63. Higgins, J. M., & McAllister, C. (2004). If you want strategic change, don't forget to change your culture artifacts. *Journal of Change Management, 4*(1), 63–73.

64. Helyar, J. (2004, October 4). Why is this man smiling? Continental's Gordon Bethune turned the airline around, guided it through 9/11, and became a great CEO. Now he's being forced out. How can this be? *Fortune*. Retrieved May 2010 from http://faculty.msb.edu/homak/homa

helpsite/webhelp/Airlines_-_Why_s_Bethune_ Smiling__Fortune_11-18-04.htm.

65. Higgins, J. M., & McAllister, C. (2004). If you want strategic change, don't forget to change your culture artifacts. *Journal of Change Management*, *4*(1), 63–73.

66. World's most admired companies. (2009, March 16). *Fortune*. Retrieved from http://archive.for tune.com/magazines/fortune/mostadmired/2009/ snapshots/2065.html; World Airline Awards for 2009. (2009). *World Airline Awards*. Retrieved from http://worldairlineawards.com/Awards_2009/ AirlineYear-2009.htm.

67. The legacy that got left on the shelf—Unilever and emerging markets. (2008, February). *The Economist*, *386*(8565), 76.

68. Unilever stock performance chart. Retrieved from http://ycharts.com/companies/UN.

69. Sull, D. N. (1999, July–August). Why good companies go bad. *Harvard Business Review*.

70. Finkelstein, S. (2003). *Why smart executives fail: And what you can learn from their mistakes*. New York: Penguin.

71. Eaton, J. (2001). Management communication: The threat of groupthink. *Corporate Communications*, *6*(4), 183–192; Kahneman, D., Lovallo, D., & Sibony, O. (2011, June). Before you make the big decision. *Harvard Business Review*, 51–60.

72. Whyte, G. (1989). Groupthink reconsidered. *Academy of Management Review*, *14*, 40–56; Neck, C. P., & Moorhead, G. (1992). Jury deliberations in the trial of *U.S. v. John DeLorean*: A case analysis of groupthink avoidance and enhanced framework. *Human Relations*, *45*(10), 1077–1091.

73. Charan, R., & Useem, J. (2002, May 22). Why companies fail. *Fortune*, 50–62.

74. Cole, M. S., Harris, S. G., & Bernerth, J. B. (2006). Exploring the implications of vision, appropriateness, and execution of organizational change. *Leadership and Organizational Development Journal*, *27*(5), 352–369.

75. Simons, G. F., et al. (1998). In S. Komives, J. Lucas, & T. R. McMahon, *Exploring leadership* (p. 54). San Francisco: Jossey-Bass.

76. Thornberry, N. (1997). A view about vision. *European Management Journal*, *15*(1), 28–34.

77. Beach, L. R. (1993). *Making the right decision* (p. 50). Englewood Cliffs, NJ: Prentice Hall.

78. Nanus, B. (1992). *Visionary leadership*. San Francisco: Jossey-Bass; Kirkpatrick, S. A., & Locke, E. A. (1996). Direct and indirect effects of three core charismatic leadership components on performance and attitudes. *Journal of Applied Psychology*, *81*, 36–51.

79. Baum, I. R., Locke, E. A., & Kirkpatrick, S. A. (1998). A longitudinal study of the relation of vision and vision communication to venture growth in entrepreneurial firms. *Journal of Applied Psychology*, *83*, 43–54.

80. Jick, T. (2003). *Managing change* (pp. 98–100). Boston: Irwin.

81. Butterworth, C. (2013, November). Leading the way. *Occupational Health*, *65*, 11.

82. Higgins, J. M., & McAllaster, C. (2004). If you want strategic change, don't forget to change your cultural artifacts. *Journal of Change Management*, *4*(1), 63–73.

83. Jick, T. (1993). The vision thing (A). In T. Jick, *Managing change* (pp. 142–148). Homewood, IL: Irwin.

84. Langeler, G. H. (1992, March–April). The vision trap. *Harvard Business Review*, 46–55.

85. Deszca, G., & Cawsey, T. (2014). Information contained in this section was collected by the authors when developing the case: Food Banks Canada and Strategic Renewal (case is reprinted in this book). Further information on Food Banks Canada can be viewed on their website: http:// www.foodbankscanada.ca/Learn-About-Hunger/ About-Hunger-in-Canada.aspx.

86. Lipton, M. (1996, Summer). Demystifying the development of an organizational vision. *Sloan Management Review*, 86.

87. Lipton, M. (1996, Summer). Demystifying the development of an organizational vision. *Sloan Management Review*, 89–91.

88. Levin, I. M. (2000). Vision revisited. *Journal of Applied Behavioral Science*, *36*(1), 91–107.

89. Kalogeridis, C. (2005). The Ford/Firestone fiasco: Coming to blows. *Radnor*, *185*(1), 22–24.

90. Healey, J. R., & Irwin, J. (2014, June 18). GM recalls 3.16 million more cars for switches. *USA Today*. Retrieved from http://www.usatoday.com/ story/money/cars/2014/06/16/gm-recall-key -switch/10629373/.

91. The National Business Hall of Fame. (1990, March 12). *Fortune*, *121*(6), 42.

92. Serwer, A. (2001, September 17). P&G's covert operation. *Fortune*, *144*(5), 42.

93. Searcey, D. (2010, April 19). Toyota agrees to $16.4 million fine. *Wall Street Journal Digital Network*, Auto Section. Retrieved May 2010 from http://online.wsj.com/article/SB10001424052748 704508904575192873543926804.html.

94. World's most admired companies. *Fortune*. Retrieved May 2010 from http://money.cnn.com/ magazines/fortune/mostadmired/2010/index .html.

95. Goss, T., Pascale, R., & Athos, A. (1993, November–December). The reinvention roller coaster: Risking the present for a powerful future. *Harvard Business Review*, 97–108.

96. McKinnon, N. (2008). We've never done it this way before: Prompting organizational change through stories. *Global Business and Organizational Excellence*, 27(2), 16–25.

97. Cranston, S., & Keller, S. (2013, January). Increasing the "meaning quotient" of work. *McKinsey Quarterly*.

98. Wheatley, M. (1994). *Leadership and the new sciences*. San Francisco: Berrett-Koehler.

99. Beach, L. R. (1993). *Making the right decision* (p. 58). Englewood Cliffs, NJ: Prentice Hall.

100. Jørgensen, H., Owen, L., & Nues, A. (2008). *Making change work*. IBM Global Services. Retrieved May 2010 from http://www-935.ibm .com/services/us/gbs/bus/pdf/gbe03100-usen -03-making-change-work.pdf; Lockwood, N. R. (2007). Leveraging employee engagement for competitive advantage: HR's strategic role. *Society for Human Resource Management Research Quarterly*. Retrieved May 2010 from http://www.improved -experience.com/doc/02_Leveraging_Employee_ Engagement_for_Competitive_Advantage2.pdf; Morgan, D. E., & Zeffane, R. (2003). Employee involvement, organizational change and trust in management. *International Journal of Human Resource Management*, 14(1), 55–75.

101. How to create a powerful vision for change. *Forbes*. Retrieved from http://www.forbes.com/sites/ johnkotter/2011/06/07/how-to-create-a-power ful-vision-for-change/.

102. Gross, A., & Minot, J. (2008, May). Meeting recruiting and retention challenges in India. *SHRM Global Forum*. Retrieved from Scribd: http://www.scribd .com/doc/10553235/Meeting-Recruiting-and -Retention-Challenges-in-India; Personal communication with G. Deszca, when visiting Infosys and Tata Consulting in March 2011.

103. Infosys to add 3,500 more employees. (2014, February 8). *The New Indian Express*. Retrieved from http://www.newindianexpress.com/cities/ thiruvananthapuram/Infosys-to-Add-3500-More -Employees/2014/02/08/article2044683.ece.

104. Dr. Martin Luther King Jr.'s "I Have a Dream" Speech. *The Martin Luther King Jr. Papers Project* at Stanford University. Retrieved May 2010 from http://www.stanford.edu/group/King/publications/ speeches/address_at_march_on_washington.pdf.

105. Sawhill, J. C., & Harmeling, S. S. (2000, March). National campaign to prevent teen pregnancy. *Harvard Business School Case Study*, 9–300–105.

106. Stohr, G. (2012, December 8). Gay marriage gets supreme court review for the first time. *Bloomberg*. Retrieved from www.bloomberg.com/news/.../gay -marriage-gets-supreme-court-review; Williams, P., & McClam, E. (2013, June 26). Supreme Court strikes down Defense of Marriage Act, paves way for gay marriage to resume in California. *NBC News*. Retrieved from http://nbcpolitics.nbcnews .com/_news/2013/06/26/19151971-supreme -court-strikes-down-defense-of-marriage-act -paves-way-for-gay-marriage-to-resume-in -california?lite.

107. Schneider, G. (2005, March 31). An unlikely meeting of the minds. *Washington Post*, p. E01.

108. Retrieved May 2010 from http://www-03.ibm .com/employment/us/diverse/index.shtml.

109. Govindarajan, V. (2010). Vijay Govindarajan's Blog: Strategic innovation, industry transformation and global leadership. Tuck School of Business at Dartmouth. Retrieved May 2010 from http:// www.vijaygovindarajan.com/2009/03/the_tata_ nano_product_or_socia.htm; Vision for Nano achieved. (2012, March 10). NDTV. Retrieved from http://www.ndtv.com/video/player/ndtv-special- ndtv-profit/vision-for-nano-achieved-says-ratan -tata/225972.

110. https://en.wikipedia.org/wiki/Tata_Nano

111. The Millennium Development Goals Report 2013. *United Nations*. Retrieved from http://www .undp.org/content/dam/undp/library/MDG/ english/mdg-report-2013-english.pdf.

112. Retrieved May 2010 from http://www.savethe children.org/programs/health/child-survival/ survive-to-5/?WT.mc_id=1109_hp_tab_s25.

113. Retrieved from http://www.globalgiving.org/ pfil/2030/projdoc.pdf.

114. Retrieved from https://www.kickstarter.com/ projects/readingrainbow/bring-reading-rainbow -back-for-every-child-everywh.

115. Latham, G. P., & Locke, E. P. (1987). How to set goals. In R. W. Beatty (Ed.), *The performance management sourcebook*. Amherst, MA: Human Resource Development Press.

116. Drawn from Jick, T. (1993). The vision thing (A). In T. Jick, *Managing change*. Homewood, IL: Irwin; Lipton, M. (1996, Summer). Demystifying the development of an organizational vision. *Sloan Management Review*, 83–92.

CHAPTER 5

1. Langton, N., Robbins, S. P., & Judge, T. A. (2010). *Organizational behaviour: Concepts, controversies,*

applications (5th Canadian ed., p. 502). Toronto: Pearson Canada.

2. Daft, R. L. (2007). *Organization theory and design* (9th ed., p. 90). Cincinnati, OH: South-Western College.

3. Walmart. (2017). *Annual report*. Retrieved from http://www.corporatereport.com/walmart/2017/ar/associates.php.

4. Kaplan, M. (2018, March 1). Walmart's ecommerce sales up 23% in fourth quarter 2017. *Practical Ecommerce*. Retrieved from https://www.practicalecommerce.com/walmarts-ecommerce-sales-23-percent-fourth-quarter-2017.

5. Cwinn, S. (2014, September 15). The scoop on Retail Link 2.0. *LinkedIn*. Retrieved from https://www.linkedin.com/pulse/20140915154156-17222406-the-scoop-on-retail-link-2-0/. What is retail link for? Competitive advantage lies in systems efficiencies. (2002). *Chain Store Age*, *78*(8), 74.

6. Bolman, L., & Deal, T. (2013). *Reframing organizations: Artistry, choice, and leadership* (5th ed.). San Francisco: Jossey-Bass.

7. Langton, N., Robbins, S. P., & Judge, T. A. (2010). *Organizational behaviour: Concepts, controversies, applications* (5th Canadian ed., pp. 500–527). Toronto: Pearson Canada.

8. For a detailed treatment of structural design dimensions, see Daft, R. L. (2007). *Organization theory and design* (9th ed.). Cincinnati, OH: South-Western College Publishing.

9. Thompson, J. D. (1967). *Organizations in action*. New York: McGraw-Hill.

10. Aragón-Correa, J. A., & Sharma, S. (2003). A contingent resource-based view of proactive corporate environmental strategy. *Academy of Management Review*, *28*(1), 71–88; Moles, C., van der Gaag, A., & Fox, J. (2010). The practice of complexity: Review, change and service improvement in NHA department. *Journal of Health Organization and Management*, *24*(2), 127–144; Davis, J. P., Eisenhardt, K. M., & Bingham, C. B. (2009). Optimal structure, market dynamism, and the strategy of simple rules. *Administrative Science Quarterly*, *54*, 413–452.

11. Daft, R. L. (2007). *Organization theory and design* (9th ed., p. 152). Cincinnati, OH: South-Western College.

12. Martínez-León, I. M., & Martínez-García, J. A. (2011, 32.5/6). The influence of organizational structure on organizational learning. *International Journal of Manpower*, 537–566; Olden, P. C. (2012, October–December). Managing mechanistic and organic structure in health care. *The Health Care Manager*.

13. Gawande, A.(November 12, 2018). Why doctors hate their computers: Digitization promises to make medical care easier and more efficient, but are screens coming between doctors and patients? *The New Yorker*. Retrieved from https://www.newyorker.com/magazine/2018/11/12/why-doctors-hate-their-computers.

14. Gandhi A., Magar, C., & Roberts, R. (2013, Winter). *McKinsey on Busines Technology*. Retrieved from https://www.mckinsey.com/~/media/mckinsey/dotcom/client_service/bto/pdf/mobt32_02-09_masscustom_r4.ashx. Tu, Q., Vonderembse, M. A., Ragu-Nathan, T. S., & Ragu-Nathan, B. (2004). Measuring modularity-based manufacturing practices and their impact on mass customization capability: A customer-driven perspective. *Decision Sciences*, *35*(2), 147–168.

15. Salvador, F., Martin de Holan, P. , & Piller, F. (2009, Spring). Cracking the code of mass customization. *MIT Sloan Management Review*. Retrieved from http://idea-space.eu:19001/up/e9a1c36ccd5c19227b26c2320bb9d547.pdf.

16. Galbraith, J. R. (1977). *Organization design*. Reading, MA: Addison-Wesley.

17. Daft, R. L. (2003). *Organization theory and design* (6th ed., pp. 204–211). Cincinnati, OH: South-Western College.

18. The 9–11 Commission. (2004). *9/11 Commission report: Final report of the National Commission on Terrorist Attacks upon the United States*. Washington, DC: Government Printing Office.

19. Keller, S., Meaney, M., & Pung, C. (2013, November). Organizing for change: McKinsey global survey results. *McKinsey and Company*; Cross, R. L., Parise, S., & Weiss, L. M. (2007, April). The role of networks in organizational change. *McKinsey Quarterly*.

20. Langton, N., Robbins, S. P., & Judge, T. A. (2010). *Organizational behaviour: Concepts, controversies, applications* (5th Canadian ed., p. 512). Toronto: Pearson Canada.

21. Goran, J.L., LaBerge, L., & Srinivansan, R. (2017, July). Culture in a digital age, *McKinsey Quarterly*. Retrieved from https://www.mckinsey.com/business-functions/digital-mckinsey/our-insights/culture-for-a-digital-age. De Snett, A., Lackey, G., & Weill, M. (2017, June). Untangling your organization's decision-making. *McKinsey Quarterly*. Retrieved from https://www.mckinsey.com/business-functions/organization/our-insights/untangling-your-organizations-decision-making. How to create an agile organization (2017). *McKinsey and Co*. https://www.mckinsey.com/business-functions/organization/

our-insights/how-to-create-an-agile-organization. Beinhocker, E. (2006, April). The adaptable organization. *McKinsey Quarterly*, 77-87.

22. McGregor, J. (2008, January 28). Case study: To adapt, ITT lets go of unpopular ratings. *Business Week*, 4068, 46.

23. Colvin, G. (2015, October 29). Microsoft and Dell are ditching employee performance reviews. *Fortune*. Retrieved from http://fortune.com/2015/10/29/microsoft-dell-performance-reviews/. Zillman, C. (2016, February 1), IBM is blowing up its annual performance review. *Fortune*. Retrieved from http://fortune.com/2016/02/01/ibm-employee-performance-reviews/.

24. Neilson, G., Martin, K.L., & Powers, E. (2008, June). The secrets to successful strategy execution. *Harvard Business Review*.

25. Survey: Partners in wealth. (2006, January 21). *The Economist*, *378*(8461), 18.

26. Farrier, T. (2013, August 29). How do the challenges with Boeing's 787 Dreamliner compare to the introductions of other aircraft? *Forbes*. Retrieved from http:// www.forbes.com./sites/quora/2013/08/29/how-do-the-challenges-with-boeings-787-dreamliner-compare-to-the-introductions-of-other-aircraft/; Kingsley-Jones, M. The Boeing 787 Dreamliner. Flightglobal. Retrieved July 3, 2014, from http:// www.flightglobal.com/feature/787dreamlines/market/; Boeing's partnership for success strains supplier relationships. (2014, February 16). *Leeham News and Comment*. Retrieved from http://leehamnews.com.2014/02/16/boeing-partnership-for-success-strains-strains-supplier-relationship/; Boeing 787 Dreamliner. *Wikipedia*. Retrieved from http//en.wikipedia.org/wiki/Boeing_787_Dreamliner. Updated.

27. Bhaskara, V. (2016, October 5). The Boeing 787 at five (part 1): The Dreamliner effect. *Airways*. Retrieved from https://airwaysmag.com/industry/the-boeing-787-at-five-one/. Bhaskara, V. (2016, October 5). The Boeing 787 at five (part 2): The Dreamliner effect. *Airways*. Retrieved from https://airwaysmag.com/industry/the-boeing-787-at-five-two/.

28. Boeing and the 787: Not so dreamy. (2009, June 24). *The Economist* online. Retrieved May 2010 from http://www.economist.com/businessfinance/displaystory.cfm?story_id=E1_TPRJQQDQ.

29. Wetzel, D. K., & Buch, K. (2009, Winter). Using a structural model to diagnose organizations and develop congruent interventions. *Organization Development Journal*, *18*(4), 9–19.

30. Outsourcing main cause for Boeing 787 Dreamliner problems. (2013, January 22). Consultancy.uk. Retrieved from https://www.consultancy.uk/news/297/outsourcing-main-cause-for-boeing-787-dreamliner-problems.

31. Yi, E. I., & Zhu, P. F. (2009, February 24). Faced with budget cuts, Harvard College Library consolidates. *Harvard Crimson*. Retrieved December 2010 from http://www.thecrimson.com/article/2009/2/24/faced-with-budget-cuts-harvard-college/.

32. Bolman, L., & Deal, T. (2008). *Reframing organizations: Artistry, choice, and leadership* (4th ed.). San Francisco: Jossey-Bass.

33. Bolman, L., & Deal, T. (2008). *Reframing organizations: Artistry, choice, and leadership* (4th ed., p. 73). San Francisco: Jossey-Bass.

34. Bolman, L., & Deal, T. (2008). *Reframing organizations: Artistry, choice, and leadership* (4th ed., p. 73). San Francisco: Jossey-Bass.

35. Bolman, L., & Deal, T. (2008). *Reframing organizations: Artistry, choice, and leadership* (4th ed., p. 74). San Francisco: Jossey-Bass.

36. Wischnevsky, J., & Damanpour, F. (2009). Radical strategic and structural change: Occurrence, antecedents and consequences. *International Journal of Technology Management*, *44*(1/2), 53.

37. LifeSpring Hospitals. *Wikipedia*. Retrieved from https://en.wikipedia.org/wiki/LifeSpring_Hospitals.

38. Masters, H., & Katrandjian, O. (2010, December 23). LifeSpring Hospitals: Bringing Maternity Care to Poor Mothers in India. *ABC News*. Retrieved from http://abcnews.go.com/Health/lifespring-hospitals-bring-maternity-care-to-poor-mothers-in-india/story?id=12459083; LifeSpring Maternity Hospital website. Retrieved from http://www.lifespring.in/; LifeSpring Hospitals. *Wikipedia*. Retrieved from http://en.wikipedia.org/wiki/LifeSpring_Hospitals; the Acumen Funds' website's description of LifeSpring was retrieved from http://acumen.org./investment/lifespring/.

39. Former Chevron Texaco executive tapped in special Labor Day board meeting. (2002, September 3). Retrieved May 2010 from http://money.cnn.com/2002/09/02/news/companies/ual/index.htm.

40. Air Canada seeking more labour concessions from unions. (2003, May 1). *CBC News*. Retrieved December 2010 from http://www.cbc.ca/money/story/2003/05/01/aircanada_030501.html.

41. Sackcloth and ashes: An entrenched dispute takes the shine off a proud airline. (2010, May 20). *The Economist*. Retrieved May 2010 from http:// www.economist.com/node/16171321.

42. Roth, D. (2002, January 22). How to cut pay, lay off 8,000 people and still have workers who love you: It's easy: Just follow the Agilent way. *Fortune*. Retrieved December 2010 from http://www.daniel roth.net/archive/2002/01/how_to_cut_pay_.html.

43. Agilent Technologies named 2017 company of the year by IBO (2018, January 16). *Bioinformatics*. Retrieved from https://globenewswire.com/news -release/2018/01/16/1290148/0/en/Agilent -Technologies-Named-2017-Company-of-the -Year-by-IBO.html.

44. Agilent Technologies. *Wikipedia*. Retrieved from https://en.wikipedia.org/wiki/Agilent_Technologies. Keysight Technologies. *Wikipedia*. Retrieved from https://en.wikipedia.org/wiki/Keysight

45. Nadler, D., Shaw, R. B., Walton, A. E., & Associates. (1994). *Discontinuous change: Leading organizational transformation*. San Francisco: Jossey-Bass.

46. Simons, R. (1995, March–April). Control in the age of empowerment. *Harvard Business Review*, 80–88; Simons, R. (1998, May–June). How risky is your company? *Harvard Business Review*, 85–94.

47. Howell, J., & Higgins, C. (1990). Champions of change: Identifying, understanding and sup- porting champions of technological innovations. *Organizational Dynamics, 19*(1), 40–55.

48. Tight, G. (1998). From experience: Securing spon- sors and funding for new product development projects—the human side of enterprise. *Journal of Product Innovation Management, 15*(1), 75–81; Harrold, D. (1999). How to get control and auto- mation projects approved. *Control Engineering, 46*(8), 34–37.

49. Harrold, D. (1999). How to get control and auto- mation projects approved. *Control Engineering, 46*(8), 34–37.

50. Drew, S. A. W. (1996). Accelerating change: Financial industry experiences with BPR. *International Journal of Bank Marketing, 14*(6), 23–35.

51. Noori, H., Deszca, G., & Munro, H. (1997). Managing the P/SDI process: Best-in-class prin- ciples and leading practices. *International Journal of Technology Management*, 245–268.

52. Dillard, J., Hunter, J., & Burgoon, M. (1984). Sequential request persuasive strategies: Meta- analysis of foot-in-the-door and door-in-the-face. *Human Communication Research, 10*, 461–488.

53. Babak, A.S., & Carol, G. (2017, May). Leading change authentically: How authentic leaders influ- ence follower responses to complex change. *Journal of Leadership and Organizational Studies*. 157-171.

54. Gladwell, M. (2000). *The tipping point: How little things can make a big difference*. New York: Little, Brown.

55. This example is drawn from Meyerson, D. E. (2001, October). Radical change, the quiet way. *Harvard Business Review*, 94–95.

56. Howell, J., & Higgins, C. (1990). Champions of change: Identifying, understanding and sup- porting champions of technological innovations. *Organizational Dynamics, 19*(1), 40–55.

57. Frost, P. J., & Egri, C. P. (1990). Influence of polit- ical action on innovation: Part II. *Leadership and Organizational Development Journal, 11*(2), 4–12.

58. Marshak, R. J. (2004). Morphing: The leading edge of organizational change in the twenty-first century. *Organizational Development Journal, 22*(3), 8–21.

59. Abrahamson, E. (2000, July–August). Change without pain. *Harvard Business Review*, 75–79.

60. Nusca, A. (2016, November 11). The man who is transforming Microsoft. Fortune. Retrieved from http://fortune.com/satya-nadella-microsoft-ceo/. Bort, J. (2015, February 3). In just one year, Satya Nadella made Microsoft so much better. *Business Insider*. Retrieved from https://www.businessin sider.com/satya-nadella-totally-changed-micro soft-2015-2. Nadella, S. (2018, April). Microsoft's next act. *McKinsey Quarterly*, Retrieved from https://www.mckinsey.com/industries/high-tech/ our-insights/microsofts-next-act.

61. Novel, J. (2018, July 20). Steve Ballmer says he and Bill Gates recommended Nadella as Microsoft's CEO, praises his performance. *CNBC*. Retrieved from https://www.cnbc.com/2018/07/19/steve -ballmer-bill-gates-recommended-nadella-as -microsoft-ceo.html. Stoller, K. (2018, October 10). The world's best employers 2018: Alphabet leads as U.S. companies dominate list. *Forbes*. Retrieved from https://www.forbes.com/sites/ kristinstoller/2018/10/10/the-worlds-best -employers-2018-alphabet-leads-as-u-s-compa nies-dominate-list/.

62. 63% of CRM initiatives fail. (2013, July 17). *Direct Marketing News*. Retrieved from http:// www.dmnews.com/63-of-crm-initiatives-fail/arti cle/303470/; Choy, J. (2003, March 17). The Cold Truth about CRM. *Asia Computer Weekly*.

63. Aiken, C. & S. Keller (April 2009). The irrational side of change management. *McKinsey Quarterly*.

64. Prosci Benchmarking Report. (2002). *Best practices in change management*. Prosci 2000, 2.

65. Tsaparis. P. (2013, February 21). Why is common sense so uncommon? *Globe and Mail* Report on Business. Retrieved from http://m.theglobeand mail.com/report-on-business/careers-leadership/ why-is-common-sense-so-uncommon/article89 36634/?service=mobile; Paul Tsaparis: Executive

profile and biography. *Bloomberg Businessweek.* Retrieved from http://investing.businessweek.com/research/stocks/people/person.asp?personid=7468530&ticker=HPQ; Canadian merger integration material drawn from Pitts, G. (2002, September 30). *Globe and Mail*, p. B3. Paul Tsaparis appointed the Chair of York's Board of Governors. (2018, September 25). *York University.* Retrieved from http://yfile.news.yorku.ca/2018/09/25/paul-tsaparis-mba-84-appointed-the-chair-of-york-universitys-volunteer-board-of-governors/.

66. Waldersee, R., & Griffiths, A. (2004). Implementing change: Matching implementation methods and change type. *Leadership and Development Journal, 25*(5), 424–434.

67. Miller, R., Casey, M., & Konchar, M. (2014, September 29). *Change your space, change your culture: How engaging workspaces lead to transformation and growth.* New Jersey: John Wiley and Sons.

68. Cameron, K., (2003, March). Organizational transformation through architecture and design: A project with Frank Gehry. *Journal of Management Inquiry, 12*(1), 88-92.

69. Mishra, K. E., Spreitzer, G. M., & Mishra, A. K. (1998, Winter). Preserving employee morale during downsizing. *Sloan Management Review*, 83–95.

70. Mishra, K. E., Spreitzer, G. M., & Mishra, A. K. (1998, Winter). Preserving employee morale during downsizing. *Sloan Management Review*, 83–95.

71. Nevis, E. C., DiBella, A. J., & Gould, J. M. (1995, Winter). Understanding organizations as learning systems. *Sloan Management Review, 36*(2), 73–85.

72. Beatty, R. W., & Ulrich, D. O. (1991, Summer). Re-energizing the mature organization. *Organizational Dynamics*, 16–31; Beer, M., & Nohria, N. (2000, May–June). Cracking the code of change. *Harvard Business Review*, 133–142.

73. Bazigos. M., De Smet, A., Gagnon, C., Aronowitz, S., McGinty, D., Weerda, K., Aghina, W., Lund, S. & Schaninger, B. (2016, May). McKinsey on organization: Agility and organization design. *McKinsey and Company.* Retrieved from https://www.mckinsey.com/~/media/mckinsey/business%20functions/organization/our%20insights/mckinsey%20on%20organization/mckinsey%20on%20organization%20agility%20and%20organization%20design.ashx. Hoyte, D. S., & Greenwood, R. A. (2007). Journey to the North Face: A guide to business transformation. *Academy of Strategic Management Journal, 6,* 91–104; Hoogervorst, J. A. P., Koopman, P. L., & van der

74. Worley, C., & Lawler, E. (2009). Building a change capacity at Capital One Financial. *Organizational Dynamics, 38*(4), 245–251.

75. Harris, M., Dopson, S., & Fitzpatrick, R. (2009). Strategic drift in international non-governmental development organizations—putting strategy in the background of organizational change. *Public Administration and Development, 29*(5), 415–428.

76. Margonelli, L. (2002, October). How IKEA designs its sexy price tags. *Business 2.0,* 106.

77. Miles, R. E., & Snow, C. C. (1992, Summer). Causes of failure in network organizations. *California Management Review, 34*(4), 53–72.

78. Morgan, J. (2012). *The collaborate organization: A strategic guide to solving your internal business challenges using emerging social and collaborative tools.* New York: McGraw-Hill.

79. Ellard, C. (2012, November 25). Do collaborative workspaces work? *Psychology Today.* Retrieved from http://www.psychologytoday.com/blog/mind-wandering/201211/do-collaborative-work-spaces-work.

80. The holes is holacracy. (2014, July 5). *The Economist.* Retrieved from http://www.economist.com/news/business/21606267-latest-big-idea-management-deserves-some-scepticism-holes-holacracy?frsc=dg%7Ce.

81. Chesbrough, H., & Brunswicker, S. (2013, May). *Managing open innovation in large firms: Survey report—Executive survey on open innovation 2013.* Stuttgart, Germany: Fraunhofer Institute for Industrial Engineering. Norskov, S., Kesting, P., & Parm. J. (2017, Iss. 2). Deliberate change without hierarchical influence? The case for collaborative OSS communities. *International Journal of Organizational Analysis,* 346-374.

82. Keller, S., Meaney, M., & Pung, C. (2013, November). Organizing for change: McKinsey global survey results. *McKinsey and Company.*

83. Martínez-León, I. M., & Martínez-García, J. A. (2011, 32.5/6). The influence of organizational structure on organizational learning. *International Journal of Manpower,* 537–566.

84. Garcia-Morales, V.J., Martin-Rojas, R., & Lardon-Lopez, M.E. (2018, Iss.3). Influence of social media technologies on organizational performance thorough knowledge and innovation. *Baltic Journal of Management,* 345-367. Cross, R. L., Parise, S., & Weiss, L. M. (2007, April). The role of networks in organizational change. *McKinsey Quarterly.*

CHAPTER 6

1. Fiegerman, S. (2016, June 15). How Yahoo derailed Tumblr after Marissa Mayer promised "not to screw it up." Mashable.com.

2. Useem, J. (2002, August 12). 3M + GE = ?: Jim McNerney thinks he can turn 3M from a good company into a great one—with a little help from his former employer, General Electric. *Fortune.* Retrieved December 2010 from http://money.cnn.com/magazines/fortune/fortune_archive/2002/08/12/327038/index.htm.

3. Piderit, S. K. (2000). Rethinking resistance and recognizing ambivalence: A multidimensional view of attitudes toward an organizational change. *Academy of Management Review,* 4(25), 783–794.

4. Bolman, L. G., & Deal, T. E. (2008). *Reframing organizations: Artistry, choice, and leadership.* San Francisco: Jossey-Bass.

5. Ringer, R. C., & Boss, R. M. (2000). Hospital professionals' use of upward tactics. *Journal of Management Issues,* 12(1), 92–108.

6. Treatment of these power-related concepts can be found in Whetten, D. A., & Cameron, K. S. (2010). *Developing management skills* (8th ed.). Englewood Cliffs, NJ: Prentice Hall.

7. Hardy, C. (1994, Winter). Power and organizational development: A framework for organizational change. *Journal of General Management,* 20, 20–42.

8. Bolman & Deal. Reframing organizations.

9. Lewin, K., Lippitt, R., & White, R. K. (1939). Patterns of aggressive behavior in experimentally created "social climates." *Journal of Social Psychology,* 10, 271–299.

10. Deal, T. E., & Kennedy, A. A. (1982). *Corporate cultures: The rites and rituals of corporate life.* New York: Penguin Books; Kotter, J. P., & Heskett, J. L. (1992). *Corporate culture and performance.* New York: The Free Press; Schein, E. H. (1992). *Organization culture and leadership.* San Francisco: Jossey-Bass.

11. Retrieved from http://www.amazon.com/s/ref=nb_sb_ss_i_3_14?url=search-alias%3Dstrip books&field-keywords=organization%20culture &sprefix=organization+c%2Cstripbooks%2C152.

12. Shani, A. B., Chandler, D., Coget, J.-F., & Lau, J. B. (2009). *Behavior in organizations: An experiential approach.* Boston: McGraw-Hill Irwin.

13. Lewin, K. (1951). *Field theory in social science.* New York: Harper and Row; Thomas, J. (1985). Force field analysis: A new way to evaluate your strategy. *Long Range Planning,* 18(6), 54–59.

14. Strebel, P. (1994, Winter). Choosing the right change path. *California Management Review,* 29–51.

15. More pain, waiting for the gain. (2006, February 11). *The Economist,* p. 58.

16. Savage, G. T., et al. (1991). Strategies for assessing and managing organizational stakeholders. *Academy of Management Executive,* 5(2), 61–75.

17. Cross, R., & Prusak, L. (2002, June). The people who make organizations go—or stop. *Harvard Business Review,* 5–12.

18. Luksha, P., personal communication to T. Cawsey.

19. Floyd, S., & Wooldridge, B. (1992). Managing the strategic consensus: The foundation of effective implementation. *Academy of Management Executive,* 6(4), 27–39.

20. Dr. Stacy Blake-Beard's fictionalized case studies present problems faced by leaders in real companies and offer solutions from experts. This one is based on a composite of incidents collected from several organizations.

CHAPTER 7

1. Howard; C., & Pierce, K. (eds.). (2014, May 28). The world's 100 most powerful women: #70 Ellen Johnson-Sirleaf. *Forbes.* Retrieved from http://www.forbes.com/power-women/; Ellen Johnson Sirleaf. *Wikipedia.* Retrieved from http://en.wikipedia.org/wiki/Ellen_Johnson_Sirleaf; Ellen Johnson Sirleaf— biographical. Nobel Peace Prize 2011. *Nobelprize.org.* Retrieved from http://www.nobelprize.org/nobel_prizes/peace/laureates/2011/johnson_sirleaf-bio.html.

2. Disney, A. (Producer), & Reticker, G. (Director). (2008). *Pray the devil back to hell* [Motion picture]. New York: Fork Films.

3. Frijda, N. H., & Mesquita, B. (2000). Beliefs through emotions. In N. H. Frijda, A. S. R. Manstead, & S. Bem (Eds.), *Emotions and beliefs: How feelings influence thoughts* (pp. 43–54). Paris: Oxford University Press.

4. Laumer, S., Maier, C., Adreas, E., & Weitzel, T. (2016, March). User personality and resistance to mandatory information systems in organizations: a theoretical model and empirical test of dispositional resistance to change. *Journal of Information Technology,* Vol. 31, Iss. 1, 67-82.

5. Kunze, F., Boehm, S., & Bruch, H. (2013). Age, resistance to change, and job performance. *Journal of Managerial Psychology,* 28(7/8), 741–760.

6. Dent, E. B., & Goldberg, S. G. (1999). Challenging resistance to change. *Journal of Applied Behavioral Science,* 35(1), 25–41.

7. Withey, M. J., & Cooper, W. H. (1989). Predicting exit, voice, loyalty, and neglect. *Administrative Science Quarterly,* 34, 521–539.

8. Jacobs, B. (2018, October 7). Top-tier candidate: Cory Booker woos Iowa's Democrats ahead of primaries. *The Guardian*. Retrieved from https://www.theguardian.com/us-news/2018/oct/07/top-tier-candidate-cory-booker-woos-iowas-democrats-ahead-of-primaries.

9. Lines, R. (2004). Influence of participation in strategic change: Resistance, organizational commitment and change goal achievement. *Journal of Change Management*, *4*(3), 193–215.

10. Nelson, J. (2013, Dec. 5). Desjardins Group's big tent approach. *Globe and Mail*.

11. Information in this example drawn from Kanter, R. M., & Malone, A. J. (2013). Monique Leroux: Leading change at Desjardins. Harvard Business School. Case 9-313-107; Nelson, J. (2012, October 5). Monique Leroux: A little bit of everything on her plate. *Globe and Mail*; Rockel, N. (2009, August 23). Monique Leroux mentors women as Desjardins chief. *Globe and Mail*.

12. Yerema, R., & Leung, K. (2017, November 6). Dejardins Group recognized as one of Canada's top 100 employers. Mediacorp Canada. Retrieved from https://content.eluta.ca/top-employer-desjardins/. Desjardins is once again recognized by mediacorp as a best employer (2015, November 9). Desjardins. Retrieved from https://www.desjardins.com/ca/about-us/newsroom/news-flash/2015110901.jsp.

13. Golob, L. (2018, May 17). Monique Leroux inducted into Canadian Business Hall of Fame. Investment Executive. Retrieved from https://www.investmentexecutive.com/news/people/monique-leroux-inducted-into-canadian-business-hall-of-fame/. 2013 Desjardins Group Annual Report. Retrieved from http://www.desjardins.com/ca/about-us/investor-relations/annual-quarterly-reports/desjardins-group/2013-annual-report/index.jsp.

14. Lines, R. (2004). Influence of participation in strategic change: Resistance, organizational commitment and change goal achievement. *Journal of Change Management*, *4*(3), 193–215.

15. Piderit, S. K. (2000). Rethinking resistance and recognizing ambivalence: A multidimensional view of attitudes toward an organizational change. *Academy of Management Review*, *25*(4), 783–794.

16. Piderit, S. K. (2000). Rethinking resistance and recognizing ambivalence: A multidimensional view of attitudes toward an organizational change. *Academy of Management Review*, *25*(4), 783–794.

17. Smith, K. K. (1982). *Groups in conflict: Prisons in disguise*. Dubuque, IA: Kendall/Hunt; Spreitzer, G. M., & Quinn, R. E. (1996). Empowering middle managers to be transformational leaders. *Journal of Applied Behavioral Science*, *32*(3), 237–261.

18. Piderit, S. K. (2000). Rethinking resistance and recognizing ambivalence: A multidimensional view of attitudes toward an organizational change. *Academy of Management Review*, *25*(4), 783–794.

19. Avery, J. B., Wernsing, T. S., & Luthans, F. (2008). Can positive employees help positive organizational change? Impact of psychological capital and emotions on relevant attitudes and behaviors. *Journal of Applied Behavioral Science*, *44*(1), 48–70; Tsirikas, A. N., Katsaros, K. K., & Nicolaidis, C. S. (2012). *Employee Relations*, *34*(2), 344–359.

20. Much of the material on ambivalence and change management is drawn from two excellent articles: Lines, R. (2005). The structure and function of attitudes toward organizational change. *Human Resource Development Review*, *4*(1), 8–32; and Piderit, S. K. (2000). Rethinking resistance and recognizing ambivalence: A multidimensional view of attitudes toward an organizational change. *Academy of Management Review*, *25*(4), 783–794.

21. Lines, R. (2004). Influence of participation in strategic change: Resistance, organizational commitment and change goal achievement. *Journal of Change Management*, *4*(3), 193–215.

22. Piderit, S. K. (2000). Rethinking resistance and recognizing ambivalence: A multidimensional view of attitudes toward an organizational change. *Academy of Management Review*, *25*(4), 783–794.

23. Sull, D. N. (1999, July–August). Why good companies go bad. *Harvard Business Review*, 42–51.

24. Festinger, L. (1957). *A theory of cognitive dissonance*. Stanford, CA: Stanford University Press.

25. Hymes, R. W. (1986). Political attitudes as social categories: A new look at selective memory. *Journal of Personality and Social Psychology*, *51*, 233–241.

26. Tormala, Z.L, & Rucker, D.D. (2015, September). How certainty transforms persuasion. *Harvard Business Review*.

27. Simoes, P. M. M., & Esposito, M. (2014). Improving change management: How communication nature influences resistance to change. *Journal of Management Development*, *33*(4), 324–341.

28. Barr, P. S., Stimpert, J. L., & Huff, A. S. (1992). Cognitive change, strategic action, and organizational renewal. *Strategic Management Journal*, *13*, 15–36; Floyd, S. W., & Wooldridge, B. (1996). *The strategic middle manager*. San Francisco: Jossey-Bass.

29. Lines, R. (2004). Influence of participation in strategic change: Resistance, organizational commitment and change goal achievement. *Journal of Change Management*, *4*(3), 193–215.

30. Peus, C., Frey, D., Gerkhardt, M., Fischer, P., & Traut-Mattausch, E. (2009). Leading and managing organizational change initiatives. *Management Review, 20*(2), 158–175; Giora, D. A., & Thomas, J. B. (1996). Identity, image, and issue interpretation: Sensemaking during strategic change in academia. *Administrative Science Quarterly, 41*, 370–403; Labianca, G., Gray, B., & Brass, D. J. (2000). A grounded model of organizational schema change during empowerment. *Organizational Science, 11*(2), 235–257; Lines, R. (2004). Influence of participation in strategic change: Resistance, organizational commitment and change goal achievement. *Journal of Change Management, 4*(3), 193–215; and Sagie, A., & Koslowsky, M. (1994). Organizational attitudes and behaviors as a function of participation in strategic and tactical decisions: An application of path–goal theory. *Journal of Organizational Behavior, 15*(1), 37–47.

31. Balogun, J., & Johnson, G. (2005). From intended strategies to unintended outcomes: The impact of change recipient sensemaking. *Organizational Studies, 26*(11), 1596.

32. Cullen, K. L., Edwards, B. D., Casper, W. C., & Gue, K. R. (2014, June). Employees' adaptability and perceptions of change-related uncertainty: Implications for perceived organizational support, job satisfaction, and performance. *Journal of Business and Psychology, 29*(2), 269–280; Paula Matos, M. S., & Esposito, M. (2014). Improving change management: How communication nature influences resistance to change. *Journal of Management Development, 33*(4), 324–341.

33. Hackman, J. R., & Oldham, G. R. (1980). *Work redesign.* Reading, MA: Addison-Wesley.

34. Gustafson, B. (2005). Plant closure "devastates" Newfoundland community. *National Fisherman, 85*(10), 11–12.

35. Gustafson, B. (2005). Plant closure "devastates" Newfoundland community. *National Fisherman, 85*(10), 11–12.

36. Gopinath, C., & Becker, T. E. (2000). Communication, procedural justice, and employee attitudes: Relationships under conditions of divestiture. *Journal of Management, 26*, 63–83.

37. Piderit, S. K. (2000). Rethinking resistance and recognizing ambivalence: A multidimensional view of attitudes toward an organizational change. *Academy of Management Review, 25*(4), 783–794.

38. Russell, R. S., Taylor, B. W., Castillo, I., & Vidyarthi, N. (2014). *Operations management: Creating value along the supply chain* (Canadian Ed.). Toronto: Wiley.

39. Reicher, A. E., Wanous, J. P., & Austin, J. T. (1997). Understanding and managing cynicism about organizational change. *Academy of Management Executive, 11*(1), 48–60.

40. Lines, R. (2004). Influence of participation in strategic change: Resistance, organizational commitment and change goal achievement. *Journal of Change Management, 4*(3), 193–215.

41. Peus, C., Frey, D., Gerkhardt, M., Fischer, P., & Traut-Mattausch, E. (2009). Leading and managing organizational change initiatives. *Management Review, 20*(2), 158–175.

42. Kickul, J., Lester, S. W., & Finkl, J. (2002). Promise breaking during organizational change: Do justice interventions make a difference? *Journal of Organizational Behavior, 23*, 469–488.

43. Watson, T. J. (1982). Group ideologies and organizational change. *Journal of Management Studies, 19*, 259–275.

44. Kotter, J. P. (1995). Leading change: Why transformation efforts fail. *Harvard Business Review, 73*(2), 59–67.

45. Kerr, S. (1995). On the folly of rewarding A, while hoping for B. *Academy of Management Executive, 9*(1), 7–14.

46. Bareil, C. (2013, Fall). Two paradigms about resistance to change. *Organizational Development Journal, 31*(3).

47. Turnley, W. H., & Feldman, D. C. (1999). The impact of psychological contract violations on exit, voice, loyalty, and neglect. *Human Relations, 52*(7), 895–922; Rousseau, D. M. (1995). *Promises in action: Psychological contracts in organizations.* Thousand Oaks, CA: Sage.

48. Matthijs Bal, P., Chiaburu, D. S., & Jansen, P. G. W. (2010). Psychological contract breach and work performance; Is social exchange a buffer or an intensifier? *Journal of Managerial Psychology, 25*(3), 252–273; Richard, O. C., McMillan-Capehart, A., Bhuian, S. N., & Taylor, E. C. (2009). Antecedents and consequences of psychological contracts: Does organizational culture really matter? *Journal of Business Research, 62*(8), 818–825.

49. Deery, S. J., Iverson, R. D., & Walsh, J. T. (2006). Toward a better understanding of psychological contract breach: A study of customer service employees. *Journal of Applied Psychology, 91*(1), 13; Suazo, M. M., Turnley, W. H., & Mai-Dalton, R. R. (2005). The role of perceived violation in determining employees' reactions to psychological contract breach. *Journal of Leadership and Organizational Studies, 12*(1), 24–36.

50. Lee, J., and Taylor, M. S. (2014, March). Dual roles in psychological contracts: When managers take both agent and principal roles. *Human Resource Management Review, 24*(1).

51. Nesterkin, D. A. (2013). Organizational change and psychological reactance. *Journal of Organizational Change Management, 26*(3), 573–594.

52. Chi-jung, F., and Chin-I, C. (2014). Unfilled expectations and promises, and behavioral outcomes. *International Journal of Organizational Analysis, 22*(1), 61–75; Chambel, M. J. (2014). Does the fulfillment of supervisor psychological contract make a difference? Attitudes of in-house and temporary agency workers. *Leadership and Organizational Development Journal, 35*(1), 20–37.

53. Edmondson, A. C. (2003). Large-scale change at the WSSC. *Harvard Business School*, 9–603–056.

54. Edmondson, A. C. (2003). Large-scale change at the WSSC. *Harvard Business School*, 9–603–056. After leading the Washington Suburban Sanitary commission, John Griffen served as secretary of Maryland's Department of Resources from 2007–2013 and was named chief of staff of Maryland's Governor O'Malley in 2013. See John Griffin named Governor O'Malley's new chief of staff (2013, April 18). *Baltimore News Journal.*

55. Kübler-Ross, E. (1969). *On death and dying*. New York: Macmillan.

56. Fink, S. L. (1967). Crisis and motivation: A theoretical model. *Archives of Physical Medicine and Rehabilitation, 48*(11), 592–597.

57. Jick, T. (2002). The recipients of change. In T. Jick & M. A. Peiperl, *Managing change: Cases and concepts* (2nd ed., pp. 299–311). New York: McGraw-Hill Higher Education.

58. Perlman, D., & Takacs, G. J. (1990). The ten stages of change. *Nursing Management, 21*(4), 33–38.

59. Piderit, S. K. (2000). Rethinking resistance and recognizing ambivalence: A multidimensional view of attitudes toward an organizational change. *Academy of Management Review, 25*(4), 783–794.

60. Kotter, J. P. (2007, January). Leading change: Why transformation efforts fail. *Harvard Business Review*, 96–103.

61. The Prosci ADKAR model. Retrieved from https://www.prosci.com/adkar/adkar-model.

62. Doherty, N., Banks, J., & Vinnicombe, S. (1996). Managing survivors: The experience of survivors in British Telecom and the British financial services sector. *Journal of Managerial Psychology, 11*(7), 51–60.

63. Bedeian, A. G., & Armenakis, A. A. (1998, February). The cesspool syndrome: How dreck floats to the top of declining organizations. *Academy of Management Executive*, 58–67; Mishra, K. E., Spreitzer, G. M., & Mishra, A. K. (1998). Preserving employee morale during downsizing. *Sloan Management Review, 39*(2), 83–95.

64. For a detailed treatment of dealing with the survivor syndrome, see Noer, D. M. (1993). *Healing the wounds*. San Francisco: Jossey-Bass.

65. Jick, T., & Peiperl, M. A. (2002). *Managing change: Cases and concepts* (2nd ed.). New York: McGraw-Hill Higher Education.

66. Personal conversation with the author.

67. Rogers, E. M. (1995). *Diffusion of innovations* (4th ed.). New York: Free Press.

68. Laumer, S., Maier, C., Adreas, E., & Weitzel, T. (2016, March). User personality and resistance to mandatory information systems in organizations: A theoretical model and empirical test of dispositional resistance to change. *Journal of Information Technology*, Vol. 31, Iss. 1, 67-82.

69. Deckop, J. R., Merriman, K. K., & Blau, G. (2004). Impact of variable risk preferences on the effectiveness of control of pay. *Journal of Occupational and Organizational Psychology, 77*(1), 63–80.

70. Oreg, S., Bayazıt, M., Vakola, M., Arciniega, L., Armenakis, A., Barkauskiene, R., . . . & van Dam, K. (2008). Dispositional resistance to change: Measurement equivalence and the link to personal values across 17 nations. *Journal of Applied Psychology, 93*(4), 935–944; Steenkamp, L. P., and Wessels, P. L. (2014). An analysis of the tolerance for ambiguity among accounting students. *International Business and Research Journal (Online), 13*(2).

71. Probst, T. M. (2003). Exploring employee outcomes of organizational restructuring: A Solomon four-group study. *Group and Organization Management, 28*(3), 416–439.

72. Tremblay, M., & Roger, A. (2004). Career plateauing reactions: The moderating role of job scope, role ambiguity and participation among Canadian managers. *International Journal of Human Resource Management, 15*(6), 996–1017.

73. Kass, S. J., Vodanovich, S. J., & Callender, A. (2001). State-trait boredom: Relationship to absenteeism, tenure, and job satisfaction. *Journal of Business and Psychology, 16*(2), 317–326.

74. Park, D., & Krishnan, H. A. (2003). Understanding the stability-change paradox: Insights for the evolutionary, adaptation, and institutional perspectives. *International Journal of Management, 20*(3), 265–270.

75. Barnett, W. P., & Sorenson, O. (2002). The Red Queen in organizational creation. *Industrial and Corporate Change, 11*(2), 289–325.

76. Kolbert, E. (2017, February 27). Why facts don't change our minds. *New Yorker Magazine*. Retrieved from https://www.newyorker.com/magazine/2017/02/27/why-facts-dont-change-our-minds.

77. Kelly, P., & Amburgey, T. (1991). Organizational inertia and momentum: A dynamic model of strategic change. *Academy of Management Journal, 34,* 591–612; Huff, J., Huff, J., & Thomas, H. (1992). Strategic renewal and the interaction of cumulative stress and inertia. *Strategic Management Journal, 13,* 55–75.

78. Kovoor-Misra, S., & Nathan, M. (2000). Timing is everything: The optimal time to learn from crises. *Review of Business, 21*(3/4), 31–36.

79. Geller, E. S. (2002). Leadership to overcome resistance to change: It takes more than consequence control. *Journal of Organizational Behavior Management, 22*(3), 29; and Brown, J., & Quarter, J. (1994). Resistance to change: The influence of social networks on the conversion of a privately-owned unionized business to a worker cooperative. *Economic and Industrial Democracy, 15*(2), 259–283.

80. Loi, R., and Lai, J. Y. M., & Lam, L. W. (2012, June). Working under a committed boss: A test of the relationship between supervisors' and subordinates' affective commitment. *Leadership Quarterly, 23*(3), 466–475.

81. Kane-Frieder, R. E., Hochwarter, W. A., Hampton, H. L., & Ferris, G. R. (2014). Supervisor political support as a buffer to subordinates' reactions to politics perceptions: A three-sample investigation. *Career Development International, 19*(1), 27–48; Sales, M. (2002, July/August). Futures thinking by middle managers: A neglected necessity. *Systems Research and Behavioral Science, 19*(4), 367; Oshry, B. (1990). Finding and using a manager's power to improve productivity. *National Productivity Review, 10*(1), 19–33.

82. Bettenhausen, K. L. (1991). Five years of groups research: What we have learned and what needs to be addressed. *Journal of Management, 17*(2), 345–381.

83. Johnson, L. (2008). Helping employees cope with change in an anxious era. *Harvard Management Update, 13*(12), 1–5.

84. Cranston, S., & Keller, S. (2015, January). Increasing the "meaning quotient" at work. *McKinsey Quarterly.* Retrieved from https://www.mckinsey.com/business-functions/organization/our-insights/increasing-the-meaning-quotient-of-work. Barash, J., Mogelof, J., & Webb, C. (2010, October). How centered leaders achieve extraordinary results. *McKinsey Quarterly.* Retrieved from https://www.mckinsey.com/featured-insights/leadership/how-centered-leaders-achieve-extraordinary-results.

85. Brenneman, G. (1998). Right away and all at once: How we saved Continental. *Harvard Business Review, 76*(5), 162–173.

86. Tyler, T. R., & De Cremer, D. (2005). Process-based leadership: Fair procedures and reactions to organizational change. *Leadership Quarterly, 16*(4), 529–545.

87. Sherman, W. S., & Garland, G. E. (2007). Where to bury the survivors? Exploring possible ex post effects of resistance to change. *S. A. M. Advanced Management Journal, 72*(1), 52–63.

88. Arthur, C. (2013, November 4). BlackBerry fires CEO Thorsten Heins as $4.7bn Fairfax rescue bid collapses. *The Guardian.* Retrieved from http://www.theguardian.com/tech nology/2013/nov/04/black berry-fires-ceo-thorsten-heins-fairfax-bid-collapses.

89. Pachner, J. (2018, March 31). The incredible shrinking company. *Globe and Mail Report on Business Magazine.* Retrieved from https://www.theglobeandmail.com/report-on-business/rob-magazine/has-john-chen-saved-blackberryyet/article38350881/.

90. Reichers, A. E., Wanous, J. P., & Austin, J. T. (1997). Understanding and managing cynicism about organizational change. *Academy of Management Executive, 11*(1), 48–60.

91. Reichers, A. E., Wanous, J. P., & Austin, J. T. (1997). Understanding and managing cynicism about organizational change. *Academy of Management Executive, 11*(1), 50–51.

92. Munduate, L., & Bennebroek Gravenhorst, K. M. (2003). Power dynamics and organisational change: An introduction. *Applied Psychology: An International Review, 52*(1), 1–13; Weick, K. E., & Quinn, R. E. (1999). Organizational change and development. *Annual Review of Psychology, 50,* 361–386; Peus, C., Frey, D., Gerkhardt, M., Fischer, P., & Traut-Mattausch, E. (2009). Leading and managing organizational change initiatives. *Management Review, 20*(2), 158–175.

93. Brown, M., & Cregan, C. (2008). Organizational change cynicism: The role of employee involvement. *Human Resource Management, 47*(4), 667–686.

94. Personal communication, 2004.

95. Kramer, R. M. (2006). The great intimidators. *Harvard Business Review, 84*(2), 88–96.

96. Sherman, W. S., & Garland, G. E. (2007). Where to bury the survivors? Exploring possible ex post effects of resistance to change. *S. A. M. Advanced Management Journal, 72*(1), 52–63.

97. Source unknown.

98. Stimson, W. A. (2005). A Deming inspired management code of ethics. *Quality Progress, 38*(2), 67–75; Farson, R., & Keyes, R. (2002). The failure-tolerant leader. *Harvard Business Review, 80*(8), 64; Casio, J. (2002). Scare tactics. *Incentive, 176*(9), 56–62.

99. Collins, J. C. (2001). *From good to great: Why some companies make the leap . . . and others don't.* New York: Harper Business.

100. Werther, W. B., Jr. (1987). Loyalty: Cross-organizational comparisons and patterns. *Leadership and Organization Development Journal, 8*(2), 3–6.

101. Deming, W. E. (1986). *Drastic changes for western management.* Madison, WI: Center for Quality and Productivity Improvement.

102. Challagalla, G. N., & Shervgani, T. A. (1996). Dimensions and types of supervisory control: Effects on salesperson performance and satisfaction. *Journal of Marketing, 60,* 89–105.

103. Appelbaum, S. H., Bregman, M., & Moroz, P. (1998). Fear as a strategy: Effects and impact within the organization. *Journal of European Industrial Training, 22*(3), 113–127.

104. Usman, A., Maqadas, F., Muhammad, K.I., & Saboor, A. (2018, Vol. 31, Iss.5). Emerging organizational parameters in implementation of organizational change. *Journal of Organizational Change Management,* 1084-1104.

105. Collins, J. C., & Porras, J. I. (1994). *Built to last: Successful habits of visionary companies.* New York: HarperCollins.

106. Kolb, D. G. (2002). Continuity, not change: The next organizational challenge. *University of Auckland Business Review, 4*(2), 1–11.

107. Balogun, J., & Johnson, G. (2005). From intended strategies to unintended outcomes: The impact of change recipient sensemaking. *Organizational Studies, 26*(11), 1573–1601.

108. Cranston, S., and Keller, S. (2013, January). Increasing the meaning quotient at work. *McKinsey Quarterly.*

109. Evans, C., Hammersley, G. O., & Robertson, M. (2001). Assessing the role and efficacy of communication strategies in times of crisis. *Journal of European Industrial Training, 25*(6), 297–309; Ashkenas, R. N., DeMonaco, L. J., & Francis, S. C. (1998). Making the deal real: How GE Capital integrates acquisitions. *Harvard Business Review, 76*(1), 165–176.

110. Difonzo, N., & Bordia, P. (1998). A tale of two corporations: Managing uncertainty during organizational change. *Human Resource Management, 37*(3–4), 295–304.

111. Bringselius, L. (2014, Spring). Employee objections to organizational change: A framework for addressing management responses. *Organizational Development Journal,* 41-54.

112. Cunha, M.P.E., Clegg, S.R., Rego, A., & Story, J. (2013, Vol. 13, No. 3). From the physics of change to realpolitik: Improvisational relations of power

and resistance. *Journal of Change Management.* 460–476.

113. Tersine, R., Harvey, M., & Buckley, M. (1997). Shifting organizational paradigms: Transitional management. *European Management Journal, 15*(1), 45–57.

114. Schneider, B., Brief, A. P., & Guzzo, R. A. (1996). Creating a climate and culture for sustainable organizational change. *Organizational Dynamics, 24*(4), 6–18.

115. Abrahamson, E. (2000, July–August). Change without pain. *Harvard Business Review,* 75–79. Driver, L. (2018, October 14). How Indra Nooyi changed the face of PepsiCo. World Finance. Retrieved from https://www.worldfinance.com/special-reports/how-indra-nooyi-changed-the-face-of-pepsico.

116. Burke, R. J. (2002). The ripple effect. *Nursing Management, 33*(2), 41–43; Weakland, J. H. (2001). Human resources holistic approach to healing downsizing survivors. *Organizational Development Journal, 19*(2), 59–69; Mishra, K. E., Spreitzer, G. M., & Mishra, A. K. (1998). Preserving employee morale during downsizing. *Sloan Management Review, 39*(2), 83–95.

117. McCann, J., Selsky, J., & Lee, J. (2009). Building agility, resilience and performance in turbulent environments. *People and Strategy, 32*(3), 44–51. Denning, S. (2018, April 24). How McKinsey embraces agile as key to managing talent. *Forbes.* Retrieved from https://www.forbes.com/sites/stevedenning/2018/04/24/how-mckinsey-embraces-agile-as-key-to-managing-talent/#4eb7fdc9cb4c.

118. Nadler, D. A., & Tushman, M. T. (1999). The organization of the future: Strategic imperatives and core competencies for the 21st century. *Organizational Dynamics, 28*(1), 45–60.

119. Meyerson, D. E. (2001, October). Radical change, the quiet way. *Harvard Business Review,* 92–100.

120. Cohen, A. R., & Bradford, D. L. (1990). *Influence without authority.* New York: Wiley; Keys, B., & Case, T. (1990). How to become an influential manager. *Academy of Management Executive, 4,* 38–49.

121. Pink, D.H. (2011). *Drive: The surprising truth about what motivates us.* New York: Riverhead Books. See also Pink's YouTube video based on the book. Retrieved from https://www.youtube.com/watch?v=u6XAPnuFjJc&list=PLOs0lcCMEHfKWAfRRmVNhb0jEMBz2i2a_.

122. Reichers, A. E., Wanous, J. P., & Austin, J. T. (1997). Understanding and managing cynicism about organizational change. *Academy of Management Executive, 11*(1), 53.

123. Adapted from Reicher, A. E., et al. (1997). Understanding and managing cynicism about organizational change. *Academy of Management Executive, 11*(1), 53.

CHAPTER 8

1. Dover, P. A. (2003). Change agents at work: Lessons from Siemens Nixdorf. *Journal of Change Management, 3*(3), 243–257.
2. Lattman, P. (2005). Rebound. *Forbes, 175*(6), 58.
3. Jac the Knife new chairman of BHP. Retrieved May 2010 from http://www.smh.com.au/business/jac-the-knife-new-chairman-of-bhp-20090804-e8mx.html.
4. Hamel, G. (2002). *Leading the revolution: How to thrive in turbulent times by making innovation a way of life.* Boston, MA: Harvard Business School Press.
5. Mass, J. (2000). Leading the revolution. *MIT Sloan Management Review, 42*(1), 95.
6. Zaccaro, S. J., & Banks, D. (2004). Leader visioning and adaptability: Bridging the gap between research and practice on developing the ability to manage change. *Human Resource Management, 43*(4), 367–380.
7. Huey, J. (1994). The new post-heroic leadership. *Fortune, 129*(4), 42. Retrieved December 2010 from http://money.cnn.com/magazines/fortune/fortune_archive/1994/02/21/78995/index.htm.
8. Jick, T., & Peiperl, M. (2003). *Managing change: Cases and concepts* (p. 362). New York: McGraw-Hill/Irwin.
9. Tandon, N. (2003). The young change agents. In T. Jick & M. Peiperl, *Managing change: Cases and concepts* (p. 428). New York: McGraw-Hill/Irwin.
10. Kanter, R. M. (2003). The enduring skills of change leaders. In T. Jick & M. Peiperl, *Managing change: Cases and concepts* (p. 429). New York: McGraw-Hill/Irwin.
11. Hammonds, K. (2001, November). Change agents: Michael J. Fox & Deborah Brooks. *Fast Company,* (52), 106.
12. Branson, C. M. (2009). Achieving organizational change through values alignment. *Journal of Educational Administration, 46*(3), 376–395.
13. Frank, J. N. (2004). Newman's Own serves up a down-home public image. *PRweek, 7*(5), 10.
14. Dickout, R. (1997). All I ever needed to know about change management I learned at engineering school. *McKinsey Quarterly, 2,* 114–121.
15. Dickout, R. (1997). All I ever needed to know about change management I learned at engineering school. *McKinsey Quarterly, 2,* 114–121.
16. Francis, H. (2003). Teamworking and change: Managing the contradictions. *Human Resource Management Journal, 13*(3), 71–90.
17. Chilton, S. (2004). Book review of *Creating leaderful organisations: How to bring out leadership in everyone. Journal of Organizational Change Management, 17*(1), 110.
18. Katzenbach, J. R. (1996). Real change. *McKinsey Quarterly, 1,* 148–163.
19. Doyle, M. (2003). From change novice to change expert. *Personnel Review, 31*(4), 465–481.
20. Appelbaum, S., Bethune, M., & Tannenbaum, R. (1999). Downsizing and the emergence of self-managed teams. *Participation and Empowerment: An International Journal, 7*(5), 109–130.
21. Kramer, R. M. (2006, February). The great intimidators. *Harvard Business Review,* 88–96.
22. Collins, J. (2001). *From good to great.* New York: HarperCollins.
23. Rubin, R., Dierdorff, E., Boomer, W., & Baldwin, T. (2009). Do leaders reap what they sow? Leader and employee outcomes of leader organizational cynicism about change. *Leadership Quarterly, 20*(5), 680–688.
24. McCall, M., & Lombardo, M. (1983). *Off the track: Why and how successful executives get derailed.* Greensboro, NC: Center for Creative Leadership.
25. Higgs, M. (2009). The good, the bad and the ugly: Leadership and narcissism. *Journal of Change Management, 9*(2), 165–178.
26. Francis, H. (2003). Teamworking and change: Managing the contradictions. *Human Resource Management Journal, 13*(3), 71–90.
27. Much of this is drawn from Jick, T., & Peiperl, M. (2003). *Managing change: Cases and concepts* (p. 362). New York: McGraw-Hill/Irwin.
28. Ilies, R., Gerhardt, M. W., & Le, H. (2004). Individual differences in leadership emergence: Integrating meta-analytic findings and behavioral genetics estimates. *International Journal of Selection and Assessment, 12*(3), 207.
29. Leban, W., & Zulauf, C. (2004). Linking emotional intelligence abilities and transformational leadership styles. *Leadership and Organization Development Journal, 25*(7/8), 554.
30. Caldwell, R. (2003). Change leaders and change managers: Different or complementary? *Leadership & Organization Development Journal, 24*(5), 285–293.
31. Higgs, M., & Rowland, D. (2005). All changes great and small: Exploring approaches to change and its leadership. *Journal of Change Management, 5*(2), 121–151.

32. Higgs, M., & Rowland, D. (2005). All changes great and small: Exploring approaches to change and its leadership. *Journal of Change Management*, 5(2), 147.

33. Kouzes, J. M., & Posner, B. Z. (2007). *The leadership challenge* (4th ed.). San Francisco: Jossey-Bass.

34. Retrieved May 2010 from http://www.ccl.org/leadership/index.aspx.

35. Criswell, C., & Martin, A. (2007). 10 trends: A study of senior executives' views on the future. Center for Creative Leadership. Retrieved December 10 from http://www.ccl.org/leadership/pdf/research/TenTrends.pdf.

36. Duck, J. D. (2001). *The change monster: The human forces that fuel or foil corporate transformation and change.* New York: Crown Business.

37. Bennis (1989), as reported in Komives, S., et al. (1998). *Exploring leadership* (p. 109). San Francisco: Jossey-Bass.

38. Cooperrider, D. L., & Whitney, D. (1998). *Collaborating for change: Appreciative Inquiry.* San Francisco: Berrett-Koehler Communications.

39. Miller, D. (2002). Successful change leaders: What makes them? What do they do that is different? *Journal of Change Management*, 2(4), 383.

40. Zaccaro, S. J., & Banks, D. (2004). Leader visioning and adaptability: Bridging the gap between research and practice on developing the ability to manage change. *Human Resource Management*, 43(4), 367–380.

41. Patton, J. R. (2003). Intuition in decisions. *Management Decision*, 41(10), 989–996.

42. Personal communication with the authors.

43. Nadler, D., & Tushman, M. (1989). Organizational frame bending. *Academy of Management Executive*, 3(3), 194–204.

44. Weick, K., & Quinn, R. (1999). Organizational change and development. *Annual Review of Psychology, 50,* 366.

45. McAdam, R., McLean, J., & Henderson, J. (2003). The strategic "pull" and operational "push" of total quality management in UK regional electricity service companies. *International Journal of Quality & Reliability Management*, 20(4/5), 436–457.

46. Kirton, M. J. (1984). Adaptors and innovators—Why new initiatives get blocked. *Long Range Planning, 17*(2), 137–143; Tushman, M. L., & O'Reilly, C. A. III. (1996). Ambidextrous organizations: Managing evolutionary and revolutionary change. *California Management Review*, 38(4), 8–30.

47. Saka, A. (2003). Internal change agents' view of the management of change problem. *Journal of Organizational Change Management*, 16(5), 480–497.

48. Hunsaker, P. (1982, September–October). Strategies for organizational change: The role of the inside change agent. *Personnel*, 18–28.

49. Wright, C. (2009). Inside out? Organizational membership, ambiguity and the ambivalent identity of the internal consultant. *British Journal of Management*, 20(3), 309–322.

50. Personal experience of the authors.

51. Saka, A. (2003). Internal change agents' view of the management of change problem. *Journal of Organizational Change Management*, 16(5), 489.

52. Personal experience of the authors.

53. Pitts, G. (2010, January 4). The fine art of managing change. *Globe and Mail.*

54. Jarrett, M. (2004). Tuning into the emotional drama of change: Extending the consultant's bandwidth. *Journal of Change Management*, 4(3), 247–258; Kilman, R. H. (1979, Spring). Problem defining and the consulting/intervention process. *California Management Review*, 26–33; Simon, A., & Kumar, V. (2001). Client's view on strategic capabilities which lead to management consulting success. *Management Decisions*, 39(5/6), 362–373.

55. Prosci Benchmarking Report. Best Practices in Change Management. (2000).

56. Adapted from Prosci Benchmarking Report. Best Practices in Change Management. (2000).

57. Worren, N., et al. (1999, September). From organizational development to change management: The emergence of a new profession. *Journal of Applied Behavioral Science,* 277.

58. Worren, N. et al. (1999, September). From organizational development to change management: The emergence of a new profession. *Journal of Applied Behavioral Science,* 277, Table 2.

59. Appelbaum, S., Bethune, M., & Tannenbaum, R. (1999). Downsizing and the emergence of self-managed teams. *Participation and Empowerment: An International Journal*, 7(5), 109–130.

60. Prosci Benchmarking Report. Best Practices in Change Management. (2000).

61. Kahn, W. A. (2004). Facilitating and undermining organizational change: A case study. *Journal of Applied Behavioral Science*, 40(1), 7–30.

62. Rooney, P. (2001, November 12). Bill Gates, chairman and chief software architect. Microsoft. *CNR.*

63. Retrieved May 2010 from http://www.newswire.ca/en/releases/archive/June2006/15/c4768.html.

64. H. Sheppard, personal communication with T. Cawsey.

65. Webber, A. M. (1999). Learning for change (an interview with Peter Senge). *Fast Company, 24.* Retrieved December 2010 from http://www.fastcompany.com/magazine/24/senge.html.

66. Senge, P. M. (1996). The leader's new work: Building learning organizations. In K. Starkey (Ed.), *How organisations learn* (pp. 288–315). London: International Thompson Business Press.

67. Gilley, A., McMillan, H., & Gilley, J. (2009). Organizational change and characteristics of leadership effectiveness. *Journal of Leadership and Organizational Studies*, 16(1), 38–47.

68. Banutu-Gomez, M. B., & Banutu-Gomez, S. M. T. (2007). Leadership and organizational change in a competitive environment. *Business Renaissance Quarterly*, 2(2), 69–90.

69. Wageman, R. (1997, Summer). Critical success factors for creating superb self-managing teams. *Organizational Dynamics*, 49–61.

70. Johnston Smith International (2000, November 22). 2000 Change Management Conference, The Change Institute, Toronto.

71. Gerstner, L. (2002). *Who says elephants can't dance?: Inside IBM's historic turnaround.* New York: HarperCollins.

72. Sheppard, P. (2003, February). Leading the Turnaround: Lou Gerstner of IBM. *Wharton Leadership Digest*, 7(5).

73. Lambert, T. (2006). Insight. *MENAFN.com.* Retrieved May 2010 from http://www.menafn.com/qn_print.asp?StroyID=129531&subl=true.

74. Katzenbach, J. (1996, July/August). From middle manager to real change leader. *Strategy and Leadership*, 34.

75. Oshry, B. (1993). Converting middle powerlessness to middle power: A systems approach. In T. Jick, *Managing change: Cases and concepts.* Homewood, IL: Irwin.

76. Howell, J., & Higgins, C. (1990, Summer). Champions of change. *Organizational Dynamics*, 40–55. Retrieved May 2010 from http://www.deloitte.com/view/en_US/us/Insights/Browse-by-Content-Type/Case-Studies/index.htm.

77. The sage of Quiznos: The skills of Greg Brenneman, a corporate-turnaround specialist, are in demand. (2008, August 28). *Economist.* Retrieved December 2010 from http://www.economist.com/node/12001911.

78. Shepard, H. (1975, November). Rules of thumb for change agents. *Organization Development Practitioner*, 1–5; Ransdell, E. (1997). Rules for Radicals. *Fast Company*, 11, 190–191; Hamel, G. (2000, July). How to start an insurrection. *Ideas@ Work*, Harvard Business Review Press.

79. Prosci Benchmarking Report. Best Practices in Change Management. (2000).

CHAPTER 9

1. Mattioli, D., & Maher, K. (2010, March 1). At 3M, innovation comes in tweaks and snips. *Wall Street Journal* (Digital Network). Retrieved May 2010 from http://online.wsj.com/article/SB1000142405274870378730457507559096304616 2.html.

2. Swanborg, R. (2010, April 30). Social networks in the enterprise: 3M's innovation process. *CIO.* Retrieved May 2010 from http://www.cio.com.au/article/344909/social_networks_enterprise_3m_innovation_process/; From Post-its to Facebras: How 3M puts innovation into practice. (2010, April 1). *Knowledge@SMU.* Retrieved May 2010 from http://knowledge.smu.edu.sg/article.cfm?articleid=1281.

3. Many 3-M press releases contain this phase. Retrieved from http://investors.3m.com/news/press-release-details/2017/3M-Reinvents-Scouring-Pad-with-New-Scotch-Brite-Dual-Purpose-Scour-Pad-96Hex/default.aspx.

4. Retrieved May 2010 from http://en.wikiquote.org/wiki/Grace_Hopper; or http://www.ideafinder.com/history/inventors/hopper.htm; or http://www.inventors.about.com/library/inventors/bl_Grace_Hopper.htm.

5. Pfeffer, J., & Sutton, R. (1999). Knowing "what" to do is not enough: Turning knowledge into action. *California Management Review*, 42(1), 83–110.

6. O'Hara, S., Murphy, L., & Reeve, S. (2007). Action learning as leverage for strategic transformation: A case study reflection. *Strategic Change*, 16(4), 177–190.

7. Sayles, L. (1993, Spring). Doing things right: A new imperative for middle managers. *Organizational Dynamics*, 10.

8. Kahan, S. (2008, October 13). Personal empowerment in difficult times. *Fast Company*. Retrieved May 2010 from http://www.fastcompany.com/blog/seth-kahan/leading-change/personal-empowerment-difficult-times.

9. Mintzberg, H., & Westley, F. (2001). Decision making: It's not what you think. *Sloan Management Review*, 42, 89–93.

10. Nohria, N. (1993). Executing change: Three generic strategies. *Harvard Business School Press #9-494-039.*

11. Waldersee, R., & Griffiths, A. (2004). Implementing change: Matching implementation methods and change type. *Leadership and Organization Development Journal*, 25(5), 424–434.

12. Beer, M., Eisenstat, R., & Spector, B. (1990, November–December). Why change programs

don't produce change. *Harvard Business Review*, 158–166.

13. Retrieved May 2010 from http://www.everyday-taichi.com/confucius-saying.html.

14. Beer, M., Eisenstat, R., & Spector, B. (1990, November–December). Why change programs don't produce change. *Harvard Business Review*, 158–166.

15. Rune, T. (2005). Organisational change management: A critical review. *Journal of Change Management*, 5(4), 375.

16. Source unknown.

17. Welbourne, T. M. (2009). Extreme strategy. *Leader to Leader*, 2009(2), 42–48.

18. Adapted from Mieszkowski, K. (1998). Change—Barbara Waugh. *Fast Company*, 20, 146.

19. Waldersee, R., & Griffiths, A. (2004). Implementing change: Matching implementation methods and change type. *Leadership and Organization Development Journal*, 25(5), 424–434.

20. Retrieved May 2010 from http://www.valuebasedmanagement.net/methods_scenario_planning.html.

21. Noori, H., Munro, H., Deszca, G., & McWilliams, B. (1999). Developing the right breakthrough product/service: An application of the umbrella methodology. Parts A and B. *International Journal of Technology Management*, 17, 544–579.

22. Wylie, I. (2002, July). There is no alternative to . . . *Fast Company*, 106–110.

23. Brown, T. (2009). *Change by design*. New York: HarperCollins.

24. Hern, A. (Dec. 19, 2018). Facebook shared private user messages with Netflix and Spotify. *The Guardian*. Retrieved from http://www.theguardian.com/technology/2018/dec/19/facebook-user-data-private-messages-netflix-spotify-amazon-microsoft-sony.

25. Cummings, T. G., & Worley, C. G. (2009). *Organization development and change*. Mason, OH: South-Western.

26. Beckhard, R., & Harris, R. (1987). *Organizational transitions* (p. 95). Reading, MA: Addison-Wesley.

27. Schein, E. (2017). *Organizational culture and leadership*. Hoboken, New Jersey: Wiley and Sons. Cameron, K.S., & Quinn, R. (2011). *Diagnosing and changing organizational culture: Based on the competing values framework* (3rd Ed.). San Francisco: John Wiley and Sons.

28. Duxbury, N., Garett-Petts, W.F., & MacLennan, D. (editors) (2015). *Cultural mapping as cultural inquiry*. Oxfordshire: Routledge. *Cultural mapping toolkit: A partnership between 2010 legacies now and creative city network of Canada* (2010). Retrieved from http://www.creativecity.ca/database/files/library/cultural_mapping-toolkit.pdf.

29. Personal communication with author.

30. Gladwell, M. (2002). *The tipping point*. New York: First Back Bay.

31. Burke, W. (2002). *Organization change: Theory and practice* (pp. 274–280). London: Sage.

32. Moore, G. (1999). *Crossing the chasm*. New York: HarperBusiness.

33. Lui, M. (2008, May 9). Clyburn sees "tipping point" to Obama. *New York Times*. Retrieved May 2010 from http://thecaucus.blogs.nytimes.com/2008/05/09/clyburn-sees-tipping-point-to-obama/; Balz, D. (2008, January 8). Obama's tipping point. *Washington Post*. Retrieved May 2010 from http://voices.washingtonpost.com/44/2008/01/obamas-tipping-point-1.html; Stanton, J. (2009, April 20). The man behind Obama's online election campaign. Web 2.0 Convergence Blogs. Retrieved May 2010 from http://www.digitalcommunitiesblogs.com/web_20_convergence/2009/04/the-man-behind-obamas-online-e.php.

34. Rigby, D., & Bilodeau, B. (2018). Management tools and trends. *Bain and Company*. Retrieved from https://www.bain.com/contentassets/f8361c5cd99e4f40bbbf83c17d6a91b9/bain_brief-management_tools_and_trends.pdf.

35. Argyris, C. (1991, May–June). Teaching smart people how to learn. *Harvard Business Review*, 104.

36. De Bono, E. (1984). *Tactics: The art and science of success* (p. 41). Toronto: Little, Brown.

37. Russo, J. E., & Schoemaker, P. J. H. (1992, Winter). Managing overconfidence. *Sloan Management Review*, 7–17.

38. Isern, J., & Pung, C. (2007). Harnessing energy to drive organizational change. *McKinsey Quarterly*, 1, 16–19.

39. Goodman, J., & Truss, C. (2004). The medium and the message: Communicating effectively during a major change initiative. *Journal of Change Management*, 4(3), 234.

40. Dutton, J., et al. (2001). Moves that matter: Issue selling and organizational change. *Academy of Management Journal*, 44(4), 716–736.

41. Kotter, J. P. (1995). Leading change: Why transformation efforts fail. *Harvard Business Review*, 73(2), 59–67.

42. Spector, B. (1989, Summer). From bogged down to fired up: Inspiring organizational change. *Sloan Management Review*, 29–34.

43. Klein, S. (1996). A management communication strategy for change. *Journal of Organizational Change Management*, 9(2), 37.

44. Birshin, M., & Kar, J. (July, 2012). Becoming more strategic: Three tips for any executive. *McKinsey Quarterly*.

45. Klein, S. (1996). A management communication strategy for change. *Journal of Organizational Change Management, 9*(2), 37.

46. Welch, J., & Welch, S. (2007). How to really shake things up: Transforming a company requires total commitment and serious stamina. *Business Week, 4061*(84), 84.

47. Goodman, J., & Truss, C. (2004). The medium and the message: Communicating effectively during a major change initiative. *Journal of Change Management, 4*(3), 234; Nelissen, P., & van Selm, M. (2008). Surviving organizational change: How management communication helps balance mixed feelings. *Corporate Communications, 13*(3), 306–318.

48. Keller, S., Meaney, M., & Pung, C. (2013, November). Organizing for change through social technologies: McKinsey global survey results. *McKinsey & Company.*

49. Daft, D., & Lengel, R. H. (1984). Information richness: A new approach to managerial behavior and organizational design. In B. Staw & R. Cummings, *Research in organizational behavior* (Vol. 6, pp. 191–233). Greenwich, CT: JAI Press.

50. Daft, D., & Lengel, R. H. (1984). Information richness: A new approach to managerial behavior and organizational design. In B. Staw & R. Cummings, *Research in organizational behavior* (Vol. 6, pp. 191–233). Greenwich, CT: JAI Press.

51. Goodman, J., & Truss, C. (2004). The medium and the message: Communicating effectively during a major change initiative. *Journal of Change Management, 4*(3), 218.

52. Klein, S. (1996). A management communication strategy for change. *Journal of Organizational Change Management, 9*(2), 34.

53. Duck, J. D. (1993, November–December). Managing change: The art of balancing. *Harvard Business Review,* 4.

54. Cranston, S., & Keller, S. (2013, January). Increasing the meaning quotient at work. *McKinsey Quarterly*; Keller, S., Meaney, M., & Pung, C. (2013, November). Organizing for change through social technologies: McKinsey global survey results. *McKinsey & Company.*

55. Peus, C., Frey, D., Gerkhardt, M., Fishcher, P., & Traut-Mattausch, E. (2009). Leading and managing organizational change initiatives. *Management Review, 20*(2), 158–175.

56. Kotter, J. P. (1995). Leading change: Why transformation efforts fail. *Harvard Business Review, 73*(2), 59–67.

57. The first six highlighted points are drawn from Kotter, J., & Schlesinger, L. (1982). Choosing strategies for change. *Harvard Business Review, 57*(2), 106–114.

58. Geller, A. (2005, February 10). As union nears win, Wal-Mart closes store. *Associated Press.* Retrieved May 2010 from http://www.commondreams.org/headlines05/0210-13.htm; Wal-Mart shutters Quebec auto shop after union win. (2008, October 16). *Montreal Gazette.* Retrieved from http://www.canada.com/finance/moneylibrary/story.html?id=01e454a4-b613-47d6-b0fa-ead56e06ec1d; Canadian Press. (2013, August 16). Only Walmart union in Canada votes to decertify. *Huff-Post Canada.* Retrieved from http://www.huffingtonpost.ca/2013/08/16/walmart-canada-union-decertifies_n_3769807.html; Blackwell, R. (2014, June 22). Supreme Court rules Walmart broke Quebec labour codes by closing store. *Global News* (2014, June 27). Retrieved from http://globalnews.ca/news/1420291/supreme-court-rules-walmart-broke-quebec-labour-code-by-closing-store/.

59. Falbe, C., & Yukl, G. (1992). Consequences for managers of using single influence tactics and combinations of tactics. *Academy of Management Journal, 35*(3), 638–652.

60. Source unknown.

61. Nutt, P. (1992). *Managing planned change* (p. 153). Toronto: Maxwell Macmillan Canada.

62. Morris, K. F., & Raben, C. S. (1999). The fundamentals of change management. In D. Nadler et al., *Discontinuous change* (pp. 57–58). San Francisco: Jossey-Bass.

63. Duck, J. D. (1993, November–December). Managing change: The art of balancing. *Harvard Business Review,* 9.

64. Ackerman, L. (1982, Summer). Transition management: An in-depth look at managing complex change. *Organizational Dynamics,* 46–66.

65. Beckhard, R., & Harris, R. (1987). *Organizational transitions* (p. 95). Reading, MA: Addison-Wesley.

66. Personal correspondence with W. Allen, Ministry of Agriculture, Food and Rural Affairs, Ontario Government.

67. For information on how to conduct an After-Action Review, see *After-action review technical guidance.* (2006). Washington, DC: U.S. Agency for International Development, PN-ADF-360. Electronic version available at http://pdf.usaid.gov/pdf_docs/PNADF360.pdf.

CHAPTER 10

1. Porter, E. (2016, March 1) Does a carbon tax work? Ask British Columbia. *The New York*

Times, retrieved from https://www.nytimes.com/2016/03/02/business/does-a-carbon-tax-work-ask-british-columbia.html. Beaty, R., Lipsey, R., & Elgie, S. (2014, July 9). The shocking truth about B.C.'s carbon tax: It works. *Globe and Mail*. Retrieved from http://www.theglobeandmail.com/globe-debate/the-insidious-truth-about-bcs-carbon-tax-it-works/article19512237/?utm_source=Shared+Article+Sent+to+User&utm_medium=E-mail:+Newsletters+/+E-Blasts+/+etc.&utm_campaign=Shared+Web+Article+Links.

2. Fred, E. (2004). Transition in the workplace. *Journal of Management Development*, 23(10), 962–964.

3. Ford, M. W., & Greer, B. M. (2005). The relationship between management control system usage and planner change achievement: An exploratory study. *Journal of Change Management*, 5(1), 29–46.

4. Ford, M. W., & Greer, B. M. (2005). The relationship between management control system usage and planner change achievement: An exploratory study. *Journal of Change Management*, 5(1), 29–46; Schreyogg, G., & Steinmann, H. (1987). Strategic control: A new perspective. *Academy of Management Review*, 12(1), 91–103; Preble, J. F. (1992). Towards a comprehensive system of strategic control. *Journal of Management Studies*, 29(4), 391–409.

5. Kotter, J. P., & Schlesinger, L. A. (2008). Choosing strategies for change. *Harvard Business Review*, 86(7–8), 130–139; Lorange, P. M., Morton, S., & Goshal, S. (1986). *Strategic control*. St. Paul, MN: West; Simons, R. (1995). Control in the age of empowerment. *Harvard Business Review*, 73(2), 80–88.

6. Kennerley, M., Neely, A., & Adams, C. (2003). Survival of the fittest: Measuring performance in a changing business environment. *Measuring Business Excellence*, 7(4), 37–43.

7. Brant, J. R. (2003). Dare to be different. *Chief Executive*, 188, 36.

8. Bond, R., Barbarika, A., & Fan, Y. (2014, October 27). Top 50 franchises for Minorities (2014). WorldFranchising.com. Retrieved from http://www.worldfranchising.com/articles/top-50-franchises-for-minorities-2014.

9. (2018, March 29). RE/MAX outsold competitors by more than 2:1 in Survey. *RE/MAX, LLC*. Retrieved from https://www.prnewswire.com/news-releases/remax-agents-on-average-outsold-competitors-by-more-than-21-in-survey-300621284.html. (2018, May 15). RE/MAX tops 120,000 agents in its first quarter. *Elite Agent epm*. Retrived from https://elite-agent.com/re-max-tops-120000-agents-in-its-first-quarter/.

10. Szamosi, L. T., & Duxbury, L. (2002). Development of a measure to assess organizational change. *Journal of Organizational Change Management*, 15(2), 184–201.

11. Harkins, P., & Hollihan, K. (2004). *Everybody wins: The story and lessons behind RE/MAX*. New York: Wiley.

12. Miller, D. (2002). Successful change leaders: What makes them? What do they do that is different? *Journal of Change Management*, 2(4), 356–368.

13. Grasso, L. P. (2006). Barriers to lean accounting. *Cost Management*, 20(2), 6–19.

14. Weber, P. S., & Weber, J. E. (2001). Changes in employee perceptions during organizational change. *Leadership and Organizational Development Journal*, 22(5/6), 291–300.

15. Nauta, A., & Sanders, K. (2001). Causes and consequences of perceived goal differences between departments within manufacturing organizations. *Journal of Occupational and Organizational Psychology*, 74(Pt. 3), 321–342; Cooke, J. A. (2003). Want real collaboration? Change your measures. *Logistics Management*, 42(1), 37–41.

16. Denton, D. K. (2002). Learning how to keep score. *Industrial Management*, 44(2), 28–33; Anonymous. (2002). Materials management benchmarks easy to find, but often measure wrong things. *Hospital Materials Management*, 27(3), 3–4.

17. Sellers, P. (1992). The dumbest marketing ploy. *Fortune*, 126(7), 88–92.

18. Kanter, R. M. (2003). Leadership and the psychology of turnarounds. *Harvard Business Review*, 81(6), 58–67.

19. Kahneman, P. (2011). *Thinking Fast and Slow*. New York: Farrer, Straus & Giroux. Kahneman, D., Lovallo, D., & Sibony, O. (2011, June). Before you make that big decision… *Harvard Business Review*. 51–60.

20. Kim, W. C., & Mauborgne, R. (2003). Fair process: Management in the knowledge economy. *Harvard Business Review*, 81(1), 127–139.

21. Favero, N., Meier, K., & O'Tool, L.J. (2016, April). Goals, trust, participation, and feedback: Linking internal management with performance outcomes. *Journal of Public Administration Research and Theory*. Vol. 26, Iss. 2. Patterson, M., Woods, S., Carroll, C., & Balain, C. (2010, October). Systematic review of the links between human resource management practices and performance. *Health Technology Assessment*, 14(51).

22. Pink, D. (2009). *Drive: The surprising truth about what motivates us*. New York: Riverhead Books.

23. Cawsey, T., & Deszca, G. Personal experience.

24. Kerr, S. (1995). On the folly of rewarding A, while hoping for B. *Academy of Management Executive*, *9*(1), 7–14.

25. Higgins, J. M., & Currie, D. M. (2004). It's time to rebalance the scorecard. *Business and Society Review*, *109*(3), 297–309.

26. Eisenhardt, K. M., & Sull, D. N. (2001). Strategy as simple rules. *Harvard Business Review*, *79*(1), 106–116.

27. Stiglitz, J. E. (2000). The contributions of the economics of information to twentieth century economics. *Quarterly Journal of Economics*, *115*(4), 1441–1478.

28. Lawson, E., & Price, C. (2003). The psychology of change management. *McKinsey Quarterly, Special Edition: Organization, 2003*.

29. Simons, R. (1995). Control in the age of empowerment. *Harvard Business Review*, *73*(2), 80–88.

30. Hoque, Z., & Chia, M. (2012). Competitive forces and the levers of control framework in a manufacturing setting. *Qualitative Research in Accounting and Management*, *9*(2), 123–145; Tero-Seppo, T. (2005, September). The interplay of different levers of control: A case study of introducing a new performance measurement system. *Management Accounting Research*, *16*(3), 293–320.

31. Kaplan, R. S., & Norton, D. P. (2000). Having trouble with your strategy? Then map it. *Harvard Business Review*, *78*(5), 167–176.

32. Kaplan, R. S., & Norton, D. P. (2004). The strategy map: Guide to aligning intangible assets. *Strategy and Leadership*, *32*(5), 10–17.

33. Interesting examples of the not-for-profit application of strategy maps in the health care sector can be found in Lee-Ching, L.C. (2009). How strategy map works for Ontario's health system. *The International Journal of Public Sector Management*, *22*(4), 349-363.

34. Cheng, M. M., & Humphreys, K. A. (2012, May). The differential improvement effects of the strategy map and scorecard perspectives on managers' strategic judgments. *The Accounting Review*, *87*(3), 899–924; González, J. J. H., Calderón, M. A., & González, J. (2012). The alignment of managers' mental models with the balanced scorecard strategy map. *Total Quality Management and Business Excellence*, *23*(5–6), 613.

35. Kaplan, R. S., & Norton, D. P. (2000). Having trouble with your strategy? Then map it. *Harvard Business Review*, *78*(5), 167–176.

36. Kaplan, R. S., & Norton, D. P. (1996). Using the balanced scorecard as a strategic management system. *Harvard Business Review*, *74*(1), 75–85.

37. Simon, R. (1999). How risky is your company? *Harvard Business Review*, *77*(3), 85–94.

38. Sirkin, H. L., Keenan, P., & Jackson, A. (2005, October). The hard side of change management. *Harvard Business Review*, *91*(9), 108–118.

CHAPTER 11

1. Barkema, H. G., et al. (2002). Management challenges in a new time. *Academy of Management Journal*, *45*(5), 916.

2. Galbraith, J. R. (2005, August). *Organizing for the future: Designing the 21st-century organization. Strategy and structure. The process will continue*. Academy of Management Annual Meeting, Hawaii.

3. Malone, T. (2005, August). *Inventing organizations*. Academy of Management Annual Meeting, Hawaii.

4. Refer to Beckhard, R., & Harris, R. T. (1987). *Organizational transitions: Managing complex change* (p. 104). Reading, MA: Addison-Wesley, for a further discussion on responsibility charting.

INDEX

importance, 354
key principles, 353
plans, 349–352, 350 (table)
skills, 285
timing, 349–350
in transition management, 358
See also Social media
Communications technology, 14–15, 408–409
Competency trap, 245
Competing values model, 70, 85–87, 86 (figure)
Complacency trap, 245
Complexity theory, 70, 90–92
Confirmation bias, 245, 378
Congruence model, 69, 71–82, 73 (figure)
Consultants
external, 296–299
internal, 295–296
Continental Airlines, 121, 250
Contingency planning, 336–338
Continuous change, 21, 23–24, 174, 211, 292, 413, 414
Continuous improvement, 256
Continuous improvers, 294
Cooperrider, D. L., 290
Corruption, 16
Coworkers, 246–249
Cranston, S., 130, 249
Creeping commitment, 172
Crises
financial (2008), 7, 17–18, 23, 101, 391
need for change and, 100, 106, 116, 117
Criswell, C., 288
Critical path methods, 340–341
CRM. *See* Customer relationship management
Cross, R., 214
Cuban Missile Crisis, 108
Cultural mapping tools, 343–344
Culture. *See* Organizational culture
Customer perspective, 385–386
Customer relationship management (CRM), 176
Cynicism, 30, 50, 111, 117, 118, 251, 379

Data collection
accuracy, 380
in change initiatives, 373, 384–385
external data, 105–106, 112, 119
internal data, 108, 119
See also Measurement and control systems
Deal, T., 152–153, 162–163, 200
De Bono, E., 348
Decision tree analysis, 336, 337 (figure)
Dell, Michael, 78, 79, 82
Dell Computers, 77–81, 82, 87, 89–90, 155
Deming, W. E., 24, 252

Demographics
aging populations, 7–9
diversity, 10–12
Departmental power, 200–202
Department of Homeland Security, 81
Design and implementation teams, 301
Design thinking, 338–339
Desjardins Group, 231–234, 252
Developmental stages of change leaders, 290, 291 (table)
Developmental strategists, 293–294
Diagnostic and steering controls systems, 381, 382
DICE framework, 392–393
Dickout, R., 284
Discontinuous/radical changes, 21, 24, 292, 328, 413, 414
Doing first strategy, 328, 329
"Do it" orientation, 324–327
Douglas, T., 112
Doyle, M., 285
Duck, Jeanie Daniel, 50–51, 56, 289
Duck's five-stage change curve, 50–51
Dunkin' Donuts, 2

Early adopters, 216–217
Early majority, 216
eBay, 120, 282
Economic environment, 16, 17–19
See also Financial crisis
Edwards, Blake, 254
Effort, 392
Egri, C. P., 173
Eigen, Peter, 16
Eisenstat, R., 330
Emergent change, 328, 329
Emotional champions, 292–293
Emotional stages, 50–51
Employees. *See* Workers
Empowerment, 327
Endothermic change, 284
Environment. *See* External environment
Environmental issues, 12–13, 102, 132
Ethics, 16–17, 348–349
Ethiopian Airlines, 161–162
Ethnic diversity, 10
Exothermic change, 284
External change agents, 296–299
External consultants, 296–299
External environment
demographics, 7–12
drivers of change, 5–19
economic, 16, 17–19
future changes, 408–410, 413
macro changes, 19–21, 20 (table)

organizational structure aligned with, 158–159
PESTEL factors, 5–7
physical, 12–13
political, 16–17
scanning, 112
technology, 13–16, 408–409, 410, 415
External stakeholders, 106–107

Facebook, 14, 29, 408
Falbe, C., 356
FedEx, 81, 124–125, 303
Financial crisis (2008), 7, 17–18, 23, 101, 391
Financial perspective, 385
Fink, S. L., 242
Fiorina, Carly, 120
Flip-flop changes, 211–212
Flow charting, 338
Floyd, S., 217
Food Banks Canada, 126
Force field analysis, 209–212, 210 (figure), 212
    (figure), 341–342
Ford Motor Company, 128, 280
Formal structures and systems
    advancing change with, 165–167, 252–253
    centralized or decentralized, 153, 414
    change acceptance and, 176–181
    change implementation and, 174–176
    change project approvals, 167–173
    complexity, 151
    defined, 150–151
    design issues, 162–165
    environmental alignment, 158–159
    future of, 410
    information-processing perspective, 155–158, 156
        (figure)
    mechanistic and organic typology, 154 (table),
        154–155, 163–164
    networks, 180
    obstacles, 326
    purposes, 74
    restructuring, 159–162, 180, 355
    strategic alignment, 158, 165
    understanding, 151, 152–155
Fox, Gretchen, 204
Fox, Michael J., 283
FOX Relocation Management Corp., 204–205
Frost, P. J., 173
Future organizations, 408–412, 411 (table)

Galbraith, J. R., 155–156, 157, 159, 161, 410
Gap analysis, 51, 53, 55–56
Garriques, Ron, 78
Gates, Bill, 109, 282, 300
Gaudet, Serge, 18

Gawande, A., 155
General Electric (GE), 118, 199, 211, 282
General Motors (GM), 6, 9, 22, 82, 102, 128–129,
    211, 379, 408
Gentile, M. C., 48, 49
Gerber, P., 69
Gerstner, Lou, 302–303, 325
Gillette, 377–378
Giving Voice to Values (GVV), 48–50
Gladden, Brian, 78
Gladwell, M., 344
GM. See General Motors
Goodman, J., 349, 352
Google, 12, 14, 29, 71, 128
Goss, T., 129
Grant, Peter, 172–173, 174
Grant, R. M., 81
Greiner, L., 88–90
Greiner's organizational growth model, 70, 87–90,
    89 (figure)
Griffiths, A., 330, 333
Groupthink, 122–123, 234
GVV. See Giving Voice to Values

H1N1 flu pandemic, 101
Hamel, G., 25, 29, 280, 306
Handy, C., 41
Handy-Dandy Vision Crafter, 127, 127 (table)
Hannon, Kerry, 9
Hardy, C., 202
Harley-Davidson, 9
Harris, R. T., 51, 110, 358
Heins, Thorsten, 251
Hewlett-Packard (Canada) Ltd., 177
Hewlett-Packard (HP), 17, 78, 120–121, 122,
    282, 333
Higgins, C., 170, 172, 173
Higgs, M., 285–286, 288
Holt, D., 112
Hopper, Grace, 326
Hotel complaint example, 39–41, 44–45,
    55–57
Howell, J., 170, 172, 173
HP. See Hewlett-Packard
Hunsaker, P., 295

IBM, 78, 133, 302–303, 325, 408
Immigration, 10
Implementation. See Action planning; Change
    implementers
Incremental/continuous changes, 21, 23–24, 174,
    211, 292, 413, 414
Individual readiness for change, 111
Influence strategies, 354–357, 357 (table)

ABOUT THE AUTHORS

Gene Deszca is professor emeritus of business administration and a former MBA director and associate director in the Lazaridis School of Business and Economics at Wilfrid Laurier University. He played a variety of leadership roles at Laurier, including the development and launch of the full-time, one-year MBA program, the executive MBA program, and the undergraduate international business concentration. He was instrumental in the development of the post-university professional accreditation programs for one of Canada's major accounting bodies and was a member of its national board of directors for several years.

Gene loves working with students and the excitement of the classroom and continues to teach graduate and executive courses, both nationally and internationally, in organizational behavior, leading organizational change, and international business. His consulting work follows similar themes for clients in both the public and private sectors, with a focus on framing and navigating organizational change and the development and delivery of executive programs to facilitate transition management. He is involved in two entrepreneurial initiatives which are in the process of scaling. The first involves software that simulates organizational disruption, for use in executive/management education (see changebydesign.com). The second organization focuses on the development and deployment of bundled hardware and software solutions (including blockchains), for use across a wide array of internet of things (IoT) applications, from smart factories to smart cities (see terepac.com).

Gene is the author or coauthor of over 100 journals, conference publications/presentations, books, monographs, cases, and technical papers. These include the books *Canadian Cases in Human Resource Management, Cases in Organizational Behaviour, Toolkit for Organizational Change* (1st ed.) and the articles *Driving Loyalty Through Time-to-Value* and *Managing the New Product Development Process: Best-in-Class Principles and Leading Practices.* He is an active case writer, and his current research focuses on organizational change and the development of high-performance enterprises.

Cynthia Ingols is a Professor of Practice, School of Business, Simmons University, Boston, Massachusetts. At the School of Business, she is the director of undergraduate programs, leads the internship program for undergraduate students, and teaches courses in organizational change, career management, and leadership. Cynthia works extensively in the business school's executive education programs where she leads Strategic Leadership for Women, a program with a global reach that strengthens the leadership skills and self-confidence of its international participants. In addition, she coaches women executives who seek interpretation of feedback from bosses, colleagues, and subordinates and then helps executives determine the actions that they might take to strengthen their leadership presence and effectiveness.

Cynthia received her doctorate from the Harvard Graduate School of Education in organization behavior and a master's degree in political science from the University of Wisconsin–Madison. She taught management communication at the Harvard Business School (HBS), managed the 65-person case writing and research staff at HBS, and taught qualitative methods courses at several Boston-area universities. She serves as an editorial member of the *Case Research Journal.* She has served on corporate boards for several organizations, including FOX RPM and Biosymposia.

Cynthia focuses her consulting work in three areas: conducting diagnostic work to promote change in organizations; developing and teaching interactive executive education programs, particularly using cases and simulations; and coaching executives to enhance their leadership capacity and careers. Cynthia's research and publications follow similar lines. Her research on executive education programs has been published in leading journals, such as *Harvard Business Review*, *Organizational Dynamics*, and *Training*. Her research work on creating innovative organizational structures and change was published in the *Design Management Journal*. She has published numerous articles about careers in journals such as the *Journal of Career Development* and *Human Resource Development Quarterly*. She coauthored two books on career management: *Take Charge of Your Career* (2005) and *A Smart, Easy Guide to* Interviewing (2003). Cynthia joined the Tupper-Gene team to publish the second and third editions of *Organizational Change: An Action-Oriented Toolkit* (2012 and 2016).

Tupper F. Cawsey was professor emeritus of business, Lazaridis School of Business and Economics, Wilfrid Laurier University. He served as editor, *Case Research Journal*, for the North American Case Research Association. He served on several boards of directors and was chair of Lutherwood's board from 2003 to 2008. Tupper was recognized nationally in 2001 as one of Canada's top five business professors by receiving the Leaders in Management Education award, sponsored by PricewaterhouseCoopers and the *National Post*. He was also the 1994 recipient of the David Bradford Educator Award, presented by the Organizational Behavior Teaching Society, and the 1990 Wilfrid Laurier University "Outstanding Teacher Award."

Tupper created the Case Track for the Administrative Sciences Association of Canada, a peer review process for cases. He is author or coauthor of over six books and monographs including *Toolkit for Organizational Change—1st Edition, Canadian Cases in Human Resource Management, Cases in Organizational Behaviour,* and several monographs including *Control Systems in Excellent Canadian Companies* and the *Career Management Guide*. Tupper has over 50 refereed journal and conference publications. In 2005, he received the Christiansen Award from the Kaufman Foundation and the North American Case Research Association (NACRA), and in 2007 his case "Board Games at Lutherwood" won the Directors College Corporate Governance Award and the Bronze Case Award at the NACRA Conference. In 2009, his case "NuComm International" won the Gold Case Award at the NACRA Conference. Tupper passed away on August 17, 2015.